20th Century Theatre

Volume I

For my mother,
Marion Busher Loney

20th Century Theatre
Volume I

by Glenn Loney

Facts On File Publications
460 Park Avenue South
New York, N.Y. 10016

20th Century Theatre

Volume I

Glenn Loney

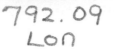

Library of Congress Cataloging in Publication Data

Loney, Glenn Meredith, 1928–
    20th century theater.

    Includes index.
    1. Theater—History—20th century. I. Title.
II. Title: Twentieth century theater.
PN2189.L65   792'.09'04   81-19587
ISBN 0-87196-463-5   AACR2
ISBN 0-87196-807-X   Vol 1.
ISBN 0-87196-808-8   Vol 2.

10 9 8 7 6 5 4 3 2 1
Printed in the United States of America

ACKNOWLEDGMENTS

BILLY ROSE THEATER COLLECTION
THE NEW YORK PUBLIC LIBRARY at LINCOLN CENTER
ASTOR, LENOX, TILDEN FOUNDATIONS
Page: 1–3, 6, 7, 9–12, 14, 17–21, 24–26, 30, 31, 35–37, 40–42, 47, 48, 52, 56,
57, 61–63, 66–68, 71, 72, 74, 75, 78, 81–84, 87, 91–94, 99–101, 105, 106,
109, 111, 112, 117, 123–125, 127, 131, 132, 139–142, 149–151, 156–158,
163, 170, 175, 176, 178, 180–182, 185–187, 190, 193, 195, 196, 198–201,
203–206, 208, 210–212, 214–216, 218, 220–224, 226–232, 234–236, 238–240,
243, 245, 247, 248, 250, 254, 256–258, 260–263, 266, 267, 271, 276, 280,
281, 284, 286, 287, 290, 293, 294, 297–299, 301, 303–305, 308–310,
312–314, 317, 321, 322, 324–327, 331, 333, 335, 337, 338, 341, 343, 346,
348, 349, 351, 352, 354, 356–358, 360, 361, 364, 365, 367, 369, 378, 383,
384, 386, 397, 398, 400, 402, 405, 411, 419, 420, 425, 432, 437, 440, 457.
THE NEW YORK PUBLIC LIBRARY, PICTURE COLLECTION
Page: 5
PLAY PICTORIAL
Editor and Publisher: B.W. Findon
London, England
Page: 27, 29, 32, 38, 44, 46, 49, 51, 54, 58, 59, 64, 65, 69, 70, 73, 76, 77, 80,
81, 85, 86, 89, 90, 95, 96, 103, 107, 119, 120, 129, 134, 136, 145, 147, 152,
155, 160, 162, 167, 169, 172, 173, 179, 184.
ANGUS McBEAN PHOTOGRAPH
HARVARD THEATER COLLECTION
Page: 207, 213, 219, 249, 255, 259, 265, 269, 278, 279, 282, 288, 296, 300,
307, 311, 318, 323, 328.
MARTHA SWOPE
Page: 371, 380, 390, 403, 404, 413, 423, 426, 442, 444, 449, 454.

Page: 34: Russell Hartley Archives For The Performing Arts
        88: Theater Collection, Museum of the City of New York
       197: Oregon Shakespearean Festival, Ashland, Oregon
       225: Collection of Glenn Loney
       242: British Tourist Authority
       252, 253, 272, 292: Eileen Darby
       270: Ben Pichot
       277: Avery Willard
       320: Tibor Hirsch
       344: Actor's Studio
       353: American Shakespeare Theater, Stratford, Conn.
       362: Joseph Costa
       375: Minnesota Theater Company
       382: Scottish Tourist Board
       387: Tom Hustler
       392: Vasco Ascolini
       393, 407: Van Williams
       395: David Byrd
       400: Kenneth Waissman and Maxine Fox Productions
       408: Stephen Moreton Prichard
       416: Stratford Festival, Stratford, Ontario
       429, 434: Paul Davis
       433: BAM Photo
       446: The National Theater
       448: Hank Kranzler
       450: Paul de Pass
       453: Donald Cooper.

We would like to acknowledge, with grateful appreciation, the Library Staff
and Pages at the New York Public Library at Lincoln Center, Billy Rose
Collection.

Preface

Twentieth Century Theatre is intended to serve two purposes: to offer an overview of theatre activity in North America and the British Isles since 1900, and to provide a "date-finder" for those who want to obtain capsule information about a particular theatre event, production, personality, or playhouse. The chronology is designed to be of use not only to the lay reader or theatre buff who wants to "dip into" the record from time to time, but also to the theatre student, journalist, critic and scholar as a research tool. Obviously it could not hope to be a complete, detailed record of 80 years of theatre. Much information had to be sacrificed to develop a one-volume study that would be accessible to a wide audience.

Twentieth Century Theatre includes all types of theatre productions in order to give a fairly representative picture of what was being produced—good and bad, popular and unpopular. The record contains a number of long-running revues, musicals, and farces. Some—or indeed many—of these may be seen as trivial in the extreme by historians and critics who take a long view of culture. This may be especially the case with those arbiters of literary taste who prefer to read plays—if they have any merit in print—rather than experience them in a theatre.

Understandably, critics and historians are interested in new ideas, new themes, new visions, new movements, new practices and new technologies. The theatre, however, remains even today a major arena of live popular entertainment. As historians, we may be fascinated by the theories of Edward Gordon Craig or the dramatic efforts of Edmund Wilson, but the fact is that the mass of successful theatrical activity is directed toward reaching and pleasing a fairly broad public, preferably for as long as possible especially if the activity is commercial and not the work of a subsidized repertory ensemble. That is why there is so much in this record concerning long runs, big successes, and memorable productions. These were what amused, excited and sometimes even inspired American and British audiences. As such then, this volume is a record of 80 years of very popular entertainment.

At the same time, in compiling the entries, I was mindful of those innovators who helped change the look, feel, quality, and spirit of the modern theatre, even though their own immediate efforts or manifestos were perhaps not much noticed or encouraged. Some may not have had success or even acceptance in the theatre marketplace, but their ideas and work, which influenced others and is now preserved in history books, deserves an honored place in a record such as this.

The selection of productions to be included has been guided by such things as length of run, reputation of the playwright, director or performers, possible controversy surrounding the play or production, or laudatory or excoriating reviews. In the case of London productions in the early decades that played in repertory or lacked long runs, recourse to John Parker's list of "Notable Productions" in *Who's Who in the Theatre* was a great help. It might be argued that the *Best Plays* series already offers an overview of Broadway and that is certainly true. But the multivolume series is not always easily accessible nor does it offer a compact guide for dates and details. It would have been very difficult to complete this survey, however, without the invaluable aid of *Best Plays* and *Theatre World*. In addition, that admirably detailed chronology, *American Musical Theatre*, and other special chronologies of genres, personalities or playhouses have been most helpful.

Twentieth Century Theatre is more than a chronology of productions. It is a valuable resource offering a broad overview of such areas as theatre censorship in Britain, America, and Canada, theatre architecture, developments in theatre management and in stage technology. There are also biographical entries, information about the inauguration of interesting theatres—and their subsequent fate as well—and even some capsule reviews of major Broadway and West End productions. In short, you will find a wider variety of entries in *Twentieth Century Theatre* than you have in any other theatre chronology.

In order to gain the overview from which this book could be assembled, it was necessary to spend almost three years in various kinds of research assisted by many friends, colleagues and students who are listed later. Teaching duties had to be adjusted and quixotic library schedules, necessitated by current severe budget and staff cutbacks, had to be observed. In some cases, the necessary sources were not available in New York but had been waiting for months in the Library of Congress to be microfilmed. In other instances, the material to be extracted was available only on microfilm, but no typewriter could be used to transcribe it. This often delayed some parts of the research or made it very difficult.

In spite of these efforts, it has not always been possible to provide some major dates and events, since records don't seem to be available. Actors as well as actresses, for instance, sometimes don't like to cite their birthdates for fear that producers may neglect them when they get older. Some actresses, in fact, get younger as the years go by. In both American and Britain—not to mention Ireland—many regional and provincial theatres have been so busy producing an attractive repertory of plays and selling seats for them they haven't had the time or the staff to maintain a complete chronological record or theatre archive. Such a chronology could be reconstructed from newspaper accounts of the theatres' work over the years, but the time and effort involved in that is tremendous. Fortunately, some press officers in British and American theatres have now prepared brief chronologies which are most helpful, as are the historical summaries they also provided.

When I began this project, it was first conceived as an American chronology. Then it was suggested that, owing to the close interaction between British and American theatre over the decades (American theatre being something of a British offspring), it would be interesting to chronicle them side by side. I told two of Britain's most knowledgeable theatre historians of the project, even asking them if they would undertake the British part. They kindly declined indicating that it would be difficult, if not impossible to accomplish. Conscious of my limitations, I have therefore enlisted many helpers and drawn on as many basic references as I could. Any errors or misinterpretations are, of course, inadvertent, and I'm eager to have them corrected for future editions.

Unlike America, there has been no continuing theatre annual in Britain covering the entire 20th century, though in various periods there have been excellent yearly surveys replete with detail. Considering the British love of theatre and what British theatre has done to enrich not only the English-speaking, but also world culture, it is surprising that there has been no such continuing publication as America's *Best Plays* chronicling the great adventures and triumphs of its stage. Apparently in the past there have not been enough regular readers willing to support such projects, so that attractive yearbooks, such as *Theatre World Annual*, or Sheridan Morley's *Theatre* have had their seasons and departed. Even the valuable monthly, *Plays and Players*, recently had a regrettable lapse in publication.

Among the British sources consulted are: *The Era Annual and Almanac*, *Whitaker's Almanac*, *Who's Who in the Theatre*, *Theatre World Annual*, *Play Pictorial*, *The Stage Yearbook*, *The Green Room Book*, *The Year's Work in Theatre*, *Drama in Britain*, *Theatre*, *Theatre Review*, and *Plays and Players*, as well as the newspapers of record, *The Times* of London and the *Sunday Times*. The detailed histories of Raymond Mander and Joe Mitchenson have also been most valuable. Scarecrow Press has recently issued a large two-volume record which is limited to the first decade of London theatre production in this century. It is impressive and exhaustive, but it doesn't indicate plots nor does it provide extracts from reviews. It does, however, indicate in what papers and on what dates reviews can be found, provided one has access to such newspaper files. Despite all these sources, some years are primarily covered by trade annuals which do not provide all the information theatre researchers could wish.

In some seasons, it is very easy to establish the runs of shows in London's West End, thanks to the diligence of editors of annuals. In other seasons, there are no complete figures readily available. Sometimes, there will be performance figures listed to the end of the season, but if the play ran into the next season, these added showings were not picked up in the next year's annual. In those years in which one has to depend on the 100-performance-plus lists offered in *Who's Who in the Theatre*, it's not easy to discover how *few* performances a less successful play may have had. Some American hits, for example, didn't achieve 100 showings in London, but it would be interesting to know whether they had 20, 40, or 80 performances.

So it has not been easy to assemble the British record, though press office chronologies from such companies as the Royal Shakespeare and the National Theatre have been most helpful. There is also an excellent new chronology and commentary called *At the Royal Court—25 Years of the English Stage Company*, that records in detail dates and data on the work of such talents as David Storey, John Osborne, Arnold Wesker, and Edward Bond.

Because time and funds prohibited much actual research in Britain, I am especially grateful for the kindness and cooperation of British colleagues and friends. Among them are Ian Macintosh of Theatre Projects, Peter Higgins of EMI, Kathleen Barker of the International Society for Theatre Research, Kay Robertson and John Lahr, an American author-critic living in London.

Through years of reporting on London theatre and covering British drama and music festivals, I've come to regard a number of talented people working in the British theatre as more than acquaintances. They have helped in the compilation of this reference through their kindness and their professional courtesy. Among them are Roger Witts of the Edinburgh Festival, Suzette Hoare of the National Theatre, David Brierley of the Royal Shakespeare, and Anne Hillier of the Chichester Festival. Dr. Levi Fox, Director of the Shakespeare Birthplace Trust, generously made the Stratford Memorial Theatre and Royal Shakespeare production records available, and Eileen Robinson did some basic research. Information on Britain's historic theatres as well as active provincial companies was forthcoming from a number of experts working at or familiar with these playhouses and ensembles. Similarly, information about drama schools, professional associations (such as British Actors Equity), technical advances, and other theatre matters was also readily provided. From such theatre groups as Glasgow's estimable Citizens', Edinburgh's Traverse, and London's Bush Theatre came almost enough information to launch a mini-book series. My great regret is that complete chronologies of such continuing theatre ventures could not be included in the present volume.

My gratitude to the many individuals, archives, and other theatre organizations that helped me gather material or verify dates must again be tinged with regret that it was simply not possible, in the compass of the present volume, to include all the entries or all the details that were developed. I hope this information can eventually be made available in a larger reference work. Special thanks are owed to Louis Rachow, who is responsible for most of the biographical entries and who made readily accessible the references in the Walter Hampden Memorial Library of the Players. My thanks also goes to such colleagues and friends as Dorothy Swerdlove and her staff at the Lincoln Center Billy Rose Theatre Collection, Mary C. Henderson of the Theatre Collection of the Museum of the City of New York, Brooks McNamara of New York University and the Shubert Archives, and Russell Hartley of the San Francisco Archives of the Performing Arts. From them I got encouragement, advice and information.

To Benito Ortolani, Chairman of Theatre at Brooklyn College, and to Stanley Waren, Provost of the CUNY Graduate Center, I owe a debt of gratitude for their counsel and assistance, especially in terms of released time and beneficial teaching schedules, and for their supply of graduate assistants. Thanks are also owed to the libraries of Brooklyn College and the Graduate Center, as well as to the New York Public Library and the library of Columbia University. Among the Brooklyn College and CUNY graduate students who were especially helpful on the project were Mark Spergel and Jo Tanner, who extracted quotes from 80 years of London and New York drama reviews. Unfortunately, most of their work could not be included owing to space limitations. Also invaluable in recording data about historic theatres were Elizabeth Swain (London theatres) and Janet Blake (New York theatres). Other students who gathered material included Tobi Stein, Antoinette Nebel, Nai-Chung Ku, Linda Wormel, Gerald Rothman, Micha Hendel, Tamar Darhi, Tom Rockenfield, Susan Falk, Lourdes Malachow, Cameron MacNeil and Pen-Hsien Li. Marilyn Daljord sorted through the many books published on both sides of the Atlantic in the last eight decades to present a sampling of important works on theatre. There are other students and former students whom I've not listed, but I value their aid.

I also have profited from the advice and research of such friends and colleagues as Paul Myers, Curator Emeritus of the Lincoln Center Theatre Collection; Garff Wilson, professor and theatre historian at the University of California at Berkeley; Norman Philbrick, former Stanford professor, historian, and archivist; Mark Sumner, Director of the Institute of Outdoor Drama; Patricia MacKay, Editor of *Theatre Crafts*, and many others working or teaching in theatre or in theatre-related areas.

Information about historic American theatres was provided by Irvin Glazer, President of the Theatre Historical Society, and by Brother Andrew Corsini, Terry Helgeson and other THS colleagues. Dates and details about various American resident theatres were tracked down by Israel Fummey, a graduate student from Ghana. I also want to thank all the press officers and archivists of various regional, professional theatres, and summer festivals for their cooperation. Unfortunately, there isn't space to list everyone.

The very important Canadian entries were largely the work of Elissa Pane and Columbine Arts Research. Heather McCallum of the Theatre Department of the Metropolitan Toronto Library also offered advice and information, as did Daniel Ladell, archivist for the Stratford Festival of Canada, and the press office of the Shaw Festival.

Very special thanks go to Judith Linn, who so tirelessly sought both representative and little-known production photos to document 80 years of theatre on both sides of the Atlantic. Brenda Zanger Greene, a former student, provided the Federal Theatre entries, based on her work in the Research Center for the Federal Theatre Project. Joseph Lieberman gave me important dates and details on New York theatre censorship. Richard Findlater's study of British censorship was invaluable. And, of course, my warmest thanks to my editor, Eleanora Schoenebaum, who so skillfully produced the finished text, and to her staff, especially Grace Ferrara and Phil Saltz. After this book has gone to press, I'm sure to remember others who have provided valuable advice and data. To all who helped this project become reality, named or unnamed, my deepest gratitude.

A further service for which I will thank anyone in advance, is the correction of any errors or major omissions which may be spotted in the published text. If the reader finds any such mistakes or believes that an important event has been left out, please write me about it. In the meantime, I trust *Twentieth Century Theatre* will be a useful "date-finder" for those who want to pinpoint a name, a theatre, a production, or an event so they can more easily locate detailed information in the reference works on which this is based. More than that, I hope this book will provide anyone who picks it up with some interesting, enjoyable glimpses of modern British-American theatre over the years.

Glenn Loney, Professor of Theatre
Brooklyn College/CUNY Graduate Center
1982

Introduction

The letter is dated February 1799. Sent from Philadelphia to London, it reads in part: "Theatricals in this new world are, I am afraid, rapidly declining, and if Providence does not assist us, I am apprehensive, from one calamity or other, we must soon fall." The writer was apparently a member of the Thomas Wignell-Alexander Reinagle Company, based in the City of Brotherly Love. His letter is a catalogue of misfortunes suffered not only in Philadelphia, but also on the road in Baltimore, Annapolis, and New York.

At that time, it cost this company about $450 to give a performance. Some nights, not even that much was recouped from ticket sales. Discouraged, this thespian correspondent observed: "I suppose the rage of the English actors for emigration has ceased. . . ." Had he been able to look into the future, he might have been amazed at the number of English actors who continued to emigrate, or at least to play New York and other major American cities, either as guest performers or as members of English ensembles.

The first stirrings of professional theatre in America were made by English actors with English repertory. This was only natural, considering that America was then a collection of English colonies, sharing a common language and sense of tradition with its mother country. After some pioneering by players such as Charles and Mary Stagg and the company of Walter Murray and Thomas Kean—about whom little is known—in 1752 the American colonies were to see their first proper London players. These were the "Company of Comedians," assembled by actor-manager Lewis Hallam. They opened in Williamsburg with Shakespeare's *The Merchant of Venice*. Eventually they became the American Company, and in 1767 they gave Thomas Godfrey's *The Prince of Parthia* its premiere. This was the first American play to have a professional production.

In the 19th century, America began to return England's theatrical generosity by sending American plays and performers across the Atlantic, not only to London, but also to provincial centers in the British Isles. Just as British talents like Dion Boucicault could make themselves at home in New York's theatre life, so could Americans adopt England as their performance base. There were, of course, some interesting rivalries and clashes. The most memorable was the 1849 Astor Place Riot, in which more than a score of people died when an infantry regiment tried to quell an angry mob threatening the Astor Place Theatre, where the English actor William Charles Macready was performing. Many in the crowd were partisans of the dynamic American actor, Edwin Forrest, whom they believed had been slighted by Macready when he appeared in England in 1845.

There was more involved in the Astor Place tragedy than popular drama criticism, not least the resentment of some New Yorkers—themselves fairly recent emigrées—toward the English, especially upper-class English. Despite changing attitudes over the years toward England and the British—often determined by economics and politics—the theatrical bond between the old land and the new remains strong even as we approach the 21st century.

Over the last eight decades two kinds of theatre exchange can be seen in the British and American theatre. Important new plays, whether premiered in New York or London, were usually produced in the other capital as soon as the celebrity and popularity of the play was established. Shrewd commercial producers have always tried to take advantage of a new play's success on Broadway or in the West End, in order to bring it—almost "pre-sold"—to the other theatre center. Supposedly, this reduced some of the financial risks. In some notable cases, as shown in the following chronology, major British plays were premiered in New York *before* they were seen in London. Bernard Shaw's *Saint Joan*, for example, was produced by the Theatre Guild on Broadway before its West End debut. In recent years, the Royal Shakespeare Company has been giving some American playwrights their world premieres in London, when it was clear that Broadway or Off-Broadway commercial managements would not. By the 1970s the sad truth was that a new British success was almost assured a rapid Broadway production in preference to a new American play. In London, the same was often said of hit American musicals. If a musical made a big splash on Broadway, it would soon be seen in the West End as well.

With the dawn of the 1980s, there was a fear among American playwrights that in the future the only serious plays that would be considered for Broadway production would be those with glowing London reviews—and that in time, the commercial theatre would abandon the drama of ideas entirely in favor of crowd-pleasing musicals and comedies. In Britain the mood is fortunately a bit more optimistic owing to the evolution in the late 1950s of several distinguished subsidized theatres, committed to short runs or repertories of both classics and challenging new dramas. Nonetheless, there was a feeling that American musicals were preferred in London's commercial theatre over any British efforts in that realm. The huge success of new works by Tim Rice and Andrew Lloyd Webber (*Jesus Christ Superstar, Evita*) finally demonstrated that a British show with elements of popular appeal and thorough professionalism could find a commercial public, though *Superstar* had to prove itself on Broadway first.

The other kind of artistic exchange which has been going on across the Atlantic for decades is the recreation of the appearance and effect of a Broadway or London staging, even though the actors are different from the original cast. That is one reason certain British directors have worked extensively in New York and elsewhere in America over the years. Another is that these men happen to be very good directors, skilled at bringing a play to life and gifted at working with actors, who are often insecure in new challenges. There are, of course, American and Canadian directors of whom the same may be said. When Harold Clurman was asked to direct in London, it was not because the producer could not find any available British talent.

Readers who dip into the first year of the first decade of this record, and follow that with a glance at the last year of the last decade, will find striking differences between 1900 and 1979 on both sides of the Atlantic. However, one thing remains constant over 80 years of British and American theatre activity: that is the popularity of Shakespeare, which can actually be seen to increase with the establishment of numerous Shakespeare Festivals—some 35 in the United States alone at last count.

At the turn of the century, the London stage was still largely dominated by talented, charismatic actor-managers, such as George Alexander and Herbert Beerbohm Tree, though the stars of older artists such as Henry Irving were on the wane. At theatres such as St. James's and His Majesty's, these actor-managers could produce new plays which suited their talents and their companies' abilities. They could allow the dramas or comedies to run their course, bringing back popular favorites from their standing repertories when a new play faltered. If they found a new, challenging drama which they felt could not hope to win even a short run, they could indulge themselves and their loyal fans in a special matinee or two. Of course these performer-managers had to make money to keep their theatres operating, but production costs were much, much less then—in rents, wages and materials—and they could afford to mount the plays, old and new, which pleased them and their publics. One flop did not close the theatre. It can be said that almost all of these managers saw themselves first as artists, rather than businessmen, and that the naked greed, which was more often the production motive on Broadway, repelled them.

London ensembles also toured their repertories to provincial cities in England, Scotland, and Ireland. A new play destined for the West End might have its initial showing in Dublin, followed by performances in Glasgow, Edinburgh, and Manchester, working its way toward London. Some troupes spent most of their performance year on the provincial circuit, with brief appearances in London, In this book, it can be seen that Frank Benson's Shakespeare ensemble played every spring in Stratford-upon-Avon, later adding a summer season, in addition to having a brief London season. Of course the record is not complete—only a sampling—and it cannot show such a troupe's entire provincial touring-year. The effect of such extensive touring, however, was to leave major provincial centers without professional companies of their own, a void which was filled in the first two decades of the century in such cities as Manchester, Liverpool, Glasgow and Birmingham, with the most notable achievement in the latter city, where Barry Jackson founded his admirable Repertory Company. Following the success of Dublin's Abbey Theatre in creating a distinctive ensemble and in producing new Irish dramas, similar efforts were made in Manchester and Birmingham, with such playwrights as John Drinkwater and Stanley Houghton emerging, as well as some of Britain's most distinguished players and directors.

Despite continental developments in new genres and styles as well as innovations in design and staging, London's theatre fare in the first decade remained a mixture of melodramas, romances, comedies, farces, thrillers, and musicals featuring attractive young ladies. Ibsen's *Ghosts* (1881) had been in existence for some time, but on both sides of the Atlantic it was still considered too shocking for commercial production. On Broadway, no producer could foresee an extended run for such a story. In London, owing to the power of the Lord Chamberlain to forbid public performances of any script he deemed offensive, there was no immediate possibility of a commercial staging. Following the adventurous continental examples of Andre Antoine's *Theatre Libre* in Paris, Otto Brahm's *Freie Buehne* in Berlin, and J. T. Grein's pioneering Independent Theatre in London, the Incorporated Stage Society in London was able for several decades to give such plays as *Ghosts* at least minimal performances—first on Sundays when professional actors were free and later at Monday matinees as well, when the Society's membership swelled. Because these were not public showings, no license was required for their presentation. But not all the plays produced by the Stage Society and other groups which followed it were necessarily under the Lord Chamberlain's ban. Some were found unobjectionable, but no commercial producer wished to stage them.

Whatever the hopes of serious writers and critics for a new serious drama to emerge in the new century, then as now, the desire to attract large audiences for long runs inevitably encouraged reductionism. Alongside such sincere local color sagas as *Caleb West* and shocking city slum portraits like *Salvation Nell*, audiences could thrill to the small town humor and leaden commonplaces of *Mrs. Wiggs of the Cabbage Patch*. Nevertheless, Shaw's crackling wit was making some inroads in London and a more sophisticated comedy was developing on Broadway, though a play such as *The New York Idea* lacks the Shavian touch.

Considering the reputation George Bernard Shaw enjoys today, it's instructive to see what stratagems were necessary to bring some of his plays to the London stage. Even during the justly admired Vedrenne-Barker management at the Royal Court (1904–1907), when Shaw himself supervised stagings of his works (usually in limited runs), his plays were not in great commercial demand, nor much admired by popular critics. Later it remained for Barry Jackson to premiere some major Shavian dramas in Birmingham before bringing them to London. In New York, Arnold Daly strove with equal effort to introduce Shaw's plays to rather indifferent audiences. That's not to say that the drama of ideas had no appeal at all to Londoners, only that its partisans were initially a small, select group.

Especially in the first decade of this century, but continuing into the second decade, British audiences were interested in the American West. Real American Indians were even imported to add authenticity to some productions. In suburban and provincial theatres, some Western melodramas also favored Mormons as subjects, particularly from the point of view of plural marriage, in spite of the fact that it was no longer a practice of the Latter Day Saints. When there wasn't an American drama of the West available, British writers would invent one. America's Eastern seaboard and mid-west proved less popular. In 1906, *The Green Room Book* noted the abundance of American plays in Britain. It also commented that American theatre people seemed to feel that the British resented American plays and performers. This was not believed to be the case in general, but some of the current plays were, for British tastes, not very good.

Today there is a popular notion that in both Britain and America before the outbreak of World War I a sort of hazy, autumnal peace existed. This may have been somewhat true among the insulated wealthy and upper-middle-class, secure in large houses with complements of minimally paid servants. And, of course, American's geographic isolation from Europe did protect it from external disturbances to a marked degree. But the period 1900–1914 was by no means a halcyon time on the continent, in Britain, or in America. What emerged in the first decade and a half was a surprising pattern of violence; hardly a month went by without some leading political, labor or social figure being attacked or assassinated. Small-scale wars disrupted the Balkans and Asia. Britain was also involved in the Boer War at the opening of this chronology. There were scenes about and references to this conflict in popular plays and entertainments. One even showed the audience film footage from the South African front. It is true though that in wartime, audiences prefer to be cheered up by shows which help them forget there's a war on; unless, of course, the war-oriented dramas and musicals are inspiring enough to generate confidence.

Over the decades, despite a constant exchange of American and British dramas and musicals, there have always been some London hits which immediately flop on Broadway—and vice versa. What often emerges from the reviews is that the play or musical in question was "too British" or "too American" to find a large audience on the other side of the Atlantic. I've not run any statistical counts, but my impression is that, on balance, American audiences have tended to admire British plays, productions and performers more often and more extravagantly than British theatregoers have liked American imports. But this is only a personal impression, reinforced in recent years by seeing so many plays and performances of both nations on both sides of the Atlantic. Readers may, however, note in the record that some major American dramatic and musical landmarks had only the briefest of runs in the West End or were instead premiered in limited runs in club theatres or by repertory ensembles. For instance, Stephen Sondheim's treatment of *Sweeney Todd*, much admired in New York, was a rapid and disastrous failure in London at the Drury Lane Theatre. And that plot was a venerable English melodrama to begin with! Similarly, some scripts hugely admired in Britain have found few fans in America.

The American theatre at the dawn of the 20th century had well-developed national touring circuits, but there were still some regional stock companies surviving. The rise in popularity of silent films in the first two decades cut their number and the later innovations of sound films and radio broadcasting—free home entertainment—dealt them a death blow. In New York there were still some producers in the mold of London's actor-managers, such as Sothern and Marlowe or Minnie Maddern Fiske, but the artistic power more often rested with producer-directors such as David Belasco, who did not perform themselves, but created and developed stars in popular productions.

However, neither the Fiskes nor the Belascos were destined to dominate the Broadway theatre nor, by extension, the American touring circuits. It was the Theatrical Syndicate, a group of theatre owners, lessors and producers, whose power became so great that they could dictate who worked where, what was to be performed, and for how long (audiences willing) in most Broadway theatres and in many playhouses across the nation. Belasco, Mrs. Fiske and others, including Sarah Bernhardt when she made one of her several "farewell tours" of the States, defied the Syndicate, joining with the young Shubert Brothers, who emerged as challengers. In time, as the record notes, the Syndicate's power was diminished and eventually broken, while the Shuberts shrewdly built a theatre empire that became perhaps even more domineering and dictatorial than that of their former foes before it too was crippled by the Great Depression.

What this meant for Broadway and the American professional theatre was that until the Depression the tastes of the surviving Shubert Brothers, Lee and J.J., dictated much of what was produced in the commercial theatre, although San Francisco and Chicago continued to function as small production centers, sending some successful shows to Broadway.

Generally the chronology during the 20s and 30s shows the same general blend of melodramas, thrillers, farces, comedies, romances, revues, and musicals—with the obligatory Shakespeare repertory seasons—to be found in West End programming. Whereas initially the major difference between British and American theatre was the dominant profit motive on Broadway contrasted with the older, more pervasive respect for the art form to be found on the London stage, gradually American influences penetrated the West End. Charles Frohman and other Americans produced on both sides of the Atlantic. By the 1930s the actor-manager was largely a memory and even in London profit making was, for some producers, becoming more important than the art and craft of the theatre.

Fortunately, on both sides of the Atlantic, theatre managers have proved fairly pragmatic. In practice, that has meant that many new ideas, new themes, formerly taboo topics, innovative production and acting styles and technological novelties—no matter what the initial resistance from producers, critics or the public—have eventually found their way to the commercial stage if they could attract a paying audience. With the gradual emergence of an American school of realism—seen in 1900 with James A. Herne's *Sag Harbor*, for instance—if producers could find a public for such plays, they would certainly produce them on Broadway. And what's more, these plays were toured endlessly on the strength of their New York reception. Ironically, in the case of *Sag Harbor*, British pragmatism backfired. When the play was produced in England, its locale was changed from its native American site to Cornwall, ostensibly to make the play more understandable to the British. It failed. But this was fairly common practice: "adapting" an American or British script for its new audience. The big Broadway musical success, *Blossom Time*, however, was a success in Britain, but under the alias of *Lilac Time*. (In Paris it was called *Chanson d'Amour*.)

It's interesting to note that the tradition of the Christmas pantomime and holiday revivals of comedies and musicals has managed to survive eight decades of modern life in London, whereas it rapidly died out in New York. Short runs, matinee performances and brief revivals have always been financially more feasible on the London stage. Christmas was evidently not an important holiday to a number of New York theatregoers.

At the beginning of the century the traditional minstrel show was vanishing from major American stages and all black shows began to appear, such as the 1903 *In Dahomey*. For decades, however, such shows were designed to amuse whites, not mixed audiences. In fact, on both sides of the Atlantic, white performers continued to impersonate blacks and orientals, especially in major roles, until the advent of such memorable actors as Paul Robeson, Charles Gilpin, and Jules Bledsoe.

The popularity of Gilbert & Sullivan and of operetta—whether of European, British, or American manufacture—influenced the development of the musical, some of which had only the most fragile of plots. Before long, the shows which were really intended as programs of songs, dances, comic sketches, and variety numbers came to be called revues, winning tremendous popularity both in London and New York. Ziegfeld's *Follies* and George White's *Scandals* were arguably the most notable, despite the excitement caused by such talents as Gertrude Lawrence in Andre Charlot's revues. Curiously, the popularity of the revue as a form lasted longer in London than it did on Broadway. Some critics have suggested that TV variety shows replaced it in the public favor in the United States.

Although musicals on Broadway and in London could have Graustarkian, romantic locales, involving young royals and peasants in amorous dalliance—plots which held their own for half a century in the affections of some theatre-goers—both American and British musicals began to have modern, topical situations and characters as well. Chorus routines, which early in the century had been largely limited to drill-team formations, began to show imaginative use of tap-dancing, soft-shoe, and later, such popular dances as the Charleston. With couples such as Vernon and Irene Castle and later Fred and Adele Astaire, ballroom dancing became the rage on stage. In the teens and the "Flaming Twenties," it was not unusual to find a critic commenting on the "dance craze," as reflected in both revues and book musicals. It has become a critical cliche to identify the 1943 American musical *Oklahoma!* as the first of the genre to integrate with great success all the performance elements—songs, story and dance—to reveal character, thought, and emotion. *Show Boat* (1927), however, is not to be ignored as an integrated musical. Nor is George Ade's *The Sultan of Sulu* (1902), whose lyrics were comically relevant to the show. In recent years, notably in *A Chorus Line* (1975) and *Dancin'* (1978), dance has assumed an ever increasing importance in musicals.

The Great War did cause a break with both the social and the theatrical past, as well as temporarily reducing greatly the number and quality of London productions. Already in the first two decades in Britain a new honesty and vitality in playwriting had originated in centers such as Dublin, Manchester, and Birmingham and the best of these works found their way to London, often performed by the troupes that premiered them. In America this development came a bit later, although the founding of "little theatres" in several regional centers was an early attempt to introduce new European ideas about drama and staging to America. The most significant American groups that provided new, impressive American drama, as well as some major performers, directors, and designers, were the Washington Square Players and the Provincetown Players, whose most notable alumnus was Eugene O'Neill.

While the sobering effects of World War I later produced such plays as *What Price Glory?* and *Journeys End*, the 1920's, until the disastrous, unexpected crash of 1929, were mostly a time of unbridled optimism, careless speculation and, often, reckless living. The theatre's entertainments reflected this, as the record shows. There were comedies, both sophisticated and daring. There were thrillers with fast-living con men and floozies. But there was also an increasingly serious drama, encouraged by the example of Shaw, Galsworthy, O'Neill, Rice, and others.

It had often been pointed out that although England had given the world its greatest playwright some four hundred years ago, the British still lacked what every civilized nation in Europe had: a subsidized National Theatre. Finally, in 1963, Britain's National Theatre was created—born at the Old Vic and later transplanted to its new home on the South Bank of the Thames. As this is written, the Americans still don't have one, while the Canadians have not only the National Theatre Center in Ottawa, but also a number of handsomely supported provincial theatres. For such theatres, of course, it's an easy matter to keep the classics alive, to try out new scripts, and to introduce important foreign dramas that would have little chance of production by commercial managements.

After the Washington Square Players had dissolved, some of their members reorganized themselves as the Theatre Guild, which distinguished itself in the decades of the 1920's, 1930's, and even the 1940's, by producing important, unknown foreign plays—including some Shaw works—as well as new, impressive American dramas. The operation—a modified repertory concept—was frequently one of juggling artistic ambitions with box-office realities, but notable achievements were made, and never with profit as the only motive. Eva Le-Gallienne, with her Civic Repertory Theatre, also tried to give New Yorkers a professional repertory company, with the best of the classics and new domestic and foreign dramas presented on 14th Street at popular prices. But it was a losing battle, since she lacked the necessary subsidies—which European playhouses even in small countries such as Sweden took for granted. In the 1930s an offshoot of the Guild, the Group Theatre, was to enrich the stage with new plays, performers and directors, imbued with the theories of Stanislavsky. Among its members were Harold Clurman, Lee Strasberg, Sanford Meisner, and Stella Adler.

In Britain, the dedication of Frank Benson and his Bensonians at the Shakespeare Memorial Theatre in Stratford-upon-Avon was rewarded by a solidly established tradition of professional Shakespeare productions in repertory, subsidized not by the state but by admiring patrons. Over the years, as tourists flocked to Stratford, successive artistic directors sustained the work of the company until it became the Royal Shakespeare Company, with homes in both Stratford and London —and at last with government subsidies as well.

At the Old Vic, Lilian Baylis was to create a home for serious drama in London, notably Shakespeare. Her work was to be ably carried forward by such gifted directors as Tyrone Guthrie, although the historic old playhouse was left in limbo at the end of the eight decades, with the collapse of the Prospect Theatre Company. Among the smaller theatres in the 1920's in London dedicated to experimental work and to plays which could not hope for commercial production were Peter Godfrey's Gate Theatre and the Barnes Theatre.

With the collapse of the American economy in 1929—and its attendant effects on Britain and Europe—even the plays and musicals of the commercial theatre in New York and London reflected wryly or angrily on the unexpected hard times. Dissidents made their anger and their programs for reform known through theatre productions. In London and in Glasgow, the Unity Theatre provided a left-leaning view, as did most of the New York groups, such as Labor Stage, Workers' Laboratory Theatre and Theatre Union. Unfortunately, the American government's first—and to date last—meaningful experiment in subsidized theatre, the Federal Theatre, was also viewed as leftist by some crucial congressmen who made sure that taxpayers' money would no longer be used to encourage such social criticism.

Despite the tremendous cost in money, effort, and human lives, World War II managed to bring the United States out of the Depression and give it a new role as a major world power, finished at last with its traditional isolationism. Britain, on the other hand, who had fought valiantly and often virtually alone against the Nazi menace, saw her Empire dissolved, her resources drained and her major cities devastated. There were some war-time theatre offerings which reflected each nation's reactions to the conflict, but the dominant fare was either morale-boosting or escapist.

In the aftermath, in Britain came a Socialist government; in America, the McCarthy anti-communist hysteria and purges. The record of productions in New York and in London pro-vides a curious counterpoint to these events. But in 1956, at the Royal Court Theatre in London, John Osborne's *Look Back in Anger* opened, with a central character lashing out verbally—if ineffectually—at all the cheats and disappointments of modern life. The play left in its wake not only some interesting Osborne imitators, but also the phrase "Angry Young Men." The Royal Court and some Off-Broadway theatres, such as the Circle in the Square, that had emerged in the 1950s as alternatives to the stifling commercialism of Broadway, were making it possible for new voices to be heard, new styles to be seen. Social protest could be projected on stage, without the restraints of profit-oriented theatre production. In 1968, with the termination of British stage censorship, nudity and other socially-oriented novelties could at last be shown in public in England, as they were in America, where they rapidly became clichés.

This commentary was intended as brief introduction to the record, not as a mini-history of 80 years. The advent of the absurd, of happenings, of the cult of Bertolt Brecht and alienation, of improvisation, of insulting the audience, of fringe theatre, Off-off Broadway theatre, pub theatre, street theatre, and alternative theatre are all so recent that it is almost indecent to mention them here, even if some are already in eclipse. To the seasoned theatre historian, however, there is very little new under the sun. The impressive growth in London in the 1970s of a number of intimate theatres, that often fed new scripts into the commercial or the major subsidized theatres, as well as the development of Off-off Broadway theatres from the early 1970s onward that made similar opportunities possible in America, may seem something quite new, until one remembers that both New York and London have long had smaller, tributary, experimental theatres. Many, however, burned themselves out in a decade or less, to be forgotten—except by archivists—and replaced by new ventures, which in their turn were hailed as innovative.

One development in the theatre in the late 1960s was something of a change. This was the protest against American military involvement in Vietnam, which generated many attacks or comments in a range of styles, notable more for their intensity or ferocity than for their cogency. Never before in either British or American theatre had there been—in time of hostilities—such outspoken use of the stage as a platform for political invective, giving force to the concept of a committed "Political Theatre"—still another aspect of the wide range of the theatre's possibilities.

As for new movements in the theatre, what ever became of verse drama? (No novelty in Shakespeare's time, nor in that of Aeschylus!) Maxwell Anderson had his day in the sun and departed. So did T. S. Eliot, who managed to impress many without enlightening most. And I must be one of the very few people who not only saw the premiere of Christopher Fry's last cyclic verse play, *A Yard of Sun*, but also rather liked it after discussing it with Fry.

It may well be true, as the French say, that the more things change, the more they remain the same. But, in the theatre, this maxim requires a bit of adjustment. For instance, in 1909, when W. H. Denny gave British readers of the *Stage Year Book* some advice on acting in America, he noted that one could live comfortably in Manhattan for $15 per week, $5 of the sum to be spent on a nice room. Denny also noted: "Take it to heart and underline it heavily, that the one aim of every soul in the business portion of the drama in America is to make money as fast as possible, and every other consideration is rendered subservient to that idea."

Read this record and see if he has a point.

20th Century Theatre
Volume I

Jan 1 *Chris and the Wonderful Lamp* (NY—Hammerstein's Victoria—Musical) Based on *Arabian Nights*, this visually oriented entertainment, with book by Glen MacDonough, has a score by John Philip Sousa. Edna Wallace Hopper is featured.

Jan 8 *Naughty Anthony* (NY—Herald Square—Comedy). Written, directed, and produced by David Belasco, this light diversion has Blanche Bates and Oliver Redpath in its cast. On March 5, it is paired with Belasco's adaptation of John Luther Long's story, *Madame Butterfly*, with Bates as Cho-Cho San, the tragic heroine.

Feb 5 *Sapho* (NY—Wallack's—Drama). Based on Alphonse Daudet's novel, this work shocks the conventional. Its star, Olga Nethersole, finds herself accused of mounting an immoral play. Nethersole plays an evil woman who seduces a pure young man and keeps him as her lover. In the end, he has a purifying influence on her and she marries the felon who is the father of her child. The play is closed after 29 performances. The *NY Times* calls the play: "objectionable, . . . coarse and vulgar . . . [Nethersole] is not fascinating or graceful, . . . " and her "awkwardness [was] never more unpleasantly in evidence than in this performance."

March 19 *The Casino Girl* (NY—Casino—Musical). With a book by Harry B. Smith and music by Ludwig Englander, Will M. Cook, Harry Mac Connell, and Arthur Nevin, this popular show features pretty girls. Its heroine, fleeing an importunate lover, opens a hat shop in Cairo. It has a run of 91 performances. Opening at London's Shaftesbury Theatre on July 11, the show is a hit, with 193 performances. Richard Carle, Marie George and Mabelle Gilman are featured.

April 9 *Quo Vadis* (NY—New York—Drama). Stanislaus Stange's six-act adaptation of Henry Sienkiewicz's best-selling novel of religous faith and persecution under Nero, opens for an initial run of 96 performances. On the same night, Jeannette Gilder's five-act adaptation is shown at the Herald Square Theatre. Her version does not find favor with the critics or the public and runs only 32 performances. On May 5 Stange's version opens at London's Adelphi Theatre. *The Era* pans the play and calls it simple entertainment.

Sep 6 *Fiddle-dee-dee* (NY—Weber and Fields' Music Hall-Musical). With music by John Stromberg, this show gives the comedy team of Joseph Weber and Lew Fields a lively, topical vehicle. *Quo Vadis* is burlesqued. It enjoys 262 performances.

Sep 10 *Arizona* (NY—Herald Square—Drama). Augustus Thomas' suspenseful western play about a lady's honor, opens

with Vincent Serrano, Eleanor Robson and Edgar Selwyn in the cast. The *NY Times* calls it "uplifting entertainment."

Sep 11 *Richard Carvel* (NY—Empire—Drama). Edward Rose dramatizes Winston Churchill's best-selling novel, set during the Revolutionary War. Charles Frohman produces. John Drew is the lead in this melodrama of love and intrigue.

Sep 17 *Caleb West* (NY—Manhattan—Drama). Michael Morton adapts F. Hopkinson Smith's best-selling novel about a master driver. Smith and Eugene Presbrey direct.

Sep 17 *The Rogers Brothers in Central Park* (NY—Hammerstein's Victoria—Musical). The popular comedy team of Gus and Max Rogers romps through what is essentially a revue by John J. McNally with songs by J. Cheever Goodwin (lyrics) and Maurice Levi (music).

Sep 27 *Sag Harbor* (NY—Republic—Drama). James A. Herne, author of American dramas dealing with ordinary people in local-color settings, opens his new play about two brothers in love with the same women. In the cast are Herne, Julia A. Herne, Chrystal Herne, Mrs. Sol Smith, William Hodge, and Lionel Barrymore. The *NY Times* calls the play "exceedingly good."

Oct 1 *David Harum* (NY—Garrick—Comedy). Adapted swiftly for the stage, Edward N. Westcott's best-selling local-color novel about a shrewd Yankee banker is an instant success, with revivals and tours continuing its popularity. William H. Crane stars.

Oct 22 *L'Aiglon* (NY—Knickerbocker—Drama). Charles Frohman presents the first New York production of Edmond Rostand's play about Napoleon's son. Maude Adams portrays the title role, originally created by Sarah Bernhardt.

Nov 10 *Florodora* (NY—Casino—Musical). This London success, with a book by Owen Hall—revised by Frank Pixley—and music by Leslie Stuart, opens to mixed reviews and a long run of 505 performances. Florodora is a Philippine island, famous for its perfume. Directed by Louis Hopper, the show rapidly becomes famed for its "Florodora Sextette": Margaret Walker, Marjorie Relyea, Daisy

Chris and the Wonderful Lamp

Greene, Vaughn Texsmith, Marie L. Wilson, and Agnes Wayburn. Initial reviews are not unanimous raves. Nursed along for the first few weeks, with daily boosts for the show in the *Sun*, it soon plays to capacity audiences ($10,000 per week), turning potential ticket-buyers away. Eventually, it runs longer than its London version, becoming the second musical to pass the 500-performance mark in New York.

Dec 10 *Janice Meredith* (NY—Wallack's—Drama). Paul L. Ford adapts his novel of a Revolutionary War romance between a young woman and her Tory father's indentured servant. Edward E. Rose aides him. The show stars Mary Mannering, whose "Janice Meredith curl" threatens the Gibson Girl hairstyle. The play runs for 92 performances.

Dec 31 *In the Palace of the King* (NY—Republic—Drama). Lorimer Stoddard adapts F. Marion Crawford's popular novel of love in the court of King Philip II of Spain. Viola Allen and E. L. Davenport are featured. William Seymour directs. It runs for 138 performances.

1900   BRITISH PREMIERES

Jan 6 *The Masked Ball* (L—Criterion—Comedy). Clyde Fitch adapts a French farce by Alexandre Bisson and Albert Carre, *La Veglione*. Though successful in NY, this London production dismays some critics because, despite an amusing beginning of merry marital mix-ups, the

heroine, Suzanne, played by Ellaline Terris, must feign intoxication at the ball, a condition thought improper for a refined young married woman, even in a farce. Terris plays opposite Seymour Hicks, as Paul Blondet.

Feb 1 *Rupert of Hentzau* (L—St. James's—

Drama). This sequel to Anthony Hope's *The Prisoner of Zenda* has Rupert trying to regain his estates. H. B. Irving has the title role. On Feb 7, producer George Alexander begins offering matinee performances of *The Prisoner of Zenda* so spectators can see the plays back-to-back.

Feb 3 *The Messenger Boy* (L—Gaiety—Musical). George Edwardes presents a new show on the old Gaiety model. Ivan Caryll and Lionel Monckton provide the score, with lyrics by Adrian Ross and Percy Greenbank. The book, about a rascally financier who tries to discredit a rival in love, is the work of James Tanner and Alfred Murray. It wins 429 performances.

Feb 10 *Face the Music* (L—Strand—Comedy). J. H. Darnley's farce about two neighbors, one a minister and one a racehorse owner, receives its West End premier. Lettice Fairfax and Vane Featherstone are in the cast. The production earns 120 performances.

March 17 *Nurse!* (L—Globe—Comedy). Clotilde Graves's farce about a hypocondriac stars Sydney Brough. Some critics find Craven's writing "very near the knuckle." She is said to be using one of women's new-found right, that of using "risky innuendo."

April 16 *Zaza* (L—Garrick—Drama). David Belasco brings his New York production—complete with Ernest Gros's realistic settings. Mrs. Leslie Carter plays the title role, created in Paris in 1898 by Rejane. Charles Stevenson plays Dufresne, the man who deceives Zaza. There are 105 performances. A London critic refers to the realism as: "simply disgusting . . . crude and mean . . . ."

April 25 *Kitty Grey* (L—Vaudeville—Comedy). Based on *Les Fetards*, this farce deals with a puritanical wife with a frisky husband. Elliss Jeffreys, Herbert Ross and Miriam Clements plays the lead. There are 107 performances.

April 25 *An American Beauty* (L—Shaftesbury—Musical). This American production has a book by Hugh Morton and score by Gustave Kerker. Edna May, Ella Snyder and Marie George are featured in this slight love story. London audiences find this play a disappointment.

April 28 *Madame Butterfly* (L—Duke of York's—Drama). David Belasco's adaptation of John Luther Long's story opens on a double-bill with the already popular comedy, *Miss Hobbs*, by Jerome K. Jerome. Despite the contrast and its tragic theme, it is an instant success. Evelyn Millard is Cho-Cho San. Allan Aynesworth plays Pinkerton.

May 2 *You Never Can Tell* (L—Strand—Comedy). George Bernard Shaw describes his work as a "Pleasant Play." Yorke Stephens plays Valentine, the dentist interested in Gloria Clandon, played by Mabel Terry Lewis. Even critics irritated by Shaw's propagandizing find much

to amuse them in the play's characters and quips. The Stage Society gave the first performance of the play at the Royalty Theatre on Nov 26, 1899. On Jan 9, 1905, the play has its Broadway premiere at the Garrick Theatre. Arnold Daly and Drina de Wolfe are featured. The production runs four months.

May 15 John Martin-Harvey re-opens London's Prince of Wales' Theatre with a triple-bill. He plays the creator of "La Marseillaise" in *Rouget de L'isle*, by Freeman Wills and A. Fitzmaurice King. He is also Ib in *Ib and Little Christina*, based by author Basil Hood on a Hans Christian Anderson tale. Cecil Clay's spoof, *A Pantomime Rehearsal*, completes the program.

May 29 *The Fantasticks* (L—Royalty—Comedy). Mrs. Patrick Campbell appears in this English adaptation of Edmond Rostand's *Les Romanesques* about two families who pretend to be Montague and Capulet in an attempt to drive their young children into marriage. George Arliss, George Du Maurier and Winifred Fraser are also in the ensemble. Rostand's play is later adapted by Tom Jones and Harvey Schmidt to become Americas longest-running musical.

Sapho

Aug 21 *English Nell* (L—Prince of Wales's—Comedy). Frank Curzon re-opens his theatre for the fall season with this Anthony Hope and Edward Rose adaptation of the novel, *Simon Dare*, about a young man torn between his affection for Nell Gwynn and another lady. Ben Webster and Marie Tempest play leads. There are 181 performances.

Aug 30 *Sweet Nell of Old Drury* (L—Hay-

market—Drama). Paul Kester offers his melodramatic tale of Nell Gwynn aiding young lovers. Fred Terry and Julia Nielson are featured.

Sep 1 *A Debt of Honour* (L—St. James's—Drama). George Alexander produces and stars in Sydney Grundy's play about a Queen's Counsel who abandons his mistress for a suitable marriage. Some critics call this play Grundy's best.

Sep 20 *The Price of Peace* (L—Drury Lane—Drama). Cecil Raleigh's "Drama of Modern Life" surprises some critics in offering a wedding service from the Book of Common Prayer and presenting the spectacle of a statesman killing a secret service agent to protect the lives of soldiers. Henry Neville, Lettice Fairfax and Vane Featherstone are in the cast.

Sep 26 *The Lackey's Carnival* (L—Duke of York's—Comedy). Henry Arthur Jones's new play about a valet who impersonates his dead master and later blackmails the widow, is compared favorably with James Townley's *High Life Below the Stairs* in its interest in domestic situations. Edith Wynne Matthison is featured.

Sep 27 *The Wedding Guest* (L—Garrick—Drama). James Barrie's play disturbs critics and audiences because its central character is a free-living, free-thinking women who complicates the lives of her former lover and his new-wedded wife. Violet Vanbrugh and H. B. Irving star. There are 100 performances.

Oct 4 *A Parlour Match* (L—Terry's—Musical). Charles Hoyt's American success bows to "uproarious applause." It is largely plotless, built around the confusions of a descendant of Captain Kidd looking for his treasure. Plot contrivances make possible a number of songs and dances and some astonishing magical effects. J. J. Dallas, Alfred Wheelan and Christopher Bruno are featured.

Oct 9 *Mrs. Dane's Defence* (L—Wyndham's—Drama). Charles Wyndham offers Henry Arthur Jones' four-act play, with himself as Sir Daniel Carteret, a distinguised judge, interested in finding out the truth about Mrs. Dane (Lena Ashwell), who has entranced his son, Lionel. Is she really a fallen women? Mary Moore is also in the cast. Both play and acting are admired, winning 209 performances.

Oct 18 *The Noble Lord* (L—Criterion—Comedy). Robert Marshall's farcical comedy is called "Gilbertian" and therefore dated, since his comic targets include Women's Rights and the notion that Irish Members of Parliament could hold the balance of political power. Ellis Jeffreys plays the heroine. One critic suggests Marshall found this in the bottom of his desk-drawer and exhumed it only because his other plays have had such success recently.

Oct 31 *Herod* (L—Her Majesty's—Drama). Stephen Phillips' tragedy shows Herod ready for any crime to carve his way to power, including the assassination of the Sanhedrin and of his wife's brother, the popular High Priest, which turns his wife against him. Herbert Beerbohm Tree produces this lavish spectacle in blank verse, and stars in the title role. Maud Jeffries is his consort, with Eleanor Calhoun as Salome.

Nov 17 *The Swashbuckler* (L—Duke of York's—Comedy). The complicated plot requires the heroine to disguise herself as a boy, to whom the hero declares his passion for the heroine. Evelyn Millard and Herbert Waring are featured. The secret of Louis N. Parker's success as a writer of romantic comedy, says one critic, is that "he is not afraid to trust the simplicity of the average playgoer."

Nov 22 *The Wisdom of the Wise* (L—St. James's—Comedy). George Alexander produces and is featured in this comedy critiquing Society.

Nov 27 *The Second in Command* (L—Haymarket—Comedy). Captain Robert Marshall makes his new play topical, with Cyril Maude as a failed officer who finds his courage in the Boer War and wins the Victoria Cross and the love of the woman he adores (Sybil Carlisle). There are 378 performances.

Dec 11 *The Happy Hypocrite* (L—Royalty—Comedy). Max Beerbohm's fantas-

Naughty Anthony

tic one-act comedy is marred slightly for some by its cynical humor, but its basic story pleases. Frank Mills plays a Regency rake with a hideous red, blotchy face. Meeting an innocent maid in a garden, he tries to make love to her. She, however, will only respond to "a saint." He buys a saintly mask and wins her. When his cronies rip off the mask, underneath is the handsome face of a young, reformed lover. Winifred Fraser plays the flower maiden.

Countess Cathleen and *The Heather Field* (the first by Yeats; the latter by Martyn) in Dublin at the Antient Concert Rooms.

Feb 19 At the Royalty Theatre in London Mrs. Patrick Campbell revives Sudermann's *Madga*, adapted by Louis N. Parker. It runs 164 performances. This is regarded as one of the finest—if not the finest—of her roles.

Feb 26 Madame Helena Modjeska opens a three-week repertory season in New York at the Fifth Avenue Theatre. The bill includes Schiller's *Mary Stuart* and three Shakespearean plays, *Macbeth*, *Twelfth Night*, and *Much Ado About Nothing*. Cecilia Loftus, John Kellard, and John T. Malone also play leading roles.

Mar 8 Directing himself and company, Johnston Forbes-Robertson stars in *Hamlet* for the first time in New York's Knickerbocker Theatre. Gertrude Elliott is Ophelia; Ian Robertson, Claudius; Leon Quartermaine, Laertes.

March 27 At London's Haymarket Theatre, Cyril Maude and Frederick Harrison revive Sheridan's *The Rivals* to plaudits from critics and audiences.

April 19 Charles Wyndham brings his production of *Cyrano de Bergerac* to London for a premiere at Wyndham's Theatre. He plays Rostand's self-sacrificing hero. Some critics suggest his role is the only reason for doing the play as the plot is otherwise not of much interest.

April 23 At Stratford-upon-Avon, the annual Shakespeare Festival opens on the poet's birthday—a Monday this year—with *As You Like It*, directed by Frank Benson. Marion Terry is Rosalind. On the following day, *Pericles* opens, with John Coleman directing and playing the title role. Also played in the Shakespeare Memorial Theatre during the short season are *Othello*, *Macbeth*, and *The Merchant of Venice*.

May 10 Eleanora Duse returns to London for a season at the Lyceum Theatre. She

1900   REVIVALS/REPERTORIES

Jan 9 At London's Haymarket Theatre, Oliver Goldsmith's *She Stoops to Conquer* pleases audiences and critics in this revival by Cyril Maude and Frederick Harrison.

Jan 10 At Her Majesty's Theatre in London, Shakespeare's *A Midsummer Night's Dream* is revived by Herbert Beerbohm Tree, who stages and also plays Bottom. Mrs. Tree and Julia Nielson are in the cast. Tree has gone to considerable expense to provide ingenious and attractive settings, costumes, and lighting, calling on the talents of set-designers Joseph Harker, Walter Hann, and Hawes Craven, as well as costume-designer Percy Anderson.

Jan 17 The New York premiere of Henrick Ibsen's play, *The Master Builder*, is given only one performance. This is followed by a one-night showing on March 2 of Alexander Ostrovsky's powerful Russian drama, *The Storm*. Both are performed at the Carnegie Lyceum Theatre.

Feb 8 At Wyndham's Theatre in London's West End, Charles Wyndham revives Arthur Wing Pinero's *Dandy Dick*, with Alfred Bishop and Violet Vanbrugh.

Feb 16 Frank Benson brings his company to London's Lyceum Theatre for a season of Shakespeare productions with his wife

and himself in many leading roles. On opening night the play is *Henry V*. On Feb 22 it is *A Midsummer Night's Dream* with Isadora Duncan as a fairy. On March 1 *Hamlet* is presented. It is succeeded by *The Rivals* and, on March 15, by *Richard II*. On March 22 the play is *Twelfth Night* and one week later it is *Antony and Cleopatra*.

Feb 19 At Dublin's Gaiety Theatre, a week-long engagement by the Irish Literary Theatre, a little-known young company, does not excite much notice with the productions of the Irish plays of George Moore, *The Bending of the Bough*; of Edward Martyn, *Maeve*, and of Alice Milligan, *The Last Feast of the Fianna*. Only later will the significance of these performances be seen as the first steps of what will become Ireland's famed Abbey Theatre. Also to be presented this year at the Gaiety will be *Diarmuid and Grania*, by W. B Yeats and Moore, performed by Frank Benson's Shakespeare troupe. Douglas Hyde's *Casadhan tSugain* is also to be presented, the first play in Gaelic ever staged in a professional theatre. W. G. Fay directs a cast of the Gaelic League Amateur Dramatic Society. Yeats, Martyn, and Augusta, Lady Gregory, have launched the Irish Literary Theatre last May (1899), with productions of *The*

opens with Sudermann's *Magda*, played in Italian, which she has performed at the Drury Lane in 1895. On May 12, Duse offers an Italian version of Pinero's *The Second Mrs. Tanqueray*, called *La Seconda Moglie*. On May 14, she gives London its first vision of her performance of D'Annunzio's *La Gioconda*.

May 22 On its way to appear at the Paris Exhibition, the Japanese Court Theatre from Tokyo performs in London at the Coronet Theatre. On the program are three traditional dramas: *Zingoro, The Loyalist,* and *The Geisha and the Knight.* One critic notes: "The whole entertainment was so odd, so *bizarre*, and so sincere in its unconscious comicality that description can but faintly reflect its excellences and its absurdities."

May 30 Herbert Beerbohm Tree offers *Rip Van Winkle* to his admirers at Her Majesty's Theatre in London. This is a new adaptation of Washington Irving's tale, not the Boucicault version so well remembered. Unfavorable comparisons are made between the two scripts, but Tree's performance as Rip is admired.

June 16 To celebrate the Lyceum company's return to London from its American tour, Henry Irving revives a beloved, nostalgic Lyceum "domestic drama," *Olivia*, with Ellen Terry in the title role. W. G. Wills' play (1878) is based on Goldsmith's novel. Fred Terry plays the town-rake who would ruin Olivia—who is fortunately restored to her anguished father, Dr. Primrose, played by Irving. The audience repeatedly gives Irving and Terry extended ovations.

June 30 At London's Savoy Theatre, the D'Oyly Carte company revives *The Pirates of Penzance.* It wins 127 performances. On Nov 7 the company revives *Patience*, with some topical updating that is frowned upon by traditionalists.

Sep 6 Herbert Beerbohm Tree re-opens. Her Majesty's Theatre, Haymarket, for the fall season with a revival of *Julius Caesar.* He casts Murray Carson in the title role, reserving Marcus Antonius for himself.

Sep 13 At London's Lyric Theatre, the "Second Edition" of the popular musical *Florodora* opens. It is the original show, with some improvements, back after the summer holidays. Ada Reeve, with new topical verse in Lady Holyrood's song, "Tact," is encored repeatedly. The show earns 455 performances in both editions.

Sep 17 At the Garden Theatre, producer Daniel Frohman presents E. H. Sothern in his first New York appearance as Hamlet. Virginia Harned is his Ophelia.

Oct 23 At New York's Academy of Music, James O'Neill opens a long-running revival of *Monte Cristo,* an adaptation of the Alexandre Dumas novel in which he stars. The audience cheered what the *NY Times* calls "a bit of the old school of acting. . . ."

Nov 26 Sarah Bernhardt and Benoit Constant Coquelin open a five-week engagement in French at the Garden Theatre in New York. Mme. Bernhardt plays two breeches-roles: *L'Aiglon* and *Hamlet*; she also impersonates Camille, Tosca and Roxanne.

Dec 22 Lewis Waller and William Mollison are hailed for the "genuine and complete success" of their staging of *Henry V* at London's Lyceum Theatre. Waller plays King Henry, with Mollison as Pistol.

Dec 26 In her native city of Birmingham, Vesta Tilley delights her many fans playing the title-role in the Christmas pantomime of *Dick Whittington.* As principal boy, she sings such songs as "The Way of the World" and the coster-song, "Happy Hampton," giving each a special character. Famed as a male-impersonator, she is widely praised in this role, making the production "the leading provincial pantomime."

Dec 26 This year in London, the Drury Lane's annual Christmas pantomime is compounded of two fairy-tales: *Sleeping Beauty and the Beast.* Dan Leno and Herbert Campbell are featured. Hickory Wood and Arthur Collins are the authors. At the Hippodrome, its first pantomime is *Cinderella*, by W. H. Risqué. The new, improved Grand Theatre re-opens with Geoffrey Thorn's *Robinson Crusoe.* Emily Stevens is St. George in the Standard's *St. George and the Dragon.* Alice Lloyd is Cinderella in the Pavilion's pantomime. Winifred Hale is Dick Whittington at the Coronet.

1900 BIRTHS/DEATHS/DEBUTS

Nov 20 American playwright Charles Hale Hoyt (b. 1860) is dead. Hoyt is acclaimed for his farcical comedies depicting typical characters in contemporary society. Among the most popular were *A Texas Steer, A Case of Wine,* and *A Trip to Chinatown,* whose 650 consecutive performances set a record in 1891.

Nov 22 Today marks the passing of Sir Arthur Sullivan (b. 1842), composer of the ever-popular scores for the Gilbert & Sullivan operettas. Sullivan's somewhat frustrated ambition was to be known as a serious musician, rather than as a purveyor of comic operas. In succeeding decades, it will be his fate to have his serious music remembered most in the selection called "The Lost Chord" and in "Onward, Christian Soldiers."

Nov 30 Author-playwright Oscar Wilde (b. 1854) dies in Paris. International fame came to Wilde with the production of his most satiric play, *The Importance of Being Earnest. Lady Windermere's Fan, A Woman of No Importance,* and *An Ideal Husband* are among his notable comedies.

1900 THEATERS/PRODUCTIONS

In Britain this year patents are granted for these theatre effects or devices, among others: B. H. Jackson's double-stages, riding on rails so that when one moves into view, the other slides into the wings; E. Downes' small revolving stage, mounted on a central spindle and ball-bearings, set in motion by an animal or a person walking on it.

Claude L. Hagen receives a U.S. patent for his system of treadmills, set at right-angles to the footlights for the chariot-race in *Ben-Hur,* as well as a patent for the three moving panoramas—one at the back of the stage and one at each side—used with the treadmills. Morgan Sherwood's patent is for an apparatus simulating a person being burned at the stake. Arden S. Fitch devises a system using two transparent screens, one behind the other, and stereopticon projectors to create the illusion of depth.

Jan 15 The London Hippodrome opens with a programme of circus and variety. Frank Matcham is the architect of this theatre, which includes a huge tank for water shows. Moss Empires Ltd. is the management. (Circus shows will cease after 1909 and between 1949 and 1951 the theatre will house the London Folies Bergeres. In 1958, it will be converted to a restaurant-cabaret, The Talk of the Town.)

Feb 1 After interior re-construction, London's St. James's Theatre re-opens with *Rupert of Hentzau.* The theatre has no boxes other than the Royal Box and one opposite; and auditorium and stage are raked; the stage has been lowered, and the roof raised, giving a stage to roof height of 74 feet.

Feb 3 This week, *The Era* reports, no less than 104 touring companies are on the road in Britain. Frank Benson's company is at the Theatre Royal, Dublin. There are three companies of *The Sign of the Cross* touring, one of them, Ben Greet's. There are also three companies each of *The Belle of New York* and the pantomime *Dick Whittington.*

Feb 23 Olga Nethersole, the star of *Sapho,* together with her leading man, Hamilton Revelle, her manager, Marcus Mayer, and

Oscar Wilde

Theodore Moss, lessee of New York's Wallack's Theatre, are arrested for public nuisance. The arrests are based on charges that the play portrays the life of a dissolute woman in a way offensive to public morals. In the course of the action, moreover, Nethersole permits Revelle to carry her up a flight of stairs in an improper manner. Robert Mackay, of the *New York World*, and the Rev. Phoebe Hanaford, have made the official complaint. On March 5, the police close the play after only 29 performances.

April 7 *Sapho* re-opens in New York for an additional run of 55 performances.

April 7 British theatre architect Frank Matcham is reported to have many irons in the fire. In some months, the Grand Theatre in Islington will reopen, with Matcham's reconstruction after the recent conflagration. Also among his projects for reconstruction or alteration are The Grand Theatre, Liverpool; the Theatre Royal, Newcastle, and the Theatre Royal, Portsmouth. New theatres will be built in Holloway, in the Pleasure Gardens, Folkestone, and in London in St. Martin's Lane for Charles Frohman.

May 24 The refurbished Novelty Theatre in London re-opens as the Great Queen Street Theatre under the management of W. S. Penley. The first production is a revival of *A Little Ray of Sunshine*.

June 15 With the 1899—1900 Broadway season closed, it's time to take stock. There have been 115 productions in some 22 theatres and performance venues. Five companies offered a total of 135 productions in repertory; 23 of these were revivals of productions already mounted. There have been 8 musicals, with one revival; 28 dramas—including two stagings of *Quo Vadis* at the same time; 25 comedies, with one revival; 8 farces, 2 one-acts, 4 comic operas, 1 vaudeville, 1 burlesque, and 3 extravaganzas. The season's last opening has been on April 30. Lack of air-conditioning in theatres and the custom of some major players to take summer vacations guarantees there will be little theatre activity on Broadway this summer.

Sep 6 Long without a proper theatre, tonight the citizens of Scotland's Perth see the opening of the City of Perth Theatre and Opera House, designed by William Alexander of Dundee. Wallace's opera, *Maritana*, is presented by J. W. Turner's English opera ensemble. This house will be badly damaged by fire in 1924.

Sep 20 Among the scenic effects admired by critics in Cecil Raleigh's *The Price of Peace* are the emergency ward of St. Thomas's Hospital, The House of Commons, the interior of Westminster Abbey, and the sinking of a yacht. Designers include Henry Emden, W. Perkins, M. Cleary, Bruce Smith, R. Caney, and Julian Hicks. The number and variety of dresses on the terraces at Niagara and in the Abbey are praised, as is the scenery, which is "beyond description," according to *The Era's* reviewer. The modelling and building up of the Abbey sets and those for the Derwent conservatory and library win praise, as does the effect of space in the Commons. The "sensational effect when the yacht slinks slowly beneath the waters will be the talk of London," readers are promised.

Sep 23 In Kansas City, Missouri, the Standard Theatre opens. It is initially dedicated to burlesque, but it will also be home to legitimate attractions over the years. In 1923, it is renamed the Missouri-Shubert, featuring repertory, vaudeville, boxing, and wrestling. Slated for demotion in 1973, it is saved and re-opens in November 1981, restored outside and reconstructed inside. Re-named the Folly Theatre in 1942, it keeps that name as a member of the League of Historic American Theatres.

Sep 27 Oscar Hammerstein opens his seventh theatre, the Republic Theatre (1,100 seats). It is located on the north side of 42 Street, west of 7th Avenue, in New York City. The stage is 35 feet wide, 32 feet deep and 75 feet to the all-motorized gridiron.

Oct 15 The Illinois Theatre opens at 65 East Jackson Street in Chicago. Designed by Wilson and Marshall, it seats 1,304. A Greek revival exterior conceals a German baroque interior. Julia Marlowe stars in Clyde Fitch's Civil War drama, *Barbara Freitchie*.

Nov *Whitaker's Almanack* lists the following London Theatres: Adelphi (Strand), Avenue (Northumberland Ave.), Britannia (Hoxton), Comedy (Panton St.), Court (Sloane Square), Covent Garden (Bow St.), Criterion (Piccadilly Circus), Daly's (Leicester Square), Drury Lane (Catherine St.), Duke of York's (St. Martin's Lane), Gaiety (Strand), Garrick (Charing Cross Rd.), Globe (Newcastle St.), Grand (Islington), Great Queen Street (Penley's), Haymarket, Her Majesty's (Tree's), London Hippodrome (Cranbourne St.), Lyceum (Wellington St.), Lyric (Shaftesbury Ave.), Olympic (Wych St.), Opera Comique (Strand), Prince of Wales's (Coventry St.), Royalty (Dean St.), Savoy (Victoria Embankment), St. James's (King), Shaftesbury (Shaftesbury Ave.), Standard (Bishopsgate), Strand (Strand), Surrey (Blackfriars Rd.), Terry's (Strand), Vaudeville (Strand), and Wyndham's (Cranbourne St.).

Nov 13 At the London Hippodrome, where novelties are always sought to vary an already varied program, Walter Gibbons combines the new "Living-pictures" with the phonograph, to give the effect of talking-pictures. As the American Comedy Four are seen to be singing "Sally in Our Alley," their voices, synchronized with the moving pictures, can be clearly heard. The phonograph also provides cheers and other sound-effects for animated pictures of a trainload of soldiers steaming out of the station. The Hippodrome gymnasts and animal acts are also good, especially the bear which shoots a pistol with great calm.

Dec There are 392 legitimate theatre productions on tour in America as of the first week of this month. In 1928, there will be only 86.

Jan 7 *The Girl from Up There* (NY—Herald Square—Musical). Hugh Morton writes the book and Gustav Kerker composes the music for this Charles Frohman "Girl" Show about a girl who has been frozen for 500 years. Edna May and Otis Harlan head the cast.

Jan 14 *When Knighthood Was in Flower* (NY—Criterion—Drama). Based on Charles Major's novel, Paul Kester's four-act dramatization brings to the stage a best-selling tale of medieval chivalry. Julia Marlowe stars in producer Charles Frohman's cast.

Jan 21 *The Climbers* (NY—Bijou—Drama). In this biting expose of high society staged by the playwright, Clyde Fitch, actress-manager Amelia Bingham achieves stardom. She is supported by Robert Edeson and Madge Carr Cook, among others. Its first scene, following a funeral, shocks because all the women appear in deep mourning, regarded as both depressing and in poor taste. On September 5, 1903 Fitch's play opens in London at the Comedy Theatre with Sydney Valentine, J.L. Mackay, Lily Hanbury and Lottie Venne in the cast.

Feb 4 *Captain Jinks of the Horse Marines* (NY—Garrick—Comedy). Both as author and director, Clyde Fitch returns in less than a fortnight. Ethel Barrymore wins stardom as Madame Trentoni, a singer, and H. Reeves Smith is Captain Jinks. Edward Unitt creates the settings and Percy Anderson the costumes. While the writer for the *NY Times* says that Ethel Barrymore: "is not a histrionic genius . . . and her good natural gifts have not yet been fully developed" he predicts that "she is a young woman who will bear a good deal of watching."

Feb 5 *Under Two Flags* (NY—Garden—Drama). Paul Potter dramatizes Ouida's popular novel for producer Charles Frohman. Blanche Bates stars in this tale of period romance, staged by David Belasco.

Feb 11 *On the Quiet* (NY—Madison Square—Comedy). Augustus Thomas' hit comedy based on a real incident, is about a man who secretly marries his fiancee despite his family's desire that he finish Yale. On September 27, 1905 the play opens in London at the Comedy Theatre. William Collier plays the leading role, supported by his American company.

Feb 25 *The Governor's Son* (NY—Savoy—Musical). George M. Cohan acts, sings, dances, and directs himself—as well as a large ensemble, including the family: Jerry J. Cohan, Nellie Cohan, and Josephine Cohan. The complicated plot is merely an excuse for Cohan's clever enlargement of the family vaudeville act. The *NY Times* praises one of its songs: "Oh, Mr. Moon" but is less enthusiastic about the show. "As a vaudeville show it was one that was rather above the average. . . ."

March 4 *To Have and To Hold* (NY—Knickerbocker—Drama). Mary Johnston's best-selling novel of the same name, is dramatized by E. F. Boddington. Producer Charles Frohman uses this drama of Colonial America as the vehicle for Robert Loraine's New York debut.

Sep 2 *The Rogers Brothers in Washington* (NY—Knickerbocker—Musical). The popular comedy team of Gus and Max Rogers star in a plot about a present given to the wrong person. Among those featured are William West, Pat Rooney and James Cherry. Ben Teal stages.

Sep 5 *Hoity Toity* (NY—Weber and Fields' Music Hall—Musical). The latest comedy revue vehicle for the team of Joe Weber and Lew Fields also features De Wolf Hopper, Lillian Russell, and Fay Templeton, in some Monte Carlo mixups with New York delicatessen owners and pretty girls. The second act is packed with burlesques of current plays. Audiences do not know that offstage Weber is no longer talking to Fields, a permanent breach. "As usual, there was a little too much of everything," says the *NY Times*.

Sep 16 *The Ladies Paradise* (NY—Metropolitan Opera House—Musical). With book by George Dance and score by Ivan Caryll, this show is notable as the first

Under Two Flags

musical comedy produced on the Met stage. In it, a young lord leads an opera-singer to the altar, over family objections. It has a ballet of 250 dancers, supporting performers such as Queenie Vassar, John Hyams and La Torjada.

Sept 23 *The Auctioneer* (NY—Bijou—Drama). David Belasco produces and directs his own play about a Jewish auctioneer on Hester Street in New York, who suddenly grows rich and is thereafter forced back into poverty by a villainous broker. It provides a debut role for David Warfield as a star and begins a long association between the producer and the performer. John Young creates the sets.

Sep 30 *The Liberty Belles* (NY—Madison Square—Musical). Klaw and Erlanger produce this Harry B. Smith show which takes place in a girls dormitory and a cooking school. Elsie Ferguson, Lotta Faust, Harry Davenport and Etta Butler are in the cast. The show runs 13 weeks.

Oct 14 *If I Were King* (NY—Garden—Drama). Produced by Daniel Frohman, this swashbuckling drama proves the first big hit for its star, E. H. Sothern, long a member of Frohman's Lyceum Theatre Stock Company. Based on the life and poems of François Villon, it is author Justin Huntly McCarthy's greatest success. His one-time wife, Cecilia Loftus, is the feminine lead. The *NY Times* terms it "one of the finest romantic pieces . . ." on the contemporary stage.

Oct 14 *The Little Duchess* (NY—Casino—Musical). Producer Florenz Ziegfeld, Jr. presents his wife, Anna Held, in a show about a duchess who is really an actress hiding from creditors. It runs for 17 weeks, followed by an extended tour. Returning to the Grand Opera House a year later, the show is so long that the plot is eliminated to allow time for the musical numbers. The book is by Harry B. Smith and score by Reginald DeKoven. George Marion stages, with sets by Ernest Albert.

Oct 28 *Eben Holden* (NY—Savoy—Drama). Edward E. Rose adapts Irving Bacheller's best-selling novel. Produced by Charles Frohman, it stars E.M. Holland.

Nov 4 *The Way of the World* (NY—Hammerstein's Victoria—Drama). Clyde Fitch's melodrama of New York social life features the introduction of an automobile in Central Park as a means of bringing characters together. Elsie de Wolfe, Frank Mills, Vincent Serrano and Alison Skipworth are in the cast.

Nov 4 *The Sleeping Beauty and the Beast* (NY—Broadway—Musical). Reworked for the American stage, this show essentially a British Christmas pantomine, is the invention of J. Hickory Wood and Arthur Collins. Notable for a long run (241 per-

Hoity Toity

formances), this Klaw and Erlanger production features ballets by Ernest D'Auban and direction by Joseph Brooks.

Nov 11 *Quality Street* (NY—Knickerbocker—Comedy). James Barrie's play about the effects of social conventions on human relationships is produced by Charles Frohman, with Maude Adams as star. It runs 64 performances.

Nov 18 *Colorado* (NY—Wallack's—Drama). Augustus Thomas's play about miners in the old West features John Albaugh, Jr., Violet Rand and Wilton Lackaye. The *NY Times* calls it "tardy and unconvincing. . . ."

Dec 2 *Alice of Old Vincennes* (NY—Garden—Drama). Edward E. Rose adapts Maurice Thompson's best-selling novel of Revolutionary War America for producer Charles Frohman. Virginia Harned has the title role. Cecil B. DeMille is also in the cast.

Dec 2 *Beaucaire* (NY—Harold Square—Comedy). Booth Tarkington and Evelyn G. Sutherland adapt Tarkington's book about a French aristocrat in disguise. Richard Mansfield directs and stars.

Dec 4 *The Girl and the Judge* (NY—Lyceum—Drama). Another Fitch drama, this Charles Frohman production stars Annie Russell. The author, as usual, stages, with sets by Edward Unitt. Fitch shows a young girl who forces her kleptomaniac mother to reveal her guilt. The mother is brought before a judge who has to choose between

his legal duty and love for the girl.

Dec 10 *The Marriage Game* (NY—Hammerstein's Victoria—Drama). Clyde Fitch adapts Emile Augier's French drama, *Le Marriage d'Olympe*, written as an answer to *La Dame aux Camelias*. A young man ruins his life by marrying a courtesan without the graces and sensitivity of a Marguerite Gauthier. The cast includes Sadie Martinot, Guy Bates Post, Junius B. Booth, Winchell Smith, and Annie Yeamans. It is panned by the *NY Times*: " . . . [the play] is undoubtedly the worst that Mr. Fitch has ever placed before the audience . . . he should be ashamed of having done so."

Dec 25 *Du Barry* (NY—Criterion—Drama). David Belasco produces and directs his play, starring his discovery and protege, Mrs. Leslie Carter. The production achieves 165 performances. "To those who assert that there is no such thing as an 'art' of acting—that the theatre is but a museum for the shrewd exploiting of the personality and idiosyncracy of the player—Mrs. Carter stands as a concrete refutation," says the *NY Times*.

Dec 30 *A Gentleman of France* (NY—Wallack's—Drama). Harriet Ford adapts Stanley Weyman's popular novel. Kyrle Bellew stars and shares staging duties with E. D. Lyons. The cast includes Edgar Selwyn, Eleanor Robson (later Mrs. August Belmont), and Frank Aiken. Liebler and Company produce the show, which lasts for 120 performances.

to a madhouse but is foiled. William Haviland plays the villain.

March 29 *The Man of Destiny* (L—Comedy—Comedy). George Bernard Shaw's sketch about the young Napoleon debuts in the West End.

April 11 *The Wilderness* (L—St. James's—Comedy). Actor-manager George Alexander stars in H.V. Esmond's play about a wealthy, mature man who hates hypocrisy and seeks love of a natural, unaffected young woman. Eva Moore plays opposite. Also in the cast are C. Aubrey Smith, Dora Barton and Julie Opp.

April 23 *The Girl from Up There* (L—Duke of York's—Musical). With its American book by Hugh Morton and its score by Gustave Kerker, this show is merely an excuse for songs and dances. Edna May heads the American cast. The show earns 102 performances.

April 25 *The Man from Blankley's* (L—Prince of Wales's—Comedy). Charles Hawtrey plays a Scottish peer who's mistaken for a man hired by a socially ambitious couple to play an aristocrat at their dinner party. Henry Ford and Fanny Brough are in the cast. F. Anstey's comedy earns 117 performances.

April 27 *The Queen's Double* (L—Garrick—Drama). Charles Cartwright's scandalous story about the "River of Diamonds," the necklace purchased for the French Queen and stolen by a swindler, has Jeanette Steer as Marie Antoinette and her double. Also in the cast are Lettice Fairfax, Mrs. Sam Sothern, Conway Tearle, and Luigi Lablache.

May 1 *The Night of the Party* (L—Avenue—Comedy). Weedon Grossmith is featured in his play about a gentleman's servant who is a 20th centruy Figaro. This is another of Grossmith's tales of the relationships between masters and servants. There are 205 performances.

May 2 *A Woman in the Case* (L—Court—Comedy). George R. Sims and Leonard Merrick have written this spritely comedy about a stolen kiss. Gertrude Kingston stars. Also in the cast are Frederick Kerr as the husband, and James Erskine as the masked wooer.

May 20 *A Royal Rival* (L—Coronet—Drama). Gerald Du Maurier bases his romantic play on Dumanoir and D'Ennery's *Don Cesar de Bazan*. The plot deals with the King of Spain and Don Cesar switching roles. Lewis Waller, Norman McKinnel and Walter Mollison are featured.

June 1 *The Silver Slipper* (L—Lyric—Musical). Owen Hall writes the book, W.H. Risque the lyrics and Leslie Stuart the music for this show which owes a nod to W.S. Gilbert's *Happy Land*. But it is mainly an excuse for lovely costumes, amusing songs and attractive dancing. There are 197 performances.

June 3 *Tally-Ho!* (L—Hippodrome—Musical). In addition to the customary

1901   BRITISH PREMIERES

Feb 6 *The Awakening* (L—St. James's—Comedy). C. Haddon Chambers depicts his hero as effete, shallow and perverse, suggesting that that is what Society admires. George Alexander stars, with Fay Davis and H.B. Irving in the cast.

Feb 11 *A Cigarette-Maker's Romance* (L—

Court—Drama). F. Marion Crawford's novel is adapted by Charles Hannan and produced by John Martin-Harvey, who stars as Count Skariatine. In a typical turn-of-the-century plot, the count has lost his memory and is working in a Munich cigarette factory, while his cousin Anton has seized his estates. Anton tries to send him

performing animals, the clowns Elton and Marcellino and other circus entertainments, the Hippodrome now offers a four-scene "hunting sketch," based on types to be found at a typical English fox-hunt. Frank Parker produces this show by W. H. Risque and Carl Kiefert.

June 17 *The Toreodor* (L—Gaiety—Musical). Edmund Payne plays a young man, looking for employment in Biarritz, who impersonates a handsome toreodor at the behest of a lovely young lady who's a Carlist revolutionary. It is the work of the successful musical team of Tanner and Nicholls (book), Ross and Greenbank (lyrics), and Caryll and Monckton (music). In the cast are George Grossmith, Jr., Claire Romaine, Sybil Arundale, and Gertie Millar. This runs 675 performances.

Aug 27 *Beckey Sharp* (L—Prince of Wales's—Drama). Marie Tempest plays the title role in this dramatization of Thackeray's *Vanity Fair*, adapted by Robert Hichens and Cosmo Gordon Lennox. Harley Granville-Barker is also in the cast. There are 169 performances.

Sep 7 *Kitty Grey* (L—Apollo—Musical). J. Smyth Pigott's comedy is turned into a musical with songs by Augustus Barrett, Howard Talbot and Lionel Monckton. There are 220 performances—twice

as many as for the comedy.

Sep 21 *Iris* (L—Garrick—Drama). Arthur Wing Pinero's five-act play has 115 performances. This is Pinero's first "Edwardian" drama, a triangle, in which Fay Davis plays a title-role of a young weak-willed widow who will lose a fortune if she marries again. She is finally thrown out by her betrayed Spanish-Jewish protector, Maldonado, played by Oscar Asche, who wrecks his flat when she is gone.

Oct 5 *A Chinese Honeymoon* (L—Strand—Musical). The show about Englishmen flirting in China, has a libretto by George Dance and a score by Howard Talbot. It has an extremely long run of 1,075 performances.

Oct 24 *The Last of the Dandies* (L—His Majesty's—Comedy). American playwright Clyde Fitch's latest work has its world premiere in London. Actor-manager Herbert Beerbohm Tree produces this comedy of manners. The show runs 103 performances, but it is not later produced in New York.

Oct 29 *Sheerluck Jones* (L—Terry's—Comedy). The title burlesques William Gillette's successful mystery melodrama, *Sherlock Holmes*. Its authors, Malcolm Watson and Edward La Serre, describe it as "drama criticism in four paragraphs."

Benson. On April 22, *King John* is played, followed the next day by *Richard II*, effectively the "Birthday Play." These are succeeded by *Henry IV, Part 2, Henry V, Henry VI, Part 2,* and *Richard III* to make a "Week of Kings." This is the first time a historical cycle has been played at the Shakespeare Memorial Theatre. Four other Benson Shakespeare productions are offered, plus Goldsmith's *She Stoops to Conquer* and Sheridan's *School for Scandal.*

May 13 Ibsen's *Pillars of Society*, translated by William Archer, has a Monday matinee performance in London at the Garrick Theatre. Oscar Asche directs and appears with Annie Webster.

June 3 Summer has come and so has Sarah Bernhardt on her annual tour to London. She opens with Rostand's *L'Aiglon*, playing the title-role, Le Duc de Reichstadt, with Constant Coquelin as Flambeau. Later, she plays Camille and Phèdre.

June 17 Mme. Rejane opens her London season of French drama at the Coronet, with *Sapho*, based on Alphonse Daudet's novel by A. Belot. On June 24, she offers *La Course de Flambeau*, by Paul Hervieu.

July 4 For the first time in Britain, *The Shogun, A Tale of Old Japan* is performed at the Criterion Theatre in London. The players are from the Imperial Court Theatre in Tokyo. The play deals with 14th century power struggles. It is preceded by *Zingoro*, in which a sculptor falls in love with a geisha. Between the plays, La Loie Fuller performs her "posture dance" to the delight of the audience.

Nov 21 The Elizabethan Stage Society presents a production of Shakespeare's *Henry V* in the theatre in London's Burlington Gardens. William Poel, the prime-mover in the Society, advocates presenting Shakespeare's works in the way they were done in the Elizabethan era.

Dec 14 Christmas is fast approaching. London's Garrick Theatre prepares for it with revivals of *Shockheaded Peter* and *The Man Who Stole the Castle*. On Dec 18, *Bluebell in Fairyland* is shown at the Vaudeville Theatre. Seymour Hicks and Ellaline Terris play the leads in this pantomime fantasy by Hicks, with music by Walter Slaughter. On Dec 19, *The Swineherd and the Princess* is featured at the Royalty Theatre. Alfred England and Avalon Collard base their holiday pantomine on Hans Christian Andersen's tale. On Dec 23, at the Avenue Theatre, *Gulliver's Travels* provides a holiday treat. Swift's satire is adapted by George Grossmith, Jr., and the music is composed by Augustus Barrett and Oscar Eve. On Dec 26, Master Vivion Thomas plays the title role in the revival of *Little Lord Fauntleroy* at the Wyndham Theatre. Frances Hodgson-Burnett's story remains popular. On Dec 26, the pantomime, *Blue Beard* is revived at the Drury Lane Theatre.

1901   REVIVALS/REPERTORIES

Jan 2 In London at the Comedy Theatre, Frank Benson revives *The Taming of the Shrew*. He and Constance Benson play Petruchio and Katharine. On Jan 19, he plays Shylock to Eleanor Calhoun's Portia in *The Merchant of Venice*. On Feb 12, the production is *Coriolanus*. On Feb 27, Benson revives *As You Like it*. These productions alternate with a season of German-language dramas.

Feb 5 For his revival of *Twelfth Night* at Her Majesty's Theatre—the name has not yet been changed—Herbert Beerbohm Tree adjusts the antiquated phrases and allusions to modern tastes. Says one critic: "He has adorned but not overloaded the piece with dressing and mounting." Tree's directorial hand is aided by Joseph Harker's impressive settings. Tree is Malvolio; Lily Brayton plays Viola, and Lionel Brough is Sir Toby Belch. Percy Anderson's costumes are described as lavish and sumptuous.

Feb 12 Marie Tempest appears in London at the Prince of Wales's Theatre in *Peg Woffington*. This is actually a reworking of Tom Taylor's well-known play, *Masks and Faces*.

Feb 27 At London's Royalty Theatre, Mrs. Patrick Campbell revives Arthur Wing Pinero's *The Notorious Mrs. Ebbsmith*. George Arliss, Gerald Du Maurier, and Winifred Fraser are also in the company.

March 4 At the New York Academy of Music, *Uncle Tom's Cabin* is revived by William A. Brady. This most popular American drama is based on Harriett Beecher Stowe's novel. Wilton Lackaye is Uncle Tom, supported by Alice Evans, Maud Raymond, and Mrs. Annie Yeamans.

March 25 Edward Gordon Craig opens a brief engagement of stage works he has directed and designed at London's Coronet Theatre. His mother, Ellen Terry, appears in *Nance Oldfield*. Also presented are Purcell's *Dido and Aeneas* and *The Masque of Love*. Martin Shaw conducts. *The Era* writes that in *Dido and Aeneas* Craig "was responsible for the crudest appointments and a setting that did nothing to help the imagination . . ."

April 15 Henry Irving revives and stars in *Coriolanus* at London's Lyceum Theatre. The production is admired as an evocation of "the power and gravity of ancient Roman government." On May 27 he gives *Robespierre*, adapted from Victorien Sardou's French play by his son Laurence Irving. On June 10 Irving plays Napoleon in a revival of Sardou and Monear's *Madame San-Gene*. Two weeks later W.G. Wills' *King Charles I* is revived.

April 15 At Stratford-upon-Avon, the annual Shakespeare Festival opens with *Much Ado About Nothing*, staged by Frank

Feb 13 On her birthday, music hall artiste Marie Lloyd bids farewell to the stage at a special tribute at the Tivoli Restaurant in London.

April 3 English theatrical impresario Richard D'Oyly Carte (b. 1844) dies in London. D'Oyly Carte encouraged the early collaboration of Gilbert and Sullivan and founded the light opera company which bears his name. The Savoy Theatre in London—the first to be lighted by electricity—was built by him.

June 2 American actor, playwright, and producer James A. Herne (b. 1839) is dead. Herne made his first appearance on stage in 1859. His first important play was *Margaret Fleming*, which starred his wife, Katharine Corcoran. Later revivals featured his daughter Chrystal in the title role. *Shore Acres*, his next play, became one of the most popular of his day.

June 18 Playwright-director Denis Johnston is born in Dublin.

Sep 7 British actor Osmond Tearle (b. 1852) dies today.

Richard D'oyly Carte

1901 THEATERS/PRODUCTIONS

In Britain this year patents are granted for these theatre effects or devices, among others: G. Purvis's endless panorama which rolls over horizontal rather than vertical rollers; A. Braatz's one-man comic horse-costume, with springs, rods, and levers to animate the hindquarters, rather than a second performer; Mariano Fortuny's system of projecting transparencies of interiors and exteriors without using lenses, instead employing light sources backed by parabolic reflectors. Fortuny, an Italian designer famed for his pleated silk gowns, also devises projection screens faced with silk, somewhat roughened in texture, to diffuse the images and angled to bounce the light off the stage floor.

U. S. patents granted this year are for: David L. Towers has designed treadmills similar to those Claude Hagen has created for *Ben-Hur*, with the refinement of dustboxes and blowers in the stage-floor for greater realism. Samuel Combs devises a system for showing a flood without wetting the scenery; the audience sees the action through a thin glass tank in which the water rises just behind the proscenium arch.

Jan 22 The Lord Chamberlain sends letters to all the London theatres licensed by his office asking that out of respect for the death of Queen Victoria no theatres shall play this evening. At the Drury Lane Theatre, the cast is in costume, but Arthur Collins, the manager, makes the announcement to the audience before the play has begun. At the Pavilion Theatre, *Cinderella* is already underway when it is halted for the sad news. Patrons have their money refunded or are given credit for a later performance.

Feb 2 Trade unionism in the theatre, reports this week's *Era*, is familiar enough to those who have toured the States but it is a new issue in British theatre. The Stage Workers' and Musicians' Unions are becoming very active, also asking support of various trades councils in winning their demands. In a dispute with the management of the Shakespeare Theatre in London's suburbs, musicians ask a minimum of 6 shillings per performance. Stage workers ask for 2 shillings a performance and 4 shillings for day-work at the theatre. In the same issue of *The Era*, "A Jaded Actor" writes to complain of unneccesary (and unpaid) rehearsals.

Feb 21 The new Apollo Theatre in London's West End has been designed by Lewen Sharp in French Renaissance style. It is decorated by T. Simpson—the sculptor—and Hubert Hooydonck, whose setdrop represents a picture from Watteau. It seats 1,200. The theatre opens with *The Belle of Bohemia*.

April 22 London's Imperial Theatre reopens after extensive refurbishing by its new owner, Lillie Langtry. The cost is said to be about £ 40,000. Frank Verity is the architect and the opening play is *A Royal Necklace*, starring Mrs. Langtry.

June 15 Looking back on the Broadway season 1900–1901 just completed, there have been at least 100 productions, with 14 revivals, in Burns Mantle's accounting. On this date, however, the *New York Dramatic Mirror* counts 144 new plays and 48 revivals, not including some 21 student shows. The *Mirror's* roster includes vaudeville productions, non-Broadway houses, and borough theatres. On Broadway, there have been 10 musicals, 2 extravaganzas, 43 dramas—with 9 revivals, 10 comedies, 7 farces—plus 4 musical farces, 4 comic operas, 2 operettas, 2 vaudevilles, 3 one-acts, and 3 burlesques. In repertory, two companies have presented 10 productions, 4 of them revivals. Productions have used some 22 performance venues.

Aug 29 Lew Dockstader's minstrel show opens the newly-renovated Princess Theatre in Toronto, Canada. Built on the site of the former Academy of Music (destroyed by fire in 1895), the Princess will host many great British and American touring companies. In the 1904–5 season, William Gillette will make his first Toronto appearance here; Forbes Robertson and Gertrude Elliott will open their second American tour here, and Mrs. Patrick Campbell is to appear in Sardou's *The Sorceress*.

Sept 11 After extensive reconstruction, supervised by Ernest Runz, The Royal Adelphi Theatre, on London's Strand, reopens as the Century Theatre, managed by Tom B. Davis. The opening production is an American musical comedy, *The Whirl of the Town*. The renovated theatre has a capacity of 1297.

Oct 7 Richard Mansfield opens Philadelphia's new Garrick Theatre, on Juniper and Chestnut Streets, with *Monsieur Beaucaire*. The theatre seats 1,516 and has a proscenium opening of 36' wide by 34' high. It is designed by Willis Hale; its cornerstone has been laid by Mansfield. Spacious, with expansive public spaces, the theatre even has a log-burning fireplace in the lobby. It is equipped with a Hook and Hastings Concert Grand Organ.

Nov 19 Today marks the founding of the Harvard Theatre Collection, one day to be regarded as the oldest theatre and dance research collection in the world.

Jan 6 *The Toreodor* (NY—Knickerbocker—Musical). With music by Ivan Caryll and Lionel Monckton, this show stars Francis Wilson. For 146 performances, audiences watch a discharged servant battle the bulls and get mixed up with a mad anarchist's bomb plots. Although this is really an English tale, set in Spain, an American "coon song" is worked into the production.

Jan 27 *Dolly Varden* (NY—Herald Square—Musical). Author Stanislaus Stange and composer Julian Edwards stage their own show with such verve that Dolly Varden becomes a fashion by-word. Lulu Glaser and Van Rensselaer Wheeler are featured. The story is from Charles Dickens's *Barnaby Rudge*, with some borrowings from *The Country Wife*. The show has 154 performances.

Jan 27 *Maid Marian* (NY—Garden—Musical). A sequel to the very popular comic opera, *Robin Hood*, this Reginald De Koven score is wedded to a Harry B. Smith book.

March 11 *The Sultan of Sulu* (Chicago—Studebaker—Musical). Author George Ade spoofs the attempts of Americans after the Spanish-American War to bring the virtues of New England schooling and U.S. moral values to Moslems in the Sulu Islands. The show opens Dec 29 on Broadway, where it has a long run.

March 17 *Soldiers of Fortune* (NY—Savoy—Drama). Playwright Augustus Thomas adapts Richard Harding Davis's adventure story to the stage. Robert Edeson stars in this production. It runs 11 weeks. This is one of the many dramatizations of popular novels to come to the New York and London stage. The trend falls off after World War I, when more original scripts are published.

May 5 *The Wild Rose* (NY—Knickerbocker—Musical). The song "My Little Gypsy Maid," sung by Irene Bentley, is introduced. The book is by Harry B. Smith

Dolly Varden

and George Hobart; the score by Ludwig Englander. In the cast are Eddie Foy, Louis Kelso, and Evelyn Florence (Nesbit). D. Frank Dodge does the settings. There are 136 performances.

June 5 *The Chaperons* (NY—New York—Musical). Music publisher Isidore Witmark composes the score; Frederic Ranken, book and lyrics. Trixie Friganza and Eva Tanguay are featured. Miss Tanguay introduces her song hit, "My Sambo." It tours extensively although it manages only 49 performances in New York. Disagreements with the Theatre Syndicate keep Witmark from ever doing another Broadway show.

July 3 *The Defender* (NY—Herald Square—Musical). With words by Allen Lowe and music by Charles Dennee, the show attracts attention, partly through Blanche Ring's interpretation of her first hit song, "In the Good Old Summertime." The plot centers around Jellie Canvas, who, trying to foil the villainous plot of Ivory D. Queers to fix a yacht race, is tied to the rails. Her rescue is shown in a Biograph film clip. Frank Smithson stages and D. Frank Dodge creates the settings.

Aug 29 *Sally in Our Alley* (NY—Broadway—Musical). This musical deals with Sally, a Jewish Miss Fix-it and her father, Izzy, who runs the Heterogeneous Emporium. The novelty song, "Under the Bamboo Tree," is introduced by the show's star, Marie Cahill. Izzy (Dan McAvoy) delights in dialect comedy and grotesque dancing. George Lederer acts as producer-director for George Hobart who wrote the book and lyrics and Ludwig Englander who wrote the score. D. Frank Dodge and Edward Unitt collaborate on the sets. Mme. C.F. Siedle designs the costumes.

Sep 1 *The Rogers Brothers in Harvard* (NY—Knickerbocker—Musical). Gus and Max Rogers go to college. A Klaw and Erlanger production. Ben Teal stages, with

the aid of Ernest Gros (sets) and F. Richard Anderson (costumes). A critic suggests that seeing the Rogers Brothers makes one realize how good Weber and Fields are.

Sep 4 *The Mummy and the Hummingbird* (NY—Empire—Drama). The play draws because of a cast including matinee idol John Drew, Guy Standing, Lionel Barrymore, Reginald Carrington, and Margaret Dale.

Sep 11 *Twirly Whirly* (NY—Weber and Fields' Music Hall—Musical). Although critics are unenthusiastic, this proves a very popular successor (244 performances) to last season's Weber and Fields revue, *Hoity Toity*. Lillian Russell sings "Come Down, Ma Evenin' Star." *The Mummy and the Hummingbird* is burlesqued. Julian Mitchell stages; John Young designs sets, and Will R. Barnes creates the costumes. Russell is Mrs. Stockson Bonds, who has just bought the local castle in Seville, where she entertains the fashionable.

Sep 22 *A Country Girl* (NY—Daly's—Musical Play). J. C. Duff stages for Augustin Daly's Musical Company. A British import, with a Lionel Monckton score, the book is by James Tanner; lyrics by Adrian Ross and Percy Greenbank. Minnie Ashley and Melville Stewart lead the cast. Walter Burridge and Henry E. Hoyt provide the set-designs. With its hero a naval officer and its comic the Rajah of Bhong, the show achieves a 14 week run.

Oct 6 *A Country Mouse* (NY—Savoy—Comedy). Arthur Law's light comedy of rural-urban contrasts provides Ethel Barrymore with another leading role. She also appears in a curtain-raiser called *Carrots*, by Jules Renard. Weber and Fields soon parody this.

Oct 27 *The Silver Slipper* (NY—Broadway—Musical). Clay Greene has adapted Owen Hall's British book. For 20 weeks, audiences see what happens when a girl

Mary of Magdala

from Venus is banished to Earth for kicking her slipper out of orbit. Edna Wallace Hopper stars. The show is produced and directed by John C. Fisher. Leslie Stuart provides the score.

Nov 3 *The Stubbornness of Geraldine* (NY—Garrick—Drama). Clyde Fitch's heroine has a problem—she is stubborn. Fitch directs a cast headed by Mary Mannering. Amy Ricard, Arthur Byron, and H. Hassard Short are also on hand. Joseph Physioc designs the settings. The play is soon parodied as *The Stickiness of Gelatine.*

Nov 12 *Mary of Magdala* (NY—Manhattan—Drama). Produced by Harrison Grey Fiske, with Mrs. Fiske and Tyrone Power, in the leads, this biblical drama is enhanced with music by Charles Puerner and choreography by Carl Marwig. The Fiskes stage, with costumes by Percy Anderson and sets by Frank Gates, E.A. Morange, and Homer Emens.

Nov 17 *The Crisis* (NY—Wallack's—Drama). The American novelist, Winston Churchill, turns his best-selling story into a four-act play. James K. Hackett stars, directs, and produces.

Nov 24 *Audrey* (NY—Madison Square—Drama). Harriet Ford and E. F. Boddington adapt Mary Johnston's popular novel for the stage. Eleanor Robson stars. Eugene O'Neill's older brother, James O'Neill, Jr. is also in the cast.

Dec 3 *The Darling of the Gods* (NY—Belasco—Drama). Playwrights David Belasco and John Luther Long use Japan as the scene of a romantic tragedy. This drama features adventure, danger, love, death by hara kiri, and celestial reunion of the dead lovers. Blanche Bates, Belasco's Butterfly stars. George Arliss is in the large cast, which includes jugglers, acrobats, and torturers. As usual, Belasco produces and directs. Its success is re-

peated in London a year later. On December 28 the play opens at His Majesty's Theatre. This Herbert Beerbohm Tree production earns a run of 168 performances.

Dec 15 *Heidelberg* (NY—Princess—Drama). Based on Wilhelm Meyer-Forster's play *Alt Heidelberg*, this Aubrey Boucicault dramatization mixes romance with nostalgia. Boucicault heads the cast. Eventually, this play will become the popular musical *The Student Prince.* On March 19, 1903, George Alexander's English version opens at the St. James's Theatre in London. In the cast are Henry Ainley, E. Lyall Sweete, Eva Moore and Elinor Aicken. There are 189 performances.

Dec 25 *The Girl with the Green Eyes* (NY—Savoy—Drama). Jealousy is the character flaw of Clyde Fitch's heroine. Clara Bloodgood is featured. Charles Frohman produces; Fitch, as is his custom, stages. Edward Unitt creates the impressive settings, including a memorable scene in the Vatican Museum. The production earns 108 performances.

Dec 29 *The Sultan of Sulu* (NY—Wallack's—Musical Comedy). George Ade makes musical fun out of the clash between the cultures of New England and the Sulu Islands, when American troops occupy after the Spanish-American War. Alfred G. Withall provides a lively score for Ade's pointed lyrics. Exotic locales are the inventions of Walter Burridge. One of the few shows launched in Chicago to find favor in New York, this lively production lasts for eight months and then tours. "The story is thickly interspersed with songs, many of which are tuneful and graceful, if all are slightly reminiscent. The composer has, however, built up a pretty theme and the music as a whole is a very close second to the libretto. At least two of the songs, 'My Sulu Lulu Loo' and 'Since I First Met You,' are as tuneful and catchy as have been heard here in a good many days of comic opera," reports the *NY Times.*

1902   BRITISH PREMIERES

Jan 18 *The Country Girl* (L—Daly's—Musical). The busy team of James Tanner, Adrian Ross, Percy Greenbank, Lionel Mockton, and Paul Rubens again collaborate on a "girl" show. Huntley Wright, Hayden Coffin, and Evie Greene are in major roles. The production is a phenomenal success, with 729 performances. *The Times* reports that: "When the curtain ultimately rose it disclosed one of the prettiest scenes of modern musical comedy—a charming Devonshire landscape.... Young Verity, a nincompoop, wants to marry Nan ... the country girl, and eventually succeeds, though she loves Challoner, who in his turn loves another country girl, Marjorie Joy ... Barry is in love with Mme. Sophie, a cheery and impudent dressmaker, and the Rajah with an Indian princess.... The book sadly needs compression, but the music is bright and cheerful, and in many respects, notably in the finish of the orchestral scoring and in the part writing of the first finale, it is on a level that is far higher than usual in musical plays. The 'Two Chicks' duet is as amusing as it is original, and all Mr. Huntley Wright's songs are likely to become popular."

Jan 27 *Mice and Men* (L—Lyric—Drama). Johnston Forbes-Robertson and Gertrude Elliott take the leads in Madeleine Lucette Ryley's new play about a gentlemen who raises a young girl on the principles of Rousseau. He later finds he has lost his heart to his ward. Although *The Times* reviewer remarks that the play is based on the most improbable circumstances, he calls it "very wholesome entertainment" and describes the girl as "one entirely fascinating character."

Feb 1 Stephen Phillips' poetic drama *Ulysses* comes to life on the stage of Her Majesty's Theatre in London, with Herbert Beerbohm Tree in the lead, supported by Lily Hanbury and Nancy Price. The production wins 150 performances and gets a rave review from *The Times.* "It is something at this time of day to find a great world-story told—in a way in which it is here told—for the first time on the English stage in the language of true poetry and with aid of all the resources of this age and the arts of plastic and music." On September 14, 1903, Phillips' play opens at New York's Garden Theatre, with Tyrone Power and Edgar Selwyn in the cast. It runs for 65 performances. The *NY Times* gives a mixed review to Power's performance which it calls "adequate."

Feb 2 *Arizona* (L—Adelphi—Drama). Augustus Thomas' American drama has Theodore Roberts and Olive May in its central roles. The staging earns 115 showings. *The Times*, reviewing the play, remarks that "whenever anyone ... does anything heroic, some one else remarks enthusiastically, 'That's Arizona!' We say ... That's Arizona!"

Feb 27 *A Country Mouse* (L—Prince of Wales's—Comedy). C. W. Somerset and Annie Hughes play the leads in Arthur Law's drama. The production gets 187 showings.

March 6 Stephen Phillips' poetic drama, *Paolo and Francesca,* is produced by George Alexander at London's St. James's Theatre, inspired by the success of Phillips' *Ulysses* at Her Majesty's Theatre. Alexander and Evelyn Millard play the doomed lovers.

March 20 *The Girl from Maxim's* (L—Criterion—Comedy). Beatrice Ferrar is the girl in this French farce.

April 2 *Merrie England* (L—Savoy—Musical). Captain Basil Hood's libretto and Edward German's score win 120 performances in this production. Walter Passmore and Rosina Brandram take the leads.

April 3 *Ben Hur* (L—Drury Lane—Drama). Gen. Lew Wallace's best-selling novel, in William Young's dramatization, is replete with all the stage machinery necessary for such effects as slaves rowing a Roman ship and a chariot race with real horses and chariots. Robert Taber and Nora Kerin are in the main roles. It earns 122 performances.

April 8 *The Little French Milliner* (L—Avenue—Comedy). Based on the French farce, *Coralie et Cie.*, Clement Scott's play is performed by a company headed by Kate Phillips and Arthur Williams. *The Wicked Uncle* is the curtain-raiser. It has 170 performances.

May 1 *Sapho* (L—Adelphi—Drama). Preceded by debate about censorship in the theatre, following its star's arrest and trial in New York for presenting the play, dramatized by Clyde Fitch from Daudet's novel, Olga Nethersole brings her current vehicle to British audiences. Frank Mills supports her both figuratively and literally. "It is Mr. Clyde Fitch's *Sapho* this time, and by no means an improvement on the original of MM. Daudet and Belot. That was lugubrious enough; this is lugubrious to excess. That was vulgar enough, but this vulgarizes vulgarity. That was long enough, but this is longer still . . . for over four hours by the clock. . . . It was a riot of superfluity. . . . A woman with swollen face and disshevelled hair is seized with spasms of eroto-mania or violent grief. She grovels at a man's feet or dashes her fist in his face or hugs him to her breast like a wild beast. And when the actress has thus wallowed and bellowed and panted and has almost worked herself into the actual throes of the frenzy she depicts, the pit 'rises' at her and the gallery cheers until it is hoarse. . . . Miss Nethersole's method . . . sets out with the determination to overdo everything . . ." according to *The Times*.

May 10 *Three Little Maids* (L—Apollo—Musical). Paul Ruben's new show draws audiences for 343 performances. The popular musical star Edna May is featured with Maurice Farkoa and G. P. Huntley.

May 22 *There and Back* (L—Prince of Wales's—Comedy). Charles Hawtrey stages George Arliss' new farce. It appears at New York's Princess Theatre on April 20, 1903, where it runs for 48 performances.

Aug 12 *The Marriage of Kitty* (L—Duke of York's—Comedy). Cosmo Gordon Lennox's adaptation from the French wins a run of 296 performances. Marie Tempest and Leonard Boyne are in the leads.

Aug 29 *There's Many a Slip* (L—Haymarket—Comedy). Cyril Maude and Winifred Emery play the main roles in Robert Marshall's version of *Bataille de Dames*, by Scribe and Legouve.

Aug 30 *If I Were King* (L—St. James's—Drama). Justin Huntly McCarthy's new "romantic play" is produced by George Alexander, who also plays the leading role of Francois Villon. Julie Opp is the feminine lead. The play runs 215 performances.

Sep 17 *Quality Street* (L—Vaudeville—Comedy). James Barrie's new play is produced by Seymour Hicks, who also has a leading role, with Ellaline Terriss and Marion Terry. It is a wistful Regency romance, with "Phoebe of the ringlets" waiting 10 years for her Valentine. The play enjoys a run of 459 performances.

Oct 2 *The Eternal City* (L—His Majesty's—Drama). Hall Caine's epic, with music by opera composer Pietro Mascagni, is produced by Herbert Beerbohm Tree, who plays a leading role, with Constance Collier and Nancy Price. The production wins 117 performances.

Oct 23 *Captain Kettle* (L—Adelphi—Drama). Malcolm Watson and Murray Carson base this play on the novel, with Carson and Esme Beringer in the main roles.

Oct 27 *My Lady Virtue* (L—Garrick—Drama). Arthur Bourchier is featured in H.V. Esmond's play. Eva Moore and Violet Vanbrugh are also in important parts.

Eleanora Duse

Nov 4 *The Admirable Critchton* (L—Duke of York's—Comedy). James Barrie's play, deals with the personality changes that transform a butler, satisfied with his station into a megomaniac when he assumes command of his former "betters" after they are shipwrecked on an island. It wins 328 performances. H.B. Irving and Irene Vanbrugh play leading roles. On November 17, 1903, Barrie's play opens at the Lyceum Theatre in New York. It achieves an 18-week run with William Gillette as the butler.

Dec 2 *The Unforseen* (L—Haymarket—Drama). Captain Robert Marshall's play has Cyril Maude in a leading role, ably supported by Allan Aynesworth, A. E. Matthews and Evelyn Millard. It earns 115 performances.

1902   REVIVALS/REPERTORIES

Jan 7 George Alexander revives Oscar Wilde's *The Importance of Being Earnest* in London at the St. James's Theatre.

Jan 13 Mrs. Patrick Campbell and her company offer a program of repertory at New York's Republic for three weeks. The repertory includes Hermann Sudermann's *Magda*, Arthur Pinero's *The Second Mrs. Tanqueray* and *The Notorious Mrs. Ebbsmith*, Bjornstjerne Bjornson's *Beyond Human Power* (NY premiere), Jose Echegaray's *Mariana* (NY premiere), and Max Beerbohm's *The Happy Hypocrite* (NY premiere).

Jan 14 Mrs. Campbell is well received. The N.Y. Times reviewer writes, "By her acting in *Magda*, Mrs. Campbell establishes her right to a prominent place on the modern stage. Occasionally, there seems a touch of monotony in her diction, a trife too much energy, whereby there is diminution of light and shade. But her rendering of the part is a great piece of acting and a rare treat." She also gives the American premiere of Maeterlinck's *Pelleas and Melisande*, at a single matinee performance at the Hammerstein Theatre. Reviews are not enthusiastic. "We are left to conjecture what is meant by it all," says the *NY Times*.

Feb 27 Henrietta Crosman's first appearance as Rosalind in *As You Like It* is at New York's Republic Theatre. Staged by Miss Crosman, it enjoys a run of 60 performances.

March 10 Edward Gordon Craig's production of *Acis and Galatea* opens at London's Great Queen Street Theatre together with a revival of *The Masque of Love*. The musical director is Martin Shaw.

April 14 At Stratford-upon-Avon, the annual Shakespeare Festival opens with *Twelfth Night*, Frank Benson directing. On Shakespeare's birthday, *Henry VIII* is offered, with Ellen Terry as Queen Katherine, her debut in this theatre. In addition to seven Benson Shakespeare productions in the Memorial Theatre, this three-week season also affords stagings of Sheridan's *The Rivals* and Bulwer-Lytton's *Richelieu*.

June 9 Sarah Bernhardt is in London to open a brief season of repertory at the Garrick Theatre. This evening's premiere is *Francesca da Rimini*. Her other productions include *Magda, Camille, Fedora, Phédre, Frou-Frou, Tosca,* and *Hamlet,* in which she appears as the Danish prince.

June 30 Constant Coquelin opens his season of French drama at London's Garrick Theatre with Rostand's *Cyrano de Bergerac*. Although Coquelin's acting is praised, the play is considered out of vogue.

Nov 4 Eleonora Duse and her Italian repertory ensemble open in New York at Hammerstein's Victoria for two weeks. Gabriele D'Annunzio's *La Città Morta, La Cioconda,* and *Francesca Da Rimini* are offered in Italian. Duse receives raves. "[Her acting] was as sound and wholesome in feeling as it was marvelously true and varied in technique," exclaims the *NY Times*.

Dec 15 At London's Lyric Theatre, *Othello* stars Johnston Forbes-Robertson. The cast includes Ben Webster, Gertrude Elliott, and Lena Ashwell.

Dec 18 Special Christmas matinees at London's Garrick Theatre are devoted to Rutland Barrington's adaptation of Charles Kingsley's *Water Babies*, a play with music. Roles are played by Kate Bishop, Edith Miller, Nellie Bowman, and Ian Maclaren.

Francisco near Fulton on Tenth. It derives its peculiar name from the fact that it's constructed in front of a Chute-the-Chutes (Roller-Coaster), which sometimes makes performances inaudible.

June 17 The London County Council Improvement Committee issues its report stating its approval of designs submitted by Ernest Runtz and based on Norman Shaw's sketch-designs, for a second Gaiety Theatre to be built on a new site at Aldwych and the Strand.

July 15 Austin Fryers of Sydenham, England, obtains a patent for a turntable or pivotal stage-section which allows for an actor to be rotated while standing on it.

Sep 29 David Belasco's New York revival of *DuBarry* boasts the use of individual dimmer controls on each borderlight and footlight. Approximately forty-five dimmers are used.

Oct 1 The International Alliance of Theatrical Stage Employees (IATSE), organized nationally on July 17, 1893, today is organized internationally, to include Canada. It is composed of approximately 950 local unions covering the United States and Canada.

Oct 27 At its 1902 American premiere in New Haven, Bernard Shaw's *Mrs. Warren's Profession* was not well received. After its first performance in New York, police arrest Arnold Daly and Mary Shaw, on charges of disorderly conduct for presenting an immoral play. After a eight month delay they are tried and acquitted.

Nov To its standard list of London theatres, *Whitaker's Almanack* adds the following playhouses: Alexander (Stoke Newington), Apollo (Shaftesbury Ave.), Borough (Stratford East), Brixton (Broadway), Camden (Camden Town), Coronet (Notting Hill), Crown (Peckham), Duchess (Balham), Fulham (Fulham Rd.), Kennington, Lyric (Hammersmith), Metropole (Camberwell), and the Shakespeare (Clapham Junction).

Dec 3 David Belasco spends a total of $78,000 on his new production, of *The Darling of the Gods*. He is intent on having it be technical and visual perfection, by his standards. Belasco is so intent on achieving the right effect for his final scene of celestial reunion that he scraps $6,500 worth of scenery and machinery, a large sum in those times. Only after two years of virtually sold-out houses does the play show its first profit of $5,000. This production also leads to Belasco's final break with the Theatrical Syndicate, in 1904, when Erlanger refuses to give Belasco a theatre for it in St. Louis for the Louisiana Purchase Exposition. Belasco leases the independent Imperial.

Dec 21 Chicago's new La Salle Theatre opens.

1902 BIRTHS/DEATHS/DEBUTS

January 13 Mrs. Patrick Campbell and George Arliss make their New York debuts in a program of repertory at the Republic.

Jan 26 Actor-director Romney Brent is born Romulo Larralde, Jr. in Saltillo, Mexico.

Feb 24 Douglas Fairbanks makes his New York debut in *Her Lord and Master* by Martha Morton.

Sep 1 Pauline Frederick makes her Broadway debut in the chorus of *The Rogers Brothers in Harvard*.

Sep 22 Producer-actor-director John Houseman is born Jacques Haussman in Bucharest, Romania.

Sep 24 Producer-director Cheryl Crawford is born in Akron, Ohio.

Oct 12 Edith Wynne Matthison makes her American debut in *Everyman*. Charles Rann Kennedy makes his stage debut in the same production.

1902 THEATERS/PRODUCTIONS

In Britain patents are granted for: J. W. Sherman's ghost-effect in which an actor housed in a black cabinet lit by incandescent lamps has his image cast from the wings onto a sheet of glass placed diagonally across the stage; O. Stoll's system of concentric stages which can revolve independently of each other, powered by an electric motor and belts; Alfred Terraine's rigid sky-dome, covering the entire acting area, top and sides, moving to the rear on tracks to permit shifting of scenery; W. Melville's rain-machine, a perforated box which permits rice or other grains to sift down, simulating stage-rain.

U.S. patents granted this year include a number of theatre-related ones. John Sherman devises a transformation effect involving a translucent screen, upstage and parallel to the footlights; in front of it but placed diagonally so scenes can be projected from the wings onto it, is a transparent screen. Rear-projections on the rear screen cause the front projections to disappear. Charles Bramhall has received a patent for his novel theatre-in-the-round (a term as yet unknown), in which the audience is slowly revolved around a center stage. Edward Snader's

patent is for his scenic arch which collapses on cue, breaking into pieces of falling masonry.

The Censorship Committee of the British Poster and Advertising Association bans the poster advertising the play, *White Slave Traffic*, showing a victim stripped to the waist and a figure with a cat-o'-nine-tails.

Laurence Housman's Nativity play, *Bethlehem*, is banned in England. The censor, George Redford, does not think it proper to depict the Holy Family on stage.

April 2 Today marks an important date in the development of an Irish theatre. W. G. Fay's Irish National Dramatic Company open the first series of productions for the newly-founded Irish National Theatre Society. The Society is to continue on a more permanent basis the work begun by the Irish Literary Theatre, instituted by W. B. Yeats, Edward Martyn, and Augusta, Lady Gregory. Performances by Fay's troupe are presented in St. Teresa's Hall, Clarendon Street, Dublin. The Society puts on two more productions later in the year.

May 1 The Chutes Theatre opens in San

Jan 21 *The Wizard of Oz* (NY—Majestic—Musical). This adaptation of L. Frank Baum's children's classic runs nearly nine months. It stars Fred Stone and David Montgomery. The opening spectacle of the cyclone which takes Dorothy's house off to Oz, staged by Julian Mitchell, is a high point. The score is by Paul Tietjens and A. Baldwin Sloane.

Jan 21 *Mr. Bluebeard* (NY—Knickerbocker—Musical). Eddie Foy is featured in this American adaptation of a British show by J. Hickory Wood and Arthur Collins. Eight composers contribute music for the score, with Jean Schwartz providing the ballet music for the pony chorus. The show runs for nearly 17 weeks.

Feb 9 *The Frisky Mrs. Johnson* (NY—Princess—Comedy). Clyde Fitch adapts *Madame Flirt*, a Parisian play, for Amelia Bingham, who produces and stars. Fitch stages, in settings by Joseph Physioc. The show has a 10 week run.

Feb 16 *The Jewel of Asia* (NY—Criterion—Musical). Blanche Ring is featured as a beauty who unties the knots of a tangled plot involving a painter who acquires a harem. Staged by George Lederer, the production runs nearly two months.

Feb 16 *Nancy Brown* (NY—Bijou—Musical). Marie Cahill plays a marriage broker who brings a supply of heiresses to the impoverished country of Bally Hoo. Frederic Ranken and George Broadhurst tailor the book to fit Cahill's talent. The score is by Henry Hadley. The show runs for 104 performances.

Feb 18 *In Dahomey* (NY—New York—Musical). Bert Williams and his partner, George Walker, are the headliners of the first full-length Broadway musical written and performed by blacks. Marion Cook composes music for Paul Laurence Dunbar's lyrics. J.A. Shipp's book has Rareback Pinkerton (Walker) fleecing Shylock Homestead (Williams) in a con-scheme to resettle poor American blacks in Dahomey. Audience applause decides the winners in an on-stage cakewalk contest. Critical praise goes to the duo rather than to the book, which judged only adequate. "The headliners were the whole show," reports the *NY Times*. In New York, the show has 53 performances but runs for 7 months later in London.

March 17 *The Prince of Pilsen* (NY—Broadway—Musical). With 18 weeks on Broadway, this show rapidly becomes popular across the nation. One or more companies are on the road and returning to New York for the next five seasons. In Nice, a Cincinnati brewer and his son are both mistaken for the real Prince of Pilsen, Carl Otto, who uses the opportunity to pass as a commoner and woo the brew-

Wizard of Oz

er's lovely daughter Nellie. The book is by Frank Pixley, the score by Gustav Luders. Notable is Luders' "The Heidelberg Stein Song," delivered *a capella*. On May 14 the following year, the play runs for 160 performances at the London's Shaftesbury Theatre. *The Times* does not like it, calling the play: "a peculiarly senseless form of theatrical entertainment."

March 23 *The Earl of Pawtucket* (NY—Manhattan—Comedy). Augustus Thomas's play about an English lord who pretends to be an American stars Lawrence D'Orsay. Kirke La Shelle produces. It runs 191 performances. The play is introduced to London at the Playhouse Theatre June 25, 1907 with Cyril Maude staring. There are 229 performances.

March 23 *Pretty Peggy* (NY—Herald Square—Comedy). Grace George heads the cast of Frances Aymar Mathews' light play. It runs for approximately 10 weeks.

April 27 *Running for Office* (NY—14th Street—Musical). Fred Niblo produces this show, with book and music by George M. Cohan. The plot concerns John Tiger's campaign to become mayor of Tigerville and marry at the same time. The Cohan family—father and mother, Jerry and Nellie, and brother and sister, George and Josephine—please some critics who wonder why it took them so long to come to Broadway. The show runs six weeks. The young George M. receives the most praise from the *NY Times* which calls him "in every way remarkable." Cohan's wife, Ethel Levey, is also in the show.

May 11 *The Runaways* (NY—Casino—Musical). Raymond Hubbell provides the score for Addision Burkhardt's book, which parodies the *Sulton of Sulu's* exotic locale. In the show, the hero is transported to a tropical island where he is made king, but must marry the widowed queen. The show runs nearly 21 weeks.

June 1 *Punch, Judy & Co.* (NY—Hammerstein's Paradise Roof Garden—Musical). Oscar Hammerstein produces and provides both book and lyrics, but not a word is spoken on stage. Bècause there is virtually no plot, everything done by an all-female cast is danced or sung. The show runs nine weeks.

Sep 1 *Three Little Maids* (NY—Daly's—Musical). These girls are daughters of a curate who prove matches for London sophisticates. Paul Rubens provides both book and music. With Maggie May, Madge Crichton, and Delia Mason, the show charms for more than four months.

Sep 7 *The Rogers Brothers in London* (NY—Knickerbocker—Musical). The Rogers Brothers pursue a diamond good luck charm through various locales. This permits them to do their standard comic "Dutch" routines, and some Cockney and blackface clowning. Herbert Gresham and Ned Wayburn stage the show. The show lasts nearly 2 months despite the *NY Times* panning it. "Everything assails the eye. Nothing truly delights it.... many ... were overheard to remark in plain terms that it was rotten," reports the reviewer.

Sep 10 *Peggy From Paris* (NY—Wallack's—Musical). George Ade's book is about a country girl who becomes pretentious after studying music in Paris. Partly because of an inferior score by William Lorraine, the show earns only 85 performances.

Sep 14 *Under Cover* (NY—Murray Hill—Comedy). Edward Harrigan writes and stars in this rollicking comedy with Annie Yeamans, Jane Elton, and Maurice Drew in the cast. It runs just over 11 weeks.

Sep 20 *Whoop-Dee-Doo* (NY—Weber and Fields's Music Hall—Musical). The team of Joseph Weber and Lew Fields are able to engage in their famous "statue" routine in this show about an innkeeper who is trying to unload his inn on two "Dutch" comics. Edgar Smith and W.T. Francis provide book and music respectively. The show runs almost 19 weeks.

Sept 28 *Her Own Way* (NY—Garrick—Drama). Maxine Elliott stars in Clyde Fitch's play about a girl loved by the hero and the wealthy villain. Fitch stages it for producer Charles Dillingham; it runs for 107 performances. The *NY Times* calls Elliott a "talented and masterly actress." On April 25, 1905, Fitch's play has its first London performance at the Lyric Theatre, however even with Elliott's talents, the play runs only three weeks.

Oct 12 *The Proud Prince* (NY—Herald Square—Drama). E.H. Sothern directs and stars in Justin Huntly McCarthy's play. Charles Frohman produces. The show has only 35 performances.

Oct 13 *Babes in Toyland* (NY—Majestic—Musical). Victor Herbert creates a score of perenniel favorites such as "Toyland" to accompany Glen MacDonough's eventful plot. The Babes, Alan and Jane, have to escape the wicked machinations of their Uncle Barnaby who wants to seize their inheritance. Shipwrecked, they find themselves in Toyland, where Mother Goose characters defend them from their villainous uncle. The show runs for six months. The *NY Times* says *Babes in Toyland* is "an achievement."

Oct 19 *The Best of Friends* (NY—Academy of Music—Drama). Charles Frohman produces Cecil Raleigh's play, with a large cast including Lionel Barrymore, May Davenport Seymour, and Tully Marshall. It runs for two months.

Nov 2 *The Office Boy* (NY—Hammerstein's Victoria—Musical). Charles Dillingham produces Harry B. Smith's version of a French farce, accompanied by the score of Ludwig Englander. Frank Daniels is featured along with Louise Gunning and Eva Tanguay. The show runs over two months.

Nov 9 *Red Feather* (NY—Lyric—Musical). This show, with a Charles Klein book, has a score by Reginald DeKoven. Florenz Ziegfeld is the producer. The story deals with a soldier who pursues a bandit only to discover that she is a countess and that he loves her. It runs 60 performances.

Nov 10 *The Pretty Sister of Jose* (NY—Empire—Comedy). Maude Adams graces this production of Frances Hodgson Burnett's play. It runs over seven weeks.

Nov 11 *Major Andre* (NY—Savoy—Drama). Clyde Fitch dramatizes and stages this story of the British spy. The cast includes Mrs. Sol Smith, Chrystal Herne and Arnold Daly. Though the play is admired by some critics it manages only 12 performances.

Dec 2 *Mother Goose* (NY—New Amsterdam—Musical). This British import is a glorified Christmas pantomime by J. Hickory Wood and Arthur Collins. George M. Cohen is among the Americans contributing songs. The cast includes Joseph Cawthorne, Pat Rooney and Viola Gillette. The show has 105 performances.

Dec 8 *Mam'selle Napoleon* (NY—Knickerbocker—Musical). Florenz Ziegfeld mounts a lavish production for his wife, Anna Held, who plays Mme. Mars, Napoleon's mistress. With a weak score by Gustav Luders, the show lasts only 43 performances.

Dec 9 *Sweet Kitty Bellairs* (NY—Belasco—Comedy). Based on the British novel, *The Bath Comedy*, this play gives David Belasco another chance to show his talents as author, director, and producer. The highly complex plot revolves around the battle for social supremacy between Kitty, darling of the visiting Irish regiment, and her adversary, Lady Bab, former queen of Bath society, in this elegant 18th century world. It runs nearly 26 weeks. Henrietta Crosman, who heads the cast, gets rave reviews. Rudolph Friml makes this production into a musical in 1917 under the title *Kitty Darlin'*. On Oct 5, 1907, the show premieres at London's Haymarket with Louis Calvert in the lead. *The Times* compares it to Donizetti's *La Figlia del Reggimento*.

Dec 28 *Glad of It* (NY—Savoy—Comedy). Clyde Fitch's play about a department store clerk who becomes a star has John Barrymore, Lucile Watson, Thomas Meighan, and Hassard Short in its cast. Variations in the plot will be used many times, especially in musicals. It runs for only four weeks.

Dec 28 *Merely Mary Ann* (NY—Garden—Comedy). Israel Zangwill's play is about Mary Ann, a domestic on the verge of marrying an improverished musician when she inherits a fortune. Too idealistic to marry for money, he leaves her. Years later, he returns to die in her arms. Eleanor Robson stars. It runs over 18 weeks. On Sep 8, 1904 it premieres at London's Duke of York's with Robson in the lead. It gets 111 performances.

Dec 29 *The Other Girl* (NY—Criterion—Comedy). Augustus Thomas's light play about a young boxer, the priest who trains him, and his efforts to marry a society girl he loves, runs for nearly five months. Performers include Elsie and Drina De Wolfe and Lionel Barrymore.

1903 BRITISH PREMIERES

Jan 21 *For Sword or Song* (L—Shaftesbury—Drama). Edward Gordon Craig designs this poetic drama by R. J. Legge, Louis Calvert, and Raymond Rose. Major roles are taken by Fred Terry and Julia Neilson.

Jan 22 *A Princess of Kensington* (L—Savoy—Musical). Captain Basil Hood creates the comic libretto, with music by Edward German. Louie Pounds, Rosina Brandram, and Walter Passmore play leading parts. The production achieves 115 performances.

Feb 7 *The Light That Failed* (L—Lyric—Drama). Rudyard Kipling's novel is adapted by George Fleming. Leading roles are taken by Johnston Forbes-Robertson, Gertrude Elliott, Aubrey Smith, Sydney Valentine, and Nina Boucicault. It earns 148 performances. On November 9 the play opens at New York's Knickerbocker, but runs for only one month.

Feb 10 *A Clean Slate* (L—Criterion—Comedy). R.C. Carton's play has Brandon Thomas in a leading role with C.W. Somerset, Robb Harwood and Katherine Compton (Carton's wife).

March 2 *Whitewashing Julie* (L—Garrick—Comedy). Arthur Bourchier has cast himself in a leading role in Henry Arthur Jones' new play about a scandal in a cathedral town: has the young widow been morganatically married to a duke? The play opens on Dec 2 at New York's Garrick Theatre where it has a run of 39 performances. The cast includes Fay Davis, Guy Standing, Louise Drew and Doris Keane.

March 14 *My Lady Molly* (L—Terry's—Musical). This show, with libretto by G.H. Jessup and score by Sidney Jones, tells the story of a couple about to be forced into an arranged marriage. Each loves another, with predictable results. Decima Moore, Sybil Arundale, Richard Green, Walter Hyde and J.T. McCallum play. The show wins 342 performances. On Jan 5, 1904 the show premieres in New York at the Daly's with Vesta Tilley in the lead. It lasts only 15 performances.

April 25 *The Medal and the Maid* (L—Lyric—Musical). The show, with book by Owen Hall and music by Sidney Jones deals with an heiress and a flower-girl who trade places, using a medallion for purposes of recognition. Lyrics are by C.H. Taylor, George Rollit and Paul Rubens. Ada Reeve, Ada Blanche and Ruth Vincent act. On Jan 11, 1904 it premieres at New York's Broadway Theatre. Here a "coon song" is interpolated to make the show more appealing to American audiences. It runs 49 performances.

April 30 *Dante* (L—Drury Lane—Drama). Laurence Irving adapts a play by Sardou and Moreau for his father, Henry Irving.

May 9 *The School Girl* (L—Prince of Wales's—Musical). Paul Potter and Henry Hamilton collaborate on the book about a convent girl's adventures in Paris. Leslie Stuart provides the score and C.H. Taylor the lyrics. Edna May and Violet Cameron are featured. The show wins 338 performances. On Sep 1, 1904, the play opens on Broadway at Daly's with a successful run of 15 weeks. Edna May is again in the cast.

May 12 *Mrs. Gorringe's Necklace* (L—Wyndham's—Comedy). Hubert Henry Davies' play is produced by Charles Wyndham, who also has a leading role. Mary Moore is Mrs. Gorringe. It wins 160 performances.

June 18 *Cousin Kate* (L—Haymarket—Comedy). Hubert Henry Davies' new play deals with a woman of the world who tries to advise her country cousin on love. Cyril Maude, Eric Lewis, A.E. Matthews, and Cyril Smith are featured in this show which runs 242 performances. On Oct 19 the play opens in New York at the Hudson with Ethel Barrymore featured. It has 44 performances and re-opens in the spring for a two week run.

Aug 31 *The Cardinal* (L—St. James—Drama). There are 105 performances for Louis N. Parker's play, with E. S. Willard featured.

Sep 2 *Billy's Little Love Affair* (L—Criterion—Comedy). H. V. Esmond's play earns 153 performances. In the cast are Allan Aynesworth and Sam Sothern.

Sep 17 *The Flood-Tide* (L—Drury Lane—Comedy). Cecil Raleigh describes his play as a melodramatic farce. In the cast are Weedon Grossmith, Mrs. Beerbohm Tree, and Claire Romaine.

Sep 24 *Little Mary* (L—Wyndham's—Drama). James Barrie describes his new stage work as "an uncomfortable play." In the cast are Gerald DuMaurier, John Hare, and Nina Boucicault. Barrie's play earns 208 performances, although *The Times* calls it "a trifle."

Oct 1 *Dolly Varden* (L—Avenue—Musical). Mabel Gilman plays the title role in this comic opera version of the Varden story. The libretto is by Stanislaus Stange, with Julian Edwards composing the score.

Oct 8 *Letty* (L—Duke of York's—Drama). Arthur Wing Pinero's new play tells the story of a shop girl, pursued by a profligate. Irene Vanbrugh is in the title role. There are 123 performances. On Sep 12, 1904, the play opens on Broadway, at the Hudson Theatre with William Faversham and Ivo Dawson. It runs nearly two months.

Oct 17 *The Duchess of Dantzig* (L—Lyric—Musical). Henry Hamilton bases his libretto on *Madame Sans-Gene*, de-scribing it as a "romantic opera." Ivan Caryll provides the score. It wins 236 performances. Holbrook Blinn, Courtice Pounds, Evie Greene, and Denis O'Sullivan are in the cast. The play is also successful in New York when it opens on Jan 16, 1905. It runs for 93 performances at Daly's.

Oct 26 *The Orchid* (L—Gaiety—Musical). George Grossmith, Jr. is featured in this story of an explorer who has found and lost a rare orchid, only to find one like it in a London flower shop. The text is by James Tanner, lyrics by Adrian Ross and Percy Greenbank and score by Ivan Caryll, Paul Rubens and Lionel Monckton. It runs 559 performances. On April 8, 1907 it opens at New York's Herald Square, with Eddie Foy in the lead. It has 178 performances.

Dec 10 *The Earl and the Girl* (L—Adelphi—Musical). Seymour Hicks provides the text and Ivan Caryll the score for this story about a fight over an inheritance. The cast includes Walter Passmore and Florence Lloyd. There are 371 performances. The actors are praised but *The Times* critic calls the musical "pointless, often tasteless...." On Nov 4, 1905 the show premieres at New York's Casino Theatre with Eddie Foy and Georgia Caine in the leads. It runs 148 performances.

Dec 21 *The Cherry Girl* (L—Vaudeville—Musical). Another "girl" show, by the team of Seymour Hicks and Ivan Caryll opens. Aubrey Hopwood augments the team. The plot, based on *Comedia dell Arte* Pierrot characters, deals with lovers temporarily foiled by a villainous family. Main roles are played by Hicks, Courtice Pounds and Ellaline Terriss. The show earns 215 performances.

Dec 23 *Madame Sherry* (L—Apollo—Musical). C.E. Hands adapts Maurice Ordonneau's French text, with English lyrics by Adrian Ross. Hugo Felix writes the score. The play opens in New York on Aug 30, 1910 at the New Amsterdam Theatre.

1903 REVIVALS/REPERTORIES

Feb 17 At His Majesty's Theatre in London, Herbert Beerbohm Tree produces an adaptation of Tolstoi's *Resurrection*, by Henry Bataille and Michael Morton. Tree and Lena Ashwell play major roles. There are 111 performances.

March 3 Ibsen's *Ghosts*, fiercely attacked by critic William Winter after its New York premiere in 1894, is revived for two weeks in New York at Mrs. Osborn's Theatre, with Mary Shaw as Mrs. Alving.

March 17 At London's Haymarket Theatre, George Colman and David Garrick's comedy, *The Clandestine Marriage*, comes to life again with the talents of Cyril Maude and Allan Aynesworth.

April 15 Edward Gordon Craig designs and directs the production of Ibsen's *The Vikings* at London's Imperial Theatre. The production is managed by his mother, Ellen Terry, who plays a leading role. *The Times* praises Terry's performance but pans the play.

April 20 At Stratford-upon-Avon, the annual Shakespeare Festival opens with Frank Benson's staging of *Hamlet*. On the playwright's birthday, the play is *The Winter's Tale*. In this two-week season, Benson also presents *Hamlet*, *Macbeth*, *The Merry Wives of Windsor*, and *A Midsummer Night's Dream*. Ben Jonson, is honored in the Memorial Theatre with a production of *Every Man in His Humour*; Phillips' *Paolo and Francsca* is also played.

May 23 With Ellen Terry as Beatrice, this revival of *Much Ado About Nothing* opens at the London Imperial Theatre. The production is designed and directed by Edward Gordon Craig.

May 23 Tom Robertson's *Caste* is revived at London's Criterion, with Marie Tempest, Ben Webster, Kate Rorke, and Gilbert Hare in leading roles.

June 15 Sarah Bernhardt opens her London season at the Adelphi with *Fedora*. Her other roles in repertory include leads in *Frou-Frou*, *Andromaque*, *Bohemos*, *La Tosca*, *Sapho*, *La Dame aux Camelias*, *Plus Que Reine*, *Phèdre*, and *Werther*.

Sep 7 Dion Boucicault's Irish drama, *Arrah-Na-Pogue*, is revived at New York's 14th Street Theatre for a run of 65 performances. Andrew Mack and Edith Barker head the cast.

Oct 5 Minnie Maddern Fiske revives Ibsen's *Hedda Gabler* for one week at the Manhattan Theatre. This is her first New York appearance in the title role. In Nov, she brings the production back for three more weeks, this time with George Arliss.

Oct 5 Eleanora Duse opens her engagement in London at the Adelphi with D'Annunzio's *La Gioconda*. On Oct 7, she shows her production of *Hedda Gabler*.

Oct 8 In Dublin, the fifth series of Irish plays, performed by W. G. Fay's company for the Irish National Theatre Society at Molesworth Hall, now opens. W. B. Yates' *The King's Threshold* is directed by Annie E. F. Horniman, who also designs and makes the costumes. J. M. Synge's *In the Shadow of the Glen* has its premiere in this fifth series program.

Oct 12 George Alexander's English version of *Heidelberg* is revived at New York's Lyric where the production lasts for one month. In this version, Richard Mans-

Babes in Toyland

field produces and stars.

Oct 26 Henry Irving opens a season of repertory at New York's Broadway Theatre with *Dante*, by Victorien Sardou and Emile Moreau. The play is translated by his son Laurence, who is in the company. Also on the bill are Irving's famed production of *The Bells*, Arthur Conan Doyle's *Waterloo*, H. R. Maxwell's *Louis XI* and Shakespeare's *The Merchant of Venice*. The *NY Times* praises Irving saying: "if ever there was a man born to play Dante on the stage it is he.... he has in full measure the simplicity, intensity, and the austere dignity of the man who lived in the shadow of his ideal of Beatrice, in the world of lofty philosophy."

Nov–Dec At Dublin's Molesworth Hall, the sixth and seventh series of Irish plays are presented by the Irish National Theatre Society, performed by W. G. Fay's ensemble.

Nov 21 Shakespeare's *A Midsummer Night's Dream* is revived as the premiere production of the new New Amsterdam Theatre. Comedian Nat C. Goodwin is Bottom. The Mendelssohn score is arranged by Victor Herbert. The run is limited to three weeks.

Dec 8 The Princess Theatre offers a trial matinee of *Candida*. This is the first professional production of George Bernard Shaw's comedy in New York. Producer Arnold Daly plays the young poet, Eugene Marchbanks, and also stages the production. Dodson Mitchell and Dorothy Donnelly play leads. On Jan 4, 1904, the play begins a regular run, for a total of 133 performances. In February, Daly adds *The Man of Destiny* to the bill. This is another New York Shaw premiere.

Dec 22 With the approach Christmas, it's time for more youthful fare: J. Knott's adaptation of *Alice Through the Looking-Glass*, with a score by Walter Tilbury, produced at Charles Wyndham's New Theatre in London. Maidie Andrews impersonates Alice. On December 23, the Adelphi presents *Little Hans Andersen*, with libretto based on his life and tales by Basil Hood. Walter Slaughter creates

the score. The Drury Lane's *Humpty Dumpty* production, on Dec 26, is the last pantomime to feature Dan Leno and Hebert Campbell. Also on this date, the Court offers matinees of *Snowdrop and the Seven Little Men*, preceded by *Br'er Fox and Br'er Rabbit*, adapted from the Uncle Remus tales by Phillip Carr, with a score by Charles Smith.

1903 BIRTHS/DEATHS/DEBUTS

April 10 Clare Boothe is born in New York City to violinist William F. Boothe.

Apr 29 British actor Stuart Robson (b. 1836) dies today.

May 26 Born in 1853, actress Agnes Ethel dies today.

May 29 Stage and screen actress Beatrice Lillie is born in Toronto, Canada.

Aug 2 Anglo-American actress Jean Margaret Davenport Lander (b. 1829) is dead in Lynn, Mass. Lander was the first actress in America to play Adrienne Lecouvreur and Marguerite Gauthier, the latter with Edwin Booth as Armand. Her

last appearance was in 1877 in Boston in her dramatization of *The Scarlet Letter*.

Aug 28 British actor Joseph Haworth (b. 1855) dies today.

Dec 2 Doris Keane makes her New York debut in *The Whitewashing of Julia* at the Garrick Theatre.

Dec 9 Jane Cowl makes her New York debut at the Belasco Theatre in *Sweet Kitty Bellairs*.

Dec 28 John Barrymore makes his Broadway debut as Corley in Clyde Fitch's *Glad of It*.

1903 THEATERS/PRODUCTIONS

In Britain this year patents are granted for: C. Planer's rear-projected scenery, using a magic-lantern and transparencies; L. J. Couch's sheave-system which permits greater flexibility in placing and moving drops.

U.S. patents granted this year include:

Edward Austen's for his setting representing a city skyline with a lake in front. The buildings are small blocks mounted on rods in a tank of shallow water. The rods can cause the buildings to tremble, crumble, and collapse in the water.

Britain's Lord Chamberlain forbids

Eleanora Duse to perform Gabriel D'Annunzio's *La Citta Morta*, even in Italian. The censor's objection is the incestuous love of a character for his sister.

Jan 1 Laura Dainty Pelham organizes the Hull House Players in Chicago, Illinois. The company of 12 dedicated amateurs presents works by dramatists who are "taken seriously by the thinking public and are who financially unpopular with the normal manager."

Jan 2 The Imperial Theatre (L) remains open while the Aquarium, of which the theatre is part, closes, prior to demolition.

Jan 21 The Majestic Theatre, on Columbus Circle in New York, opens with a version of *The Wizard of Oz*. The theatre is owned by William Randolph Hearst and his associates, who think it wise to pioneer development in areas north of Times Square. Their gamble proves unsuccessful and the area is soon referred to as the "Arctic Circle." During the next four-and-one-half decades the theatre is

Proud Prince

converted to a motion-picture house, returns to presenting live drama, and then showcases burlesque. In 1944, the theatre is renamed the International, but in 1949, it is taken over by the National Broadcasting Company for use as a television studio. It is torn down in 1954, to make way for the New York Coliseum.

Feb 10 The Criterion Theatre in Piccadilly Circus re-opens, after re-modeling, with *A Clean Slate*. The original theatre had opened in 1874. Frank Curzon is the manager of this 645 seat theatre.

March 2 *The Times* of London is unable to provide its readers with a review of Henry Arthur Jones' new drama *Whitewashing Julia*. *The Times'* drama critic has been refused admission to the Garrick Theatre.

March 12 The New Theatre, a three-tier

house with a capacity of 877, opens in St. Martin's Lane in London. Charles Wyndham has built the theatre; Claude Ponsonby advised on the Louis XVI interior. The opening production is *Rosemary*, starring Charles Wyndham and Mary Moore.

March 14 The third series of Irish National Theatre Society productions opens in Dublin at Molesworth Hall. On May 2, the Society shows its productions for the first time in London, at the Queen Gate Hall, South Kensington.

May 30 The Buxton Opera House, designed by architect Frank Matcham, opens tonight in the spa-town of Buxton, near Birmingham. The handsome new house is opens with Frank Stayton's *Mrs. Willoughby's Kiss*. There are 1200 seats in the theatre, which is cooled in warm weather by a "Sunburner," a gasolier in the center of the auditorium's ceiling which provides some illumination but which is more useful in drawing up cool air from vents under the seats. Inside and

out, the theatre is an attractive blending of Beaux Arts style and Art Nouveau detailing.

June 15 At the end of the current 1902–1903 Broadway season, 26 theatres and performance spaces have accomodated a total of 99 productions. Of these, ten have been musicals, 40 of them plays—with six revivals, 7 musical plays, 2 musical farces, 20 comedies, 2 farces, 5 comic operas—two of them revivals, 2 extravaganzas, 1 vaudeville, and two one-acts. There have been three shows in repertory. The last opening of the season has been on June 8.

June 16 Harry W. Bishop of San Fransisco obtains a patent for a revolving stage on which several stage settings may be placed and rotated into the view of the audience.

July 4 The closing performance of the

Gaiety Theatre on the Strand is followed by a valedictory speech by Sir Henry Irving and the singing of *Auld Lang Syne*. The new Gaiety Theatre at Aldwych and the Strand is nearing completion.

Oct 13 The New Amsterdam Theatre (1,700 seats) managed by Klaw and Erlanger, opens on West 42nd Street in New York City, with *A Midsummer Night's Dream*. The architects are Herts and Tallant. The architectural style is Art Nouveau. The stage is 100 ft. × 60 ft. with a 40 ft. proscenium width. There is also a rooftop theatre seating 700.

Oct 26 The new Gaiety Theatre opens at Aldwych and the Strand with a production of *The Orchid*. King Edward VII and Queen Alexandra are in the audience.

Oct 29 The Hudson Theatre opens with Ethel Barrymore in *Cousin Kate*. The theatre is on the north side of 44th Street, between 6th Avenue and Broadway, in New York City. The facade is simply treated in the Renaissance style.

Nov 2 Minnie Maddern Fiske opens in the new Majestic Theatre in Toronto, Canada with *Mary of Magdalen*. Rebuilt from the remains of the old Toronto Opera House (gutted by fire in March 1903), the Majestic, along with Shea's and the Star, serves the large Toronto audience for vaudeville, burlesque, and popular melodrama.

Nov 2 The Lyric Theatre in New York City opens on West 42nd Street, with *Old Heidelberg*. This is the first New York theatre built by the Shuberts.

Nov 2 The New Lyceum (later called the Lyceum), on New York's West 45th St, is designed by Herts and Tallant and owned by producer Daniel Frohman. It opens with *The Proud Prince*. The Lyceum suffers hard times in the Depression, but survives. In the late 1960's, the APA-Phoenix Repertory Company takes up residence. In the 1970's, it is given Landmark status.

Nov 23 Chicago's fire-proof Iroquois Theatre opens. The latest engineering innovations and safety devices have been employed in the design.

Dec 30 Chicago's Iroquois Theatre is devastated by fire during a performance by Eddie Foy in *Mr. Bluebeard*. Panic, crowding, and suffocation cause the worst losses and injuries. 602 people die.

Jan 5 *The Virginian* (NY—Manhattan—Drama). Owen Wister, with the aid of Kirke La Shelle, adapts his best-selling novel of adventure in the Far West for the stage. It runs over 17 weeks. Dustin Farnum stars.

Jan 19 *The Secret of Polichinelle* (NY—Madison Square—Comedy). Pierre Wolff's play uses *Commedia dell'arte* characters for its inspiration. James K. Hackett produces and directs. The production runs nearly 16 weeks.

Feb 10 *The Pit* (NY—Lyric—Drama). Channing Pollock adapts Frank Norris' strong indictment of the commodities market for the stage. In the cast are Wilton Lackaye and Douglas Fairbanks. William A. Brady's production runs for 77 performances.

Feb 22 *The Yankee Consul* (NY—Broadway—Musical). Henry Blossom, Jr. creates the book and lyrics, with a score by Alfred Robyn. Raymond Hitchcock stars as an American consul who gets mixed up in a marriage-for-revenge plan and a threatened Latin American revolution. The arrival of the U.S. Navy—often seen in contemporary musicals—quells the rebellion. George Marion stages. The production runs over 14 weeks.

April 2 *Piff! Paff! Pouf!* (NY—Casino—Musical). Eddie Foy stars as one of four suitors who will help Augustus Melon (Joseph Miron) to inherit his late wife's fortune by marrying off his daughter. This is the first full score composed for Broadway by Jean Schwartz, partnered by William Jerome with lyrics. There is a "Radium Dance," in which chorines in luminescent costumes jump glowing ropes. The show, a considerable hit, runs for 33 weeks.

April 4 *The Dictator* (NY—Criterion—Comedy). Richard Harding Davis gives a serious title to his lively farce about a Central American "banana republic." The play contains such elements as mistaken identity, revolution, counter-revolution and a military *coup d'etat* to make the plot interesting. It features John Barrymore, William Collier and Thomas Meighan. The play runs nearly two months. On May 3, 1905, Davis's play opens in London at the Comedy Theatre with William Collier and his company. Collier plays the lead.

May 23 *The Southerners* (NY—New York—Musical). Eddie Leonard puts on blackface to play Uncle Daniel in this musical about life in the antebellum South. This is the first time an entire black chorus is used in a show with a white cast. The score is by black composer Will Marion Cook. The show has only 36 performances. The *NY Times* reports that: "When the chorus of real live coons walked in for the cakewalk last night at the New York Theatre, mingling with the white members of the cast, there were those in the audience who trembled in their seats, as if expecting another Pelée explosion. It was only a year ago that the entire cast of a farce at the Madison Square struck because a single gentleman of color was engaged to play the part of a negro porter, and held out until the said gentleman was utterly cast out. . . . It was rumored that he [Will Marion Cook, the Negro composer] had supplied his darky aides with safety razors. . . . The proscenium boxes, it is true, were reported to be filled with lily whites who had retreated before the thunderstorm. One blonde in particular there was who had refused to be associated with black. But even she smiled and looked polite. Mr. Cook's revolution was brought off triumphantly."

June 6 *A Little Bit of Everything* (NY—Aerial Gardens/New Amsterdam—Revue). This popular summer show (120 performances) mingles Offenbach with vaudeville. Fay Templeton and Peter Dailey head the troupe, directed by Herbert Gresham and Ned Wayburn. Richard Marston designs the settings.

Aug 23 *The Isle of Spice* (NY—Majestic—Musical). Yet another show set on a tropical island, this features Bompopka, King of Nicobar, who puts his wives away in a Tomb of Silence when they reach the age of 35. The U.S. Navy arrives in time to get things right. The customary military drill is provided by 17 U.S. Marines (real ones) from the Brooklyn Navy Yard. The show, staged by Gus Sohlke, originated in Chicago. It runs 10 weeks.

Sep 3 *Mrs. Wiggs of the Cabbage Patch* (NY—Savoy—Comedy). Alice Heggan Rice's best-sellers, *Mrs. Wiggs* and *Lovey Mary*, become a very successful play about the triumph of optimism and hard work over poverty. Madge Carr Cook stars with Mabel Taliaferro and Edith Story. Oscar Eagle does the staging and also plays Mr. Wiggs. The show has a run of nearly 19 weeks. It arrives in London on April 27, 1907, with Cook as Mrs. Wiggs. The production wins 268 showings. *The Times* critics call Cook's acting, "nothing short of perfect."

Sep 5 *A Madcap Princess* (NY—Knickerbocker—Musical). Harry B. Smith bases his libretto on the stage version of the best-selling Charles Major novel, *When Knighthood Was in Flower*. In the story, Mary Tudor (Lulu Glaser) defies her brother, Henry VIII, and elopes with Charles Brandon. Ludwig Englander provides the score; Edward Temple, the direction and Homer Emens and Edward Unitt, the settings. The show runs only six weeks.

Sep 5 *The Rogers Brothers in Paris* (NY—

The Virginian

New Amsterdam—Musical). The brothers call this a "vaudeville farce," for it has the thinnest of plots. There is an auto race on stage with two real cars racing around a painted Place de la Concorde. Ned Wayburn and Herbert Gresham stage the ensemble, including Gus and Max Rogers, Josephine Cohan and Fred Niblo. The production manages a nine week run.

Sep 20 *The College Widow* (NY—Garden—Comedy). George Ade creates a popular play about the efforts of a winsome girl to keep a football hero from deserting her father's college for another school which might defeat them. The show with staging by George Marion and sets by Walter Burridge, runs for almost 35 weeks.

Sep 26 *The Music Master* (NY—Belasco—Comedy). David Warfield, directed by David Belasco, realizes one of his most notable roles as Anton Van Barwig, the master. Charles Klein is the playwright; the production runs nearly nine months.

Sep 26 *How He Lied To Her Husband* (NY—Berkeley Lyceum—Comedy). For one week only, Arnold Daly plays the lover in the world premiere of this parody of *Candida*, which George Bernard Shaw has written for Daly. On February 28, 1905 Shaw's play opens at the Court Theatre in London featuring Harley Granville Barker, Gertrude Kingston, and A. G. Poulton. Also on the bill are W.B. Yeats'

The Pot of Broth and Arthur Schnitzler's *In the Hospital*. Because the triple-bill is judged a failure, Shaw refuses to accept royalties from the Vedrenne-Barker management. Critic Desmond McCarthy describes Shaw's play as, "knock-about satire . . . a seedy kind of fun." He finds Shaw's characters "as contemptible as they are ridiculous, and yet real enough to make you believe in them."

Oct 3 *Love's Lottery* (NY—Broadway—Musical). This show is clearly a vehicle for the non-operatic debut of Mme. Ernestine Schumann-Heink. It lasts 50 performances, more a tribute to the star's drawing power than to the libretto and score of Stanislaus Stange and Julian Ed-

The College Widow

wards. Schumann-Heink portrays a German laundress in the England of 1818, who wins a lottery and the affection of a sergeant.

Oct 10 *The Sho-gun* (NY—Wallack's—Musical). With a book by humorists George Ade and a score by Gustav Luders, this show, takes Americans to Ka-Choo, the presumed capital of Korea. The Goo-Goo Chewing Gum King has come from America to persuade the Sho-gun to chew his product. Before the tangled events can end in disaster, the U.S. Navy appears to

straighten things out. George Marion directs characters with names such as Flai-Hai, Hanki-Panki, Omee-Omi, and Hunni-Bun. The show runs nearly 16 weeks.

Oct 10 *The Sorceress* (NY—New Amsterdam—Drama). Mrs. Patrick Campbell stars in Victorien Sardou's play, translated by Louis N. Parker. The production manages only 36 performances.

Oct 20 *Higgledy-Piggledy* (NY—Weber's Musical Hall—Revue). Joseph Weber, having broken with his partner Lew Fields, joins Florenz Ziegfeld to produce this thinly plotted show featuring two "Dutch" Americans touring Europe. Marie Dressler, playing Weber's daughter, is cheered singing "A Great Big Girl Like Me." Anna Held is starred as a Parisian lovely. George Marion directs; Sam Marion stages the dances. The show runs for 23 weeks.

Oct 24 *Granny* (NY—Lyceum—Drama). Clyde Fitch adapts the French play of Georges Mitchell as a vehicle for Mrs. G. H. Gilbert to make her farewell to the stage. At the close of each performance, she reads a poem written for her by Fitch, who also stages the show. The company plays three weeks in New York, moving on to Chicago, where four days after the opening, Mrs. Gilbert dies, at the age of 83.

Nov 7 *Little Johnny Jones* (NY—Liberty—Musical). George M. Cohan stars for the first time on Broadway in this show which he has written (book, lyrics, music) and staged. Cohan is an American jockey in England, the "Yankee Doodle Boy," but his reputation is smirched by a villain. As his ship sails for home, he stays behind to clear himself, singing "Give My Regards to Broadway" to the passengers. An impressive transformation scene shows the passage of time until a rocket goes up from the ship to signal that evidence exonerating him has been found. Cohan's parents and his wife, Ethel Levey, are on hand. The *NY Times* reports that: "*Little Johnny Jones* has even less dramatic reason for existence than did *The Governor's Son*, with which the Cohan family first invaded the legitimate."

Nov 14 *Humpty Dumpty* (NY—New (NY—New Amsterdam—Musical). John McNally adapts this British Christmas pantomime by J. Hickory Wood and Arthur Collins. Bob Cole and Rosamond Johnson's songs are especially admired, including "Sambo and Dinah," which tells how "dusky lovers bill and coo." Ned Wayburn and Herbert Gresham do the staging, with ballets by Ernest D'Auban.

Led by Frank Moulan, the cast draws the public for almost 17 weeks.

Nov 15 *Sunday* (NY—Hudson—Drama). Ethel Barrymore is featured in Thomas Raceward's play. With sets by Joseph Physioc and Ernest Gros and staging by William Seymour, the production enjoys a 10-week run.

Nov 21 *The Two Roses* (NY—Broadway—Musical). Stanislaus Stange decides to turn Goldsmith's *She Stoops To Conquer* from classic play to short-run (29 performances) musical. Ludwig Englander and Gustav Kerker devise a score. Fritzi Scheff, as Rose, must carry the show. She receives her biggest applause when she interpolates some arias from her operatic repertoire.

Nov 21 *Woodland* (NY—New York—Musical). From Chicago comes an unusual production with book and lyrics by Frank Pixley, and music by Gustav Luders. All the characters are birds such as Miss Nightingale, Prince Eagle, Blue Jay, and the King of the Birds. The show runs ten weeks.

Dec 5 *It Happened in Nordland* (NY—Lew Field's—Musical). The American Ambassadress (Marie Cahill) is a double for the mysteriously vanished Queen of Nordland. She stands in until the Queen returns, finding her long-lost brother (Lew Fields) in the process. Spectacles are lavish, especially a carnival scene. Victor Herbert composes an attractive score, but he fails to forbid interpolations by the stars. Cahill's additions infuriate him and she leaves the show after 154 performances. Blanche Ring replaces her.

Dec 12 *Leah Kleschna* (NY—Manhattan—Drama). Produced by Minnie Maddern Fiske and Harrison Grey Fiske, C.M.S. McLellan's play is rewritten with a happy ending for Mrs. Fiske who plays the title role. The story is about a thief who reforms. In the cast also are John Mason, George Arliss, Etienne Girardot, Charles Terry, and Mary Maddern. The play runs 131 performances. The *NY Times* praises Mrs. Fiske's acting as "marked by that exceptional quality of intellectual analysis which creates and sustains interest in everything she attempts." On May 2, 1905 the show has its London premiere at the New Theatre. It runs 186 performances. The cast which receives raves includes Lena Ashwell as Leah. Others are Charles Warner, Leonard Boyne, and Herbert Waring.

1904 BRITISH PREMIERES

Jan 19 *Joseph Entangled* (L—Haymarket—Comedy). Henry Arthur Jones' new play wins 137 performances. Cyril Maude, Herbert Waring, Sam Sothern, Ellis Jeffreys, Beatrice Ferrar, Mrs. Charles Cal-

vert, and Winifred Arthur Jones are in the ensemble.

Jan 20 *The Duke of Killicrankie* (L—Criterion—Comedy). Captain Robert Marshall's farcical play boasts a cast includ-

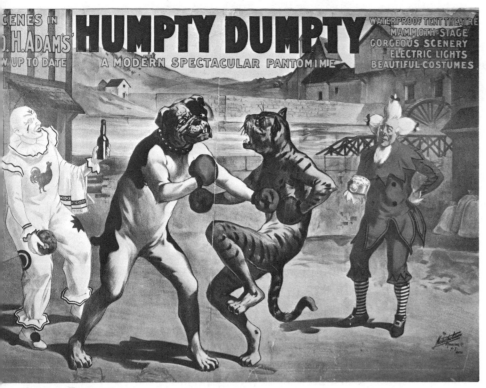

HUMPTY DUMPTY

O.H. ADAMS' A MODERN SPECTACULAR PANTOMIME

SCENES IN ... UP TO DATE

WATERPROOF TENT THEATRE
MAMMOTH STAGE
GORGEOUS SCENERY
ELECTRIC LIGHTS
BEAUTIFUL COSTUMES

Humpty Dumpty

ing Weedon Grossmith, Graham Browne, Marie Illington, and Eva Moore. It achieves 328 performances. With John Drew in the lead role, this play opens on Sep 5, at New York's Empire Theatre. It has a 16-week run.

Feb 10 *The Love Birds* (L—Savoy—Musical). George Grossmith's new musical comedy re-opens the Savoy. Raymond Roze contributes the score. In the company are Lottie Venne, Blanche Ring, Kate Cutler, Lawrence Grossmith, and Bertram Wallis.

Feb 18 *A Man of Honour* (L—Avenue—Drama). W. Somerset Maugham offers some social dissection in this play about a gentlemen engaged in a missionary effort to uplift a woman of low breeding. Marriage is his means, but when she discovers he doesn't really love her but is only trying to reform her, she drowns herself. He is horrified, but nonetheless rejoices in his regained freedom. The *Times* reviewer writes: "the play strikes us as powerful; and we feel a certain grim attraction, even fascination, in it by reason of its close and unflinching observation of some of the more sordid aspects of our poor human nature."

March 5 *The Cingalee* (L—Daly's—Musical). There are 385 performances for this tale of love on the other side of the world. James Tanner provides the book; Lionel Monckton is credited with the music, and lyrics are provided by Adrian Ross, Percy Greenbank, and Paul Rubens. In the major roles are Huntley Wright, Hayden Coffin, Fred Kaye, Willie Warde, Isabel Jay, Sybil Arundale, and Gracie Leigh. The reviewer for *The Times* finds the plot too

trivial and unimportant to be worth the trouble of the unravelling.

April 14 *Saturday to Monday* (L—St. James's—Comedy). Frederick Fenn and Richard Pryer's new piece is called an "irresponsible comedy." George Alexander heads the cast, with A. Vane Tempest, E. Vivian Reynolds, Elinor Aickin, Beatrice Forbes Robertson, and Lilian Braithwaite also in the cast. It earns 100 performances.

April 16 *The Wheat King* (L—Apollo—Drama). *The Pit*, Frank Norris' American novel, exposing the effects of stockmarket manipulations is adapted by Mrs. Ashton Johnson and Miss Elliott Page. Murray Carson and Esme Beringer play.

May 3 *Harlequin and the Fairy's Dilemma* (L—Garrick—Comedy). W. S. Gilbert reworks some traditional materials and characters. Actor-manager Arthur Bourchier takes a lead, along with Violet Vanbrugh, Jessie Bateman, Dorothy Grimston, Sydney Valentine, and Jerrold Robertshaw.

May 18 *Veronique* (L—Apollo—Musical). The play, based on André Messager's French opera, gets a British book by Henry Hamilton and lyrics by Lilian Eldee and Percy Greenbank. With a company including Rosina Brandram, Ruth Vincent, Kitty Gordon, George Graves, and Lawrence Rea, the production runs 495 performances.

June 18 *Sergeant Brue* (L—Strand—Musical). Liza Lehman creates the score for Owen Hall's libretto. The story is about a young man, Brue, who must earn promotion to sergeant in order to get a large

bequest. Willie Edouin, Arthur Williams, Olive Morrel, Zena Dare, and Ethel Irving are in the cast. The show enjoys 280 performances. This London hit repeats its success, with a 19-week run following its opening on April 24, 1905 at New York's Knickerbocker Theatre. Frank Daniels has the lead and Blanche Ring interpolates "My Irish Molly O" to audience cheers.

Sep 9 *The Catch of the Season* (L—Vaudeville—Musical). Actor-manager Seymour Hicks plays the lead in this new musical which he has written in collaboration with Cosmo Gordon Hamilton. It is a variation on the Cinderella story. Zena Dare, Rosina Filippi, and Ethel Matthews are also in the company. The show wins a long run of 621 performances. On August 28, 1905, this London hit opens at New York's Daly Theatre with a run of 13 weeks. Edna May stars. Ben Teal stages, in settings by Ernest Gros. The play has been padded out with numerous American song interpolations.

Oct 6 *His Majesty's Servant* (L—Imperial—Drama). This romantic play, by Sarah Barnwell Elliott and Maud Hosford, wins 126 performances. Lewis Waller, H. V. Esmond, Norman McKinnel, Evelyn Millard, and Mary Rorke are in the main roles.

Oct 12 *A Wife Without a Smile* (L—Wyndham's—Comedy). Arthur Wing Pinero's new play is interpreted by Dion Boucicault, G. M. Grahame, Lettice Fairfax, Dorothy Grimston, and Margaret Illington. The unsmiling wife has the misfortune to be newly wed to a husband who thinks he has a fine sense of humor. Some critics object to a dancing doll, attached to the ceiling, to signal activity in the bedroom above; it's vulgar. On Dec 19, the play premieres in New York at the Criterion Theatre but only runs 16 performances. The cast includes Margaret Illington and Elsie De Wolfe.

Oct 31 *The Walls of Jericho* (L—Garrick—Drama). Alfred Sutro's attack on high society is produced by Arthur Bourchier, who also plays a leading part, with other major roles taken by Sydney Valentine, Muriel Béaumont, and Violet Vanbrugh. The production earns an impressive run of 423 performances. *The Times* reviewer, however, criticizes the work for its prejudiced picture of the upper class. Sutro's play is also a hit in New York. It opens on Sep 25, 1905 at the Savoy, with a cast headed by James K. Hackett, who also stages. Mary Mannering and Harriet Otis Dellenbaugh are also in the ensemble. Joseph Physioc designs the sets.

Aug 30 *Beauty and the Barge* (L—New—Comedy). Cyril Maude, Kenneth Douglas, Jessie Bateman, and Mrs. Charles Calvert take major roles in this farce about a flirtatious sea captain by W. W. Jacobs and Louis N. Parker. The production achieves 219 performances. The *Times* praises the play's: "fresh, homely, slightly tarry flavour. . . . It is a new flavour in the theatre, which sorely needs the introduction of new flavours, and the taste of it sent the audience last night into paroxysms of delight."

Nov 1 *John Bull's Other Island* (L—Court—Comedy). George Bernard Shaw's "new and unpublished play" opens in a series of six November matinees. Troublesome Ireland is the "other" island. The play's emphasis is on the contrast between an Englishman and an Irishman. Under the Vedrenne-Barker management of the Royal Court Theatre, Granville Barker, Louis Calvert and Nigel Playfair play. Ellen O'Malley plays Judy. *The Times* reports: "The play delights us . . . by its able dialectic. Its interlocutors never shirk a point or swerve from it; every side gets a fair hearing . . . on the other hand the play is a disappointment because of its willful, perverse disregard of anything like construction. . . . A rivulet of 'story' meanders through a meadow of 'Shawisms' and trickles dry long before the curtain descends."

Nov 14 *The Freedom of Suzanne* (L—Criterion—Comedy). Cosmo Gordon Lennox writes a light comedy, which is animated by Allan Aynesworth and Marie Tempest. It earns 156 performances.

Dec 17 *Lady Madcap* (L—Prince of Wales's—Musical). This show about an aristocratic young woman who masquerades as a maid to meet sturdy yeomen, has a score by Paul Rubens and a libretto by Rubens and N. Newnham Davies. Adrienne Augarde and G.P. Huntley take the leads.

Dec 27 *Peter Pan, Or the Boy Who Wouldn't Grow Up* (L—Duke of York's—Comedy). James Barrie's fantasy of Never-Never Land—with the eternal boy, Peter; a fairy, Tinkerbell; a family of flying children, the Darlings; and the infamous Captain Hook—instantly charms audiences. In the cast are Nina Boucicault (Peter), Gerald Du Maurier, Hilda Trevelyan, Dorothea Baird, Pauline Chase, George Shelton, and young George Hersee. The production runs for 145 performances. It becomes an annual event, featuring popular actresses as Peter. It receives a glowing review in the *Times*: "The whole affair is a delicious frolic, touched with the lightest of hands, full of quiet wisdom and sweet charity, under its surface of wild fun, and here and there not without a place for a furtive tear. It is lucky in its players. For Miss Nina Boucicault, as Peter Pan, knows well how to blend pathos with frolicsomeness. . . . As for Mr. Gerald Du Maurier we know not whether we like him best as the respectable, black-coated Mr. Darling or as the luridly melodramatic Pirate King or as the momentary mimic of Sir Henry Irving, as Mr. Beerbohm Tree, and Mr. Martin Harvey." *Peter Pan* opens in New York on November 6, 1905 at the Empire. Here Barrie's play repeats its London success, complete with flying apparatus for Maude Adams as Peter and for the Darling children. Ernest Lawford is Hook, and Jane Wren, Tinker Bell. The initial run lasts for 223 performances, followed by tours and revivals.

1904 REVIVALS/REPERTORIES

Jan 4 *Lew Dockstader's Mistrels* fullfill a month's engagment at New York's Victoria Theatre. In the traditional minstrel format, Dockstader and fellow performers manage to spoof a variety of New York fads and foibles, including the Mayor and gossip at Sherry's. Also in the company are Carroll Johnson, Eddie Leonard, John Daly, Max Schenck, and Bert White.

Jan 14 The eighth series of Irish plays, produced by W. G. Fay and company for the Irish National Theatre Society, opens in Dublin at Molesworth Hall.

Jan 18 For three weeks, Ada Rehan and Otis Skinner appear in repertory at New York's Lyric Theatre, offering Shakespeare's *The Taming of the Shrew*, *The Merchant of Venice*, and Sheridan's *The School for Scandal*. This engagement is produced by Liebler & Company. Immediately following it, Sam S. Shubert moves the *Shrew* and *Scandal* productions to the Liberty Theatre, where each has a week's run, Otis Skinner having been replaced by Charles Richman.

Feb 8 Charles Frohman presents Viola Allen as Viola in Shakespeare's *Twelfth Night* for a two-week run at New York's Knickerbocker Theatre. On February 22, Frohman replaces this company with the Ben Greet ensemble for two weeks. The play remains the same, but this time Edith Wynne Matthison is Viola, and Greet, who also directs, is Malvolio.

Feb 17 At the Royal Court Theatre in London's Sloane Square, *Romeo and Juliet* comes to life again with Charles Lander and Thirza Norman. On April 8, *Two Gentlemen of Verona* returns to the stage, with Norman Acton Bond, William Devereaux, and others. *Timon of Athens* is revived on May 18. These are J.H. Leigh's efforts to provide a London season of Shakespeare, soon to be upstaged by the Vedrenne-Barker productions of Shaw and other moderns at the Court Theatre.

Feb 25 The Irish National Theatre Society premieres J. M. Synge's *Riders to the Sea* in Dublin at Molesworth Hall. In March the Society will present Yeats' *The King's Threshold* and Synge's *Riders to the Sea* and *In the Shadow of the Glen* at London's Royalty Theatre.

March 1 Richard Mansfield opens his New York season of repertory, at the New Amsterdam. *Ivan the Terrible*, by Alexis Tolstoi, has its American premiere that night and runs for two weeks. In an additional two weeks, Mansfield offers *Ivan*, *Old Heidelberg*, *Beau Brummell*, *A Parisian Romance*, *Beaucaire*, and *Dr. Jekyll and Mr. Hyde*.

March 28 That popular 19th century melodrama, *The Two Orphans*, is revived for 7 weeks at the New Amsterdam Theatre in New York to tumultuous applause. Grace George and Margaret Illington are the unfortunate orphans. William Seymour directs.

March 28 Henrik Ibsen's play, *Rosmersholm* has its Broadway premiere at the Princess Theatre. Although the actors call themselves The Century Players, they are clearly survivors of the National Theatre Company which preceded them. William Morris stars with Florence Kahn. Panned by the *NY Times* for both its poor acting and crude adaptation of the text, it runs for eight performances.

April 15 Ibsen's *Pillars of Society* is presented for one matinee at New York's Lyric Theatre. Wilton Lackaye, Maude Wilson, and George Kelley lead the cast.

April 18 At New York's Harlem Opera House, *Camille*, by Dumas fils, is revived for one week, with Virginia Harned and William Courtenay as Marguerite and Armand. With some cast changes, this troupe plays a further week in May at the Garrick Theatre.

April 18 Charles Frohman revives *Camille* at the Hudson Theatre in New York, with Margaret Anglin and Henry Miller as Marguerite and Armand. This runs for two weeks.

April 18 At Stratford-upon-Avon, the annual Shakespeare Festival opens with *The Merchant of Venice*, directed by Frank Benson. On April 23, there is a matinee of *Hamlet*, followed by *As You Like It* in the evening. During the three-week season, Benson's players offer 11 other Shakespearean dramas in the Memorial Theatre. An added dramatic dividend is the staging of the *Oresteian Trilogy* of Aeschylus.

April 26 At London's Royal Court Theatre, Bernard Shaw's *Candida* is presented in a series of six matinee performances. Kate Rorke is Candida, with Granville Barker as Marchbanks and Norman McKinnel as Candida's pastor-husband, Morell. The audience shouts "author" and rapidly vacates the theatre to catch a glimpse of Shaw next door on the Underground platform. This production is a prelude to the formation of the Vedrenne-Barker management at the Court, which will last until 1907.

May 16 Julia Marlowe and Tyrone Power appear as Parthenia and Ingomar in a special matinee of *Ingomar*, produced by Charles Frohman at his Empire Theatre in New York.

June 13 At London's Prince of Wales's

Theatre, Mme. Rejane opens a two-week season of her French repertoire with *Zaza*.

June 20 At His Majesty's Theatre, Sarah Bernhardt opens her London season with Sardou's *La Sorciere*.

Sep 12 Franklin Thompson revives the popular local-color drama of Denman Thompson and George Ryer, *The Old Homestead*, for almost eight weeks at the New York Theatre. Thompson appears with Annie and Venie Thompson.

Oct 17 Charles Frohman presents E. H. Sothern and Julia Marlowe, together for the first time in a program of Shakespeare revivals. The plays are *Hamlet*, *Romeo and Juliet*, and *Much Ado About Nothing*. Mrs. Sol Smith plays Juliet's Nurse.

Oct 18 At the Royal Court Theatre in London, the new Vedrenne-Barker management offers Gilbert Murray's translation of *The Hippolytus* of Euripides for six matinee performances. Ben Webster acts with Edyth Olive. On Nov 15, they begin six matinees of Maeterlinck's *Aglavaine and Selysette*, translated by Alfred Sutro. Edyth Olive and Thyrza Norman act. Two weeks later Shaw's *Candida* returns for 10 performances. On Dec 23 Granville-Barker plays Pierrot in *Prunella: Or, Love in a Dutch Garden*, which he has written with Laurence Houseman. Thyrza Norman and Lewis Casson are in the cast.

Nov 7 The celebrated French actress, Gabrielle Rejane, opens a month of repertory in French at the Lyric Theatre in New York. Among the productions are *Amoureuse*, *Lolotte*, *La Robe Rouge* (Brieux), *La Petite Marquise*, *La Dame aux Camelias* (Dumas, fils), *Incognito*, *L'Hirondelle*, *Ma Cousine*, *Sapho* (Daudet), *La Douleureuse*, *La Parisienne* (Becque), *La Passerelle*, and *Zaza*. In her ensemble are Suzanne Avril and Jeannin Kelm.

Nov 19 In London, Oscar Wilde's *Lady Windermere's Fan* is revived at the St. James's Theatre.

Nov 21 At London's Royalty Theatre, the Mermaid Society begins a series of productions of neglected Jacobean and Restoration plays with Ford's *The Broken Heart*. On November 28, Vanbrugh's *The Confederacy* is staged. On December 5, the play is *The Maid's Tragedy*, by Beaumont and Fletcher. On December 26, the Mermaid Society offers Beaumont and Fletcher's *The Knight of the Burning Pestle*.

Nov 28 Nance O'Neil is featured in this Manhattan premiere of Hermann Sudermann's German play, *The Fires of St. John*. It runs a week.

Nov 29 At London's Adelphi Theatre, Oscar Asche and Lily Brayton play Petruchio and Katherine in a revival of *The Taming of the Shrew*.

Dec 5 Robert B. Mantell opens a fortnight's repertory of *Othello*, *Richard III*, and Bulwer-Lytton's *Richelieu* at New York's Princess Theatre. Marie Booth

Russell plays opposite him.

Dec 21 The holiday season pervades London's West End. At the Garrick Theatre, the children's pantomime treat is *Little Black Sambo and Little White Barbara*, by Rutland Barrington. The curtain-raiser at these matinees is Tom Gallon's *Lady Jane's Christmas Party*.

Dec 24 At the Casino Theatre in New York, *Lady Teazle* opens, with score by A. Baldwin Sloane, music by John Kendrick Bangs and Roderic Penfield, based on Sheridan's *The School for Scandal*. Lillian Russell stars. The 86 chorus girls outnumber the 57 performances. Sam S.

Shubert and R. H. Burnside direct.

Dec 26 It's Boxing Day in London. At the Drury Lane, Hickory Wood and Arthur Collins' pantomime opens. It's called *The White Cat*.

Dec 26 Charles Frohman revives James Barrie's *The Little Minister* for 73 performances at New York's Empire with Maude Adams starring.

Dec 27 In Dublin, the new Abbey Theatre, opens with the Irish National Theatre Society's productions of Yeats' *On Baile's Strand*, Lady Gregory's *Spreading the News*, and a revival of Yeats' *Cathleen Ni Houlihan*.

1904 BIRTHS/DEATHS/DEBUTS

Jan 13 Oliver Messel is born in London, England.

Feb 15 Future English designer Elizabeth Montgomery, of Motley fame, is born in Oxfordshire, England.

Feb 21 American actor Owen Fawcett (b. 1839) dies.

Mar 26 American actor Dan Daly (b. 1858) dies.

April 28 British actress Nellie Farren (b. 1846) dies today.

May 14 Ethel Barrymore appears on the London stage at Wyndham's Theatre in *Cynthia*, a Hubert Henry Davies' play.

June 10 New York drama critic and author Laurence Hutton is dead at age 60. Among his many published works are *Curiosities of the American Stage* and *Other Times and Other Seasons*. He also edited the five-volume *American Actors Series* (1881–82).

July 22 British actor-manager-playwright Wilson Barrett (b. 1847) dies.

Aug 4 Drama critic Harold Hobson is born

in Yorkshire, England.

Sep 19 The Broadway premiere of *Mr. Wix of Wickham* is notable because it marks the debut of composer Jerome Kern, who contributes some songs to the score. Julian Eltinge also makes his debut here as a female impersonator. Edward E. Rice, long associated with the American musical theatre—co-author of *Evangeline* and *Adonis*—ends his producing career with this show.

Oct 6 Producer-director Alfred de Liagre is born in Passaic, New Jersey.

Nov 28 Czech actress Francesca Janauschek dies at the Actor's Fund Home at age 74. Janauschek made her debut in Prague in 1846, and two years later became leading lady of the Frankfurt Stadttheater. She toured extensively in Europe and the United States. In 1873 she undertook to play in English, appearing in a number of Shakespearean roles.

Dec 2 Born in 1822, the American actress Mrs. G. H. Gilbert dies.

1904 THEATERS/PRODUCTIONS

In Britain this year patents are granted for: De Dio Boggie's scenic background, painted to resemble a picture-postcard album, with the picture areas open to display tableaux-vivants; I. N. Lyons' device for raising and lowering scenic drops, using a shaft and drum, driven by worm-gears and motor, with batten-cables winding around the drum. This is only one of a number of patents for improved, mechanized means of flying scenery, doing away with flymen.

U.S. patents granted this year include: Edward Austen's device in which an iceberg or an island seems to float along on a body of water. Edgar Healy has devised a rainbow effect, projected by a group of stereopticons. Isabelle Green—better known to her fans as Belle LaVerde—pat-

ents a costume with concealable luminescent panels. When these are revealed under proper illumination, she seems transformed into an insect.

At the present time, the Shubert Brothers are producing shows which play in theatres controlled or owned by the Theatrical Syndicate, as well as in their own theatres. Shubert theatres are booked through the Klaw and Erlanger Exchange. The Syndicate is operating a virtual monopoly, setting terms to please its operators, rather than to accomodate producers who are working on relatively slim profit-margins. Currently, the Shuberts control 15 theatres, employing 1,200 people and paying $65,000 weekly in salaries.

LYRIC THEATRE

SAM S. AND LEE SHUBERT INC. MANAGERS

REGINALD DE KOVEN
PROPRIETOR

Lyric Theater Program

Following last year's tragic fire at the Iroquois Theatre in Chicago, the structure has been renovated and renamed Hyde & Behman's Theatre. Designed by Benjamin Marshall, the house seats 1,724. In 1905, it will become the Colonial Theatre. It will be razed in 1925, to be replaced by the Oriental Theatre, opening in 1926.

Founded in 1899, the Stage Society is now incorporated in London. Among its members are James Barrie, Gilbert Murray, and G. B. and Charlotte Shaw.

After witnessing a private performance by the Stage Society of Leo Tolstoi's *The Power of Darkness*, Britain's Lord Chamberlain relents and grants a license for public performance, although the play has already been widely staged abroad. His censors have previously regarded the drama as a sordid display of crime and immorality. The play's moral purpose is explained to the Lord Chamberlain after the performance.

March 18 Tonight marks the 1,000th performance of *A Chinese Honeymoon* at London's Strand Theatre.

June 15 At the end of this Broadway season, there have been a total of 126 productions in some 30 different theatre spaces. 18 have been revivals. Three companies played 12 repertory productions, 7 of them revivals. There have been 18 musicals, 1 minstrel show, 3 extra-vaganzas, 4 comic operas, 2 operettas, and 2 musical plays, as well as 1 vaudeville and one burlesque each. There were 52 dramas produced, 6 of them revivals, with *Camille* offered by two ensembles at the same time. Comedy has been represented by 22 shows, 3 of them revivals. There were also five farces and 3 one-acts.

Aug 4 A patent is granted for the creation of a new theatre in Dublin, the Abbey Theatre, dedicated to Irish plays and classical plays translated from continental languages. On Dec 25 the Abbey opens in what was formerly the Mechanic's Institute. The building has been purchased for W. B. Yeats and the Irish National Theatre Society by a generous patron, Annie E. F. Horniman. The Abbey will soon earn an international reputation for its plays and its players. Later, in 1907, tiring of this "singularly ungrateful theatrical Cinderella," Horniman will move herself and her fortune to Manchester where she will build a new repertory company of note.

Aug 31 *The Times* of London begins publishing cast lists accompanying its reviews of West End premieres. Only major characters are listed, and no directors, designers, or producers are cited.

Fall At the opening of the new theatre season in Chicago, these are the major operating theatres: the Auditorium, the Powers, the Illinois, the Grand Opera House, the Garrick, the Studebaker, McVickers, the Chicago Opera House, Hyde & Behman's, the Olympic, the Great Northern, the Music Hall, the La Salle, Cleveland's, the Columbus, the Alhambra, the Academy of Music, the Bijou, the Haymarket, the People's, the Criterion, and the Bush Temple.

Oct 18 With the opening of Gilbert Murray's version of *Hippolytus* at London's Royal Court Theatre, the Vedrenne-Barker management begins a series of productions—32 plays in all, for a total of 988 separate performances—which will come to a close on June 29, 1907. John E. Vedrenne handles the business affairs, with Harley Granville Barker as artistic manager, advised by George Bernard Shaw. There are no stars in this theatre, and even classics are produced as though they have been written for modern audiences. Truth in acting and simplicity in production are hallmarks of the work. Shaw is represented by 11 plays. Other playwrights performed include Maeterlinck, Masefield, Hauptmann, Schnitzler, Yeats, Ibsen, and Galsworthy.

Dec Curious about the number of chorus girls in the Shubert musical, *Lady Teazle*, the *New York World* conducts a survey among the 86 beauties. When they work, which is seldom more than 20 weeks per year, they receive $18 per week. Being in a show chorus is, however, often only a means to an end. 48 of the girls questioned admit they have "independent means." Furs and jewels are the boast of 78 chorines. Seven own new, expensive automobiles; another seven are driven to the theatre in carriages. Not all chorus girls (and boys) are kept; for a number, this exposure may lead to better opportunities on stage.

Dec 12 Harrison Grey Fiske and Minnie Maddern Fiske have bought and refurbished the Manhattan Theater to give them a New York home, because the Theatrical Trust has frozen them out.

Dec 15 Chicago's new Orchestra Hall is dedicated. Designed by D. H. Burnham, it seats 2,580. Much later, in 1966, it will be refurbished. In 1981, the architectural firm of Skidmore, Owings, and Merrill will devise a thorough renovation of the hall.

Dec 24 The London Coliseum opens as a variety house in St. Martin's Lane. The building has been designed by Frank Matcham in Italian Renaissance style. The capacity is 2,358, and the theatre now supercedes the Drury Lane as the largest in London. It has stalls, dress circle, grand tier and balcony. The program notes that it is "the only theatre in Europe which provides lifts to take the audience to the upper parts of the building," which include a Terrace Tea Room at the top. There is also a cupola supporting a revolving globe which bears electric letters spelling COLISEUM. (Complaints will soon stop the sign from revolving). Oswald Stoll is in charge of the theatre, which will present four two-hour performances daily on its three-sectioned revolving stage.

Dec 31 The new Lyceum Theatre in London opens as a music hall with a twice-nightly variety bill. Bertie Crewe has designed this 2,814 seat theatre, managed by Thomas Barrasford. It is on the site of the old Lyceum, built in 1834 and demolished earlier this year, except for the portico and rear walls which have been preserved.

Jan 2 *Cousin Billy* (NY—Criterion—Comedy). Clyde Fitch adapts a farce by Eugene Labiche. With Francis Wilson and May Robson in leading roles, it achieves 76 performances. Fitch, as is his custom, directs, with settings by Ernest Gros, Homer Emens, and Edward G. Unitt.

Jan 9 *You Never Can Tell*, See L premiere, 1900.

Jan 11 *Adrea* (NY—Belasco—Drama). David Belasco presents his star, Mrs. Leslie Carter, in this play he has co-authored with John Luther Long. The large cast includes Tyrone Power, J. Harry Benrimo, and Charles Stevenson. Belasco, as usual, produces and directs. The production runs for 123 performances.

Jan 14 *Fantana* (NY—Lyric—Musical). Robert B. Smith sketches the dialogue and lyrics to a Raymond Hubbell score. Sam S. Schubert contributes the plot-line about a vineyard owner who tries to teach viticulture to the Japanese and eventually has to be rescued by the U.S. Navy. Douglas Fairbanks, Julia Sanderson and Adele Ritchie are in the large cast. After a Chicago tryout, the show runs more than 37 weeks on Broadway.

Jan 16 *The Duchess of Dantzig*. See L premiere, 1903.

Jan 24 *Buster Brown* (NY—Majestic—Comedy). Playwrights Charles Newman and George Totten Smith bring the cartoon character to the stage. The play runs 95 performances.

Jan 30 *Strongheart* (NY—Hudson—Comedy). William C. DeMille writes this play, which runs for 98 performances prior to touring. Robert Edeson heads the cast.

Jan 31 *The Woman in the Case* (NY—Herald Square—Drama). Clyde Fitch's play about a woman who tried to save her husband from a false charge of homicide features Blanche Walsh. It enjoys 89 performances.

Feb 20 *The Education of Mr. Pipp* (NY—Liberty—Comedy). Augustus Thomas makes a play out of a series of pictures by illustrator Charles Dana Gibson, creator of the Gibson Girl. Digby Bell and Kate Denin Wilson play. The show runs nearly ten weeks.

April 12 *A Yankee Circus on Mars* (NY—Hippodrome—Musical). This extravaganza, held together by George Hobert's thin plot-line opens the Hippodrome. Essentially, the book is an excuse for some grand spectacles and impressive circus acts. Now as in future years, the Hippodrome has a policy of two shows a day. This premiere plays 15 weeks, followed by a summer closure, and 176 more performances when it reopens.

April 24 *Sergeant Brue*. See L premiere, 1904.

May 1 *The Rollicking Girl* (NY—Herald Square—Musical). This show with book and score by Sydney Rosenfeld and W.T. Francis, respectively, tells the tale of a nervous bride-to-be who runs away to hide out with a wig-maker. Both of them want to have stage careers, but the girl returns to her groom. Sam Bernard plays Schmaltz, the wig-maker, like a "Dutch comic," something he has learned from Weber and Fields. The show runs for half a year.

June 5 *Lifting the Lid* (NY—New Amsterdam Aerial Gardens—Revue). Described as a "musical travesty," this show credits Jean Schwartz and William Jerome with lyrics and music. Yet its entire second act is made up of borrowings from Gilbert and Sullivan. Eddie Leonard, Fay Templeton, and Virginia Earle appear. Ned Wayburn does the musical staging. It runs 14 weeks.

June 12 *When We Were Forty-One* (NY—New York Roof Theatre—Revue). This burlesque parodies H. V. Esmond's *When We Were Twenty-One*. Harry Bulger, as a mad Dr. Hasler, wants to put everyone over 41 to sleep. Percy and Elsie Janis also appear. Gus Edwards creates a score for Robert B. Smith's book. It runs two months.

Aug 28 *The Ham Tree* (NY—New York—Musical). James McIntyre and Thomas Heath, a popular blackface team, impersonate a rajah and his minister of state to get free room-and-board when they are stranded in a small town. The book is by George Hobart, the music and lyrics by William Jerome and Jean Schwartz.

Sep 4 *The Rogers Brothers in Ireland* (NY—Liberty—Musical). These "Dutch" comedians make an appeal to Irish audiences by singing Irish songs in German dialect. They plan to steal the Blarney Stone, exhibit it in America, and use the money to free Ireland. With Max Hoffmann's music and some attractive settings—a view of the Lakes of Killarney is especially praised—the show pleases for 106 performances.

Sep 5 *Man and Superman* (NY—Hudson—Comedy). Shaw's genetic satire has its American premiere. It features Robert Loraine, Fay Davis and Edward Abeles. It runs for six months. The *NY Times* praises it saying, ". . . we may denounce him as the most inconsistent of men, but we must admit that there is a kind of joy in his inconsistency. He may build only to cast down, but we stand back amazed at the process of his building and share with a childlike sort of pleasure the overturning of the edifice."

Sep 27 *Just Out of College* (NY—Lyceum—Comedy). George Ade writes this play with its accent on youth. The show is staged by William Seymour, Among the cast are Ward Sinclair, Frances Comstock, George Irving, Jack Devereaux and Tully Marshall. It runs nearly two months.

Oct 2 *Happyland* (NY—Lyric—Musical). DeWolf Hopper is a comic King who is too happy. So, to create some unhappiness, he orders everyone to marry. The score is by Reginald DeKoven. This production tallies a total of 17 weeks.

Oct 3 *The Man on the Box* (NY—Madison Square—Comedy). Grace Livingson Furniss adapts Harold McGrath's popular novel. It features Henry E. Dixey, Carlotta

Buster Brown

The Squaw Man

Nillson and Marie Nordstrom. The show runs for 111 performances.

Oct 23 *The Squaw Man* (NY—Wallack—Drama). In Edwin Milton Royle's tale of interracial love, Nat-U-Ritch, the hero's Indian wife, commits suicide rather than burden him as he faces returning to England. The cast includes William Faversham, William S. Hart, and Selina Fetter Royle, the author's wife.

Oct 24 *Wonderland* (NY—Majestic—Musical). A Grimm fairy-tale is the basis for this sequel to *Babes in Toyland*. The indifferent score is by Victor Herbert. Critics admire a two-man comic horse more than Glen MacDonough's libretto. Nonetheless, the show runs for more than nine weeks and tours for nearly two years.

Oct 30 *Moonshine* (NY—Liberty—Musical). Edwin Royle writes this show with George Hobart. Marie Cahill stars as a woman who, at the Henley Regatta, plays detective to save the man she loves. She is admired in such interpolated songs as "The Conjure Man" and "Robinson Crusoe's Isle."

Nov 4 *The Earl and the Girl*. See L premiere, 1903

Nov 14 *The Girl of the Golden West* (NY—Belasco—Drama). Blanche Bates, as Minnie, the saloon-keeper and sweetheart of the mines, is partnered by Robert Hilliard as her fugitive lover, Dick Johnson. Frank Keenan is Jack Rance, the pursuing sheriff who also wants Minnie. Belasco, who has worked as an actor during the Comstock Lode boom in Virginia City, Nevada, writes, directs, and produces. The NY Times praises the atmosphere of the play.

Nov 20 *The Lion and the Mouse* (NY—Lyceum—Drama). Charles Klein's play is a formula melodrama that is also intended as a social comment on political corruption. On May 22, 1906 the play premieres in London at the Duke of York Theatre. It runs for two weeks, with Edward Breese and Margaret Illington in the leads.

Dec 13 *A Society Circus* (NY—Hippodrome—Musical). Thompson and Dundy return with a second edition of lavish spectacle. Lady Volumnia gives a party as the framework for the succession of elaborate scenes and unusual variety acts. For the "Song of the Flowers," the audience is sprayed with perfume while the huge chorus makes itself into a floral bouquet. "Motoring in Mid-Air" salutes the newly devised airplane. The show runs for 596 performances, playing two-a-day. Arthur Voegtlin designs the spectacles.

Dec 14 *Dorothy Vernon of Haddon Hall* (NY—New York—Drama). Paul Kester adapts Charles Major's best-selling novel of the time of Elizabeth I. It runs only five weeks. On April 14, 1906 it premieres at London's New Theatre with the title *Dorothy o' the Hall*. Julia Neilson and Fred Terry star.

Dec 25 *Mlle. Modiste* (NY—Knickerbocker—Musical). Fritzi Scheff stars as Fifi, the hat-shop salesgirl who becomes an opera star. Her singing is criticized but Victor Herbert's score, Henry Blossom's book and lyrics are much admired. "Kiss Me Again," "The Time and the Place and the Girl," "I Want What I Want When I Want It" all become popular and remain so. Fred Latham stages; Homer Emens designs the attractive settings.

1905　　BRITISH PREMIERES

Jan 5 *The Scarlet Pimpernel* (L—New—Comedy). This tale of adventure called a "romantic comedy" is about an English nobleman who smuggles French aristocrats out of Revolutionary France. It earns for 123 performances, with 120 more in December revival. Fred Terry and his wife Julia Neilson take the leads.

Jan 5 *The Talk of the Town* (L—Lyric—Musical). This musical comedy by Seymour Hicks—with songs by Charles Taylor, H. E. Haines, Hamish McCann, and Evelyn Baker—has a 100 performance run. Walter Passmore Robert Evett, Agnes Fraser, Olive Morrell, and Sydney Fairbrother appear.

Feb 21 *Mr. Hopkinson* (L—Avenue—Comedy). R. C. Carton's farce draws audiences for 163 performances. His wife, Katherine Compton, is in one of the leads, with Annie Hughes, Ellen O'Malley, James Welch, Frederick Kerr, and Henry Kemble.

Feb 28 *How He Lied to Her Husband*. See NY premiere, 1904.

April 5 *Alice Sit-by-the-Fire* (L—Duke of York's—Comedy). James Barrie's new play, subtitled *A Page from a Daughter's Diary*, deals with a girl who knows about life only from the plays she sees. In the company are Ellen Terry, Irene Vanbrugh, Lettice Farifax, Hilda Trevelyan, C. Aubrey Smith and Kenneth Douglas. There is also a Barrie curtain-raiser, *Pantaloon*, which Barrie calls "a plea for an ancient family." The show has 115 performances. The same program premieres in New York at the Criterion on Christmas Day 1905. In *Alice*, a young Ethel Barrymore plays a middle-aged woman, using a choker of pearls to age herself. John Barrymore appears in a small role. In *Pantaloon*, brother Lionel Barrymore plays the title-role, with John Barrymore as Clown. The production runs for over 10 weeks.

April 29 *The Little Michus* (L—Daly's—Musical). Andre Messager's operetta is adapted by Henry Hamilton, with English lyrics by Percy Greenbank of the Vanloo and Duval libretto. It is a variation on the Prince and the Pauper. Adrienne Augarde, Mabel Green, Willie Edouin, and Robert Evett play leading parts. It wins 401 performances. *The Times* reports that the operatta "goes rather heavily and long; . . . [but] there are many characteristic and attractive [numbers]."

May 30 *The Spring Chicken* (L—Gaiety—Musical). The French farce, *Coquin de Printemps*, is the inspiration for actor-author George Grossmith, Jr. Lyrics are by Adrian Ross and Percy Greenbank; by Ivan Caryll and Lionel Monckton. The substance of the farce is the recapture by several wives of errant husbands in a scheme involving sleeping-draughts. Heading the cast are Gertie Millar, George Grossmith, Jr., Connie Ediss, Kate Cutler, and Lionel Mackinder. The show runs 401 performances. *The Times* writes: "The music . . . is not always so happy as it was in *The Orchid*, but many of the incidental numbers leaped straight into success." This show opens on October 8, 1906 at New York's Daly Theatre. In the cast are the talented dancers Bessie McCoy and Blanche Deyo, as well as Adele Rowland. Moving twice to other theatres, it has a total of 115 performances, with Richard Carle in the lead.

Aug 28 *The Blue Moon* (L—Lyric—Musical). There are 185 performances for this show, with a book by Harold Ellis, revised by A. M. Thompson. Lyrics and music are by Percy Greenbank, Paul Rubens, and Howard Talbot. Billie Burke, Florence Smithson, Carrie Moore, Willie Edouin, and Walter Passmore are in leading roles.

Sep 4 *Oliver Twist* (L—His Majesty's—Drama). J. Comyns Carr adapts Dickens' novel for the stage in five acts. With tryouts it runs 114 performances. Major roles are played by actor-manager Herbert Beerbohm Tree, Lyn Harding, and Constance Collier.

Sep 7 *The Prodigal Son* (L—Drury Lane—Drama). Hall Caine's new play is based on the Biblical theme. George Alexander plays the leading role in this adaptation from Caine's popular novel. It wins 105 performances.

Sep 23 *The Conqueror* (L—Scala—Drama). This dramatic fantasy by R.E. Fyffe (actually the Duchess of Sutherland) is about a military victor who falls in love with a young girl who loves another and eventually kills the conqueror. Johnston Forbes Robertson and his wife, Gertrude Elliott, star. *The Times* pans it saying: "Pretty ladies prattle pretty blank verses to pretty gentlemen, or listen to pretty choruses. . . . the total impression is tra-la-la (played on a guitar with nice pink ribbons). Rough truths about such work as this would be ungallant. . . ."

Sep 27 *On the Quiet.* See NY premiere, 1901.

Oct 24 *Captain Drew on Leave* (L—New—Comedy). Hubert Henry Davies' four-act play has Charles Wyndham in the lead, with Marion Terry, Louis Calvert, Vane Tempest, and Mary Moore in major roles. It wins 154 performances.

Nov 7 *The Voysey Inheritance* (L—Court—Drama). Harley Granville Barker's five-act play opens for a series of six special matinees. The interplay of characters in the family is the dominant interest in this study of corruption. The cast includes A. E. George, Dennis Eadie, Grace Edwin, Florence Haydon, Eugene Mayeur, Edmund Gwenn, and Alexandra Carlisle.

Nov 14 *Mr. Popple (of Ippleton)* (L—Apollo—Musical). Paul Rubens' comedy wins 173 performances. Ethel Irving and G. P. Huntley play the leads.

Mr. Popple

1905 REVIVALS/REPERTORIES

Jan 5 Gerhart Hauptmann's *Die Weber* is offered in the German season at London's Great Queen Street Theatre. Fischer and Jarno's *Ein Rabensvater* follows; then Kadelburg and Shoenthan's *Zwei Gluckliche Tage*, Hauptmann's *Rose Bernd*, Fulda's *Maskerade*, L'Arronge's *Mein Leopold*, Holbe's *Der Strom*, Ibsen's *Die Wildente* (*The Wild Duck*), Schowronnek's *Ein Palast Revolution*, and Blumenthal and Kadelburg's *Zwei Wappen*, closing the season.

Jan 21 Eugen Tschirikoff's Russian play, *The Chosen People*, is presented by the St. Petersburg Dramatic Company at London's Avenue Theatre.

March 21 At the Royal Court Theatre in London, the Vedrenne-Barker management presents Gerhart Hauptmann's *The Thieves' Comedy* with Rosina Filippi. On April 11, Gilbert Murray's translation of Euripides' *The Trojan Women* has 8 matinees with Edith Wynne-Matthison, Gertrude Kingston and Edyth Olive. George Bernard Shaw's *John Bull's Other Island* begins a three-week run of evening and matinee performances on May 1. The next day Shaw's *You Never Can Tell* begins nine matinees. On May 22 his *Candida* opens for a three-week run. The following day *Man and Superman* begins a series of 12 special matinees. Shaw's *You Never Can Tell* is given another three-week run starting June 12. On Sep 11 *John Bull's Other Island* is brought back for evening performances. On Oct 23 *Man and Superman* becomes an evening attraction.

March 20 Richard Mansfield is at New York's New Amsterdam Theatre for nearly a month. Among the plays offered are Fitch's *Beau Brummell* and Tolstoi's *Ivan the Terrible*. On April 10, Mansfield premieres Moliere's *The Misanthrope*, advertising it as the first performance in English.

March 27 Minnie Maddern Fiske offers three matinees of three one-act plays she has written: *A Light from St. Agnes*, *The Eyes of the Heart*, and *The Rose*. George Arliss, Robert V. Ferguson, Mary Maddern, and Charles Terry are in the casts.

April 3 Dion Boucicault's 19th century comedy, *London Assurance*, has a four-week revival at New York's Knickerbocker Theatre. Ida Conquest, Ben Webster, and Ellis Jeffreys appear.

April 4 H. B. Irving plays Hamlet in Otho Stuart's revival at London's Adelphi Theatre. On July 4, Frank Benson presents *The Comedy of Errors*. Otho Stuart returns on November 25 to present *A Midsummer Night's Dream*.

April 17 Oliver Goldsmith's 18th century comedy, *She Stoops to Conquer*, is revived at New York's New Amsterdam Theatre for three weeks. The cast includes Eleanor Robson, Isabel Irving, and Kyrle Bellew.

April 24 At Stratford-upon-Avon, the annual Shakespeare Festival opens with *The Merchant of Venice*. Originally, this was to have been Sir Henry Irving's production, with Irving as Shylock, but illness has forced cancellation. Frank Benson plays Shylock instead in his own company's production. On April 25, *The Comedy of Errors* is revived for the first time since 1884. During the three-week season in the Memorial Theatre, Marlowe's *Edward II* is also played.

April 29 Henry Irving presents his last London season, this time at the Drury Lane Theatre. Tennyson's *Becket* is the first offering, followed by *The Merchant of Venice* on May 22. On June 5, Irving presents *Waterloo*, a one-act play by Arthur Conan Doyle. On the next day, he opens *Louis XI*, a Dion Boucicault adaptation of Casimir Delavigne's French drama.

May 23 Eleonora Duse begins her season in London's new Waldorf Theatre, with Pinero's *La Seconda Moglie*, the Italian version of *The Second Mrs. Tanqueray*.

June 5 Mme. Rejane opens her London season of French dramas at the Terry Theatre with Pierre Wolff's *L'Age d'Aimer*. She also presents Meilhac and Halevy's *La Petite Marquise*, Nicodemi's *L'Hirondelle*, Sardou's *Madame Sans-Gêne*, and Grasac and Croisset's *La Passerelle*.

June 7 Constant Coquelin opens his London season of his French repertoire at the Shaftesbury Theatre with *L'Abbe Constantin*, by Hector Cremieux and Pierre Decour. On June 9, he plays Albert Capus' *Notre Jeunesse*.

Sep 11 Arnold Daly continues his efforts to popularize George Bernard Shaw in

America with a month of repertory at New York's Garrick Theatre. The plays include *Candida, The Man of Destiny, How He Lied To Her Husband, You Never Can Tell, John Bull's Other Island* (American premiere), and *Mrs. Warren's Profession* (New York premiere). Mary Shaw, Chrystal Herne, Winchell Smith, Dodson Mitchell, and Mabel Taliaferro join Daly in the ensemble.

Sep 16 Mr. and Mrs. Kendal open their London season with Ernest Hendrie's play *Dick Hope*, at the St. James Theatre in London. On October 12, they follow it with *The Housekeeper*, a three-act farce by Metcalfe Wood and Beatrice Heron-Maxwell.

Sep 26 At London's Royal Court Theatre, the Vedrenne-Barker management offers six special matinee performances of St. John Hankin's *The Return of the Prodigal*. A.E. Matthews acts. On Oct 17 Ibsen's *The Wild Duck* begins six matinees with a cast including Granville Barker, Agnes Thomas, Edmund Gwen, Mathe-son Lang and Lewis Casson.

Oct 23 Maurice Maeterlinck's *Monna Vanna*, runs over six weeks, with Bertha Kalich as Monna. Harrison Gray Fiske produces the drama at the Fiske's own Broadway theatre, the Manhattan.

Nov 27 At the St. George Hall in London, the Dublin Theatre Society opens a repertory of Irish plays. J. M. Synge's *The Well of the Saints*, Augusta, Lady Gregory's *Spreading the News*, W. B. Yeats' *On Baile's Strand*, Padraic Colum's *The Land*, and William Boyle's *The Building Fund* are presented.

Dec 18 Olga Nethersole stars in Henry Hamilton's adaptation of *Carmen* at New York's Herald Square Theatre.

Dec 23 The new Aldwych Theatre in London's West End opens with a new edition of *Bluebell in Fairyland*, featuring Mr. and Mrs. Seymour Hicks (Ellaline Terriss). Hicks has also devised the libretto, with songs by Aubrey Hopwood and Charles Taylor, for this Christmas Pantomime.

1905 BIRTHS/DEATHS/DEBUTS

Jan 25 Admired actress Ada Nielson (b. 1846) dies.

March 11 Tonight there is a command performance of George Bernard Shaw's comedy, *John Bull's Other Island*, at London's Royal Court Theatre. In the cast of the command performance are Louis Calvert, A. E. George, Ellen O'Malley, and Granville Barker. The play has been given a series of nine special matinee performances by the Vedrenne-Barker management in February, but the King insists on this revival. He laughs so hard he breaks the expensive chair provided for him. His royal approval puts the Crown's seal on Shaw as Britain's foremost playwright. Shaw refuses a royalty, calling the performance "unauthorized." London producers, after years of neglect, beseige him with offers. He smiles only on Vedrenne-Barker and Arnold Daly who gave *Candida* a success in New York in 1904. These managers are to pay only 10 percent royalty; the rest, if permitted to stage a Shaw play, must pay 25 percent.

March 7 A. M. Palmer (b. 1839), a distinguished American producer and theatre manager, dies. Palmer is perhaps best known as the innovative manager of New York's Union Square Theatre.

March 26 Maurice Barrymore (b. 1848) dies. This English-born actor has sired Ethel, John, and Lionel Barrymore—later to be fondly burlesqued as the American theatre's "Royal Family."

April 23 American actor and producer Joseph Jefferson (b. 1829) dies in Palm Beach. Noted for his comic roles, Jefferson is primarily identified with *Rip Van Winkle*, which he and Boucicault adapted in 1865, and in which he continued to act for the remainder of his career. In 1893 Jefferson succeeded Edwin Booth as president of The Players.

May 12 Just as the three Shubert brothers are beginning to establish themselves solidly in New York theatre production as foes of the entrenched Theatrical Syndicate, Sam Shubert, (b. 1875) dies. His surviving brothers, Lee and J.J., will honor him in naming many of the Shubert Theatres they are to build across the United States.

May 14 Jessie Bartlett Davis (b. 1861), the dynamic, admired American actress dies.

May 16 Kirke LaShelle (b. 1863) who made a career as librettist, lyricist, and manager, dies.

May 22 Bertha Kalich, star of the Yiddish theatre, makes her debut in an English-speaking role as Fedora, in Sardou's drama. It is revived for one week in New York at the American Theatre.

Aug 28 A young juggler, W.C. Fields, plays Sherlock Baffles in *The Ham Tree* at the New York Theatre on Broadway.

Aug 31 Sanford Meisner is born in Brooklyn, N.Y.

Sep 13 The popular American author-actor-manager William Gillette is one of those U.S. talents who are welcomed in Britain. Today, he opens his London season at the Duke of York's Theatre with his comedy, *Clarice*, which he's already tried out in Liverpool at the Shakespeare Theatre. On October 3, he adds a "fantasy in about one-tenth of an act," called *The Painful Predicament of Sherlock Holmes*. On October 17, he revives his big success, *Sherlock Holmes*.

Oct 13 Actor-manager Sir Henry Irving (b. 1838) dies in Bradford, England. Irving began management of the Lyceum Theatre in 1878, playing Hamlet. He remained with the Lyceum for the next 23 years where he acted in and produced *The Merchant of Venice, Othello, Faust*, Tennyson's *Becket*, and numerous others. Irving was knighted in 1895, the first actor to receive this honor.

Nov 6 Maude Adams makes her debut as Peter Pan at New York's Empire Theatre with such acclaim that the play is extended throughout the entire 1905–1906 season.

Nov 23 Actor-manager Daniel Bandmann (b. 1840) dies. Born in Germany, he made his career in the United States.

Dec 4 Sarah Bernhardt holds a press conference at the Chateau Frontenac in Quebec City, Canada to respond to press and clergy criticisms of her repertorie on this North American tour. (The Archbishops of Montreal and Quebec threaten excommunication to any Catholic attending her performances of such pieces as Sardou's *La Sorcière*.) Mlle. Bernhardt responds in kind, saying that although agriculture seems to have prospered in Canada, nothing else has, since there are no writers, no sculptors, no poets, etc. At tonight's performance of *Camille*, La Divine Sarah is booed and pelted with rotten eggs.

1905 THEATERS/PRODUCTIONS

In Britain this year patents are granted for: M. Kruse's design for three-dimensional settings with the elements decreasing in size upstage to give a greater feeling of depth. This is an adaptation of the two-dimensional painted forced perspectives of the baroque stage.

U.S. patents are granted to Samuel Del Vall who has invented a stage device for flash fires; Neilson Burgess who patents an apparatus which can simulate the effect and sound of large crowds, as at the racetrack in the grandstand; and George Mullen whose device is a fake piano with an open back and doors in the front and sides for comic entrances.

Oliver Morosco, a West Coast theatre manager based in Los Angeles, begins producing plays with a view to possible transfer to Broadway when they prove successful. Between 1905 and 1922, he will premiere some 84 plays at the Burbank Theatre, including J. Hartley Manners' *Peg O'My Heart*, in 1912 and Anne Nichols' *Abie's Irish Rose*.

This year in France, official censorship

of plays is ended, although it is to continue across the Channel in Britain for decades yet. Eugene Brieux, dramatist of contemporary moral and social problems, is a leader in the fight to defeat censorship.

Jan 2 The Theatre Royal, Haymarket, reopens after complete interior reconstruction, supervised by C. Stanley Peach. The capacity is now 906. The new managers are Frederick Harrison and Cyril Maude, whose opening presentation is *Beauty and the Barge*, with *That Brute Simmons* as a curtain raiser. (The first theatre on this site opened in 1720.)

Jan 4 The new Royalty Theatre, enlarged and redecorated, is reopened as the Theatre Francaise in London, by Gaston Meyer. Mme. Rejane's season is the first upon the rechristened stage, beginning with Edouard Pailleron's *La Souris (The Bat)*. There are an astonishing number of French productions offered during the year at this playhouse.

Feb With the success of their special matinee performances of plays by George Bernard Shaw and others, John E. Vedrenne forms a partnership with Harley Granville Barker to lease the Royal Court Theatre and present a repertory of matinee and evening performances of important modern and classic plays. They agree to take only £20 per week salary—an advance on box-office receipts—and limit production costs of each play to £200. The stock company members are initially to receive only £3 per week.

Feb 4 In Dublin, the Irish National Theatre Society is now officially incorporated.

April 12 Frederick Thompson and Elmer Dundy—creators of Luna Park at Coney Island—open their new theatre, the Hippodrome. On the east side of Sixth Avenue at 43rd Street, it is the eastern boundary of New York's theatre district. It is also the largest legitimate theatre in the world, holding 5,000 spectators. Its stage is nearly a block wide and is 110 feet deep, making possible a variety of amazing spectacular scenes. It employs 78 electricians, a permanent ballet of 200, with 400 chorus girls and 100 chorus boys. Unfortunately, the house is so large that only those near the stage can hear the lyrics of the songs. Shows thus emphasize the spectacular. The cost of operations far outweighs income, and the owners sell their building. Subsequently, the Keith-Albee vaudeville chain try in vain to make a profit. Billy Rose's 1935 production, *Jumbo*, closes the playhouse. In 1939, the building is torn down, but the site is not developed until 1952. A skyscraper and a garage currently occupy the space.

April 12 One of the segments of the new New York Hippodrome's opening attraction, *A Yankee Circus on Mars*, is *Andersonville: A Story of Wilson's Raiders*.

In its final scene, says the *NY Times*, ". . . realism truly runs riot. A great lake in the foreground has filled with water to the depth of fourteen feet and into this during the battle plunge men who swim the stream under fire. As a climax a troop of cavalry dashes on, the riders urge their horses into the water, and all swim across to safety."

May 13 London's Royal Strand Theatre closes with the final performance of Howard Talbot's musical *Miss Wingrove*.

May 22 The Waldorf Theatre opens with *Il Maestro Capella* and *I Pagliacci*. W.G.R. Sprague has designed this 1,028 seat theatre as a twin for the Aldwych theatre. It is the last three-tier theatre to be built in London. Henry Russell is the manager of this theatre, built by the Waldorf Theatre Syndicate and leased for 21 years by America's Shubert Brothers. The opera performances will alternate with plays performed by Eleanora Duse and her company. In 1909, the name of the theatre will be changed to the Strand; between 1911 and 1913, it will be called the Whitney, and will then revert to The Strand.

June 15 A grand total of 157 productions are tallied at the end of the 1904–05 Broadway season, using some 33 theatre spaces. Seven repertory companies have presented a total of 40 shows, including 11 one-acts and 12 revivals. There have been 34 dramas, 7 of them revivals. Comedies numbered 38, with six revivals. Other productions included 5 farces, 1 burlesque, 1 vaudeville, 7 one-acts, 4 extravaganzas, 1 operetta, 6 comic operas—3 of them revivals, 1 musical farce, 7 musicals, 2 revues, and 10 musical plays.

July 15 Angered at monopolistic policies of the Theatrical Syndicate, the Shubert Brothers break off business relations with it and form an alliance with David Belasco and Harrison Grey and Minnie Maddern Fiske.

Aug Various business interests of the Shuberts are incorporated as Sam S. and Lee Shubert, Inc. The authorized capital of the firm is listed as $1,400,000.

Sep The New York Public Library removes Bernard Shaw's *Man and Superman* from the public shelves of the Library to the "reserve section." The "restricted circulation" is judged necessary to keep the work away from children, since they would not understand Shaw's attacks on social conditions.

Sep 14 Philadelphia's Lyric Theatre opens.

Sep 23 The new Scala Theatre has its gala opening in London.

Oct 16 As of this date, 18 more theatres are added to the Shubert circuit, which has been growing steadily since Shuberts have broken with the Theatrical Syndicate.

Nov 14 A new lighting effect is seen during the premiere of *Girl of the Golden West*. The front curtain becomes translucent gradually, when lit from behind. Louis Hartmann, David Belasco's associate, is credited.

Dec There are 369 legitimate theatre productions on tour in America as of the first week of this month. In 1928, there will be only 86.

Dec The London Coliseum, built in 1904 (Frank Matcham, architect) as a house for music and dancing, this month comes under the jurisdiction of the Lord Chamberlain's office. Now it is possible to present a Christmas Pantomime in the big theatre, and Arthur Shirley's is the one chosen.

Dec 5 Part of Charing Cross Station collapses onto the Royal Avenue Theatre, currently undergoing major reconstruction. Six are killed and 26 injured.

Scarlet Pimpernel

Dec 23 The Aldwych Theatre opens in London. It is a two-tiered Georgian-style theatre, with a capacity of 1,024, and is managed by Charles Frohman. The opening production is a musical dream play, *Blue Bell*.

Dec 26 During a performance of the Christmas Pantomime, *Aladdin*, part of the flown scenery falls 40 feet from the flies, striking musical director, John Jones, on the head. It renders him unconscious, and he is not able to return to work. In March 1906, a jury awards him £ 350 damages.

29

Jan 1 *Forty-five Minutes from Broadway* (NY—New Amsterdam—Musical). This musical, about a fight over a will, has Donald Brian, Fay Templeton and Victor Moore. Author-director George M. Cohan's songs include "Mary Is a Grand Old Name." Moving from Chicago to New York, the show runs for 90 performances and tours.

Jan 1 *Twiddle-Twaddle* (NY—Weber's Music Hall—Revue) Weber uses his "Dutch" dialect comedy and burlesques current shows and fashions in this sprightly revue. Marie Dressler does a parody of a Spanish dance. Aubrey Boucicault, Trixie Friganza and Charles Bigelow are in the ensemble. Al Holbrook stages and Ernest Albert creates the sets. The show runs for 169 performances.

Jan 8 *The Clansman* (NY—Liberty—Drama). Thomas Dixon, Jr., combines his popular novels, *The Leopard's Spots* and *The Clansman*, to make this play sympathetic to the purposes of the Ku Klux Klan. Holbrook Blinn is in the company. The production has only 51 performances.

Jan 16 *The Vanderbilt Cup* (NY—Broadway—Musical). Sydney Rosenfeld's book capitalizes on the vogue for auto racing. Raymond Peck contributes the lyrics for Robert Hood Bowers' music. Elsie Janis plays Dorothy, who wins the Cup despite vile intrigues against her. The show enjoys a total run of 183 performances.

Jan 22 *The Galloper* (NY—Garden—Comedy). Richard Harding Davis's lively farce offers Raymond Hitchcock, E. L. Davenport, and Nanette Comstock. George Marion directs, with Walter Burridge providing sets. It runs for almost ten weeks.

Feb 12 *George Washington, Jr.* (NY—Herald Square—Musical). George M. Cohan writes, directs and composes. Sam H. Harris produces. Cohan, supported by his father, mother and wife, is a patriotic young American who rejects his anglophile father. "It's a Grand Old Flag" is the show's hit song. The show runs only 10 weeks in New York but does very well on tour, returning in 1907 for four weeks.

Feb 12 *The Duel* (NY—Hudson—Drama). Otis Skinner is the Abbe Daniel in Louis N. Parker's adaptation of Henri Lavedan's French original. Fay Davis and Guy Standing also play. This runs over nine weeks.

Feb 20 *Abyssinia* (NY—Majestic—Musical). Bert Williams, who has composed the music with Will Marion Cook, plays Rastus, who wins a lottery and decides to visit his putative ancestral homeland, taking along Jasmine Jenkins (George Walker). Comic mishaps nearly spell their doom in the book by J. A. Shipp and Alex Rogers. While American blacks speak minstrel-talk, Africans speak the King's English in this show. It runs only 31 performances.

Feb 26 *Brown of Harvard* (NY—Princess—Comedy). Rida Johnson Young's play enjoys a total of 149 performances. It has incidental music by Melville Ellis, who set Young's "When Love is Young" lyrics to music.

March 1 *The Redskin* (NY—Liberty—Drama). William A. Brady obtains the services of ten Sioux Indians for this play. Brady produces and directs a cast which includes Tyrone Power, Albert Bruning, and Lionel Adams. It has 26 performances.

April 9, 1906 *The Social Whirl* (NY—Casino—Musical). Charles Doty and Joseph Herbert write the book about three married men embarrassed by a gossip item. Gustav Kerker writes the score and Herbert the lyrics. R.H. Burnside stages. Maude Raymond sings a coon song about a black who has to dance when he hears a band. The show has 195 performances.

April 16 *The Free Lance* (NY—New Amsterdam—Musical). John Philip Sousa's show has a book by Harry B. Smith. In it, a duke orders his son to marry but he and his intended refuse, flee and take on peasant disguises. Herbert Gresham stages. The show musters only 35 performances.

May 12 *Raffles, the Amateur Cracksman* (NY—Princess—Comedy). The popular stories of Raffles, the gentlemanly thief, are made into a play by their creator E.W. Hornung, assisted by Eugene Presbrey. The show runs 21 performances. It premieres at London's Comedy on May 12, 1906 with Gerald Du Maurier in the lead. Here the show runs for 351 performances.

May 28 *His Honor the Mayor* (NY—New York—Musical). This musical, about a not so honorable mayor, stars Blanche Ring. She is supported by a pony ballet, an eccentric dancer and a unicyclist. "Waltz Me Around Again, Willie" is a popular song with audiences. The show runs 13 weeks.

June 25 *Mamzelle Champagne* (NY—Madison Square Garden Roof—Revue). This musical, with book and lyrics by Edgar Allen Woolf, is actually a Columbia University Varsity Show, its all-male cast replaced with a professional company. Without the female impersonation, some of the lines fall flat, but the show enjoys a run of over seven weeks. This success has little to do with the production but a lot to do with the murder of Stanford White, which occurs during the second act of the show.

Aug 30 *About Town* (NY—Herald Square—Revue). Joseph Herbert devises the book and lyrics for this Lew Fields show. The score is by Melville Ellis and Raymond Hubbell. Lawrence Grossmith, Edna Wallace Hopper and Louise Dresser play. The story is an excuse for the variety numbers and chorus routines, one in which some of the dancers tear off parts of their costumes, startling some of the audience. It has 138 performances.

Aug 30 *The Hypocrites* (NY—Hudson—Drama). Henry Arthur Jones' British play features Richard Bennett, Doris Keane, and John Glendinning. It runs 209 performances.

Sep 3 *His House in Order* (NY—Empire—Comedy). Arthur Wing Pinero's play provides a vehicle for John Drew, with Margaret Illington, Leona Powers, and Lena Halliday, among others. It runs nearly 16 weeks.

Sep 11 *Clothes* (NY—Manhattan—Drama). Grace George stars in this tale by Channing Pollock and Avery Hopwood. Douglas Fairbanks is also in the cast.

Sep 24 *The Prince of India* (NY—Broadway—Drama). J.I.C. Clarke adapts General Lew Wallace's novel for the stage. The cast includes William and Marshall Farnum, Sam S. Harris, Julie Herne and Adele Davis. It runs slightly over nine weeks.

Sept 24 *The Red Mill* (NY—Knickerbocker—Musical). David Montgomery and Fred Stone star as two broke Americans who help a Dutch girl win her true love. Henry Blossom creates the plot and lyrics to Victor Herbert's score. Among the hits are "Every Day is Ladies' Day With Me." and "Because You're You." The show runs 274 performances.

Oct 1 *Popularity* (NY—Wallack's—Comedy). This George M. Cohan play manages only three weeks run.

Clothes

Brown of Harvard

Oct 3 *The Great Divide* (NY—Princess—Drama). Playwright William Vaughn Moody deals with differences between America's East and West. Margaret Anglin and Henry Miller star. The drama enjoys a total of 357 performances.

Oct 3 *The Genius* (NY—Bijou—Comedy). Brothers William C. and Cecil B. de Mille collaborate on a farcical vehicle for comic Nat C. Goodwin. It runs slightly longer than a month.

Oct 17 *The Three of Us* (NY—Madison Square—Comedy). Rachel Crothers' play about a girl and her two brothers protecting their claim to a gold mine, attracts audiences for 227 performances. Carlotta Nillson as the girl is praised. "... she is unquestionably the cleverest of the younger actresses of our stage," says the *NY Times.*

Oct 22 *The House of Mirth* (NY—Savoy—Drama). Clyde Fitch and Edith Wharton collaborate on a dramatization of Wharton's best-selling novel. Fay Davis stars. It has only 14 performances. The *NY Times* complains that the play is "doleful" and does not have many laughs, apparently missing the point that the Wharton title is ironic.

Oct 22 *The Rich Mr. Hoggenheimer* (NY—Wallack's—Musical). Harry B. Smith's book and lyrics join Ludwig Englander's score and interpolations by Jerome Kern, Kenneth Clark and Jean Schwartz. The book tells about a man who goes to America to spy on his son, in love with a poor but deserving girl. Sam Bernard stars. The show runs for 187 performances.

Oct 30 *Caesar and Cleopatra* (NY—New Amsterdam—Comedy). George Bernard Shaw's play stars Johnston Forbes-Robertson and Gertrude Elliott. It runs 49 performances.

Nov 19 *The New York Idea* (NY—Lyric—Comedy). Langdon Mitchell's play about a sophisticated young Manhattan couple who break up and then make up stars Minnie Maddern Fiske and John Mason. Harrison Grey Fiske stages. It runs for 66 performances. On Nov 19, 1907 the play opens at London's Queen's Theatre with Fred Kerr and Ellis Jeffreys in the cast.

Nov 27 *The Parisian Model* (NY—Broadway—Musical). Harry B. Smith provides book and lyrics to Max Hoffman's score. Anna Held plays an artist's model who inherits a fortune mysteriously. Under the "personal direction" of Florenz Ziegfeld, director Julian Mitchell contrives a series of production numbers in lavish costumes and settings to show off the Held talents. The show has 179 performances.

Nov 27 *The Rose of the Rancho* (NY—Belasco—Drama). Producer-director David Belasco collaborates with Richard Walton Tully on this western play. Featuring Frances Starr, the cast also includes Charles Richman, Frank Losee, Jane Cowl, and J. Harry Benrimo. It has a total run of 45 weeks.

Nov 28 *Pioneer Days* (NY—Hippodrome–Musical). This show is actually three separate entertainments: a one-act circus, an "operatic extravaganza" called *Neptune's Daughter,* and the titular melodrama, showing Belasco's Golden West much magnified. A band of Sioux Indians is used. Mermaids dive into the Hippodrome tank and disappear, thanks to a ridge around the orchestra edge of the tank which permits them to exit, breathing and unseen. Manuel Klein provides the music. The show runs for 288 performances.

Dec 4 *The Man of the Hour* (NY—Savoy—Drama). Playwright George Broadhurst's new work is hailed as his best effort. Audiences agree, keeping it running for 479 performances. In its cast are Douglas Fairbanks and Harriet Otis Dellenbaugh. Fairbanks plays a reformer, out to expose the corruption of City Hall. Although no specific reference is made to Tammany Hall in the playtext, the Tammany theme-song of the Democartic party machine is played at the close of each performance. The Mayor of New York is angered by the play, but the controversy only makes it more popular.

Dec 24 *Dream City* (NY—Weber's—Musical). Edgar Smith's fable deals with the efforts of a developer to get a farmer to sell his farm at Malaria Center, Long Island. Joe Weber and Otis Harlan star. Victor Herbert's score is acclaimed by the *Tribune* as "a triumph of musical fooling." His afterpiece, *The Magic Knight,* a spoof on Wagner is especially admired. The show has 102 performances.

Dec 25 *The Student King* (NY—Garden—Musical). Reginald DeKoven's light opera about a student who finds that he is a prince manages only five weeks run. Henry Coote plays the prince.

Dec 31 *Brewster's Millions* (NY—New Amsterdam—Comedy). Winchell Smith and Byron Ongley adapt George Barr McCutcheon's story about a young man who must spend a million dollars in order to inherit millions. John Drew Devereaux is in the cast as is George Spelvin, the first appearance of this fictitious actor, a favorite of Smiths's. It runs for 163 performances. On May 1, 1907 it opens at London's Hicks Theatre with George Du Maurier as Brewster. It runs for 321 performances.

Dec 31 *Caught in the Rain* (NY—Garrick—Comedy). William Collier and Grant Stewart appear in the play they have written about an arranged marriage and its comic complications. The show runs 161 performances.

1906   BRITISH PREMIERES

Jan 13 *The Little Cherub* (L—Prince of Wales's—Musical). With Adrian Ross lyrics, Ivan Caryll score, and Owen Hall book, this show stars Zena Dare. The story is about a girl who must charm a pompous earl to marry his son. It runs for 114 performances. On Aug 6 it opens on Broadway at the Criterion Theatre and runs 155 performances. An interpolation composed by Marie Doro, "The Doggie in Our Yard," proves a hit.

Jan 24 *The Heroic Stubbs* (L—Terry's—Comedy). Estelle Winwood is in the cast of this Henry Arthur Jones play which lasts only a month. James Welch plays a romantic Bond Street bootmaker.

Jan 25 *Nero* (L—His Majesty's—Drama). Stephen Phillips' heroic verse drama stars Herbert Beerbohm Tree and Mrs. Tree. It has a two month run.

Feb 1 *His House in Order* (L—St. James's—Comedy). Arthur Wing Pinero offers serious overtones to his comedy about a young married woman's conflict with the living and the dead. The play runs for 430 performances. Irene Vanbrugh's Nina is much admired. Nigel Playfair, Iris Hawkins, and George Alexander are also in the company.

March 3 *Brigadier Gerard* (L—Imperial—Comedy). Arthur Conan Doyle's romantic comedy stars Lewis Waller. It runs for 118 performances. On Nov 5, 1906, it premieres at New York's Savoy where it lasts only 16 performances.

March 19 *The Beauty of Bath* (L—Aldwych—Musical). Seymour Hicks stars in the musical for which he and Cosmo Hamilton have written the book. The story deals with two brothers in love with the same girl, who change roles to confuse her. Herbert Haines composes the score, with lyrics by Charles Taylor. It enjoys a run of 287 performanes. Bert Sinden, Marguerite Leslie, and Ellaline Terriss play. *The Times* critic complains that the production buries the play.

April 5 *Josephine* (L—Comedy—Comedy). James Barrie's play about a man who wears skirts to impersonate Josephine, a political personality, stars Dion Boucicault. Critics object to the political comment and note that there are moments of poor taste.

April 11 *The Belle of Mayfair* (L—Vaudeville—Musical). Edna May, stars in this musical with a score by Leslie Stuart and a book by H.E. Brookfield and Cosmo Hamilton. The book deals with the familiar story of a girl who fears her father's opposition to her marriage. It runs for 416 performances. On Dec 3 this London success opens at New York's Daly's Theatre and runs for 140 performances. In the cast are Irene Bentley, Christie MacDonald, and Bessie Clayton.

April 14 *The Dairymaids* (L—Apollo—Musical). Paul Rubens and Frank Tours provide the score. Rubens and Arthur Wimperis provide lyrics. The book, by A.M. Thompson and Robert Courtneidge, tells the story of two love-smitten lords who disguise themselves as girls to be near their loves. Walter Passmore, Agnes Fraser, Gracie Leigh, Florence Smithson and Carrie Moore are in the cast. It runs 239 performances. On Aug 26, 1907 the

show premieres at New York's Criterion Theatre with Julia Sanderson and Huntley Wright featured. It runs nearly 11 weeks.

May 21 *Shore Acres* (L—Waldorf—Drama). James A. Herne's American drama, hailed in the U.S. for its believable characters and emancipation from European influence premieres in England. It runs for barely three weeks, despite the best efforts of Cyril Maude. A possible explanation is the change of locale from rural America to Cornwall.

May 29 *Colonel Newcome* (L—His Majesty's—Drama). Thackeray's novel, *The Newcomes*, provides Michael Morton with his play and Beerbohm Tree with his starring role. It is withdrawn on July 7, and revived on October 29, only to close finally on November 17. Marion Terry, Mrs. Tree, Lilian Braithwaite, Basil Gill, and Lyn Harding are in the cast.

June 20 *See-See* (L—Prince of Wales's—Musical). Charles Brookfield devises the book for this "Chinese comic opera," with Adrian Ross lyrics and Sidney Jones score. Denise Orme is See-See. The show has 152 performances.

Aug 9 *Amasis* (L—New—Musical). This comic treatment of an ancient Egyptian fable has book by Frederick Fenn and score by Philip Michael Faraday. Ruth Vincent and Ruthland Barrington have the leads. It runs for 200 performances.

Sep 3 *Toddles* (L—Duke of York's—Comedy). Cyril Maude and Gertrude Kingston are in this Clyde Fitch adaptation of *Triplepatte*, a French farce by Tristan Bernard and Andre Godfernaux. It runs for 335 performances. On March 16, 1908 it premieres at New York's Garrick Theatre with John Barrymore and Pauline Frederick in the leads. The show has only a two-week run.

Sep 12 *Peter's Mother* (L—Wyndham's—Drama). Marion Terry, A. E. Matthews, and Alice Beet animate Mrs. Henry de la Pasture's play for 182 performances. It is paired with *The Sixth Commandment*, a one-act drama which has Walter Hampden in its cast.

Sep 20 *The Bondman* (L—Drury Lane—

The Merveilleuses

Drama). Hall Caine adapts his novel for a cast including Mrs. Patrick Campbell Henry Neville, Frank Cooper, Lionel Brough, and Marie Illington. It has 145 performances.

Oct 17 *Robin Hood* (L—Lyric—Drama). Henry Hamilton and William Devereaux's play features Lewis Waller, Helen Leyton and Philip Cunningham. Devereaux also acts. There are 162 performances.

Oct 27 *The Merveilleuses* (L—Daly's—Musical). Victorien Sardou devises the plot, to a Hugo Felix score. Basil Hood provides the English text, with lyrics by Adrian Ross, for this *opera buffe*. There are 196 performances. Denise Orme, Evie Greene, and Robert Evett play leading roles.

Dec 12 *The Vicar of Wakefield* (L—Prince of Wales's—Musical). Lawrence Houseman fashions a libretto from Goldsmith's novel, with a score by Liza Lehmann. After a Manchester tryout, the show is brought to life in the West End, by players such as David Bispham, Isabel Jay, Edith Clegg, and Amy Martin.

Dec 26 *Sinbad* (L—Drury Lane—Pantomime). J. Hickory Wood and Arthur Collins rework the Sinbad story, to music by J. M. Glover. Walter Passmore stars. Also on hand are Rosamund Bury, Marie George, Queenie Leighton, and Alec Davison. There are 128 performances.

1906   REVIVALS/REPERTORIES

Jan 1 At London's Royal Court Theatre, the Vedrenne-Barker management brings back Shaw's *Major Barbara* after its successful matinees. On Jan 16 *Electra* is given six matinees. The management offers six matinees of two one-act plays *A Question of Age*, by R.V. Harcourt and *The Convict on the Hearth*, by Frederick Fenn on Feb 6. They are not popular, so Shaw's *Major Barbara* is substituted for the last four matinees. On Feb 12 Granville Barker's *The Voysey Inheritance* begins a four week run. There are six matinees of another double-bill: *Pan and the Young Shepherd* and *The Youngest of the Angels*, both by Maurice Hewlett beginning on Feb 27. Shaw's *Captain Brassbound's Conversion* has six special matinee performances beginning on March 20. It runs again—for 12 weeks—beginning on April 16. On March 26 Gilbert Murray's version of Euripides' *Hippolytus* opens for a two-week run. *Prunella*, by Laurence Houseman and Granville-Barker has 12 matinees beginning April 24. On July 9 Shaw's *You Never Can Tell* is revived for a summer run.

Jan 4 London's season of French-language theatre is launched at the New Royalty by Madame Rejane, appearing in *Souris, Heureuse,* and *La Rafale.* Over 40 different plays are offered, most modern favorites. In the summer, Coquelin, father and son, provide a varied bill, with several Moliere classics.

Feb 17 Oliver Goldsmith's classic 18th century comedy, *She Stoops To Conquer* is revived at London's Waldorf Theatre. Cyril Maude, Sydney Brough, and Winifred Emery play.

March 19 Brandon Thomas's lively farce, *Charley's Aunt,* is revived in New York at the Manhattan Theatre. It stars Etienne Girardot. The revival runs for ten weeks.

April 23 At Stratford-upon-Avon, the annual Shakespeare Festival opens with *Much Ado About Nothing,* staged by Frank Benson. Building on the Benson Company's 1901 production of *Henry VI, Part 2,* for the first time Benson offers the cycle of *Henry VI, Parts 1, 2,* and *3* this season. Lasting three weeks, the program includes ten other Shakespearean dramas in the Memorial Theatre, as well as revivals of Sheridan's *The Rivals,* Goldsmith's *She Stoops to Conquer,* and Bulwer-Lytton's *Richelieu.*

Sep 17 At London's Royal Court Theatre, the managers, J.E. Vedrenne and Harley Granville Barker, revive George Bernard Shaw's *John Bull's Other Island* for six weeks. Beginning Sep 25 there are eight matinees of John Galsworthy's *The Silver Box.* On Oct 23 St. John Hankin's comedy *The Charity That Begins at Home* begins eight matinees. On Oct 29 Vedrenne and Granville Barker bring back *Man and Superman.* Shaw's drama, *The Doctor's Dilemma* is given eight matinees beginning Nov 20. On Dec 31 this is revived for six weeks of regular performances.

Oct 1 From London comes the H. B. Irving–Dorothea Baird Repertory for a four-week season of plays. The fare includes *Paolo and Francesca* (Phillips), *King Rene's Daughter* (Phipps), *The Lyons Mail* (Reade), *Charles I* (Wills), *Markheim* (Courtney/Stevenson), and *Mauricette* (Irving/Picard) for New Yorkers.

Oct 22 Shakespeare's seldom performed *Cymbeline* is revived at New York's Astor Theatre, with Viola Allen, Henry Hadfield and Alison Skipworth. The production runs for a month.

Nov 12 In a series of nine New York matinees, Henry Miller produces Robert Browning's poetic play, *Pippa Passes.* The cast includes Mabel Taliaferro, Robert Cummings, Henry B. Walthall, and Eleonora Leigh.

Dec 18 *Peter Pan* is revived for the holiday season at The Duke of York's Theatre in London. Gerald Du Maurier is Captain Hook, with Pauline Chase as Peter and Hilda Trevelyan as Wendy. There are 102 performances.

Dec 20 *Alice in Wonderland* appears for the holidays as a musical extravaganza, playing matinées at the Prince of Wales's Theatre in London. Florrie Arnold is the March Hare; Carmen Silva is the Lily, and Marie Studholme is Alice.

Dec 27 Herbert Beerbohm Tree revives *Antony and Cleopatra* at His Majesty's Theatre in London. Constance Collier and Basil Gill also appear.

1906 BIRTHS/DEATHS/DEBUTS

April 5 In the House of Commons, A. E. W. Mason, Britain's first actor-MP, delivers his maiden speech. His election to Parliament is seen by the theatre community as a victory, in giving theatre concerns an advocate in the Commons.

April 19 Actress-singer Constance Carpenter is born in Bath, England.

April At the Duke of York's Theatre in London, Charles Frohman organizes a benefit for victims of the San Francisco Earthquake. Under the patronage of the American Ambassador, it realizes a large sum which Frohman augments from his own funds.

June 12 At the Theatre Royal, Drury Lane, Ellen Terry celebrates her Golden Jubilee with a gala benefit.

June 21 At the Garrick Club in London, over 60 theatre people gather to honor Charles Frohman for his services to the stage, the performer, and dramatic literature.

June 25 Brooding that his wife, the showgirl Evelyn Nesbit, has been Stanford White's mistress, Harry K. Thaw shoots him dead during the second act of *Mamzelle Champagne* at the Madison Square Roof Garden. Pleading insanity, Thaw evades punishment.

Oct 1 The H.B. Irving—Dorothea Baird Repertory makes its New York debut with a four-week season of plays.

1906 THEATERS/PRODUCTIONS

In Britain this year patents granted include W. Hagedorn's water tank for drowning or mysterious emergences from water, with an air-dome concealed at its base so the actor can breathe.

U.S. patents are granted to Bernard J. Fagan who invents a device which makes inanimate objects dance about and Henry C. Barrow who devises a system for instantly dropping scenery that catches fire to the stage-floor and smothering it with an asbestos cover.

This year, as a direct result of a moralists' campaign, the London County Council bans so-called "living statuary," also known as *poses plastiques* and *tableaux vivants,* in which the performers appear in the nude. For half a century, this has been permitted on the London stage, provided the *poseuses* do not move. By the 1930's nudity is again permitted under special regulations set by the Lord Chamberlain's Office.

London County Council surveys reveal that there is a total of 57 premises within the county for the regular presentation of stage plays. Two—Drury Lane and Covent Garden—operate under letters patent from the Crown. Forty-four are under the licensing jurisdiction of the Lord Chamberlain, who must censor playscripts. The remaining 11 are supervised by the LCC. Total seating is 71,015, with assesed tax value total of £139,808. There are also 46 music halls and theatres. Halls of concerts, dances, and exhibitions number another 248. Total London seating capacity for public entertainments is estimated at 312,000 minimally.

Jan 1 The Majestic Theatre opens today in Chicago. It seats 1,969 and is dedicated to vaudeville. E. P. Krause is the designer. In 1945, this playhouse will become the Shubert Theatre.

Jan 1 George M. Cohan, working with producers Klaw and Erlanger, manages to bring his new show, *Forty-five Minutes from Broadway,* to Broadway for only $10,000. This is recouped in the first week of the popular show's run.

Jan 4 After interior reconstruction and remodelling of the frontage, London's Royalty Theatre re-opens with *La Souris,* starring Réjane.

Jan 8 During the opening of *The Clansman* at New York's Liberty Theatre, pamphlets are distributed denouncing the play's racism. The distributers are hurried off by the police. The *NY Times* reports that the "large and noisy audience without discrimination vigorously applauded every highly flavored sentiment [of the play]."

Jan 10 The Illuminating Engineering Society (IES) is founded. It is dedicated to the advancement of the theory and practice of lighting technology.

Jan 29 The Holborn Empire Theatre in London opens under the management of

Walter Gibbons.

April 18 San Francisco is suddenly struck by a great earthquake, followed by a disastrous fire. Ten of the city's theatres are rapidly and totally destroyed, never to be restored to use. They are the Grand Opera House, the Tivoli Opera House #3, the Majestic Theatre, the Alhambra Theatre, the California Bush Street Theatre, the Alcazar Theatre, the Orpheum Theatre, Fisher's Theatre, the Columbia Theatre and the Central Theatre. Only the Chutes Theatre remains.

April 19 As soon as reports of the deaths and destruction of the San Francisco earthquake are received, theatre people organize benefits and make donations Sarah Bernhardt, in Chicago, rents a tent and organizes a benefit tour which will take her to San Francisco. George M. Cohan sells newspapers in Wall Street to aid the sufferers, getting as much as a thousand dollars a paper. Boston suspends its Sunday ban on performances so James K. Hackett can give a benefit.

court to stop a publisher from printing and selling postal cards which show her attired in a nightgown and other scanty costumes. The cards are forgeries, in that her head has been printed attached to the body of another female model. The publishers contend that cards are not libellous, as Millar claims, but in fact depict attire which an actress such as Gertie Millar might possibly be expected to wear "in the course of her professional career."

June 15 On Broadway this season, 32 theatres have sheltered a total of 118 productions, 12 of them revivals. There were six productions offered in repertory, four of those being revivals. There have been 51 dramas, with 4 revivals included; 10 comedies, with 1 revival; 10 farces, 10 musicals, 1 revue, 8 musical plays, 1 musical farce, 4 comic operas, 1 operetta, and 5 extravaganzas. There have been 10 one-acts, and 1 vaudeville.

June 16 The Imperial Theatre London closes down after the final performance of *Boy O'Carroll*.

electric sign.

October 6 Begun before San Francisco's quake and fire last April, the Colonial Theatre opens tonight. A capstone on its facade bears the date "1905."

Oct 18 "Actor's Day" is initiated, with George Lewis, George Sims, and Squire Bancroft as trustees. The object of the Day is that in every British theatre once a year, actors should perform without wages to provide money for their funds and charities. The third Thursday in October is chosen as the day.

Nov 6 The New Theatre opens in New York City on Central Park West and 62 Street. It is intended to be the home of a privately funded "National Theatre." The stage contains a 64-foot revolving stage, built at a cost of $250,000. The theatre will close, a failure in only two years, and be reopened as the Century Theatre.

Dec Gaining ground in their war with the Theatrical Syndicate, the Shuberts close the year with some 59 theatres in New York and elsewhere in the United States booked on their circuit. About two-thirds of the playhouses are actually owned or leased by the Shuberts. The rest are owned and managed by allies in the attempt to break the Syndicate's oppressive monopoly.

Dec 8 With Phyllis Dare—a 16-year-old Edwardian beauty—as Cinderella, the new King's Theatre in Edinburgh opens. Its boxes are elaborately wrought with plaster figures and painted in rose, white, and gold. Originally the theatre auditorium has, in addition to the stalls, three levels of balcony seating. In 1956, these will be reduced to two levels.

Dec 10 In Bury St. Edmunds, the Theatre Royal, initially opened on Oct 13, 1819 and designed by William Wilkins, now re-opens after a "refurbishing" by architect Bertie Crewe.

Dec 26 The Hicks Theatre in London opens with *The Beauty of Bath*, transferred from the Aldwych. W.G.R. Sprague has designed the new theatre with its Louis XVI interior, capacity 907, and Charles Frohman is the manager. (In 1909 the name of the theatre will be changed to the Globe Theatre, perpetuating the name of the Globe theatre on Newcastle Street, demolished in 1902).

San Francisco Earthquake

May 13 San Francisco's Chutes Theatre, now opens as the Orpheum Theatre and will continue operating with that name until January 20, 1907.

June In court, in a suit against Charles Frohman and others, Karri Thomas establishes the professional status of a "Gibson Girl." Employed at £ 3 per week for *The Catch of the Season* (1904) at the Vaudeville, she was given two weeks' notice. She contends she should have had a run-of-the-play contract, since she spoke two lines: "I am a perfect wonder at spotting winners," and "I never lose at bridge." Charles Cruikshanks, secretary of the Actors' Association, testifies for her. The jury agrees, awarding her £ 200.

June Popular star Gertie Millar goes to

Aug 18 In Edinburgh, Andrew Carnegie sets the foundation stone for the projected new King's Theatre, to be constructed by W. S. Cruikshank and Company. A. Stewart Cruikshank, son of the builder, is chosen to manage the theatre.

Aug 30 Arthur Bourchier, manager of the Garrick, bans critics from the premiere of *The Morals of Marcus*, noting that they may review the play when he is ready to invite them. The author and actors are denied reviews because of his action and Bourchier finally apologizes.

Sep 24 Producer Charles Dillingham erects a huge mill outside the New York Knickerbocker Theatre for the play, *The Red Mill*. It is illuminated and its sails revolve, making it Broadway's first moving

Jan 7 *The Truth* (NY—Criterion—Comedy). Written for Clara Bloodgood, who plays Beckey Warder, a girl who has difficulty telling the truth, this Clyde Fitch play runs only 34 performances. It is directed by the playwright. On April 6 Fitch's play opens at the Comedy Theatre in London. Marie Tempest and Dion Boucicault are in the cast. *The Times* praises Tempest's acting.

Jan 19 *Salomy Jane* (NY—Liberty—Comedy). Paul Armstrong adapts Bret Harte's western short story, *Salomy Jane's Kiss.* It features Eleanor Robson, H.B. Warner, Holbrook Blinn and Ada Dwyer. Staged by Hugh Ford, it runs for over 15 weeks.

Feb 18 *The Tattooed Man* (NY—Criterion—Musical). Victor Herbert's score combines with a book by Harry B. Smith and A.N.C. Fowler. Frank Daniels stars in this Arabian nights story of spurned love. The run is limited to 59 performances owing to a fire in the adjacent New York Theater. The show makes it up with a year-and-a-half on the road.

March 7 *Widower's Houses* (NY—Herald Square—Comedy). This American premiere of George Bernard Shaw's play is offered by the Shuberts at special matinees, for 16 performances. Effie Shannon and Herbert Kelcey are featured.

March 11 *The Spoilers* (NY—New York—Drama). Rex Beach, aided by James MacArthur, dramatizes his popular novel. It runs for only two weeks.

April 8 *The Orchid.* See L premiere, 1903.

April 12 *Comtesse Coquette* (NY—Bijou—Comedy). This Roberto Bracco romance is translated by Dirce St. Cyr and Grace Isabel Colbron. Alla Nazimova stars. The play runs over nine weeks.

May 20 *Fascinating Flora* (NY—Casino—Musical). R. H. Burnside and Joseph Herbert collaborate on the book in which Flora (Adele Ritchie) leaves her home-loving husband for a possible operatic career. Her hopes are dashed but all ends well. Burnside stages, with dances by Jack Mason. The show, with a Gustav Kerker score, and many interpolations, runs for 113 performances.

July 8 *Ziegfeld Follies of 1907* (NY—New York Roof—Revue). The thin plot thread shows Pocahontas and John Smith in modern America, complete with impersonations of Teddy Roosevelt and other celebrities. Harry B. Smith devises the book, the title perhaps deriving from his column, "Follies of the Day." The music is by many composers. This first edition costs only $13,000 to mount, runs for 70 performances, tours briefly, and makes a lot of money.

Aug 5 *The Time, the Place, and the Girl* (NY—Wallack's—Musical). This story of

Salomy Jane

love in a sanatorium is written by Will Hough and Frank Adams. Joseph Howard writes the lyrics and score. Although this show had 400 performances in Chicago, it manages only a month on Broadway.

Aug 6 *The Shoo-Fly Regiment* (NY—Bijou—Musical). This all-black musical, intended primarily for white audiences, shows a black regiment winning a battle in the Spanish-American War. Despite a book by Bob Cole, lyrics by James W. Johnson, music by J. Rosamond Johnson, and a lively cast, the show lasts only two weeks.

Aug 12 *A Yankee Tourist* (NY—Astor—Musical). Based on Richard Harding Davis' *The Galloper,* this book tells of a suitor who pretends to be a famous war correspondent, as Davis actually is, in order to stay near his nurse-fiancee. Raymond Hitchcock and Flora Zabelle star. Wallace Beery is also in the cast and takes over the lead just before the national tour. Lyrics are by Wallace Irwin, music by Alfred Robyn, William Jerome and Jean Schwartz. The show runs 103 performances.

Aug 26 *The Round Up* (NY—New Amsterdam—Drama) Edmund Day's formula melodrama of villainy in the Wild West premieres with Maclyn Arbuckle, Orme Caldara and Julia Dean. It achieves 155 performances.

Aug 31 *My Wife* (NY—Empire—Comedy). John Drew stars in this Michael Morton adaptation of a French original. He is supported by Billie Burke, Dorothy Tennant, and Morton Selten. The play has 129 performances.

Sep 2 *The Rogers Brothers in Panama* (NY—Broadway—Musical). Capitalizing on the drama of building the Panama Canal, the brothers, Gus and Max, create a lively mixture of mistaken identities and adventure. Music is by Max Hoffman. Ben Teal stages and Pat Rooney arranges the dances. The show has a run of 71 performances.

Sep 2 *Anna Karenina* (NY—Herald Square—Drama). Virginia Harned plays the doomed heroine of Tolstoi's novel in this adaptation by Thomas Broadhurst. The production runs nearly six weeks.

Sep 9 *The Thief* (NY—Lyceum—Drama). Haddon Chambers adapts Henri Bernstein's French play for a total of 281 performances. Kyrle Bellew and Margaret Illington are featured. On November 12 the play opens at London's St. James's Theatre. In this Cosmo Gordon-Lennox adaptation, Lilian Braithwaite, Irene Vanbrugh and Reginald Owen appear. The play wins 186 performances.

Sep 30 *The Evangelist* (NY—Knickerbocker—Drama). British dramatist Henry Arthur Jones' play is staged by William Seymour; the cast includes May Davenport Seymour, Edith Taliaferro, Conway Tearle, and Howard Kyle. It wins only 19 performances.

Oct 1 *The Girl Behind the Counter* (NY—Herald Square—Musical). Edgar Smith Americanizes this British show for Lew Fields. As Henry Schniff, Fields wants to help his stepdaughter marry an American boy instead of the English title favored by her mother. Howard Talbot's score is enriched by interpolating Paul Lincke's already popular "The Glow-Worm." Fields resists this, insisting music-publisher Edward Marks pay him $1,000 if the song fails to stop the show. Every evening it has dozens of encores. The show runs almost 33 weeks.

Oct 7 *The Gay White Way* (NY—Casino—Revue). The search for the person de-

The Time, the Place and the Girl

picted in a headless photograph takes detective Jefferson De Angelis on a tour of Manhattan which provides unusual locales for a variety of vaudeville turns. He and Blanche Ring parody *The Great Divide* and the sawmill scene in *Blue Jeans*. R. H. Burnside stages; the show runs for 105 performances.

Oct 10 *Hip! Hip! Hooray!* (NY—Weber's—Musical). Somewhere between a revue and a musical, the show's plot by Edgar Smith permits Joe Weber to cavort at Doolittle College with side-kick Dick Bernard, as a pair of "Dutch" comics. Their love interests are played by Valeska Suratt and Bessie Clayton. The show, with Gus Edwards' music, lasts only two months.

Oct 16 *A Grand Army Man* (NY—Stuyvesant—Drama). David Belasco produces and directs. He has developed the play with Pauline Phelps and Marion Short. David Warfield stars. Also in the company are Jane Cowl and Antoinette Perry. The play enjoys 149 performances.

Oct 19 *The Top of the World* (NY—Majestic—Musical). Mark Swan's book has Jack Frost freezing folks he doesn't like. A clever American unfreezes them and lets love take its course. James O'Dea contributes lyrics to the score of Manuel Klein and Anne Caldwell (Mrs. O'Dea). The show pleases for 156 performances.

Nov 11 *The Christian Pilgrim* (NY—Liberty—Drama). John Bunyan's *Pilgrim's Progress* is the source of this play by James MacArthur, with music by William Furst. Henrietta Crosman and Tyrone Power star. It runs 14 performances.

Nov 18 *The Witching Hour* (NY—Hackett—Drama). Augustus Thomas's play draws upon his experiences with Washington Irving Bishop, a popular mind-reader, to use telepathy and hypnotism for dramatic effect in this tale of the troubles of Jack Brookfield, the gentleman gambler. John Mason stars with Russ

Whytal, Jennie Eustace, Ethel Winthrop, and George Nash. It plays nearly 27 weeks with a subsequent profitable tour.

Nov 25 *The Auto Race* (NY—Hippodrome—Musical). Manuel Klein provides the music and aids Edward Temple with the book for this auto-race story. The show includes a naval battle, a "Four Seasons Ballet" and a circus. Temple stages with Arthur Voegtlin responsible for the impressive settings. It plays two-a-day for 312 performances.

Dec 3 *The Talk of New York* (NY—Knickerbocker—Musical). George M. Cohan returns as author and director, and, with Sam H. Harris, as producer. Victor Moore repeats his Kid Burns character from *Forty-Five Minutes From Broadway*. Gertrude Vanderbilt plays a lady blackmailer, who is exposed by the Kid. Her shocked fiance shoots her, but the Kid takes the blame. All is sorted out at the close. It has 157 performances.

Dec 3 *The Warrens of Virginia* (NY—Belasco—Drama). Mary Pickford stars in this William C. deMille play about a Southern belle in love with a Northern soldier during the Civil War. Cecil B. deMille, Frank Keenan and Emma Dunn also star. Belasco stages and the production runs for 190 performances.

Dec 16 *A Knight for a Day* (NY—Wallack's—Musical). This Robert B. Smith book is a reworking of *Mamselle Sallie*. May Vokes and John Slavin lead the mirth, with Sallie Fisher and Percy Bronson providing the romance. Raymond Hubbell writes the score. The show achieves a 22-week run.

Dec 30 *The Comet* (NY—Bijou—Drama). Owen Johnson's first play deals with a woman who falls in love with her former lover's son, who eventually commits suicide. It stars Alla Nazimova. The play runs for seven weeks.

1907   BRITISH PREMIERES

Jan 10 *Nelly Neil* (L—Aldwych—Musical). With a score by Ivan Caryll, C. M. S. McLellan's story features Edna May. There are 107 performances.

Jan 31 *Miss Hook of Holland* (L—Prince of Wales's—Musical). G.P. Huntly and Eva Kelly star in this "Dutch musical incident" about a brewer's daughter who loves a bandmaster. The program announces that the chatter is by Paul Rubens and Austen Hurgon, with jingles and tunes by Rubens as well. There are 462 performances. On Dec 31 the play premieres in New York at the Criterion Theatre with Christie McDonald in the cast. It is staged by T. Reynolds. The play runs for 119 performances.

Feb 10 *The Cassilis Engagement* (L—Imperial—Comedy). St. John Hankin writes an amusement about a women who gets her son to break his engagement to a bookmaker's daughter. Evelyn Weeden and Langhorne Burton are featured.

March 2 *My Darling* (L—Hicks'—Musical). P. G. Wodehouse contributes some "additional lyrics" to Seymour Hicks and Herbert Haines' book. Marie Studholme is Joy Blossom.

March 9 *The Rising of the Moon* (Dublin—Abbey—Drama). Lady Gregory's play

about Irish insurgency opens with Arthur Sinclair and J. M. Kerrigan in the ensemble.

March 30 *Tom Jones* (Manchester—Prince's—Musical). Edward German composes the score for this adaptation of Henry Fielding's novel. In its Manchester premiere, C. Hayden Coffin plays Tom Jones. It arrives in London at the Apollo on April 17. There are 110 performances. On Nov 11 the play opens at New York's Astor Theatre with Van Rennselaer Wheeler and Louise Gunning. Robert Courtneidge and German stage the work. It runs more than eight weeks.

April 24 *Jeanne D'Arc* (L—Waldorf—Drama). Percy MacKaye's American version of the Joan of Arc story features E. H. Sothern, Walter Hampden, and Julia Marlowe—as the Maid.

April 25 *Mr. George* (L—Vaudeville—Comedy). Comedian Charles Hawtrey and young Billie Burke animate Louis N. Parker's play.

April 27 *Mrs. Wiggs of the Cabbage Patch* See NY premiere, 1904.

May 1 *Brewster's Millions* See NY premiere, 1906.

May 13 *When Knighthood Was in Flower* (L—Waldorf—Drama). Charles Major's adaptation of this best-selling American novel arrives in London. *The Times* calls the play "egregious nonsense."

May 15 *The Girls of Gottenberg* (L—Gaiety—Musical). Another musical by those frequent collaborators Ivan Caryll and Lionel Monckton (music) and Adrian Ross and Basil Hood (lyrics), this show features George Grossmith, Jr., as co-author and actor. The comedy tells of the attempt of Prince Otto to take a town populated only by women. Gertie Millar, Gladys Cooper, and May de Sousa are also in the company. There are 303 performances. It opens Sep 2, 1908, in New York at the Knickerbocker Theatre for 103 showings.

June 8 *The Merry Widow* (L—Daly's—Musical). Franz Lehar's operetta appears in London with lyrics by Adrian Ross—and a controversy between Edward Morton and Captain Basil Hood over authorship of the English book. Morton's name is withdrawn from the program. The story is about a Prince, who is ordered to court a widow to keep her millions in the nation's treasury. Although coolly received in Vienna at its 1905 premiere, it is an immediate hit in London. There are 778 performances. Its success follows to New York, where it opens on Oct 21 at the New Amsterdam. Donald Brian is the Prince. The show runs for 416 performances. It revives the vogue for operetta and discourages comic operas, English musicals, and native American works until World War I changes the cultural and political climate

June 25 *The Earl of Pawtucket.* See NY premiere, 1903.

Sep 11 *The Gay Gordons* (L—Aldwych—Musical). P. G. Wodehouse contributes lyrics to this show by Seymour Hicks, with music by Guy Jones and other lyrics by Henry Hamilton, Arthur Wimperis, and C. H. Bovill. Hicks head a cast which includes Zena Dare and Ellaline Terriss. There are 229 performances.

Oct 9 *Sweet Kitty Bellairs.* See NY premiere, 1903.

Oct 26 *Lady Frederick* (L—Court—Com-

The Warrens of Virginia

edy). Ethel Irving stars in W. Somerset Maugham's play about an older woman who is prepared to wed a wealthy young man to repair her sagging finances. There are 422 performances. *The Times* reports that Maugham: ". . . has an easy style, a gift for inventing epigrams as well as for opportunity remembering them . . . a not unpleasant vein of cynical worldliness. . . ."

Nov 25 *Caesar and Cleopatra* (L—Savoy—Drama). George Bernard Shaw's "history" play opens in the West End, after a premiere at the Grand Theatre, Leeds, in September. Johnstone Forbes-Robertson, Gertrude Elliott, Philip Tonge, and Elizabeth Watson play. *The Times* suggests that Offenbach contribute music to the play since the play lacks a story.

Dec 23 *Is Marriage a Failure?* (L—Terry's—Comedy). From the Royal Theatre in Worthing, where it opened, Russell Vaun and Alban Atwood's farce finally reaches London. Atwood, Clayton Greene, Fred Volpe, and Beatrice Selwyn are in the troupe. Produced and directed by David Belasco, this play opens on Aug 24, 1909, at New York's Belasco Theatre with Jane Cowl and Blanche Yurka in the cast.

for a limited season. The repertoire is mainly Shakespeare: *Macbeth, As You Like It, Julius Caesar, Twelfth Night, Much Ado About Nothing,* and *The Merchant of Venice. Everyman,* and *Masks and Faces,* by Charles Reade and T. Taylor complete the bill. With Greet are Sybil Thorndike, Percy Waram, Sydney Greenstreet, and Julia Perkins.

March 9 For just over three weeks, Shaw's *Mrs. Warren's Profession* is revived in New York, with Mary Shaw again in the title role. This production is at the Manhattan Theatre.

March 18 Ermete Novelli makes his New York debut with his company from Italy for a four-week engagement at New York's Lyric Theatre. In the large repertoire of plays are: *King Lear, The Merchant of Venice, Othello, Hamlet, The Taming of the Shrew, Oedipus Rex,* Goldoni's *Il Burbero Benefico* and *Il Ratto Sabine,* Dumas' *Kean,* and *Mia Moglie Non Ha Chic,* among others. Novelli wins praises from the *NY Times* which reports: "He illustrates very convincingly that naturalism . . . is understood and developed on the latin stage. . . . In much of the comedy Novelli plays directly to the audience, literally taking them into his confidence, making them a part of this experience."

April 22 At Stratford-upon-Avon, the annual Shakespeare Festival opens with *Coriolanus.* Frank Benson stages his company in the drama, following it on April 23, with *Love's Labour's Lost.* Ten other plays by the Bard are presented during the three-week season in the Memorial Theatre. Garrick's *The Country Girl* is also played; Morrison and Stewart's *Don Quixote* and *The Peacemaker* are in the program as well. Critics find this season the most memorable to date.

June 10 The Abbey Theatre of Dublin presents *The Playboy of the Western World* at London's Great Queen Street Theatre. The next day they introduce Synge's *Ri-*

1907   REVIVALS/REPERTORIES

Jan 8 At London's Court Theatre the Vedrenne-Barker management gives eight special matinee performances of *The Campden Wonder* by John Masefield and *The Reformer* by Cyril Harcourt. On Feb 5 it premieres George Bernard Shaw's *The Philanderer.* On June 4 Shaw's *Don Juan in Hell* and *The Man of Destiny* are presented.

Jan 22 The D'Oyly Carte revives Gilbert and Sullivan's *The Gondoliers* at London's Savoy Theatre, with Marie Wilson as Casilda and Louie Rene as the Duchess of Plaza-Toro.

Jan 28 Ellen Terry and her ensemble begin a three-week engagement of Charles Frohman productions. The repertory includes *Nance Oldfield, The Good Hope,* and Shaw's *Captain Brassbound's Conversion.* It is the New York premiere of the Shaw play.

Feb 22 At Dublin's Abbey Theatre the ensemble stages Lady Gregory's new comedy, *The Jackdaw,* with Sara Allgood in the cast. On April 20 Wilfred Scawen Blunt's verse-drama, *Fand,* premieres.

March 4 Ben Greet and his ensemble return to New York at the Garden Theatre

ders to the Sea, Yeats' The Shadowy Waters, and Lady Gregory's The Jackdaw. On June 12, the bill includes Lady Gregory's The Gaol Gate, The Rising of the Moon, and Hyacinth Halvey, with Yeats' On Baile's Strand. Yeats' Cathleen-ni-Houlihan and The Hour Glass are performed on the 13th and 14th. The Times reports that: "Time and success do not seem to spoil the members of this Irish company. The old hush and stillness which was noticed on their first appearances is rarely broken, and the musical talk goes rippling on with as little movement as possible to disturb it, yet with no loss of dramatic effect. Consequently there is no call to say who acted best or better. All acted well."

Tom Jones

June 12 Margaret Mayo adapts Victorien Sardou's lively comedy Divorons, at the Duke of York's. Grace George is featured, and Sadie Jerome is also in the cast.

Sep 16 J. Sheridan Knowles' 19th century drama, Virginius, is revived at New York's Lyric Theatre, with James O'Neill. The NY Times describes the play as "old fash-

ioned."

Oct 15 Arnold Daly offers a two-month repertory season of one-act plays, some by Yeats and Shaw, in New York, with a company including himself, Annie Yeamans, Margaret Wycherly, Holbrook Blinn, and Helen Ware. He also sponsors Madame Hanako, the Japanese tragedienne, with her own company at the Berkeley in a series of plays: A Japanese Doll, A Japanese Lady, A Japanese Ophelia, and The Spy of the Government. At the end of this program, Daly revives Shaw's Candida for 30 performances. The NY Times calls Mme. Hanako: ". . . a curious creature." "At times she suggests an animated doll, at others a writhing, suffering little animal. . . . her exhibit is interesting when it is not too harrowing, too positively sickening, as in the final moments of her play, The Martyr, where she commits harakari. . . ."

Oct 25 Sara Bernhardt plays the lead in Le Reviel, by Paul Hervieu. It is presented at London's Royalty Theatre.

Nov 4 Members of the Comedie Française open at London's Royalty Theatre with Chacun sa Vie. Henri Meilhac's Margot (1890) is offered on November 11.

Nov 21 In Dublin, the Abbey Players premiere The Unicorn from the Stars by W.B. Yeats and Lady Gregory.

Dec 23 The Christmas pantomime season opens with productions of Alice in Wonderland (Apollo), The Forty Thieves (Crystal Palace), and Robinson Crusoe (Lyceum). On December 24 more pantomines open: Humpty Dumpty (Coronet, Cinderella (Shakespeare), and Little Red Riding Hood (Elephant and Castle). On December 26 a host of Christmas pantomimes open: Aladdin (Adelphi), Babes in the Wood (Borough, Drury Lane, Kingston), Jack and the Beanstalk (Britannia, Crown), Mother Goose (Broadway), Dick Whittington (Camden), Robinson Crusoe (Fulham, Royal, Croydon), Sinbad (Dalston, Edmonton, King's), Cinderella (Kennington), Little Red Riding Hood (Marlborough, Artillery, Woolwich), and Puss In Boots (West London).

rian Joseph Knight (b. 1829) is dead. Knight wrote for the Athenaeum, covering the early performances of Henry Irving and Ellen Terry.

Aug 26 Huntley Wright, a British patter expert makes his debut in The Dairymaids at New York's Criterion Theatre.

Aug 30 American actor Richard Mansfield (b. 1854) dies in New London, Conn. Mansfield's extensive repertoire included Cyrano de Bergerac and Dr. Jekyll and Mr. Hyde, in addition to his Shakespearean characterizations. He was the first to produce Shaw in America, and in the 1906–1907 season he presented the first English production of Ibsen's Peer Gynt, playing the title role.

Girls of Gottenberg

Sep 16 David Kessler makes his debut on the English-speaking stage in The Spell by Samuel Shipman. Kessler is already noted on the Yiddish stage.

Nov 9 John Hare and Charles Santley are made new knights in King Edward VII's Birthday Honours List.

Dec 1 Theatrical producer Herman Levin is born in Philadelphia.

Dec 3 Mary Pickford makes her New York debut at the Belasco Theatre in William C. deMille's The Warrens of Virginia.

Dec 18 Playwright Christopher Fry is born Christopher Fry Harris in Bristol, England.

In Britain patents are granted for G. W. S. Poole's system of flats with rolled painted canvas at the top of each. When the canvas is unrolled, the room or scene previously disclosed now seems to be upside down. Rolling the canvas up again reverses the scene.

In the U.S. Anton Karst and A. V. Gilsa, German inventors, patent a theatre-structure concept, which has stage and audi-

1907 BIRTHS/DEATHS/DEBUTS

Feb 8 Ray Middleton is born in Chicago, Illinois.

Feb 25 Playwright Mary Chase, nee Mary Coyle, is born in West Denver, Colorado, to flour salesman Frank Coyle and his wife.

March 11 Gladys Hanson makes her debut in the play, The Spoilers at Broadway's New York Theatre.

March 23 The distinguished actor Richard Mansfield makes his last appearance on the stage. He plays Baron Chevrial in A Parisian Romance, at the New Am-

sterdam Theatre in New York.

April 8 Rida Johnson Young's The Boys of Company "B" opens at New York's Lyceum Theatre. The comedy is light entertainment featuring Arnold Daly, to be replaced in six weeks by John Barrymore. In the cast also are Mack Sennett, later to create the Keystone Cops. Florence Nash makes her debut. It runs for three months.

May 13 Writer-playwright Daphne du Maurier is born to actor Gerald and actress Muriel (Beaumont) du Maurier.

June 23 English drama critic and histo-

torium as separate buildings, with a thin space between which can instantly be filled with a wall of water in case of fire in either building. Richard Stanley's design makes it possible by mechanical means to effect a lighting transformation from a scene in a copper-shop to a living-room without removing any of the props. The Great Lafayette's patent protects his production of a lion hunt on stage, followed by the capture of a live lion, and the apparent feeding of a real person to the lion.

In Manchester, Annie E. F. Horniman founds a new provincial repertory theatre ensemble dedicated to the "new drama." She begins her operations in the Midland Hotel Theatre, actually a ballroom.

Anxious not to offend the Japanese Emperor, whose son the Crown Prince is visiting England, Lord Althorp, the Lord Chamberlain, bans performances of Gilbert & Sullivan's operetta, *The Mikado*. This despite the fact that the work is a Japanese favorite, and the music is being played aboard Japanese warships. The librettist, W. S. Gilbert, complains that the ban has been imposed without warning. He is reported, by Mrs. D'Oyly Carte, to have protested at the censor's office, "weeping for two hours on end." The ban is lifted in 1908. The operetta has been performed for two decades previous to this ban.

Charlotte Shaw, wife of the controversial playwright Bernard Shaw, translates Eugene Brieuxs' controversial French drama, *Maternite*. Fellow members of the Stage Society submit it for censorship. It is rapidly rejected with the comment: "Inform whoever is responsible for the play that it will *never* be licensed in England."

Harley Granville Barker refuses to make requested changes in his drama *Waste*. As a result, the Lord Chamberlain's Office refuses to license it for public performance. One of the offending details in the play is reference to an abortion, leading to the death of the patient. But Granville Barker has already staged *Votes for Women*, with just such a reference and no licensing difficulties. In November 1907 *Waste* is performed privately at London's Imperial Theatre. Not until 1920, with a completely rewritten text, will *Waste* be licensed. In 1907, Edward Garnett's *The Breaking Point* is also banned. It features an unmarried heroine, in love with a married man and afraid of pregnancy. She commits suicide.

The Lord Chamberlain has refused a permit licensing performance of Eugene Brieux's controversial French drama, *Les Hannetons*, by the Stage Society. His censor is offended by a line: "The first time we met, I told you I'd had a lover: that

was a lie." Performance permission is given when the original French line is retranslated as "I'd not been straight," replacing "I'd had a lover."

Jan 1 London's first Yiddish Music Hall opens. It is the Princess, in Christian Street, Whitechapel.

Jan 21 Yesterday, it was the Orpheum Theatre. Today it takes back its original name, the Chutes Theatre. Al Jolson is the star tonight. The theatre will continue operating until June 1909 in San Francisco.

Jan 28 The Playhouse opens on Charing Cross Road with a transfer of *Toddles*. It was formerly known as The Royal Avenue Theatre. Cyril Maude is the manager of this 678-seat theatre designed by Detmar Blow and Ferdinand Billeray. In 1951 it will become a live audience TV studio. Before this conversion it is the theatre that has the last painted canvas backdrop in London.

Feb 1 At London's St. James's Theatre, *His House in Order* has its 400th performance.

Feb 14 *Raffles* has its 300 performance at London's Comedy Theatre.

Feb 18 The Walker Theatre opens in Winnipeg, Manitoba, Canada with Henry Savage's Grand Opera Company in *Madame Butterfly*. Owner C. P. Walker lures the best touring companies of the day by offering runs in his chain of theatres from Winnipeg to Minneapolis. In April, the Walker Theatre will present the Canadian premiere of Shaw's *Mrs. Warren's Profession*.

March 10 Herbert Beerbohm Tree, speaking to the Incorporated Stage Society, calls for cheaper ticket prices, considering the stiff competition theatre has to face from the lower-priced music hall entertainments—where smoking is also freely allowed. Stall—or orchestra—seats at a standard 10s. 6d., he insists, are too expensive for many. At the same time, he admits, theatre rentals and production costs have never been so high.

March 18 San Francisco's New Alcazar Theatre opens, replacing the 1885 theatre of the same name, built by Michael H. De Young, publisher of the *San Francisco Chronicle*. It's designed by H. G. Corwin and sited at the corner of Sutter and Steiner Streets. It closes as a legitimate theatre on Nov 26, 1911, with a minstrel show, going through many changes until it's torn down in 1979. In later years, it functions mainly as a cinema.

March 30 The 500th performance of *The Scarlet Pimpernel* occurs at London's New Theatre.

April Both the Shubert Brothers and the Syndicate have shown marked interest in

vaudeville. "Advanced Vaudeville," the Syndicate has been calling its production and booking proposals. Now the two groups join forces to form the U.S. Amusement Company, with A. L. Erlanger as president, Lee Shubert as vice-president, and Marc Klaw as treasurer. The initial capitalization is set at $50,000,000, some of it represented by theatres and leases, not by cash. For the Syndicate, Klaw and Erlanger control 51% of the stock, with the Shuberts in control of 42%. The remainder is held by others.

April 10 The Edison Manufacturing Company and the National Phonographic Company deny that they have infringed Isadore Newmark's copyright on a show song, "The Paralytic Hotel." They admit that they have recorded the song and sold the cylinders but insist that the copyright covers only sheet-music which can be read. Phonograph cylinders, they demonstrate, cannot be read; only heard. Mr. Justice Sutton agrees with them and orders Newmark to pay costs of the English court hearings.

May 6 A majority votes to exclude actor-managers from the Actors' Association in London.

May 17 The new Hippodrome Theatre opens in Portsmouth, England.

June The Play Actors Society is formed, by active members of the Actors' Association, to promote the production of the plays of Shakespeare and other poetic dramas without the aids of scenery or special costumes.

June 15 The 1906–07 Broadway season is closed. There have been a total of 25 revivals in a grand total of 142 productions. 20 revivals have swelled the total of 35 repertory company offerings. Other productions tallied as follows: musicals—13, revues—2, musical plays—4, musical farces—1, comic operas—4, operettas—1, minstrel shows—1, extravaganzas—5, comedies—25, farces—3, dramas—46—with four revivals and two competing productions of *The Kreutzer Sonata*, and one-acts—2. The productions have been presented in 32 different theatre spaces.

July 27 George Bernard Shaw offers to back the proposed Vedrenne-Barker management of London's Savoy Theatre with £2,000. Despite his criticisms of the two men's work at the Royal Court, he has been a staunch supporter, then as now. Unfortunately, the move to the Savoy will not prove profitable. Finally, in March 1911, the partnership will end in debt.

Aug 26 Mark Swan's *Top o' the World* opens the new Royal Alexandra Theatre in Toronto, Canada. Designed by John Lyle for $750,000, the 1,800-seat proscenium house will have an unbroken record of never losing money in any season. The first Toronto theatre to be built in the 20th century, it is named for Queen Alexandra, the consort of King Edward VII. The Theatre is granted a Royal Patent. A beautiful example of Edwardian design, the outer lobby is Italian marble, and the inner lobby is panelled in rosewood.

Sep 2 Philadelphia celebrates the opening of the Forrest Theatre. The opening show is *Advanced Vaudeville*, to be followed in November with Hazel Dawn in *The Pink Lady*. Architect Benjamin Marshall has designed a house so spacious that 50% more patrons could have been accomodated. As now seated, it holds 1,846 and has a proscenium opening of 42 feet wide by 36 feet high and a stage 93 feet wide by 49 feet deep and 26 dressing-rooms. Located at Broad and Sansom Streets, the theatre is the most lavishly decorated and furnished of its time. It is to be the home of many major productions, either on their way to Broadway or on tour. Curtains screening off the balcony and loges can make the house look more intimate. The orchestra seating is sloped below grade, with ramped entrances. In 1927, the playhouse will be torn down.

Sep 26 Philadelphia has a new theatre, the Adelphi. It opens with *Hip Hip Hooray*, featuring Joe Weber. It has 1,341 seats and a twin-facade with the adjacent Lyric

Theatre, which thus become known as "The Twin Theatres." It has a proscenium opening of 31 feet wide by 31 feet high. Later operated by the Shuberts, it will be demolished in 1937.

Oct Obviously angered by the attempt of the Syndicate and the Shuberts to become involved in the production and booking of vaudeville—as well as legitimate theatre, which they already dominate—vaudeville theatre owners and managers this month announce the formation of a circuit of some 30 theatres in which they propose to tour legitimate productions, offering competition to their apparent adversaries, the U.S. Amusement Company, run by the Syndicate and the Shuberts. As a result of this challenge, the U.S. Amusement Company agrees to dissolve; its principals pledging to keep their hands off vaudeville for 15 years. In return, the United Booking Office—which handles vaudeville bookings—pays them $250,000 and assumes all unexpired artists' contracts.

Oct 2 The newly-formed Pilgrim Players present *The Interlude of Youth*, a morality play. This amateur group is to be the embryo of the Birmingham Repertory Company.

Oct 8 The Actors' Union registers itself officially as a Trade Union. Its aims are to seek fair minimum wages, freedom from

abuses, peaceable negotiation, and unity in obtaining goals in Britain.

Oct 8 The Queen's Theatre, Shaftesbury Avenue, London opens with *The Sugar Bowl*. Herbert Sleath is the manager of this 989 seat theatre, designed by W.G.R. Sprague (The Queen's Theatre in Longacre closed in 1887).

Oct 9 After partial re-construction to the designs of Frederick W. Foster, London's Great Queen Street Theatre re-opens under the name of the Kingsway Theatre under the management of Lena Ashwell.

Oct 16 David Belasco opens the Stuyvesant Theatre (1,000 seats), on West 44th Street in New York City, with David Warfield in a new play, *A Grand Army Man*, by Belasco, Phelps, and Short. The theatre, renamed the Belasco in 1910 has a permanent dimmer-board with 65 dimmers. The theatre costs $750,000. After Belasco's death it is leased to Katharine Cornell, Elmer Rice, and the Shuberts. In the early 1950's, it is used as an NBC radio playhouse, but returns to producing legitimate theatre in 1953 under Shubert control.

Oct 27 A group of some 71 authors send a letter to the London *Times* denouncing the censorship functions of the Lord Chamberlain in these terms: "An office autocratic in procedure, opposed to the spirit of the Constitution, contrary to common justice and to common sense." A deputation is also sent to the Prime Minister to protest. Bernard Shaw's *The Shewing Up of Blanco Posnet* is an immediate cause of the protest. Augusta, Lady Gregory, has staged it in Dublin at the Abbey Theatre, followed by a private performance in London, sponsored by the Stage Society. The British censor, however, refuses a license for public performance. Only in 1916 may it be licensed, with changes required.

Dec 2 In Newcastle-on-Tyne, the Olympia Theatre is destroyed by fire. In Burnley, on the same day, the New Palace and Hippodrome open.

Dec 10 At Queen's Hall in London, actress Vane Featherstone holds her annual tea party in aid of the Theatrical Ladies' Guild and Mrs. C. L. Carson's Christmas Dinner Fund.

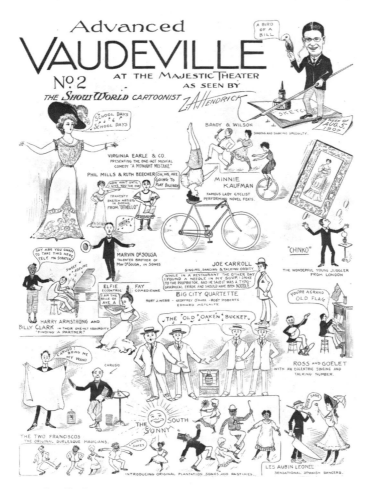

Vaudeville Cartoon

Jan 2 *The Merry Widow Burlesque* (NY—Weber's Music Hall—Musical). Joe Weber uses the original music from *The Merry Widow* in this parody. George V. Hobart writes the book. Lulu Glaser stars. It runs 156 performances.

Jan 15 *The Jesters* (NY—Empire—Drama). Charles Frohman provides Maude Adams with a starring role in this translation of Miguel Zamacois' poetic drama. William Seymour stages, and sets are by Ernest Gros, costumes by Dazian. The production runs for 53 performances. The *NY Times* says her acting has "a fine sense of delicate values."

Jan 27 *A Waltz Dream* (NY—Broadway—Operetta). In this operetta Edward Johnson plays a young man married to a foreign princess and longing for his homeland. Magda Dahl plays opposite him. Also in the cast is Joseph W. Herbert, who has provided the English book and lyrics. Oscar Straus provides the score. Herbert Gresham stages, with settings by Homer Emens and costumes by F. Richard Anderson. The show runs for 111 performances. It premieres in London on March 7 at the Hicks. With George Grossmith, Jr. and Mary Gary, there are 146 performances.

Jan 28 *The Soul Kiss* (NY—New York—Musical). In this musical comedy, Ralph Herz, as J. Lucifer Mephisto, tempts a sculptor (Cecil Lean) to be unfaithful with a series of famous beauties. Adeline Genee, as "The Dancer," claims his heart. Harry B. Smith provides the book and Maurice Levi and others the music. Florenz Ziegfeld produces. The show enjoys a run of over 15 weeks.

Feb 3 *Bandana Land* (NY—Majestic—Musical). Bert Williams and George Walker team up in this lively tale of some black promoters outwitting a tram company in the process of buying some farmland. Book and lyrics are by J.A. Shipp and Alex Rogers. The score is by Will Marion Cook. The authors stage the action but Ada Overton Walker stages the musical numbers. The comedy, highlighted by a Williams and Walker cakewalk which stops the show, runs over 11 weeks.

Feb 3 *Fifty Miles from Boston* (NY—Garrick—Musical). This show salutes Edward Harrigan of Harrigan and Hart. Cohan names a central character after him, composes a hit song, "H-A-Double-R-I-G-A-N," and invites him to the opening. In the show Harrigan, played by George Parson, is smitten with Sadie, played by Edna Wallace Hopper, but she loves a baseball star. Cohan's play runs only four weeks.

Feb 24 *Nearly a Hero* (NY—Casino—Musical Comedy). "Dutch" comic Sam Bernard is arrested by mistake, causing

Nearly a Hero

some amusing mixups. Ethel Levey, Ada Lewis, Zelda Sears, and Elizabeth Brice contribute vocal and dancing talents. Audiences come for 116 performances, despite the weak Harry B. Smith book.

Feb 25 *Paid in Full* (NY—Astor—Drama). Eugene Waller's play tells the story of a young man who embezzles in order to improve his situation. His wife helps him settle the matter but then leaves him because of his criminal conduct. The cast includes Tully Marshall, Hattie Russell and Lillian Albertson. The drama runs for 167 performances. It premieres in London on Sep 8 at the Aldwych. Robert Loraine and Hilda Antony appear.

March 23 *Girls* (NY—Daly's—Comedy). Clyde Fitch reworks a play by Hugo Holtz. Featuring Laura Nelson Hall and Leslie Kenyon, this play runs two months. On Sep 10, 1913, it premieres at London's Prince of Wales's Theatre with a cast including Dorothy Fane, Daisy Thimm, Esme Beringer, and Enid Bell. It doesn't last the month.

March 23 *The Servant in the House* (NY—Savoy—Drama). Charles Rann Kennedy's play, in which the servant represents Christ, is produced by Henry Miller. The cast includes Tyrone Power, Walter Hampden, Charles Dalton and Edith Wynne Mathson. It runs for 10 weeks, followed by extensive touring. On Oct 25, 1909, it premieres at the Adelphi in London with Mathson and Miller in the cast.

April 6 *The Royal Mounted* (NY—Garrick—Drama). Cecil B. and William C. de Mille write this drama of the Canadian Mounties. C. B. deMille and Cyril Scott (a featured player) do the staging. It runs for only four weeks.

April 20 *The Yankee Prince* (NY—Knickerbocker—Musical). All the Cohans save George M. Cohan's wife Ethel are in this show which Cohan wrote, composed, staged, and produced (with Sam Harris). Donald Crisp is also on hand. This is yet another tale of an American parent in Europe, looking for a title to marry his daughter. The show runs only 28 performances.

June 15 *Three Twins* (NY—Herald Square—Musical). "Cuddle Up a Little Closer, Lovie Mine" becomes a hit in this long-running show (nearly nine months). Bessie McCoy is coy as a girl in love with a twin who has a slightly crazy duplicate. The lyrics are by Otto Hauerbach, later changed to Harbach, and the score is the work of Karl Hoschna.

June 15 *Ziegfeld Follies of 1908* (NY—Jardin de Paris—Revue). Adam and Eve survey the achievements of their children. One of these triumphs is digging a tunnel from Manhattan to New Jersey, where Zeigfeld's glamorous chorines are seen as giant mosquitoes. Nora Bayes scores a hit with an interpolated song, written with her husband Jack Norworth, "Shine On, Harvest Moon." Harry B. Smith provides the plotline, with a score by Maurice Levi. It runs for 15 weeks.

Aug 10 *The Traveling Salesman* (NY—Liberty—Comedy). James Forbes' play with a cast including Gertrude Coghlan, John Tansy, Maud B. Sinclair, and Frances

Traveling Salesman

Golden Fuller, runs 35 weeks.

Aug 17 *The Man from Home* (NY—Astor—Comedy). This play by Booth Tarkington and Harry Leon Wilson based on their experiences watching Americans in Europe, is intended to poke gentle fun at the displaced travelers longing for home. Instead of laughing at them, audiences cheer their pro-American, anti-European comments for a run of 496 performances on Broadway and ultimately nearly six years of touring. William Hodge stars.

Aug 18 *The Devil* (NY—Garden—Comedy). Henry W. Savage produces Ferenc Molnar's play, believing, as does Harrison Gray Fiske, that he has the American rights. The confusions which lead to two premieres on the same night are caused by misunderstandings generated by the lack of a copyright agreement between America and Hungary. Savage's version runs 87 performances, with Edwin Stevens playing a broadly comic devil. Also in the cast is Theodosia de Cappet, later to become the celebrated film vamp, Theda Bara. On the same night Fiske produces and directs this play in a different translation. It stars George Arliss as the Devil. Arliss is subtle and sardonic for 175 performances.

Aug 31 *Algeria* (NY—Broadhurst—Musical). Victor Herbert devises the score and Glen MacDonough the book. His song, "Rose of the World," is immediately popular, unlike the plot of a lovelorn sultana and some Foreign Legionaires. George Marion both stages and performs. Producer Frank McKee closes the show after only six weeks.

Sep 2 *The Girls of Gottenburg* See L premiere, 1907.

Sep 5 *Sporting Days* (NY—Hippodrome—Musical). In addition to the circus treats in this edition of the annual Hippodrome show is a technically amazing presentation, "The Battle of the Skies," supposedly fought in 1950. The show, playing two-a-day, runs 448 performances.

Sep 7 *Wildfire* (NY—Liberty—Comedy). Lillian Russell scores a success in this play about a woman who foils an attempt to fix a horse race. The comedy is by George Broadhurst and George Hobart. Will Archie as the jockey is the hit of the evening. The show runs for two months.

Sep 22 *The Fighting Hope* (NY—Stuyvesant—Drama). David Belasco produces and stages William Hurlburt's play, featuring Blanche Bates. The production achieves 231 performances.

Sep 28 *Mlle. Mischief* (NY—Lyric—Musical). This Viennese operetta is reworked by Sydney Rosenfeld as a vehicle for Lulu Glaser. The plot device is her bet that she can behave as a soldier for 24 hours in a barracks without being detected. The show runs three months. Ned Wayburn stages the musical numbers and J. C. Huffman the remainder of the material.

Sep 29 *A Gentleman from Mississippi* (NY—Bijou—Drama). Douglas Fairbanks is featured in this play by Harrison Rhodes and Thomas Wise, who is also in the cast. It has 407 performances.

Oct 5 *The American Idea* (NY—New York—Musical). George M. Cohan sends two Brooklyn millionaires to Paris, where they hope their daughters will marry counts. This show manages a two months' run and a tour, but critics find it repetitive of other Cohan chauvinistic musicals.

Oct 20 *Little Nemo* (NY—New Amsterdam—Musical). Based on Winsor McCay's comic-strips, Harry B. Smith's book takes Nemo on a series of colorfully mounted adventures in Slumberland. Victor Herbert provides the score for a series of handsome scenes such as a weather factory with a ballet of human raindrops. Master Gabriel, supposedly a midget, plays the youthful hero Nemo. Joseph Cawthorn, Harry Kelly, and Billy B. Van clown and cavort for 111 performances. Improvising one night, Cawthorn coins the word "Whiffenpoof," later adopted at Yale.

Oct 29 *Samson* (NY—Criterion—Drama). Charles Frohman presents this Henri Bernstein opus starring Constance Collier, Pauline Frederick, and William Gillette. It runs for 152 performances. Bernstein's production comes to London on Feb 3, 1909, with Violet Vanbrugh, Leon Quartermaine, Charles Bryant, Marie Illington, and Edith Latimer in the cast. It runs for 120 performances.

Nov 2 *Via Wireless* (NY—Liberty—Drama). Winchell Smith joins Paul Armstrong to write this play and helps Frederic Thompson stage it. The show includes Smith's favorite fictional performer, George Spelvin, in the cast. Eventually, Spelvin is to become a comic designation for an actor when he appears in a second role in the same play, and not just plays by Winchell Smith. The show runs 11 weeks.

Nov 17 *Salvation Nell* (NY—Hackett—Drama). Edward Sheldon's strong drama of life among the downtrodden features Minnie Maddern Fiske. Harrison Grey Fiske produces and shares directing tasks with his wife. The play runs for 71 performances. *Theatre Magazine* praises Mrs. Fiske's acting as "absolutely true to life."

Nov 23 *The Patriot* (NY—Garrick—Comedy). J. Hartley Manners writes a light farce. William Collier stars and directs. His family is in the cast. The show runs nearly five months.

Nov 30 *The Blue Mouse* (NY—Lyric—Comedy). Clyde Fitch adapts a German farce by Alexander Engel and Julius Horst and stages it with Mabel Barrison, Harry

Little Nemo

Conor, and Rosa Cooke. The production runs 29 weeks.

Nov 30 *Miss Innocence* (NY—New York—Musical). Produced by Florenz Ziegfeld, this comedy is about a girl, played by Anna Held, who, accompanied by a handsome Army officer (Lawrence D'Orsay) goes to Paris to find her parents. Harry B. Smith writes the book and Ludwig Englander composes most of the score, although there are interpolations such as "Shine On, Harvest Moon." T. B. McDonald creates the lavish settings and Julian Mitchell directs. The show runs for 176 performances.

Nov 30 *The Prima Donna* (NY—Knickerbocker—Musical). Fritzi Scheff is the prima donna of the Paris Opera who wins the heart of an officer who is also a count. The show, with a Victor Herbert score and a Henry Blossom book, runs for nine weeks.

Dec 7 *The Queen of the Moulin Rouge* (NY—Circle—Musical). Princess Marotz (Flora Parker) goes to Paris to rekindle her fiance's interest as the lady of the show's title. This long run—five months—is credited not to the Paul M. Potter story, nor even to the music of John T. Hall, but to the lively can-can sequences, spritely staging, and some chorines disrobing behind a transparent curtain. Carter De Haven and Patricia Collinge are in the company, as is Frank X. Bushman, later to be a cinema hero as Francis X. Bushman.

1908   BRITISH PREMIERES

Feb 12 *Diana of Dobson's* (L—Kingsway—Comedy). Cicely Hamilton's popular play about a poor young girl, employed in a sweatshop who reforms playboy, runs for 141 performances. Lena Ashwell is Diana. The play is a denunciation of sweatshops as well as people who value only money.

March 23 *The Bride of Lammermoor* (Glasgow—King's—Drama). Stephen Phillips' adaptation of Scott's novel opens with Martin Harvey.

March 26 *The High Bid* (Edinburgh—Lyceum—Comedy). Henry James' play opens with Johnston Forbes-Robertson and Gertrude Elliott in the leading roles.

March 26 *Jack Straw* (L—Vaudeville—Comedy). W. Somerset Maugham's comedy about an archduke masquerading as a waiter who is masquerading as an archduke stars Charles Hawtrey. The cast includes Vane Featherston, Lottie Venne and Dagmar Wiehe. The play runs for 321 performances. On Sep 14 it premieres at New York's Empire theater with John Drew. The production enjoys 112 performances.

April 18 *A Fearful Joy* (L—Haymarket—Comedy). Lillie Langtry stars in Sydney Grundy's farce about an elderly husband deceived by his wife and her young lover. It is an adaptation of *Le Plus Heureux de Trois* by Labiche and Gondinet. Allan Aynesworth and Lily Grundy also play. *The Times* reports that Langtry failed to make much of her character.

April 25 *Havana* (L—Gaiety—Musical). This musical has a book by George Grossmith, Jr., and Graham Hill. Leslie Stuart provides the score, with lyrics by Adrian Ross and George Arthurs. Lawrence Grossmith plays Don Adolfo, who is to marry Consuelo, played by Evie Greene. The Don sings "Cupid's Telephone." The play runs for 211 performances. On Feb 11, 1909 the play premieres in New York at the Casino with James T. Powers in the lead. It runs 34 weeks.

May 9 *The Thunderbolt* (L—St. James's—Drama). Arthur Wing Pinero's play about an attempt to prevent a woman from inheriting a fortune, features Louis Calvert and Reginald Owens. Stella Campbell, daughter of Mrs. Pat Campbell, plays the lead.

May 11 *Butterflies* (L—Apollo—Musical). The musical, with a book by W. J. Locke, is based on the comedy *The Palace of Puck*. It is a variation on *A Midsummer Night's Dream*. It runs for 217 performances. *The Times* calls the musical "jolly" but complains that the lavish costumes and entertainments get in the way.

May 12 *Getting Married* (L—Haymarket—Comedy). George Bernard Shaw's talky comedy has a matinee performance, with a cast including Fanny Brough, Beryl Faber, Mary Rorke, Marie Löhr, Henry Ainley, and Robert Loraine. On Nov 6, 1916, the play has its New York premiere, produced and staged by William Faversham, who also plays the Bishop of Chelsea. It runs for 112 performances at the Booth Theatre.

May 24 *Nan* (L—Royalty—Drama). John Masefield's tragedy about a girl whose innocent father is hanged for stealing features Lillah McCarthy in the title role. It is given at a Sunday matinee. On Feb 17, 1920 the play opens in New York's 39th Street Theatre with Alexandra Carlisle. It has only four matinees.

June 13 *The Explorer* (L—Lyric—Drama). W. Somerset Maugham's play has Lewis Waller as Alexander Mackenzie, the explorer in question. Eva Moore, Mary Rorke, and Evelyn Millard play the women in the drama. On May 19, 1909, Maugham's revised version is premiered at the Lyric; Waller still plays the lead.

June 16 *The Flag Lieutenant* (L—Play-house—Comedy). This "naval comedy" is by Major W. P. Drury and Leo Trevor. Cyril Maude plays the title-role, the real hero who saves a British garrison on Crete from the Bashi-Bazouks, but who lets his Major have the credit, risking himself the charge of cowardice. The play runs for 381 performances.

Sep 1 *The Passing of the Third Floor Back* (L—St. James's—Comedy). Jerome K. Jerome's idle fancy is a "modern morality," play showing the Mysterious Stranger in the Third Floor Back bringing out the best qualities in formerly shabby characters. Johnston Forbes-Robertson stars with Gertrude Elliott. It has 186 performances. *The Times* complaining that the figures are all black and white writes that, "Mr. Jerome's play is written for the simple and the sentimental and the optimistic . . . ."

Sep 3 *What Every Woman Knows* (L—Duke of York's—Comedy). James Barrie's chronicle of the ways in which the quiet but determined woman helps husband John to political success attracts audiences for 384 performances. Gerald Du Maurier and Hilda Trevelyan lead. On December 23 the show arrives at New York's Empire Theater with Maude Adams and Richard Bennett in the leads. The show runs six months.

Sep 3 *The King of Cadonia* (L—Prince of Wales's—Musical). Frederick Lonsdale's musical has lyrics by Adrian Ross and score by Sidney Jones. Bertram Wallis plays the title-role of a handsome king who foils a conspiracy against the throne by joining the conspirators. Isabel Jay and Huntley Wright also play. There are 330 performances.

Oct 6 *Bellamy the Magnificent* (L—New—Comedy). Charles Wyndham plays the title-role in Roy Horniman's "satirical comedy" on the morals of Mayfair. Kate Cutler and Robert Loraine also appear.

Oct 12 *Lady Epping's Lawsuit* (L—Criterion—Comedy). Hubert Henry Davies' play has Mary Moore and John Toke. Mr. and Mrs. Sam Sothern are also in the cast.

Oct 24 *The Belle of Brittany* (L—Queen's—Musical). This comic opera by Leedham Bantock and P.J. Barrow has songs by Percy Greenbank, Howard Talbot and Marie Horne. It is about a belle who falls in love with an heir. She sings "Daffodil Time," with a bevy of daffodil girls. Lawrence Rea appears with Walter Passmore and George Graves. It has 147 performances.

Nov 17 *Nell Gwynne, the Player* (L—New—Comedy). Jean Aylwin plays the actress-mistress of Charles II (Charles Quartermaine), with Edith Olive as her rival.

Feb 3 The Sicilian Players, headed by Giovanni Grasso and Mimi Aguglia Ferrau, open at London's Shaftesbury Theatre with Luigi Capuana's *Malia.* Before they close on March 14, they will have played *Cavalleria Rusticana, La Zolfara, La Figlia di Jorio, Juan Jose, Morte Civile, Rusidda, La Lupa,* and *Feudalismo.*

Feb 6 Ine Cameron opens a repertory season at London's Royalty with Dion Boucicault's American drama, *Rip Van Winkle,* with Fred Storey as Rip. Later, he is Skylock to her Portia. She is also Juliet to Paul Lovett's Romeo.

Feb 8 The Irish National Theatre of Dublin present W.B. Yeats' *A Pot of Broth.* This is later replaced by Lady Gregory's *The Rising of the Moon.*

Feb 8 Olga Nethersole brings her repertory to Daly's Theatre in Manhattan for three weeks. The program includes Fitch's *Sapho,* Sudermann's *Magda,* Dumas' *Camille,* Pinero's *The Second Mrs. Tanqueray,* Scribe and Legouve's *Adrienne Lecouvreur,* as well as *Carmen*—with incidental music—and *I Pagliacci,* also with music.

Feb 11 Mrs. Patrick Campbell presents Hugo von Hofmannstahl's *Electra,* pre-ceded by a 16th century Japanese play, *The Flower of Yamato,* for nine performances at New York's Garden Theatre. She is supported by her daughter, Stella, Ben Webster, Mrs. Beerbohm Tree, Charles Dalton, and Edgar Kent.

Feb 11 At London's Royal Court Theatre, the Vedrenne-Barker management brings back Bernard Shaw's *You Never Can Tell* for a seven-week run. On April 8, John Galsworthy's *The Silver Box* has a three-week run. St. John Hankin's *The Return of the Prodigal* is revived on April 29. It is replaced on May 10 with *Votes for Women!* On May 27, Shaw's *Man and Superman* is returned for a five-week run.

Feb 17 Frank Benson opens his season at London's Coronet Theatre with *Much Ado About Nothing.* Mrs. Benson is his Beatrice. In March, he is Don Quixote in a version by G. E. Morrison, with George R. Weir as his Sancho Panza.

Feb 17 For two weeks, Henry Ludlowe and his ensemble play *Richard III* and *The Merchant of Venice* in New York at the Bijou Theatre.

March 2 Vera Komisarzhevsky brings her Russian ensemble and her repertory to Daly's Theatre in New York for three weeks. Among them are Maeterlinck's *Sister Beatrice* and *The Miracle of St. Anthony;* Ibsen's *A Doll's House* and *The Master Builder;* Ostrovsky's *The Dowerless Bride, A Child of Nature;* Sudermann's *The Battle of the Butterflies,* and *The Fires of St. John;* and Gorky's *The Children of the Sun.* The *NY Times* reports that there is no great insight in Komisarzhevsky's acting and complains that: "There is little variety to her expression, while her resource is limited, and, generally conventional."

March 14 Shakespeare's *Romeo and Juliet* is revived at London's Lyceum, with Matheson Lang as Romeo and Nora Kerin as Juliet. The last performance is on May 30.

March 21 Paris' famous theatre of horrors, the Grand Guignol, begins a brief engagement at London's Shaftesbury Theatre, with a mixed program of farces and shock plays. *The Times* reports that ". . . the laborious efforts . . . to make the flesh creep produced little else than mild amusement."

April 4 Herbert Beerbohm Tree revives *The Merchant of Venice,* but his interpretation of Shylock offends some because "he is a Jew behaving as a Jew must needs behave in an anti-Semitic environment." In his production at His Majesty's in London, Alexandra Carlisle is Portia.

April 12 William Archer's translation of Gerhart Hauptmann's German "dream poem," *Hannele,* has a brief run at London's Scala Theatre. Winifred Mayo plays the pathetic Hannele. On December 8, Herbert Beerhohm Tree offers the play for "Afternoon Theatre," with Marie Löhr as Hannele.

April 20 At Stratford-upon-Avon, the annual Shakespeare Festival opens with *Much Ado About Nothing,* directed by Frank Benson. On April 23 *A Midsummer Night's Dream* is presented in the Memorial Theatre. Notable in this season is the William Poel production of *Measure for Measure,* performed by the Horniman company from Manchester; this play is never played by Benson's troupe. Garrick's *The Country Girl* is repeated from last season. Also played are *Dr. Johnson* and *Monsieur de Paris* during the three-week season.

April 27 Hans Andersen opens a short season of German-language theatre at London's Royalty Theatre. The program is made up of Gustav Kadelburg's farce, *Der Weg zur Hölle,* G. E. Lessing's 18th century classic, *Minna von Barnhelm,* and Richard Skowronnek's farce *Panne.*

April 28 At London's Savoy Theatre, the D'Oyly Carte Opera Company revives Gilbert & Sullivan's *The Mikado,* with Henry Lytton in the title-role and Straf-

Butterflies

ford Moss. On July 14, *H. M. S. Pinafore* is revived, followed on Oct 19 by *Iolanthe*. *The Pirates of Penzance* opens on Dec 1.

May 5 Suzanne Depres appears for a fortnight at the Shaftesbury Theatre in London in a French repertoire which includes Ibsen's *Doll's House* and *La Robe Rouge*, *Denise*, *La Rafale*, *Le Detour*, and *Poil de Carotte*. (The last play interpreted by Gertrude Elliott and Forbes-Robertson, is known in London as *Carrots*).

May 18 From Paris, Mme. Bartet comes to the Shaftesbury in London for a two-week season of French plays, chosen from works by Dumas fils, Hervieu, de Musset, Marivaux, and Racine.

June 8 At London's Aldwych Theatre, Oscar Asche and Lily Brayton open their season with Frank Stayton's *The Two Pins*, a "comedy of the Middle Ages." This is followed by a revival of *The Taming of the Shrew*.

June 15 Coquelin opens a four-week season of French drama at His Majesty's Theatre in London. In the repertoire are: *Le Bourgeois Gentilhomme*, *Le Voyage de Monsieur Perrichon*, *Les Romanesques*, *L'Eté de St. Martin*, *Le Mariage de Figaro*, *Cyrano de Bergerac*, *Le Bons Villageois*, *Tartuffe*, *La Joie Fait Peur*, *Les Precieuses Ridicules*, and *L'Anglais tel qu'on le Parle*, among other plays.

June 29 Severin-Mars offers a short season of French repertory at London's Royalty Theatre. *Octave*, *Un Honnéte Homme*, *Fleur d'Oranger*, and *La Derniere Soirée de Brummel* compose the bill.

July 6 Shakespeare in the Botanic Gardens is a London summer treat. The production is *The Tempest*, with Patrick Kirwan as Caliban and Reginald Maurice as Prospero.

July 14 At the Lyceum Theatre in London, a triple-bill offers William S. Gilbert's "original play" of *Rosencrantz and Guildenstern*, with Gilbert as King Claudius and Marion Terry as Gertrude. The title-roles are taken by Nigel Playfair and James Hearn. Also performed are *A Matter-of-Fact Husband*, by John Cutler, K. C., and Tristan Bernard's French farce, *French as He Is Spoke*.

Aug 3 George M. Cohan and Sam Harris present the *Cohan and Harris Minstrels* for a limited engagement of three weeks at the New York Theatre. Cohan is not on stage, but Eddie Leonard is. So are George Evans and the famed female impersonator, Julian Eltinge, who performs a Salome dance. A Cohan one-act musical, *The Belle of the Barbers' Ball*, is a second-act feature.

Sep 5 At London's His Majesty's Theatre, Herbert Beerbohm Tree produces a new version of Goethe's *Faust*, adapted by Stephen Phillips and J. Comyns Carr. There are 113 performances, with Tree as Mephistopheles.

Sep 9 John Martin Harvey opens his London season at the Adelphi Theatre with *The Conspiracy* and *The Corsican Brothers*, from Alexandre Dumas' novel. On Sep 14, Martin Harvey offers *The House of Pierre*, a one-act play by Julie Opp Faversham and Kate Jordan; on Sep 21, Basil Hood's *Ib and Little Christina;* on Sep 28, the play is *A Tragedy of Truth*, by Rosamund Langbridge. On Oct 5, Stephen Phillips' *The Last Heir*, based on Scott's *The Bride of Lammermoor*, has its London premiere, with Martin Harvey and Nina De Silva. On Oct 26 he revives his great success, *The Only Way*, based on Dickens' *A Tale of Two Cities*.

Sep 21 James K. Hackett and his ensemble visit Broadway for a four-week engagement at the Hackett Theatre. For the first three weeks, Anthony Hope's *The Prisoner of Zenda* is revived, followed by *The Crisis*.

Oct 15 At London's Shaftesbury Theatre, H. B. Irving revives that venerable melodrama, *The Lyons Mail*, adapted from Moreau's French original by Charles Reade. *The Sergeant of Hussars* is the curtain-raiser. The production earns 128 performances. Irving and his wife, Dorothea Baird, play leading roles.

Nov 10 At London's Royal Court Theatre, Gilbert Murray offers his version of Euripides' *The Bacchae* in rhymed verse. Lillah McCarthy, Esme Percy and Winifred Mayo appear.

Nov 25 Lewis Waller revives Shakespeare's *Henry V*, playing the title-role at London's Lyric Theatre.

Nov 27 At London's New Theatre, Mrs. Patrick Campbell produces W. B. Yeats' *Deirdre* and Hugo von Hofmannstahl's *Electra*. She plays both title-roles, supported by Alan Patrick Campbell, and Stella Patrick Campbell. Sara Allgood plays Clytemnestra and a Musician in the Yeats drama.

Dec 19 The holiday season approaches with the opening of *Pinkie and the Fairies*, at London's His Majesty's Theatre. Frederic Norton has composed the music to accompany W. Graham Robertson's words. On Dec 21, the Coronet Theatre opens its *Dick Whittington* pantomime; On the 23, the Lyceum offers *Little Red Riding Hood*, and the *Cinderella* opens at the Adelphi and at the Pavilion. At the Drury Lane, on Dec 26, *Dick Whittington*, with Queenie Leighton as plucky Dick, is on view.

1908   BIRTHS/DEATHS/DEBUTS

Jan 28 Adeline Genee makes her New York debut in *The Soul Kiss*. With real hounds, Genee and the chorus perform an elegant hunting ballet.

Feb 2 William S. Gilbert, comic opera librettist, is honored at a dinner at London's Savoy Hotel.

April 14 Britain's beloved stage comedian, Willie Edouin (b. 1846), dies today.

May 26 Robert Morley is born in Semley, Wiltshire, England.

June 19 Mildred Natwick is born in Baltimore, Maryland.

July 12 Actor Milton Berle is born Milton Berlinger in New York City.

Aug 4 American playwright Bronson Howard (b. Oct 7, 1842) dies in Avon-by-the-Sea, N.J. Howard's first serious play, *Saratoga*, was produced by Augustin Daly in 1870. The more successful of his later plays was *The Henrietta* and *Shenandoah*. In 1891 he founded the American Dramatists Club, the first playwrights organization.

Aug 22 Ruth Shepley makes her debut in *All For A Girl* at the Bijou theater in New York.

Sep 26 Actor Willian Farren (b. 1826) dies.

Oct 19 Gus Rogers, of the popular American "Dutch" comedy duo, The Rogers Brothers, today dies. Born in 1869, he appeared in such shows as *The Rogers Brothers Go to Washington, . . . to Harvard*, and *. . . to Paris*.

Nov 17 Today marks the death of Lydia Thompson, famed for her buxom dancing troupe of "British Blondes," which delighted Victorian dandies and shocked moralists with their curvacious plumpness barely concealed by pink tights. Born in 1836, Thompson is to be remembered long after her passing, named by some critics as the inspiration for what was later to develop as burlesque—without the 19th century requisite of parody.

Dec 14 Laurence Naismith is born Laurence Bernard Johnson in Thames-Ditton, England.

1908   THEATERS/PRODUCTIONS

In Britain this year a patent is granted for A. E. Robbins' detachable doorknob for stagedoors, to prevent canvas flats from being damaged when scenery is moved or stored.

In the U.S. George Schneider patents a scene-shifting system based on the ancient Greek device of the three-sided sce-

King of Cadonia

nic *periaktoi*. (Others patent versions of the periaktoi as well in this decade). Italy's Mariano Fortuny, devises a cloth cyclorama curving over the stage and supported by means of evacuating air from the metal frame behind it.

Edward Lytton, stage manager of Wyndham's Theatre, puts his new invention into operation for *The Early Worm*. Powered by a 4 hp Siemens motor, Lytton's skillfully designed system of cogs, shafts, drums, and wire cables makes it possible to change all kinds of flown scenery rapidly and inexpensively. Changeover for a new production takes about an hour. Hemp ropes are eliminated, as are some stagehands. Frank Curzon is installing this system in the Prince of Wales's Theatre. Annie Horniman's Manchester Repertory Theatre is established in the Gaiety Theatre, the first provincial theatre in Britain to have every seat numbered and reserved. The house is simply decorated in white and red; nothing is garish, befitting the Horniman Quaker ancestry. She is to develop a regional school of playwrights here: Harold Brighouse, Allan Monkhouse, and Stanley Houghton. Her company will include at different times such talents as Sybil Thorndike, Lewis Casson, Edyth Goodall, Esme Percy, Ada King, Milton Rosmer, and Herbert Lomas. By 1917, the war will have seriously curtailed the company. By the early 1920's, the Gaiety will be only a cinema.

Jan With the dissolution of the U.S. Amusement Company, the Shubert brothers regain control of the theatres they had assigned to the company. Once more they have their own circuit for touring their own productions and booking those of others.

Jan 13 In Boyertown, Pennsylvania, 167 lives are lost when the Rhoades Opera House burns.

Jan 20 The Irish National Theatre of Dublin give their first performance in New York with Lady Gregory's play, *Twenty*

Days in the Shade at the Savoy.

Feb 9 Family burlesque and vaudeville will be the fare of Chicago's newest theatre, the Star and Garter, opening today at 815 West Madison Ave. It accomodates 2,000 spectators. It will finally close in Sep 1971, followed in 1972 by demolition.

Feb 25 Playwright James Barrie, with a deputation including W. S. Gilbert, Alfred Sutro, Gilbert Murray, Arthur Wing Pinero, W. H. Hudson, Henry James, Granville Barker, and Comyns Carr, confront Herbert Gladstone at the Home Office with a petition signed by 71 notables in the arts, demanding the abolition of licensing of plays. The group insists that the original purpose of the Licensing Act was political though it is now perverted to socalled moral ends. Censorship, they maintain, is contrary to common sense and common justice; it is also an autocratic procedure, contrary to the spirit of the Constitution.

March 18 Two theatres are destroyed by fire; one of them is the Olympic, in Springfield, Illinois; the other is the Opera House in New London, Missouri.

March 25 At London's Drury Lane Theatre, a fire destroys the stage and the flies. The auditorium is spared because of a fire-resistant curtain.

June 15 At the close of the current 1907–8 Broadway season, 30 theatres have been used to present a total of 132 productions. 34 shows have been repertory offerings, mostly revivals, with 13 of the productions one-acts. There have been 43 dramas, with 2 revivals; 13 comedies, 4 farces, 15 musicals, 3 revues, 4 musical plays, 3 musical farces, 4 comic operas, 2 operettas, 4 extravaganzas, 1 burlesque, and 2 one-acts, one of them a revival. The *NY Times*, which seldom prints such tallies, runs its own count of 225 new plays "of all classes." 118 have been offered in recognized producing houses (Broadway), 61 in "combination" houses, 21 in stock houses, and 25 by dramatic schools.

July 23 Because the Lord Chamberlain's office has refused to license for public performances, Elinor Glyn's drama, based on her notorious and popular novel, *Three Weeks*, is produced privately at London's Adelphi Theatre.

Aug 2 In a report titled "Some Fortunes in Playwriting," the *NY Times* comments: ". . . any capitalist, or group of capitalists or investors acquiring about six moderately good plays or musical comedies are bound to make a fortune out of them . . . and there seems to be practically no risk in such a venture."

Aug–Sep London's Imperial Theatre, opened in 1876 as the Aquarium Theatre, is torn down in sections, its interiors promised for a reconstruction of the Albert Theatre in Canning Town. In 1901, Lillie Langtry spent thousands recon-

structing the theatre, allowing only the original outer walls to remain. But her management, as well as those of Herbert Waring and Ellen Terry, did not succeed, nor did that of Lewis Waller. Part of Ellen Terry's problem, it is said, was her partial dependence on the extreme views of her son, Gordon Craig, on staging and scenery.

Sep 6 The Comedy Theatre, on West 41 Street in New York, opens with a production of *The Melting Pot*, by Israel Zangwill. Owned by the Shuberts, the Comedy briefly houses the Washington Square Players, and in 1916 and 1917 respectively, it serves as the site for New York premiere performances by Katharine Cornell and monologist Ruth Draper. In 1937, it is used as the home of Orson Welles' Mercury Theatre. From 1934–41, the Yiddish theatre group, the Artef Company, lease the building. The Comedy is torn down in 1942.

Sep 26 In Brooklyn, New York, the new Fulton Theatre opens.

Nov The Shuberts withdraw from the recently organized National Association of Theatrical Producing Managers. They are annoyed at its delay in dealing with their charges against Florenz Ziegfeld, who has, they insist, lured the popular singer Nora Bayes from their employ to his.

Nov 12 The Park Theatre burns in Brooklyn, New York.

Dec 14 Tonight is the Grand Opening Night of the new Watford Palace of Varieties, with two performances nightly, at 7 and 9 p.m. Tickets range from 4 pence to 1/6d. Sylvester and Mason are the first managers. Among the artists to appear in the early years are Charlie Chaplin, Stan Laurel, Marie Lloyd, Fred Karno's Company, and the Seymour Hicks troupe. During World War I, variety is alternated with legitimate plays. Bob Hope is booed off the stage. In 1964, the theatre is to pass from private ownership to control of the Watford Civic Theatre Trust, sponsored by the Borough of Watford.

Dec 22 The Herald Square Theatre in New York is damaged by fire tonight. The successful run of the musical, *Three Twins*, is halted, to be resumed on Jan 18, 1909 at the Majestic Theatre.

Dec 30 The Maxine Elliott Theatre (900 seats) on West 39 Street in New York opens with *The Chaperon*, a comedy by Marion Fairfax. Elliott stars. It runs for 62 performances. At Elliott's instructions, the actors' dressing rooms include such uncommon conveniences as running water, carpeting, curtained windows, and full-length mirrors. As the theatre center moves north of 42 Street, activities at the theatre decrease. In 1936, the Federal Theatre Project leases the building for a season. The Columbia Broadcasting System takes over the space until 1959, when it is demolished to make way for a garment-district building.

Jan 19 *The Easiest Way* (NY—Belasco/Stuyvesant—Drama). At his own theatre, shortly to become just the Belasco, David Belasco produces and stages Eugene Walter's controversial play. The theme is the moral compromises women of the period must make to support themselves adequately. The *NY Times* praises it saying, "With so few economic options for women, the blame is more society's, the play suggests, than that of the women's weak morals." On Feb 10, 1912 the play opens in London with Sarah Brooke at the Globe Theatre.

Feb 1 *The Fair Co-ed* (NY—Knickerbocker—Musical). George Ade writes the book and lyrics, and Gustav Luders provides the score. William Rock arranges the dances. Starring Elsie Janis as the only girl enrolled at Bingham College, the show deals with the problems of keeping her fiance, played by Arthur Stanford, from flunking out, since her father's will requires her to marry a graduate of Bingham. The show, directed by Fred G. Latham, runs 17 weeks.

Feb 1 *The Third Degree* (NY—Hudson—Drama). Charles Klein's play, with a cast including Wallace Eddinger and Helen Ware, excites interest for 21 weeks.

Feb 22 *A Woman's Way* (NY—Hackett—Comedy). William A. Brady produces and stages this piece by Thompson Buchanan. Grace George stars supported by Robert Warwick, Dorothy Tennant, and Reginald Carrington. The play runs for 112 performances.

March 15 *Votes for Women* (NY—Wallack's—Drama). Suffragettes and their demands to vote attract attention. Mary Shaw leads the cast. Endorsed by George Bernard Shaw, this play was first performed in England. It runs for two weeks.

March 24 *A Fool There Was* (NY—Liberty—Drama). Porter Emerson Brown's shipboard morality play features Robert Hilliard and Nannette Comstock. It runs for 93 performances.

April 10 *The Beauty Spot* (NY—Herald Square—Musical). This show, with Reginald De Koven's score and Joseph W. Herbert's book, runs for 137 performances. Heading the cast are Jefferson De Angelis and Marguerite Clark.

April 12 *The Climax* (NY—Weber's Drama). Edward Locke's play, about a young woman with ambitions to be an opera star, bows. It has 240 performances. The *NY Times* reports that "Although the play . . . is somewhat lacking in probability in the last analysis, as an entertainment it is decidedly pleasant and unusual."

April 12 *The Happy Marriage* (NY—Garrick—Comedy). Clyde Fitch's new play,

staged by the author, provides Doris Keane with a starring role. Also in the cast as Dudley Digges, Albert Hackett, and Grace Goodall.

May 3 *The Red Moon* (NY—Majestic—Musical). J. Rosamond Johnson provides the score, praised even by those critics not especially fond of shows with all-black casts. Bob Cole's book tells the tale of a black Minnehaha (Abbie Mitchell) on and off the reservation. Cole and Johnson play two comical con men, Slim Brown and Plunk Green. The production lasts only four weeks.

May 22 *The Midnight Sons* (NY—Broadway—Musical). With a score by Raymond Hubell and a book by Glen MacDonough, this show, intended for summer audiences, runs for nearly eight months. Its strengths are such talents as Vernon Castle, with his unusual dances, and Blanche Ring, who interpolates "I've Got Rings on My Fingers," the big hit of the show. Ned Wayburn's staging, opening with a theatre audience on stage watching a performance, facing the real audience is impressive.

June 14 *Ziegfeld Follies of 1909* (NY—Jardin de Paris—Revue). Harry B. Smith's book, with Maurice Levi's score and some interpolations provide the excuse for some lovely ladies and lavish production numbers. The show has only 64 performances, depsite such novelties as Lillian Lorraine piloting an airship over the heads of the audience. Nora Bayes, Jack Norworth, Sophie Tucker, Bessie Clayton, Rosie Greene, and Annabelle Whitford are also on hand.

Aug 24 *Is Matrimony a Failure?* (NY—Belasco—Comedy). Leo Ditrichstein adapts a German comedy by Blumenthal and Kadelberg. Jane Cowl and Blanche Yurka are in the cast. The show is produced and directed by David Belasco.

Aug 26 *Arsene Lupin* (NY—Lyceum—Drama). Charles Frohman gives New Yorkers a look at this French play by Francis de Croisset and Maurice Leblanc. It runs 144 performances. On Aug 30 the play opens in London, with Gerald Du Maurier, Dennis Eadie and Alexandra Carlisle in the cast. It is given 199 performances at the Duke of York's Theatre. *The Times* complains that the play does not continually amuse.

Aug 30 *In Hayti* (NY—Circle—Musical). McIntyre and Heath, the popular blackface duo, have designs on the Presidency of Haiti. Chorus girls, dressed like roosters, chant about "Chicken," and the comics carry live chickens through the show. After 56 performances on Broadway, it goes on tour.

Sep 4 *A Trip to Japan* (NY—Hippo-

Sophie Tucker (Ziegfeld Follies)

drome—Musical). Produced, written, and staged by R. H. Burnside, this "melodrama with music" concerns the hiring of a circus so the Japanese can conceal shipments of submarines to Japan. The book is only an excuse for elaborate scenic effects. It runs for 447 performances.

Sep 4 *The Fortune Hunters* (NY—Gaiety—Comedy). Winchell Smith writes and directs this show about a man who must marry a wealthy woman. It is a vehicle for John Barrymore. The show has 345 performances. The *NY Times* reports that "Mr. Barrymore, who it is to be hoped is now lost to musical comedy forever, gave indisputable signs last night of grown and growing powers."

Sep 5 *The Melting Pot* (NY—Comedy—Drama). Israel Zangwill's play, with Sheridan Block, John Blair, Chrystal Herne, and Leonora von Ottinger, tells of a young Jewish boy in love with a gentile girl. It runs 136 performances. The *NY Times* pans it, calling the show "sentimental trash masquerading as a human document . . ."

Sep 5 *Smith* (NY—Empire—Comedy). Another W. Somerset Maugham work, this Charles Frohman production mingles Americans and Britons such as John Drew, Lewis Casson, Sybil Thorndyke, Hassard Short, and Mary Boland, as Smith. William Seymour stages.

Sep 6 *The Dollar Princess* (NY—Knickerbocker—Musical). This tuneful tale of the taming of a female typist is more operetta than musical thanks to the music of Leo Fall. Valli Valli and Donald Brian star. It runs for 288 performances.

Sep 13 *The Chocolate Soldier* (NY—Lyric—Musical). Although Bernard Shaw was already mocking romantic notions

Harvest Moon

about heroism in war in *Arms and the Man*, this musical adaptation, with an Oscar Straus score, is itself described as an "unauthorized parody." The play's characters are differently named than Shaw's and its plot, also divergent, is filled with the kind of details Shaw was rebelling against when he wrote his comedy. Stanislaus Stange adapts the German text of Bernauer and Jacobson. Straus' score includes such favorites as "My Hero." With Ida Brooks Hunt and J.E. Gardner singing the leads, the show enjoys a run of 296 performances. Later it becomes a revival standard. On Sep 10, 1910 it opens in London at the Lyric Theatre, with Constance Drever, Roland Cunningham, Alexis, and C.H. Workman in the cast. The show runs for 500 performances.

Sep 20 *The Awakening of Helena Richie* (NY—Savoy—Drama). Based on Margaret Deland's popular novel, the play provides an effective starring role for Margaret Anglin.

Sep 27 *The White Sisters* (NY—Daly—Drama). Hugh Ford stages this play by F. Marion Crawford and Walter Hackett. Despite the presence of Viola Allen, James O'Neill, and William Farnum, it has only 48 performances.

Oct 11 *The Man Who Owns Broadway* (NY—New York—Musical). Based on his earlier unpopular play, *Popularity*, this George M. Cohan show has Raymond Hitchcock playing a Cohan-like role of a brash young musical star who overcomes intrigues to win an heiress. Produced by Cohan and Harris, the musical is written and staged by Cohan.

Oct 15 *The Harvest Moon* (NY—Garrick—Drama). In this Augustus Thomas play, evil suggestions are planted in the mind of a young American actress, threatening her career and romance. Although this difficult theme draws audiences only for 91 performances, critic Arthur Hobson Quinn calls the drama an artistic success.

Nov 1 *Mr. Lode of Koal* (NY—Majestic—Musical). Bert Williams, shipwrecked on island, finds himself proclaimed king. Despite music by Williams and J. Rosamond Johnson and book and lyrics by J. A. Shipp and Alexander Rogers, Williams' performance is the only audience magnet. In this production Williams begins to develop the monologues which are to distinguish his appearances later in his career. The show runs for only 40 performances.

Nov 10 *Seven Days* (NY—Astor—Comedy). Mary Roberts Rinehart and Avery Hopwood collaborate on this complicated farce about a man who tries to hide his divorce from a relative. The show runs 397 performances. The *NY Times* reports: "there is hardly a dull moment."

Nov 22 *Old Dutch* (NY—Herald Square—Musical). Edgar Smith adapts a German comedy about an inventor seeking anonymity with his daughter in the Tyrol. George Hobart puts words to Victor Herbert's music. The show is stolen by two miming children, one of them Helen Hayes, making her Broadway debut. Vernon Castle is also in the cast.

Dec 4 *The Nigger* (NY—New—Drama). Edward Sheldon's melodrama concerns a white supremacist governor who learns that he is part black.

Gertie Millar stars as a shop girl who is angered when she finds out that her love is a nobleman. George Grossman, Jr., and J. Edward Fraser appear. The show runs for 636 performances.

Jan 27 *An Englishman's Home* (L—Wyndham's—Drama). This play is credited on the program to "A Patriot," actually Major Du Maurier. A young man scoffs at volunteer soldiers until England is attacked. Lawrence Grossmith, Charles Rock and Elaine Inescort lead. There are 157 performances. Some critics suggest it could happen in earnest. One calls for recruiting sergeants in the gallery and pit. On March 22 it premieres at New York's Criterion with William Hawtrey starring. It runs only five weeks.

March 9 *Strife* (L—Duke of York's—Drama). John Galsworthy's study of the destructive clash between a labor leader and a company manager during a strike, and its effects on workers' families, has a cast including Lillah McCarthy, Norman McKinnel and Edmund Gwenn. On Nov 17, the play joins the New Theatre repertory in New York.

April 13 *Mr. Preedy and the Countess* (L—Criterion—Comedy). R. C. Carton's farce about the troubles of a young man, engaged to a middle class girl, who shelters a countess, wins 237 showings. Katherine Compton (Mrs. Carton) stars with Weedon Grossmith.

April 17 *The Devil* (L—Adelphi—Comedy). Ferenc Molnar's Hungarian play gets an English translation from Henry Hamilton. Lyn Harding stars.

April 28 *The Arcadians* (L—Shaftesbury—Musical). This comic opera by Mark Ambient and A. M. Thompson, is a tale of fictional Arcadians trying futilely to teach the English their ways. In the cast are Dan Rolyat and Florence Smithson. The music is by Lionel Monckton and Howard Talbot. Arthur Wimperis has written the lyrics. The show, a great favorite, runs for over 800 performances. On Jan 17, 1910, it premieres in New York at the Liberty Theatre, where it runs for 136 performances. Frank Moulan stars.

June 15 *The Fires of Fate* (L—Lyric—Drama). Arthur Conan Doyle calls his play, which is based on his book *The Tragedy of the Korosko*, a "Modern Morality." Lewis Waller stars with A.E. George, Auriol Lee, and Evelyn D'Alroy. It earns 121 performances.

July 6 *His Borrowed Plumes* (L—Hicks—Comedy). Jennie Jerome (Mrs. George Cornwallis-West) is the playwright. The leading lady is Mrs. Patrick Campbell. Her daughter Stella is in the cast, as are Henry Ainley, Dawson Milward, Sara Allgood, Winifred Fraser, Annie Hughes, and Gertrude Kingston.

Sep 1 *Madame X* (L—Globe—Drama). This is an adaptation of Alexandre Bisson's French courtroom drama. In the ensem-

1909 BRITISH PREMIERES

Jan 7 *Henry of Navarre* (L—New—Drama). William Devereaux's romance tells of the French Court under the domination of Catherine de Medici. Fred Terry, Julia Nielson, Malcolm Cherry and Tita Brand play. The drama runs 223 performances.

Jan 9 *Penelope* (L—Comedy—Comedy). W. Somerset Maugham's play has Marie

Tempest in the leading role and it earns 246 performances. In December, it will open in New York for a run of only four weeks.

Jan 23 *Our Miss Gibbs* (L—Gaiety—Musical). George Edwardes produces this show with songs by Adrian Ross, Percy Greenbank, Ivan Caryll and Lionel Monckton.

ble are Lena Ashwell, Winifred Harris, Sydney Valentine, O. P. Heggie, and Edmund Gwenn.

Sep 1 *Dear Little Denmark* (L—Prince of Wales's—Musical). The show has "chatter, jingles, and music" by Paul Rubens. Isabel Jay stars as a burgomaster's daughter engaged to a clockwinder but in love with a bell-founder. Bertram Wallis and Huntley Wright also play. The show has 109 performances.

Sep 2 *Mid-Channel* (L—St. James's—Drama). Arthur Wing Pinero's play has Lyn Harding and Irene Vanbrugh as Theodore and Zoe Blundell, whose marriage is in trouble. On Jan 31, 1910 Pinero's play opens in New York's Empire Theatre with Ethel Barrymore. It runs for 96 performances. Later, it is considered one of Pinero's best dramas.

Sep 9 *The Whip* (L—Drury Lane—Drama). Cecil Raleigh and Henry Hamilton's new melodrama is about efforts to prevent the killing of a race horse. Audiences thrill to the scenes of Bruce Smith, Harry Emden and R. McClery which include a train crash complete with traveling panorama effect. Cyril Keightly, Vincent Clive, Jessie Bateman and Nancy Price lead. The production wins 112 performances this fall. Revived in March, it achieves 277 more.

Sep 16 *The Brass Bottle* (L—Vaudeville—Comedy). F. Anstey's farce on the Aladdin theme earns 244 performances. Lawrence Grossmith plays the hero, Horace Ventimore.

Sep 25 *The Dollar Princess* (L—Daly's—Musical). Leo Fall's score supports with the story by Willner and Gruenbaum. Basil Hood writes the book and Adrian Ross the lyrics. The show deals with an American oil king whose domestic staff is composed of impoverished European aristocrats—with predictable romantic entanglements. Joseph Coyne, Lily Elsie, Robert Michaelis and Emmy Wehlen play. There are 423 performances. *The Times* reports that "*The Dollar Princess* is an ambitious (we almost said pretentious) work, which hardly justifies its ambition as yet."

Sep 27 *Happy Hooligan* (L—Lyric, Hammersmith—Comedy). The "American Extravaganza," with music by Alexander Humphries, has George Richie in the title-role.

Sep 29 *The Mountaineers* (L—Savoy—Musical). Guy Eden and Reginald Somerville collaborate on the book for this "Romantic Comic Opera," with Somerville also contributing the score.

Sep 30 *Smith* (L—Comedy—Comedy). W. Somerset Maugham's entertainment wins 168 performances. Marie Löhr stars with Robert Loraine.

Oct 12 *Don* (L—Haymarket—Comedy). Rudolf Besier's play, about a young man engaged to be married, who shelters a woman running from her fanatical husband, has James Hearn, Ellen O'Malley, Norman McKinnel, and Charles Quartermaine. It earns 288 performances.

Oct 13 *Sir Walter Raleigh* (L—Lyric—Drama). William Devereux's play is shown 181 times, with Winifred Emery as Queen Elizabeth and Lewis Waller as Raleigh.

Oct 21 *The Little Damozel* (L—Wyndham's—Drama). Monckton Hoffe's play tells the story of a damozel who fears her husband does not really love her. Charles Hawtrey stars. The play runs for 191 performances.

Dec 15 *Fallen Fairies* (L—Savoy—Musical). W.S. Gilbert uses *The Wicked World* as source material for this two-act opera, with a score by Edward German.

Dec 27 *The Bad Girl of the Family* (L—Aldwych—Drama). Frederick Melville's play, previewed in a suburban theatre, achieves a run of 452 performances.

Dec 27 *The House of Temperley* (L—Adelphi—Drama). Author Arthur Conan Doyle calls his play a melodrama of the ring. Ben Webster plays Sir Charles Temperley, on the road to ruin because of the evil advice of the unscrupulous gamester, Sir John Hawker, played by Charles Rock. Only a duel can clean the slate. Edmund Gwenn, Reginald Davis, and Dorothea Desmond also play. There are 161 performances.

the Bastille, playing the dual roles of Louis XIV and Phillippe Marchiali. On September 4, Lang offers Justin Huntly McCarthy's *The Proud Prince*, playing King Robert of Sicily.

March 20 Charles Hawtrey opens his London season at the Royalty Theatre with *The Noble Spaniard*, adapted from the French by W. Somerset Maugham. He plays the Duke of Hermanos. On May 27, he presents Arnold Bennett's *What the Public Wants*, with Ben Webster, E. Holman Clark, Louis Calvert, and Margaret Halstan in the company.

April 7 In London at His Majesty's Theatre, Herbert Beerbohm Tree revives Sheridan's *The School for Scandal*. He plays Sir Peter Teazle, opposite Marie Löhr as Lady Teazle.

April 12 At London's Royal Court Theatre, Gerald Lawrence and Fay Davis open their season of Shakespeare productions with *As You Like It*, followed by *Romeo and Juliet*, *The Merchant of Venice*, and *Twelfth Night*.

House of Temperley

April 19 At Stratford-upon-Avon, the annual Shakespeare Festival opens with *Julius Caesar*. Frank Benson stages his company in the play. On Shakespeare's birthday, he revives *Cymbeline*. There are 13 other plays by Shakespeare in the festival program, plus four Mystery Plays from the Chester Cycle, *Richelieu*, *The Passing of the Third Floor Back*, H.O. Nicholson's *The Midnight Bridal*, and Hannah Cowley's *The Belle's Strategem* in the Memorial Theatre.

April 27 Laurence Irving and his wife, Mabel Hackney, appear in the first of two New York matinees at the Hackett Theatre of Eugene Brieux's French drama, *The Incubus*. Irving has translated the play.

May 7 Arthur Bourchier revives *Macbeth* at London's Garrick Theatre, where he is actor-manager. His wife, Violet Vanbrugh, plays Lady Macbeth. On May 11, Lewis Waller revives *Henry IV, Part 1* at the Lyric Theatre, featuring himself as Hotspur, with Louis Calvert as Falstaff and Minnie Griffen as Mistress Quickly.

June 7 The Irish National Theatre Society

1909   REVIVALS/REPERTORIES

Jan 18 At London's Savoy Theatre, Gilbert & Sullivan's *The Gondoliers* is revived. On March 1, *The Yeoman of the Guard* is revived.

Feb 8 At London's Shaftesbury Theatre, H. B. (Henry) Irving, son of the distinguished actor-manager, Henry Irving, opens his brief season with a revival of *Hamlet*. On February 15, he revives W. G. Wills' *Charles I*, following that with *Louis XI*, adapted by Dion Boucicault from Casimir Delavigne's drama, on February

22. His wife, Dorothea Baird, plays opposite, appearing first as Ophelia, then as Henrietta Maria.

Feb 26 At London's Royal Court Theatre, Eleanore Driller opens her short German-language season with Heinrich von Kleist's *Das Kaethchen von Heilbronn*, in which she plays the title-role.

March 13 At London's Lyceum Theatre, Matheson Lang revives *Hamlet*, playing the title-role. On May 13, Lang produces Norman Forbes' drama, *The Prisoner of*

begins a short season of Irish plays in London at the Royal Court Theatre with a double-bill of J. M. Synge's *The Playboy of the Western World* and Lady Gregory's one-act tragedy, *Dervorgilla*. On June 8, the triple-bill is Synge's *The Well of the Saints*, Yeats' *Kathleen ni Houlihan*, and Gregory's *The Workinghouse Ward*. On June 9, Synge's *Riders to the Sea*, Gregory's *Hyacinth Halvey*, and Norreys Connell's *An Imaginary Conversation* are performed.

June 21 Lucien Guitry brings his company from his Theatre de la Renaissance in Paris, opening tonight with *L'Assommoir*, a stage version of Zola's novel. Jeanne Desclos plays Nana. On June 23, he presents Henri Bernstein's *Le Voleur*, and, on June 25, Paul Bourget's *L'Emigre*. On June 28, the plays are Moliere's *Bourgeois Gentilhomme* and Anatole France's *Crainquebille*, followed by *La Massière*, by Jules Lemaitre, on June 30, and Bernstein's *Samson* on July 2 in London.

June 21 The Shakespeare Festival commences in London at His Majesty's Theatre with a revival of *The Merry Wives of Windsor*. Herbert Beerbohm Tree, the actor-manager of the theatre, plays Falstaff. For a fortnight, the fest continues, with *Twelfth Night*, *Julius Caesar*, *Hamlet*, *Richard III*, *The Merchant of Venice*, and *Macbeth*.

Aug 25 After the efforts of Augusta, Lady Gregory, to have the Lord Chamberlain license Bernard Shaw's *The Shewing-Up of Blanco Posnet*—which he had refused to do—the play finally opens in Dublin at the Abbey Theatre.

Sep 9 At London's Haymarket Theatre, Norman McKinnel appears as King Lear.

Sep 14 At His Majesty's Theatre Herbert Beerbohm Tree plays the High Priest in *False Gods*, J.B. Fagan's adaptation of Eugene Brieux's play, *La Foi*. On Nov 8 Tree revives Paul M. Potter's *Trilby*. On Nov 25 Tree plays Beethoven in Louis N. Parker's version of Rene Fauchois' play.

Sep 22 H. B. Irving revives *The Bells*—adapted from the French drama, *Le Juif Polonais*, at London's Queen's Theatre.

Nov 6 *Antony and Cleopatra* inaugurates the impressive new New Theatre of Winthrop Ames, later to be called the Century. In the repertory ensemble are E.H. Sothern, Julia Marlowe, Pedro de Cordoba, Louis Calvert, Albert Bruning, Robert Homans, Beatrice Forbes-Robertson, Guy Bates Post, Florence Reed, Annie Russell, Matheson Lang, Grace George, and Leah Bateman-Hunter, among others in New York.

Nov 30 Stella Patrick Campbell acts in George Alexander's revival of Oscar Wilde's *The Importance of Being Earnest* in London at the St. James's.

Nov 30 At the Afternoon Theatre preformance in London at His Majesty's Theatre, Lydia Yavorskaya (Princess Bar-

iatinsky) and her Russian company play the Alexandre Dumas, fils drama, *La Dame aux Camelias*, followed by the fifth act of Alexander Ostrovsky's *Vassilissa Melentieva*—seen now for the first time in England. On Dec 7, she plays Hedda in Ibsen's *Hedda Gabler*, and on Dec 9, she is Mlle. Y., opposite Mrs. Beerbohm Tree, as Mme. X, in Strindberg's *The Stronger Woman*.

Dec 16 *Pinkie and the Fairies* is revived for the Christmas season at His Majesty's Theatre. On Dec 20 *Peter Pan* is revived at the Duke of York's Theatre. On the 23rd, the Lyceum offers *Aladdin*, while a more splendid version is presented at the Drury Lane on Dec 27. *Cinderella* is played at the Crystal Palace, the Elephant and Castle, and the Strand Theatre.

1909 BIRTHS/DEATHS/DEBUTS

Jan 16 Ethel Merman is born Ethel Zimmerman in Astoria, N.Y.

Feb 11 John Albaugh, Sr. (b. 1848) dies. Albaugh, a distinguished American actor-manager, with his wife, formed an admired acting-duo in the late 19th century.

March 13 Actress Ina Claire makes her New York City stage debut in an impersonation of the Scottish performer, Sir Harry Lauder, at the American Music Hall.

March 24 Ireland's gifted poet-playwright John Millington Synge dies today, deeply mourned by his colleagues in the Irish National Theatre movement. Born in 1871, he journeyed to Ireland's barren Arran Islands to capture the speech and customs of countryfolk in *The Playboy of the Western World*, which enraged Irish patriots at its Dublin premiere.

April 9 Choreographer-actor-director-dancer Robert Helpmann is born in Mount Gambier, Southern Australia.

April 13 *How the Vote Was Won*, a "Suffragist Play," which has a limited run at

London's Royalty Theatre, wins the support of a number of popular performers who join the cast: Beatrice Forbes-Robertson, Nigel Playfair, Auriol Lee, Athene Seyler, Winifred Mayo and O.P. Heggie.

April 27 American actress and author Olive Logan (b. 1839) dies.

April 29 Actor Tom Ewell is born Yewell Tompkins in Owensboro, Kentucky.

Sep 4 Failing to rally from an appendicitis operation, American playwright Clyde Fitch (b. 1865) dies in Chalons-sur-Marne, France. Of Fitch's 36 original plays, *Captain Jinks of the Horse Marines*, *The Girl With the Green Eyes*, *The City*, and *The Truth* were among those which brought him international acclaim. His other works include adaptations of the plays of Sardou and Edith Wharton's *The House of Mirth*.

Oct 23 American player William H. Crompton (b. 1843) dies.

Nov 22 Helen Hayes makes her Broadway debut in *Old Dutch*.

1909 THEATERS/PRODUCTIONS

Between 1895 and this year, only 30 plays of some 8,000 submitted to the Lord Chamberlain's Office for censorship have been denied a license for public performance.

Bernard Shaw's one-act play, *Press Cuttings*, is banned by the Lord Chamberlain's office. The censor's basic objection is to Shaw's main characters, Prime Minister Balsquith and War Minister Mitchener. The names are too close to those of real politicians: Balfour, Asquith, Milner, and Kitchener.

In Britain this year patents are granted for: A. H. Moorhouse's stage-noise cabinet, operated by external levers which produce sounds such as horses hooves, bells, sirens, and so on; C. Tritschler's stage-grass, made from animal skins, with the hair dyed to the desired hue of green or brown; S. Lafayette's endless belt of cutout soldiers, set behind a scenic wall, to give the effect of troops marching by.

Antoine Salle of Paris gets a U.S. patent for his apparatus which makes it possible

to project the image of a living actor onto a miniature stage: it's done with mirrors. Israel Weingarden and Asa Cummings invent a device which permits a mechanical eagle—with flapping wings and electrically powered eyes—to fly and even to carry a body in its talons.

Jan Britain's *The Era Almanack and Annual* provides a list of current New York theatres: American, Astor, Belasco, Bijou, Broadway, Casino, Circle, Criterion, Daly's, Empire, Fourteenth Street, Garden, Garrick, Grand Street, Hackett, Herald Square, Hippodrome, Hudson, Knickerbocker, Liberty, Lincoln Square, Lyceum, Lyric, Madison Square, Majestic, Metropolis, New Amsterdam, New York, New York Roof Garden, Savoy, Stuyvesant, Thalia, Third Avenue, Wallack's West End, Weber's and Yorkville.

March 1 American themes are popular in Britain's theatres. This evening Ben Landeck's adaptation of Bret Harte's *The Luck of Roaring Camp* opens in London's Fulham Theatre, while in Harwich, at the

Prince's Theatre, the show is *Rags*, "A Western American Musical Drama."

March 24 Despite her sadness occasioned by the untimely passing today of Ireland's gifted playwright, J. M. Synge, her friend and colleague, Aug. Lady Gregory, a founder of the Irish Theatre movement, does verbal battle with Dublin Castle, seat of British authority in Ireland, because Britain's Lord Chamberlain has refused a license for the performance of George Bernard Shaw's *The Shewing-Up of Blanco Posnet*.

April In Glasgow, Alfred Wareing opens the Scottish Repertory Theatre, the Citizen's Theatre. Sixteen new plays are presented in the first four seasons, but none of them becomes a foundation stone of a new Scottish drama. The outbreak of war brings Wareing's venture to a close.

April 25 Adrian Ross, lyricist for the George Edwardes production of *Havana* at London's Gaiety Theatre, notes that musicals now are of two types: "comedy with music" and "variety with a thread of story." With the success of German and Viennese operettas, however, musicals are returning to something akin to comic opera. Ross's lyrics have been suggested by characters, situations, and plot action. Only one or two specialty numbers, not connected with the plot, have been used. For choruses and ensembles, the music has been composed first, but not for duets and comic songs.

May 1 On this date, the Shuberts' agreement with the Syndicate, which led to formation of the U.S. Amusement Company, formally expires. From this time forward, the theatrical map of the United States changes from day to day, as individual theatre-owners shift their alliances from Syndicate to Shuberts—and back, on occasion. Sam S. and Lee Shubert's former allies, Belasco and the Fiskes, now side with the Syndicate, partly because it controls more theatres appropriate for their productions and partly because they feel the Shuberts deserted them when the U.S. Amusement Company was formed. James K. Hackett also leaves the Shuberts for the Syndicate.

May 2 Producer Lee Shubert tells the *NY Times* that the author of a successful play can now earn, in one season, a royalty ranging from $30,000 to as much as $100,000. Shubert notes that the average seasonal box-office gross in New York is $600,000 per week. With a 40-week season, the total is $24 million.

May 22 J. J. Shubert tells the *NY Dramatic Mirror* that the Shubert organization is now in a position to play 40 weeks, coast-to-coast, owing to theatres they own outright or control. In the coming season, the Shuberts will control 100 attractions. Sixty of them will be produced by the Shuberts; the remaining forty will be Shubert bookings for other producers. (Thus far, the Shuberts have not been very suc-

cessful in winning control of small-town theatres, so they try another tack by making handsome offers to neglected theatres. This leads to the announcement of an "Open Door Policy" by many owners and managers.)

June 15 Broadway's 1908–09 season comes to its close, with a grand total of 110 productions presented in 31 theatre spaces. Yesterday marked the last opening of the season. Among the productions have been 16 musicals, 3 revues, 7 musical plays, 2 comic operas, 2 operettas, 2 extravaganzas, 1 opera—a revival, and 1 minstrel show. Dramas have numbered 45, with one revival and two productions of *The Devil* simultaneously playing. There have been 26 comedies, 3 farces—with one revival, and 2 one-acts.

June 15 Looking back from a much later vantage point, drama critic Burns Mantle and his assistant, Garrison Sherwood, select ten *Best Plays* for the decade of Broadway seasons which ends today. They are Fitch's *Barbara Frietchie*, Fitch's *The Climbers*, McCarthy's *If I Were King*, Belasco's *The Darling of the Gods*, Ade's *The County Chairman*, McLellan's *Leah Kleschna*, Royle's *The Squaw Man*, Moody's *The Great Divide*, Thomas' *The Witching Hour*, and Tarkington and Wilson's *The Man From Home*.

July The Shubert Theatrical Company of New York increases its captial stock from $800,000 to $1,000,000, raising it again in a year hence to $1,500,00. At this time, and for some three to four years hence, the war between the Shuberts and the Theatrical Syndicate for dominance in control, booking, and production for American theatres remains at its fiercest, after which the Shuberts will assume the dominant position, becoming a virtual monopoly, quite as ruthless as the Syndicate has been in its time of power.

July 18 Writing in the *NY Times*, Adolph Klauber presents some statistics on theatre production. Nationally, on a seasonal basis, direct investment totals $100 million, of which $40 million goes for rents and leases of theatre buildings, etc. $20 million covers salaries of actors. $38 million is needed for support salaries and operating costs. Only $2 million is invested in production aspects such as sets, costumes, lights, and props. Currently there are some 25,000 actors, with about 5,000 chorus girls in New York City. Actors' wages weekly range from a low of $10 to a high of $250, averaging about $20, with $18 for chorus. Musicians get $25 per week.

July 29 The Joint Select Committee on Censorship opens its hearings in London today. Members of the House of Lords and the House of Common join under the leadership of Herbert Samuel, a Liberal lawyer, to study the Lord Chamberlain's functions as a censor and licensor of plays, in response to numerous protests from

Our Miss Gibbs

authors, producers, and others. On Nov 2, it will issue its report in nearly half-a-million words. Among its findings: "With dramas of certain class, it is only after performance, and by reference to their effect upon the audience, that a final opinion as to their propriety can be reached."

Aug 16 For two weeks, the *Cohan and Harris Minstrels* return to Broadway. At the New York Theatre, audiences are offered clog dances and minstrel songs such as "Down Where the Watermelon Grows." This is the last appearance of a traditional minstrel show in mid-town Manhattan.

Sep 1 The Hicks Theatre, renamed the Globe, presents its first production in the "new" house.

Sep 4 The Gaiety Theatre, at 1547 Broadway in New York, opens with *The Fortune Hunter*. Producers Klaw and Erlanger build the theatre to spotlight actor George M. Cohan. In the late 1920's, the theatre is leased out as a movie house and then as a burlesque house. After the demise of burlesque in the 1940's, the theatre reverts to showing films, becoming the Victoria.

Oct 28 The Cort Theatre, designed by J. E. O. Pridmore, opens in Chicago. It seats 962 and has an Italian "Atmospheric" interior. It will be razed in 1934.

Nov 8 The New Theatre on Central Park West between 62 and 63 Streets in New York, designed by Carrere and Hastings, opens with Shakespeare's *Antony and Cleopatra*. Built as a subsidized theatre, putting art above profits, its idealism lasts two seasons. It becomes the Century Theatre, housing large-scale musicals and spectacles, and later is the home of the Century Opera Company. In 1930, the theatre is torn down and replaced by an apartment building.

Dec 29 In Boston, a climactic oath—"You're a goddam liar"—in Clyde Fitch's *The City* has been banned. Now, in New York, it is used without action from the police. At the premiere, it is reported that several people have fainted on hearing this blasphemous expression. One of them is said to be a drama critic.

Tillie's Nightmare

Jan 10 *The Old Town* (NY—Globe—Musical). This George Ade (book) and Gustav Luders (music) show is designed for the talents of Montgomery and Stone, as two out-of-work circus performers pursuing old sweethearts. Producer Charles Dillingham stresses spectacle with Homer Emens' sets. It lasts for 171 performances.

Jan 17 *The Arcadians* See L premiere, 1909.

Jan 19 *The Faith Healer* (NY—Savoy—Drama). Despite the efforts of Henry Miller, Jessie Bonstelle, and Laura Hope Crews, William Vaughn Moody's challenging drama of the conflict between the demands of a humane mission and personal love has only six performances. Later it is much admired by critics such as Authur Hobson Quinn.

Jan 21 *Alias Jimmy Valentine* (NY—Wallack's—Drama). Based on O. Henry's short-story, *A Retrieved Reformation*, this adaptation by Paul Armstrong enjoys a run of 155 performances. Laurette Taylor plays. Edward E. Rose directs. On March 29, it opens London's Comedy Theatre with Gerald Du Maurier and Alexandra Carlisle in the cast. It runs 149 performances.

Jan 24 *Mrs. Dot* (NY—Lyceum—Comedy). W. Somerset Maugham's comedy stars Billie Burke. It runs 72 performances.

Jan 31 *Mid-Channel* See L premiere, 1909.

Feb 8 *A Man's World* (NY—Comedy—Drama). Playwright Rachel Crothers stages her study of a woman writer, surrounded by dependent fellow-artists, who refuses to accept the double standard in morality. Mary Mannering stars.

Feb 10 *The Yankee Girl* (NY—Herald Square—Musical). Blanche Ring carries this insipid tale of anti-American intrigue. It is produced by Lew Fields. Ring's interpolation of "I've Got Rings on My Fingers" delights audiences. Before its twelve-week Broadway run, the show has been touring. After its New York engagement, it returns to the road.

May 5 *Tillie's Nightmare* (NY—Herald Square—Musical). Marie Dressler is Tillie in Lew Fields' production of this show. Edgar Smith writes the book and A. Baldwin Sloane the music. Staged by Ned Wayburn, it has 77 performances.

June 4 *The Summer Widowers* (NY—Broadway—Musical). Lew Fields doubles as producer and star in a slight show with a score by the A. Baldwin Sloane and lyrics by Glen Macdonough. This "musical panorama in seven views" also features Vernon Castle and Irene Franklin, as well as Alice Dovey and Helen Hayes.

June 20 *The Ziegfeld Follies of 1910* (NY—Jardin de Paris—Revue). Two debuts mark this new edition of the Follies: those of Bert Williams and Fanny Brice. Williams, a major black performer, is the first to be accepted into the Follies. Anna Held appears as a comet—on film.

Aug 23 *Baby Mine* (NY—Daly's—Comedy). Margaret Mayo's play, produced by William A. Brady, is about a pathological liar who must convince her husband he is a father. The show runs for 287 performances. The *NY Times* gleefully reports ". . . funny it certain is—one of the funniest farces this town has ever seen."

Aug 30 *Madame Sherry* See L premiere, 1903.

Aug 30 *The Country Boy* (NY—Liberty—Comedy). Edgar Selwyn stages his own script for audiences who throng to 143 performances.

Sep 3 *The International Cup, The Ballet of Niagara,* and *The Earthquake* (NY—Hippodrome—Musical). The Shuberts produce writer-director R. H. Burnside's three event entertainment which emphasizes spectacle: a yacht sinking, lions and elephants cavorting on stage. Playing two-a-day, the show has a good run.

Sep 19 *Get-Rich Quick Wallingford* (NY—Gaiety—Comedy). George M. Cohan writes and directs this comedy based on George Randolph Chester's novel of a con man who reforms. Cohen produces with Sam Harris. It runs 424 performances.

Sep 26 *Alma, Where Do You Live?* (NY—Weber's—Musical). George Hobart adapts the French text of Paul Harve; Jean Briquet provides the lively score to this story of rivals who try to cheat a man out of his inheritance. Joe Weber produces and directs. It runs 232 performances.

Oct 3 *Rebecca of Sunnybrook Farm* (NY—Republic—Comedy). Kate Douglas Wiggin's best-selling novel is adapted for the stage. The novel and play help establish sub-genre of children's literature, later parodied in *Auntie Mame*. This show runs 216 performances and subsequently tours. On Sep 2, 1912, this American adaptation opens at London's Globe Theatre with Edith Taliaferro, Marie Day, and Nanette Foster in the cast.

Oct 4 *The Concert* (NY—Belasco—Comedy). Leo Ditrichstein adapts Hermann Bahr's German-language success for producer-director Belasco. To curb an amorous pianist-husband who has affairs with his students, his wife turns the tables. The show runs 264 performances. On Aug 28, 1911, it opens at London's Duke of York's Theatre with Henry Ainley, Irene Vanbrugh, Nell Carter, and Florence Edney.

Oct 31 *The Gamblers* (NY—Maxine Elliott's—Drama). Playwright Charles Klein provides a tense melodrama dealing with the world of finance, as popularly imagined. It runs 192 performances.

Nov 7 *Naughty Marietta* (NY—New York—Musical). This "comic opera" with melodrama overtones mingles love and adventure. The book is by Rida Johnson Young. Oscar Hammerstein commissions Victor Herbert's score which includes "Tramp! Tramp! Tramp!", "I'm Falling in Love with Someone" and "Ah, Sweet Mystery of Life." Emma Trentini and Orville Harrold star. Gaetano Merola conducts.

Nov 15 *Nobody's Widow* (NY—Hudson—Comedy). Producer-director David Belasco stars Blanche Bates in this Avery Hopwood work about a woman reunited with the husband she thought dead. It enjoys 215 performances. The *NY Times* praises it saying, "As Mr. Hopwood's brilliant little comedy has been staged so it is acted with complete understanding and perfect art by Miss Bates."

Dec 21 *The City* (NY—Lyric—Drama). Walter Hampden and Helen Holmes are the lovers in Clyde Fitch's posthumously produced play staged by John Emerson with a cast picked by Fitch. Critics acclaim this study of the city's effect on small-town people as Fitch's strongest work.

Dec 26 *The Spring Maid* (NY—Liberty—Musical). Adapted from a German operetta, with music by Heinrich Reinhardt, the central interest is a charming young lady who becomes an attendant at the Karlsbad Spa in order to win her love. Christine MacDonald and Tom McNaughton play. The show has 192 performances.

Jan 20 *Dame Nature* (L—Garrick—Drama). Frederick Fenn adapts Henri Bataille's *La Femme Nu*, about a housekeeper who is deserted by a painter once he becomes famous. Ethel Irving, Nancy Price and Ernest Leicester star. It runs 112 performances.

Feb 1 *The O'Flynn* (L—His Majesty's—Drama). Herbert Beerbohm Tree plays the title role in Justin Huntly McCarthy's play involving the man who would be a Catholic king of England, James II (C. H. Croker-King).

Feb 19 *The Balkan Princess* (L—Prince of Wales's—Musical). Frederick Lonsdale and Frank Curzon, who is the theatre's manager, collaborate on the book with a score and lyrics by Paul Rubens. Arthur Wimperis assists on lyrics. The story tells of a princess who is rejected by a count with radical ideas. Bertram Wallis and Isabel Jay star with Hazel Dawn and Lauri de Frece in the cast. Curzon stages. The sets are by Joseph Harker. The show has 176 performances. The show opens on Feb 9, 1911 at New York's Herald Square Theatre. Louis Gunning and Christine Nielson star. The show runs 108 performances.

Feb 24 *The Tenth Man* (L—Globe—Drama). W. Somerset Maugham's play is produced by actor-manager Arthur Bourchier, with George Winter, Frances Dillon and Daisy Markham.

April 14 *The Naked Truth* (L—Wyndham's—Comedy). Charles Hawtrey directs and stars in this farce about a ring that forces its wearer to tell the truth. The play is by George Paston (pen name of Evelyn Symonds) and W.B. Maxwell. Phyllis Embury appears. The show earns 173 performances.

June 4 *The Girl in the Train* (L—Vaudeville—Musical). Victor Leon's German text for *Die Geschiedene Frau* (*The Divorced Woman*) is adapted, with lyrics by Adrian Ross for Leo Fall's original score. The story is about a woman who sues for divorce when she thinks her husband has been unfaithful. "Memories" and "I Wonder" are among the songs. Edward Royce stages with Alfred Terraine's settings. The show wins 340 performances.

June 4 *The Speckled Band* (L—Adelphi—Drama). Arthur Conan Doyle dramatizes his short-story; H.A. Saintsbury stars. There are 169 performances.

June 28 *Priscilla Runs Away* (L—Haymarket—Comedy). Elizabeth Arnim's four-act romance deals with a princess who longs for the simple life, but when she gets it, it is a disaster. Phyllis Nielson-Terry leads with Charles Maude and E. Lyall Swete. Norman McKinnel directs. The show runs 192 performances.

Sep 3 *Nobody's Daughter* (L—Wyndham's—Drama). Evelyn Symonds, under the pen-name of George Paston offers this story of a young woman, deserted by her parents, who is raised by another. Rosalie Toller, Gerald Du Maurier and Lilian Braithwaite play. Du Maurier directs. The show runs 185 performances.

Sep 10 *The Man from Mexico* (L—Strand—Comedy). H. A. Souchette's farce arrives in the West End, after provincial tryouts. It earns 150 performances, with Harry Parker, George Giddens, Jean Harkness, and Gladys Harvey in the cast.

Sep 10 *The Chocolate Soldier* See NY premiere, 1909.

Oct 1 *Inconstant George* (L—Prince of Wales's—Comedy). Gladys Unger adapts *L'Ane de Buridan* by Flers and Caillavet. Charles Hawtrey plays the fickle lover with C. Aubrey Smith and Doris Lytton in the cast. There are 218 performances.

Oct 15 *Grace* (L—Duke of York's—Drama). Irene Vanbrugh stars in W. Somerset Maugham's play about a bored wife of a "county" husband. Dennis Eadie and Lillah McCarthy also appear. Dion Boucicault directs.

Oct 21 *Mrs. Skeffington* (L—Queen's—Comedy). Cosmo Hamilton's "Episode in Cavalry Barracks" has Arthur Lewis as General Thurlow. Ellen O'Malley, Beryl Faber, and Estelle Winwood are also in the cast.

Nov 5 *The Quaker Girl* (L—Adelphi—Musical). James Tanner's book is about a young Quaker girl rebelling against the sect's restrictions. Gertie Millar, Joseph Coyne and Elsie Spain play. The score is by Lionel Monckton with lyrics by Adrian Ross and Percy Greenbank. Producer George Edwardes has J.A.E. Malone do the staging with Willie Warde arranging dances and chorus. Settings are by Joseph Harker, A. Terraine and Paquereau. The production has 536 performances.

Nov 14 *The Unwritten Law* (L—Garrick—Drama). There are 104 performances for this adaptation by Laurence Irving of Dostoievsky's *Crime and Punishment*. Irving stars.

Nov 19 *Eccentric Lord Comberdene* (L—St. James's—Comedy). R.C. Carton parodies adventure novels in the wild tale of a Russian Grand Duchess attempting to leave England and return to her homeland. Katherine Compton, Rita Jolivet, and producer George Alexander are in the cast.

Dec 14 *The Princess Clementina* (L—Queen's—Drama). A.E.W. Mason and George Pleydell adapt Mason's novel. Stella Patrick Campbell leads with Eille Norwood, Nigel Playfair, H.B. Irving, Charles Wogan and Dorothea Baird. There are 106 performances.

1910 REVIVALS/REPERTORIES

Jan 17 *The Ben Greet Repertory* opens at the Garden Theatre with some classics: *Everyman*, *Macbeth*, *Julius Caesar*, *The Tempest*, *A Midsummer Night's Dream*, *The Merchant of Venice*, *Dr. Faustus*, *She Stoops to Conquer*, and *The Rivals*. Contemporary works are *The Palace of Truth* (W. S. Gilbert), *Three Wonder Tales* (Rose M. O'Neil), and *Little Town of Bethelhem* (Katrina Trask).

Jan 26 The New Theatre Company in New York begins its classic and modern repertory with *Twelfth Night* featuring Annie Russell, Louis Calvert and Matheson Lang. On March 28 *The Winter's Tale* with Edith Wynne Matthison is added. Maurice Maeterlinck's *The Blue Bird* begins the company's second season on Oct 1. This production is so popular that repertory is temporarily abandoned. On Nov 7 repertory begins again with Louis Calvert in *Falstaff*. On Dec 5 the company produces Maeterlinck's *Mary Magdalene* with Olga Nethersole. It manages only 16 performances.

Jan 29 J. Comyns Carr adapts Robert Louis Stevenson's popular horror story, *Dr. Jekyll and Mr. Hyde*, presented at the Queen's Theatre in London. H.B. Irving and Dorothea Baird star. There is an after-piece called *The Plumbers*, written by Harry Grattan, who plays "Erb."

Feb 7 At the Academy of Music, the *Sothern and Marlowe Repertory* offers four weeks—plus a later two weeks—of Shakespeare: *Hamlet*, *As You Like It*, *The Taming of the Shrew*, *Romeo and Juliet*, *The Merchant of Venice*, and *Twelfth Night*. E. H. Sothern and Julia Marlowe star in this Manhattan visit.

Feb 10 At the Abbey Theatre in Dublin, W. B. Yeats' play, *The Green Helmet* is produced. J. M. Kerrigan, Sara Allgood, and Ambrose Power appear. The play is part of Yeats' Cuchulain Cycle.

Feb 19 The Sicilian Players come to London's Lyric Theatre. *Omerta—The Law of Silence*— follows a revival of *Feudalismo*, which opens the engagement. Giovanni Grasso and his ensemble also play G. Cognetti's *Basso Porto* on March 4; *Pietra Fra Pietre* (Sudermann's *Stein unter Steinen*), on March 8; *Festa d'Aderno*. on March 11; and Shakespeare's *Otello*, in a Sicilian version, on March 21.

Feb 21 Charles Frohman experiments with repertory at the Duke of York's. He opens with John Galsworthy's drama *Justice*.

Dame Nature

Two days later he shows George Bernard Shaw's *Misalliance*. On March 1, Frohman offers James Barrie's *The Twelve-Pound Look* and *Old Friends* and George Meredith's *The Sentimentalists*. On March 9 Harley Granville-Barker's *The Madras House* joins the repertory. On April 7 Pinero's *Trelawny of the "Wells"* is revived. This is followed on April 13 by Houseman-Granville Barker's *Prunella*. On May 17 Elizabeth Baker's *Chains* is produced.

March 28 The London Shakespeare Festival gets underway at His Majesty's Theatre with Herbert Beerbohm Tree and company in *The Merry Wives of Windsor*, followed on April 2 with Tree's *Julius Caesar* and on April 7 with *Twelfth Night* and on the 11th with Tree's *Hamlet*. On April 12, Norman McKinnel and company present *King Lear*. On April 13, *The Merchant of Venice* is offered by Arthur Bourchier and troupe. On April 14, H. B. Irving plays Hamlet. On April 18, Frank Benson and ensemble present *The Taming of the Shrew*, followed on the 19th by their *Coriolanus*. The Elizabethan Stage Society mounts *Two Gentlemen of Verona* on April 20. Lewis Waller and company present *Henry V* on April 21. On April 25, Tree returns with his troupe to present their version of *The Merchant of Venice*, followed by *Richard II* on April 27.

April 4 In London at the Lyric Theatre, Lewis Waller revives Sheridan's *The Rivals*, playing Captain Absolute.

April 13 In Dublin at the Threatre Royal, John Martin Harvey presents his production of *Richard III*, with himself in the title role. On May 28, he opens the production in London at the Lyceum Theatre.

April 18 Alla Nazimova stars in the first New York production of Ibsen's *Little Eyolf*. The Shuberts produce.

April 22 At Stratford-upon-Avon, the annual Shakespeare Festival opens with *Hamlet* starring Herbert Beerbohm Tree. In the evening, Frank Benson presents *The Taming of the Shrew*. On April 23 Benson revives *The Two Gentlemen of Verona*. Among other plays presented are *Richard III*, with Genevieve Ward and *The Merchant of Venice*, with Ellen Terry. On May 6, Edward VII dies, cutting short the festival.

May 3 Forty "old Bensonians" present a special matinee at the Shakespeare Memorial Theater in Stratford-upon-Avon, performing scenes from *The Merchant of Venice*, *A Midsummer Night's Dream*, and *The Taming of the Shrew*.

May 5 In Dublin at the Abbey Theatre, Padraic Colum's new play, *Thomas Muskerry*, features Arthur Sinclair in the title-role. Described as a "drama of Irish life," it is interpreted by a company including J. M. Kerrigan, Sara Allgood, and Maire O'Neill. On May 19, S. L. Robinson's *Harvest* is premiered by the Abbey players.

May 30 W. B. Yeats' *Deirdre of the Sorrows* has its London premiere at the Court Theatre, performed by the Abbey Theatre ensemble from Dublin. Maire O'Neill plays the title-role. On June 1, Lady Gregory's play, *The Image*, has its London premiere, paired with *The Rising of the Moon*. Other productions shown include William Boyle's *The Eloquent Dempsy* and *The Building Fund*, Lord Dunsany's *The Glittering Gate*, Padraic Colum's *Thomas Muskerry*, Yeats' *The Green Helmet*, and S. L. Robinson's *Harvest* and *The Cross Roads*. The company includes Sara Allgood, J. M. Kerrigan, Arthur Sinclair, and Fred O'Donovan, among others.

July 25 In Edinburgh, at the Lyceum Theatre, Dickson Moffat impersonates the Scots poet, Robert Burns, in *A Nicht wi' Burns*, by George Reston Malloch.

July 25 At Stratford-upon-Avon, this is the first summer festival season. Director Frank Benson offers *The Winter's Tale* as the first production. Other plays include *Julius Caesar*, *Macbeth*, *Henry V*, *Twelfth Night*, *As You Like It*, *Richard II*, *Hamlet*, *The Merry Wives of Windsor*, and Charles Reade's *Masks and Faces*. A special treat is the premiere of the prize play, *The Piper*, by the American playwright, Josephine Preston Peabody.

Aug 1 London is very interested in the problems of American Indians married to whites. Today *His Indian Wife*, by Emma Litchfield opens at the Elephant and Castle Theatre. It follows by 11 days the revival of Edwin Milton Royle's *A White Man*.

Sep 1 Herbert Beerbohm Tree presents Shakespeare's *Henry VIII* at His Majesty's Theatre in London. Violet Vanbrugh, Laura Cowie and Clarence Derwent are also in the large cast.

Sep 29 In Dublin at the Abbey Theatre, J. J. Ray's new play, *The Casting-Out of Martin Whelan*, has it world premiere. Fred O'Donovan plays the lead.

Nov 10 In Dublin at the Abbey Theatre, Lady Gregory's comedy *The Full Moon*, has its premiere.

Dec 5 E. H. Sothern and Julia Marlowe return with a season of Shakespeare repertory. At the Broadway Theatre, they offer *Hamlet*, *Macbeth*, *Romeo and Juliet*, and *As You Like It*.

Dec 5 Playwright-actor William Gillette opens a series of revivals of his own plays at the Empire Theatre, under Charles Frohman management. On the roster are *Held by the Enemy*, *Sherlock Holmes*, *The Private Secretary*, *Too Much Johnson*, and *Secret Service* for New Yorkers.

Dec 5 At a special matinee at London's Aldwych Theatre, the Stage Society produces John Masefield's *Pompey the Great*, a three-act tragedy, with Herbert Grimwood.

Dec 5 Madame Sarah Bernhardt and her company arrive at the Globe Theatre for four weeks of repertory. Lou Tellegen makes his New York debut in the ensemble. Played in French, the rep includes Racine's *Phèdre*, Rostand's *L'Aiglon* and *La Samaritaine*, Sardou's *La Sorciere* and *Tosca*, Daudet's *Sapho*, Dumas fils' *La Dame aux Camelias*, Bisson's *La Femme X*, Benelli's *La Beffa*, Zamacois' *Les Bouffons*, Moreau's *Le Proces de Jeanne d'Arc*, and de Kay's *Judas*. Berhardt's acting, according to critics, defies age.

Dec 19 *Old Heidelberg* is revived by the New Theatre Company in New York.

Dec 20 Christmas is near, and *Our Little Cinderella*, staged at the Playhouse, is the first holiday entertainment to open. Margery Maude and Cyril Maude star. *Cinderellas* open in the next few days at the Coronet, the Broadway, New Cross; the Lyric, Hammersmith; and the Lyceum Theatres.

Dec 21 Frank Benson brings his production of the Stratford Festival prize play *The Piper*, to the St. James's in London. The play, based on the Pied Piper legend, is by Josephine Preston Peabody. He stars. It opens on Jan 30, 1911 at New York's New Theatre, with Edith Wynne Matthison in the lead. On March 19, 1920 the play is revived at the Fulton Theatre for a one week run.

Dec 26 At London's Drury Lane, the big Christmas pantomime this season is *Jack and the Beanstalk*, by J. Hickory Wood, Frank Dix, and Arthur Collins, who is also the theatre's manager. J. M. Glover provides the score. The Penders provide an interpolated traditional Harlequinade. Dolly Castles is Jack, with George Graves as a pantomime "dame" playing Jack's mother.

Dec 27 In New York, the New Theatre ensemble revives Sheridan's *The School for Scandal* with Grace George and Louis Calvert.

1910 BIRTHS/DEATHS/DEBUTS

Jan 2 Born in 1847, the American actress Agnes Booth dies today. The wife of Junius Brutus Booth, Jr., she was also Edwin Booth's sister-in-law.

Jan 10 Peggy Wood makes her New York debut in *The Old Town* at New York's Globe Theatre.

Jan 26 Lotta Faust (b. 1881) an actress of some note dies today.

March 5 American actor Louis James (b. 1842) dies in Helena, Mont. James made his debut in 1863, later joining Mrs. John Drew at Philadelphia's Arch Street Theatre. In 1871 he joined Daly at the 5th Avenue Theatre. From 1880 to 1885 he was leading man with Lawrence Barrett.

March 21 American actor Clark Creston, (b. 1866) dies today.

May 2 The popular stage perfomer, Lottie Collins (b. 1866) dies today.

June 18 Actor, songwriter, singer and dancer Avon Long is born in Baltimore, Maryland.

June 20 Fanny Brice makes her debut in Florenz Ziegfeld's *Follies*.

July 18 Singing-waiter Irving Berlin makes his first New York City appearance singing his own songs in the revue, *Up and Down Broadway* at the Casino Theatre.

Oct 30 English actress Henrietta Hodson is dead at age 69. Hodson made her first appearance on stage in Glasgow and Greenock, where she was in the same company as the young Henry Irving. In 1871 she played Imogen in *Cymbeline* and retired seven years later. She was instrumental in introducing Lily Langtry to the stage.

Dec 4 Future composer Alex North is born in Chester, Pennsylvania.

Dec 27 Actor Frank Worthing (b. 1866) dies in Detroit. Born in Scotland, Worthing began his professional career as assistant prompter in an English stock cmpany. In 1890 he joined Mrs. Patrick Campbell's Company. After a season with Olga Nethersole in America, he was engaged by Augustin Daly and played leading roles opposite Ada Rehan.

1910 THEATERS/PRODUCTIONS

In Britain this year patents are for Edward Gordon Craig's setting of a series of folding, double-hinged screens, preferably painted white or pale yellow, which can be arranged in various angles of perspective to suggest interior and exterior locales; rollers can be attached to the screens for swifter changes in their arrangement; Craig is to patent his screens in the U.S. in 1912; F. Siviter's design for a giant chicken, operated by an actor inside, but adaptable in principle to any large animal or human.

U.S. patents are granted this year to Harry Rochez who has invented a means of having a group of musical instruments on stage seem to play themselves. George Byrne patents an electrical system which makes sparks fly between two performers when they come in contact. Frank Thomas's effect, with an actor moving between screens on which water images are projected, can simulate swimming or drowning. Rubin Denny gets a patent for a cabinet with mirrors in which an actor is concealed, with only the image of his head visible. Even that can be made to disappear. John Sullivan's effect is that of a train moving along a track, parallel with the footlights, disappearing into the wings.

The Censorship Committee of the British Poster and Advertising Association in London bans Julius Price's poster for the Daly's Theatre revue, *An Artist's Model*, until the artist makes the picture of the scantily clothed model acceptable by "a much enlarged paillette."

Jan 10 The Columbia Theatre, designed by the architects Bliss and Favel, opens in San Francisco. The exterior is a blend of neo-classic and baroque elements. The auditorium is neo-classic, with seating for 1,456 in an orchestra and two balconies. The opening production is *Father and the Boys*, starring William Crane. In 1924, it will become the Geary Theatre.

Jan 10 The Globe Theatre, at 1555 Broadway in New York, opens with *The Old Town*, by George Ade and George Luders. In 1931, the owner, Charles Dillingham, loses his theatre, and it becomes a movie house. In 1958, the theatre opens with a new main entrance, on West 46 Street, and a new name, the Lunt-Fontanne.

May Declaring their right to book whatever attractions they see fit, some 1,200 owner-managers of American small-town theatres form the National Theatre Owners' Association. This means these playhouses are open to the Shuberts, as they are to the Syndicate. Meanwhile, the Shuberts continue to buy and lease theatres in New York (Maxine Elliott's and the Metropolitan) and across the country (Seattle—the Alhambra; San Francisco—the American, Detroit—the Whitney; Wilkes-Barre—the Nesbit and the Grand Opera House, etc.). The Shuberts are also building their own theatres in cities limited to one-week bookings.

May 7 Today marks the death of Edward VII, but Dublin's Abbey Theatre does not honor the occasion by closing. This action causes Annie E. F. Horniman to sever her connection with the theatre, whose premises she has paid for as a gift to the Irish Theatre movement.

May 28 The *NY Dramatic Mirror*, tallying the Broadway season from 1909–10, lists a total of 288 productions in Broadway and other theatres, with 152 of them new. 37 have had more than 75 showings; 20 have passed the 100-mark, and only 7 have had more than 200 performances.

Fall At the beginning of the new theatre season, there are some 1,520 American theatres available for booking legitimate productions on tour. This figure does not include the theatres in major cities such as New York, Boston, Chicago, Philadelphia, St. Louis, and San Francisco.

Fall At the opening of this Broadway season, Lee and J. J. Shubert have some 70 theatres in New York and around America under their direct control by virtue of ownership or leases. In addition, they have exclusive booking contracts with many more theatres, as well as favorable access to most of the one-night-stand theatres. They have also become a formidable production organization, having at present no less than 50 dramatic and musical companies playing New York or touring under their direct management.

Oct 8 Terry's Theatre on the Strand in London closes after the last performance of *The Rejuvenation of Aunt Mary*.

Oct 10 Producer-playwright David Belasco reopens his Stuyvesant Theatre, on West 44 Street in New York, as the Belasco. The opening show is his production of *The Concert*.

Oct 11 London's Little Theatre opens with Cavendish Morton's production of *Lysistrata*. The designers of the theatre are Hayward and Maynard, who have reconstructed the old Coutts Bank to create a theatre with no galleries or tiers and with a capacity of 250.

Dec There are 236 legitimate theatre touring productions in America as of the first week of this month. In 1928, there will be only 86, but in 1900, there were 392.

Dec 26 The Wimbledon Theatre in London opens with the pantomime, *Jack and Jill*. Cecil Masey and Roy Young have designed this 2,000-seat theatre as a touring house. The manager is J.B. Mullholland.

Dec 26 The London Palladium opens on Argyll Street, on the site of the former National Skating Palace (1895), Hegler's Grand Cirque (1871), and the old Argyll House. Frank Matcham is the designer of the 2325-seat theatre which opens with a variety program, including the one-act play, *The Conspiracy*.

Jan 2 *The Slim Princess* (NY—Globe—Musical). Henry Blossom provides book and lyrics; Leslie Stuart the music (with the help of Victor Herbert) for this musical about a princess who is too thin. Elsie Janis stars. Charles Dillingham produces.

Jan 17 *The Scarecrow* (NY—Garrick—Drama). Using Hawthorne's tale, *Feathertop*, Percy MacKaye dramatizes the plight of a scarecrow when he falls in love with young woman. Although this Edgar Selwyn-staged production has only 23 performances, it is admired abroad and seen in French and German versions, including one by Max Reinhardt.

Jan 23 *Chanticler* (NY—Knickerbocker—Drama). Louis N. Parker adapts Edmond Rostand's poetic allegory with Maude Adams in the lead. Charles Frohman produces. The show runs 96 performances.

Jan 30 *The Boss* (NY—Astor—Drama). Edward Sheldon's play offers the strongly drawn character of Michael Regan, a tough, tricky contractor and politician, who nonetheless has standards and courage. Holbrook Blinn stars and shares directing credits with William A. Brady.

Chanticler

Feb 13 *The Twelve Pound Look* (NY—Empire—Comedy). Ethel Barrymore is the alert young typewriter-girl in James Barrie's one-act play. It is preceded by a revival of Barrie's *Alice-Sit-by-the-Fire*, also with Barrymore. Charles Frohman produces.

March 13 *As a Man Thinks* (NY—Nazimova's 39th Street—Drama). Augustus Thomas stages his own drama about a man cured through mental healing. Chrystal Herne and John Mason are featured. The Shuberts produce.

March 13 *The Pink Lady* (NY—New Amsterdam—Musical). This complicated plot of lovers' mix-ups has a score by Ivan Caryll. It is staged by Julian Mitchell. Hazel Dawn is featured. The show runs 312 performances.

March 14 *Thais* (NY—Criterion—Drama). Based on the Anatole France tale, Paul Wilstach's play is notable for its leads: Constance Collier and Tyrone Power. (Sidney Greenstreet also has a small part.) "It was, in fact, a night of deserved triumph for Miss Constance Collier and Tyrone Power," reports the *NY Times*.

March 20 *La Belle Paree* (NY—Winter Garden—Musical). Described as a "Jumble of Jollity," this show opens the new Winter Garden for 104 performances. The undistinguished score is by Jerome Kern and Frank Tours. Al Jolson, a newcomer, sings "Paris Is a Paradise for Coons," in blackface.

April 3 *Mrs. Bumpstead-Leigh* (NY—Lyceum—Comedy). Harry James Smith's play about a woman anxious to conceal her mid-continent past under a veneer of British manners becomes a vehicle for Mrs. Minnie Maddern Fiske. Mrs. Fiske and her producer-husband, Harrison Gray Fiske direct.

April 27 A triple bill opens at the Folies Bergere Theatre in New York. It is comprised of *Hell*, "a profane burlesque;" *Temptation*, a ballet by Alfredo Curti; and *Gaby*, a "satirical revuette in three scenes." In the cast: Ada Lewis, Otis Harlan, Mayme Kelso, Leslie Leigh, and Ethel Levy, spoofing Gaby Deslys. It plays 92 performances.

June 26 *The Ziegfeld Follies of 1911* (NY—Jardin de Paris—Revue). This is the first time Ziegfeld's name is officially in the Follies title. Leon Errol makes his debut, joining Follies favorites such as Bert Williams, Fanny Brice, Lillian Lorraine, and the Dolly Sisters. Julian Mitchell stages.

Aug 10 *The Real Thing* (NY—Maxine Elliott—Comedy). Henrietta Crosman, with Frank Mills, Minnie Dupree, and others, animates Catherine Chisholm Cushing's play for 60 performances.

Aug 19 *Hello, Paris* (NY—Folies Bergere—Revue). This is Jesse Lasky and Henry Harris' last attempt to make a success of the Folies. In this midnight show, Harry Pilcer is featured, with songs by J. Rosamond Johnson.

Aug 28 *The Siren* (NY—Knickerbocker—Musical). This comedy, with a Leo Fall score and a Harry B. Smith adaptation of the Stein and Willner German-language original, tells how the police employ a young lady to discover whether a young marquis is writing satires about the government. Donald Brian and Julia Sanderson star. It runs for 136 performances.

Sep 2 *Around the World* (NY—Hippodrome—Musical). A search for a lost diamond is the excuse for the current sequence of astonishing scenes at the Hippodrome. Carroll Fleming provides the book and staging, with lyrics and music by Manuel Klein. Playing two performances a day, the show has 445 performances.

Sep 11 *The Fascinating Widow* (NY—Liberty—Musical). Julian Eltinge, playing Hal Blake, disguises himself as the widow, Mrs. Monte, to expose a two-timing rival of his financee. The book is by Otto Hauerbach, with a Kerry Mills score.

Sep 18 *Disraeli* (NY—Wallack's—Drama). George Arliss creates a memorable role—one he is to repeat with great success in the cinema—in Louis N. Parker's study of the British prime minister. The production runs for 280 performances. On April 4, 1916 it premieres at London's Royalty with Dennis Eadie in the title role. It is shown 128 times.

Sep 19 *The Woman* (NY—Republic—Drama). David Belasco produces and stages William C. deMille's melodrama about political corruption. It runs for 247 performances.

Sept 25 *The Little Millionaire* (NY—Cohen—Musical). George M. Cohan authors, directs, produces (with Sam H. Harris) and stars in this story of a father and son who must marry to fulfill terms of a will. The show runs 192 performances.

Sep 26 *Bought and Paid For* (NY—Playhouse—Drama). George Broadhurst's drama about a wealthy man who eventually wins the love of his wife has 431 performances.

Oct 5 *The Never Homes* (NY—Broadway—Musical). Glen MacDonough's book, E. Ray Goetz's lyrics and A. Baldwin Sloane's score poke fun at feminists. Lew Fields produces. Will Archie and Helen Hayes are in the cast. The show has only 92 performances.

Oct 17 *The Return of Peter Grimm* (NY—Belasco—Drama). Belasco stages his own play about a man who is brought back from the dead. It is a vehicle for Richard Mansfield.

Oct 17 *Gypsy Love* (NY—Globe—Musical). Harry B. and Robert B. Smith adapt Franz Lehar's *Ziegeunerliebe*. Marguerite Sylva stars. The show has only 31 performances.

Oct 19 *The Enchantress* (NY—New York—Musical). Victor Herbert provides the music for this story of an adventurer who falls in love with a prince. Kitty Gordon stars. Frederick Latham stages. The show has 72 performances followed by a long tour.

Oct 21 *The Garden of Allah* (NY—Century—Drama). Alexander Salvini, Mary Mannering, and others help authors Robert Hichens and Mary Anderson bring the novel to life on stage, Hugh Ford directs. 241 performances are their reward.

Nov 20 *Vera Violetta* (NY—Winter Garden—Musical). The title refers to the heroine's enchanting perfume. Gaby Deslys and Harry Pilcer stop the show with "The Gaby Glide." Blackface waiter Al Jolson is called on for repeated encores. It has 112 performances.

1911   BRITISH PREMIERES

Jan 19 *Preserving Mr. Panmure* (L—Comedy—Comedy). Arthur Wing Pinero's play about a stolen kiss has an all-star cast including Dion Boucicault and Marie Löhr. On Feb 27, 1912 it opens at New York's Lyceum Theatre. Gertrude Elliott and Lumsden Hare star. It runs only 31 performances.

Feb 1 *The Witness for the Defence* (L—St. James's—Drama). George Alexander heads the cast in A.E.W. Mason's taut play. There are 150 performances. On Dec 4 it premieres at New York's Empire Theatre with Ethel Barrymore featured.

Feb 2 *The Popinjay* (L—New—Drama). Boyle Lawrence and Frederick Mouillet adapt Alphonse Daudet's *Les Rois en Exil*. Fred Terry and Julia Nielson star. There are 147 performances.

Feb 16 *Mr. Jarvis* (L—Wyndham's—Drama). *Madam, Will You Walk?*, Beth Ellis' novel, comes to the stage in this version by Leon Lion and Malcolm Cherry. Henrietta Watson, H. V. Esmond and Gerald Du Maurier perform.

Feb 21 *Bardelys the Magnificent* (L—Globe—Comedy). Rafael Sabatini has provided the story for this romantic comedy, adapted by Henry Hamilton. Ashton Pearse and Lewis Waller are in the cast.

Feb 22 *Baby Mine* (L—Criterion—Comedy). The farcical plot conceived by Margaret Mayo has Zoie desperately trying to get an adoptive baby to cement her childless marriage. Weedon Grossmith and Iris Hoey perform. William A. Brady, the New York producer, has mounted this production which runs 345 performances.

Feb 23 *The Lily* (L—Kingsway—Drama). David Belasco's adaptation of *Le Lys*, by Pierre Woolfe and Gaston Leroux stars Laurence Irving.

Feb 24 *Loaves and Fishes* (L—Duke of York's—Comedy). W. Somerset Maugham's four-act satire is animated by Robert Loraine and Ellis Jeffreys.

March 4 *Peggy* (L—Gaiety—Musical). George Grossmith, Jr. adapts Xanroff and Guerin's play *L'Amorcage*. Songs are the work of C.H. Bovill and Leslie Stuart. The plot, say the critics, is of no consequence. Phyllis Dare stars. There are 270 performances.

March 11 At London's Little Theatre, Harley Granville Barker offers a program of short plays adapted from Arthur Schnitzler's *Conversations of Anatol*. They are: *A Christmas Present, An Episode, Ask No Questions and You'll Hear No Stories, A Farewell Supper,* and *The Wedding Morning.*

March 22 *Lady Patricia* (L—Haymarket—Comedy). Mrs. Patrick Campbell is the lady in question. The show earns 100 performances.

March 29 *Passers-By* (L—Wyndham's—Comedy). Playwright C. Haddon Chambers uses what he calls "the long arm of coincidence" to reunite two unjustly and long separated lovers. Irene Vanbrugh plays. It runs for 163 performances.

April 18 *A Butterfly on the Wheel* (L—Globe—Drama). There are 119 performances of this four-act play by Edward Hemmerde and Francis Neilson. On Jan 9, 1912, Lewis Waller's production of this play opens at New York's 39th Street Theatre with Charles Quartermaine in the cast. It runs for 191 performances.

April 19 *Kismet* (L—Garrick—Drama). Edward Knoblauch's story of a rescue from a harem stars Oscar Asche and Lily Brayton. This lavish production has 328 performances. On Christmas Day the play opens at New York's Knickerbocker Theatre with Otis Skinner starring. Harrison

Grey Fiske stages. The show has 184 performances and successive tours.

April 19 *Fanny's First Play* (L—Little—Comedy). George Bernard Shaw's "Easy Play in Three Acts" deal with two children of respectable families who are thrown into jail for boisterous behavior. Shiel Barry and Lillah McCarthy are featured. The show runs 624 performances. On September 16, 1912 Shaw's play opens at the Comedy Theatre in New York and is given 256 performances. Harley Granville Barker stages.

May 20 *The Count of Luxembourg* (L—Daly's—Musical). Franz Lehar's tuneful score has an English flavor after Basil Hood has reworked the original libretto. Lyrics are by Adrian Ross and Hood. Bertram Wallis and Lily Elsie are featured in this story of disguised love. There are 340 performances. On September 16, 1912 the play opens in New York at the New Amsterdam Theatre. Glenn MacDonough Americanizes the libretto and Herbert Gresham stages. With new lyrics by Adrian Ross and Basil Hood, the show manages 120 performances.

May 29 *A Trip to Brighton* (L—New—Comedy). W. Somerset Maugham labels this farce a "Comedietta." Sam Sothern and Mary Moore appear. Maugham has adapted it from a French original by M. Tarride.

June 29 *Pomander Walk* (L—Playhouse—Comedy). Louis N. Parker's play is cast with performers such as Winifred Emery, Margery Maude, Norman Forbes, Reginald Owen, and Cyril Maude.

July 4 *Bunty Pulls the Strings* (L—Playhouse—Comedy). Graham Moffat's "Scottish Comedy" has its premiere at a matinee. The author and his wife star in this story of a girl who saves her father from being blackmailed into marriage. The show runs for 617 performances. On October 10th Moffat's play opens on Broadway at the Comedy Theatre. The play runs for 391 performances. William A. Brady and the Shuberts co-produce. The *NY Times* asserts, "It is inevitable that Mr. Moffat should be compared to Mr. J.M. Barrie, but neither of them will be the loser by comparison."

Sep 9 *The Mousme* (L—Shaftesbury—Musical). Alex Thompson and Robert Courtneidge write an oriental fantasy, with a score by Lionel Monckton and Howard Talbot. Arthur Wimperis and Percy Greenbank provide the lyrics. Florence Smithson and Eric Maturin play leads. There are 209 performances.

Sep 12 *The Perplexed Husband* (L—Wyndham's—Comedy). Alfred Sutro's play, with Gerald Du Maurier heading the cast, wins 154 performances. On Sep 2, 1912 it is premiered at New York's Empire Theatre with John Drew opposite Mary Boland. It runs 10 weeks.

Sep 14 *The Hope* (L—Drury Lane—Drama). Cecil Raleigh and Henry Ham-

The Garden of Allah

ilton star in this melodrama about the trials of two lovers. Arthur Collins produces. Cyril Keightley and Evelyn D'Alroy are featured. There are 102 performances.

Sep 30 *The Spring Maid* (L—Whitney—Musical). Julius Wilhelm and A.M. Willner's play is adapted by C.H.E. Brookfield with music by Heinrich Reinhardt. Marise Fairy and Courtice Pounds are in the cast.

Oct 6 *The Honeymoon* (L—Royalty—Comedy). Marie Tempest plays Flora Lloyd in Arnold Bennett's new play. There are 126 performances.

Nov 4 *The Glad Eye* (L—Globe—Comedy). Jose Levy adapts *Le Zebre*, a French farce by Armont and Nancey. The play is about two women who hire a detective to catch their husbands who slip off for gay adventures. Auriol Lee, Daisy Markham, Lawrence Grossmith and H. Marsh Allen have leads.

Dec 9 *Bella Donna* (L—St. James's—Drama). This play is adapted from Robert Hichens' novel by J.B. Fagan. Mrs. Patrick Campbell plays an opportunist who tries to poison her husband. Lydia Branscombe and George Alexander also play. There are 253 performances. On November 11, 1912 it opens at the Empire Theatre on Broadway with Alla Nazimova in the lead. The play runs nine weeks.

Peggy

1911   REVIVALS/REPERTORIES

Jan 7 At the New Theatre near Manhattan's Columbus Circle, *Vanity Fair* enters the repertory, with Marie Tempest as Becky Sharp. On the 30th, Josephine Preston Peabody's *The Piper*, the Stratford Prize Play, opens with Edith Wynne Matthison in the title role. Mary Austin's Indian play, *The Arrow Maker*, bows on Feb 27. On Sep 15, the theatre is called the Century, as Maeterlinck's *The Blue Bird* is revived, a show which premiered here less than a year ago, before the New had failed as a costly experiment in repertory.

Jan 12 In Dublin, the Abbey Theatre players premiere Lady Gregory's one-act "tragic comedy," *The Deliverer*.

Jan 15 At the Royal Opera, Covent Garden, Professor Max Reinhardt stages Gilbert Murray's translation of Sophocles' *Oedipus Rex*. John Martin Harvey and Lillah McCarthy star.

Jan 26 Lord Dunsany's play, *King Argimenes and the Unknown Warrior*, is produced in Dublin at the Abbey Theatre. Fred O'Donovan plays the king.

Jan 26 William Archer's translation of Henrik Ibsen's *John Gabriel Borkman* has a brief showing in London at the Court Theatre. James Hearn is Borkman.

Feb 25 Oscar Asche and Lily Brayton open their London season at the Garrick Theatre with a revival of *The Merry Wives of Windsor*.

Feb 26 Henrik Ibsen's Norwegian dramatic poem, *Peer Gynt*, is staged by Catherine Lewis for the Ibsen Club at London's Rehearsal Theatre.

Feb 27 Oscar Wilde's one-act tragedy, *Salome*, is performed privately by the New Players at London's Court Theatre. Herbert Grimwood is Herod, with Edyth Olive as Herodias, and Adeline Bourne as Salome. It has been banned because of its obscenity.

March 13 "Potted" versions of *Inconstant George*, *Henry VIII*, and *Count Hannibal* take the stage of London's Apollo Theatre as the parodic portion of Pelissier's Follies' entertainment. On June 7, the burlesques are of *The Chocolate Soldier* and *The Witness for the Defence*. On August 29, *Kismet* and a Grand Guignol sketch are shown.

March 30 In Dublin at the Abbey Theatre, St. John Ervine has the world premiere of his four-act drama, *Mixed Marriage*. In the cast are Maire O'Neill, Arthur Sinclair, and J. M. Kerrigan.

April 4 At London's Lyceum Theatre, Algernon Charles Swinburne's tragedy, *Atalanta in Calydon*, is revived and staged by Elsie Fogerty.

April 17 At Stratford-upon-Avon, the annual Shakespeare Festival opens with *The Merry Wives of Windsor*, followed by *The Merchant of Venice*, and *Twelfth Night*. The "Birthday Play" is *Much Ado About Nothing*. Other productions offered by Frank Benson and company include *Henry V*, *Julius Caesar*, *Macbeth*, *As You Like It*, *Romeo and Juliet*, *A Midsummer Night's Dream*, *Richard III*, Sheridan's *The Critic*, Peabody's *The Piper*, and four plays from the Chester Mystery Cycle. At the close of the season, the Irish Players from the Abbey Theatre in Dublin offer a repertory of their productions, including Synge's *The Playboy of the Western World*.

April 17 At His Majesty's Theatre in London, *A Midsummer Night's Dream* is revived, with Arthur Bourchier playing Bottom. Gerald Lawrence is Theseus. Oberon and Titania are played by Evelyn D'Alroy and Margery Maude.

April 17 Robert B. Mantell begins a season of repertory in New York at Daly's Theatre, including *Richelieu*, *Louis XI*, *Richard III*, *King Lear*, *As You Like It*, *The Merchant of Venice*, *Hamlet*, *Othello*, *Romeo and Juliet*, *Macbeth*, and *Julius Caesar*. Mantell is the leading man.

May 11 At London's New Theatre, Phyllis Nielson-Terry plays Rosalind in her production of *As You Like It*.

May 18 Bernard Shaw's *Arms and the Man* is revived in London at the Criterion Theatre. Arnold Daly and Margaret Halstan play leads.

May 22 At His Majesty's Theatre, Herbert Beerbohm Tree opens the London Shakespeare Festival with his production of *Julius Caesar*. On May 29, Oscar Asche and Lily Brayton are featured in *As You Like It*. On June 1, the play is *The Merchant of Venice*; on June 5, *Twelfth Night*; on June 9, *The Taming of the Shrew*, with Frank Benson and company; on June 12, Tree's production of *Henry VIII*; on June 20, the Benson troupe in *Richard III*, and on July 3, *The Merry Wives of Windsor*.

May 29 Anton Chekhov's four-act play, *The Cherry Orchard* in Constance Garnett's translation, has a special matinee performance. It is produced by the Stage Society.

June 5 From Dublin, the Abbey Theatre ensemble comes to London's Court Theatre. George Fitzmaurice's *The Pie Dish* opens today. On June 7, St. John Ervine's four-act *Mixed Marriage* is performed. On the following day, the play is T. C. Murray's *Birthright*. On June 12, Arthur Sinclair plays Scapin in Lady Gregory's three-act translation of Molière's short play, *The Rogueries of Scapin*. *The Casting-Out of Martin Whelan* is presented on June 14. On June 15, Lady Gregory's *The Full Moon* is offered; on June 19, William Boyle's *The Mineral Workers* and Lennox Robinson's *The Clancy Name*.

July 3 E. H. Sothern and Julia Marlowe return to New York to offer another Shakespeare repertory season, at the Broadway Theatre. On the program: *Macbeth*, *The Taming of the Shrew*, *Hamlet*, *The Merchant of Venice*, *Romeo and Juliet*, *Twelfth Night*.

July 11 Mrs. Patrick Campbell is Melisande to Martin Harvey's Pelleas in matinee revival performances of Maeterlinck's poetic fantasy.

July 22 In Stratford-upon-Avon, the second summer season of Shakespeare's plays is performed at the Memorial Theatre by Frank Benson's company. Randle Ayrton and Baliol Holloway debut with the troupe. In the repertory are *A Midsummer Night's Dream, Henry V, Richard II, The Merchant of Venice, Romeo and Juliet, As You Like It, The Taming of the Shrew, Hamlet,* and *The Tempest.*

July 23 August Strindberg's *The Father* has its first British performance in London at the Rehearsal Theatre. It is performed by the Adelphi Play Society.

Aug 11 At Oxford's New Theatre, the Elizabethan Stage Society presents Schiller's *Wallenstein* and scenes from *The Piccolomini,* another play in the Wallenstein Trilogy.

Aug. 21 John Kellerhd opens a reportory program at the Irving Place Theatre in New York. *Oedipus Rex, Hamlet, Macbeth,* and *The Merchant of Venice* are featured.

Sep 2 Fred Terry produces a new "arrangement" of *Romeo and Juliet* in London at the New Theatre, with Vernon Steel and Phyllis Nielson-Terry as the young lovers.

Sep 4 In Dublin, a number of new plays are opening. Tonight, it's *A Hospital Ward,* by J. Malachi Muldoon, at the Queen's Theatre, as well as Mary Costello's *The Comedy of Aideen* and Joahanna Redmond's *Pro Patria.* At the Abbey Theatre tonight, William Boyle's *The Love Charm* has its premiere.

Sep 5 In London at His Majesty's Theatre, Herbert Tree again plays the title-role in a revival of *Macbeth,* with Violet Vanbrugh as his lady.

Sep 28 Bernard Shaw's *Man and Superman* is revived in London at the Criterion Theatre, with Robert Loraine and Pauline Chase.

Oct 5 At London's Savoy Theatre, Max Reinhardt's German-speaking cast presents the "Wordless Musical Play," *Sumurun,* with Leopoldine Konstantin as the Beautiful Slave. The plot has been devised by Friedrich Freska; music by Victor Hollander. This is the Berlin Deutsches Theater production, with Reinhardt's best actors: Conradi, Rothauser, Lotz, Tiedemann, Matray, Von Derp, and Scholz. The staging is admired for the vivid pageant of colors, moving swiftly from scene to scene against a simple white background.

Oct 14 Oscar Wilde's *Lady Windermere's Fan* is revived at London's St. James's Theatre. Marion Terry and Lilian Braithwaite play leads.

Nov 8 At a special matinee at His Majesty's Theatre, Israel Zangwill's four-act drama, *The War God,* is shown to London theatre-goers, with Charles Maude.

Nov 20 Sothern and Marlowe return with their Shakespeare repertory, this time playing the Manhattan Opera House, adding *As You Like It* to the roster of productions shown in July.

Nov 20 The Irish Players make their premiere apparance in New York at the Maxine Elliott Theatre. The repertory includes several plays by J. M. Synge: *The Well of the Saints, The Shadow of the Glen, Riders to the Sea,* and *The Playboy of the Western World.* By Lady Gregory are *Hyacinth Halvey, The Jackdaw, Spreading the News, The Image, The Workhouse Ward, The Gaol Gate,* and *The Rising of the Moon.* Other plays in the repertory are W.B. Yeats' *Cathleen ni Houlihan,* Lennox Robinson's *Harvest,* St. John Ervine's *Mixed Marriage,* William Boyle's *The Building Fund* and *The Mineral Workers,* T. C. Murray's *Birthright,* Johanna Redmond's *Falsely True,* and George Bernard Shaw's *The Shewing Up of Blanco Posnet.* In the ensemble are Sara Allgood, Arthur Sinclair, Cathleen Nesbitt, and Una O'Connor, among others.

Nov 26 At London's Savoy Theatre, the Pioneer Players give a special performance of an unlicensed play, Laurence Houseman's *Pains and Penalties: The Defence of Queen Caroline.* It has been banned because it deals with royalty in an unflattering way.

Dec 11 At the Shakespeare Theatre in London's Clapham district, *Through Death Valley; Or, the Mormon Peril* opens. Joseph Le Brandt's four-act drama has Jack Fortescue in a leading role.

Dec 14 The holidays are coming, so London's Aldwych Theatre prepares for the onslaught of juvenile audiences with *The Golden Land of Fairy Tales.* The original German text is translated, but Heinrich Berte's score is retained. In the company are Maud Cressall, Florrie Lewis, Alfred Latell, Mary Glynn, and Shakespeare Stewart. On December 21 Roger Quilter

composes the music for the fairy-play, *Where the Rainbow Ends,* with text by Clifford Mills and John Ramsey. London's Savoy Theatre produces the work for Christmas audiences. On December 23, Pauline Chase is Peter Pan at the Duke of York's in London. At the Coronet, Myra Hammond plays Robin Hood in *The Babes in the Wood.* At the Britannia, Marie Kendall stars in *Goodie Two Shoes.* Other

The Hope

openings today are the Camden Theatre's *Babes in Toyland,* with Leslie Ross and Will Meaton, and J. Hickory Wood and Fred Bowyer's *Mother Goose* at the Crystal Palace. On December 26 a new pantomime opens at London's Drury Lane Theatre, *Hop O' My Thumb,* by George R. Sims, Frank Dix, and Arthur Collins, the theatre's manager. Renee Mayer plays the title-role. Stanley Lupino plays the cat at the Lyceum in its version of *Dick Whittington,* Other theatres showing this tale are the Broadway and the Shakespeare. Also on view: *Cinderella* (Brixton, Dalston, Kennington), *Jack and the Beanstalk* (Lyric, Hammersmith), and *Robinson Crusoe* (Elephant and Castle).

Dec 26 *The Three Musketeers* is the premiere production of the New Prince's Theatre in Shaftesbury Avenue.

1911 BIRTHS/DEATHS/DEBUTS

Jan 15 Producer-director Cy Feuer is born in New York.

Jan 27 Billed as Alfred Willmore, Irish actor, director, playwright, and designer Micheal MacLiammoir makes his first stage appearance as King Goldfish in *The Goldfish* at the Little Theatre in London.

Jan 30 Hugh Marlowe is born Hugh Herbert Hipple in Philadelphia, Pennsylvania.

Feb 9 Alice Brady makes her debut under the stage name Marie Rose in *The Balkan Princess.*

March 13 Actress Hazel Dawn makes her Broadway debut in the musical comedy, *The Pink Lady,* at the New Amsterdam Theatre.

June 6 Edward Harrigan (b. 1844), actor, playwright, manager, dies today. Harrigan, with his partner Tony Hart, will be best remembered for his comic lowlife portraits of New York City folk in his Mulligan Guards productions.

Sep 22 Mae West makes her New York debut at the Folies Bergere Theatre in *A la Broadway.*

Sep 27 French star Gaby Deslys makes her American debut in *The Revue of Revues* at the Winter Garden.

Oct 2 Former mining engineer assayer and mineralogist Henry Hull makes his New York acting debut as Henry Steele in the A. E. W. Mason comedy, *Green Stockings,* at the 39th Street Theatre.

Nov 2 Once one of London's most lovely leading ladies, Kyrle Bellew (b. 1855) dies.

Dec 20 The American actress Rose Eytinge (b. 1835) dies this day.

Dec 22 Actor, producer, and playwright, Wright Lorimer (b. 1874) dies.

1911 THEATERS/PRODUCTIONS

In Britain this year patents are granted for C. S. Culver's imitation automobile, rigged so that its bonnet (hood) will blow off as if in an explosion.

In the U.S. Claude L. Hagen patents his system of flying drops, with buckets of sand in which the weight can be varied to match the weight of the scenery. Menlo Moore's device can suspend an actor over the audience.

The Censorship Committee of the British Poster and Advertising Association bans the poster advertising the play, *Pleasures Of A Gay City*, which shows a victim stripped to the waist and a figure with a cat-o'-nine-tails. The poster was also banned in 1902 by same Committee.

Britain's Lord Chamberlain refuses to license Sophocles' *Oedipus Rex* for public performance.

Jan 1 Chicago's new Blackstone Theatre opens today. It's designed by Marshal and Fox for a site at 60 East Balboa Street. It has 1,200 seats.

Jan 23 *Chanticler* opens at New York's Knickerbocker Theatre. In this production, a scrim-translucency effect never before seen has been created by the architect J. Monroe Hewlett and Bassett Jones.

Feb 13 George M. Cohan's Theatre, at 1482 Broadway in New York, opens with *Get-Rich-Quick Wallingford*. Built as part of the Fitzgerald Building, the theatre and building are eventually bought by Joe Leblang. The theatre closes in 1932, and is razed along with the Fitzgerald Building in 1938.

Feb 26 The Columbia Theatre opens today in Chicago. It is designed by architect J. E. O. Pridmore. Intended for burlesque and music hall presentations, it seats 1,550. In 1923, it will become the Adelphi Theatre. It will be razed in 1974.

March 19 The Des Moines Theatre in Iowa burns, a total loss at $44,500, $2,600 of which is covered by insurance.

March 20 The Winter Garden (1,800 seats) opens on Broadway at 50 Street in New York City. The theatre is built by the Shuberts for musical theatre.

April 3 Bertha Kalish opens in J. Gordin's *The Kreutzer Sonata* at the Royal Alexandra Theatre in Toronto, Canada. The Toronto Police Morality Squad charges that the final scene (a double murder) is too violent for public view, and although a detailed account of the scene is printed in local papers, the management decides to lower the curtain during the violent scene, raising it a few moments later for the final lines of the play. Madame Kalish never plays Toronto again.

April 11 At London's Scala Theatre, Charles Urban's season commences, with *Castles in the Air* using Kinemacolor pictures.

April 15 William A. Brady opens The Playhouse with the production of *Sauce for the Goose*, starring his wife, Grace George. The theatre is on West 48 Street in New York City.

April 27 The Folies Bergere, on West 46 Street in New York, owned by producers Henry B. Harris and Jesse Lasky and designed by Herts and Tallant, opens with *Hell, Temptation, and Gaby*. Designed as a theatre-restaurant, on Oct 11 it opens as a regular Broadway house is renamed the Fulton. In 1955, it is renamed Helen Hayes Theatre. It is razed in 1982.

May 31 Surveying the Broadway season just past, the *NY Dramatic Mirror* tallies some 366 productions, with 150 of them new productions. 32 shows have had more than 100 performances; only 9 have passed the 200-performances mark. The *Mirror's* count runs from May 22, 1910, to May 27, 1911. In *Best Plays*, Burns Mantle and Garrison P. Sherwood provide a breakdown by genres, though their new-production total is slightly different. With a base of 36 theatres—much smaller than the number the *Mirror* uses—they list 52 dramas, 41 comedies, 20 musicals, 4 revues, 4 operas, 4 operettas, 3 Shakespearean revivals, 3 repertory offerings, 1 ballet, and 1 burlesque.

June 10 *Driving a Girl to Destruction* closes at the Star Theatre, Liverpool, marking its demise as a melodrama house. It will now be reconstructed and become the home of the newly-formed Liverpool Repertory Company.

Aug In Stratford-upon-Avon, a "syndicate" called Benson Ltd. takes over control of the finances of the Shakespeare Memorial Theatre.

Sep 17 In *The Return of Peter Grim* at New York's Belasco Theatre, Louis Hartmann introduces the incandescent followspot.

Sep 23 Dublin's Abbey Theatre, founded by W. B. Yeats and Augusta, Lady Gregory, among others, begins its first American tour with this evening's performance in Boston.

Nov As in Dublin, so in New York: militant Irish, believing themselves and their nation maligned by John Millington Synge's *The Playboy of the Western World*, provoke a noisy disturbance. The performance comes to its end with many driven from the theatre and ten arrested. Boston has already noisily protested the play. Irish in other cities on the Abbey Theatre's tour are not to be outdone in showing their patriotism.

Nov This month Charles Brookfield joins George Redford in the Lord Chamberlain's Office, censoring and licensing plays for public production. Brookfield is named Joint Examiner of Plays. In December, Redford is to retire, replaced by an *Observer* drama critic, Ernest Bendall. Brookfield's appointment, though he has been a minor actor and is the author of forty plays, excites protest for he is known to be a foe to modern English drama. This month after a private performance of *Pains and Penalties* at the Savoy Theatre, Brookfield's appointment is attacked and the Lord Chamberlain is censured by the audience, addressed by Harley Ganville Barker. The play deals with the ill treatment by George IV of his detested queen, Caroline.

Nov 6 The Victoria Palace in London opens with a variety entertainment, including the one-act play, *The Deputy Sheriff*. The 1565-seat theatre is on the site of the former Royal Standard Music Hall, and has been designed by Frank Matcham. Alfred Butt is the manager.

Nov 11 In Liverpool, the Liverpool Playhouse opens, with a production of *The Admirable Crichton*, after a preliminary season which began with Galsworthy's *Strife* in a temporary home. Basil Dean stages both plays for this new provincial repertory theatre, owned by 1,300 shareholders. Not only will this company provide Liverpool with the best of the London plays, but it will also develop new playwrights from the Midlands and send productions to London.

Dec 23 San Franciscans are fond of the name Alcazar, apparently. Tonight the third theatre of that name opens. Inside and out, its architecture and decoration are Moorish, in keeping with its name. In August 1922, it changes its name to the Wilkes-Alcazar Company. It's torn down in the 1960's to make way for a garage which takes its name.

Dec 25 In Richmond, Virginia, the new Empire Theatre opens, a home for vaudeville and legitimate theatre, designed by Louis Legnaioli and built by Moses Lafayette Hofheimer.

Dec 26 The New Prince's Theatre opens on Shaftesbury Avenue in London with *The Three Musketeers*, transferred from the Lyceum. Bertie Crewe is the designer of this 1,250 seat theatre. After three years, the theatre will be known as The Prince's Theatre.

Jan 8 *Over the River* (NY—Globe—Musical). John Golden composes the score for Ziegfeld and Dillingham's production. It stars Eddie Foy as a man who tells his wife he's off to Mexico, when he actually has to go to jail. It runs 120 performances.

Jan 8 *The Bird of Paradise* (NY—Daly's—Drama). Richard Walton Tully's drama of interracial love features Laurette Taylor, Virginia Reynolds, Guy Bates Post and Herbert Fargeon. Tully does the staging. It runs 112 performances. On Sep 11, 1919 it premieres at London's Lyric with Lily Moa, Diamond Kekona and William Kamoku in the cast. It runs 312 performances.

Jan 8 *The Talker* (NY—Harris—Drama). Author Marion Fairfax stages this popular drama about a wife who sees herself as a New Woman; she's eager to pursue her own life. In the cast are Pauline Lord, Lillian Albertson, and Tully Marshall. It achieves 144 performances.

Jan 16 *Sumurun* (NY—Casino—Spectacle). Max Reinhardt brings the entire Berlin cast, with all of the Deutsches Theatre's sets and costumes, to recreate his wordless spectacle. Composer Victor Hollaender conducts the score. Ernst Stern's visualizations are potent. "The Reinhardt method is more graphic than the Italian pantomime, which not infrequently expresses itself in symbols which cannot be understood without some previous knowledge of the art."

Jan 22 *Elevating a Husband* (NY—Liberty—Comedy). Edward Everett Horton, Conway Tearle, Jessie Carter, and others are directed by Gustav von Seyfferitz in this play by Clara Lipman and Samuel Shipman. It runs for 120 performances.

Jan 29 *The Trail of the Lonesome Pine* (NY—New Amsterdam—Drama). John Fox, Jr.'s popular novel of southern hill country is adapted by Eugene Walter. William S. Hart is in the cast.

Jan 29 *Officer 666* (NY—Gaiety—Comedy). Augustin MacHugh's melodramatic farce about mistaken identities, with a bogus policeman and a larcenous art expert is produced by George M. Cohan and Sam H. Harris. It features Francis D. McGinn. It runs for 192 performances. On Oct 30 the play opens at London's Globe Theatre. There are 110 performances.

Feb 8 *Hokey-pokey* and *Bunty, Bulls and Strings* (NY—Broadway—Musical). This is the Jubilee of Weber and Fields. They celebrate their reunion in this loosely structured play which burlesques the season's successful plays.

Feb 26 *Oliver Twist* (NY—New Amsterdam—Drama). Charles Dickens' novel is adapted by J. Comyns Carr. The cast includes Robert Vivian, Marie Doro, Fuller Mellish, Nat C. Goodwin, and Constance Collier.

March 5 *Whirl of Society* (NY—Winter Garden—Revue). This revue in three parts, is a showcase for the Shuberts' new star, Al Jolson. *A Night with the Pierrots* is a ragtime burlesque of Reinhardt's *Sumurun*. The show includes an "operatic mimodrama," *Sesostra*, also inspired by *Sumurun*.

March 19 *The Flower of the Palace of Han* (NY—Little—Drama). Adapted from the Chinese by Charles Rann Kennedy and Louis Laloy, this tale is also produced by Winthrop Ames. It stars Edith Wynne Matthison.

April 11 *A Winsome Widow* (NY—Moulin Rouge—Musical). Although this is based on Charles Hoyt's *A Trip to Chinatown*, it proves more of a vaudeville. Producer Flo Ziegfeld gives it lavish staging. Mae West is noticed for the first time. Raymond Hubell provides the score, with interpolations from other composers.

April 15 *The Wall Street Girl* (NY—Cohan—Musical). Blanche Ring and Will Rogers play in this tale of a women who saves her father from ruin with a mine in Nevada. Margaret Mayo and Edgar Selwyn have devised the book. It runs for seven weeks.

July 22 *The Passing Show of 1912* (NY—Winter Garden—Revue). Devised to keep the Garden filled when Jolson is on vacation, this show stresses short parodies of current Broadway hits, lovely chorus girls and impressive settings. In the cast are Eugene and Willie Howard, Jobyna Howland, Charlotte Greenwood, and Trixie Friganza.

Aug 3 *Hanky Panky* (NY—Broadway—Musical). Christine Nielson stars in this show with a score by A. Baldwin Sloane. Lew Fields produces.

Aug 31 *Under Many Flags* (NY—Hippodrome—Musical). Capt. Alan Strong flies from the White House lawn around the world in this Carroll Fleming story with music by Manuel Klein. Fleming also stages. With two performances a day, it garners 445 showings.

Sep 10 *The Governor's Lady* (NY—Republic—Drama). David Belasco stages Alice Bradley's play for 135 performances.

Sep 11 *Within the Law* (NY—Eltinge—Drama). Bayard Veiller writes a taut play about a girl, wrongly sent to prison, who vows revenge within the law. Jane Cowl, William B. Mack and Georgia Lawrence appear. Holbrook Blinn stages. It achieves 541 performances. The *NY Times* criticizes the play asking, ". . . How [Veiller] dared have the play performed during the present demoralized condition of the po-

Officer 666

lice force is a matter he must settle with his own conscience." On May 24, 1913 Veiller's play opens at London's Haymarket Theatre. It is adapted by Frederick Fenn and Arthur Wimperis and runs for 427 performances. In the cast are Frederick Ross, E. Lyall Swete, Mabel Burnege, Leon Lion, Edyth Goodall, and Mabel Russell. Herbert Beerbohm Tree produces, with sets by Joseph Harker and R.C. McCleery.

Sep 16 *Fanny's First Play* See L premiere, 1911.

Sep 23 *Broadway Jones* (NY—Cohan—Comedy). There are 176 performances for George M. Cohan's new show, featuring the author-director as Jackson Jones. Father and Mother Cohan are also on hand. After a tour of the provincial theatres, Cohan's play arrives in London's West End on Feb 3, 1914, where it wins 159 performances and a 1916 revival of 114 performances.

Sep 30 *Oh! Oh! Delphine* (NY—Knickerbocker—Musical). C.M.S. McLellan's adaptation of the French farce *Villa Primrose* has a score by Ivan Caryll. The show, about reserve officers in mixups with wives and mistresses, runs 285 performances. On February 18, 1913 this British play opens at London's Shaftesbury Theatre. Iris Hoey stars. Producer Robert Courtneidge engages Walter Hann, R.C. McCleery, and Conrad Tritschler to design the lavish interiors and exteriors for the handsomely costumed show. There are 174 performances.

Oct 14 *The Affairs of Anatol* (NY—Little—Comedy) John Barrymore is Arthur Schnitzler's debonair Viennese amoralist. The show runs for 72 performances.

Oct 21 *The Ziegfeld Follies of 1912* (NY—Moulin Rouge—Revue). As usual, the show features beautiful girls in elaborate costumes and comics—this time Bert Williams and Leon Errol. It runs 11 weeks.

Oct 28 *The Lady of the Slipper* (NY—Globe—Musical). Victor Herbert provides the score, James O'Dea the lyrics and Anne Caldwell and Lawrence McCarty the book for this Cinderella story. Producer Charles Dillingham mounts the musical lavishly. It has a run of 232 performances—the second longest run of the season.

Nov 4 *The Yellow Jacket* (NY—Fulton—Drama). The mysterious Orient is evoked in this tale by George Hazleton and J. Harry Benrimo. It runs ten weeks and tours extensively.

Nov 13 *The Red Petticoat* (NY—Daly's—Musical). Jerome Kern creates the score for this musicalization of Rida Johnson Young's *Next*, a flop in 1911. Helen Lowell is a barber who gets her man in a Nevada mining-town. The show runs for 61 performances.

Nov 21 *Roly Poly* and *Without the Law* (NY—Broadway—Revue). Weber and Fields go to Raatenbad, where Bijou Fitzsimmons (Marie Dressler) pursues Fields. Nora Bayes sings "When It's Apple Blossom Time in Normandy." The evening ends with a parody of *Within the Law*, but the show attracts audiences only for 60 performances.

Nov 22 *The Whip* (NY—Manhattan Opera House—Drama). Cecil Raleigh and Henry Hamilton's melodramatic plot is interpreted by Lumsden Hare, Robert Jarman, Marie Illington, and others. It enjoys 163 performances.

Dec 2 *The Firefly* (NY—Lyric—Musical). Otto Hauerbach's book and lyrics tell a tale of contemporary New York in which an Italian streetsinger disguises herself as a boy to be near the wealthy man she loves. Rudolf Friml provides the music. Emma Trentini, Craig Campbell and Audrey Maple play. The show wins 120 performances.

Dec 20 *Peg o' My Heart* (NY—Cort—Comedy). J. Hartley Manners creates a play and a role which becomes identified with his wife, Laurette Taylor, the Peg of the title, a winsome young orphan who changes the lives of those around her. Manners stages and Oliver Morosco produces this show. It runs for 603 performances, followed by tours and revivals. On Oct 10, 1914, the play opens at London's Comedy Theatre, with Laurette Taylor as Peg. There are 710 performances and two 1916 revivals. *The Times* reports that Taylor, "is something to be seen."

Dec 25 *Stop Thief* (NY—Gaiety—Comedy). Frank Bacon and William Boyd help bring Carlyle Moore's farcial tale to life for 149 performances.

Peg O' My Heart

1912 BRITISH PREMIERES

Jan 30 *The Pigeon* (L—Royalty—Comedy). John Galsworthy's fantasy in three acts has Whitford Kane as Christopher Wellwyn and Gladys Cooper as Ann. On March 12, Galsworthy's work is produced by Winthrop Ames at New York's Little Theatre. It runs 64 performances.

Feb 1 *The Bear-Leaders* (L—Comedy—Comedy). R.C. Carton's farce about two young aristocrats, engaged to others, who fall in love has Katharine Compton (Carton's wife). It earns 200 performances.

Feb 17 *The "Mind the Paint" Girl* (L—Duke of York's—Comedy). Arthur Wing Pinero's four-act entertainment stars Marie Löhr. It earns 126 performances. The show is later burlesqued as *The "Mind the Gate" Girl*, premiering on May 21 at His Majesty's. On September 9th the play opens on Broadway at the Lyceum Theatre. Dion G. Boucicault stages it. It runs for 136 performances.

Feb 24 *The Sunshine Girl* (L—Gaiety—Musical). This show is primarily by Paul Rubens, assisted on the book by Cecil Raleigh and on lyrics by Arthur Wimperis. The story is about a man who will inherit a soap factory if he doesn't marry for five years. Basil Foster, Phyllis Dare and George Grossmith, Jr. lead. On Feb 13,

1913 the play comes to New York's Knickerbocker Theatre where it wins a 20 week engagement.

Feb 28 *The Monk and the Woman* (L—Lyceum—Drama). Frederick Melville's melodrama features William Lugg as Father Ignatius. It wins 150 performances.

March 5 *Milestones* (L—Royalty—Drama) Arnold Bennett and Edward Knoblauch collaborate on this play about accepting change. Gladys Cooper plays a lead. It runs 607 performances. On Sep 17 the play premieres at New York's Liberty Theatre where it runs for 215 performances.

March 6 *Kipps* (L—Vaudeville—Comedy). H. G. Wells' novel is translated to the stage by Wells and Rudolf Besier. O.B. Clarence and Christine Silver appear.

March 27 *The Yellow Jacket* (L—Duke of York's—Drama). This Chinese fable by George Hazleton and J. Harry Benrimo—with music by William Furst—has 154 performances.

April 11 *The Pink Lady* (L—Globe—Musical). C. M. S. McLelland had adapted this show from its French original, *Le Satyre*, by Berr and Guillemand. Hazel Dawn

and Jean Crane sing. There are 124 performances.

April 11 *At the Barn* (L—Prince of Wales's—Comedy) Anthony P. Wharton's play sing Marie Tempest. There are 181 performances.

May 11 *Princess Caprice* (L—Shaftesbury—Musical). The Leo Fall operetta was originally known as *Der Liebe Augustin*. The British book is by Alex Thompson, with lyrics by Percy Greenbank, A. Scott Craven, and Harry Beswick. Robert Courtneidge produces. Cicely Courtneidge sings with Courtice Pounds, Fred Leslie, Harry Welchman, and Clara Evelyn. There are 265 performances.

May 25 *Autumn Manoevres* (L—Adelphi—Musical). Emmerich Kalman's operetta has a British libretto by Henry Hamilton and lyrics by Percy Greenbank. J.A.E. Malone stages this story about a man dispossessed from his ancestral home. Robert Evett and Phyllis LeGrand are leads.

June 1 *Gipsy Love* (L—Daly's—Musical). Franz Lehar's operetta gets a British libretto from Basil Hood. Sari Petrass plays the headstrong Ilona who deserts her Hussar officer fiance (Webster Millar) for the attractions of the vain gipsy musician, Jozsi (Robert Michaelis). Edward Royce stages for producer George Edwardes, with sets by Joseph Harker and E. H. Ryan. Adrian Ross provides English lyrics for songs such as "The Looking Glass." There are 299 performances.

June 17 *Hindle Wakes* (L—Aldwych—Drama). Stanley Houghton's play features Sybil Thorndike. It wins 108 performances. On Dec 9 it opens in New York at the Maxime Theatre where it runs for only four weeks.

June 17 *Find the Woman* (L—Garrick—Comedy). Charles Klein's four-act play tells the story of a man whose wife clears him of a murder charge. It stars Arthur Bourchier and Violet Vanbrugh. It earns 189 performances.

Aug 12 *Ready Money* (L—New—Comedy). There are 282 performances of James Montgomery's play, with a cast including Allan Aynesworth, Kenneth Douglas, May Whitty, Hilda Anthony, and Dorothy Thomas. In this American play, Aynesworth is a master-counterfeiter who loans some bogus $1,000 bills to a financially pressed young mine-owner (Douglas). The fake money restores confidence in the mine's investors, but leads to the arrest of the counterfiter, whose philosophy is: "For its size, there is nothing that can be seen further from afar than a thousand-dollar note!"

Aug 31 *Little Miss Llewelyn* (L—Vaudeville—Comedy). The French play, *Le Mariage de Mlle. Beulemans*, by Fonson and Wicheler, is the basis for this light entertainment. Hilda Trevelyan stars. There are 192 performances.

Sep 3 *Drake* (L—His Majesty's—Drama). Lyn Harding plays Sir Francis Drake opposite Phyllis Nielson-Terry as Queen Elizabeth. Louis N. Parker's historical epic wins 220 performances.

Sep 5 *The Girl in the Taxi* (L—Lyric—Musical). This production makes Yvonne Arnaud a star. She plays a pretty, flirtatious wife, the winner of an award for virtue, who has come to Paris and promptly finds herself involved with other men than her husband. Arthur Playfair also sings. The melodies of this Palais Royal musical are by Jean Gilbert. Frederick Fenn and Arthur Wimperis have adapted the original text of Georg Okonhowski for British audiences. The Lyric's director, P. Michael Faraday has done the staging. There are 385 performances.

Oct 3 *Doormats* (L—Wyndham's—Comedy). Hubert Henry Davies has a hit with this farce about the experiences of two married couples, in each of which one member is dominant and the other is the "doormat." The cast is headed by Gerald Du Maurier. Marie Löhr and Nina Boucicault are also in the ensemble. It earns 186 performances.

Oct 14 In London at the Duke of York's Theatre, the triple-bill offers Bernard Shaw's "demonstration," *Overruled;* Arthur Wing Pinero's *The Widow of Wasdale Head*, and James M. Barrie's *Rosalind*.

Oct 19 *The Dancing Mistress* (L—Adelphi—Musical). This show, about a lovely young dancing mistress at a fashionable English girls' school, has a score by Lionel Monckton, lyrics by Adrian Ross and Percy Greenbank and book by James Tanner. Gertie Millar stars. J.A.E. Malone stages for producer George Edwardes. It runs 242 performances.

Dec 23 *Hello! Ragtime* (L—Hippodrome—Revue). Taking its title from the popular musical form, the revue runs 451 performances.

Lennox Robinson's new play, *Patriots*, opens with a cast including J. M. Kerrigan, Sara Allgood, Arthur Sinclair, Kathleen Drago, and Fred O'Donovan. On April 15, the play is Joseph Campbell's *Judgement*.

April 22 At Stratford-upon-Avon, the annual Shakespeare Festival opens with *The Merchant of Venice. Antony and Cleopatra* is performed on April 23. Other plays offered are *Henry V, A Midsummer Night's Dream, Hamlet, Romeo and Juliet, Coriolanus, The Taming of the Shew, Julius Caesar, Twelfth Night, Richard III,* Goldsmith's *She Stoops to Conquer*, and Maeterlinck's *Pelleas and Melisande*. Frank Benson and his compnay present the plays.

April 28 At London's Little Theatre, the Adelphi Play Society offers a bill of three short plays: Strindberg's *Miss Julia*, Tolstoi's *The Cause of It All*, and Clifford Bax's *The Poetasters of Ispahan*.

May 1 A French company presents Alexandre Bisson's *L'Heroique le Cardunois*, a three-act comedy, at London's Little Theatre. On May 9, *La Rampe*, by Henri de Rothschild, is presented. On May 20, Alfred Capus' *Les Maris de Leontine* takes the stage.

May 6 Richard Le Gallienne's tragedy, *Orestes*, is produced in London at Kensington's Boudoir Theatre. Edyth Olive and Rathmel Wilson star.

May 6 William A. Brady and the Shuberts revive Gilbert and Sullivan's *Patience* at the Lyric in New York. In June, at the Casino Theatre, they also revive *The Pirates of Penzance, H. M. S. Pinafore*, and *The Mikado*.

May 6 Annie Horniman's Manchester Repertory Company offers Gilbert Cannan's play, *Mary's Wedding*, at London's Coronet Theatre. On May 7, they present J. Sackville Martin's comedy, *A Question of Property*. On May 8, they produce Cannan's *Miles Dixon* and Stanely Houghton's *The Younger Generation*. On May

---

1912   REVIVALS/REPERTORIES

March 11 At the New Prince's Theatre, the Stage Society presents two short plays: August Strindberg's *Creditors* and Hermann Bahr's *The Fool and the Wise Man*. This is the first performance in English of the Strindberg opus.

March 16 With the performance of *King Ahaz*, a Yiddish opera, the new Yiddish Theatre is opened in London's East End. The music-drama is the work of Samuel Alman. On June 5, Israel Zangwill's *The Melting Pot* will be produced.

March 17 Maurice Maeterlinck's *Mary Magdalene* is presented for the first time in England at London's Rehearsal Club Theatre. Pax Robertson and Henry J. Robinson star.

March 19 At London's Kingsway Theatre, Euripides' *Iphigenia in Tauris*, as translated by Gilbert Murray, is produced by Harley Granville Barker.

March 31 Chekhov's *The Seagull* has its London premiere at the Little. Gertrude Kingston, Lawrence Anderson and Lydia Yavorska are featured.

April 9 At London's His Majesty's Theatre, Herbert Tree stars in *Othello*, supported by Lawrence Irving and Phyllis Nielson-Terry. On May 20, *The Merchant of Venice* is the Tree opening production, followed by *Twelfth Night* (May 23) and *Henry VIII* (May 27).

April 11 In Dublin at the Abbey Theatre,

The Perplexed Husband

Sunshine Girl

14, the plays are George Calderon's *The Little Stone House* and Sackville Martin's *Cupid and the Styx*. On May 24, Allan Monkhouse's *Mary Broome* is presented.

June 10 Dublin's Abbey Theatre ensemble comes to London's Royal Court for a season of Irish drama, opening with Lennox Robinson's *Patriots*. On June 20, T. C. Murray's *Maurice Harte* is offered, followed on the 27th, by William Boyle's *Family Failing*. On July 11, W. B. Yeats' *The Countess Cathleen* opens, accompanied by an Irish operetta, *The Rebel*, and a play, *The Hanging Outlook*.

Aug 7 At Stratford-upon-Avon, the summer season of Shakespeare plays begins at the Memorial Theatre with a program including *Othello*, *Henry V*, *Antony and Cleopatra*, *A Midsummer Night's Dream*, *The Merry Wives of Windsor*, Sheridan's *The Rivals*, McCarthy's *If I Were King*, and *The Interlude of Youth*, a medieval morality play, staged by Barry Jackson.

Aug 24 In London's East End, the Pavilion Theatre reopens with Leo Tolstoi's tragedy in six tableaux, *A Living Corpse*. On October 18, a Yiddish opera in four acts, *The Two Savants*, premieres. It is based on Schiller's *Die Raeuber*.

Sep 2 For the first time in England, Jean Marvin's "Romance of the Golden West" is performed at the Opera House, Northampton. Called *The Cow-Puncher*, the play is peopled with such characters as Seattle Ike and Dublin Tim. On September 16, Prairie Joe and Great Hawk take the stage in Manchester at the King's Theatre, in Mrs. F. G. Kimberley's *The Prairie Outlaw*.

Sep 21 At London's Savoy Theatre, *The Winter's Tale* comes to life again, with Henry Ainley as the jealous King Leontes.

Nov 8 At London's Court Theatre, Mary Morrison's translation of Gerhart Hauptmann's *Lonely Lives* is staged, with Clarence Derwent. On November 11, Henrik Ibsen's *Brand* has its first British production.

Nov 11 Annie Russell and her Old English Comedy Company revive Oliver Goldsmith's *She Stoops To Conquer* in New York at the 39th Street Theatre. This is played in repertory with *Much Ado About Nothing* and Sheridan's *The Rivals*.

Nov 15 At London's Savoy Theatre, Harley Granville Barker unveils his attractively stylized production of *Twelfth Night*, featuring his wife, Lillah McCarthy as Viola. Designer Norman Wilkinson's sets are praised for subtle use of colors as well as elegant simplicity. B. W. Findon, in *Play Pictorial* calls it: "A performance of sheer delight, wonder and surprise."

Nov 21 In Dublin, the company of the Abbey Theatre premieres Lady Gregory's *Damer's Gold* and W. B. Yeats' *The Hour Glass*.

Dec 26 In London's heart and its outer regions, many pantomimes open on this Boxing Day, except for the Kingsway Theatre, which revives Bernard Shaw's *John Bull's Other Island*. Pantomimes include *Cinderella* (Prince's, Wimbledon, Coronet), *Aladdin* (Broadway, West London, Brixton, Marlborough, Kennington), *Mother Goose* (Borough, Woolwich Opera House), *Forty Thieves* (Lyceum), *The Sleeping Beauty* (Drury Lane), *The Magic Bell* (London Opera House), *Wonderful Grandmother* (Manchester Gaiety), *Fifinella* (Liverpool Repertory), and *A Little Christmas Miracle* (Dublin Abbey Theatre).

1912 BIRTHS/DEATHS/DEBUTS

April 22 Comedians Ed Gallagher and Al Shean make their debut in *The Rose Maid* at New York's Globe Theatre. Shean's nephews, The Marx Brothers, will later win stardom.

May 26 Playwright Henry Ephron is born in New York City.

May 30 Actor Hugh Griffith is born in Anglesey, North Wales.

June 21 Mary McCarthy is born in Seattle, Washington.

July 24 Theatre-designer and engineering consultant George Izenour is born in New Brighton, Pennsylvania.

Aug 8 Daniel Manor is born in Brooklyn, N.Y.

Aug 15 Actress Wendy Hiller is born in Bramhall, Cheshire, England.

Nov 13 Playwright Eugene Ionesco is born in Slatina, Romania.

Dec 16 English actor-manager George Rignold is dead at age 74. Rignold became famous as a producing manager in Australia in the 1880s. He also made a name with his spectacular Shakespearean productions at Her Majesty's Theatre in Sydney, which he opened in 1886. Marc Antony, Bottom, Master Ford, Macbeth, and Othello were among Rignold's notable roles.

1912 THEATERS/PRODUCTIONS

In Britain patents are granted for: T. R. Barrett's scenic system of a treadmill between railroad tracks, with the end coach of a train protruding from the wings and a moving scenic panorama behind, so an actor will seem to be running to catch the train; G. Bennie's stage-ship, mounted on rockers, so it will seem to roll and pitch in a storm; N. Linton's rain-effect, with tinsel outside a window agitated and illuminated; R. C. Oldham and S. T. Skinner's system of constructing scenic flats with detachable canvas, so one frame may be used for various scenes in the same production, and so there will be less chance of tearing the fabric or damaging the painting in transit or storage. The popularity of melodramas, spectacles, and stage realism are the direct stimuli for the detailed special effects being patented in this and the past decade.

In the U.S. Alden McMurtry patents a device which makes sparks jump from one part of a performer's body to another. Daniel Troy devises a costume made of fluorescent material, overlaid with ordinary material, so that it will seem to change when put under ultra-violet light. John C. Spikes' idea has musical instruments either concealed or built into the props and furniture of a meat-market stage-setting.

The Authors League of America is formed by a group of writers seeking to act in concert to protect rights of book and magazine writers.

Joseph Urban, a designer from Austria, opens the Urban Scenic Studio in New York City. Urban introduces new scene painting techniques such as a pointillist method of scene-painting and the use of dyes to create a more transluscent drop.

From 1852 up to this year, 19,304 "stage plays" have been submitted to the Lord Chamberlain's Office for licensing for public performance. In this time, only 103 scripts have been denied approval.

Jan The Lord Chamberlain denies a permit for public performance to Israel Zangwill's *The Next Religion*. Among the offenses are such lines as: "The real Good Friday would be that which brought the cure for cancer." This month, in addition to his long-standing function of licensing plays for public performance, the Lord Chamberlain begins to censor and license plays or sketches for performance in music-halls within his area of competence.

Jan 2 The Toy Theatre in Boston, Massachusetts opens its doors for its initial performance. On the bill are: *Two Out of Time* by Oliver Hereford; *In His House* by George Middleton; and *Press Cuttings* by George Bernard Shaw. The theatre is a converted stable seating 130 people. The group was founded by Jane Gale.

Jan 18 The cast of the Abbey Theatre's Dublin production of Synge's *The Playboy of the Western World* is arrested in Philadelphia, Pennsylvania, for performing "immoral or indecent plays."

Feb Eden Phillpotts' first play, based on his popular novel, *The Secret Woman*, is in rehearsal in London at the Kingsway Theatre. Despite this fact, the Lord Chamberlain threatens to refuse a performance license unless the playwright removes offensive lines, however, Chamberlain declines to reveal which lines may not be heard by British audiences.

March 12 The Little Theatre opens on West 44 Street in New York City. The theatre, built by Winthrop Ames for experimental works, has only 299 seats. The limited number of seats ensures financial difficulties for a playhouse in the Broadway area.

April 1 Chicago has a new theatre. It is the Palace Music Hall, with 1,500 seats. Later its name will be changed to the Erlanger Theatre. In 1962, it will be razed.

May 1 The Pittsburgh Academy burns at a loss of $50,000. The Theatre has been used as a burlesque house and was to be closed anyway.

May 29 The *NY Dramatic Mirror*, counting the past Broadway season tallies a total of 400 productions in Broadway and other New York theatres. Of these, 163 have been new productions. 62 have had more than 50 showings; 35 have passed the 100-mark, and 9 have had more than 200 performances. In *Best Plays*, authors Mantle and Sherwood, using a base of 45 Broadway playhouses, offer a breakdown of productions as follows: 51 dramas, 40 comedies, 33 musicals, 3 revues, 6 operas, 5 operettas, 2 Shakespearean revivals, and 4 repertory offerings.

June More than 60 playwrights, along with other theatre folk, have now signed a petition to the King, protesting continuation of censorship of plays by the Lord Chamberlain and his aides.

Aug 12 The 48th Street Theatre in New York opens with the production, *Just Like John*. In 1937, the theatre is renamed the Windsor, and leased to Labor Stage, under the auspices of the International Ladies Garment Workers Union. In 1943, the theatre reverts to its original name. In 1944, the Pulitzer Prize winner *Harvey*, by Mary Chase, opens and runs for four years. In 1955, after the theatre is severely damaged by the collapse of a water-tower atop its roof, it is torn down.

Sep 11 The Eltinge Theatre, at 236 West 42nd Street in New York, presents its first production, *Within the Law*. Producer Al H. Woods names the theatre for one of his stars, Julian Eltinge, a popular female impersonator. During the Depression, Woods loses his theatre. In the 1930's, it serves briefly as a burlesques house, but is soon converted to a motion-picture house called the Empire.

Sep 16 In the Earl's Court Exhibition Hall, *A Posy on a Ring* is produced in the "Olde Globe Theatre," designed by the noted architect Edward Lutyens. The play is a tabloid version of Thomas Middleton's comedy, *A Chaste Maid in Cheapside*. Theatre and play are part of a round of festivities—including dinners and balls with guests in Shakespearean character costumes—titled "Shakespeare's England." A prime-mover in these activities, designed to raise money for a National Theatre, is the American-born Jennie Jerome, mother of Winston Churchill and widow of Randolph Churchill. She is also a playwright.

Oct 15 After a brief closing for construction of a balcony and demolition of the seven original boxes, London's Little Theatre re-opens with *Captain Brassbound's Conversion*.

Dec 20 The Cort Theatre, on West 48 Street in New York, owned by West Coast theatre-operator John Cort and designed by Edward B. Corey, opens with J. Hartley Manners' *Peg o' My Heart*. Considered a "lucky house," it shelters many hit shows, including *Merton of the Movies*, *Room Service*, *Sunrise at Campobello*, *The Shrike*, and *The Diary of Anne Frank*. In the early 1970's, it is used by CBS as the TV home for the "Merv Griffin Show," but returns to presenting dramas.

Gipsy Love

Jan 8 *A Good Little Devil* (NY—Republic—Comedy). Austin Strong has adapted the script from the French of Rosemonde Gerard and Maurice Rostand. Mary Pickford and Lillian Gish are in the ensemble. It earns 131 performances.

Jan 11 *Joseph and His Brethern* (NY—Century—Drama). Louis N. Parker adapts this biblical tale with James O'Neill and Franklyn Pangborn in the leads. It runs 121 performances. On Sep 2 it opens at London's His Majesty's with Beerbohm Tree and George Relph. There are 154 performances.

Feb 6 *The Honeymoon Express* (NY—Winter Garden—Musical). This comedy about an attempt to reunite a bride with her new spouse stars Al Jolson and Gaby Deslys. Fanny Brice and Harry Fox are also in the cast. The show runs for 158 performances.

Feb 10 *Romance* (NY—Maxine Elliott—Drama). Edward Sheldon's sentimental plot tells of a young man, destined to become a bishop, who loves an opera star. Doris Keane stars. It enjoys a 21-week run.

March 3 *The American Maid* (NY—Broadway—Musical). John Philips Sousa's last attempt on Broadway, this show is a reworking of his 1893 unproduced work, *The Glass Blowers*. The hero is now a Spanish-American War veteran. Films of combat sequences are shown, accompanied by Sousa marches. It runs two weeks.

March 14 *Damaged Goods* (NY—Fulton—Drama). Eugene Brieux's controversial play about venereal disease is given one matinee performance by producer-actors Richard Bennett, Wilton Lackaye, Margaret Wycherly and Laura Burt. It attracts so much interest that it begins a regular run a month later, tallying 66 performances.

April 7 *The Purple Road* (NY—Liberty—Musical). Valli Valli plays Wanda, who, unsuspecting, is wooed and won by a disguised Napoleon (Harrison Brockbank). This book and lyrics are by de Gresac and Duncan, with score by Reinhardt and Peters. There are 136 performances.

June 5 *All Aboard* (NY—44th Street Roof Garden—Musical). This is Lew Fields' summer special, with Fields as a seedy sailor who dreams of an evening full of vaudeville acts.

June 16 *The Ziegfeld Follies of 1913* (NY—New Amsterdam—Revue). Ann Pennington's dancing talents are unveiled for *Follies* audiences. Suffragettes are spoofed—in ragtime.

July 24 *The Passing Show of 1913* (NY—Winter Garden—Revue). The frame of this revue is the visit of Peg o' My Heart to Broadway, involving her in parodies of currently popular shows. In the company are John Charles Thomas, Edward Begley, and Charlotte Greenwood. Harold Atteridge provides script and lyrics for the score of Jean Schwartz and A. W. Brown.

Aug 16 *Potash and Perlmutter* (NY—Cohan—Comedy). Based on a series of *Saturday Evening Post* dialect stories, this dramatization by Montague Glass runs for 441 performances. Alexander Carr and Barney Bernard star. On April 14, 1914 the show premieres at London's Queen's Theatre with Robert Leonard and Augustus Yorke in the leads. It runs 665 performances.

Aug 19 *Believe Me, Zantipee* (NY—39th Street—Comedy). This play by Frederick Ballard wins the Harvard Prize. In the cast are John Barrymore and Henry Hull. It runs 10 weeks.

Aug 21 *The Family Cupboard* (NY—Playhouse—Drama). Owen Davis's play is staged by John Cromwell. William Morris, Alice Brady and Irene Fenwick are featured. It has 140 performances.

Aug 28 *Adele* (NY—Longacre—Musical). Paul Herve's book and Jean Briquet's score are reworked by Adolf Philipp and Edward A. Paulton. Georgia Caine, Natalie Alt, and Hal Forde animate a plot about a French girl who falls in love with the son of her father's business rival. There are 196 performances.

Aug 30 *America* (NY—Hippodrome—Musical). Someone is trying to steal the plans to the Panama Canal! The chase runs through a number of impressive scenic effects. The 360-performance run is a disappointment, a falling-off from previous years of two-a-day presentations.

Sep 4 *The Temperamental Journey* (NY—Belasco—Comedy). Leo Ditrichstein adapts *Pour Vivre Hereux* for American audiences. He plays Jacques Dupont. Josephine Victor and Cora Witherspoon are also in this Belasco production. There are 124 performances.

Sep 8 *Sweethearts* (NY—New Amsterdam—Musical). Still another Victor Herbert musical. The book tells the romantic tale of a princess who recovers her throne and wins her love. Christine MacDonald is Sylvia, a part with its near two-octave range that is created for her. Herbert's score, especially in the quality of its orchestration, rises to the level of grand opera at times, says the *Tribune*.

Sep 22 *Seven Keys to Baldpate* (NY—Astor—Comedy). Based on Earl Derr Biggers' novel, this comedy thriller by George M. Cohan stars Wallace Eddinger. It runs for 320 performances.

Sep 25 *Half an Hour* (NY—Lyceum—Comedy). James Barrie's play about a

Romance

woman who must retrieve a letter announcing she is going to leave her husband stars Grace George.

Nov 10 *The Little Cafe* (NY—New Amsterdam—Musical). Based on Tristan Bernard's French farce, this show has a score by Ivan Caryll. It is about a waiter who falls in love with a demi-mondaine but eventually marries a nice girl. Hazel Dawn sings. The show runs for 144 performances.

Nov 11 *The Madcap Duchess* (NY—Globe—Musical). This period piece permits its wild teen-age duchess heroine (Ann Swinburne) to assume various disguises in pursuit of her prince (Glenn Hall). Victor Herbert provides a delicate score. David Stevens and Justin H. McCarthy have based the book and lyrics on McCarthy's best-seller *Seraphica*, the show runs only for 71 performances.

Nov 19 *Grumpy* (NY—Wallack's—Comedy). Cyril Maude stars in this story of a lawyer who comes out of retirement to solve a crime. The show, with script by Horace Hodges and T. Wigney Percival, runs 181 performaces. On May 13, 1914 it premieres at London's New Theatre with Maude again in the lead. It runs 151 performances.

Nov 25 *The Misleading Lady* (NY—Fulton—Drama). Charles Goddard and Paul Dickey write this story of a woman who tricks a man into proposing marriage just for a joke. It runs 183 performances. On Sep 6, 1916 the show premieres at London's Playhouse Theatre with Gladys Cooper in the cast. In has a 239 performance run.

Dec 8 *The Things That Count* (NY—Maxine Elliott—Drama). John Cromwell stages a cast which includes Edna Wallace Hopper, Wallace Erskine, and Alice Brady. William A. Brady produces. The production wins 224 performances.

Dec 10 *High Jinks* (NY—Lyric—Musical). With a thin plot based on Leo Ditrichstein's 1905 success, *Before and After*, the real interest in the show is the Rudolf Friml score. The music suggests operetta, but the events suggest a series of vaudeville turns. Manna Zucca and Burrell Barbaretto play in this Arthur Hammerstein production, which has 213 performances.

Dec 23 *The Secret* (NY—Belasco—Drama). Henri Bernstein's French play is produced and directed by David Belasco. Frances Starr, Robert Warwick, and Basil

Gill lead. It runs for 143 performances.

Dec 25 *The Land of Promise* (NY—Lyceum—Drama). W. Somerset Maugham's play features Billie Burke, Lumsden Hare and Lillian Kingsbury. It runs 76 performances.

Dec 30 *The Philanderer* (NY—Little—Comedy). A Winthrop Ames production, the direction of the show is credited to its author, George Bernard Shaw, and Harley Granville Barker. Charles Maude, Reginald Besant, and Mary Lawton are in the company.

1913 BRITISH PREMIERES

Jan 9 *General John Regan* (L—Apollo—Comedy). This Irish comedy is about an American visitor (Henry Wenham) to an Irish village who convinces the rest into erecting a monument to a non-existent native. Charles Hawtrey stars with Cathleen Nesbit. Although credited to "George A. Birmingham," the play has actually been written by a novice Irish playwright, the Rev. J. O. Hannay. It earns 275 performances.

Jan 18 *Turandot, Princess of China* (L—St. James's—Drama). Jethro Bithell adapts the German text with music by Ferruccio Busoni. Evelyn D'Alroy stars in this imposing production which is called "unprecedented" by some critics.

Jan 22 *The Headmaster* (L—Playhouse—Comedy). There are 164 performances for this play by W. T. Coleby and Edward Knoblauch. Cyril Maude stars.

March 22 Tonight at London's Drury Lane

Seven Keys to Baldpate

Theatre, which he helped open in 1889, Johnston Forbes-Robertson opens his farewell season, playing opposite his wife, Gertrude Elliott. The play is *Hamlet*. On March 24, they play Jerome K. Jerome's *The Passing of the Third Floor Back* and *The Sacrament of Judas*, adapted by Louis N. Parker from the French. On March 31, the play is *The Light That Failed*, based on Kipling's novel by adapter George Fleming. *Mice and Men*, by Madeleine Lucette Ryley is revived on April 7, followed by Bernard Shaw's *Caesar and Cleopatra* on April 14; *The Merchant of Venice*, on May 5, and *Othello*, on May 19.

March 25 *The Great Adventure* (L—Kingsway—Comedy). Arnold Bennett's story about a painter who masquerades as his valet to protect his privacy has a cast including Henry Ainley, Clarence Derwent and Guy Rathbone. It runs 673 performances.

April 2 *Typhoon* (L—Haymarket—Drama). Melchoir Lengyel's four-act Hungarian epic deals with "the conflict over old traditions of the Orient and new western concepts of morality." Laurence Irving, Claude Rains and Mabel Hackney lead. There are 204 performances.

April 5 *The Girl on the Film* (L—Gaiety—Musical). James Tanner adapts the German libretto of Bernauer and Schanzer. Adrian Ross provides lyrics for music by Walter Killo, Willy Bredschneider, and Albert Sirmay. Emmy Whelen plays as the girl who takes over for the star who walks out on the film. The show runs 232 performances.

May 17 *The Marriage Market* (L—Daly's—Musical). Gladys Unger adapts this Brody and Martos libretto. Victor Jacobi's score has lyrics by Adrian Ross and Arthur Anderson. The thin plot involves an heiress who wants to join the cowboys' mock auction of young ladies to meet the son of her father's enemy. The show wins 423 performances.

May 22 *Croesus* (L—Garrick—Drama). Henri de Rothschild's play stars actor-manager Arthur Bourchier.

May 24 *Within the Law* See NY premiere, 1912.

May 28 *Oh, I Say!* (L—Criterion—Comedy). This French farce, adapted by Sydney Blow and Douglas Hoare, tells of an embarrassed groom who discovers the apartment he's taken for the honeymoon actually belongs to an old flame. James Welch and Sybil De Bray lead. The show wins 288 performances.

July 17 *The Barrier* (L—Strand—Drama). Philip Hubbard adapts Rex Beach's novel. The title refers to the taboo against marriage between a white man and a girl of the Alaskan wilderness who is half white, half Indian. Matheson Lang stars and also directs.

Aug 28 *The Picture of Dorian Gray* (L—Vaudeville—Drama). Oscar Wilde's novel is translated to the stage in three acts and a prologue, by G. Constant Lounsbery, with Lou Tellegen as Gray.

Sep 1 *Androcles and the Lion* (L—St. James's—Drama). George Bernard Shaw's play, based on the classic fable, has O. P. Heggie, Edward Sillward and Leon Quartermaine. *The Times* reports that it is "all good fun... and not peculiarly and quintessentially Shavian fun."

Sep 6 *The Ever Open Door* (L—Aldwych—Drama). There are 156 showings of this four-act "drama of London life," by George Sims and H. H. Herbert.

Sep 11 *Sealed Orders* (L—Drury Lane—Drama). This fall's Drury Lane melodrama of blackmail is crafted by Cecil Raleigh and Henry Hamilton for manager Arthur Collins. C. M. Hallard stars. There are 160 repetitions.

Sep 13 *Never Say Die* (L—Apollo—Comedy). W. H. Post's farce about a man who is given a month to live stars Charles Hawtrey. There are 216 showings.

Sep 16 *The Fugitive* (L—Court—Drama). John Galsworthy's new four-act play opens with a cast including Nigel Playfair and Estelle Winwood.

Sep 18 *Mary Goes First* (L—Playhouse—Comedy). Henry Arthur Jones' play has Marie Tempest in the lead. It earns 152 performances.

Sep 25 *The Pearl Girl* (L—Shaftesbury—Musical). Basil Hood's book has music by Hugo Felix and Howard Talbot. The story is of a girl who impersonates a millionairess. Cecily Courtneidge and Harry Welchman star. The show runs 245 performances.

Oct 18 *The Girl from Utah* (L—Adelphi—Musical). With Sidney Jones, James Tanner, Adrian Ross and Percy Greenbank, Paul Rubens writes music, plot and verse for this show. It is staged by J. E. A. Malone for George Edwardes. Ina Claire stars as the Utah girl pursued by a polygamous Mormon. The show runs 105 performances. On Aug 24, 1914, it reaches New York's Knickerbocker Theatre with Julia Sanderson in the lead. The show has 120 performances.

Nov 4 *The Pursuit of Pamela* (L—Royalty—Comedy). C. B. Fernald's play earns 123 performances, with Gladys Cooper in the lead.

Nov 13 *Great Catherine* (L—Vaudeville—Comedy). George Bernard Shaw's satiric sketch on Russian Court life in the XVIII century opens with Gertrude Kingston and Edmond Breon in the leads.

Nov 22 *Who's the Lady?* (L—Garrick—Comedy). José Levy adapts the French farce by Henniquin and Veber, *Madame la Présidente,* for producer Louis Meyer.

Gaby Deslys stars. There are 180 performances.

Nov 29 *Mr. Wu* (L—Strand—Drama). This play, by Harry Vernon and Harold Owen tells story is about a Chinese merchant whose daughter is seduced by the son of a British merchant. Matheson Lang stars. There are 408 performances.

Dec 23 *Hullo! Tango* (L—Hippodrome—Revue). The Hippodrome celebrates the holidays with a new revue. It wins 485 performances, with two-a-day performances.

Wales's Theatre.

May 12 From their home in Manchester at the Gaiety Theatre, Annie Horniman's repertory players come to London's Royal Court for a season, opening with Galsworthy's *The Pigeon* and Casey's *More Respectable.* On May 15, they offer *The Whispering Well,* by Frank Rose; on May 19, St. John Ervine's *Jane Clegg* Calderon's *The Little Stone House,* and Björnson's *The Newly-Married Couple;* on May 22, Masefield's *The Tragedy of Nan;* on May 26, Housman and Barker's *Prunella* and Chapin's *Elaine.*

May 16 At the Liverpool Repertory Theatre, a double-bill is produced: J. S. M. Tombs' *Emily* and John Reynolds' *Pauline.*

May 27 W. Somerset Maugham adapts Moliere's *Le Bourgeois Gentilhomme* for British audiences as *The Perfect Gentleman.* Herbert Tree and Phyllis Nielson-Terry play. On June 9, Tree revives *The Merchant of Venice.* On June 16, the play is *Twelfth Night* with Tree as Malvolio. On June 23, Tree plays Marcus Antonius in *Julius Caesar.* He is Mercutio in *Romeo and Juliet* on June 30.

June 2 From Dublin's Abbey Theatre come the players of the Irish National Theatre Society to perform St. John Ervine's *The Magnanimous Lover,* at London's Court Theatre. On June 12, they offer scenes from Moliere's *The Miser;* on the 28th, George Fitzmaurice's *The Magic Glasses* and his *The Country Dressmaker;* on June 30, the play is R. G. Ray's *The Gombeen Man.* On July 10, they perform Radbindranath Tagore's two-act play, *The Post Office.*

June 4 Mrs Patrick Campbell stars in George Alexander's revival of Arthur Wing Pinero's *The Second Mrs. Tanqueray* at London's St. James's.

June 9 At London's New Theatre, a French season opens with *L'Habit Vert,* by de Flers and de Caillavet. Jeanne Granier heads the cast. On June 23, Henri Bernstein's *Le Secret* is performed.

Aug 2 The summer season of Shakespeare's plays in Stratford-upon-Avon at the Memorial Theatre opens with *The Merchant of Venice,* followed by *As You Like It, Hamlet, King John, Richard II, The Merry Wives of Windsor, Much Ado About Nothing, Romeo and Juliet, The Taming of the Shrew, Twelfth Night, Henry IV, Part 2,* Bulwer-Lytton's *Richelieu,* John Masefield's *The Tragedy of Pompey the Great,* and Shaw's *The Devil's Disciple.* The Norwich Players offer *The Drama of Job* and the Dunmow Players present *The Tinker's Wedding.*

Aug 4 In Manchester at the Gaiety Theatre, the repertory company introduces Lord Dunsany's *The Lost Silk Hat.* On Aug 11, the company presents Lechmere Worrall's *Other People's Babies* and R. Murray Gilchrist's *The Moor Gates.* On Aug 18, *The Death of Chopin* by Leonard

1913   REVIVALS/REPERTORIES

Jan 20 British interest in Western America focuses on three groups: Red Indians, Cowboys, and Mormons. Tonight, at the Theatre Royal, Woolwich, the play is Edwin George's *At the Mercy of the Mormons.*

Jan 23 Dublin's Abbey Theatre presents G. Sidney Paternoster's *The Dean of St. Patrick's,* about Dean Jonathan Swift.

Feb 1 At the Gaiety Theatre in Manchester, Annie Horniman's repertory ensemble opens *Westward Ho!,* adapted by Peggy Webling from Charles Kingsley's novel.

Feb 13 Laurence Irving stars in William Archer's translation of Henrick Ibsen's *The Pretenders.* It is given at London's Haymarket Theatre.

Feb 15 The Birmingham Repertory Company, under the directorship of Barry Jackson, opens its first season with *Twelfth Night.*

March 10 The Stage Society presents a Schnitzler double-bill at London's Aldwych Theatre: *Comtesse Mitzi* and *The Green Cockatoo.* H. A. Hertz translates the first; Penelope Wheeler, the second.

March 14 Under Holbrook Blinn's direction, the Princess Players offer a repertory of one-act plays at New York's Princess Theatre. Works of William C. deMille, Edward Ellis, and Edgar Wallace are presented.

March 22 In Manchester at the Gaiety Theatre, Annie Horniman's repertory company premiere Frank Rose's *The Whispering Well,* with music by J. H. Foulds. Sybil Thorndike is in the cast.

March 22 At London's Prince's Theatre, E. Harcourt Williams and Lillian Hallows play the young lovers in *Romeo and Juliet.*

March 31 Max Reinhardt's spectacular production of *The Miracle* opens at the Liverpool Olympia. Patricia Bostock and Bertha Clifton star.

April 21 At Stratford-upon-Avon, the annual Shakespeare Festival opens with *Richard II. Henry IV, Part 2* is presented on April 23. Other productions by Frank Benson's company include *Henry V, Richard III, Much Ado About Nothing, As You Like It, Hamlet,* Sheridan's *The Rivals,* Shaw's *The Devil's Disciple,* and William Poel's production of *Troilus and Cressida,* featuring him, Edith Evans, and Hermione Gingold. In this four-week season, the Birmingham Repertory offers its production of *The Silver Box.* The students of Stratford's King Edward VI Grammar School present their staging of *Henry V.*

April 21 At Manchester's Gaiety, Annie Horniman's repertory company presents St. John Ervine's *Jane Clegg,* with Sybil Thorndike in the title role.

April 21 William A. Brady and the Shuberts begin a series of Casino Theatre revivals of Gilbert and Sullivan comic operas: *The Mikado, H. M. S. Pinafore,* and *Iolanthe.*

April 24 In Dublin the Abbey Theatre presents *Broken Faith* and *The Magic Glasses.*

May 4 The Mountain Play Association begins presenting original plays as well as famous favorites every summer in Mount Tamalpais, Marin County, California.

May 10 John Martin Harvey stars in his production of *The Taming of the Shrew* and on June 10 he plays in Edward Knoblauch's *The Faun* at London's Prince of

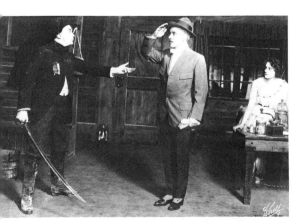

Misleading Lady

Marriage Market

Inkster premieres. On the 25, they perform an adaptation of John Fletcher's *The Elder Brother*.

Aug 30 The Birmingham Repertory Theatre opens its second season with Shaw's *You Never Can Tell*. On Sep 20, they perform *The Death of Tintagiles* and *A Farewell Performance*. On Nov 11, Gilbert Murray's translation of Euripides' *Medea* is staged.

Sep 1 Charles Frohman revives *Much Ado About Nothing* at the New York Empire. John Drew, Laura Hope Crews, Mary Boland, and Frank Kemble Cooper play.

Sep 1 In Manchester at the Gaiety Theatre, the repertory is enlarged with *Wind o' the Moors*, by L. du Garde Peach. On Sep 15, Laura Walker acts in Eva Lewes' *Mary Latimer, Nun*. John Turner's one-act play, *Account Rendered*, opens on Sep 22, paired with Eden Phillpotts' *Hiatus* and Elizabeth Baker's *The Price of Thomas Scott*, with Brember Wills as Scott and Sybil Thorndike as Annie Scott. On the 29, Thorndike plays in Allan Monkhouse's *Nothing Like Leather*. On Oct 6 Eden Phillpotts' *The Shadow* opens and on the 13, *Julius Caesar*. On Nov 28, H. M. Richardson's *The Awakening Woman* is on view.

Sep 22 E. H. Sothern and Julia Marlowe come to the Manhattan Opera House to play some of their Shakespeare repertory, with Justin Huntley McCarthy's *If I Were King* added.

Sep 27 Under Holbrook Blinn's direction, the *Princess Players* open their second season at the Princess Theatre in New York. George Jean Nathan's *The Eternal Mystery* is in the repertory. Other plays include: *The Black Mask, The Bride, En Deshabille, Russia, Felice, A Pair of White Gloves, Fear, Hari-Kari, The Neglected Lady, The Hard Man, The Kiss in the Dark, The Fountain,* and *It Can Be Done.*

Sep 29 Johnston Forbes-Robertson and Gertrude Elliott bring a program of revivals to the Shubert Theatre in New York for three months. In addition—*Hamlet, Othello, The Merchant of Venice*—the large ensemble also performs Shaw's *Caesar and Cleopatra* and such dramas as *The Light That Failed, Mice and Men,* and *The Passing of the Third Floor Back.*

Oct 22 At the Liverpool Repertory Theatre, Eden Phillpott's *The Mother* premieres. On Nov 19 the company presents *The Game*, by Harold Brighouse.

Nov 20 In Dublin at the Abbey Theatre, St. John Ervine's *The Critics; Or, a New Play at the Abbey Theatre* is presented.

Dec 1 John Pollack adapts Tolstoi's *Anna Karenina* at London's Ambassador's Theatre. Lydia Yavorska plays the lead.

Dec 26 It's Boxing Day and time for Christmas pantomimes to open all over Britain. At London's Playhouse Theatre, Frances Hodgson Burnett's *Little Lord Fauntleroy* is revived. At the Savoy Theatre, the production treat is *Alice in Wonderland. A Midsummer Night's Dream* is at the Coronet Theatre. *Peter Pan* is again at the Duke of York's Theatre.

Dec 26 At London's Shaftesbury Theatre, *Henry V* is played by Frank Benson and his troupe. There are also revivals of *Raffles* (Wyndham's) and *Charley's Aunt* (Prince of Wales's).

1913 BIRTHS/DEATHS/DEBUTS

Jan 8 Stage and screen actress Lillian Gish makes her New York debut as Marjanie in the 3-act fairy play, *A Good Little Devil*, by Rosemonde Gerard and Maurice Rostand, at the Republic Theatre. Gish comes to Broadway after numerous cross-country tours beginning at age five in 1904.

Jan 18 Danny Kaye, actor-comedian-conductor, is born David Daniel Kominski in Brooklyn, N.Y.

March 22 Karl Malden is born Mladew Sekulovich in Chicago, Illinois.

March 26 Winston Churchill's mother, formerly Lady Randolph Churchill and now Mrs. George Cornwallis-West, offers her four-act play, *The Bill*, for audiences at Glasgow's Royalty Theatre.

May 4 Future playwright Carroll Moore is born in Somerville, Mass.

June 7 N. Richard Nash is born Nathaniel Richard Nusbaum in Philadelphia.

June 16 American actress Della Fox (b. 1872) dies.

July 10 British actor-playwright Aubrey Boucicault (b. 1869), a member of a distinguished theatre family with roots in Ireland is dead.

Sep 25 Harry Gabriel Pelissier dies at age 39. The noted English actor, composer, and producer originated the Apollo Theatre's successful *Pelissier Follies* which had their beginnings at English seaside resorts. He was the first husband of actress Fay Compton.

Oct 28 Director-actor-producer-playwright Peter Glenville is born in London.

Nov 24 American actor Edmund Milton Holland (b. 1848) dies in New York City. Holland was with Joseph Jefferson in the first New York production of *Rip Van Winkle*, and as E. Milton, became a member of Wallack's company where he stayed for 13 years, later reverting to his family name. He had just joined Belasco's company. His father was the English actor, George Holland.

Nov 25 Director-producer-playwright George Abbott makes his stage debut as Babe Merrill in *The Misleading Lady*, by Charles Goddard and Paul Dickey, at the Fulton Theatre in New York.

Dec 1 Mary Martin is born in Weatherford, Texas.

Dec 11 English dramatist (William) Stanley Houghton is dead at age 32. Houghton is considered the best of the so-called Manchester School of realistic playwrights, much influenced by Ibsen.

In Britain this year patents are granted for: Langdon McCormick's scenic illusion of a train coming toward the audience from a distance; McCormick's approaching train, seen by night, in which moving panoramas of tracks on each side divide to reveal more and more of an engine front, whose headlight has an iris which makes the light seem to come ever closer; McCormick's effect of a ship approaching or sailing away; McCormick's illusion of a tree burning. This has been a big year for Langdon McCormick, and these aren't all his theatre patents this time round.

In the U.S. George Kunkel and George Williams patent a system of knock-down stage-flats, with detachable canvas surfaces and folding frames. Director-playwright Richard Walton Tully patents his volcano-effect, used in his spectacle *Bird of Paradise*. Alden McMurtry devises an effect of a large sheet of music on which electrical sparks light up each printed note when that note is played by performers. The Actor's Fidelity League (AFL) is founded in New York. The league is an independent organization of actors advocating freedom for the individual "consistent with the square deal." Some actors disparage the group as tools of the theatre managers calling them "fidos."

Jan 23 Built for the comedy team Weber and Fields, the Weber and Fields Music Hall, on West 44th Street in New York, opens with *The Man with Three Wives*. The Shuberts soon take possession of the building and rename it the 44th Street Theatre. The building also houses a basement café and a roof theatre, which presents small-scale revues, musicals, and plays. In 1945, the building is purchased by the *NY Times*, and demolished to make way for an extension to the newspaper's plant.

Feb Abe Erlanger and Lee Shubert make a kind of peace in the theatre war in four cities where they own or control competing theatres: Chicago, St. Louis, Boston, and Philadelphia. Harmful competition will be reduced by regulating the number of attractions booked in each city and the number of theatres available for performance. This agreement does not, however, affect theatres in New York or other major American cities.

March 14 *Damaged Goods*, Eugene Brieux's French drama about the spread of venereal disease, banned in Britain, cannot find a Broadway producer. Today's special matinee has been made possible by the sponsorship of Wilton Lackaye, Richard Bennett, and others, with Edward L. Bernays, co-editor of *The Medical Review of Reviews*, as its director. There is clerical protest, followed by a second matinee of March 17. Finally, in April, public performance are permitted.

May In London, theatre and music critics join forces to form The Critics' Circle, affiliated with the Institute of Journalists. The organization is to further professional interests in the performing arts, as well as to foster social intercourse.

May 1 The Longacre Theatre, on West 48th Street in New York, built by baseball magnate H. H. Frazee and designed by Henry B. Herts, opens with the production of *Are You A Crook?* by William J. Hurlbut and Frances Whitehouse. It presents many musical comedies, melodramas, and the avant-garde drama *Rhinoceros*. It survives a decade as a radio and television playhouse from 1943–53, to return to legitimate theatre productions.

May 3 The last performance on the stage of the old Chicago Opera House, designed by Cobb and Frost and opened in 1885, takes place today.

May 20 American composer W. Legrand Howland's first play, *Deborah*, has its world premiere at the Princess Theatre in Toronto, Canada. The theme of the play is expressed in the line "Every woman, married or single, has the right to motherhood." The local censor asks that the word "single" be removed, but even this is not enough for a group of concerned citizens called The Committee of Forty, who insist that the cast be charged with performing an immoral stage performance. Box office receipts go up 100% before the week is out, and the judge decides the play is indeed moral.

May 26 Actor's Equity Association (AEA) is founded. AEA is the labor union that negotiates minimum conditions and enforces members' contracts for all professional performers in the legitimate theatre in the U. S.

June 5 The Ambassadors Theatre, just off Shaftesbury Avenue in London, opens with Monckton Hoffe's play, *Panthea*. W.G.R. Sprague has designed the theatre, capacity 453, and Durrant Swan is the manager. The stalls of the theatre are below ground level to accommodate height restrictions because of low-standing neighboring buildings.

June 18 Today the *New York Dramatic Mirror* prints its accounting of the season running from June 1, 1912, through June 1, 1913. There have been 170 productions, with 110 of them dramas and playlets, 31 of them musicals, and 29, comedies. In *Best Plays*, authors Mantle and Sherwood, basing their count on performances in 54 theatres, make possible the following tally: 69 dramas, 46 comedies, 18 musicals, 6 revues, 9 operas, 6 operettas, 6 Shakespearean revivals, 1 burlesque, and three repertory shows. All of which illustrates the difficulties of counting and sorting, as well as relying on such tallies.

Who's the Lady

July Writing in this month's *American Magazine*, Julian Johnson sums up the position of the brothers Shubert on the American theatrical scene. These former managers of "opryhouses" in upstate New York, he notes, now control 15 theatres in New York alone, with three more to be added soon. In addition, the Shuberts furnish attractions to a thousand theatres throughout the United States, as well as owning theatres in major American cities coast-to-coast and employing 7,000 people in their theatres and offices. Plans are being drawn, Johnson reveals, to build Hippodromes on the New York model in London and in Berlin. A typical Shubert weekly gross income is over a million dollars.

Oct 2 The Shubert Theatre (1,400 seats) opens on West 44th Street in New York City. The theatre, designed by Henry B. Harris, is dedicated to the memory of Sam S. Shubert. The British actor Johnston Forbes-Robertson gives his farewell performance as Hamlet on opening night.

Oct 16 The Booth Theatre opens on West 45th Street in New York City, built by Winthrop Ames. The opening performance is the first American production of *The Great Adventure*. The new Booth Theatre commemorates the original Booth (1869–1883), located at West 23rd Street and 6th Avenue. Ames' father had an interest in the old Booth.

Jan 5 *The Legend of Leonora* (NY—Empire—Comedy). Maude Adams stars in James Barrie's new comedy about a woman on trial for pushing a man out of a train.

Jan 10 *The Whirl of the World* (NY—Winter Garden—Revue). This revue is composer Sigmund Romberg's Broadway debut. It runs for 161 performances.

Jan 12 *The Queen of the Movies* (NY—Winter Garden—Musical). Jean Gilbert provides the music for this show about a mad professor who wants to suppress films. Valli Valli stars. The show runs 13 weeks.

Jan13 *Sari* (NY—Liberty—Musical). Emmerich Kalman writes the score for this musical about a gypsy girl who resolves a conflict between her relatives. Mitzi Hajos stars. The play runs 151 performances.

Jan 20 *The Yellow Ticket* (NY—Eltinge—Drama). Hugh Ford stages Michael Morton's play starring John Barrymore. It runs 183 performances.

Feb 24 *Too Many Cooks* (NY—39th Street—Comedy). John Cromwell stages Frank Craven's play which runs for 223 performances.

March 16 *The Crinoline Girl* (NY—Knickerbocker—Musical). Otto Hauerbach devises the book and Percy Wenrich the songs. Famed female impersonator Julian Eltinge creates the lyrics and stars in this show which runs 11 weeks.

June 1 *The Ziegfeld Follies of 1914* (NY—New Amsterdam—Revue). Ed Wynn performs some comedy routines. Leon Errol dances and helps Ziegfeld stage. Raymond Hubbell's score is undistinguished. It has 112 performances.

June 10 *The Passing Show of 1914* (NY—Winter Garden—Revue). Sigmund Romberg creates the score, with interpolations from Harry Carrol. Marilyn Miller makes her first legitimate stage appearance, winning attention for her impersation of female impersonator Julian Eltinge. The show runs for 133 performances.

Aug 14 *Twin Beds* (NY—Fulton—Comedy). Margaret Mayo stages the farce she and Salisbury Field have written. It runs for 411 performances.

Aug 19 *On Trial* (NY—Candler—Drama). Author Hopkins produces and directs Elmer Reizenstein's (later Rice) script. The play is hailed as a pivotal development in American drama. The audiences wait to find out why a defendant has pleaded guilt to murder when it is suspected he is shielding someone. It enjoys 365 performances. "... not orthodox but it works," reports the *NY Times*. On April 29, 1915 the show opens at London's Lyric where it wins 174 performances.

Aug 24 *The Girl from Utah* See L premiere, 1913.

Aug 26 *Under Cover* (NY—Cort—Drama). Roi Cooper Megrue's story of an under cover customs agent has Harry Crosby, Ralph Morgan and George Stevens. It receives 349 performances. It opens at London's Strand on Jan 17, 1917 where it wins 192 performances. Matheson Lang stars.

Sep 5 *War of the World* (NY—Hippodrome—Musical). Arthur Voegtlin devises this show with Manuel Klein's music and lyrics. The show runs only 229 performances, a failure in Hippodrome terms, playing two-a-day.

Sep 8 *It Pays to Advertise* (NY—Cohan—Comedy). Louise Drew, Grant Mitchell and W.J. Brady are in this Roi Cooper Megrue and Walter Hackett farce about a soap magnate whose son goes into competition with him. The show has a 399-performance run.

Sep 28 *The Hawk* (NY—Shubert—Drama). William Faversham stages and stars in the play by Francis De Croisset. It runs for 136 performances.

Sep 28 *Daddy Long-Legs* (NY—Gaiety—Comedy). Jean Webster's best-selling novel about an orphan befriended by a wealthy man stars Ruth Chatterton. It runs 264 performances. On May 29, 1916, it opens at London's Duke of York's Theatre. The cast includes Renee Kelly, Jean Cadell, Fay Davis and Charles Waldron. Kelly wins praise as the orphan girl. The play runs for 514 performances.

Oct 10 *Dancing Around* (NY—Winter Garden—Revue). With a slender story-line which vanishes midway, the show is carried by blackface singer Al Jolson. Sigmund Romberg and Harry Carroll provide the score.

Oct 20 *Chin-Chin* (NY—Globe—Musical). Ivan Caryll provides the score for this reworking of an English Christmas pantomine. The show runs 295 performances in a depressed season.

Oct 27 *Experience* (NY—Booth—Drama). George V. Hobart's book combines with music by Silvio Hein and Max Bendix. It runs 225 performances.

Nov 2 *The Only Girl* (NY—39th Street—Musical). Adapted by Henry Blossom from Frank Mandel's comedy, *Our Wives*, the plot details the fates of four friends who vow to remain bachelors. Victor Herbert's score includes "When You're Away." The show runs 240 performances. On Sep 25, 1915 it opens at London's Apollo, where it runs 107 times.

Dec 1 *Polygamy* (NY—Playhouse—Drama). This Harvey O'Higgins and Harriet Ford play about Mormons runs 159 performances.

Dec 8 *Watch Your Step* (NY—New Amsterdam—Musical). Composer Irving Berlin advertises this show as ragtime. The plot is the meagre excuse for dancing led by Vernon and Irene Castle. The show runs for 175 performances.

Dec 22 *The Song of Songs* (NY—Eltinge—Drama). Edward Sheldon bases his play on Herman Sudermann's novel. It runs 191 performances.

Dec 24 *The Lie* (NY—Harris—Drama). Henry Arthur Jones's play features C. Aubrey Smith and Margaret Illington. It is given 172 performances. On Oct 13, 1923 it premieres at London's New Theatre with Sybil Thorndike and Robert Horton. Here it has 187 showings.

Dec 25 *Hello Broadway* (NY—Astor—Revue). Creator-director George M. Cohan signals a new era in Broadway musical theatre revues. His cast bring on and strike sets, speeding up the pace of the production. The leads include Peggy Wood and Louise Dresser. The show runs 123 performances.

Yellow Ticket

Jan 28 *The Music Cure* (L—Little—Comedy). George Bernard Shaw's one-act farce features Madge McIntosh.

Feb 3 *Broadway Jones* See NY premiere, 1912.

Feb 7 *After the Girl* (L—Gaiety—Musical). Producer George Edwardes offers a "revusical comedy" in two acts by Paul Rubens with lyrics by Percy Greenbank. The thin plot deals with a father chasing his runaway daughter (Isobel Elsom). It earns 105 performances.

Feb 26 *The Land of Promise* (L—Duke of York's—Drama). W. Somerset Maugham writes about a woman who will not desert her husband despite living in poor conditions. There are several violent physical encounters between the couple. *The Times* denounces the violence, which had been met by applause.

April 11 *Pygmalion* (L—His Majesty's—Comedy). George Bernard Shaw's tale of speech expert Henry Higgins' transformation of a Covent Garden flower-seller, Eliza Doolittle, into a gracious lady wins 118 performances. Mrs. Patrick Campbell as Liza and Herbert Tree as Higgins star. *The Times*, reports, "As for the play, it is certainly to be seen; but it will live (if it lives) for its parts rather than its whole." Mrs. Campbell brings the show to Broadway in October where it runs for only 72 performances.

April 14 *Potash and Perlmutter* See NY premiere, 1913.

April 16 *Mam'selle Tralala* (L—Lyric—Musical). Arthur Wimperis and Hartley Carrick adapt this story by Georg Okonkowski and Leo Leipziger. Jean Gilbert supplies the music and Yvonne Arnaud stars. The show runs 105 performances.

April 20 *The Passing Show* (L—Palace—Revue). Alfred Butt's show has P. L. Fler's staging of travesties, sketches, and musical numbers. Arthur Wimperis has devised the book, with a score by Herman Finck. It wins 351 performances.

April 23 *My Lady's Dress* (L—Royalty—Drama). Playwright Edward Knoblauch tells the tale of a woman who imagines the laborers whose work have gone into her dress. Frank Vernon directs a cast starring Gladys Cooper and Dennis Eadie.

June 4 *The Cinema Star* (L—Shaftesbury—Musical). Jack Hulbert and Harry Graham adapt *Die Kino-Koenigin* by Georg Okonkowski and Julius Freund. Robert Courtneidge produces and Jean Gilbert writes the music. It gets 109 performances.

Sep 26 *England Expects* [Every Man To Do His Duty] (L—London Opera House—Drama). The show is designed by its authors, Seymour Hicks and Edward Knoblauch, to awaken the patriotic spirit. They call the show a "military sketch, in five scenes."

Oct 10 *Peg O' My Heart*. See NY premiere, 1912.

Oct 26 *Philip The King* (Bristol—Theatre Royal—Drama). John Masefield's verse drama opens with Brember Wills as Philip II of Spain and Muriel Pratt as the Infanta.

Oct 29 *The New Shylock* (L—Lyric—Comedy). Herman Scheffauer's comedy of New York ghetto life stars Louis Calvert. It does not have a long run.

Nov 25 *The Dynasts* (L—Kingsway—Drama). Harley Granville Barker's acting version of Thomas Hardy's epic drama features Clarence Derwent, Henry Ainley and Esme Beringer.

Dec 10 *The Man Who Stayed Home* (L—Royalty—Comedy). In September, Lord Kitchener has called for a million soldiers. This hero doesn't volunteer, but serves at home by unmasking a ring of German spies at an East Coast holiday resort. Eille Norwood stages. There are 584 performances.

Daddy Longlegs

Jan 11 At London's Savoy, the Pioneer Players perform the medieval religious drama *Paphnutius*, by Hroswitha. Ellen Terry stars.

Jan 27 At London's Little Theatre, William Poel revives *Hamlet*, with Esme Percy in the lead.

Feb 9 *Othello* returns to New York at the Lyric Theatre, with William Faversham staging himself as Iago. R. D. MacLean is Othello.

March 16 Margaret Anglin directs and stars in *Twelfth Night*, *The Taming of the Shrew* and *As Your Like It* at New York's Hudson Theatre. Later she revives Oscar Wilde's *Lady Windermere's Fan*. Sidney Greenstreet, Eric Blind and Pedro de Cordoba are in the company.

April 9 Instead of the usual musical spectacular, *H. M. S. Pinafore* is staged for 89 two-a-day performances at New York's huge Hippodrome Theatre.

April 11 In London at the Little Theatre, Joel Chandler Harris' American Uncle Remus characters come to life in Mrs. Percy Dearmer's "musical frolic," *Brer Rabbit and Mr. Fox*. Martin Shaw creates the score.

April 14 Winthrop Ames revives Clyde Fitch's *The Truth*, at his Little Theatre in New York. Conway Tearle and Grace George take leading roles.

April 22 At Stratford-upon-Avon, the annual Shakespeare Festival opens with *A Midsummer Night's Dream*. Frank Benson and his company are still on their American tour, so Patrick Kirwan has directed this season. The "Birthday Play" is *Much Ado About Nothing*. Other plays in the repertory include *The Comedy of Errors*, *Twelfth Night*, *Hamlet*, *As You Like It*, *The Merchant of Venice*, Henry Porter's *The Two Angry Women of Abington*, and Nathaniel Field's *A Woman Is a Weathercock*.

May 10 Guy Rathbone produces and plays in Chekhov's *Uncle Vanya* in this Stage Society production.

May 11 Charles Frohman revives Sardou's *A Scrap of Paper* at his Empire Theatre in New York. For four weeks, Ethel Barrymore, John Drew and Mary Boland appear.

June 11 Charles Marlowe's farce, *When Knights Were Bold*, is revived in London at the Apollo Theatre for a run of 244 performances. In the months that follow, as Britain becomes more deeply involved in the Great War, revivals—rather than costly new productions—will become a staple of the theatre.

June 26 At London's Royal Court Theatre, a brief season of Roland Pertwee plays gets underway with: *Swank*, *Falling Upstairs*, and two other short plays, *Vantage Out* and *The Return of Imray*.

July 4 The first licensed English performance of Ibsen's *Ghosts* is given at London's Haymarket.

July 21 The first licensed performance of Maurice Maeterlinck's drama, *Monna Vanna*, is premiered at London's Queen's.

Aug 1 At Stratford-upon-Avon, Frank Benson and his company, returned from their American tour, open a four-week season of Shakespeare's plays with *Much Ado About Nothing*. Also offered are *Hamlet, Richard II, Henry IV, Part 2, Henry V, The Merry Wives of Windsor, The Merchant of Venice, Twelfth Night, Julius Caesar, As You Like It, The Taming of the Shrew*, and *Romeo and Juliet*. The Birmingham Repertory brings its productions of Wilde's *The Importance of Being Earnest, The Return of the Prodigal*, and Goldsmith's *She Stoops To Conquer*.

Aug 17 The German menace is pinpointed at London's Palladium in Edmund Goulding's, *God Save the King*. On Oct 12, at the Palace in Southampton Fred Ellis's *God Save the Empire* is shown. That night at the Palladium in London, the special feature is a one-act War Episode, *For France*, by J. O. Francis. *The German Spy* is offered at the Grand Theatre in Mansfield on Aug 24.

Aug 29 The Birmingham Repertory Theatre opens its third season with Galsworthy's *The Eldest Son*.

Oct 5 For the first time under Lilian Baylis's management, Shakespeare's *The Taming of the Shrew* is produced at London's Old Vic Theatre. Other firsts this year are their productions of *Hamlet* (Oct 12) and *The Merchant of Venice* (Oct 26); *The Tempest* (Nov 9), *The Merry Wives of Windsor* (Nov 16), *The Comedy of Errors* (Nov 30), *Twelfth Night* (Dec 7), and *A Midsummer Night's Dream* (Dec 21). By 1923, Baylis will have offered the complete canon of 37 plays.

Oct 13 F. Jay's short historical drama, *The Cobweb*, opens at Dublin's Abbey Theatre.

Oct 17 Holbrook Blinn returns with the Princess Players to Manhattan's Princess

Theatre. Among the playwrights represented are George Ade, Henry Arthur Jones, Edgar Wallace, and Stanley Houghton.

Oct 20 William Gillette revives Sardou's *Diplomacy* on Broadway at the Empire

Theatre for 63 performances.

Dec 21 This Christmas season, there are few cheerful entertainments. James Barrie offers a short war play, *Der Tag*, at the London Coliseum. His *Peter Pan* is revived at the Duke of York's on Dec 24.

1914 BIRTHS/DEATHS/DEBUTS

March 7 Director-actor-producer Morton DaCosta is born Morton Tecosky in Philadelphia, Pennsylvania.

April 17 American actor-manager Arthur McKee Rankin (b. 1841) is dead in San Francisco. Rankin made his first appearance in 1861 at Rochester, New York under the name George Henley. In 1877 he produced, and acted in *The Danites*, which he made famous throughout the world. During 1910 and 1911 Rankin appeared at many variety theatres in *The White Slaver*.

April 22 Playwright Jan de Hartog is born in Haarlem, Holland.

May 11 Actress Ruth Donnelly makes her Broadway debut as a Telephone Operator in Owen Davis and Arthur Somers Roche's *A Scrap of Paper* at the Criterion Theatre.

May 29 English actor and playwright Lawrence Sidney Irving (b. 1871) drowns in the St. Lawrence River in Canada. Irving, the younger son of Sir Henry, first appeared with the Bensonians in 1891. He was the author of a number of plays, of which the most successful was *The Unwritten Law*. Irving also wrote the tragedy, *Peter the Great*, for his father.

Aug 4 After playing the first two houses at the Holborn Empire Theatre in London, Maud Tiffany disappears, never to be heard of again.

Oct 4 *New Yorker* theatre critic Brendan Gill is born in Hartford, Connecticut.

Nov 10 English dramatist Cecil Raleigh (b. 1856) is dead. Raleigh was drama critic for *Vanity Fair, The Lady*, and *Sporting Times*. Among his numerous plays are *Sporting Life, The White Heather, The Sins of Society*, and *The Sunshine Girl*.

Nov 13 Playwright William Gibson is born in New York City.

Dec 3 Tanya Moiseiwitsch is born in London to pianist Benno Moiseiwitsch.

1914 THEATERS/PRODUCTIONS

In Britain this year a patent is granted for F. D. Thomas' complicated effect of a boat full of actors rolling in a heavy sea, accomplished by three projections on a large screen, curved from the stage-floor at the footlights upstage into the flies, with the boat in a rocking-cradle, set in the middle of it.

G. S. Street joins Ernest Bendall as an Examiner of Plays in the Lord Chamberlain's Office. In 1920 he becomes the chief Examiner. Street is later to write that his work has actually protected authors and managers from more direct attacks by groups who value their immunity from being shocked more than they respect the art of the dramatist.

April 20 Tonight marks the inauguration of Boston's new Wilbur Theatre, designed by architect Clarence Blackall, who has chosen a facade that imitates a colonial house. The initial production is Edward Sheldon's *Romance*, starring Doris Keane. This is a Shubert Theatre, commissioned by the Shubert brothers. Its most productive theatre-life will be from 1914–18, and from 1939–45. Important pre-Broadway tryouts will play here; *A Long Day's Journey into Night* and *Our Town* will have their world premieres at the Wilbur Theatre.

June 24 The *NY Dramatic Mirror* today announces that 176 productions have been presented in the past season. The breakdown is as follows: 29 musicals, 36 revivals, 20 melodramas, 50 comedies, 18 dramas, 14 farces, 10 tragedies, 3 spectacles, 6 vaudevilles, and 26 playlets. For the same period, *Best Plays* authors Burns Mantle and Garrison P. Sherwood, basing their figures on productions in 54 Broadway venues, make possible a tally of 45 dramas, 45 comedies, 24 musicals, 7 revues, 3 operas, 3 operettas, 5 Shakesperean revivals, and 4 repertory productions.

Nov 10 The Punch and Judy Theatre, at 153 West 49th Street in New York, opens with *The Marriage of Columbine*. Designed by architects Murphy and Dana, the theatre has a standard-sized stage but a limited seating capacity of 299 seats. In 1926, the owner, actor-manager Charles Hopkins, renames the theatre for himself. Since 1933, as the World Theatre, it has been a motion-picture house.

Dec 22 The Bandbox Theatre (299 seats) opens at 205 East 57th Street in New York City. Formerly the Adolph Phillipps Theatre, it is to be used by its manager, Douglas Wood, to produce five experimental works a season for a subscription audience.

The Man Who Stayed Home

Jan 25 *90 in the Shade* (NY—Knicker-bocker—Musical). Jerome Kern creates the score and Guy Bolton the book for this show about an American playboy who goes to the Philippines to pursue amorous adventures. Richard Carle and Marie Cahill star. The unpaid actors refuse to perform after 40 showings, closing it down.

Jan 26 *Marie-Odile* (NY—Belasco—Drama). David Belasco produces and directs Edward Knoblauch's play about a foundling raised by nuns. It has 119 performances. On June 8 it is premiered at His Majesty's in London with Marie Lohr in the starring role. The production survives only a month.

Feb 4 *The White Feather* (NY—Comedy—Drama). John Cromwell stages this British drama of seeming cowardice. Coauthors are Lechmere Warrall and J. E. Harold Terry. William A. Brady produces. Leslie Faber plays a young Englishman who seems to be avoiding military service. Actually he's spying on German agents. The play runs 140 times.

Feb 18 *Maid in America* (NY—Winter Garden—Revue). Sigmund Romberg and Harry Carroll provide the music and Harold Atteridge the "song cues" for this war-oriented show. In the company are Blossom Seeley, Nora Bayes and Joe Jackson. It has a run of 108 performances.

March 2 *The Peasant Girl* (NY—44th Street—Musical). Emma Trentini and Clifton Crawford play in this story of a waif who struggles to become an opera star. Rudolph Friml adds melodies to this European import. The show has 111 performances.

April 20 *Nobody Home* (NY—Princess—Musical). With a Jerome Kern score and book by Guy Bolton and Paul Rubens, this is the first of a series of "Princess Musicals." A series of mix-ups lead to wedding bells at the close. The show runs 135 performances.

May 29 *The Passing Show of 1915* (NY—Winter Garden—Revue). Among the other pieces in this show is one in which Marilyn Miller parodies Clifton Crawford and Mary Pickford. It runs 145 performances.

June 21 *The Ziegfeld Follies of 1915* (NY—New Amsterdam—Revue). This edition is distinguished by Joseph Urban's designs. W. C. Fields talks for the first time and does his billiard act. Ed Wynn directs a mock film from the audience.

Aug 5 *The Blue Paradise* (NY—Casino—Musical). Sigmund Romberg reworks Edmund Eysler's score for this story about a young man who discovers that his old sweetheart is a shrew. Vivienne Segal charms. It runs for 356 performances.

Aug 10 *The Boomerang* (NY—Belasco—Comedy). David Belasco produces Winchel Smith and Victor Mapes' script about a man consumed with jealousy. It runs 495 performances.

Sep 1 *The House of Glass* (NY—Candler—Drama). Max Marcin's play, produced by Cohan and Harris, runs 245 performances.

Sep 13 *Hit-the-Trail-Holiday* (NY—Astor—Comedy). Guy Bolton and George Middleton give George M. Cohan the idea for this farce about a small town in the throes of a revival. It runs 336 performances.

Sep 29 *The Princess Pat* (NY—Cort—Musical). Victor Herbert creates the score of this tale of Europeans in love mix-ups. Henry Blossom provides book and lyrics. Eleanor Painter stars. The "Neapolitan Love Song" becomes a hit. The show plays for 158 performances.

Oct 14 *Alone at Last* (NY—Schubert—Musical). Jose Collins and John Charles Thomas star in Franz Lehar's operetta. It runs 180 performances.

Oct 19 *Our Mrs. McChesney* (NY—Lyceum—Comedy). George Hobart helps Edna Ferber adapt her McChesney stories for the stage. Ethel Barrymore stars. It runs 151 performances.

Oct 21 *Abe and Mawruss* (NY—Lyric—Comedy). Roi Cooper Megrue assists Montague Glass in reworking his Potash and Perlmutter stories for Broadway. This dialect comedy, with Barney Bernard and Julius Tannen, proves so popular that it runs for 196 performances. In January 1916, it is retitled *Potash and Perlmutter in Society*.

Nov 2 *Hobson's Choice* (NY—Princess—Comedy). Harold Brighouse's play tells of a daughter who defeats her dictatorial father. Viola Roach and Harold de Becker lead. The show earns 135 performances.

Nov 10 *The Great Lover* (NY—Longacre—Comedy). Leo Ditrichstein and Frederick and Fanny Hatton write this comedy about romantic problems in the opera world. It has 245 performances. On Oct 2, 1920 it opens at London's Shaftesbury where it is again successful—238 performances.

Dec 1 *Treasure Island* (NY—Punch and Judy—Drama). Jules E. Goodman adapts

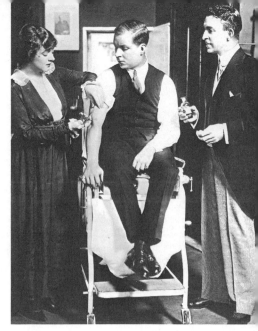

Boomerang

Robert Louis Stevenson's classic tale of a brave boy and lusty pirates. It runs for 205 performances, with Charles Hopkins as producer, player, and co-director.

Dec 14 *The Weavers* (NY—Garden—Drama). Gerhardt Hauptmann's German classic, translated by Mary Morrison, opens for a run of 87 performances.

Dec 23 *Katinka* (NY—44th Street—Musical). Rudolf Friml provides the score and Otto Hauerbach the book and lyrics for this musical about love intrigues among Russians in Vienna. It continues for 220 performances. On Aug 30, 1923 it opens at London's Shaftesbury where it runs for 108 performances.

Dec 23 *Very Good, Eddie* (NY—Princess—Musical). The second "Princess Musical" has another Jerome Kern score, with book by Guy Bolton and Philip Bartholomae. It is based on the latter's *Over Night*. The show is seen as an effective break with the operetta tradition, setting a standard for succeeding American musicals. It runs 341 performances. On May 18, 1918, it opens at London's Palace Theatre where it has only 46 performances.

Dec 25 *Stop! Look! Listen!* (NY—Globe—Musical). Irving Berlin provides lyrics and music for Harry B. Smith's book about a chorus girl who becomes a star. Berlin's "I Love a Piano" becomes a hit. Marion Davies, Gaby Deslys and Harry Pilcer play. The show runs for 105 performances.

Feb 11 *Searchlights* (L—Savoy—Drama). Horace Vachell's drama of a man changed by war has H.B. Irving and Fay Davis. It runs 105 performances.

March 9 *The Passing Show of 1915* (L—Palace—Revue). Herman Finck writes the music and Arthur Wimperis and Hartley Carrick the book and lyrics for this revue with Elsie Janis and Arthur Playfair. This show wins only 143 performances, in contrast to last year's which ran for 351.

March 19 *5064 Gerrard!* (L—Alhambra—

Revue). Gaby Deslys and Beatrice Lillie are in this review with sketches by Cosmo Gordon Lennox, C.H. Bovill and Robert Hale and music by Willy Redstone and Max Darewski. It runs for 194 performances.

April 20 *Quinney's* (L—Haymarket—Comedy). Henry Ainley appears in Horace Vachell's comedy about an antiques dealer. It runs for 284 performances.

April 24 *Betty* (L—Daly's—Musical). Frederick Lonsdale and Gladys Unger devise the book, with score by Paul Rubens, who is aided on the lyrics by Adrian Ross. Winifred Barnes stars as Betty, a kitchenmaid who marries a nobleman. The show runs for 391 performances.

April 28 *Tonight's the Night* (L—Gaiety—Musical). Based on the old hit, *Pink Dominoes*, this show's book is by Fred Thompson and the score by Paul Rubens. "They Didn't Believe Me" is the major duet in this story of two women who test their men's fidelity. The show has 460 performances.

April 29 *On Trial*. See NY premiere, 1914.

June 1 *Armageddon* (L—New—Drama). Stephen Phillips' drama of Hell stars John Martin Harvey and Nina de Silva.

June 9 *Gamblers All* (L—Wyndham's—Drama). May Martindale's play revolves around a woman addicted to gambling. Charles France, Gerald Du Maurier, and Lewis Waller are in the cast. The play receives 93 performances.

June 18 *More* (L—Ambassadors'—Revue). This revue, with sketches and lyrics by Harry Grattan and music by Edward Jones, stars Alice Delysia. British ideas of the U.S. and Japanese melodrama are

Treasure Island

among the topics of parody or song. It runs for 376 performances.

July 16 *All Scotch* (L—Apollo—Revue). Harry Grattan creates this revue with Herman Darewski sharing credits for the music.

July 23 *Peter Ibbetson* (L—His Majesty's—Drama). John Raphael adapts George Du Maurier's novel about two lovers who meet only in spirit. Owen Nares plays the title role. He is assisted by Eva Le Gallienne and Constance Collier.

Sep 1 *The Big Drum* (L—St. James's—Comedy). George Alexander stars in Arthur Wing Pinero's new comedy. It wins 111 performances.

Sep 4 *The Ware Case* (L—Wyndham's—Drama). Gerald Du Maurier and Marie Lohr star in George Pleydell's drama of a guilty man who convinces a jury of his innocence. It runs 209 performances.

Oct 6 *Romance* (L—Duke of York's—Drama). This American play by Edward Sheldon is a tremendous hit, with 1,049 performances. The popular American star, Doris Keane, plays Mme. Margherita Cavallini, with Owen Nares as Thomas Armstrong, rector of St. Giles in New York and forty years later the Bishop, looking back on his love for the opera singer. A. E. Anson stages and plays the role of the banker, Van Tuyl.

Oct 16 *The Case of Lady Camber* (L—

Savoy—Drama). Horace Vechell's drama of a nurse thought to have poisoned her patient, has May Stuart, Ben Webster and Kate Bishop. It runs 191 performances.

Oct 21 A double bill of *The Best Man*, by Daisy McGooch and Cecil James, and *Stop Thief!* a three-act farce by Carlyle Moore, earns a run of 151 performances in London at the New Theatre. Marie Illington and Frederick Volpe are in the cast. On Oct 14 the production premiered in York at the Theatre Royal.

Oct 27 *A Little Bit of Fluff* (L—Criterion—Comedy). Walter Ellis writes a lively farce about a milksop who tries to protect a neighbor who has been out on an amorous adventure. Ernest Thesiger leads. The show runs 1,241 performances.

Nov 3 *Tina* (L—Adelphi—Musical). Paul Rubens collaborates with Harry Graham on the book and Hayden Wood on the score of this musical about an impoverished duke who seeks the heart and fortune of an heiress. The show features Godfrey Tearle. It has 277 performances.

Dec 9 *Who Is He?* (L—Haymarket—Comedy). Following the success earlier in the season at this theatre of his comedy, *Quinneys'*, Horace Vachell is rewarded with a run of 157 performances for this light entertainment. It's based on a novel by Mrs. Belloc Lowndes. Henry Ainley appears.

1915   REVIVALS/REPERTORIES

Jan All over Britain, patriotic fervor is being whipped up, especially in theatres and music halls, with plays, revues, sketches, and tableaux. Some pertinent titles are: *American Diplomacy, Are We Downhearted? Boys of the Bull Dog Breed, Brave Women Who Wait, The Clarion Call, The Contemptible Little Army, A Daughter of Belgium, The Day Before the Day, The Deserter, Empty Sleeve, The Enemy in Our Midst, The Eve of Liege, For All Eternity, For King and Country, For Mother Country, For Russia, For Serbia.*

Jan 4 Jane Delmar heads a French cast at the Criterion Theatre in *La Demoiselle de Magasin*, by Jean Fonson and Fernand Wicheler. On January 25, the play is Fonson's *La Kommandatur*, followed on February 22 with *Zonneslag et Cie.*, a comedy-vaudeville by Gustave Libeau and Maurice Saye. On March 8, *La Flambee*, by Henry Kistemaeckers is presented.

Jan 8 At London's Garrick Theatre, French drama in the original and in translation occupies the stage most of the season. Tonight, the play is translated as *A Daughter of England*, with Marga la Rubia playing Sylvia Chetwynd in a confrontation at the French-German border. The Grand Guignol Theatre of Paris opens its season at the Garrick on July 19, with

a program of *La Porte Close* (Robert Francheville), *Bloomfield et Cie.* (G. Fabri/Leon Frapie), *Mirette a ses Raisons* (Romain Cadus), *La Delaissee* (Max Maurey), *Asile de Nuit* (Maurey), *The Grip* (J. Sartene), *Le Piege* (Achaume/Armaury), *The Mask* (F. T. Jesse/H. M. Harwood), *Depuis Six Mois* (Maurey), *Compiegne* (L. Buteaux), *Le Pharmacién* (Maurey), *The Vampire* (Vylars/Silvestre), *La Derniere Torture* (de Lorde/Morel), and *Y'a d'Jolies Femmes*, a French revue by Celval and Charley.

Jan 12 Owing partly to the war-inspired interest in the French allies, there is a remarkable increase in the number of French plays presented in London, especially by French companies acting in French. Tonight at the Cosmopolis, the play is *Jalousie*, by Alexandre Bisson and Adolphe Leclercq. On May 14, *La Passarelle* is revived at this theatre.

Jan 19 Emile Verhaeren's *Le Cloitre*, is presented in London at the Kingsway Theatre. In the summer, beginning on July 19, the troupe offers a season of plays by Georges Courteline (*La Commissaire est Bon Enfant* and *La Paix Chez Soi*) and Tristan Bernard (*Le Seul Bandit du Village* and *Le Captif.*)

Jan 25 At London's Old Vic Theatre, Lil-

Passing Show of 1915

lian Baylis presents Shakespeare's *Macbeth* staged by Ben Greet. On Feb 8, Estelle Stead and Andrew Leigh offer the Baylis Vic its first *As You Like It*. On March 1 the Baylis premiere is *The Winter's Tale*, followed on March 22 by *Othello*, both Ben Greet productions new at the Baylis Vic. On April 26, Fisher White offers a production of *Julius Caesar*. Ben Greet offers three further Baylis Shakespeare premieres: *Romeo and Juliet*, *Henry V*, and *Richard III*, on Oct 11, Oct 25, and Nov 22.

Jan 26 Now in its fourth season, the Liverpool Repertory Company starts its "real rep" experiment: tonight and Tuesday: Ronald Jean's *Two and Two*; Wednesday afternoon and evening: *Twelfth Night*; Thursday: *The Importance of Being Earnest*; Friday: *Two and Two*; Saturday matinee: *Twelfth Night* and Saturday evening, *Earnest* again.

Jan 27 Harley Granville Barker stages a repertory of Anatole France's *The Man Who Married a Dumb Wife* and Bernard Shaw's *Androcles and the Lion*. It is the New York premiere of *Androcles*, at Wallack's Theatre. Robert Edmond Jones designs the sets for the France play and is immediately recognized by the critics as a major new talent. In Feb, *A Midsummer Night's Dream* is added to the repertory.

Feb 1 Robert B. Mantell opens a series of repertory classics at 44th Street Theatre in New York, presented by William A. Brady. Bulwer-Lytton's *Richelieu* and Mattheus's *Louis XI* take turns with *Othello*, *King Lear*, *Romeo and Juliet*, *Julius Caesar*, *Macbeth*, *King John*, *Hamlet*, *Richard III*, and *The Merchant of Venice* for a month's engagement.

Feb 2 Sheridan's *The School for Scandal* is revived at the Royal Opera, Covent Garden for a special Royal Matinee. The huge cast is an honor roll of British theatre. It includes Herbert Tree and Irene Vanbrugh.

Feb 10 In Dublin at the Abbey Theatre the Irish Players present *The Dreamers*, Lennox Robinson's three-act historical drama, with Fred O'Donovan and Sara Allgood. On April 8, Lady Gregory's melodrama, *Shanwalla*, is premiered, with Kathleen Drago, J. M. Kerrigan and Arthur Sinclair. On Nov. 15, the play is *For the Land She Loved*, an Irish melodrama by P. J. Bourke. On Nov 30, St. John Ervine's *John Ferguson* has its premiere. Much later it will be a notable Theatre Guild production on Broadway.

Feb 19 The *Washington Square Players* open their first season of one-act plays at New York's Bandbox Theatre. Playwrights include Chekhov, Maeterlinck, Andreyev, Philip Moeller, and John Reed. Some of the American authors are in the large company, as well as performers such as Helen Westley, Alice Harrington, and William Pennington.

Feb 24 In this wartime season, revivals are the rule at London's Lyceum Theatre. Tonight the production is *The Three Musketeers*, followed on March 31, by the revival of *A Royal Divorce*. The next attraction, on May 22, is C. Watson Mill's patriotic four-act play, *In Time of War*, which is replaced on July 14, with *Her Forbidden Marriage*, again a revival. On Sep 29, the revival is *Between Two Women*.

Feb 27 On the home front, there are stringent economies everywhere. Theatre programs grow thinner; there are fewer new productions. In London at the Aldwych Theatre, a revival of the successful Drury Lane melodrama, *The Whip*, opens tonight. For the rest of the year, the Aldwych offers only revivals: on April 19, *Florodora*; on May 22, *The Dairymaids*; on July 31, *Pete*; on Oct 9, *The Prodigal Son*.

March 24 In Liverpool at the Repertory Theatre, the show is Ronald Jeans' seven-scene burlesque of a Music Hall revue, called *Hello, Repertory!*, which sounds suspiciously like Joe Peterman's current series of revues, such as *Hello! Brixton!* and *Hello! Plymouth!* On Oct 19, the Rep offers a Welsh play by Dorothea Evans, *The Call (Yr Alwad)*, with Doris Lloyd,

Eileen Thorndike, and others.

April 5 The Garrick Producing Company begins a repertory season in New York at the Garrick Theatre with Bernard Shaw's *You Never Can Tell*. A month later, *Arms and the Man* joins it, followed by *Candida*.

April 12 At London's Royal Court Theatre, the realities of the war in France are brought home with the production of *Alsace*, a three-act drama in French, with a cast headed by Mme. Réjane. On July 13, *Remember Louvain*, by Captain R. W. Mockridge, is presented. On Oct 18, the play is *Patachon*, by Maurice Hennequin and Felix Duquesnel, acted by a French ensemble.

April 19 William A. Brady opens a season of Gilbert and Sullivan revivals in New York at the 48th Street Theatre. George Abbott, De Wolf Hopper, and Alice Brady are in the ensemble. The repertory offers *The Mikado*, *The Sorcerer*, *Iolanthe*, *The Yeoman of the Guard*, *H. M. S. Pinafore*, and *Trial by Jury*.

April 19 At Stratford-upon-Avon, the annual Shakespeare Festival opens, though menaced by wartime economies, with *Julius Caesar*. For Shakespeare's birthday, Frank Benson offers *Henry V* in the Memorial Theatre. Other productions in the repertory include *Romeo and Juliet*, *The Merry Wives of Windsor*, *The Merchant of Venice*, *The Taming of the Shrew*, *Hamlet*, *Coriolanus*, *Twelfth Night*, and *Richard III*.

June 14 At London's Coronet Theatre, a season of French drama played in repertory in the original language opens, lasting into July. Among the plays offered—most of them one-act dramas—are *Une Femme Charmante* (Andre Mycho), *Le Baiser dans la Nuit* (Maurice Level), *Le Chauffeur* (Max Maurey), *Le Triangle* (Alfred Sutro), *La Recommandation* (Maurey), *Au Coin Joli* (Frederic Boutet), *Cent Lignes Emues* (Charles Torquet), *La Revenante* (Jean d'Aguzay), *Gardiens du Phare* (Paul Autier/Paul Cioquemin), *La Bonheur* (Pierre Veber), *Rosalie* (Maurey), *Le Poison Hindou* (Eugene Joullot/Andre Peyre), *M. Jean* (Georges Nanteuil), and *Sous la Lumiere Rouge* (Level).

July 31 The four-week summer season of Shakespeare's plays in the Memorial Theatre in Stratford-upon-Avon opens. The repertory offered by Frank Benson and his company includes *The Taming of the Shrew*, *The Merry Wives of Windsor*, *Hamlet*, *Henry IV, Part 2*, *Henry V*, *Richard III*, *As You Like It*, *Twelfth Night*, *Romeo and Juliet*, and Phillips' *Paolo and Francesca*. The Birmingham Repertory presents a triple-bill of *How He Lied to Her Husband*, *The Storm*, and *The Liar*.

Sep 28 Grace George, with her New York Playhouse Company, opens a season of repertory at the Playhouse. The program includes the American premiere of Bernard Shaw's *Major Barbara*, with George in the title role. The other plays are Langdon Mitchell's *The New York Idea*, Henry Arthur Jones' *The Liars*, James B. Fagan's *The Earth*, and Shaw's *Captain Brassbound's Conversion*. The season lasts until April 29, 1916.

Oct 4 The *Washington Square Players* return for their second Broadway season, again with one-act plays and also Chekhov's *The Sea Gull*. Among the shorter plays are *Helena's Husband*, by Philip Moeller; *Literature*, by Arthur Schnitzler; *The Antick*, by Percy MacKaye; *Interior*, by Mauriece Maeterlinck; *Overtones*, by Alice Gerstenberg; *The Tenor*, by Frank Wedekind; *Whims*, by Alfred de Musset, and *The Clod*, by Lewis Beach. The season lasts until May 31, 1916.

Nov 29 E. H. Sothern produces *Our American Cousin*, the play Abraham Lincoln saw when John Wilkes Booth assassinated him. It is revived at New York's

Booth Theatre with Sothern Mather and Blanche Yurka in the leads.

Dec 4 In Birmingham at Barry Jackson's Theatre, John Masefield, offers his "Japanese tragedy," *The Faithful*. Jackson and Felix Aylmer are in the cast.

Dec 6 At the St. James's Theatre in London, Matheson Lang revives Shakespeare's *The Merchant of Venice*. On Dec 20, at the Royal Court, Frank Benson revives *A Midsummer Night's Dream*.

Dec 24 Despite the hardships of wartime, Christmas pantomimes manage to survive. Today, *Alice in Wonderland* opens at the Duke of York's Theatre in London. On Dec 27, *Where the Rainbow Ends* is presented at the Garrick Theatre. *Peter Pan* is presented at the New Theatre; *Puss in Boots*, at the Drury Lane; *Robinson Crusoe*, at the Lyceum, and *Babes in the Wood*, at the Aldwych Theatre.

Tina

their listings on 61 Broadway venues. There have been 80 dramas, 43 comedies, 21 musicals, 2 revues, 8 operettas, 2 Shakespearean revivals, and 1 repertory offering.

Summer George Cram Cook and his wife, Susan Glaspell form the nucleus of what is to become the Provincetown Players, later famed for premiering many of Eugene O'Neill's plays.

July 14 Under the direction of Stuart Walker, the Portmanteau Theatre opens its premiere dress rehearsal to the public. Dedicated to "youth and the eternal spirit of joy," the program includes three pieces: *The Triplet*, *A Fan and Two Candlesticks*, and *Six Who Pass While the Lentils Boil*. A feature of the program is the introduction of Walker's "portable settings" which he can pack up and carry away in ten boxes.

October Chicago's Studebaker Theatre has been having financial difficulties. Until 1906, it has been successful as a legitimate playhouse. Vaudeville has followed, then closure. This month the theatre re-opens with "Two Dollar Movies." This program will also fail.

Nov 17 In Baraboo, Wisconsin, the Al Ringling Theatre opens, designed by C. W. and G. L. Rapp of Chicago as a 1/3 scale copy of the opera theatre in the Palace of Versailles. There are 874 seats in this jewel-box theatre, with its 26 Corinthian columns decorating the auditorium, with a mural-painted oval ceiling and 17 boxes spaced between columns. Florence Webber stars in *Lady Luxury*, a comic opera at tonight's opening performance. From 1915–27, this stage will welcome a number of stars in shows from Broadway, via Minneapolis. After Baraboo, the shows move to Chicago. This theatre serves the Ringlings in what is the winter home of the famed Ringling Brothers and Barnum and Bailey Circus. The entire theatre, with its rich decorations has cost $100,000.

Dec There are 95 legitimate theatre productions on tour in America as of the first week of this month. The popularity of motion-pictures is quite clear; in 1900, there were 392 touring shows at this time.

1915　BIRTHS/DEATHS/DEBUTS

March 19 Patricia Morison is born in New York to playwright-actor William Morison.

May 7 American producer-manager Charles Frohman (b. 1860) drowns in the sinking of the *Lusitania*. Frohman's first success came in 1888–89 with the production of Bronson Howard's *Shenandoah*. In 1893 he opened the Empire Theatre with his own stock company. He was the brother of Daniel and Gustave Frohman.

May 7 American playwright Charles Klein (b. 1867) drowns in the sinking of the *Lusitania*. Klein wrote *The Auctioneer* and *The Music Master* for production by David Belasco. At his death he was play-reader

for Charles Frohman.

July 4 Playwright-director Jerome Lawrence is born in Cleveland, Ohio.

July 17 The U.S. actress Sarah Kemble LeMoyne (b. 1859) dies.

Aug 30 American playwright and adaptor Paul Armstrong (b. 1869) dies.

Oct 31 Blanche Walsh (b. 1873) praised for roles such as Margaret in Clyde Fitch's *The Woman in the Case*, dies.

Dec 31 The noted Italian actor, Tomasso Salvini, (b. 1829) is dead. He was acclaimed on both sides of the Atlantic, even though he performed in Italian, often supported by English-speaking ensembles.

1915　THEATERS/PRODUCTIONS

Alexander Wayrich receives a U.S. patent for an apparatus which makes it possible for a variety of scenes, set in booths moved on tracks, to appear and disappear. Two scenes can even be superimposed, using mirrors and screens, so that they seem ghostly.

Jan 27 *The Man Who Married a Dumb Wife* opens at Wallack's Theatre in New York, produced by Harley Granville Barker. The setting is designed by Robert Edmund Jones, who is the first American scene designer to work in the fashion of Appia and Craig on Broadway. His setting has an abstract simplicity which is to become a kind of manifesto against traditional realism on stage.

Feb 12 The Neighborhood Playhouse opens at 466 Grand Street in New York. It is funded by Alice and Irene Lewisohn, noted for their arts and education phi-

lanthropies.

May 25 The Little Theatre in London closes after the final performance of the Abbey Theatre's season there. It will not re-open until 1920.

June 16 Today, the *NY Dramatic Mirror* offers a provisional tally of the Broadway season just past, but the count runs from June 1, 1914 through June 15, 1915—more than a calendar year. There have been 187 productions, of which 35 won over 100 performances. Breakdown by types is as follows: 49 comedies, 32 musicals, 31 dramas, 30 playlets, 12 tragedies, 23 melodramas, 8 farces, and 2 miscellaneous productions. From season to season, there are inconsistencies in the *Mirror's* categories, as well as in its calendar. Burns Mantle and Garrison P. Sherwood, authors of the *Best Plays* covering this decade, have different categories and base

1916 AMERICAN PREMIERES

Jan 10 *Sybil* (NY—Liberty—Musical). With a score by Victor Jacobi, this musical tells the tale of a prima donna who disguises herself as a duchess to save her hussar. It features Julia Sanderson, Donald Brian and Joseph Cawthorn. The show runs 21 weeks. On Feb 19, 1921 it opens at London's Daly's Theatre with Jose Collins in the title role. There are 347 performances.

Jan 17 *The Cinderella Man* (NY—Hudson—Comedy). Frank Bacon, Lucille LaVerne and Burton Churchill are featured in Edward Childs Carpenter's play, which earns 192 performances. On June 12, 1919 it opens at London's Queen's Theatre with Owen Nares, Annie Esmond and Renee Kelly. Here it has 257 performances.

Jan 18 *Erstwhile Susan* (NY—Gaiety—Comedy). Based on Helen Martin's popular novel, *Barnabetta*, this play is a vehicle for Mrs. Fiske who is directed by her husband. It achieves 167 performances.

Feb 9 *The Cohan Revue of 1916* (NY—Astor—Revue). Cohan's revue satirizes war fervor and *Major Barbara*. The show runs 165 performances.

Feb 17 *Robinson Crusoe, Jr.* (NY—Winter Garden—Musical). Sigmund Romberg provides the score for this show about a man who dreams he is Crusoe. Al Jolson interpolates his favorite songs. It runs for 139 performances.

Feb 28 *Pom-pom* (NY—Cohan—Musical). Hugo Felix provides the score for this show about a prima donna kidnapped by pickpockets. Mitzi Hajos stars. The show runs 16 weeks.

May 24 *Caliban of the Yellow Sands* (NY—Lewisohn Stadium—Drama). Percy MacKaye's pageant involves New York school students and a large cast of noted performers for 10 performances.

June 12 *The Ziegfeld Follies of 1916* (NY—New Amsterdam—Revue). With book and lyrics by George Hobart and Gene Buck, this edition of the Follies has a Shakespearean theme. Bert Williams, Fanny Brice and Ina Claire play. The show runs for 112 performances.

June 22 *The Passing Show of 1916* (NY—Winter Garden—Revue). More topical than before, this edition stresses patriotism and satire. Ed Wynn helps orchestrate the fun. Sigmund Romberg and Otto Motzan concoct the score, with newcomer George Gershwin getting credit with Romberg on "The Making of a Girl."

Aug 8 *Seven Chances* (NY—Cohan—Comedy). David Belasco produces and stages this Roi Cooper Megrue play with a cast including Frank Craven, Otto Kruger, and Carroll McComas. It runs for 151 performances.

Aug 18 *Turn to the Right!* (NY—Gaiety—Comedy). Winchell Smith and John E. Hazzard write this comedy about a convict who reforms. It wins 435 performances.

Sep 2 *The Man Who Came Back* (NY—Playhouse—Drama). Adapted from a story by John F. Wilson, this play achieves 457 performances. The cast includes Henry Hull. On April 8, 1920 it premieres at London's Oxford with a cast including Henry Wenman and Lilian Braithwaite. It has 196 showings.

Sep 6 *Pierrot the Prodigal* (NY—Booth—Drama). The Prodigal Son tale is retold as a commedia pantomime, with music. It has 165 performances.

Sep 11 *Flora Bella* (NY—Casino—Musical). This show deals with a princess who pretends to be a non-existent sister to a reawaken her husband's interest in her. With opera star Lina Abarbanell, it achieves 112 performances.

Sept 14 *Nothing But the Truth* (NY—Longacre—Comedy). Using Fred Isham's novel, James Montgomery writes a comedy about a man who vows to tell no lies for one day. William Collier and Ned A. Sparks star. It runs 332 performances. On Feb 5, 1918 it premieres at London's Savoy where it runs for 578 performances.

Sep 18 *Pollyanna* (NY—Hudson—Comedy). Catherine Chisholm Cushing's treatment of Eleanor Porter's novel wins 112 performances.

Sep 25 *Upstairs and Down* (NY—Cort—Comedy). Frederic and Fanny Hatton's comedy lasts for 40 weeks on Broadway. Leo Carillo is in the cast.

Sep 25 *Miss Springtime* (NY—New Amsterdam—Musical). This musical has a score by Emmerich Kalman, book by Guy Bolton and lyrics by P. G. Wodehouse. It stars Sari Pentrass. The show achieves 224 performances.

Oct 23 *So Long, Letty* (NY—Shubert—Musical). Featuring the long-legged dancing of Charlotte Greenwood, this show has music and lyrics by Earl Carroll, and a book by Oliver Morosco and Elmer Harris. Morosco is also producer and director. It runs 12 weeks on Broadway.

Oct 23 *Come Out of the Kitchen* (NY—Cohan—Comedy). A. E. Thomas adapts Alice Duer Miller's popular novel. Henry Miller produces. Ruth Chatterton and William Boyd are in the cast.

Oct 26 *Major Pendennis* (NY—Criterion—Comedy). Langdon Mitchell's play, based on Thackeray's novel, stars John Drew. It runs 12 weeks.

Oct 26 *The Show of Wonders* (NY—Winter Garden—Musical). This revue has music by Sigmund Romberg, Otto Motzan and Herman Timberg. Marilyn Miller stars. The show runs 209 performances.

Oct 30 *Old Lady 31* (NY—39th Street—Drama). Rachel Crothers directs her play, suggested by a novel of Louise Forsslund. It has a 20-week run.

Oct 31 *Good Gracious Annabelle* (NY—Republic—Comedy). Clare Kummer's play is hailed as a harbinger of a new kind of American sophisticated comedy. Walter Hampden, Roland Young and Lola Fisher head the cast. It earns 111 performances.

Nov 6 *The Century Girl* (NY—Century—Revue). Florenz Ziegfeld and Charles Dillingham stage a lavish show. Designed by Joseph Urban, it has a staircase which becomes a Ziegfeld trademark. Victor Herbert and Irving Berlin contribute the music. With artists such as Hazel Dawn and Leon Errol, the show has 200 performances. It is the last such revue in America to take its name from the theatre in which it plays.

Nov 13 *Captain Kidd, Jr.* (NY—Cohan and

Turn to the Right

Century Girl

Harris—Comedy). Edith Taliaferro, Zelda Sears, and Otto Kruger appear in Rida Johnson Young's farce. It runs for 16 weeks.

Nov 20 *The Thirteenth Chair* (NY—48th Street—Drama). Bayard Veiller's thriller stars Margaret Wycherly. It runs for 41 weeks.

Dec 6 *Her Soldier Boy* (NY—Astor—Mus- ical). Rida Johnson Young adapts her book to Emmerich Kalman's score, with additional music by Sigmund Romberg. "Pack Up Your Troubles," an interpolation, is a big hit in this story of a soldier returning from war. The show runs 198 performances. On June 26, 1918 it opens at London's Apollo where it runs for 372 performances.

1916 BRITISH PREMIERES

Jan 27 *Please Help Emily* (L—Play- house—Comedy). H. M. Harwood's farce, similar to a Feydeau piece, stars Gladys Cooper. There are 213 performances.

Jan 29 *Tiger's Cub* (L—Garrick—Drama). George Potter's play about a man who comes to Alaska to find his father's killer has Madge Titheradge and Basil Gill. H. A. Saintsbury directs. There are 201 per- formances.

Feb 8 *Caroline* (L—New—Comedy). W. Somerset Maugham's light comedy stars Irene Vanbrugh. It earns 141 perfor- mances.

March 1 *My Lady Frayle* (L—Shaftes- bury—Musical). Arthur Wimperis and Max Pemberton write this version of the Faust theme. Howard Talbot and Herman Finck provide the score, with lyrics by Wimperis. Margot Joyce and J. V. Bryant star. The show runs 130 performances.

March 16 *A Kiss for Cinderella* (L— Wyndham's—Comedy). James Barrie's "fancy" stars Hilda Trevelyan and Gerald Du Maurier. It earns 156 performances.

March 22 *The Barton Mystery* (L—Sa- voy—Drama). Walter Hackett's play stars H. B. Irving. It runs 165 performances.

March 30 *Mr. Manhattan* (L—Prince of Wales's—Musical). The book is by Fred Thompson and C. H. Bovill with music by Howard Talbot and lyrics by Ralph Roberts. Raymond Hitchcock stars. This show earns 221 performances.

April 4 *Disraeli*. See NY premiere, 1911.

April 19 *The Bing Boys Are Here* (L— Alhambra—Revue). George Grossmith and Fred Thompson write this story of the Bing brothers in London. The score is by Nat Ayer. George Robey and Alfred Lester star. There are 378 performances.

May 13 *The Happy Day* (L—Daly's— Musical). Seymour Hicks writes the book about a queen reluctant to marry the prince to whom she is betrothed. The score is by Paul Rubens and Sydney Jones; lyrics by Rubens and Adrian Ross. Jose Collins stars. It runs for 241 performances.

May 29 *Daddy Long-Legs*. See NY pre- miere, 1914.

June 5 *Pell-Mell* (L—Ambassadors—Re- vue). C. B. Cochran's show has been de- vised by Fred Thompson and Morris Harvey, with a score by Nat Ayer and lyrics by Clifford Grey and Hugh Wright. Alice Delysia stars. There are 298 per- formances.

June 19 *Razzle-Dazzle* (L—Drury Lane— Revue). There are 408 performances for this show by Albert de Courville, Wal Pink, and Basil Hastings, with a score by Herman Darewski and Manuel Klein. William Wilson stages.

June 22 *Hobson's Choice* (L—Apollo— Comedy). Harold Brighouse's story of an obstinate shoe-merchant father, a deter- mined, clever daughter, and the sensible shoe-maker she marries comes to the West End for a run of 246 performances. Nor- man McKinnel, Edyth Goodall, and Re- ginald Fry play the leading roles.

June 29 *Some (More) Samples* (L—Vau- deville—Revue). J. W. Tate provides the score and Clifford Harris the lyrics for Harry Grattan's show. It receives 278 per- formances.

Aug 24 *High-Jinks* (L—Adelphi—Musi- cal). Frederick Lonsdale adapts this Aus- tralian farce about a flirtatious doctor. W. H. Berry plays. Jerome Kern is among the show's four composers. There are 383 performances.

Aug 31 *Chu-Chin-Chow* (L—His Majes- ty's—Musical). Oscar Asche devises and stars in this sumptuous fantasy of the Far East. Frederic Norton composes the mu- sic. It wins 2,238 showings. On Oct 22, 1917 it premieres at New York's Man- hattan Opera House with Tyrone Power. It runs for 208 performances. This is very successful by New York standards.

Sep 4 *The Girl from Ciro's* (L—Garrick— Comedy). Jose Levy adapts Pierre Veber's farce about people who lead double lives. H. V. Esmond is featured. It earns 202 performances.

Sep 5 *Her Husband's Wife* (L—New— Comedy). Marie Lohr and Allan Aynes- worth play in A. E. Thomas's comedy. It runs for 121 performances.

Sep 6 *The Misleading Lady*. See NY pre- miere, 1913.

Sep 14 *The Light Blues* (L—Shaftes- bury—Musical). Mark Ambient and Jack Hulbert devise this story of love during May Week. Adrian Ross provides the lyr- ics and Howard Talbot and Herman Finck the score. Stanley Logan, Cicely Court- neidge, and Noel Coward appear.

Sep 19 *Theodore & Co.* (L—Gaiety—Mus- ical). Jerome Kern and Ivor Novello create the music; Adrian Ross and Clifford Gray the lyrics. H. M. Harwood and George Grossmith adapt a French play about an aristocratic confidence man. Austin Mel- ford and Leslie Henson lead. It has 503 performances.

Sep 27 *The Best of Luck* (L—Drury Lane— Drama). This is the Drury Lane's seasonal spectacular. The authors are Arthur Col- lins, Henry Hamilton, and the late Cecil Raleigh. In the large cast are Madge Tith- eradge and C. M. Hallard.

Oct 18 *Home on Leave* (L—Royalty— Comedy). Edward Knoblauch—who has Anglicized his name to Knoblock—wins 145 performances for this three-act ve- hicle for Dennis Eadie and Marie Löhr.

Nov 6 *Vanity Fair* (L—Palace—Revue). Herman Finck composes the score and Arthur Wimperis and Percy Greenbank the lyrics in this burlesque of popular plays. Arthur Playfair and Nelson Keys are featured. It achieves 265 performances.

Nov 23 *Houp La!* (L—St. Martin's—Musical). Fred Thompson and Hugh Wright develop this story about a bankrupt circus owner who thinks his luck has changed. Wright and Percy Greenbank provide lyrics for music by Nat Ayer and Howard Talbot. Gertie Millar stars. There are 108 performances.

Dec 6 *London Pride* (L—Wyndham's—Drama). This is a "London play for London people," and at the same time a comment on English attitudes toward the war. Gladys Unger and A. Neil Lyons are the authors. There are 280 performances.

Dec 22 *Three Cheers* (L—Shaftesbury—Revue). Harry Grattan takes script credit, with music by Herman Darewski and lyrics by Adrian Ross. There are 190 performances.

Disraeli

1916   REVIVALS/REPERTORIES

Jan 31 Lilian Baylis, as manager of London's Old Vic Theatre, continues the series of Shakespeare premieres. Tonight, Ben Greet presents *Much Ado About Nothing*. Later in the year, he offers three more Baylis Shakespeare premieres: *Henry VIII* (Sep 30), *Richard II* (Nov 20), and *The Two Gentlemen of Verona* (Dec 4).

Feb 7 James K. Hackett stages and stars in a revival of *Macbeth* at New York's Criterion Theatre.

March 14 Herbert Beerbohm Tree revives Shakespeare's *King Henry VIII*, playing Cardinal Wolsey. It is staged at the New Amsterdam Theatre. In May, Beerbohm Tree revives *The Merchant of Venice* and *The Merry Wives of Windsor* in New York.

April 24 At Stratford-upon-Avon, *Henry V* and *The Merchant of Venice* are offered on the same day in the last regular Shakespeare Festival until the Great War is over. Other productions presented by Frank Benson include *All's Well That Ends Well*, *King John*, *A Midsummer Night's Dream*, *Twelfth Night*, and *The Taming of the Shrew*.

April 24 The Drama Society revives Shakespeare's *The Tempest* at New York's Century Theatre for six weeks. Louis Calvert stars.

April 24 Arnold Daly revives Clyde Fitch's *Beau Brummell*, at New York's Cort Theatre. He plays the title role.

April 24 Margaret Anglin revives Oscar Wilde's *A Woman of No Importance* at the Fulton Theatre in New York, for seven weeks.

May 1 At the Comedy Theatre in London, revues account for all the new seasonal productions. Tonight it's *Half-past Eight*, "one of those musical things," with score by Paul Rubens and book by Rubens and C. H. Bovill. It runs for 143 performances. This show is followed by *This and That*, on Sep 15, a revue by J. W. Tate (music) and Clifford Harris and Valentine (lyrics). *Samples* is revived on Oct 24.

May 2 To commemorate the tercentenary of Shakespeare' death, the company from the Memorial Theatre in Stratford-upon-Avon presents *Julius Caesar* with Frank Benson in a special matinee at the Drury Lane Theatre. This is followed by a pageant of Shakespearian characters. Three days later Benson presents nine scenes from the Bard's plays at Stratford. Among the cast are Gladys Cooper, Irene Vanbrugh, Ben Greet and Ellen Terry.

May 8 John Martin Harvey stars in *Hamlet* at His Majesty's in London. On May 15 he stars in *The Taming of the Shrew*. On May 22 he leads the cast of *Richard III*. *Henry V* opens on May 29.

July 29 At Stratford-upon-Avon in the Memorial Theatre, a young company from the Old Vic, under the direction of Ben Greet, presents a four-week season of Shakespeare, taking over from Frank Benson who customarily provides the productions. (He and his actress-wife Constance are in France, running a canteen for the French Red Cross.) In the repertory are *The Comedy of Errors*, *Othello*, *Much Ado About Nothing*, *The Tempest*, *The Winter's Tale*, *Two Gentlemen of Verona*, *Hamlet*, *Henry VIII*, *Macbeth* and Sheridan's *The Rivals*. Sybil Thorndike, Robert Atkins, Russell Thorndike, and William Stack are in the ensemble.

Aug 30 The *Washington Square Players* return for a repertory season at New York's Comedy Theatre. Most of the plays are one or two-act dramas, but during the last three weeks of May 1917, they present a production of Ibsen's *Ghosts*. Among the American plays are Susan Glaspell's *Trifles* and Lawrence Langner's *Another Way Out*.

Sep 16 The Birmingham Repertory Theatre opens its fifth season with Goldsmith's *The Good-Natured Man*. On Oct 7, it presents the world premiere of the anonymously written *The Inca of Perusalem*. Later George Bernard Shaw acknowledges authorship.

Oct 9 At London's historic Old Vic Ben Greet presents *The Comedy of Errors*.

Oct 10 David Belasco revives *The Music Master*, by Charles Klein, with David Warfield repeating the role he created in 1904. This production, at New York's Knickerbocker Theatre, runs for 159 performances.

Nov 6 Producers Klaw and Erlanger revive General Lew Wallace's *Ben-Hur* at the Manhattan Opera House in New York.

Nov 12 At the Aldwych Theatre, the French Players present Alfred de Musset's *A Quoi Revient les Jeunes Filles* for the first time in London. Ernest Thesiger stars.

Nov 27 Stuart Walker's Portmanteau Theatre opens at New York's 39th Street Theatre. In the repertory are Walker's own plays, *Six Who Pass While the Lentils Boil*, *The Very Naked Boy*, *Nevertheless*, and *The Trimplet*. Lord Dunsany's *The Gods of the Mountain*, *The Golden Doom*, and *King Argimenes and the Unknown Warrior* are also included in the program.

Nov 29 The Liverpool Repertory Company presents Zola's *Therese Raquin*.

Dec 4 Sarah Bernhardt returns to New York for a three-week engagement at Charles Frohman's Empire Theatre. In her repertory are two plays co-authored by her son, Maurice Bernhardt, *La Morte de Cleopatre* (with Henri Cain) and *Hecube* (with Rene Clarence). She also performs the sixth act of *L'Aiglon*, the last act of *La Dame aux Camelias*, an arrangement of *L'Holocauste*, and a version of the trial scene from *The Merchant of Venice*, titled *Shylock*.

Dec 18 Gertrude Kingston and her company present a repertory of five plays in New York at the Maxine Elliott Theatre. Two are New York premieres: Bernard Shaw's *Great Catherine* and *Overruled*. The other plays are Shaw's *How He Lied To Her Husband*, Lord Dunsany's *The Queen's Enemies*, and *The Inca of Perusalem*, by "a Fellow of the Royal Society of Literature."

Feb 28 Novelist and playwright Henry James (b. 1843) dies in London. Born in New York, James became a British subject in 1915. Few of his plays have been successfully produced. He is chiefly remembered for his novels and theatrical essays.

April 11 Author, playwright, and correspondent Richard Harding Davis (b. 1864) dies in Mt. Kisco, N.Y. Noted primarily for his journalistic writings and short stories, Davis also wrote 25 plays, of which the most popular were *Ranson's Folly*, *The Dictator*, and *Miss Civilization*.

April 24 Members of the Abbey Theatre ensemble take part in the Easter Uprising in Dublin. Among them are Ellen Bushell, Barney Murphy, Helena Moloney, Arthur Shields, and Peadar Kearney, author of Ireland's National Anthem. Sean Connolly, of the Abbey, is killed in action.

May 13 American actress Clare Louise Kellogg (b. 1842) dies today.

July 16 American playwright and author John Howard Lawson's play, *Servant-Master-Lover*, is produced in Los Angeles. It is his first to receive a professional production.

Sep 11 Actress-producer Janet Achurch dies at age 59. Her grandparents, Mr. and Mrs. Achurch Ward, were the friends and contemporaries of the Kemble family and Mrs. Siddons. She made her first appearance at the Olympic Theatre on Jan 8, 1883, in the farce, *Betsy Baker*, under the management of Genevieve Ward.

Sept 14 Playwright-critic-educator Eric Bentley is born in Bolton, England

Theodore & Co.

1916 THEATERS/PRODUCTIONS

In Britain patents are granted for B. M. Giroux's curtain painted to resemble a volcano and containing means for producing tremors, smoke, and landslides; J. L. Carter's theatrical appliance for producing the illusion of mounted troops cresting a hill and advancing toward the audience; A. B. Hector's Color Music device by which intensity of light can be controlled by piano-key electrical contacts.

Stephen Goldoni receives two U.S. patents for making sparks when a performer dances. One is composed of electrically charged floor mats, activated by special dancing shoes. The other involves an abrasive wheel, set in motion by the dancer's weight. Frank D. Thomas receives a patent for his method of combining three-dimensional scenic objects and projections.

May 24 Designers Robert Edmund Jones and Joseph Urban collaborate on *Caliban of the Yellow Sands*, which opens in Lewisohn Stadium at City College in New York. A significant development created by Jones and Urban for this production is a highly efficient long-throw floodlight, necessary for this outdoor production.

July 1 This date is past the end of the current Broadway season, but it is the cut-off date used by the *NY Dramatic Mirror* for its annual tally. Counting from June 15, 1915 through July 1, 1916, there have been 150 productions, with 37 of them running more than 100 performances. 120 have been new productions, divided among such categories as 42 comedies, 31 dramas, 26 musicals, 22 playlets, 10 melodramas, 10 farces, 6 tragedies, and 3 miscellaneous offerings. There have been 30 revivals as well. Following the play genre designations cited in *Best Plays*, by Burns Mantle and Garrison P. Sherwood, the breakdown, based on shows in 62 theatres, is 63 dramas, 44 comedies, 11 musicals, 7 revues, 4 operas, 2 operettas, and 6 Shakespearean revivals.

Aug 26 With the close of the summer Shakespeare season, the Memorial Theatre in Stratford-upon-Avon ceases to be the annual home of festival productions of Shakespeare's plays until the spring of 1919. During the balance of the wartime emergency, the theatre will be used by army amateur performers. It will also house two pageants and a patriotic melodrama.

Nov 23 The St. Martin's Theatre opens, just off Shaftesbury Avenue, London with *Houp La!* W. G. R. Sprague is the designer of this English Georgian style, 550-seat theatre, which is managed by C. B. Cochran.

Dec 1 The Provincetown Playhouse opens at 139 MacDougal Street in New York City. The small playhouse will be used by a group of artists organized by George Cram Cook to do new experimental work. The young playwright Eugene O'Neill is a member of the Company.

Dec 26 It's Boxing Day again—and also St. Stephens'—and time for Christmas pantomime openings in central and suburban theatres. Wartime economies have cut down the number and the lavishness of the shows, but Drury Lane mounts the Sims, Dix, and Collins *Puss in Boots*. At the Globe, *Where the Rainbow Ends* opens, with *Alice in Wonderland* coming back to life at the Savoy.

Chu Chin Chow

Jan 15 *Love o'Mike* (NY—Shubert—Musical). Another Jerome Kern score enriches the inane plot of house-party crushes and phony heroics. J. H. Benrimo stages Clifton Webb, Peggy Wood and Lawrence Grossmith star.

Feb 1 *The Wanderer* (NY—Manhattan Opera House—Drama). Producers F. Ray Comstock, Morris Gest and William Elliott present a play based on the bibilical tale of the Prodigal Son. James O'Neill, Florence Reed and Lionel Braham star. It runs for 108 performances.

Feb 5 *A Successful Calamity* (NY—Booth—Comedy). Clare Kummer's play, produced and directed by Arthur Hopkins, has Roland Young, William Gillette, Estelle Winwood and William Devereaux. It achieves 144 performances.

Feb 20 *Oh, Boy!* (NY—Princess—Musical). Jerome Kern provides the score (including "Till the Clouds Roll By") for the Guy Bolton and P.G. Wodehouse musical about newlyweds who must hide their marriage. The show runs 463 performances.

March 12 *Our Betters* (NY—Hudson—Comedy). W. Somerset Maugham's comedy about title-hungry Americans and fortune-hungry titled Englishmen has Chrystal Hearne, Rose Coghlan and Leonore Harris. It runs for 14 weeks. On Sep 19, 1923, the show premieres at London's Globe where it runs for 548 performances.

March 19 *Eileen* (NY—Shubert—Musical). Despite a Victor Herbert score including "Thine Alone" and favorable notices, this show musters only an eight-week run. Walter Scanlan and Grace Breen lead. Its story of an Irish revolutionary pales beside the real war in Europe, with the *City of Memphis*, and *Illinois*, and the *Vigilancia* sunk by German U-boats the previous day.

April 17 *Peter Ibbetson* (NY—Republic—Drama). Gerald DuMaurier's novel comes to the stage, with John Barrymore in the title role. Lionel Barrymore, Madge Evans, Constance Collier, Nina Varesa, and Laura Hope Crews are also in the cast. The show has only 71 performances.

April 26 *The Passing Show of 1917* (NY—Winter Garden—Revue). "Goodbye Broadway, Hello France!" helps set the tone for this wartime edition. DeWolf Hopper competes with Chic Sale for laughs. The basic score is by Sigmund Romberg, with interpolations. The show has 196 performances.

May 14 *The New World, Old Friends,* and *The Old Lady Shows Her Medals* (NY—Empire—Dramas). A triple-bill of plays by James Barrie is premiered on Broadway. B. Iden Payne stages, with actors such as Norman Trevor, Winifred Fraser, and Lyn Harding. They run for six weeks.

June 7 *Hitchy-Koo* (NY—Cohan and Harris—Revue). Some war songs and a first-act Wedding Album finale are part of this show with a score by E. Ray Goetz, who also drafts some of the lyrics. Leon Errol, Irene Bordoni, Frances White, and Raymond Hitchcock lead the cast.

June 12 *The Ziegfeld Follies of 1917* (NY—New Amsterdam—Revue). Raymond Hubbell and Dave Stamper write the music, with a finale by Victor Herbert. Book and lyrics are by Gene Buck and George Hobart. Will Rogers, Fannie Brice and W. C. Fields are in the cast.

Aug 15 *Business Before Pleasure* (NY—Eltinge—Comedy). This sequel in the lives of Abe Potash and Mawruss Perlmutter is written by Montague Glass and Jules Eckert. "Gus" Yorke and Robert Leonard are featured. It runs 357 performances. On April 21, 1919 the show premieres at London's Savoy with the two American comedians in the lead. The production wins 207 performances.

Aug 16 *Maytime* (NY—Shubert—Musical). Sigmund Romberg writes the score for this Rida Johnson Young adaptation of a German work about love in old New York. It runs for 492 performances.

Aug 22 *Eyes of Youth* (NY—Maxine Elliott—Comedy). Marjorie Rambeau stars in this play by Charles Guernon and Max Marcin. It achieves 414 performances. On Sep 2, 1918 it premieres at London's St. James's with Dorothy Paget. It has 384 performances.

Aug 23 *Cheer Up* (NY—Hippodrome—Revue). Producer Charles Dillingham offers horses diving into a pool and a cornfield transformed into a poppy field. Raymond Hubbell provides the songs, with John Golden the lyrics. Playing two-a-day, it tallies 456 performances.

Aug 27 *A Tailor Made Man* (NY—Cohan and Harris—Comedy). Harry James Smith's light satire on social foibles runs for 398 performances. Grant Mitchell, Minna Gale Haynes, and Lotta Linthicum appear.

Aug 28 *Leave It To Jane* (NY—Longacre—Musical). Guy Bolton and P. G. Wodehouse adapt George Ade's popular play, *The College Widow*, with a Jerome Kern score. Edith Hallor is Jane. The show runs 167 performances.

Sep 3 *The Masquerader* (NY—Lyric—Drama). John H. Booth adapts Katherine C. Thurston's novel. Louis Calvert and Guy Bates Post are in the cast. It achieves 160 performances.

Sep 6 *Polly with a Past* (NY—Belasco—Comedy). Guy Bolton and George Middleton concoct this Cinderella story. Ina

Maytime

Claire stars with Herbert Yost and H. Reeves Smith. It runs 315 performances. On June 4, 1921 the show opens at London's St. James's with Edna Best and Noel Coward in the leads. It achieves 110 performances.

Sep 24 *The Riviera Girl* (NY—New Amsterdam—Musical). Emmerich Kalman's operetta *Czardasfurstin* receives new book and lyrics by Guy Bolton and P.G. Wodehouse. Jerome Kern adds new songs. Gene Lockhart, Juliette Day and Louis Casavant are in the ensemble. Wartime enmities are blamed for its poor run—78 performances.

Sep 24 *Lombardi, Ltd.* (NY—Morosco—Comedy). Oliver Morosco produces and Clifford Brooke directs this British amusement, featuring Leo Carillo. The comedy runs for 296 performances.

Oct 3 *Tiger Rose* (NY—Lyceum—Drama). David Belasco produces and directs Willard Mack's play about a girl who loves a Mountie. Lenore Ulrich and Pedro de Cordoba are featured. The show has 384 performances. It premieres at London's Savoy on Oct 16, 1919 with Marjorie Campbell as Rose. Here, the show earns 142 performances.

Oct 16 *Jack O'Lantern* (NY—Globe—Musical). Fred Stone stars as a simple fellow who saves two children. Ivan Caryll writes the score and Anne Caldwell and R.H. Burnside the book. The show achieves 265 performances.

Oct 22 *Chu-Chin-Chow* See L Premiere, 1916.

Nov 5 *Miss 1917* (NY—Century—Revue). Book and lyrics are by Guy Bolton and P.G. Wodehouse, in an obvious attempt to repeat the success of *The Century Girl*. Victor Herbert provides the score, with some interpolations by Jerome Kern. Lew Fields, Irene Castle and Marion Davies are among the cast. The show has a disappointing run of six weeks.

Nov 19 *Odds and Ends of 1917* (NY—Bijou—Revue). With a first-act finale featuring famous couples such as Antony and Cleopatra, this slight show, with a score by Bide Dudley, John Godfrey, and James Byrnes, earns 112 performances.

Nov 28 *Over the Top* (NY—44th Street Roof—Revue). With such topical fare as an attack on a German trench by American planes, this show runs almost 10 weeks. Sigmund Romberg provides the score. Justine Johnson stars.

Dec 20 *Flo-Flo* (NY—Cort—Musical). John Cort produces Silvio Hein's musical with a number of variety acts, including some Yiddish comedy. The show enjoys 220 performances.

Dec 24 *Parlor, Bedroom, and Bath* (NY—Republic—Comedy). 232 performances reward this farce by C. W. Bell and Mark Swan. In the cast are Helen Menken, Francine Larrimore, and May Vallen.

Dec 25 *Going Up* (NY—Liberty—Musical). Based on James Montgomery's story, *The Aviator*, this farce has music by Louis Hirsch and book and lyrics by Otto Harbach. Frank Craven and Edith Day star. The show earns 351 performances.

Dec 25 *Why Marry?* (NY—Astor—Comedy). Jesse Lynch Williams' work is seen as a clever defense for the new woman who wants to mate without marriage. Lotus Robb, Beatrice Beckley and Estelle Winwood play with Nat C. Goodwin. The play wins 120 performances and the first Pulitzer Prize for drama. The *NY Times*

Tiger Rose

reports "Short of Shaw, no one has ventilated such a subject with such telling satire and explosive humor. And there are certain respects in which, as it seemed, the play surpasses even Shaw." On May 22, 1918 the show opens at London's Gaity where it runs for 574 performances. On May 12, 1920 the play is revived at the Comedy Theatre in London with Dorothy Tetley, Edward Combermere, Henrietta Watson, C. Aubrey Smith, and Nigel Bruce—as a footman.

1917 BRITISH PREMIERES

Jan 17 *Under Cover*. See NY premiere, 1914.

Jan 25 *The Aristocrat* (L—St. James's—Drama). Louis N. Parker's drama takes place in France during the time of Louis II. George Alexander and Mary Glynne lead. The play runs 150 performances.

Feb 1 *Anthony in Wonderland* (L—Prince of Wales's—Comedy). Monckton Hoffe calls his four-act play a "fantastic comedy." Charles Hawtrey stars. It runs for 114 performances.

Feb 10 *The Maid of the Mountains* (L—Daly's—Musical). Frederick Lonsdale's book tells of the leader of a band of brigands and his love. Harold Fraser-Simson and Harry Graham provide the music and lyrics. Arthur Wontner and Jose Collins star. It has 1,345 performances.

Feb 14 *Seven Days' Leave* (L—Lyceum—Drama). Walter Howard's story of a British naval captain on home leave who manages to sink a German submarine with the aid of a friend taps a vein of public sentiment. With Hilda Vaughan and Alfred Paumier in the cast, it runs for 715 performances. On Jan 17, 1918 it premieres in New York, where it gets only 156 performances.

March 3 *Remnant* (L—Royalty—Drama). Michael Morton adapts Dario Niccodemi's play about a waif who helps a young man make good. It provides leading roles for Dennis Eadie and Marie Lohr. There are 124 performances.

March 14 *General Post* (L—Haymarket—Comedy). J.E.H. Terry writes a play about a young man who rises in the army during the war. Norman McKinnel, George Tully and Madge Titheradge perform. There are 532 performances.

March 17 *Damaged Goods* (L—St. Martin's—Drama). Eugene Brieux's *Les Avaries*, is translated by John Pollock. The play, which deals with a young man with syphilis, is staged by J.B. Fagan "For Adults Only." Basset Roe, Nora Wynne and J. Fisher appear. The show, previously refused a license by the censors, runs 281 performances. *The Times* reports, "It touches with urgency and good sense . . ."

Dec 31 *The Cohan Revue of 1918* (NY—New Amsterdam—Revue). George M. Cohan and Irving Berlin pool some songs to create the score. Nora Bayes and Charles Winninger jest. This is the last attempt Cohan will make to continue the Weber and Fields revue tradition.

Dec 31 *Happiness* (NY—Criterion—Comedy). J. Hartley Manners, as author and director, again presents his wife, Laurette Taylor. The show earns 136 performances.

March 29 *Suzette* (L—Globe—Musical). All the players have characters in this show by Austen Hurgon and George Arthurs, but it's really more of a revue, featuring the popular Gaby Deslys, partnered by Harry Pilcer. Max Darewski composes, with lyrics by Arthurs. Also in the company are Yvan Servais, Stanley Lupino, May Wilkins, and Eric Masters. The show runs for 255 performances.

April 7 *Wurzle-Flummery* (L—New—Comedy). A.A. Milne offers this light comedy, which is admired by several critics as a promise of even better things to come. The cast includes Nigel Playfair, Dion Boucicault, and Helen Haye.

April 26 *Cheep!* (L—Vaudeville—Revue). Harry Grattan creates this revue with Beatrice Lillie in the cast. It shows 483 times.

May 5 *Bubbly* (L—Comedy—Revue). Andre Charlot presents this show which burlesques a variety of current theatre styles. J.H. Turner provides the book, with music by Philip Braham. Arthur Playfair and Phyllis Monkman are in the large cast.

May 23 *Inside the Lines* (L—Apollo—Drama). Earl Derr Biggers writes about a possible spy in the British navy. Eille Norwood, Frederick Ross and Ida Adams play. The play, with a surprise ending, runs for 421 performances.

June 8 *The Three Daughters of Monsieur Dupont* (L—Ambassadors—Drama). St. John Hankin adapts Eugene Brieux's French play about the fate of three women. The Lord Chamberlain had long banned it because it deals with the issue of birth control. Ethel Irving, Italia Conti and Aimee de Burgh star. The show has 158 performances.

June 8 *Smile* (L—Garrick—Revue). There are 206 performances of this show by Albert de Courville and Wal Pink. Frederick Chappelle provides the score.

Aug 4 *The Better 'Ole* (L—Oxford—Musical). Bruce Bairnsfather and Arthur Elliot base this on the popular cartoon character, Old Bill (Arthur Bourchier), calling it a "fragment from France, in two explosions, seven splinters, and a gas attack." The music and lyrics are the work of Her-

Flo Flo

man Darewski and James Hurd, respectively. The cast includes Sinclair Cotter, Tom Woottwell, Herbert Young, Madge Burdett, Peggie Foster, and Germaine Arnaux. There are 811 performances.

Aug 21 *Billeted* (L—Royalty—Comedy). F. Tennyson Jesse and H. M. Harwood collaborate on this war-time farce, which earns 236 performances. Dennis Eadie and Dawson Milward are featured.

Aug 22 *Carminetta* (L—Prince of Wales's—Musical). Monckton Hoffe reworks this show initially devised by Andre Borde and C.A. Carpenter. Lyrics are by Douglas Furber and extra songs by Herman Finck and Herman Darewski. Alice Delysia stars in this confrontation of English officers and gypsy women. The show runs for 260 performances.

Aug 23 *The Invisible Foe* (L—Savoy—Drama). Walter Hackett's play is able to attract audiences for 129 performances. H. B. Irving stars.

Sep 6 *Arlette* (L—Shaftesbury—Musical). Jose Levy translates and Austen Hurgon and George Arthurs adapts this French operetta about a girl who captures a prince's heart. The music, by Vieu and Le Feuvre, is enhanced by Ivor Novello tunes. Winifred Barnes stars. It runs for 260 performances.

Sep 12 *The Yellow Ticket* (L—Playhouse—Drama). Michael Morton's play about a Jewish woman trying to go to England stars Gladys Cooper and Arthur Wontner. It earns 234 showings.

Sep 14 *The Boy* (L—Adelphi—Musical). Arthur Wing Pinero's *The Magistrate* becomes a musical comedy, with book by Fred Thompson and score by Lionel Monckton and Howard Talbot. Lyrics are by Adrian Ross and Percy Greenbank. Donald Calthrop plays as a flirtatious 19-year-old kept in an Eton jacket by his age-conscious mother. The play enjoys 801 performances.

Oct 10 *The Saving Grace* (L—Garrick—Comedy). Charles Hawtrey stars and directs C. Haddon Chambers's play about an officer trying to marry his niece off to a wealthy playboy (played by Noel Coward). There are 166 performances.

Oct 16 *The Thirteenth Chair* (L—Duke of York's—Drama). There are 246 performances of Bayard Veiller's "whodunit" with Mrs. Patrick Campbell in the lead.

Oct 17 *Dear Brutus* (L—Wyndham's—Comedy). James Barrie's comedy about choices people make has Gerald Du Maurier, Sam Sothern and Norman Forbes. The production wins 365 showings.

Dec 22 *The Beauty Spot* (L—Gaiety—Musical). Arthur Anderson adapts this French show with music by J.W. Tate. Tom Walls and Maisie Gay are in the large cast. It has 152 performances.

Dec 31 *Sleeping Partners* (L—St. Martin's—Comedy). This is a "Garden of Eden Episode," adapted from the French of Sacha Guitry by Seymour Hicks. It earns a run of 129 performances, with Hicks, Madge Lessing, Stanley Turnbull, and William Home composing the entire cast.

is adapted from Leo Tolstoi's short story, *What Men Live By*. It's played in London at the St. James's Theatre, in an Academy of Dramatic Arts matinee.

April 15 In London at the Garrick Theatre, the French Players offer Eugene Brieux's comedy, *Blanchette*, with Georgette Meyrald in the title-role.

April 16 Robert B. Mantell returns to New York to present two weeks of Shakespeare at the 44th Street Theatre. In the repertory are *Julius Caesar, King Lear, Hamlet, Macbeth, King Richard III*, and *The Merchant of Venice*. Bulwer-Lytton's *Richelieu* alternates with the Bard's works.

April 26 H. B. Irving revives *Hamlet*, playing the title-role in London at the Savoy Theatre. On May 19, the great 19th century success of Irving's father, Henry Irving, *The Bells*, is revived. As a curtain-raiser, Conan Doyle's *The Story of Waterloo* is paired with it.

May 12 The Birmingham Repertory Theatre gives Synge's *The Tinker's Wedding* its first production since its 1909 premiere in the London Court Theatre matinee series.

June 10 The Pioneer Players come to London's Strand Theatre to present a translation of Paul Claudel's *The Tidings Brought to Mary*. On July 12, their production is *Three Weeks*, Roy Horniman's adaptation of Elinor Glyn's novel, with Jerrold Robertshaw and Marga La Rudia.

June 12 Eddie Cantor debuts in blackface in *The Ziegfeld Follies of 1917*.

July 1 The Stage Society gives a special production of Henry James's *The Outcry*.

Sep 1 The Birmingham Repertory Theatre opens its sixth season with Wilde's *Lady Windermere's Fan*.

Sep 1 Madame Sarah Bernhardt returns to Broadway, bringing the same repertory she offered last season. Her ensemble is at the Knickerbocker Theatre for two weeks.

Sep 29 The cycle of Shakespeare's 37 plays presented by Lilian Baylis at London's Old Vic Theatre continues with premieres of *King John* and *Henry IV, Part II* (Oct 29), both are produced by Ben Greet.

Oct 31 The Washington Square Players open their season in New York at the Comedy Theatre. Two full-length British plays are presented: Miles Malleson's *Youth* and George Bernard Shaw's *Mrs. Warren's Profession*. A large program of one-act plays is offered, including Eugene O'Neill's *In the Zone*, Theresa Helburn's *Enter the Hero*, Elmer (Rice) Reizenstein's *The Home of the Free*, Zona Gale's *Neighbors*, and George Cram Cook and Susan Glaspell's *Suppressed Desires*. The large ensemble has Louis Calvert, Walter Hampden, Gareth Hughes, and Mme. Yorska as guests for a production of Oscar Wilde's *Salome*. Others in the company are Katherine Cornell, Sam Jaffe and Edna St. Vincent Millay. " 'In

1917 REVIVALS/REPERTORIES

Feb 2 In Dublin, new plays are shown at the Tivoli, Empire, the Queen's, and other venues, but the Abbey Theatre is still home of a dedicated ensemble producing new Irish dramas. Tonight the play is *Fox and Geese*, by the Misses Day and Cummins, with Arthur Shields, May Craig, and others. On April 25, R. J. Ray's *The Strong Hand* is premiered, with Maureen Delany in the cast. On Sep 24, the troupe offers Seumas O'Kelly's *The Parnellite*. On Oct 30, the play is John Barnwall's *The Bacac* with Peter Nolan, Irene Kelly and others. On Nov 20, the company performs Her-

bert Farjeon's *Friends*. In Dec, on the 11th, Micheal MacLiammhoir and Barry Fitzgerald appear in *Blight*.

Feb 15 At London's Haymarket, the Stage Society offers a special program of Anatol France plays: *The Comedy of the Man Who Married a Dumb Wife* and *Au Petit Bonheur*.

Feb 25 At the Garrick Theatre in London, the Stage Society trys out John Masefield's verse drama, *Good Friday*, with H. Athol Forde and Dorothy Green.

April 3 Miles Malleson's play, *Michael*,

the Zone' was of a very high order, both as a thriller and as a document in human character and emotion. . . . Katherine Cornell disclosed a personality of distinguished spirits, marked intelligence, and increasing skill," reports the *NY Times*.

Nov 18 Yvonne Arnaud plays La Perichole, with Arthur Viroux as the Bishop of Lima in Prosper Merimee's *La Carosse du Saint-Sacrament*. This is one of the productions of the French Players' season in London at the Pavilion. They also offer *L'Amiral*, a comedy by Jacques Normand. At the Aldwych Theatre, on December 17, J. T. Grein has his own French Players perform *Le Fourberies de Nerine*, by Theodore de Banville, and *Jean III*, by Sacha Guitry.

Nov 27 Jacques Copeau has brought his much-admired Theatre du Vieux-Colombier from Paris to Manhattan for a season of performances which will extend into April 1918. The ensemble opens the engagement on this date with Copeau's *L'Impromptu du Vieux-Colombier* and Moliere's *Les Fourberies de Scapin*, followed on Dec 5 by Becque's *Navette*, Moliere's *La Jalousie du Barbouille*, and Merimee's *La Carosse du Saint-Sacre-*

ment. On the 11th, de Musset's *Barberine* and Renard's *Le Pain de Menage* open, followed on Christmas Day by Shakespeare's *La Nuit des Rois* or *Twelfth Night*.

Dec 16 At London's Criterion Theatre, the Pioneer Players present a triple-bill composed of Bernard Shaw's *Inca of Perusalem*, W. F. Casey's *Insurrection*, and a Japanese marionette-play, *Kanawa*, played by live actors.

Dec 20 James M. Barrie's *A Kiss for Cinderella* is revived for the holidays at London's Queen's Theatre. On Dec 24, the New Theatre presents a revival of *Peter Pan*. On Dec 26, the Theatre Royal, Drury Lane, presents *Aladdin*, with book by Anstey, Dix, and Collins, and music by Glover and Gideon. *The Wonder Tales* is presented at London's Ambassadors' Theatre, adapted by Rose O'Neill and Ethel Weltch from Nathaniel Hawthorne's book of stories. Pandora, Midas, and Baucis and Philemon are among the characters recreated.

Dec 24 Charles Frohman's office revives the Dumas fils, drama, *The Lady of the Camellias* at the Empire Theatre in New York. Ethel Barrymore stars.

signed in modules, which can be rearranged according to the needs of the production.

Jan 16 Condemned and closed as a German concern in 1915, Bechstein Hall today is re-opened for performances as Wigmore Hall.

Feb 5 The Morosco Theatre (905 seats) opens on West 45 Street in New York City. The theatre is built for Oliver Morosco, the successful West Coast producer, by the Shuberts. Morosco opens the theatre with *Canary Cottage*, a musical revue.

April 12 The Bijou Theatre (650 seats) opens on West 45 Street in New York City. The theatre, built by the Shuberts, is the smallest theatre in the Times Square area. It is razed Feb 1982, to make way for the new multi-story Portman Hotel.

Maid of the Mountains

1917   BIRTHS/DEATHS/DEBUTS

April 9 Drama critic-playwright Henry Hewes is born in Boston, Massachusetts.

April 20 The American actor-producer David Montgomery (b. 1870) dies today.

June 20 Actor Digby Valentine Bell (b. 1851) is dead.

June 30 Drama critic and author William Winter (b. 1836) is dead at age 80. Winter served on the staff of the New York *Tribune* from 1865 to 1909. He was the most conspicuous figure in American dramatic criticism of the period. He also wrote biographies of Henry Irving, Joseph Jefferson, Edwin Booth, Ada Rehan, David Belasco, and others.

Nov 6 English actor-manager William Hunter Kendal (b. 1843) is dead. Kendal played in the provinces appearing with

the Keans, G. V. Brooke, and Helen Faucit. While engaged at the Haymarket, he married actress Margaret Robinson. The Kendals went into partnership with Sir John Hare at the St. James's Theatre in 1879 where they played leading parts.

Nov 7 Because of anti-German sentiment, Otto Hauerbach has changed his name. The program for *Kitty Darlin'*, premiering tonight, announces that Otto Harbach has written the lyrics.

Nov 28 Fred and Adele Astaire make their Broadway debut in the musical revue, *Over the Top*, at the 44th Street Roof Theatre.

Dec 1 John Merivale is born to actor Philip Merivale and actress Viva Birkett in Toronto, Canada.

1917   THEATERS/PRODUCTIONS

In Britain patents are granted for: P. H. Boggis' flame effects produced by a series of streamers agitated from below by an air current; A. Collins' portable rotating spiral staircase for stage use.

John H. M. Dudley receives a U.S. patent for a scenic effect of the great guns of a warship, one turret being able to pivot out over the audience. This is just the sort of spectacle beloved of audiences at New York's Hippodrome Theatre. Frederick M. Smith has devised a system of gears and

pulleys for rolling scenic borders above the stage for rapid deployment and removal.

The Cleveland Play House, with actress Katherine Wick Kelly as one of its leading forces, acquires its first real home, an old Protestant church building in Cleveland, Ohio.

Jan 1 Sam Hume becomes the manager of The Arts and Crafts Theatre in Detroit, Michigan. He brings with him his innovation of adjustable scenery: scenery de-

May Despite the exploding bombs and shells in London's West End, theatre ensembles continue to perform calmly. Although there is a special wartime Entertainment Tax, audiences continue to patronize the theatres, though Henry Arthur Jones' *The Pacifists*, a recent failure, may have been hurt by this. Music Halls have virtually disappeared from the West End, except for variety programs at the Coliseum. The Alhambra and the Empire are now houses for sophisticated revues, and the Palace programs musical comedy. The Tivoli is now a patch of bare ground in the Strand. One has to go to Holborn or South-West to the Victoria for music hall entertainment. Near Waterloo Station, in the Old Vic (formerly Emma Cons' Royal Victorian Coffee Music Hall), plays are performed three nights and two matinees per week.

Bubbly

May 15 The Birmingham Repertory Theatre's performance of Synge's *The Tinker's Wedding* is disrupted by a rioting group objecting to the play's portrayal of the Catholic priesthood. As a result, the rest of the week's performances are sold out.

June 9 For the Broadway season this year, the *NY Dramatic Mirror* tallies 173 total productions, with 146 of them new and 42 of them achieving more than 100 performances. In the *Mirror's* count, which covers more than a year, there have been 25 musicals and 28 revivals, which suggests that the total production count should be 174. For the same season, Burns Mantle and Garrison P. Sherwood, authors of *Best Plays*, base their listings on 63 theatres, with 65 dramas, 55 comedies, 17 musicals, 5 revues, 3 operas, 1 operetta, 1 Shakespeare revival, and 3 repertory offerings.

Aug Capt. M. W. Plunkett selects men from all branches to form the 3rd Canadian Division Concert Party to entertain at the front in France. Named for the divisional symbol, The Dumbells (sic) perform gallows humor sketches, such as one about a real estate agent selling lots on Vimy Ridge with "free gas" and cellar already excavated. The Dumbells play in France and Belgium before a 4-week run in London in 1918. The group stays together after the war, performing successful revues which tour Canada. On May 9, 1921, their *Biff, Bing, Bang* is a hit at the Ambassador Theatre in New York City. They disband in 1929.

Oct 10 The Plymouth Theatre (1,000 seats) opens on West 45 Street in New York City. William Gillette stars in the Clare Kummer comedy, *A Successful Calamity*, which has opened a year earlier. Arthur Hopkins is the manager of this, the eighth playhouse on the block bounded by Broadway and 44 and 45 Streets.

Oct 22 Philadelphia issues a demolition permit for the Chestnut Street Theatre, opened in 1863 under the management of William Wheatley. Seating 1,189, it has recently been used as a stock playhouse, although Edwin Forrest and Sarah Bernhardt have both played here. Today, the demolition permit is granted.

Nov 5 Today Chicago's Studebaker Theatre re-opens after a $100,000 remodeling, designed by Andrew N. Rebori, later to become noted for his Art Deco stylings. A successful legitimate house in the first decade of the century, the Studebaker had fallen on hard times, reduced to vaudeville and films, both of which have failed. Now it is restored to legitimate use, with an enlarged stage and improved production facilities. Eventually it will be entered in the National Register of Historic Places, as Chicago's oldest legitimate theatre.

Nov 20 The Pasadena Community Playhouse, founded by Gilmor Brown, presents at the Shakespeare Club House its first series of plays. Among those plays to be presented this week are *The Song of Lady Lotus Eyes*, *The Critic*, *Pierre Patelin*, *The Neighbors*, and *The Man From Home*.

Dec 22 Since 1913, there has been an unofficial—though intermittently broken—truce between the Theatrical Syndicate forces and those of the Shubert organization. Today, however, the *New York Dramatic Mirror* comments: "It is generally felt that another theatrical war has been inevitable for some time. . . ." The spark for this renewal of hostilities is the action of Klaw and Erlanger and the Nirdlingers to enjoin the Shuberts from presenting first-class attractions in Philadelphia at the Chestnut Street Opera House. The 1913 agreement between the Shuberts and the Syndicate has limited first-class shows to the Forrest, Garrick, Broad Street, Adelphia, and Lyric Theatres. In the ensuing battle of suit and counter-suit over accountings for monies and similar matters, the Shuberts gain control of even more theatres and become more securely entrenched as the major force in American theatre production and operation.

The Saving Grace

Jan 22 *Seventeen* (NY—Booth—Comedy). Stanislaus Stange and Stannard Mears adapt Booth Tarkington's novel about teenage America. Ruth Gordon and Paul Kelly are in the cast. It runs for 225 performances. On Oct 20, 1925 it appears at London's Ambassadors where it gets only 14 performances.

Feb 1 *Oh, Lady! Lady!* (NY—Princess—Musical). Jerome Kern writes the score and Guy Bolton and P.G. Wodehouse the book and lyrics for this show about a jewel theft. Florence Shirley and Carl Randall are in the cast. The play runs 219 performances.

Feb 14 *Sinbad* (NY—Winter Garden—Musical). Al Jolson dominates this show, which begins in a Long Island dog show and rapidly removes to more exotic climes and settings. It runs for over twenty weeks. Late in the run, Jolson's big hit song, "My Mammy," is introduced. On tour, "Swanee," with lyrics by Irving Caesar and music by George Gershwin, is interpolated.

Feb 18 *The Copperhead* (NY—Shubert—Drama). Augustus Thomas' tense drama of the Civil War, based on a Frederick Landis story, achieves a 15-week run. Lionel Barrymore stars.

May 9 *The Kiss Burglar* (NY—Cohan—Musical). Glen MacDonough writes the book and lyrics and Raymond Hubbell the score for this show about a man who steals kisses from a duchess. Fay Bainter stars. The show runs 100 performances.

June 18 *The Ziegfeld Follies of 1918* (NY—New Amsterdam—Revue). Will Rogers, W.C. Fields, Ann Pennington, Eddie Cantor and Marilyn Miller are in this edition of the *Follies*. It is the last *Follies* for Lillian Lorraine. The show has 151 performances.

July 22 *Friendly Enemies* (NY—Hudson—Comedy). Samuel Shipman and Aaron Hoffman tell the story of a German-American transformed from a sympathizer of the Kaiser to a supporter of the American war effort. It runs 440 performances.

July 25 *The Passing Show of 1918* (NY—Winter Garden—Revue). Sigmund Romberg and Jean Schwartz compose the songs for this show which includes Fred and Adele Astaire, Frank Fay and Charles Ruggles. It has 124 performances.

Aug 13 *Three Faces East* (NY—Cohan and Harris—Drama). Anthony Paul Kelly's play about Germans trying to assassinate British leaders attracts patrons for 335 performances.

Aug 19 *Yip Yip Yaphank* (NY—Century—Revue). This soldier show from Camp Upton gives to American World War I's second most popular song, "Oh, How I Hate to Get Up in the Morning." The show, depicting rookie life, is notable for its score by Sergeant Irving Berlin. It runs for four weeks.

Aug 22 *Everything* (NY—Hippodrome—Revue). Irving Berlin and John Philip Sousa provide the songs and John Golden and others the lyrics. Among the performers are Harry Houdini and DeWolf Hopper. Playing two-a-day, the show manages 461 performances.

Aug 26 *Where Poppies Bloom* (NY—Republic—Drama). Roi Cooper Megrue reworks the French play by Henri Kistemaekers to make a melodrama of the war experience in Flanders fields. Marjorie Rambeau, Louis Stone, and Pedro de Cordoba are in the cast. The production runs for 104 performances.

Aug 26 *Lightnin'* (NY—Gaiety—Comedy). Frank Bacon and Winchell Smith write this tale of Lightnin' Bill Jones—slow-witted and slow-moving—who owns a hotel straddling the California-Nevada border, to the delight of guests in legal trouble. Bacon creates his memorable role as Jones. The show has 1,291 performances. On Jan 27, 1925, it opens at London's Shaftesbury with Horace Hodges in the lead. But it has only 151 showings.

Sep 5 *Daddies* (NY—Belasco—Comedy). John Hobble's amusement runs for almost 43 weeks, with a cast including Jeanne Eagels and George Abbott. David Belasco produces and directs.

Sep 9 *Forever After* (NY—Central—Drama). Owen Davis' story of a dying soldier opens the Central Theatre and enjoys a long run of 312 performances. The cast is headed by Alice Brady, John Warner, and Conrad Nagel. William A. Brady produces, and Frank Hatch directs.

Sep 19 *Tea for Three* (NY—Maxine Elliott—Comedy). Roi Cooper Megrue stages his own script, which runs for 300 performances.

Oct 4 *Sometime* (NY—Shubert—Musical). Mae West vamps an innocent man, causing his fiancee to refuse to see him for five years. This show, by Rida Johnson Young, with music by Rudolf Friml, has one of the earliest uses of dramatic flashback technique. Ed Wynn stars in this show which runs 283 performances.

Oct 5 *Sleeping Partners* (NY—Bijou—Comedy). Sacha Guitry's Parisian farce is translated for American tastes. It runs for 20 weeks, with a cast of H. B. Warner, Irene Bordoni, Guy Favieres, and Arthur Lewis.

Oct 19 *The Better 'Ole* (NY—Greenwich Village—Musical). The Charles Coburns produce and perform in this show, based on cartoonist Bruce Bairnsfeather's character of Old Bill. Perdical Knight and Herman Darewski are credited with the score, but much of the music is interpolated old favorites. The show runs 353 performances.

Oct 23 *The Riddle: Woman* (NY—Harris—Drama). Charlotte Wells and Dorothy Donnelly collaborate on this play which runs over 20 weeks. In the cast are Robert Edeson, Chrystal Herne, and Bertha Kalich.

Oct 31 *Three Wise Fools* (NY—Criterion—Drama). Austin Strong's play about the Three Musketeers as old men features Helen Menken, Claude Gillingwater and Harry Davenport. It runs 316 performances. On July 12, 1919 it opens at London's Comedy with Charles Glenney, Herbert Ross, Arthur Lewis and Margaret Bannerman in the cast. There are 303 showings.

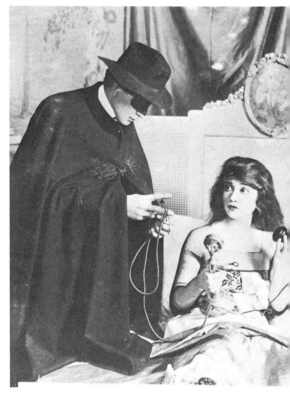

The Kiss Burglar

Nov 4 *The Canary* (NY—Globe—Musical). Harry B. Smith writes the words and Ivan Caryll the music for this story about a man who has accidently swallowed a diamond. The score is padded out with numbers from Irving Berlin, Jerome Kern and Harry Tierney. Joseph Cawthorne and Julia Sanderson star. It runs 152 performances.

Nov 11 *Home Again* (NY—Playhouse—Comedy). Opening on the day of armistice in Europe, this peaceful play is based on the stories and folk-poems of James Whitcomb Riley, the "Hoosier Poet." It

Empire Theatre

runs only five weeks.

Nov 12 *Tiger! Tiger!* (NY—Belasco—Drama). Edward Knoblock's play wins 183 performances, the cast includes Wallace Erskine, Dorothy Cumming, and Lionel Atwill. David Belasco produces and directs.

Nov 18 *The Betrothal* (NY—Shubert—Drama). Winthrop Ames produces Maurice Maeterlinck's drama focusing on a man's relationship to his ancestors and descendants, a Blue Bird sequel. The production runs for 25 weeks.

Nov 27 *Oh, My Dear!* (NY—Princess—Musical). The last of the Princess musicals, Guy Bolton and P.G. Wodehouse create a book which involves some Big City types stranded on a health farm. Louis Hirsch writes an indifferent score. The show runs 189 performances.

Dec 23 *Atta Boy* (NY—Lexington—Revue). Another soldier show, this one mounted by men from the Aberdeen Proving Ground. Mocking the routine of army life, with female impersonations typical of such shows, its timing is wrong. The war is over, and audiences have lost interest. It musters only a three-week run.

Dec 23 *Dear Brutus* (NY—Empire—Comedy). James Barrie's play is staged by B. Iden Payne, with a cast including Helen Hayes, Louis Calvert, William Gillette, and Violet Kemble Cooper. It runs for 23 weeks.

Dec 23 *Listen Lester* (NY—Knickerbocker—Musical). Harry Cort and George Stoddart create this book and lyrics and Harold Orlob the score for this story of a man trying to recover some indiscreet letters. Hansford Wilson, Gertrude Vanderbilt, Ada Mae Weeks and Clifton Webb are in the cast. It runs 272 performances.

Dec 23 *Somebody's Sweetheart* (NY—Central—Musical). Arthur Hammerstein produces and stages this show about a gypsy in love with a man engaged to another. Antonio Bafunno writes the score and Alonzo Prince the lyrics. It runs 224 performances.

Dec 24 *A Prince There Was* (NY—Cohan—Comedy). George M. Cohan writes, produces, and stars in this show. Marie Vernon and Jessie Ralph are also in the cast, for 159 performances.

Dec 25 *East Is West* (NY—Astor—Comedy). Samuel Shipman and John Hymer's play is about a flirtatious oriental who marries an American. But things turn out well for that time—she discovers she is Spanish not oriental. Fay Bainter and Lester Lonergan star. It runs 680 performances.

Dec 26 *A Little Journey* (NY—Little—Comedy). Rachel Crothers's play about a society girl who, having lost her fortune, goes out west to join her brother, earns 252 performances. Crothers stages a cast including Jobyna Howland and Edward Lester.

earlier Bing Boys show, there is a thread of plot on which to string sketches, dances and songs. It runs 562 performances.

Feb 21 *The Lilac Domino* (L—Empire—Musical). This show is not to be confused with its contemporary, *The Purple Mask*. It comes from America (produced in 1914 at the Forty-Fourth Street Theatre), with a book by Harry B. Smith—rewritten for London by S. J. A. Fitzgerald. The score is the work of Charles Cuvillier. It wins 747 performances, with a successful revival in another war-time, 1944. Among the company are Dallas Anderson, Josephine Earle, A. Stewart Piggott, Vincent Sullivan, Edwin Wilson and Andrée Corday.

March 7 *Box o' Tricks* (L—Hippodrome—Musical). This colorful, inventive revue by Albert de Courville and Wal Pink wins 625 performances. Dave Stamper and Frederick Chappelle provide the score. De Courville produces, with the American director choreographer, Ned Wayburn, doing the staging. In the company are Cicely Debenham and Tom McNaughton.

March 30 *The Prime Minister* (L—Royalty—Drama). Hall Caine's melodrama concerns the sacrifice a woman makes for love. Ethel Irving stars. It runs only 66 performances.

March 30 *By Pigeon Post* (L—Garrick—Drama). Austin Page's melodrama has a war background. The novelty is women playing doctors and chauffeurs. Madge Titheradge plays. There are 378 showings.

May 15 *Tabs* (L—Vaudeville—Revue). Harry Grattan's new show earns 268 performances, with Ronald Jeans helping on sketches and lyrics. The music is largely by Ivor Novello, with Gwladys Dillon staging dances and production numbers. The cast is adorned by Beatrice Lillie.

May 30 *The Man from Toronto* (L—Royalty—Comedy). Douglas Murray's play about a mistress masquerading as a maid

1918   BRITISH PREMIERES

Jan 5 *Out of Hell* (L—Ambassadors'—Drama). Frances Ivor and H. Brough Robertson play the double roles of mothers and sons on both sides of the war. Herbert Thoma's play earns only a four-week run. The play opens on Aug 20 at New York's Eltinge Theatre with Shelly Hull and Effie Shannon. It runs 21 weeks.

Jan 26 *Love in a Cottage* (L—Globe—Comedy). Marie Löhr is in W. Somerset Maugham's new comedy. It runs 128 performances.

Feb 16 *The Bing Boys on Broadway* (L—Alhambra—Revue). Songs are by Clifford Grey and Nat Ayre, Harry Vernon produces with Gus Sohlke staging. As in the

has 486 performances. Players include Iris Hoey and Eric Lewis.

June 1 *Tails Up* (L—Comedy—Musical). Philip Braham writes the score and High Wright and Davy Burnaby the lyrics for this show which includes Teddy Gerard and Arthur Playfair. It runs 467 performances.

June 20 *You Never Know, Y'Know* (L—Criterion—Comedy). This is an adaptation of Feydeau's *Puce a l'Oreille*, involving a wife fearful of her husband's possible philandering. Rex London and Enid Sass play leads. There are 351 performances.

June 21 *Nurse Benson* (L—Globe—Comedy). R.C. Carton and Justin Huntly McCarthy collaborate on this play about a pair of schemers. Blanche Stanley has the title role. There are 324 performances.

July 4 *The Hidden Hand* (L—Strand—Drama). Laurence Cowen's spy melodrama features Lewis Mannering and William Stack. It runs for 165 performances.

July 10 *The Purple Mask* (L—Lyric—Comedy). Matheson Lang directs and stars in this adaptation of Armont and Manoussi's *Le Chevailier au Masque*, the story of a French royalist in 1804. It has 365 performances.

July 11 *The Chinese Puzzle* (L—New—Drama). Lion M. Lion and Marion Bower write a drama of a Chinese diplomat who takes the blame for revealing secret negotiations rather than destroy the happiness of a friend. Lion and John Howell lead the cast. It earns a total of 145 performances.

July 20 *The Title* (L—Royalty—Comedy). Arnold Bennett writes a story of a man who doesn't want to be named in the New Year's Honours List but accepts a knighthood to please his wife. C. Aubrey Smith and Eva Moore are in leading roles. There

are 285 performances.

Aug 1 *The Freedom of the Seas* (L—Haymarket—Drama). Walter Hackett's drama of romance and treachery on the high seas has Dennis Eadie, Randle Ayrton and James Carew. There are 226 performances.

Aug 3 *As You Were* (L—London Pavilion—Musical). Arthur Wimperis writes the book and lyrics and Harman Darewski and Edouard Mathe the score for this revue about a millionaire who goes back in time. Alice Delysia, Leon Morton and John Humphries are in the cast. The show achieves 484 performances.

Aug 5 *The Luck of the Navy* (L—Queen's—Drama). Mrs. Clifford Mills uses the British Navy as background for her thriller. Percy Hutchison and Patrick Ludlow are in the cast. There are 289 performances.

Aug 29 *The Law Divine* (L—Wyndham's—Comedy). H.V. Esmond stars in his own play about a man, wounded in war, who is neglected by his wife, so busy "doing her bit for the war-effort." The show wins 368 performances.

Sep 18 *Roxana* (L—Lyric—Comedy). Doris Keane stars in Avery Hopwood's variation on the theme of *Taming of the Shrew*. There are 219 performances.

Sep 25 *Hullo! America* (L—Palace—Revue). Clifford Gray and Herman Finck provide the songs and J.H. Turner the book for this revue starring Elsie Janis. There are 358 performances.

Oct 2 *The Female Hun* (L—Lyceum—

Drama). Walter Melville's play about a British officer married to a woman loyal to Germany includes Herbert Mansfield and Leslie Carter. There are 225 performances.

Nov 7 *The Officers' Mess* (L—St. Martin's—Musical). Sydney Blow and Douglas Hoare call their book a musical farce. Philip Braham provides the score of this musical. A large company includes Evan Thomas, Elsie Stevens and Roger Livesey. The show has 200 performances.

Nov 28 *US* (L—Ambassadors'—Revue). This is described as a "song show." Songs are from a variety of composers. In the company are Lee White, Clay Smith and Monty Wolfe. It wins 812 performances.

Dec 7 *Scandal* (L—Strand—Comedy). Kyrle Bellew and Noel Coward act in Cosmo Hamilton's comedy about a woman who pretends to be married to a gentleman. It runs 238 performances. On Sep 12, 1919 the show opens at New York's 39th Street Theatre with Francine Larrimore and Charles Cherry. It tallies 318 performances.

Dec 20 *Buzz-Buzz* (L—Vaudeville—Revue). There are 612 showings of this Arthur Wimperis and Ronald Jeans revue, with music by Herman Darewski. A new name, Gertrude Lawrence, is in the cast.

Dec 23 *In the Night Watch* (L—Oxford—Drama). Michael Morton writes of a wife who helps clear her husband at a naval court martial. The cast includes Dennis Wyndham and Madge Titheradge. There are 215 performances.

1918 REVIVALS/REPERTORIES

Jan 7 Swedish playwright Hjalmar Bergman's *Karen* is presented at New York's Greenwich Village Theatre.

Jan 8 Jacques Copeau's Theatre du Vieux-Colombier continues its New York engagement with Curel's *La Nouvelle Idole* (11) tonight, followed on the 23 by Copeau and Croué's *Les Frères Karamazov* (14) and on the 31 by Marivaux's *La Surprise de l'Amour* (7). On Feb 7, Villeroy's *La Traverse* (12) opens, with Renard's *Poil de Carotte* (12). Mirbeau's *Le Mauvais Bergere* (9) is played on the 20. On March 5, Meilhac and Halevy's *La Petite Marquise* (14) and Moliere's *L'Amour Medecin* (14) are offered, with Moliere's *L'Avare* (11) opening on March 19. On April 2, the company presents three plays: Courteline's *La Paix Chez Soi* (3), Martin du Gard's *Le Testament du Pere Leleu* (3), and Porto-Riche's *La Chance de Françoise* (3).

Jan 29 In Dublin at the Abbey Theatre, where W. B. Yeats and Lady Gregory are Directors, her play, *Hanrahan's Oath*, a one-act comedy, opens. Other new plays produced during the season include Rose McKenna's *Aliens* (March 12), Christian Callister's *Little Bit of Youth* (May 28), Charles McEvoy's *Her Ladyship* (June 24), Edward Barrett's *The Grabber* (Nov 12),

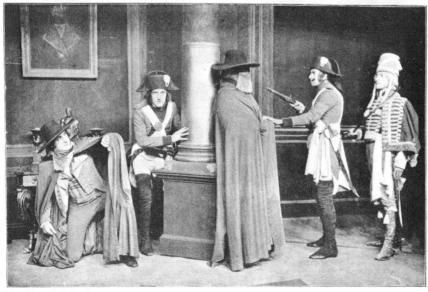

The Purple Mask

and Dorothy McArdle's *Atonement* (Dec. 17).

Jan 19 *Everyman* is revived for two matinees at the Cort Theatre in New York. Edith Wynne Matthison, Constance Bennett, and Charles Rann Kennedy are in the company. A week later, the group gives two matinees of *The Merchant of Venice*.

Feb 18 At London's Old Vic Theatre, Shakespeare's *King Lear*, staged by Ben Greet, is presented, continuing the cycle of the Bard's plays, produced under the management of Lilian Baylis. Other Baylis Shakespeare firsts this year are *Cybeline* (Mar 4), *Measure for Measure* (Oct 7), and *Love's Labour's Lost* (Dec 9). The last two are staged by George R. Foss.

Feb 18 Madge Mc Intosh and H.K. Ayliff play in *Realities*, the "new Ibsen play" presented at London's Royal Court Theatre by Austin Fryers.

March 11 Ibsen's *The Wild Duck* receives its New York English-language premiere at Plymouth Theatre. Alla Nazimova and Lionel Atwill star.

April 1 Arthur Sinclair and his Irish Players—the company of the Abbey Theatre in Dublin—open a season of more than a month at London's Royal Court Theatre with *Tactics* and *Fox and Geese* the first week. *Duty*, *The Coiner*, and *The Building Fund* are the second week's triple-bill. On the third week, Synge's *The Playboy of the Western World* is presented; it plays till the end of the engagement.

April 5 Laurette Taylor begins a series of matinees at New York's Criterion Theatre, in which she stars in scenes from Shakespeare. Lynn Fontanne is in the cast.

April 18 The Greenwich Village Players offer a program of three one-act plays for a month at the Greenwich Village Theatre. They are Eugene O'Neill's *'Ile*, Harold Brighouse's *The Maid of France*, and Arthur Schnitzler's *The Big Scene*. On May 20, Susan Glaspell's *A Woman's Honor* replaces the Schnitzler play, and the run is extended until June 1.

May 13 Ibsen's *The Master Builder* is revived at the Royal Court Theatre for two weeks in Leigh Lovel's season.

Aug 31 The Birmingham Repertory Theatre opens its seventh season with *Milestones*, by Arnold Bennett and Edward Knoblock.

Sep 16 Oscar Wilde's *An Ideal Husband* is revived for a ten-weeks' run in New York at the Comedy Theatre. Cyril Harcourt, Julian L'Estrange, and Constance Collier are in the ensemble.

Oct 3 John Barrymore stars in Arthur Hopkin's staging of Tolstoi's *Redemption* at New York's Plymouth Theatre.

Oct 12 John Drinkwater's *Abraham Lincoln*, premieres at the Birmingham Repertory Theatre and becomes its most successful and acclaimed production to date,

The Freedom of the Seas

later transferring to the West End and to Broadway.

Oct 14 In New York, Jacques Copeau's Paris-based Theatre de Vieux-Colombier opens its second consecutive season with Bernstein's *Le Secret* (8) followed on the 21 by Beaumarchais' *Le Mariage de Figaro* (16), and on the 28 by Brieux's *Blanchette* (8). On Nov 4, Donnay's *Georgette Lemeunier* (8) is played, with France's *Crainquebille* (8) and Clemenceau's *La Voile du Bonheur* (8) on the 11. Dumas'

La Femme de Claude (8) is presented on Nov 18, followed by Moliere's *Le Medecin Malgre Lui* (8) and Banville's *La Gringoire* (8) on the 25. Ibsen's *Rosmersholm* (8) is played on Dec 2, with Augier and Sandeau's *Le Gendre de M. Poirier* (8) on the 9. On the 16, it's de Musset's *Les Caprices de Marianne* (8) and Bernard's *Fardeau de la Liberte* (8), followed on the 23 by Rostand's *Les Romanesques* (8) and Moliere's *La Jalousie du Barbouille* (8), and on the 30, by Courteline's *Boubouroche* (8) and Hervieu's *L'Enigme* (8).

Oct 25 At London's "Old Vic," home of Shakespeare revivals and productions of neglected operas, the 100th anniversary is today observed, with Queen Mary and Princess Mary in attendance.

Nov 4 Robert B. Mantell returns to Broadway with his repertory of plays, staying at the 44th Street Theatre until Dec 21. The bill includes Edward Bulwer-Lytton's *Richelieu* and H. V. Mattheus's adaptation of Casimir Delavigne's *Louis XI*. Shakespeare is represented by *Hamlet*, *Othello*, *Macbeth*, *Richard III*, *The Merchant of Venice*, and *Romeo and Juliet*.

Dec 26 It's Boxing Day and at London's Drury Lane Theatre, the traditional pantomime is *The Babes in the Woods*. At the Lyceum, *Cinderella* opens today. At the New Theatre, the traditional holiday treat, J. M. Barrie's *Peter Pan*, has been running since Dec 19. On the 16, the Garrick has revived Thomas' *Charley's Aunt* for holiday audiences.

1918   BIRTHS/DEATHS/DEBUTS

Feb 2 American author and critic Leander Richardson (b. 1856) is dead. Richardson was editor of the *New York Dramatic News* from 1891 to 1896. *The Millionaire* and *Under the City Lamps* are among his dramatic works.

Feb 15 Vernon Castle (b. 1887) has won international fame on the stage, especially with his partner Irene, as a creator and performer of stylish ballroom dances. Today he passes on.

March 16 Actor-manager Sir George Alexander (b. 1858) dies in London. Sir George joined Henry Irving's Lyceum Company in 1880. In 1889 he took a theatre of his own, producing plays by Oscar Wilde and Sir Arthur Wing Pinero. His most successful role was the dual one of the king and Rassendyll in *The Prisoner of Zenda*. He was knighted in 1911.

March 22 The American actress Maggie Mitchell (b. 1832) dies.

May 18 English actor W. L. Abingdon (William Lepper Pilgrim) is dead at age 59 in New York City. Abingdon appeared as Professor Moriarty in William Gillette's *Sherlock Holmes* at London's Lyceum Theatre in 1901. His American per-

formances included stints in vaudeville.

June 14 Dorothy McGuire is born in Omaha, Nebraska.

Aug 13 French-American actress Anna Held (b. 1873) is dead. Held made her first American appearance in 1896 at the Herald Square Theatre in *A Parlor Match*. She played in numerous musical comedies, among them *Miss Innocence*, *The Little Duchess*, and *The Parisian Model*. She was the first wife of Florenz Ziegfeld.

Aug 31 Lyricist, producer, and playwright Alan Jay Lerner is born in New York City.

Oct 15 Playwright-director Robert E. Lee is born in Elyria, Ohio.

Nov 20 American scene and costume designer Kate Drain weds playwright John Howard Lawson.

Dec 2 The famed French playwright Edmond Rostand (b. 1868) is dead. He will be best remembered for his romantic masterpiece *Cyrano de Bergerac*, though he also wrote *L'Aiglon* for Sarah Bernhardt, and other romantic dramas popular in their time.

Dec 27 British actor Frank Kemble Cooper (b. 1847) dies today.

In Britain patents are granted for: Falconbridge and Lewsley's mechanism for controlling the curtain and lights simultaneously; C. H. Dent's pivoted levers attached to a turning drum to simulate horses' hooves galloping.

Howard Thurston, the popular magician, receives a U.S. patent for a special cabinet for use in his act. The director-playwright Richard Walton Tully gets three patents. Two are for devices allowing one actor to replace another on stage without being detected easily. One of these is a trick-sofa with a hinged back. He also has devised an effect of drifting fog, using scrims and "sidewardly moving lights."

In Dublin, William Butler Yeats, Lennox Robinson, and James Stephens found the Dublin Drama League, for the purpose of producing seasons of dramas of international repute at the Abbey Theatre. This work will continue intermittently for the ensuing decade.

Jan Owing to war-time problems, Annie Horniman's British repertory company has had to be disbanded at the Gaiety Theatre in Manchester. Nonetheless, in the coming season she will attempt to keep the theatre active with touring attractions and special productions. Some of her former troupe—Irene Rooke, Mrs. A. B. Tapping, and Douglas Gordon—form an ensemble to present a six-week season of revivals of *Humpty Dumpty*, *Miss Hobbs*, and *Lady Huntsworth's Experiment*. From Sep 23 to Nov 2, Dion Boucicault and Irene Vanbrugh present *Caroline*, *Trelawny of the "Wells,"* *Belinda*, and *His Excellency the Governor*, with a specially organised company for the Gaiety.

Jan 15 In Chicago, the Chicago Theatre is destroyed by fire.

Jan 18 The Norworth Theatre, on West 48 Street in New York, named for composer Jack Norworth and designed by DeRosa and Pereira, opens with *Odds and Ends of 1917*. Norworth gives up management of the theatre four months after the opening, and the theatre is renamed the Belmont. Playwright Philip Barry's first New York show, *You and I*, opens here. In 1951, the theatre is torn down and replaced by a commercial building.

March 11 The Woods Theatre, designed by Marshall and Fox, opens in Chicago at 50 West Randolph. It seats 1,200 people. In 1932, it will convert to a cinema and in 1980 will still be functioning as such.

April 1 Henry Miller's Theatre (1,000 seats) opens in New York City. The theatre has been designed for the comfort of the spectators with the latest staging techniques by the popular actor-manager, Henry Miller.

May With the departure for war of no less than 12 members of the Washington Square Players, recently based at the Comedy Theatre, the group decides to disband.

Aug 1 The *NY Dramatic Mirror* notes 190 total productions given in New York in the past season. Perhaps the war overseas has pre-empted journalists' attention; the *NY Times* and *Variety* do not offer a seasonal tally or breakdown by genres. The *Mirror* presents no breakdowns. In *Best Plays*, authors Burns Mantle and Garrison P. Sherwood, basing their listings on 70 theatres, note 68 dramas produced, 64 comedies, 25 musicals, 11 revues, 2 operettas, 3 Shakespearean revivals, and 3 repertory offerings.

Aug 3 After conversion to a theatre, the London Pavilion opens with the revue *As You Were*. Charles B. Cochran is the manager of this 1,080 seat theatre which has been a music hall since 1884.

Aug 26 In Philadelphia, the Sam S. Shubert Theatre opens, designed by Herbert J. Krapp. On the site of the Horticultural Hall, the theatre retains the marble staircase of that structure. Seating 1,913, it has a proscenium opening of 46 feet wide by 27 feet high. Producer Morris Gest, to honor his late friend, Sam Shubert, opens the house with his production of *Chu Chin Chow*.

Fall At the outset of this new season in New York, the Shubert brothers control 18 of the city's theatres, with 5 in Boston, 4 in Philadelphia, 3 in Chicago, and 2 each in San Francisco, Pittsburgh, Providence, and Washington, D. C. They also have theatres in almost all cities booked as one-week stands. The Selwyns and Al Woods join forces with the Shuberts; other New York theatre-owners and producers allied with the Syndicate stand fast.

Sep 9 The Central Theatre, at Broadway and 47 Streets in New York, designed by Herbert J. Krapp, opens with the production *Forever After*, by Owen Davis. By 1928, the theatre converts to a motion-picture house, then to a showcase house for Minsky's burlesques. In the 1950s, under the name Holiday, it briefly returns to presenting plays. It becomes a film house named the Forum.

Nov Frederick B. Adam, in conjuction with Roscoe E. Major, installs their first switching preset switchboard in the Illinois Theatre in Chicago. This switchboard allows pre-setting dimmers at various levels.

Nov Frederick H. Koch, who has recently accepted a teaching post at the University of North Carolina organizes the Carolina Playmakers. The Playmakers will produce plays written by students at the university, emphasizing regional themes.

They perform at a local high school.

Nov 4 After this date, every one of the members of American Actors' Equity Association must insist on the Standard Contract, agreed upon a year ago by AEA and the Theatre Managers' Association. 12,000 members, including 47 stars, have signed a pledge to insist on this contract. During the past year, the AEA has formally affiliated with the British and Australian Associations. When members are "at liberty," the AEA now puts their names on a weekly list sent to managers and producers.

Irving Berlin

Nov 23 The Actors' Association in London, prodded by Sydney Valentine and various actor complaints of abuses by theatre managers in wages and contracts, decides to become a real trade union, rather than a limited liability company. Immediately, demands are made for contractual minimum wages and a flat payment weekly for rehearsals—hitherto unpaid, at a time when all other theatre personnel have been paid during rehearsals. £ 3 is to be the minimum for both rehearsals and playing on a weekly basis. In September, collective bargaining, chaired by J. E. Vedrenne, has brought National Association of Theatrical Employees members raises from £ 1 per week to 6 shillings a performance.

Dec There are only 25 legitimate theatre productions on tour in America as of the first week of this month. Two major causes are the growth of motion-pictures and national concern about Americans overseas, fighting in France. In 1900, there were 392 touring shows at this time of year.

Jan 13 *Cappy Ricks* (NY—Morosco—Comedy). Edward Rose turns Peter B. Kyne's novel of a salty old sea captain into a play. Rose and Franklin Underwood stage. It runs 128 performances.

Jan 14 *The Woman in Room 13* (NY—Booth—Drama). Samuel Shipman and Max Marcin write this thriller which achieves 175 performances. On Nov 4, 1929 it opens at London's Garrick where it has only a short run.

Jan 15 *Up in Mabel's Room* (NY—Eltinge—Comedy). Wilson Collison and Otto Harbach devise this popular farce with a cast including Enid Markey and Hazel Dawn. It has 229 performances.

Feb 3 *The Velvet Lady* (NY—New Amsterdam—Musical). Victor Herbert's "Life and Love" is a popular number in his new score. The lady appears in the closing minutes of the musical to unravel a mix-up about lost love-letters and stolen jewels and save a young couple's marriage. The show has 136 performances.

Feb 10 *Augustus Does His Bit* (NY—Comedy—Comedy). George Bernard Shaw's one-act play bows in New York. It is followed by John T. Foote's *Toby's Bow*. The show has 144 performances.

Feb 10 *Please Get Married* (NY—Little—Comedy). Ernest Truex heads the cast of this farce by James Cullen and Lewis Browne. Oliver Morosco produces. It runs for 20 weeks.

Feb 12 *Monte Cristo, Jr.* (NY—Winter Garden—Revue). This popular spectacle involves a young man who, while reading the Dumas novel, dreams that he and his friends are reliving the tale. The score is by Sigmund Romberg and Jean Schwartz. Chic Sale, Charles Purcell and Ralph Herz play. It runs for 254 performances.

Feb 17 *The Royal Vagabond* (NY—Cohan and Harris—Musical). Described as a "Cohanized Opera Comique," the show spoofs operetta themes and mannerisms. Cohan and Irving Berlin add to Anselm Goetzel's undistinguished score. Tessa Kosta, Fred Santley and Dorothy Dickson are in the cast. It has 208 performances.

March 24 *Tumble In* (NY—Selwyn—Musical). Rudolf Friml devises the score, with book and lyrics by Otto Harbach. The show, with Charles Ruggles, Claire Nagel, Zelda Sears, and Virginia Hammond in the ensemble, runs for four months.

April 8 *Come Along* (NY—Nora Bayes—Musical). John Nelson provides the music and lyrics for this show about a Red Cross nurse who goes to France and finds her lover wounded. Regina Richards and Paul Frawley head the cast. This show is a casualty of the Armistice. It has only 47 performances.

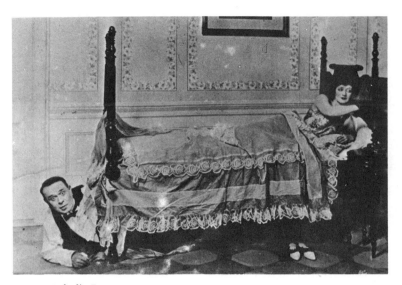

Up in Mabel's Room

April 9 *The Jest* (NY—Plymouth—Drama). John and Lionel Barrymore win a run of 179 performances, directed by Arthur Hopkins, in Sem Benelli's Italian tale. Burns Mantle selects this as one of the season's ten *Best Plays*.

May 13 *John Ferguson* (NY—Garrick—Drama). St. John Ervine's tragedy of hard life in Ireland is the Theatre Guild's first success. Augustin Duncan stages and plays the title role. The show runs for 177 performances. On Feb 23, 1920 it opens at the Lyric, Hammersmith, for a run of only 65 performances. William Rea has the title role.

May 26 *La, La, Lucille* (NY—Henry Miller—Musical). "The incarnation of jazz," says the *NY Times* of George Gershwin's first full Broadway score. Fred Jackson's farcical book shows the mix-ups which occur when a young dentist tries to set up an adulterous scene so he can divorce his wife. The show has 104 performances.

June 2 *Scandals of 1919* (NY—Liberty—Revue). George White produces and directs his first *Scandals*. With Arthur Jackson, he also devises the book and lyrics. The music is by Richard Whiting. White joins Ann Pennington, with whom he has danced in the *Follies*, in shimmying and tapping.

June 10 *A Lonely Romeo* (NY—Shubert—Musical). The actors' strike is to close this show when it reaches the 87 performance mark. It is a vehicle for Lew Fields, who collaborates on the book with Harry B. Smith. Fields portrays a married man who is a hatter by day and a "cabaret fiend" by night. Smith's brother Robert provides lyrics for Malvin Franklin's score. "Any Old Place with You," a Rodgers and Hart song is interpolated. Herbert Fields is also in the cast.

June 28 *At 9:45* (NY—Playhouse—Drama). Owen Davis's murder mystery uses George Backus, Clifford Dempsey and Nedda Harrigan. It runs for 139 performances. On Dec 22, 1925 it premieres at London's Comedy with a cast including Frederick Forrest, Alison Leggatt and Dorothy Tetley. It earns 126 showings.

July 15 *Greenwich Village Follies* (NY—Greenwich Village—Revue). John Murray Anderson inaugurates the first edition of this lively show, which moves uptown after six weeks for a total run of 232 performances. Bessie McCoy Davis parodies the forthcoming Prohibition era, among other topical spoofs.

July 17 *Shubert Gaieties of 1919* (NY—44th Street—Revue). Gilda Gray, the shimmy queen, is in the troupe, as are Ted Lorraine, Clayton and White, and Billie Williams. The show runs for 87 performances. This summer show is interrupted by the actors' strike, after which George Jessel replaces Henry Lewis in the ensemble.

July 28 *A Voice in the Dark* (NY—Republic—Drama). A deaf lady has seen a murder; she re-enacts it in pantomime. The accused replays the scene with dialogue to exonerate herself. A blind man, has overheard the killer's admission of the crime; this is recreated in the dark. With actors such as Olive Wyndham and William Boyd in leading roles, these theatrical effects attract audiences for almost 17 weeks.

Aug 5 *The Challenge* (NY—Selwyn—Drama). Eugene Walter's play about a young socialist converted to capitalism has Allan Dinehart, Jessie Glendenning and Holbrook Blinn. The production runs nine weeks.

Aug 6 *The Red Dawn* (NY—39th Street—Drama). Thomas Dixon, apologist for the

Ku Klux Klan, responds to the political upheavals in Russia with a vision of a soviet established on an island off the coast of California. The arrival of a U.S. warship and a change of heart by the visionary who originated the idea frustrate the plan. Opening just before the Equity strike, the show has only five performances.

Aug 23 *Happy Days* (NY—Hippodrome—Musical). Producer Charles Dillingham offers the usual mixture of circus acts, vaudeville and elaborate stage effects. The company walks out on Aug 28 to support Equity's strike, but the show eventually has 452 performances.

Sep 12 *Civilian Clothes* (NY—Morosco—Comedy). Florence Lanham and Thurston Hall animate this comedy about a woman who marries a soldier only to find him unimpressive in civilian clothes. The play runs almost 19 weeks.

Sep 12 *Scandal.* See L premiere, 1918.

Sep 13 *Adam and Eva* (NY—Longacre—Comedy). Guy Bolton and George Middleton write this story of a man who teaches a wealthy family self-reliance. Otto Kruger and Ruth Shepley play. The show has 312 performances.

Sep 20 *Clarence* (NY—Hudson—Comedy). Booth Tarkington's comedy about a diffident entomologist who teaches a family persistence and values has a cast including Alfred Lunt, Mary Boland, Helen Hayes and Glenn Hunter. There are 300 performances.

Sep 25 *Roly-Boly Eyes* (NY—Knickerbocker—Musical). This show is a vehicle for black-face comic Eddie Leonard. He plays Billy Leonard who runs away from home when he's framed for a crime he didn't commit. He later returns to vindication and to sing "Ida, Sweet as Apple Cider" to his girl (Queenie Smith). The show enjoys 100 performances.

Sep 30 *The Gold Diggers* (NY—Lyceum—Comedy). Ina Claire stars in Avery Hopwood's play about a chorus girl, kept by a gentleman, who tries to protect her ward. The show runs 282 performances. On Dec 14, 1926 it opens at London's Lyric with Tallulah Bankhead in the lead. It wins 180 showings.

Oct 2 *The Ziegfeld Midnight Frolic* (NY—New Amsterdam Roof—Revue). Gene Buck provides lyrics for Dave Stamper's score. Ned Wayburn stages the sketches and songs. Ted Lewis, Fanny Brice, Chic Sale, W. C. Fields, and Irene Barker are featured. The show has 75 performances.

Oct 2 *The Storm* (NY—48th Street—Drama). Edward Arnold, Robert Rendel and Helen MacKellar are featured in Langdon McCormick's tale of a woman, trapped in a cabin by a snowstorm, who cannot choose between two suitors. The show runs 282 performances.

Oct 6 *The Girl in the Limousine* (NY—Eltinge—Comedy). Avery Hopwood and Wilson Collison devise this farce. Tony, robbed in a taxi, is dumped in Betty's room. Her aunt, mistakenly thinking him Betty's husband, orders him to get into bed with Betty, who has the flu. All ends without morality being offended. Charles Ruggles, Doris Kenyon, and Zelda Sears are in the company. This show runs for 137 performances.

Oct 6 *Declasse* (NY—Empire—Drama). Ethel Barrymore has her greatest success to date in Zoe Akins's play about a lady who is married to a titled butcher but whose heart lies elsewhere. The show runs for 257 performances. The *NY Times* reports ". . . there are no decently reticent adjectives that will . . . do justice to such great occasions as the playing of Ethel Barrymore."

Oct 7 *Apple Blossoms* (NY—Globe—Musical). Fritz Kreisler and Victor Jacobi write the score and William LeBaron the book for this show about a couple who marry but secretly resolve to pursue Bohemian lives. John Charles Thomas and Wilda Bennett play the couple. Fred and Adele Astaire dance. There are 256 performances.

Oct 13 *The Little Whopper* (NY—Casino—Musical). Rudolf Friml provides the score for Otto Harbach's book about a girl who finds herself in the wrong man's hotel room. Vivienne Segal stars. It runs 224 performances.

Oct 14 *His Honor, Abe Potash* (NY—Bijou—Comedy). Montague Glass and Jules E. Goodman offer further adventures of half of the Potash and Perlmutter duo. Barney Bernard stars as Abe whom politicians try to use after he wins a mayoralty. The show runs 215 performances.

Oct 23 *The Passing Show of 1919* (NY—Winter Garden—Revue). Lee and J. J. Shubert, lacking the flair of a Ziegfeld or Anderson, offer a bevy of beautiful girls but not much wit or sparkle. The Avon Comedy Four includes Smith and Dale, who perform "The Doctor's Office," later adapted in Neil Simon's *The Sunshine Boys.* The show enjoys 280 performances.

Nov 10 *Wedding Bells* (NY—Harris—Comedy). Salisbury Field writes this comedy about a man about to marry who loves another. Wallace Eddinger, Jessie Glendenning and Margaret Lawrence are featured. It runs 21 weeks.

Nov 11 *The Magic Melody* (NY—Shubert—Musical). Composer Sigmund Romberg becomes his own co-producer—with Max Wilner—in an effort to free himself from banal librettos provided by the Shuberts. This tale of a son reunited with his mother after years apart is not an improvement. Charles Purcell, Carmel Myers, Julia Dean and Tom McNaughton are in the cast. It runs 143 performances.

Nov 18 *Irene* (NY—Vanderbilt—Musical). James Montgomery provides the book and Harry Tierney and Joe McCarthy the music for this story of a shop girl who charms a wealthy young man. Edith Day and Bobbie Watson are featured. It runs seven months during this season and 428 performances in 1920–21. On April 7, 1920 it comes to London's Empire with Edith Day and Robert Hale. Here it wins 399 showings.

Nov 19 *The Son-Daughter* (NY—Belasco—Drama). David Belasco and George Scarborough write about the "New China" from a New York vantage point. Lenore Ulric, Thomas Findlay and Albert Bruning are featured. The show runs 223 performances.

Nov 24 *Aphrodite* (NY—Century—Musical). Henri Febrier and Anselm Goetzel write the music for this show which is short on plot and long on spectacle. Michael Fokine choreographs. The large cast includes Dorothy Dalton and Mildred Walker. The show runs over 18 weeks.

Nov 25 *The Rise of Silas Lapham* (NY—Garrick—Comedy). Lillian Sabine dramatizes William Dean Howell's popular novel showing Silas's discovery that there are other values than wealth and social position. James K. Hackett stars. The show runs nearly six weeks.

Dec 2 *One Night in Rome* (NY—Criterion—Drama). J. Hartley Manners creates a role for his wife, Laurette Taylor, in which she impersonates an Italian fortune-teller, *L'Enigme*, who forces a young Englishman to discover real depth in his character and to acknowledge his love for her. The production has 107 performances.

Dec 3 *My Lady Friends* (NY—Comedy—Comedy). This slight farce has Clifton

John Furguson

93

Smilin' Through

Crawford as a rich Bible publisher who likes to help penniless and pretty young women. The show runs 214 performances.

Dec 15 *Abraham Lincoln* (NY—Cort—Drama). John Drinkwater recreates the Lincoln legend from 1860 to his assassination at Ford's Theatre. Frank McGlyn is Lincoln. There are 193 performances.

Dec 19 *The Sign on the Door* (NY—Republic—Drama). Channing Pollock's melodrama is about a man who unwittingly implicates his wife in murder. It runs 187 performances. On Sep 1, 1921 the show premieres at London's Playhouse with Gladys Cooper in the cast. It wins 306 showings.

Dec 19 *For the Defense* (NY—Playhouse—Drama). Elmer Rice concocts a melodrama involving the shooting of a sinister hypnotist and the subsequent trial of an innocent girl, the beloved of the young district attorney. Winifred Lenihan and Richard Bennett play. The production has 77 performances.

Dec 22 *Night Lodging* (NY—Plymouth—Drama). Maxim Gorki's *The Lower Depths* runs only 14 performances, but it offers Edward G. Robinson as Satin and Pauline Lord as Nastia. Arthur Hopkins is the producer.

Dec 22 *The Famous Mrs. Fair* (NY—Henry Miller's—Drama). James Forbes's play about a liberated woman who rediscovers her family has Margalo Gillmore in the title role. It wins 183 performances.

Dec 30 *Smilin' Through* (NY—Broadhurst—Drama). The spirits of a murdered sweetheart and the hero's mother cause an old man to soften his opposition to the young man's marriage to his niece. In the cast are Orme Caldera, Jane Cowl, Henry Stephenson, Elaine Inescort, and others. The play runs for 175 performances.

1919   BRITISH PREMIERES

Jan 27 *Oh, Joy* (L—Kingsway—Musical). Jerome Kern provides the score. The book by Guy Bolton and P.G. Wodehouse tells of a man whose elopement causes all sorts of complications. Tom Powers and Dot Temple are featured along with Beatrice Lillie. There are 167 performances.

March 8 *The House of Peril* (L—Queen's—Drama). Horace Vachell bases his thriller about stolen pearls on Mrs. Belloc Lowndes's novel. *The Chink in the Ar-*

mour. Emily Brooke, Norman McKinnel, Annie Schletter and Margaret Halstan are featured. It runs 107 performances.

March 25 *Joy-Bells* (L—Hippodrome—Revue). The American musical director, Ned Wayburn, stages this nineteen-scene show, featuring such talents as George Robey, Fred Allandale and Anita Elson. Frederick Chappelle composes the score, with book and lyrics by Albert de Courville, Wal Pink, and T. J. Gray. The show

has 712 performances.

March 27 *Caesar's Wife* (L—Royalty—Drama). W. Somerset Maugham's drama of a young wife who loves another has Fay Compton, George Relph and C. Aubrey Smith. There are 241 performances.

April 3 *Our Mr. Hepplewhite* (L—Criterion—Comedy). Gladys Unger's play about a grande dame's rebellious children has Arthur Wontner in the title role. There are 239 performances.

April 19 *Monsieur Beaucaire* (L—Prince's—Musical). Based on Booth Tarkington's novella and play, this "romantic opera" has a score by Andre Messager and libretto and lyrics by Adrian Ross and Frederick Lonsdale. Marion Green is Beaucaire, the disguised Duc d'Orleans, wooing English ladies as the barber of Bath. It runs 221 performances. On Dec 11, it premieres at New York's New Amsterdam with Green repeating his role. Here it runs for almost 18 weeks.

April 21 *The Very Idea* (L—St. Martin's—Comedy). William LeBaron's farce wins a run of 255 performances—with a midsummer break. The cast includes Donald Calthrop, Mary Glynne, Dora Barton, and Juliette Jose.

May 20 *Kissing Time* (L—Winter Garden—Musical). Guy Bolton and P.G. Wodehouse base their book on *Madame et son Filleul* by Hennequin and Weber. The music is by Ivan Caryll. Complications arise from the wartime practice in France of ladies carrying on correspondence with "godsons" at the front to boost their morale. Yvonne Arnaud and George Grossmith are featured. Staged by Felix Edwardes, the show earns 430 performances.

June 7 *Victory* (L—Globe—Drama). Joseph Conrad provides the literary substance for B. M. Hastings' dramatization. Marie Lohr, usually in comic roles, plays Lena. The production runs just over ten weeks.

June 9 *A Temporary Gentleman* (L—Oxford—Drama). Gordon Ash plays a clerk promoted in war-time to officer ranks. When the war is over, he doesn't want to be a clerk again, and he suffers some hard knocks learning he was only a "temporary" gentleman. Pauline Hugen also plays. H. F. Maltby writes and stages the play for producers Jay and Littler. There are 265 performances.

June 12 *The Cinderella Man.* See NY premiere, 1916.

July 10 *Tilly of Bloomsbury* (L—Apollo—Comedy). Ian Hay's play is based on his popular novel about a girl who tries to impress her future mother-in-law. Mary Glynne is Tilly. The show runs 414 performances.

Aug 20 *Home and Beauty* (L—Playhouse—Comedy). W. Somerset Maugham offers a new farce about a man, presumably lost in the war, who comes back to find his wife married to his best friend. Gladys Cooper and Charles Hawtrey are featured. There are 235 performances.

Aug 28 *Bran Pie* (L—Prince of Wales's—Revue). Andre Charlot's new revue has no plot. It features Beatrice Lillie and Jack Hurlbut. It achieves 414 performances.

Sep 8 *The Choice* (L—Wyndham's—Drama). Alfred Sutro writes about an older man who loses his young fiancee when he refuses to pardon the misconduct of a war hero. Gerald Du Maurier stars and stages. The cast includes Viola Tree and Leon Quartermaine. It runs 316 performances.

Sep 9 *Eastward Ho* (L—Alhambra—Musical). Actor-author Oscar Asche collaborates with Dornford Yates on book and lyrics. With Grace Torrens and John Ansell's score and Asche's staging, the show wins 124 performances. In the large cast are Violet Loraine, Ralph Lynn and Peggy Kurton.

Sep 11 *The Bird of Paradise.* See NY premiere, 1912.

Sep 12 *The Great Day* (L—Drury Lane—Drama). Louis N. Parker and George Sims concoct the annual Drury Lane melodrama, with incidental music by J. M. Glover. In the company are Sybil Thorndike, Frederick Ross, Violet Paget and Aubrey Fitzgerald. There are 98 performances.

Sep 13 *Who's Hooper?* (L—Adelphi—Musical). Fred Thompson adapts Arthur Wing Pinero's *In Chancery* for this show about an amnesia victim. Music is by Ivor Novello and Howard Talbot. Clifford Grey provides the lyrics for songs such as "A Ladies' Man." W.H. Berry and Violet

Blythe are featured. There are 349 performances.

Sep 17 *Afgar* (L—London Pavilion—Musical). Fred Thompson and Worton David provide the book, Douglas Furber the lyrics and Charles Cuvillier the score for this story about a girl who seeks to win the single-hearted affection of her lord, despite the lovely harem he keeps for show. Alice Delysia and John Humphries are featured. The show runs 300 performances.

Sep 25 *Baby Bunting* (L—Shaftesbury—Musical). Ronald Squire plays Bunny Bunting, who must acquire a wife and child to win an inheritance in this Fred Thompson-Worton David adaptation of Nicholls and Lestocq's play, *Jane.* Songs are by Clifford Grey and Nat Ayer. There are 213 performances.

Oct 8 *The Kiss Call* (L—Gaiety—Musical). The latest Gaiety show is based on a French farce, Gavault and Berr's *Le Coup de Telephone.* Fred Thompson does the adaptation. Ivan Caryll composes, with lyrics from Percy Greenbank, Adrian Ross and Clifford Grey. In the ensemble are

Evelyn Laye, Binnie Hale, G. P. Huntley and Austin Melford. It has 176 performances.

Oct 16 *Tiger Rose.* See NY premiere, 1917.

Nov 11 *Lord Richard in the Pantry* (L—Criterion—Comedy). Sydney Blow and Douglas Hoare adapt Martha Swayne's popular novel about a lord who rents his home and becomes a butler. Cyril Maude has the title role. There are 576 performances.

Dec 23 *The Whirligig* (L—Palace—Revue). Maisie Gay, Emma Trentini, Yetta Rianza, Jack Morrison and Billy Leonard are featured in this show devised by Albert de Courville, Wal Pink, and Edgar Wallace, with music by Frederick Chappelle. De Courville stages, with choreography by Jack Mason. The show wins 441 performances.

Dec 31 *In the Night* (L—Kingsway—Drama). Cyril Harcourt adapts a French play by Sommi Picenardi about a young wife married to an unsympathetic older husband. Jessie Winter, Alfred Drayton and Reginald Owen are featured. There are 139 performances.

1919 REVIVALS/REPERTORIES

Jan 6 Jacques Copeau and his company from Paris's Theatre de Vieux-Colombier continue their New York engagement with Moliere's *L'Avare* (8) and on the 13, Vigny's *Chatterton* (8), followed on the 20 by Copeau and Croue's *Les Freres Karamazov* (8) and Corneille's *Le Menteur* (8) on Jan 27. On Feb 3, *L'Ami Fritz* (8), by Erckmann and Chatrian, opens, followed

on the 10 by Maeterlinck's *Pelleas et Melisande* (8). MacKaye's American drama, *Washington* (8), opens on Feb 17, as does La Fontaine's *La Coupe Enchantée* (9). On the 24, Shakespeare's *La Nuit des Rois* (7) is played, followed on March 3 by Capus *La Veine* (16). Moliere's *Le Misanthrope* (8) is opened on March 17, the company's final production in this season.

Jan 12 The Incorporated Stage Society, of which George Bernard Shaw is a member, begins its London season of matinee productions with Vanbrugh's *The Provok'd Wife,* played by Margaret Halstan, Hubert Carter, and Lewis Casson, among others. On March 9, H. F. Rubinstein's *The Spirit of Parsifal Robinson* is shown. On April 13, the play is John Masefield's Japanese tragedy, *The Faithful.* On May 25, a double-bill of Yeats and Swinburne is presented. All these productions are staged at the King's Hall, Covent Garden.

Jan 15 Stuart Walker brings his Portmanteau Theatre to New York's Punch and Judy Theatre for a repertory season running through March 22. The repertoire includes five plays by Lord Dunsany, Walker's own *The Very Naked Boy* and the *Book of Job.*

Feb 9 At London's King's Hall, Covent Garden, the Pioneer Players present an American play by Susan Glaspell, *Trifles.* Other plays in their seasonal program include Miles Malleson's *The Artist,* Paul Claudel's *The Hostage,* and Herman Heijerman's *The Rising Sun.*

Kissing Time

March 11 In Dublin at the Abbey Theatre, the new play is *The Rebellion in Bally-cullen* (Brinsley McNamara). On April 21, it's *The Dragon* (Lady Gregory), a "wonder play," with Barry Fitzgerald and Arthur Shields. On April 27, Leonid Andreyev's *The Pretty Sabine Women* is premiered. On May 20, the play is *The Curate of St. Chad's* (Constance P. Anderson). On Aug 4, Fitzgerald and Maureen Delany appear in *Brady* (Mrs. Theodore Maynard). On Aug 2, it's *The Saint* (Desmond Fitzgerald). On Sep 30, the drama is *The Labour Leader* (Daniel Corkery). On Oct 7, it's *Meadow Sweet* (Seamas Kelly). On the 14, the play is *The Queer Ones* (Con O'Leary). On Nov 25, the offering is *The Enchanted Trousers* (Gideon Cusley). On Dec 14, the Leinster Players present a drama of the Irish Midlands, *The Curse of the Country* (Thomas King Moylan).

March 17 At London's Royal Court Theatre, J. B. Fagan revives Sheridan's *The School for Scandal* for a run of 65 performances. Arthur Whitby and Mary Grey are featured. On May 26, Fagan opens a production of *Twelfth Night* which has only seven performances. On Oct 9, he revives *The Merchant of Venice*, which achieves a run of 109 performances. Maurice Moscovitch is Shylock. Mary Grey and Edith Evans are Portia and Nerissa.

March 17 Philip Moeller's *Moliere* is presented at New York's Liberty Theatre with Henry Miller in the title role.

March 22 The Tsar of All the Russias is no more, and some British theatre-people look toward the East with apprehension. At the Temperance Hall in Tredegar, the warning is Ronald Grahame's seven-scene shocker, *The Bolshevik Peril*. Later, on Nov 22, at St. Mary's Hall in Putney, Francois Tussaud's melodrama, *The Bolshevik*, is played.

March 28 At London's Garrick Theatre, Robert Loraine revives and stars in Rostand's *Cyrano de Bergerac*. Stella Mervyn Campbell is his Roxanne. The production is a critical and audience success, running for 226 performances.

March 31 Continuing the cycle of Shakespearean play premieres begun in 1914, at the Old Vic in London, Lilian Baylis, the manageress now offers the George R. Foss production of *Henry IV, Part 1*.

April 12 Doris Keane revives *Romeo and Juliet* at London's Lyric Theatre for a run of 73 performances. Ellen Terry plays Nurse to her Juliet, with Basil Sydney as Romeo and Reginald Denham as Paris.

April 19 The newly organized Theatre Guild presents its first production, *The Bonds of Interest* at New York's Garrick. John Garrett Underhill translates Jacinto Benavente's play, based on *commedia dell'arte* characters and situations. Edna St. Vincent Millay is Columbine and

Baby Bunting

Dudley Digges, Polchinelle. The production runs a month.

April 22 In Stratford-upon-Avon, *As You Like It*, from Nigel Playfair's Lyric Theatre, Hammersmith, helps reopen the Shakespeare Memorial Theatre for the Shakespeare Festival which has been curtailed during the Great War. The next day two productions are presented: *Coriolanus* and *Twelfth Night*. The latter is a Court Theatre production. Other plays include *The Merry Wives of Windsor*, *Richard III*, *The Taming of the Shrew*, and Shaw's *Candida*, produced by the Lyric, Hammersmith.

April 28 Kalidasa's Sanskrit masterpiece, *Shakuntala*, runs for slightly over a month in an English version presented at New York's Greenwich Village Theatre.

May 5 At the Elephant and Castle Theatre in London, the drama is *Her Honour at Stake*, by Patrick Gore. Later in the season, on Oct 13, the premiere is *Her Life of Pleasure*, by Mrs. F. G. Kimberley.

May 17 At London's Lyceum Theatre, a revival of Hugh Morton and Gustave Kerker's 1898 musical success, *The Belle of New York*, runs for 97 performances.

June 2 At London's Elephant and Castle Theatre, the juxtaposition of attractions continues to be titillating. Tonight the play is *Love's Young Dream*, by Eva Elwes. On July 7, the drama is *Love Without Licence*, a "romance of the South Seas."

June 3 William Poel, the dedicated apostle of Elizabethan stagings for Elizabe-than plays, offers an abridged version of *The Comedy of Errors* in London at the Apothecaries' Hall. It's performed by children of the South Hackney Central School.

July 1 London's Incorporated Stage Society opens its 21 Season, but the first production is delayed until Oct 19, when Herbert Trench's *Napoleon* is shown at the Queen's Theatre. A. E. George plays Napoleon. M. Willson Disher's *Joan of Memories* follows. On Dec 14, Henry James' *The Reprobate* is shown at the Royal Court, staged by Allan Wade.

Aug 2 At the Memorial Theatre in Stratford-upon-Avon, the first summer season of Shakespeare productions since the end of the Great War is launched with *The Merry Wives of Windsor*. Also in the repertory are *Julius Caesar*, *Romeo and Juliet*, *The Tempest*, *The Winter's Tale*, and *A Midsummer Night's Dream*. This is the debut of the New Shakespeare Company, under the direction of W. (Walter) Bridges Adams.

Aug 4 At London's Savoy Theatre, the first Army entertainers of the recent war, Les Rouges et Noirs, present a special revue, *Splinters*, for 36 performances.

Aug 30 The Birmingham Repertory Theatre opens its eighth season with Beaumont and Fletcher's *The Knight of the Burning Pestle*.

Sep 1 In Liverpool, at the Playhouse, William Hurlbut's American light comedy, *Over Sunday*, is produced, with Clive

Brook and Iris Hoey in leading roles.

Sep 29 Rupert D'Oyly Carte begins a series of Gilbert & Sullivan revivals in London at the Prince's Theatre. *The Gondoliers* is the initial offering, followed by *Iolanthe*, *The Mikado*, *Patience*, and *The Yeoman of the Guard*.

Oct 6 E. H. Sothern and Julia Marlowe offer two weeks of Shakespearean repertory at New York's Shubert Theatre. The dramas are *Hamlet*, *Twelfth Night*, and *The Taming of the Shrew*.

Nov 3 Manchester shows its interest in Shakespeare this fall. Tonight Frank Benson's Stratford company present *The Merchant of Venice* at the New Queen's Theatre. On Nov 6, at the Royal Theatre, Fred Terry opens his production of *Much Ado About Nothing*, playing Benedick opposite Violet Farebrother as Beatrice. On Dec 26, at the Gaiety Theatre, the New Shakespeare Company presents *The Merry Wives of Windsor*. In the latter troupe are such players as Ernest Thesiger, Baliol Holloway, Dorothy Green, William Calvert, Constance Pelissier, and James Whale.

Nov 8 The Birmingham Repertory presents Carroll Aiken's *The God of Gods* with Susan Richmond featured.

Nov 10 Marion de Forest's American dramatization of Louisa May Alcott's popular novel, *Little Women*, has a matinee premiere at London's New Theatre. It has 35 performances. Katharine Cornell plays Jo, with Joyce Carey as Meg.

Nov 10 At a matinee in London at the Duke of York's Theatre, Maurice Froyez presents a revival of Moliere's *Le Bourgeois Gentilhomme*. On Nov 25, *Le Malade Imaginaire* is presented.

Nov 11 Lennox Robinson's *The Lost Leader*, about a man who insists he is Parnell, premieres at New York's Greenwich Village Theatre. The production has 31 performances.

Nov 14 Sybil Thorndike plays the title-role in the ancient Hindu drama, *Shakuntala*, adapted for the stage by Lawrence Binyon and K. N. Das Gupta, at London's Winter Garden Theatre.

Nov 23 At the Lyric, Hammersmith, the Phoenix Society—an offshoot of the Stage Society, dedicated to reviving old classics—produces John Webster's Jacobean tragedy, *The Duchess of Malfi*. For their first season, planned for 1919–1920, the program chosen also includes Dryden's *Marriage a la Mode*, Heywood's *The Fair Maid of the West*, Otway's *Don Carlos*, and Jonson's *Volpone*.

Dec 13 At London's Scala Theatre, where F. C. Nettlefold has been presenting a series of revivals, including W. S. Gilbert's *Pygmalion and Galatea*, Bulwer-Lytton's *The Lady of Lyons*, and Mark Ambient's *The Net*, he now stages a revival of *Othello* for 31 performances.

Dec 20 *Fifinella*, a fantasy by Barry Jackson and Basil Dean is presented for the holiday season at London's Scala. Vera Lennox has the title role, the Queen of Summer Fairies.

Dec 26 Boxing Day again—and time for the traditional Christmas pantomimes all over London and in the provinces. At Drury Lane, the spectacular show is *Cinderella*. Fewer West End theatres now offer pantos, for these children's holiday treats interrupt the long-running successes. At the Holborn Empire, *Little Women* is given in matinee performances. Some theatres don't wait for Boxing Day to open Christmas shows: at the New, *Peter Pan* opens on Dec 18; at the Royalty, *Charley's Aunt* opens on the 16; at the Victoria Palace, *Where the Rainbow Ends* opens on the 20. At the Metropolitan, *Bluebell in Fairyland* doesn't open until Dec 29. At London's Empire Theatre, Victor Herbert's musical, *The Red Mill*, opens with Little Tich and Ray Kay as Connor and Kidder, the comic leads.

Dec 26 At London's Royal Opera House, Covent Garden, John Martin Harvey revives *Hamlet*.

1919 BIRTHS/DEATHS/DEBUTS

Jan 1 American comedian Richard Knowles (b. 1858) dies in London. Knowles started his career in Leadville, Colorado, in the mid-1870's. In 1891 he went to London where he remained a music hall favorite until his death. Knowles' best remembered songs are *Girlie, Girlie* and *Brighton*.

Jan 12 Actor-manager Sir Charles Wyndham (b. 1837) is dead. Sir Charles had frequently acted as an amateur before making his professional appearance at the Old Royalty Theatre in 1862. In 1874, he inaugurated the famous series of Crystal Palace matinées. Wyndham was knighted by King Edward on the occasion of his Coronation in 1902.

Jan 20 Alex Nicol is born in Ossining, N.Y.

Jan 23 Playwright-author Millard Lampell is born in Paterson, N.J.

Jan 31 American actor Nat C. Goodwin (b. 1857) dies in New York City. Goodwin's career as a vaudeville comedian began at Tony Pastor's Opera House in New York in 1875. Although best known for his comic roles, he was also a success in Augustus Thomas' *In Mizzoura* and Clyde Fitch's *Nathan Hale*. A book of reminiscences, *Nat Goodwin's Book*, was published in 1914. He was married to Maxine Elliott.

March 14 Playwright Thomas Wolfe makes a student debut today as the Carolina Playmakers offer their first bill of one-act plays in the "Play-House." Wolfe plays the title-role in his play, *The Return of Buck Gavin*.

March 29 Stage and screen actress Eileen Heckart is born in Columbus, Ohio.

April 29 Actress-singer Celeste Holm is born in New York City.

Aug 12 Playwright, director, and television-producer Peter Luke is born in St. Albans, Hertfordshire, England.

Aug 30 Noel Coward makes his debut with the Birmingham Repertory Company, appearing in the initial production of the new season, *The Knight of the Burning Pestle*.

Oct 15 Jan Miner is born in Boston, Massachusetts.

Oct 17 English actor, producer, and author Henry Brodribb Irving (b. 1870) is dead. Irving, the elder son of Sir Henry, made his first appearance on stage under Sir John Hare in 1891. In the course of his career he revived many of his father's roles, both in England and America.

Nov 13 English actor Lionel Rignold is dead at age 69. Rignold made his first West End appearance in 1883 as King Kosmos in *A Trip to the Moon*. Mr. Pineapple in *A Chinese Honeymoon* and Pink in *What the Butler Saw* were two of his most popular roles. Rignold was a director of the Royal General Theatrical Fund.

Dec 11 Joe Masteroff is born in Philadelphia, Pa.

1919 THEATERS/PRODUCTIONS

In Britain patents are granted for: C. J. Tritschler's searchlight apparatus of a light in a box with a slit the same shape as the projected beam; Tritschler's effect of an airship appearing in the night sky, catching fire, and crashing.

William and Louise Johnson earn a U.S. patent for their fake phonograph cabinet with an open bottom and a hole in the top—where the turntable should be—allowing an actor's head to protrude. The device has its novelty-value, especially in vaudeville, but will not prove helpful in staging *King Lear*. Frederick Rockwell and Wilbur Davis have developed a system in which *details* of scenery are painted on a projection screen, with the general outlines projected.

This year *Drama*, a quarterly theatre review, makes its appearance, sponsored by the British Theatre Association. London and provincial theatre work is surveyed.

Looking back on the 1918 season, E. A. Baughan, writing in Britain's *The Stage Year Book*, notes that two Boche air-raids last February emptied the theatres for at least a week. He observes: "The theatre has been a most accurate barometer of the state of the war. When the news was bad, the theatres were empty; when the news was good, they filled again; and at the end of 1918 a stall [orchestra-seat] was more difficult to buy than a box of matches. We were lifted on a wave of theatrical prosperity." That's not been the case artistically, however. Quite the reverse, says Baughan, calling 1918 a "barren season." Although the Great War has been the worst the world has ever seen and though it has brought about changes in society, the British drama has failed to reflect that. Instead, the war-plays have been thinly disguised "crook-melodramas." Perhaps native playwrights are still too close to this titanic struggle, surmises Baughan. In future, though, they should examine the war from the point of view of the social upheaval it has set in motion.

Since its founding in 1912, the Authors League of America has found itself involved in protecting authors' rights both in print and in performance. To simplify matters, this year two subsidiary groups are formed: The Authors Guild and The Dramatists Guild (DG).

With the founding of the British Theatre Association, the members begin a long dedication to the aims announced this year by Geoffrey Whitworth: "To assist the development of the art of the theatre and to promote a right relationship between drama and the life of the community." It establishes an extensive theatre library, and develops an effective Information Service.

Jan During the war-period just past, the fifty-three theatres in Manhattan and the Bronx have seldom been empty of attractions for long. A six-year agreement between the Shuberts and Klaw and Erlanger for pooling booking arrangements has been terminated, reopening stiff competition. Producers who book through the Shuberts include W. A. Brady, Arthur Hammerstein, Oliver Morosco, Elizabeth Marbury; Comstock, Elliott, and Gest; R. W. Tully, and Arthur Hopkins. Klaw and Erlanger book David Belasco, Cohan and Harris, the Charles Frohman Company, George C. Tyler, H. W. Savage, and Charles Dillingham. A. H. Woods and the Selwyns have booked New York theatres with both managements. The 10 per cent War Tax on theatre tickets has not deterred theatre attendance. Travel restrictions have cut down regional touring, with a resultant increase in local stock companies.

It is reported in *The Stage Year Book* that the imposition of income taxes in the United States reveals 914 members of the theatre profession (actors, singers, and musicians) to have average incomes as high as $12,000. Five artists have incomes in excess of $150,000.

Feb 1 The New Middlesex Theatre of Varieties in London, which opened in Oct 30, 1911 closes. It will re-open in May as The Winter Garden Theatre.

May 20 Designer Claude Bragdon breaks with the realistic conventions of the early 20th century with his set design for *Hamlet*, produced by the American actor-manager Walter Hampden. The setting consists of neutral draperies, steps, and levels, and movable units which can be rearranged quickly, while maintaining a unity of style in the production.

June 15 At the close of the current Broadway season, *Best Plays* authors Burns Mantle and Garrison P. Sherwood make possible play tallies by type, basing their listings on 75 theatre venues. There have been 45 dramas, 60 comedies, 29 musicals, 4 revues, 1 opera, 1 operetta, 3 Shakespearean revivals, and 3 repertory offerings. Mantle and Sherwood also choose ten representative Broadway plays for the decade—1909–1919. The choices include Walter's *The Easiest Way*, Smith's *Mrs. Bumpstead-Leigh*, Parker's *Disraeli*, Sheldon's *Romance*, Cohan's *Seven Keys to Baldpate*, Reizenstein's (Rice's) *On Trial*, Anspacher's *The Unchastened Woman*, Kummer's *Good Gracious Annabelle*, Williams' *Why Marry?* and Ervine's *John Ferguson*.

June 23 In Edinburgh, the King's Theatre is damaged by fire.

July 18 The Association Actors and Artistes of America (AAAA) is organized. Known as the "Four A's," it will be the parent organization of all the performing arts trade unions. The following organizations are affiliated with the four A's: Actors' Equity Association (AEA), American Federation of Television and Radio Artists (AFTRA), American Guild of Musical Artists (AGMA), Guild of Variety Artists (GVA), Screen Actors Guild (SAG), among others.

Aug 7 Actors' Equity Association, now allied with the American Federation of Labor, calls a strike, to last for five weeks and to settle long-standing grievances with theatre producers and managers. Among the demands are: 1) eight performances to constitute a week's work, 2) extra pay for extra performances, 3) pay for playing, 4) pay for extra rehearsals, 5) full pay for pre-holiday weeks. Public sympathy seems to be with the actors, many of whom are favorites. The settlement is described as a "peace without victory." The season begins with relatively little bitterness and no reprisals.

Aug 7 George M. Cohan, who is both an actor and a manager, sides with the theatre managers in the Equity strike. He helps form an Actors' Fidelity Association, called the "Fidos" by Equity opponents, to frustrate the strike's aims. Actors who are uneasy about mixing art with organized labor join Cohan. After the dispute between Equity and the Producing Managers' Association is settled September 6, Cohan is gradually to find that his action has hurt him in the eyes of many performers.

Sep The added costs imposed by meeting Equity demands to settle the strike, forces raising of ticket-prices. From the Civil War until World War I, ticket prices have ranged from $1.50 to a $2 top, with many poorer seats quite inexpensive. In this 1919 season, most musicals now must charge $2.50 or $3 for their best seats. (In 1917, musicals could be mounted for $20,000 to $30,000, although the *Ziegfeld Follies* then cost $88,000. In 1919, the *Follies* cost Ziegfeld $170,000 to stage, but this reflected more his lavish taste than gradually increasing production costs.)

Sep 27 The Broadhurst Theatre, on West 44 Street in New York, named for playwright George Broadhurst, presents its first production, Shaw's *Misalliance*. It is designed by Herbert J. Krapp. The Shuberts and Broadhurst share management of the theatre for a brief time. Two Pulitzer Prize winners, Sidney Kingsley's *Men in White* and the musical *Fiorello*, written by Jerome Weidman and George Abbott, with music by Jerry Bock and lyrics by Sheldon Harnick, enjoy long runs here.

Nov 24 A six-night run of Galsworthy's *The Silver Box* opens at the Oxford Street Settlement in Shipton Street, Sheffield England, marking the formation of a dramatic group under the directorship of Herbert M. Prentice. It proves to be the beginning of the Sheffield Rep.

Dec 1 At the Art Institute of Chicago, *The Drama of the Nativity and the Massacre of the Innocents* opens. The designer, Herman Rosse, successfully uses front projections as an integral part of the production concept. Using two full-size curtains (55' wide) for the motifs, Rosse projects diamond shapes all over, to create a scenic change in the multi-scene show.

Dec 29 The Lafayette Players of New York, a black troupe, open Philadelphia's newest theatre, called the Dunbar Theatre, after poet Paul Lawrence Dunbar. The house will later be known as the Lincoln Theatre. The initial production is *Within the Law*. The theatre seats 1,400 and is devoted to black productions for black audiences. Reviewers compare its features favorably with the nearby Shubert Theatre. Later, it will play films as well as stage productions. It is to be demolished in the 1950's.

Jan 5 *Always You* (NY—Central—Musical). Oscar Hammerstein gives Broadway his first book and lyrics. The story is about a man who forgets his promise to marry a French girl but later rediscovers his love. Herbert Stothart writes the score. Walter Scanlan and Helen Ford are featured. The show runs slightly longer than two months.

Jan 13 *The Passion Flower* (NY—Greenwich Village—Drama). Jacinto Benavente's Spanish tragedy deals with a man in love with his step-daughter, whose fiancé he has slain. Charles Waldron, Nance O'Neil, and Edna Walton are in the cast. This smouldering tale runs for 18 weeks.

Jan 15 *The Power of Darkness* (NY—Garrick—Drama). The Theatre Guild produces Leo Tolstoi's dark drama of "sin fastening on sin." Ida Rauh and Marjorie Vonnegut play the women who drive Nikita (Arthur Hohl) deeper and deeper into crime. The production has a five-week run.

Jan 27 *As You Were* (NY—Central—Musical). Labeled a revue, Arthur Wimperis's show has an amusing story-line, in which Sam Bernard plays a husband, plagued by his extravagant wife—who is able to travel back into history to meet Cleopatra, Helen of Troy, and other beauties. They are all alike, so he settles for his wife (Irene Bordoni). Clifton Webb plays all the historical lovers. The show has 143 performances.

Feb 2 *The Night Boat* (NY—Liberty—Musical). Jerome Kern's lively score complements Anne Caldwell's book and lyrics. John Hazzard is featured as a restive husband who pretends to be captain of an Albany night boat to get away from wife and mother-in-law. The show runs over 18 weeks.

Feb 2 *Beyond the Horizon* (NY—Morosco—Drama). Eugene O'Neill's first full-length drama features Richard Bennett and Robert Kelly as the two Mayo brothers, in love with the same girl (Elsie Rizer). The drama wins the Pulitzer Prize. The *NY Times* says "... the only reason for not calling *Beyond the Horizon* a great play is the natural gingerliness in which a reviewer uses that word ..."

Feb 23 *The Letter of the Law* (NY—Criterion—Drama). Eugene Brieux's *La Robe Rouge* is adapted, with Lionel Barrymore as Mouzon, the magistrate so eager for promotion that he tries to browbeat a peasant into admission of murder. This strong drama runs just over 11 weeks.

Feb 23 *Sacred and Profane Love* (NY—Morosco—Drama). Carlotta, seven years after a night of love with Emilio, a famed pianist, finds he has become a drug addict and failure in Paris. She redeems him. Elsie Ferguson and Jose Ruben play the

leading roles in this Arnold Bennett drama. It runs for 11 weeks.

Feb 23 *Jane Clegg* (NY—Garrick—Drama). St. John Ervine.'s play, about a wife with a weak husband, has Margaret Wycherly in the title role. She is supported by Helen Westley, Dudley Digges, Henry Travers, and others in this Theatre Guild production. The show runs 112 performances.

March 8 *Ziegfeld Girls of 1920* (NY—New Amsterdam Roof—Revue). Among the talents in this show are Fannie Brice, W. C. Fields, and Lillian Lorraine. It enjoys 78 performances.

March 19 *What's In a Name?* (NY—Maxine Elliott—Revue). The lovely settings and costumes by James Reynolds delight for 87 performances. One scene has dancers posed like porcelain figurines in 18th century dress atop a giant music-box. John Murray Anderson produces and provides some of the lyrics and sketches.

June 7 *Scandals of 1920* (NY—Globe—Revue). George White and Ann Pennington dance to a George Gershwin score. Others in the show include Ethel Delmar, Peggy Dolan, Lou Holtz, and George "Doc" Rockwell. White produces and collaborates on the book with Andy Rice. Sketches are topical (Prohibition) and general (politics).

June 22 *The Ziegfeld Follies of 1920* (NY—New Amsterdam—Revue). Contributing music and lyrics are Gene Buck, Irving Berlin, Dave Stamper, Joseph McCarthy, Harry Tierney, and Victor Herbert. Fanny Brice delights with "I'm an Indian." Moran and Mack perform in blackface as the Two Black Crows. Also on hand are W. C. Fields, Charles Winninger, and Van and Schenck.

July 27 *Poor Little Ritz Girl* (NY—Central—Musical). Lew Fields produces the first full-length professional show by Richard Rodgers and Lorenz Hart. Some of their songs are replaced during the tryouts with works by Sigmund Romberg and Alex Gerber. Florence Webber and Charles Purcell sing the leads. Lulu McConnell adds some humor. The traditional story deals with a poor chorus girl who unwittingly rents an apartment belonging to a wealthy baritone. All ends well for 119 performances.

July 30 *Opportunity* (NY—48th Street—Drama). Playwright Owen Davis invents a Wall Street office-boy who makes a million in steel investments, marries the office stenographer, takes up with a vamp, loses all, has a nervous breakdown, and returns to his loyal wife. Nita Naldi is featured. The show runs for 138 performances.

Aug 9 *Ladies Night* (NY—Eltinge—Comedy). Avery Hopwood and Charlton An-

Night Boat

drews write this farce about a man trying to hide in a Turkish Bath on Ladies Night. It runs for 360 performances. The show comes to London's Aldwych on Nov 1, 1933 in an adapted version by Austin Melford and Douglas Furber. It achieves 165 performances.

Aug 9 *Good Times* (NY—Hippodrome—Musical). "The Wedding of the Dancing Doll" is one of the colorful numbers in the current Hippodrome spectacular, devised by R. H. Burnside, with music by Raymond Hubbell. This Charles Dillingham production tallies 456 performances, playing two-a-day.

Aug 16 *Enter Madame* (NY—Garrick—Comedy). Brock Pemberton directs and produces Gilda Varesi and Dolly Burne's play, which runs for nearly 11 months. Varesi plays a tempestuous opera star whose husband orders her to give up her career.

Aug 17 *Spanish Love* (NY—Maxine Elliott—Drama). Avery Hopwood and Mary Roberts Rinehart team up to adapt a Spanish tale about two intense Spaniards in love with the same girl. William Powell and Maria Ascarra play. It runs 308 performances.

Aug 23 *The Bat* (NY—Morosco—Drama). Mary Roberts Rinehardt and Avery Hopwood collaborate on this mystery which has long-lasting success, especially in amateur theatres. The story tells of a woman who rents the home of a deceased banker who may have stolen money. Strange noises and surprising murders occur. On Jan 23, 1922, it opens at the St. James's in London where it runs for 327 performances.

Aug 30 *The Bad Man* (NY—Comedy—Comedy). Porter Brown's satiric play deals with Pancho (Holbrook Blinn), who, with some ardent banditry, helps Gil Jones, a returned veteran, save his Arizona ranch from foreclosure and also helps him win his girl. Lester Lonergan stages. The play runs over 42 weeks. The play premieres in London on March 3, 1923, at the New Theatre with Matheson Lang as the bandit; he is also producer and director. Included in the cast are H. O. Nicholson, William Hallman, W. Boyd Davis, Alfred Drayton, and Florence Saunders. There are 111 performances.

Aug 30 *The Greenwich Village Follies of 1920* (NY—Greenwich Village—Revue). Bert Savoy does broad female impersonations. Phil Baker plays his accordion. The score is by A. Baldwin Sloane, with some lyrics by John Murray Anderson. Soon transferred uptown, the production has 192 performances.

Sep 6 *Honeydew* (NY—Casino—Musical). The celebrated violinist, Efrem Zimbalist, provides the score for Joseph Herbert's book and lyrics. Henry Honeydew composes song-cycles on the love-life of insects. His father-in-law, who has married Henry's first wife, is an insect exterminator. Complications ensue. The show has 231 performances in the season and continues running.

Sep 7 *The Woman of Bronze* (NY—Frazee—Drama). In this play by Paul Kester, Margaret Anglin plays the wife of a sculptor (John Halliday) who is unfaithful. He leaves her but returns to create a masterpiece. This play runs for nearly 32 weeks.

Sep 13 *Welcome Stranger* (NY—Cohan and Harris—Comedy). Aaron Hoffman's play is about a Jewish entrepreneur whose hard work and enterprise change a town's attitudes. It runs for 309 performances. On Oct 19, 1921, it opens at London's Lyric, with Henry Green. The play is shown 224 times.

Sep 27 *The Tavern* (NY—Cohan—Comedy). George M. Cohan casts Arnold Daly as The Vagabond in Cora Dick Gantt's burlesque melodrama. The production is set in a tavern where some unusual characters gather, threatened by various forces. Matters are resolved when sanitarium keepers come to take some of them back to confinement. The production runs 32 weeks.

Sep 29 *Three Live Ghosts* (NY—Greenwich Village—Comedy). Returning from a German POW camp after the war, three soldiers find themselves reported dead. Frederick Isham has devised some good reasons for their not being able to correct the mistake. The production runs for 250 performances.

Sep 30 *The Mirage* (NY—Times Square—Drama). The Selwyn brothers produce Edgar Selwyn's melodrama about a girl from Erie Pa. who becomes a kept woman in New York. Florence Reed is the girl. The production runs a profitable 192 performances.

Scandals of 1920

Oct 5 *Tip Top* (NY—Globe—Musical). The sketchy book by Anne Caldwell and R. H. Burnside provides an excuse for the star, Fred Stone, to show his skill as a novelty dancer and comedian, as well as demonstrate marksmanship and bullwhip expertise. Also on hand are Oscar Ragland, the Duncan Sisters (Vivian and Rosetta), Gus Minton, and Princess White Deer. Ivan Caryll composes the score. The show runs 246 performances.

Oct 12 *The Meanest Man in the World* (NY—Hudson—Comedy). George M. Cohan produces Augustin MacHugh's play about a man (Frank Thomas) who believes that riches come through being selfish, but a pretty girl (Marion Coakley) convinces him otherwise. The show runs over 25 weeks.

Oct 18 *Mary* (NY—Knickerbocker—Musical). George M. Cohan produces this show. It's written by Otto Harbach and Frank Mandel, with a Lou Hirsch score that is much admired. In try-outs known as *The House That Jack Built*, the show deals with Jack's plans to build mobile homes, and Mary's hopes to win him. The production runs nearly seven months and has four road companies.

Oct 19 *Hitchy-Koo 1920* (NY—New Amsterdam—Revue). Raymond Hitchcock, Julia Sanderson, Florence O'Denishawn, and Grace Moore evoke nostalgia for the New York "we used to know." Jerome Kern composes the score. The show, staged by Ned Wayburn, runs for 71 performances.

Oct 20 *The First Year* (NY—Little—Comedy). Frank Craven stars in the play he has written. It is about a woman who finds the first year of marriage is rocky and she leaves her husband. It is an immediate success—tickets for the entire season selling out after the second week. The production has 278 performances in the season and continues running. On Nov

29, 1926, the play opens at London's Apollo. Ernest Truex, the American actor, is praised as Thomas Tucker. Phyllis Povah, George Curzon, and Mary Rorke are also in the cast. There are 180 performances.

Nov 1 *The Emperor Jones* (NY—Neighborhood Playhouse—Drama). The Provincetown Players produce Eugene O'Neill's eight-scene drama about the fears and fall of a black emperor of an anonymous West Indian island. Charles Gilpin has a personal triumph in the title-role. There are 204 performances. On Sep 10, 1925, it opens at London's Ambassadors with Paul Robeson in the lead. It has only 43 performances.

Nov 8 *Afgar* (NY—Central—Musical). The continental beauty, Alice Delysia, scantily but fetchingly clad, is Zaydee, a harem beauty who unionizes her fellow inmates. This show wins 171 performances.

Nov 10 *Heartbreak House* (NY—Garrick—Drama). George Bernard Shaw's allegory of Britain before and during World War I earns 125 performances in this Theatre Guild production. Helen Westley, Albert Perry, and Lucille Watson are among the cast. The *NY Times* reports that the play "is quite the larkiest and most amusing one that Shaw has written in many a year . . ." On Oct 18, 1921, it plays at London's Court with Brember Wills, Edith Evans, James Dale and Mary Grey. There are 63 performances.

Nov 23 *Rollo's Wild Oat* (NY—Punch and Judy—Comedy). Clare Kummer's play, features Roland Young as stage-struck Rollo who uses his own money to hire a theatre and actors so he can play Hamlet. The show runs for almost seven months.

Nov 29 *The Broken Wing* (NY—48th Street—Comedy). Inez Plummer plays the Mexican girl, Inez, who dreams of a "gringo husband" and gets her wish when an American aviator crashes his plane into her foster-father's house. In the cast are George Abbott, Louis Wolheim and Mary Worth. The production runs nearly 22 weeks.

Dec 14 *Lady Billy* (NY—Liberty—Musical). Zelda Sears, also an actress and director, writes book and lyrics for this story about a lady who disguises herself as a boy to show tourists through her castle. She also appears as a ghost. An American takes an interest in her, suggesting she go to the states as a boy-soprano. She marries him. Harold Levey provides the score. The popular star, Mitzi (Hajos), is Lady Billy. Boyd Marshall is the American. Sydney Greenstreet is also in the cast.

Dec 21 *Sally* (NY—New Amsterdam—Musical). Marilyn Miller has the title role as a poor dishwasher who subs for a truant prima ballerina and breaks into the Ziegfeld Follies. Jerome Kern's score includes "Look for the Silver Lining" and "Wild Rose." The show runs 507 performances. On Sep 10, 1921, it premieres at London's

Winter Garden with Dorothy Dickson as Sally. There are 383 performances.

Dec 23 *Deburau* (NY—Belasco—Comedy). Sacha Guitry's play features Lionel Atwill with Elsie Mackay. Lavishly mounted, the production recreates the world of the 19th century pantomimist and famed Pierrot. The show runs for more than 23 weeks. On Nov 3, 1921, it opens at London's Ambassadors with Robert Loraine in the title-role. A failure, it has only 28 showings.

Dec 27 *Miss Lulu Bett* (NY—Belmont—Comedy). Zona Gale's play concerns a spinster drudge in her sister's home. In jest, her brother-in-law, a magistrate, "marries" her to his visiting brother. It turns out to be legal and, eventually, lasting. The play runs the season and beyond, winning the $1,000 Pulitzer Prize.

Dec 27 *Diff'rent* (NY—Provincetown Playhouse—Drama). Eugene O'Neill's play opens in Greenwich Village but is soon moved uptown to the Princess Theatre. James Light, as Captain Caleb Williams, is not different from other men; he has had affairs. Disappointed in him, Emma Crosby (Mary Blair) remains single for 30 years. Finally, she offers herself to a young soldier just back from the Great War. The Captain, stunned, kills himself. She follows him. The play has 100 performances.

Dec 29 *The Passing Show of 1921* (NY—Winter Garden—Revue). With a Jean Schwartz score, the show runs for 200 performances, featuring Willie and Eugene Howard. Marie Dressler is in the revue for a short time.

Ambassadors'—Drama). Playwright H. M. Harwood tackles politics and politicians with wit and insight. Cathleen Nesbitt and Norman McKinnel have leading roles. With a split run between the Ambassadors' and the Kingsway Theatre, the play has a total run of 222 performances.

April 21 *The Skin Game* (L—St. Martin's—Drama). John Galsworthy's play, about a man whose antagonism over the use of neighboring property is really related to much larger issues of personality and position, features Athole Stewart. It runs for 349 showings. On Oct 20, it opens at Broadway's Bijou.

May 15 *A Southern Maid* (L—Daly's—Musical). Jose Collins plays the captivating Dolores, beloved of the bandit Francesco del Fuego (Bertram Wallis) and of Sir Willoughby Rawdon (Claude Flemming), a Santiago plantation owner. True love triumphs for 306 performances. The book is by Dion C. Calthrop and Harry Graham, with score by Harold Fraser-Simson and lyrics by Graham and Adrian Ross. Ivor Novello also contributes some songs. Among the numbers are "Love's Cigarette," "Dark Grows the Sky," and "My Way of Love." Dorothy Monkman and Gwendoline Brogden play Juanita and Chiquita.

June 1 *Johnny Jones* (L—Alhambra—Musical). Playing the title-role, comedian George Robey calls this a "Robey Salad, with musical dressing." Ivy St. Helier plays his sister Sue, who joins him in singing "A Little House, a Little Home." There are 349 performances, with the show's book by Harry Vernon, and most of the songs by Clifford Grey and Charles Cuvillier.

June 16 *Jig-Saw* (L—Hippodrome—Revue). There are 307 performances of this show, devised by Albert De Courville, Wal Pink and Edgar Wallace, with music by Frederick Chappelle and E. A. Horan. Laddie Cliff, Stanley Lupino, Daphne Pollard, Nancy Gibbs, Phil Lester, the Dooley Boys, and the Dolly Sisters are in the cast.

1920   BRITISH PREMIERES

Jan 5 *Mr. Pim Passes By* (L—New—Comedy). A. A. Milne writes a role for Irene Vanbrugh, shown as a widow of a convicted forger—who is later reported alive—and now the wife of a country man (Ben Webster). Dion Boucicault plays the aged Mr. Pim. This play has been seen earlier in Manchester at the Gaiety Theatre (Dec 1, 1919). In London, there are 246 performances. The New York Theatre Guild production, opening at the Garrick on Feb 28, 1921, earns a run of almost 16 weeks, with a cast including Laura Hope Crews, Dudley Digges, and Phyllis Povah.

Feb 12 *Wild Geese* (L—Comedy—Musical). Jack Buchanan, Elsie Carlisle, Olive Groves, and Phyllis Monkman are in the cast of this show by Ronald Jeans. Charles Cuvillier supplies the music. The show earns 112 performances.

Feb 24 *The Young Visiters* (L—Court—Comedy). Daisy Ashford's youthful attempt to write a sophisticated tale is adapted by Margaret Mackenzie and Mrs. George Norman, preserving the fun and naivety. Audrey Cameron plays Daisy. Ben Field is Mr. Salteena. The production wins a run of 105 performances.

Feb 26 *Mary Rose* (L—Haymarket—Drama). J. M. Barrie's play about a woman who disappears briefly in the Scottish islands as a girl and later, as a woman, vanishes again, to return much later as a ghostly presence, features Fay Compton in the title role. It runs for 398 performances. On Dec 22, 1920, the show reaches New York's Empire, with Ruth Chatterton as Mary Rose. It runs 16 weeks.

March 15 *Come Out of the Kitchen* (L—Strand—Comedy). Alice Deur Miller's novel, adapted by A. E. Thomas, began its stage life in 1916 at the Columbia (Geary) in San Francisco. In the West End, with Gertrude Elliott playing the charm-

ing Olivia, it wins 111 performances. Like the successful *Lord Richard in the Pantry*, it shows the gentry, having let the house, going below stairs to wait on the temporary tenants.

March 26 *Just Fancy!* (L—Vaudeville—Revue). This show earns 332 performances for producer Cosmo Gordon Lennox. The company includes Ralph Lynn, Betty Chester, Walter Williams, Margaret Bannerman, Fred Groves, Dan O'Neill, Bob Cory, Phyllis Asche, and others. Arthur Wimperis devises book and lyrics, with a score by Herman Darewski.

March 29 *The Young Person in Pink* (L—Haymarket—Comedy). Gertrude Jennings' play earns a run of 216 performances and two transfers. Ben Webster stages this tale of an amnesiac who falls in love with a man engaged to an older woman. Joyce Carey, Donald Calthorpe, and Violet Vanbrugh are in the cast.

April 5 *Paddy the Next Best Thing* (L—Savoy—Comedy). Peggy O'Neil, the American actress, charms audiences as Patricia (Paddy) Adair, raised as a tomboy by her father, who longs for a boy. Her fiancé must perform four feats before he can win her over. There are 867 performances of this Gayer Mackay and Robert Ord comedy, based on Gertrude Page's novel.

April 7 *Irene.* See NY premiere, 1919.

April 8 *The Man Who Came Back.* See NY premiere, 1916.

April 16 *The Blue Lagoon* (L—Prince of Wales's—Drama). Harold French and Faith Celli play two teenagers marooned on a desert island where they discover their affection for each other. Norman MacOwan and Charlton Mann have adapted the novel of H. De Vere Stacpoole. There are 263 performances.

April 20 *The Grain of Mustard Seed* (L—

Miss Lulu Bett

June 24 *The Garden of Allah* (L—Drury Lane—Drama). Producer Arthur Collins stages another Drury Lane melodrama. Mary Anderson and Robert Hichens have adapted his novel to give stage life to the amorous adventures depicted by Godfrey Tearle (Boris Androvsky) and Madge Titheradge (Domini Enfilden). Although this play has been premiered in 1911 in New York at the Century Theatre, its thrills are new to the London audiences which throng the theatre for 359 performances.

July 7 *Brown Sugar* (L—Garrick—Comedy). Edna Best has a success in Lady Arthur Lever's artificial comedy, in which Best, as a chorus girl with a heart of gold but a slum background, marries Lord Sloane (Herbert Marshall) and has to prove herself to his aristocratic parents (Eric Lewis and Henrietta Watson). There are 266 performances.

July 10 *At the Villa Rose* (L—Strand—Drama). A. E. W. Mason's play enjoys a run of 126 performances, ending Nov 13, and followed a month later by a 23-performance revival. Kyrle Bellew plays Celia Harland, with a cast including Arthur Bourchier, Miriam Lewes, George Zucco, Norman Page, and Hutin Britton.

July 14 *My Old Dutch* (L—Lyceum—Comedy). Albert Chevalier recreates one of his gallery of cockney characters in this play Arthur Shirely and he have devised. He sings such songs as "My Old Dutch." Alice Bowers, by the play's end, becomes his "Old Dutch." There are 186 performances.

July 15 *French Leave* (L—Globe—Comedy). There are 283 performances of Reginald Berkeley's light entertainment, essentially a war-time military farce, in which a wife (Renee Kelly), posing as a Parisian opera star, visits her husband near the front. A. Hylton Allan plays the distraught officer-husband, who finds his disguised wife has captivated his commanding general and his sub-lieutenant.

July 21 *I'll Leave It To You* (L—New—Comedy). Noel Coward's light comedy comes to London after a premiere in May at the Gaiety in Manchester. He plays Bobbie, with a cast including Stella Jesse, Muriel Pope, Douglas Jeffries, and Moya Nugent. There are 37 performances.

Aug 9 *The Unknown* (L—Adlwych—Drama). W. Somerset Maugham's play, produced by Viola Tree, who plays Mrs. Wharton, has only 77 performances. It dwells on the evils of the late war and questions some accepted ideas about religion and the Deity. In the company among others are Haidee Wright, Charles France, Leslie Faber, Basil Rathbone, and Ellen O'Malley, as the heroine.

Sep 1 *The Prude's Fall* (L—Wyndham's—Drama). Gerald Du Maurier plays Captain Le Briquet in this play by Rudolf Besier and May Edginton, which achieves 229 performances. The captain declares his love for Mrs. Audley, an engaged widow (Emily Brooke). She accepts, even though he offers no promise of marriage. Later, he humiliates her, his intention always having been to teach her a lesson for her prudish behavior toward a former woman-friend.

Sep 4 *London, Paris, and New York* (L—Pavilion—Revue). There are 366 performances of this show with Arthur Wimperis book and lyrics and Herman Darewski score. In the ensemble are Albert Bruno, "June," Nellie Taylor, Hugh Wakefield, Nelson Keys, and Georgia O'Ramey, among others.

Sep 9 *The Wandering Jew* (L—New—Comedy). Matheson Lang produces, stages (with A. W. Tyrer), and stars in this E. Temple Thurston dramatization of the old legend of the Jew who, having cursed Christ on Calvary, has been doomed to wander. He perishes at the stake, condemned by the Inquisitors. The cast includes Hutin Britton, Lillah McCarthy, W. F. Grant, George Skillan, and Dorothy Holmes-Gore. There are 390 performances.

Sep 18 *A Night Out* (L—Winter Garden—Musical). Adapted from Feydeau and Desvallieres' *L'Hotel du Libre Exchange*, this show, by Arthur Miller and George Grossmith, wins 309 performances. The songs are the work of Clifford Grey (lyrics) and Willie Redstone (music). Lesley Henson heads the cast. Henson plays a house-bound sculptor-husband who arranges a farcical, disastrous evening at the notorious Hotel Pimlico when his wife's away.

Oct 2 *The Great Lover*. See NY premiere, 1915.

Oct 7 *The Naughty Princess* (L—Adelphi—Musical). There are 280 performances for this show, based on Barde's *La Reine Joyeuse*, by J. H. Turner, with songs by Adrian Ross (lyrics) and Charles Cuvillier (music). W. H. Berry plays the King of Panoplia, off to Paris where his daughter (Lily St. John), has run away—with her companion (Amy Augarde) and a bogus painter (George Grossmith) who is really a prince.

Oct 18 *The Romantic Age* (L—Comedy—Comedy). A. A. Milne's play about a woman who is looking for a knight in shining armor features Barbara Hoffe. John Williams and Arthur Wontner are also in the cast. There are 126 showings. On Nov 14, 1922, it opens at New York's Comedy with Margalo Gillmore. It has only 21 performances.

Dec 1 *A Little Dutch Girl* (L—Lyric—Musical). Maggie Teyte plays a princess, in disguise as a Dutch serving-maid, who captures the heart of a reluctant prince (Martin Iredale). The score is the work of Emmerich Kalman, with lyrics by Harry Graham, who has fashioned the book with Hicks. There are 207 performances.

Dec 13 *It's All Wrong* (L—Queen's—Revue). Elsie Janis stars in this show she's concocted—contributing sketches, lyrics, and music, but aided by others as well, such as composer Herman Finck. There are 112 showings.

Dec 16 *Jumble Sale* (L—Vaudeville—Revue). There are 176 performances of this show, featuring Binnie Hale, Phyllis Titmuss, Joyce Barbour, Walter Williams, Eric Blore, and others. J. H. Turner provides the book, with songs by Philip Braham and Reginald Arkell.

Dec 23 *The Charm School* (L—Comedy—Comedy). Alice Duer Miller and Robert Milton adapt her popular novel for a run of 155 showings. Owen Nares, Keneth Kent, Maggie Albanesi. Lena Halliday, and Sydney Fairbrother, among others, animate the play.

1920   REVIVALS/REPERTORIES

Jan 5 Matheson Lang's adaptation of a French work, Le *Chevalier au Masque* opens in New York at the Booth Theatre. It is called *The Purple Mask* and details a series of daring exploits of the Count de Trevieres (Leo Ditrichstein) in attempting to oppose Napoleon. The production runs for over 17 weeks.

Jan 6 In Dublin at the Abbey Theatre, Lady Gregory's *The Golden Apple* opens. On Feb 19, E. Barrington's *The Daemon in the House* is premiered. On March 28, the play is T. W. Kerrigan's *The Visitant*. The new play on May 23 is Moireen Fox's *The Fire-Bringers*. On Sep 7, Frank J. H. O'Donnell's *The Drifters* is produced, followed on the 21 by Fergus O'Nolan's *A Royal Alliance*. On Oct 5, a new play *The Serf*, is shown. On the 12, St. John Ervine's play, *The Island of Saints: How to Get Out It*, is on the bill. On Nov 30, the new production is Brinsley MacNamara's *The Land for the People*.

Jan 9 In London at the St. James's Theatre, producer Gilbert Miller revives Shakespeare's *Julius Caesar*, with Clifton Boyne as Casear. There are 83 performances.

Jan 15 At London's Little Theatre, the Grand Guignol Players offer H. F. Maltby's *What Did Her Husband Say?* for a run of 121 performances. It's paired with *The Medium*, which is kept in the bill for 85 showings.

Jan 18 At the Lyric, Hammersmith, the French Players offer a production of Henri Bernstein's *Le Secret*. On Feb 29, the play is Francois de Croisset's *Le Bonheur, Mesdames*.

Jan 31 At London's Royalty Theatre, managers Eadie and Curzon revive J. M.

A Night Out

Barrie's *The Admirable Crichton* for a run of 135 performances.

Feb 2 Frank Benson and company offer a week's performances of *Hamlet* at St. Martin's Theatre in London.

Feb 5 At London's New Theatre, Matheson Lang opens *Carnival*, which he and H. C. M. Hardinge have adapted from the Italian drama, *Sirocco*. He plays Silvio, with Hilda Bayley, Dennis Neilson-Terry, Dorothy Fane, Ivy Pike, and others in the cast. The production has 188 performances. On Feb 11, he begins a series of Wednesday matinees at which he plays Othello to Arthur Bourchier's Iago, with Hilda Bayley as Desdemona and Hutin Britton as Emilia.

Feb 6 Constance Collier revives John Raphael's adaptation of George Du Maurier's novel, *Peter Ibbetson*, playing Mary, Duchess of Towers, to Basil Rathbone's Ibbetson in London at the Savoy Theatre. With an April break and a theatre-move, the run totals 114 performances.

Feb 8 Dryden's Restoration comedy *Marriage a la mode* is presented by the Phoenix Society at the Lyric, Hammersmith. The Society revives Heywood's 1617 comedy, *The Fair Maid of the West*, on April 11. On Nov 28, the Society offers Thomas Otway's 1682 *Venice Preserved*.

March 1 Walter Hampden produces Percy Mackaye's "Ballad Play," *George Washington*, which was originally intended to be performed outdoors at festivals. Hampden plays the Founding Father at various stages in his career. The production runs for two weeks in New York.

March 6 John Barrymore plays Shakespeare's tragic monarch *Richard III*, under the aegis of Arthur Hopkins at New York's Plymouth Theatre. Barrymore eventually has to withdraw, suffering from nervous tension. Critics praise not only Hopkins' sensitive direction but also the effective settings of Robert Edmond Jones. The *NY Times* extols Barrymore's acting.

March 8 At a London matinee at the Court Theatre, the Arts Theatre presents Anton Chekhov's *The Three Sisters*.

March 14 At the Lyric, Hammersmith, John Galsworthy's duologue, *Defeat*, is performed by the Curtain Group and the People's Theatre Society.

March 22 Maurice Browne produces the Gilbert Murray translation of Euripides' *Medea* in New York at the Garrick Theatre, for a two-week run. Ellen Van Volkenburg is the vengeful Medea.

March 24 The annual Columbia University Varsity Show opens in the Grand Ballroom of the Hotel Astor for a run of four performances only. It is notable because it boasts the first full score by Richard Rodgers, with lyrics by Lorenz Hart, and additional lyrics by Oscar Hammerstein II. Called *Fly With Me*, it has an all-male cast and is set 50 years in the future (1970) at Bolsheviky U, a socialist college in a city very like Manhattan.

March 25 The musical *The Shop Girl* (1894) is revived in London at the Gaiety Theatre for a run of 327 performances.

March 28 At the Lyric Theatre, Hammersmith, George Kaiser's Expressionist drama, *From Morn to Midnight*, is produced by the Incorporated Stage Society. Edith Evans, and Irene Rathbone are in the cast.

April 5 J. J. Shubert revives *Florodora* at the Century Theatre in New York.

April 12 *Coriolanus*, produced and staged by Russell Thorndike and Charles Warburton for Lilian Baylis at London's Old Vic Theatre, continues the Shakespeare cycle.

April 13 Gogol's Russian comedy, *The Government Inspector*, opens in London at the Duke of York's Theatre for a brief run of 30 performances. Claude Rains is featured.

April 19 With W. Bridges Adams directing and designing, the spring season of Shakespeare productions opens in Stratford-upon-Avon. *The Merchant of Venice* is the premiere play. *Cymbeline* is the "birthday play" in the three-week season at the Memorial Theatre. Other plays include *Much Ado About Nothing*, *The Taming of the Shrew*, *Richard II*, and *Hamlet*.

May 11 At London's Aldwych Theatre, Sacha Guitry opens a season of French plays, ending June 12.

June 5 At the Lyric Theatre, Hammersmith, Nigel Playfair revives John Gay's 1727 ballad opera, *The Beggar's Opera*, for a total run of 1,469 performances. C. Lovat Fraser designs the sets, costumes, and act-drop with a stylized simplicity. In the company are Frederick Ranalow, Frederic Austin, Sylvia Nelis, and Elsie French.

July 12 At the London Coliseum, Hugo Rumbold presents Jean Cocteau's *Nothing-Doing Bar*, with music by Darius Milhaud.

July 19 With a six-week season, the longest to date, the summer repertory of Shakespearean productions opens in the Memorial Theatre at Stratford-upon-Avon. The plays are *Cymbeline*, *The Merchant of Venice*, *Much Ado About Nothing*, *The Taming of the Shrew*, *Richard II*, *Hamlet*, *Henry V*, *As You Like It*, *Macbeth*, and *Twelfth Night*.

Sep 4 The Birmingham Repertory Theatre (BR) opens its ninth season with L. P. Brown's *The Potter's Shop*.

Sep 23 George Bernard Shaw's 1900 *You Never Can Tell* is revived in Hampstead by the Everyman Company. Two months later, on Nov 22, Leon Lion and Louis Calvert offer the first of six matinee performances of the play at the Garrick Theatre.

Sep 23 At London's Aldwych Theatre, Ethel Irving has a four-week run in the title-role of Sardou's *La Tosca*, with Lyn Harding as Baron Scarpia and Gerald Lawrence as Cavaradossi.

Sep 28 At London's Garrick Theatre, Ernest Hutchinson's "play of today" opens, titled *The Right To Strike*. With transfers to the Lyric and the Queen's, it manages 83 performances.

Oct 4 At New York's Garrick Theatre, the Theatre Guild offers David Pinski's *The Treasure*, about Russian villagers tearing up a cemetery, searching for gold coins. The production lasts only five weeks. In the cast are Celia Adler, Dudley Digges, Jennie Moscowitz, Edgar Stehli, Henry Travers, and others.

Oct 4 In a series of special matinees at London's Strand Theatre, the New Shakespeare Company gives 34 performances of Shakespeare's *Henry V*.

Nov 2 James K. Hackett plays the title-role in the Scottish tragedy—*Macbeth*—at London's Aldwych Theatre, with Mrs. Patrick Campbell as Lady Macbeth. There are 30 repetitions of the production.

Nov 13 In London, at the Royalty Theatre, G. Martinez Sierra's Spanish play, *The Romantic Young Lady*, receives 68 performances. In the cast, among others, are Dennis Eadie, Mary Rorke, and Joyce Carey.

Dec 4 At London's Royal Court Theatre, J. B. Fagan offers a revival of Shakespeare's *A Midsummer Night's Dream* which achieves 94 performances.

Dec 19 The Stage Society presents George Bernard Shaw's *O'Flaherty, V. C.* at the Lyric, Hammersmith, with Arthur Sinclair in the title-role. Sara Allgood plays Mrs. O'Flaherty. The play has already been seen in New York on June 21.

Dec 27 A successful London revival of John Gay's *The Beggar's Opera* is imported with a British cast to play at the Greenwich Village Theatre. It lasts 37 performances.

Jan 16 Composer, conductor, and critic Reginald de Koven (b. 1859) is dead in Chicago. De Koven wrote over 150 songs and instrumental works in addition to two operas with librettos by Percy MacKaye: *The Canterbury Pilgrims* and *Rip Van Winkle.* He is best known for his operettas, of which *Robin Hood* was most successful.

Feb 12 With *He and She*, Rachel Crothers reworks her earlier play, *The Herfords*, (1911). She directs and also plays her heroine, Ann Herford, who nearly ruins her marriage by winning a design prize which finally goes to her husband, played by Cyril Keightley. The production runs only 28 performances at New York's Little Theatre.• In 1980, it is revived at the Brooklyn Academy of Music by the BAM Company.

April 5 Spurned by producers because of his role in the Equity strike, Ed Wynn packages his own show, *The Ed Wynn Carnival* in New York. The ensemble includes Marion Davies, but Wynn's lisping clowning and ridiculous inventions are the core of the fun.

April 20 American drama critic Robinson Locke (b. 1856) is dead in Toledo, Ohio. Locke, critic and publisher of the *Toledo Blade*, was noted for his comprehensive scrapbook collection on the American theatre dating back to 1870.

May 10 Producer Claire Nichtern is born Claire Joseph in New York City.

May 11 American author, critic, and playwright William Dean Howells (b. 1837) dies in New York City. As critic, Howells encouraged the work of Ned Harrigan, James A. Herne, and Clyde Fitch. His plays include *A Counterfeit Presentment*, *Yorick's Love*, *The Garroters*, and *The Mouse Trap.*

May 17 Future composer-lyricist Bob Merrill is born in Atlantic City, New Jersey.

May 22 American playwright Hal Reid is dead at age 60. Reid's plays include *The German Emigrants*, *The Singing Girl from Killarney*, *From Broadway to Bowery*, *The Nazarene*, and *The Kentuckian.* In 1912 he was appointed Censor to the Universal Film Corporation.

June 18 American actor George Anderson Brown dies in Providence, Rhode Island, at age 81. Brown was the oldest member of the Boston Opera Company.

July 19 Actress Nera Rosa dies in New York at age 80. Rosa gained recognition as Frochard in *The Two Orphans.*

Aug 10 American actor James O'Neill (b. Nov 15, 1847) dies in New London, Connecticut. O'Neill performed with Adelaide Neilson and Edwin Booth. His portrayal of Edmond Dantes in *The Count of Monte Cristo* is O'Neill's chief claim to fame. His son, Eugene, is a playwright.

Sep 14 Future actress Kay Medford is born Kathleen Patricia Regan in New York City.

Sep 24 Magician John W. Sergent dies in New York at age 67. Sergent was founder of the Society of American Magicians.

Oct 22 American actor Oliver Doud Byron (b. 1842) dies in Long Branch, New Jersey. One of the best known tragedians of the 1890s, Byron supported Edwin Booth, Mrs. Scott-Siddons, and other stars. He made his debut in *Nicholas Nickleby*, with Joseph Jefferson in 1856. He married Mary Kate Rehan, sister of Ada Rehan. His son Arthur is an actor.

Nov 17 Noted in the Yiddish theatre, actor Jacob Ben-Ami appears in his first English-speaking role as Peter Krumback in Sven Lange's *Samson and Delilah* at the Greenwich Village Theatre. Ben-Ami began his acting career with the Russian theatre in Minsk in 1907.

Nov 21 Future actor Ralph Meeker is born Ralph Rathgeber in Minneapolis, Minnesota.

1920 THEATERS/PRODUCTIONS

In Britain patents are granted for: A. B. Klein's keyboard-controlled projection of any desired color of the spectrum, once artificial light has been broken up by a prism; N. DeBoudkowsky's method of painting several pictures—in different colors—on the same surface, rendering each separately visible by changing the hue of the illumination.

Ferdinand Oebbecke receives a U.S. patent for inventing a system whereby lenses make possible the projection of images of a live stage production onto a ground-glass screen. The moving images are then interrupted rapidly to simulate the effect of a motion-picture. Imitation imitates imitation.

Feb 24 J. E. Vedrenne and Frank Vernon launch their managership of the newly restored Little Theatre—damaged by war-time bombs—in London with Eva Moore in the title-role of Edward Knoblock's *Mumsee*, a French mother of five children, one of whom betrays France during the Great War but expiates his crime with a patriotic, heroic death. The war is over, and the play achieves only 38 performances. Theatre seating capacity has been increased to 377.

May 11 A counterweighted curtain-opening mechanism, which is operated by a winch, is patented in the U.S. by William Lemle.

June 15 Taking stock of the 1919–20 Broadway season, there have been 150 new plays, both legitimate and musicals, with some 50 theatres in which to produce them. Six shows had over 300 performances; 14 had more than 200 showings, and 26 had runs of more than 100 performances. *Lightnin'* is now the longest-running play, with 800 performances. Thanks to profits from war-time investments, there are now more independent producers. Film companies are also becoming involved in production. Three theatres have been taken over by cinema magnates, with a view to producing plays in them which can then be turned into profitable films. Ethel Barrymore's *Declassee* has been financed in this manner. Critic Burns Mantle inaugurates his annual compilation of the Broadway season, picking ten *Best Plays* and providing statistics, cast lists, and synopses of the rest of the productions. He admits that new plays are also produced in Chicago and Boston, as well as other American cities, but insists that the best always reach Broadway. For the current season, Mantle's best are: Drinkwater's *Abraham Lincoln*, O'Neill's *Beyond the Horizon*, Forbes' *The Famous Mrs. Fair*, Tarkington's *Clarence*, Ervine's *Jane Clegg*, Akins' *Declasse*, Middleton/Bolton's *Adam and Eva*, Benelli's *The Jest*, Field's *Wedding Bells*, and Butler's *Mamma's Affair.*

Nov 18 The Apollo Theatre, on West 42 Street in New York, originally designed by Eugene DeRosa, in 1910, as a combination motion-picture and vaudeville house, known as the Bryant, reopens as a legitimate theatre, with *Jimmie*, by Oscar Hammerstein II. Among its tenants are George White's *Scandals* and Minsky's burlesque shows. From 1937–78, it is used to show films. It reopens as a legitimate theatre in 1979.

Dec There are 42 legitimate theatre productions on tour in America as of the first week of this month. In 1900, there were 392.

Shuffle Along

Jan 18 *The Green Goddess* (NY—Booth—Drama). William Archer's play is well received, running beyond the season. George Arliss plays the Rajah of Rukh, ruler of a mythical kingdom in Asia. Ronald Coleman plays a Temple Priest. On Sep 6, 1923 it opens in London at St. James's Theatre with George Arliss, Owen Roughwood and George Relph in the company. Gilbert Miller and Winthrop Ames produce. There are 417 performances. *The Times* calls it "thrilling" and praises Arliss as acting with "immense gusto and authority."

Feb 8 *The Ziegfeld 9 O'Clock Frolic* (NY—Danse de Follies—Revue). With the advent of Prohibition, the speakeasies are stealing away the audiences for revues. This show has only 35 performances, despite such performers as Anna Wheaton, Oscar Shaw, Frank Farnum, and Princess White Deer.

Feb 11 *The Rose Girl* (NY—Ambassador—Musical). With an Anselm Goetzl score and a book about a perfume factory girl who runs off to Paris, pursued by a Count. This old-fashioned show runs nearly 14 weeks.

Feb 28 *Mr. Pim Passes By.* See L premiere, 1920.

March 2 *Nice People* (NY—Klaw—Comedy). Rachel Crothers supervises the production of her four-act play, which has an impressive trio in major roles: Tallulah Bankhead, Katherine Cornell, and Francine Larrimore. Larrimore, as a headstrong, rich young debutante finds she is willing to give up her fortune to marry a decent young man who despises New York society. The production runs 15 weeks.

April 18 *Clair de Lune* (NY—Empire—Drama). John and Ethel Barrymore join forces to bring this play by Michael Strange to life. Strange is really Mrs. John Barrymore. The plot is based on Victor Hugo's *The Man Who Laughed.* The play has a two-month run, thanks to its large, distinguished cast—Dennis King, Henry Daniell, and Violet Kemble Cooper, among others.

April 20 *Liliom* (NY—Garrick—Drama). Ferenc Molnar's Hungarian fantasy deals with the colorful, feckless drifter, Liliom, who is given a chance after a careless, wasted life to come back to earth to help his daughter. Joseph Schildkraut and Eva LeGallienne star. It runs just over two months in the Theatre Guild production.

May 10 *The Last Waltz* (NY—Century—Musical). Oscar Straus's score ensures the success of this production. Its original Balkan plot is adapted to make the hero an American navy officer. Walter Woolf and Eleanor Painter star with Ruth Hills, Ted Lorraine, James Barton, and Beatrice and Marcella Swanson.

May 23 *Shuffle Along* (NY—63rd Street Music Hall—Musical). This all-black show, with score and lyrics by Eubie Blake and Noble Sissle, including the hit, "I'm Just Wild About Harry," is a slow-starter, but eventually has 504 performances on Broadway. Blake is at the piano, and in the troupe are the librettists, Flournoy Miller and Aubrey Lyles, as well as Sissle, Lottie Gee, and Billy Williams. Corruption is stamped out in Jimtown, with a lot of tap, soft-shoe, and buck-and-wing dances as accompaniment.

June 1 *Gold* (NY—Frazee—Drama). Eugene O'Neill's four act play tells of the tragedy engulfing a sea captain (Willard Mack) obsessed with buried treasure. There are six performances. On Nov 9, 1926, it premieres in Liverpool at the Playhouse. It is given by the Repertory Company. In the cast are Herbert Lomas, Robert Speaight, and Rex Harrison.

June 20 *Goat Alley* (NY—Bijou—Drama). An all-black cast animates Ernest Culbertson's "drama of primitive love and life." Lillian McKee plays Lucy Belle Dorsey, a hard-working girl who is forced into prostitution to survive when her man is jailed. Released, he abandons her and her child. Cecil Owen stages this slice of life in the black ghetto of Washington, D.C. It runs only five performances.

June 21 *The Ziegfeld Follies of 1921* (NY—Globe—Revue). Florenz Ziegfeld pays a quarter of a million dollars to mount this show, with Joseph Urban sets and James Reynolds costumes recreating a Persian Court and the Versailles gardens. Fanny Brice introduces "My Man" and "Second Hand Rose." Brice, Raymond Hitchcock, and W. C. Fields spoof the Barrymores in a burlesque of *Camille.* Music is provided by Victor Herbert, Rudolf Friml, and Dave Stamper.

July 11 *George White's Scandals* (NY—Liberty—Revue). This summer show has a three-month run. It features White and Ann Pennington as dancers, with Lester Allen also offering fancy footwork. The score is by George Gershwin.

Aug 1 *Getting Gertie's Garter* (NY—Republic—Comedy). A married man must retrieve a diamond studded garter he gave last year to a newly married woman. Avery Hopwood and Wilson Collison have devised the play, which runs 15 weeks.

Aug 9 *Tangerine* (NY—Casino—Musical). Guy Bolton and Philip Bartholomae write the book, Howard Johnston the lyrics, and Carlo Sanders the score. When some husbands, jailed for not paying alimony, are freed, they go to Tangerine, a South Sea isle where women do all the work. Doing man's work tires the American women, who are glad to reconcile with their men. This show, staged by George Marion and Bert French, runs for 42 weeks.

Aug 13 *Dulcy* (NY—Frazee—Comedy). Lynn Fontanne plays Dulcinea Smith, full of bromides but eager to help everyone. Her desire to help her husband in business nearly causes disaster, but all ends well. Also in the cast are Howard Lindsay and Elliott Nugent. Lindsay stages the show, which runs for nearly 31 weeks. The authors are George S. Kaufman and Marc Connelly. On Nov 20, 1923, *Dulcy* premieres at London's Criterion Theatre, but even with Renee Kelly as Dulcy, it can't earn more than 30 performances in the West End. Jessie Bateman and Morton Selten are also in the ensemble.

Aug 23 *The Detour* (NY—Astor—Drama). Although Owen Davis' play has only a six-week run, its subject and treatment are admired by some critics. Effie Shannon plays a Long Island farm woman who has been saving butter and egg money so her daughter (Angela McCahill) can study art. Her husband forbids it. The wife rebels, only to learn that her daughter has no talent. The family settles back into its accustomed routine. Augustin Duncan directs and plays the father.

Aug 25 *Six-Cylinder Love* (NY—Sam H. Harris—Comedy). Donald Meek plays Richard Burton, whose family has been living beyond its means. The show runs the entire season and beyond. In the cast also are Hedda Hopper, Eleanor Gordon, and Ernest Truex. Sam Forrest stages.

Aug 30 *Back Pay* (NY—Eltinge—Drama). Fannie Hurst's play runs almost ten weeks. Helen MacKellar plays a girl reared in a brothel, who runs off to New York, where she becomes an elegant kept-woman. She is reformed by her girlhood love.

Aug 31 *Daddy's Gone A-Hunting* (NY—Plymouth—Drama). Frank Conroy plays a husband who returns from studying art in Paris, determined to be "free" of his wife and daughter. Nothing can reclaim him, so the wife (Marjorie Rambeau) is

Six Cylinder Love

left in despair. Zoe Akins' drama runs four months.

Aug 31 *The Greenwich Village Follies* (NY—Shubert—Revue). Opening uptown instead of in the Village, this edition runs 167 performances. Ted Lewis' jazz band plays the music, much of it by Carey Morgan, though not the hit song, "Three O'Clock in the Morning" (Terris/Robeldo). Joe E. Brown appears with vaudeville partner James Watts.

Sep 3 *Get Together* (NY—Hippodrome—Revue). The annual two-a-day spectacle at the huge Hippodrome enjoys 397 performances, featuring the choreography and dancing of Michael Fokine. The ballet is called *The Thunderbird*, considered inferior to his *The Firebird*. Charlotte dances an ice-ballet on skates. R. H. Burnside stages the variety numbers, including such treats as Jocko, the Juggling Crow.

Sep 5 *The Hero* (NY—Belmont—Drama). Gilbert Emery's play enjoys a ten-week run, with a cast including Fania Marinoff, Richard Bennett, and Blanche Friderici. The hero is a liar, seducer and thief who is just back from the war. He is a strong contrast to his decent, plodding brother Andrew who has stayed home and tried to solve the family problems. The play is admired by critics, but the public seems tired of themes connected with the war and returning veterans.

Sep 12 *The Circle.* See L premiere, 1921.

Sep 15 *The White-Headed Boy* (NY—Henry Miller—Comedy). Arthur Shields plays Denis, the spoiled son for whom the rest of the family must sacrifice. J. B. Fagan stages. Lennox Robinson's Irish comedy runs nearly eight weeks.

Sep 19 *Bluebeard's Eighth Wife* (NY—Ritz—Comedy). Arthur Wimperis adapts Alfred Savoir's French play, with Ina Claire featured. There are 155 performances. On Aug 26, 1922, it opens at London's Queen's with Norman McKinnel, Henry Ford, C. M. Hallard, Madge Titheradge, Doris MacIntyre, Peggy Rush, and others. It plays 478 times.

Sep 22 *The Music Box Revue* (NY—Music Box—Revue). Irving Berlin opens the handsome, intimate theatre Sam Harris has built for him with a more intimate

form of revue. "Say It With Music" becomes the signature song for these revues. William Collier is the MC, with Sam Bernard and Rene Riano kidding the dance craze. Staged by Hassard Short, the show runs through the season and beyond.

Sep 29 *Blossom Time* (NY—Ambassador—Musical). With a Franz Schubert score, adapted by Sigmond Romberg, and Dorothy Donnelly's reworking of the libretto of Heinrich Berte's *Das Dreimädlerhaus*, this is to be one of the Schubert's greatest successes. Bertram Peacock is Schubert; Olga Cook plays Mitzi. There will be two companies on Broadway at the same time as well as 14 troupes on the road. In London, it's known as *Lilac Time.*

Oct 3 *The O'Brien Girl* (NY—Liberty—Musical). A run of nearly 21 weeks is given this show, which has book and lyrics by Otto Harbach and Frank Mandel. The score is by Lou Hirsch. Elizabeth Hines plays an Irish stenographer who spends all her money on an Adirondack vacation, where she meets and wins a handsome young scion of a wealthy family. George M. Cohan produces.

Oct 3 *Thank You* (NY—Longacre—Comedy). Tom Cushing and Winchell Smith's play runs for 257 performances during the season. Edith King plays a girl raised in Paris who helps her minister-uncle shame his penny pinching Connecticut congregation into treating him with respect.

Oct 5 *Main Street* (NY—National—Drama). Sinclair Lewis's best-selling novel of Carol Kennicott's encounter with the midwestern drabness and narrowness of Gopher Prairie, enjoys an 86-performance run, in this dramatization by Harvey O'Higgins and Harriet Ford. Alma Tell plays Carol.

Oct 6 *Bombo* (NY—Jolson's 59th Street—Revue). Lavishly mounted, this Shubert show stars Al Jolson as Bombo, a blackface servant to Christopher Columbus. The Sigmund Romberg score is enhanced by interpolations such as "April Showers" and "Toot, Toot, Tootsie!" It runs the season. "California, Here I Come" is added by Jolson on tour.

Oct 10 *A Bill of Divorcement.* See L premiere, 1921.

Oct 17 *The Claw* (NY—Broadhurst—Drama). Henri Bernstein's French play, adapted by Louis Wolheim and E. D. Dunn, provides a vehicle for Lionel Barrymore, as a socialist politician who is compromised and ruined by his much younger wife, who then deserts him. He drops dead just before he is to defend himself in the Chamber of Deputies, with a mob howling outside. Arthur Hopkins produces and stages the production which lasts for 115 performances.

Oct 18 *The Demi-Virgin* (NY—Times Square—Comedy). Gloria Graham (Hazel

Dawn) is a movie-star, newly married to leading-man Wally Dean (Glenn Anders). An old flame, stirring Wally's embers on the wedding night, singes Gloria enough to sue for divorce before she's really tried marriage. Avery Hopwood adapts the play from a French original. During the season, it has 268 performances, thanks in part to a strip-poker scene and attendant calls for stage censorship. The *NY Times* refuses to print the show's title in its ad columns.

Nov 1 *Good Morning, Dearie* (NY—Globe—Musical). Billy Van Cortlandt (Oscar Shaw) marries a millinery shop-clerk (Louise Groody), after they foil a robbery by her gangster ex-lover. Anne Caldwell invents the story and lyrics for a Jerome Kern score. The show runs 33 weeks.

Nov 1 *The Grand Duke* (NY—Lyceum—Comedy). David Belasco produces and stages Sacha Guitry's Parisian play about a Russian Grand Duke who does a good turn for a former mistress and his unacknowledged son by marrying them off to a wealthy French plumber and his daughter. Lionel Atwill and Lina Abarbanell star. The show runs for 131 performances.

Nov 2 *Anna Christie* (NY—Vanderbilt—Drama). Eugene O'Neill's play of waterfront life has 177 performances. Arthur Hopkins produces and stages, with Pauline Lord, George Marion, and Frank Shannon in the leads. " 'Anna Christie' might be described as a work which towers above most of the plays in town, but which falls short of stature and the perfection reached by Eugene O'Neill in some of his earlier work," says the *NY Times.* With the original cast premiering in London on April 10, 1923, O'Neill's play wins 102 performances at the Strand Theatre. C. B. Cochran produces. Writing in *Play Pictorial*, editor B. W. Findon praises the acting: "It certainly is a most wonderful and absorbing performance, not only for the intrinsic merits of the play itself, but for the splendid representation which is given by Miss Pauline Lord . . ."

Nov 7 *The Perfect Fool* (NY—George M. Cohan—Revue). Ed Wynn returns to Broadway with a lively show built around Wynn's bizarre characterizations and inventions. The book, lyrics, music, and staging are all by Ed Wynn. The show runs through the season with 256 performances.

Nov 10 *The Straw* (NY—Greenwich Village—Drama). Margalo Gillmore plays Eileen Carmody, a girl whose only chance of surviving tuberculosis is the fragile hope that a young newsman (Otto Kruger) loves her. Eugene O'Neill's play has only 20 performances.

Nov 17 *Ziegfeld's Midnight Frolic* (NY—New Amsterdam Roof—Revue). Gene Buck and Dave Stamper provide music and lyrics for a company including Will

Rogers, Leon Errol, Gloria Foy, and Carlos and Inez. The post-theatre show runs 123 performances. Cynics insist it would have run longer if liquor could have been served.

Nov 29 *Kiki* (NY—Belasco—Comedy). David Belasco has adapted this Andre Picard farce, which he now produces and stages. Lenore Ulric has the title role of a girl of the Parisian streets who has kept herself pure for the music hall manager she loves. The show runs beyond the season. On Aug 2, 1923, the play, now called *Enter Kiki*, opens at London's Playhouse with Gladys Cooper in the title role. There are 155 showings.

Dec 5 *The Hand of the Potter* (NY—Provincetown—Drama). This tragedy which ranges from the lavish Upper East Side to the poverty-stricken Lower East Side is the handiwork of novelist Theodore Dreiser. It has 21 performances.

Dec 12 *The Mountain Man* (NY—Maxine Elliott—Comedy). Sidney Blackmer plays a Virginia mountaineer who goes off to France, vowing to shoot the presumed French lover of his intended. After service with the A. E. F., he returns to claim his girl. This Clare Kummer play runs for 163 performances. Catherine Dale Owen is the girl.

Dec 21 *Bulldog Drummond*. See L premiere, 1921.

Dec 23 *The Dover Road* (NY—Bijou—Comedy). A. A. Milne's comic notion is to force eloping couples—waylayed by Mr. Latimer (Charles Cherry) for a sojourn at his home—to see each other as they really are *before* they get married. The show runs through the season and beyond. On June 7, 1922, it premieres in London at the Haymarket Theatre, with Athene Seyler, Allan Aynesworth, John Deverell, and others in the cast. Charles Hawtrey stages. The play wins 267 showings in the West End.

1921 BRITISH PREMIERES

Jan 8 *The Betrothal* (L—Gaiety—Drama). This is Maurice Maeterlinck's sequel to *The Bluebird*. Tyltyl (Bobbie Andrews) is older now, and the Fairy Berylune (Winifred Emery) leads him on a quest this time not for happiness but for true love. Charles Ricketts designs and Harley Granville Barker stages. C. Armstrong Gibbs composes the score. Gladys Cooper, Ivan Berlyn, and Stella Campbell are in the ensemble. There are 111 showings.

Jan 13 *A Safety Match* (L—Strand—Drama). Ian Hay adapts his own novel for the stage. The cast, includes Herbert Marshall, Kyrle Bellew, Arthur Bourchier, Franklyn Bellamy and Phyllis Relph. It wins 222 performances.

Jan 17 *League of Notions* (L—New Oxford—Revue). C. B. Cochran's new show's title puns on the League of Nations, but the sketches have no such ambitions. Most of them provide handsome frames for the beauties and talents of the Dolly Sisters, Jennie and Rosie. John Murray Anderson stages and creates the book, with Augustus Barratt, the composer. There are 357 performances.

Feb 19 *Sybil*. See NY premiere, 1916.

March 3 *The Circle* (L—Haymarket—Comedy). W. Somerset Maugham's new play features a pair of young lovers (Leon Quartermaine and Fay Compton) who plan to elope—despite her previous marital commitments—just as her neglectful husband's mother (Lottie Venne) had done 30 years ago. There are 180 performances. On Sep 12, it opens at the Selwyn Theatre in New York, with John Drew and Mrs. Leslie Carter in the cast. The production attracts audiences for nearly 22 weeks. Part of the attraction is Mrs. Carter's return to the New York stage after seven years of retirement in France, as well as the return of Drew after two years absence.

March 14 *A Bill of Divorcement* (L—St. Martin's—Drama). Clemence Dane's play about a woman who wants to divorce the husband she has not seen for years to marry another, wins 409 showings. Lilian Braithwaite plays the lead, with C. Aubrey Smith, Ian Hunter, Meggie Albanesi, and Agnes Thomas in the cast. Katherine Cornell is featured when the play opens in New York on Oct 10, at the George M. Cohan Theatre. The show runs for 173 performances. Basil Dean directs.

March 29 *Bulldog Drummond* (L—Wyndham's—Drama). "Sapper" creates this four-act tale of adventure about Capt. Hugh Drummond (Gerald Du Maurier) who foils a gang of kidnappers. There are 428 performances. Some critics suggest that the dramatic action owes much to film-techniques. Also among the cast are Alfred Drayton, Ronald Squire, Basil Foster, Dorothy Overend, and Emily Brooke. In its New York premiere on Dec 21, A. E. Matthews plays Capt. Drummond, at the Knickerbocker Theatre. The show runs for five months.

April 14 *The Peep-Show* (L—Hippodrome—Revue). This show wins 417 performances, with players such as Mona Vivian, Stanley Lupino, Annie Croft, Desiree Ellinger, and Leslie Sarony.

May 13 *Pins and Needles* (L—Royalty—Revue). This "revue with points" manages 240 showings, with Edmund Gwenn, Alfred Lester, Mai Bacon, Jack Morrison, Madge White, Alfred Austin, and Billie Hill in the ensemble. Albert Courville directs and devises sketches with Wal Pink. Frederick Chappelle creates the score, with lyrics by various hands.

May 26 *The Gipsy Princess* (L—Prince of Wales's—Musical). Sari Petras plays Sylva in Emmerich Kalman's operetta. Book and lyrics for English audiences are provided by Arthur Miller and Arthur Stanley. The cast includes Billie Leonard, Phyllis Titmuss, Harry Cole, Mark Lester, and Maxine Hinton. There are 204 performances.

May 30 *If* (L—Ambassador's—Drama). Lord Dunsany's fantasy allows John Beal (Henry Ainley) to relive the last ten years of his life—this time, involving romance and dangers in the mountains of Persia, instead of a married suburban existence. But it's all a dream. Marda Vanne and Gladys Cooper also star. There are 178 performances of this Nigel Playfair production.

June 2 *A Family Man* (L—Comedy—Comedy). John Galsworthy's play—with a cast including Auriol Lee, Norman McKinnel, and Mary Barton—has only 51 showings. On May 30, Galsworthy's *The First and the Last* has had a matinee performance at the Aldwych, with Owen Nares, Meggie Albanesi, and Malcolm Keen.

June 11 *Out To Win* (L—Shaftesbury—Drama). George Tully plays two roles in this suspense drama by Roland Pertwee and Dion Calthrop. As Anthony, he is on the run from crooks who want to know where his newly discovered radium lode is located. As Richard, a look-alike decoy, he's captured and tortured by the would-be thieves. The authors and producer Robert Courtneidge stage, strongly assisted by the scenery and stage-tricks of designer R. C. McCleery. Madge Compton, Edith Evans, Hilda Bayley, Charles France, Eric Maturin, Fred Lewis, and others are in the cast. There are 121 performances.

The Betrothal

July 19 *Ambrose Applejohn's Adventure* (L—Criterion—Comedy). Walter Hackett's play is about a man in possession of a map showing buried treasure. It is first known as *Spanish Treasure*. Charles Hawtrey stars with Marion Lorne, Mona Harrison, Hilda Moore, Annie Esmond, and Leslie Faber. The show lasts for 454 performances.

Aug 9 *The Edge o' Beyond* (L—Garrick—Drama). Gertrude Page's popular novel is adapted by Roy Horniman and Ruby Miller, who plays the central role of Dinah, a woman who goes out to Rhodesia to find her mate. Basil Rathbone is her admirer. Doris Lloyd, Reginald Hunter, Marie Mitchell, and Martin Lewis are in the cast. The production lasts for 194 performances.

Sep 8 *Woman to Woman* (L—Globe—Drama). Michael Morton's play has been seen in America first. Now it opens for a run of 116 performances, with a cast including Arthur Wontner, Wilette Kershaw, Louise Regnis, and Athole Stewart.

Sep 10 *Sally*. See NY premiere, 1920.

Oct 5 *The Golden Moth* (L—Adelphi—Musical). Ivor Novello provides the score for Fred Thompson and P. G. Wodehouse's tale of adventure, which runs for 281 performances. Robert Michaelis and W. H. Berry play leads. Also in the cast are Cecily Debenham, Sylvia Leslie, and Fred Maguire.

Oct 11 *A to Z* (L—Prince of Wales's—Revue). Featured in this show are the Trix Sisters, one of whom (Helen) also contributes to the libretto, with Dion Titheradge and Ronald Jeans, and to the score, with Ivor Novello. There are 433 performances. The ensemble includes Gertrude Lawrence, Jack Buchanan, George Hestor, Herbert Ross, and Phyllis Haye.

Oct 15 *Cairo* (L—His Majesty's—Musical). Oscar Asche, creator of *Chu Chin Chow*, devises the action, and Percy Fletcher, the music. Asche also produces and acts Ali Shar, a strolling player. There are 267 showings.

Oct 17 *Fun of the Fayre* (L—Pavilion—Revue). There are 230 performances of this show, which has sketches by J. H. Turner and songs by Augustus Barratt. June and Clifton Webb sing "Whose Baby?" Frank Collins stages a company including the Dolly Sisters, Henry Caine, Jo Monkhouse, Evelyn Laye, Walter Williams, and Morris Harvey.

Oct 18 *Heartbreak House*. See NY premiere, 1920.

Oct 19 *Welcome Stranger*. See NY premiere, 1920.

Nov 3 *Deburau*. See NY premiere, 1920.

Nov 16 *The Faithful Heart* (L—Comedy—Comedy). There are 194 performances of Monckton Hoffe's play, with Mary Odette playing a mother and also a daughter, abandoned by Waverley Ango (Godfrey Tearle). After a lapse of 20 years and the death of the mother, he has to choose between his love for a fiancée (Molly Kerr) or his sense of duty and affection toward the daughter he deserted.

Dec 20 *The Truth About Blayds* (L—Globe—Drama). A. A. Milne's play, about a revered old poet who, at the point of death, reveals the poems for which he's celebrated were written by a friend long dead, enjoys a run of 124 performances. The cast includes Norman McKinnel, Irene Vanbrugh, Irene Rooke, Dion Boucicault, and Faith Celli. On March 14, 1922, it opens in New York at the Booth Theatre, running through and beyond the season. Winthrop Ames stages a cast including Leslie Howard, O. P. Heggie (Blayds), and Frieda Inescourt.

Dec 24 *Pot Luck* (L—Vaudeville—Revue). Beatrice Lillie and Jack Hulbert head this show, attracting audiences for 286 performances. Ronald Jeans and Dion Titheradge devise the sketches, with music by a variety of composers.

1921   REVIVALS/REPERTORIES

Jan 16 Fritz Leiber opens a season of Shakespearean drama. He stars as Macbeth, Romeo, and Marc Anthony, at New York's 48th Street Theatre.

Jan 17 At London's Little Theatre, the Grand Guignol troupe, with Sybil and Russell Thorndike, Lewis Casson, and others, opens its season with *The Shortest Story of All* and *The Person Unknown*, for 72 performances. On March 28, they offer *Gaspers, The Love Child, Seven Blind Men, Dead Men's Pool, The Kill*, and *The Chemist* for 104 showings. There are 117 performances of the next program on June 29, which includes *Latitude 15 Deg. S, The Vigil, Rounding the Triangle, The Old Women*, and *Shepherd's Pie*. 119 performances are possible with the next bill on Oct 12: *Haricot Beans, The Unseen Fear, The Old Story*, and *E. and O. E.*, though *Fear* is dropped midway in the run. On Nov 28, *Crime* is presented for 65 performances.

Jan 30 At the Lyric Theatre, Hammersmith, the Phoenix revives Ben Jonson's *Volpone*. On April 24, it revives another old play, William Rowley's Jacobean drama, *The Witch of Edmonton*.

Feb 2 In London at the Aldwych Theatre, *The Tempest* is revived for a six-week run by manager Viola Tree who plays Juno. Prospero is Henry Ainley, with Joyce Carey as Miranda, and Louis Calvert as Caliban.

Feb 14 The Erlanger management revives J. Hartley Manners' *Peg O' My Heart*, with Laurette Taylor repeating her role as Peg, for 11 weeks on Broadway.

Feb 17 At London's Royal Court Theatre, J. B. Fagan opens a production of Shakespeare's *Henry IV, Part 2*, which runs for 62 performances. This is followed by his revival of *Othello*, seen 68 times. Frank Cellier plays King Henry, with Basil Rathbone as Prince Hal. Godfrey Tearle is Othello, to Madge Titheradge's Desdemona. Rathbone is Iago.

Feb 17 Producer-director Arthur Hopkins revives *Macbeth* at New York's Apollo Theatre with Lionel Barrymore and Julia Arthur. The production has only 28 performances.

Feb 28 Edward Sheldon's *Romance*, a romantic comedy, is revived by the Shuberts at the Playhouse in New York. With Doris Keane in the lead, it enjoys 106 performances.

Feb 28 A bill of one-act comedies by Clare Kummer is presented at five matinees at the Punch and Judy Theatre in New York. The plays are *Chinese Love, The Robbery, Bridges, The Choir Rehearsal*. In the ensemble are Sidney Blackmer, J. M. Kerrigan, Ruth Gilmore, and Mary Ellison.

March 14 At the Everyman Theatre in Hampstead, George Bernard Shaw's one-acts, *How He Lied To Her Husband, The Dark Lady of the Sonnets*, and *The Shewing-Up of Blanco Posnet*, are revived. On April 18, Shaw's *Major Barbara* is produced, followed on May 23 by *Man and Superman*.

March 20 At the Lyric, Hammersmith, the Phoenix revives Congreve's Restoration comedy, *Love for Love*. On Nov 13 the Phoenix revives *The Maid's Tragedy* by Beaumont and Fletcher.

March 28 Sybil Thorndike is admired as the wife of a barbarous, hunt-loving husband in Maurice Level's *The Kill*. This is the third series of plays at the London Grand Guignol (Little Theatre). Russell Thorndike plays the lover, who has a heart-attack as they are planning to elope. Her husband (Lauderdale Maitland) returns and throws the unconscious man out the window to be devoured by his wolfhounds. There are 104 performances of the play, judged by some to be morbid, without being "frightful." There are five other plays on the bill, some deliberately horrific; others are comic, to relieve the tension.

April 4 Sarah Bernhardt comes to London—with a wooden leg—to play Louis Verneuil's *Daniel* at the Prince's Theatre. The play has just premiered in English at the St. James's in January, with Claude Rains playing the title-role now filled by Bernhardt. On April 26th, Andre Brule brings his French troupe to the same house for a season of dramas including *Le Coeur Dispose, L'Epervier, Arsene Lupin, Coeur de Lilas*, and *Coeur de Moineau*.

April 17 Margaret Anglin plays Clytemnestra for one matinee only at the Manhattan Opera House. The play is Euripides' *Iphigenia in Aulis*; Mary Flower is Iphigenia.

April 19 Walter Hampden revives *Macbeth* at New York's Broadhurst Theatre for six performances. Mary Hall is his Lady Macbeth.

April 19 It's been a long time since a real burlesque of a serious play has been shown in London. Tonight, the production is *Faust on Toast*, devised by Frith Shephard and Adrian Ross. Jack Buchanan Renee Mayer, Maisie Gay, and Robert Hale play the leads. The show is suspended after just two weeks. A revised version opens May 12, lasting only three weeks.

April 23 *Anthony and Cleopatra* is the "birthday play" at the Memorial Theatre in Stratford-upon-Avon. Under the direction of W. Bridges Adams, other productions include *Richard III*, *A Midsummer Nights Dream*, *As You Like It*. *Henry IV, Part 2*, *Macbeth*, *The Merry Wives of Windsor*, and Sheridan's *The School for Scandal*.

April 23 The Birmingham Repertory Theatre presents a matinee of *Henry IV, Part 1* and an evening performance of *Henry IV, Part 2* as a celebration of Shakespeare's birthday.

May 9 Robert Atkins directs Shakespeare's *Pericles* for Lilian Baylis at London's Old Vic Theatre, continuing the cycle begun in 1914 and which will end in 1923 when all 37 of the Bard's plays will have been performed. On November 28, Atkins stages *All's Well That Ends Well* for Baylis.

June 15 Eugene O'Neill's *In the Zone* is produced by the London's Everyman Theatre in Hampstead.

June 27 This is the first London season of *The Co-Optimists*, a spritely revue by a company which affects Pierrot costumes. The show wins a run of 500 performances at the Royalty Theatre.

July 6 John Drinkwater's drama *Abraham Lincoln*, already highly praised by British critics, is revived in London at the Lyceum Theatre, moving to the Scala, for a total run of 173 performances.

July 18 The Shakespeare Memorial Theatre in Stratford-upon-Avon opens its seven-week summer season, its longest to date. The plays include *Antony and Cleopatra*, *Richard III*, *A Midsummer Night's Dream*, *As You Like It*, *Henry IV, Part 2*, *Macbeth*, *The Merry Wives of Windsor*, and Sheridan's *The School for Scandal*, all revived from the spring season. In addition, the Dutch actor Louis Bouwmeester appears as Shylock in *The Merchant of Venice*; *The Winter's Tale* is also offered. Marie Slade and Company provide an all-female cast in *Henry V*.

Sep 2 Nikita Balieff's *Chauve-Souris* ("Bat") Cabaret from Moscow opens at the London Pavilion. It later transfers to the Apollo Theatre, for a total run of 74 performances.

Sep 9 J. B. Fagan revives George Bernard Shaw's *John Bull's Other Island* for 43 performances at London's Royal Court Theatre.

Theater Guild

Sep 21 David Belasco revives his psychic drama, *The Return of Peter Grimm*, starring its original hero, David Warfield, for a run of nearly ten weeks at New York's Belasco Theatre.

Oct E. H. Sothern and Julia Marlowe return to New York for a stint of Shakespearean repertory running into December. *Twelfth Night*, *The Taming of the Shrew*, and *The Merchant of Venice* are offered.

Oct 3 At London's Prince's Theatre, the D'Oyly Carte Opera Company begins a season of Gilbert & Sullivan revivals.

Oct 4 At the Everyman Theatre in Hampstead, Eugene O'Neill's *Diff'rent* is produced. The American play, *Suppressed Desires*, is also presented.

Nov 28 The Theatre Guild produces a five-week run of two short French plays, *The Wife with the Smile*, by Andre Obey and Denys Amiel, and *Boubouroche*, by Georges Courteline, at New York's Garrick Theatre. In the company are Arnold Daly, Blanche Yurka, Catherine Proctor, and Philip Loeb, among others.

Dec 12 At London's Old Vic, the resident company presents August Strindberg's *Advent*. In the "Morality" play are Rupert Harvey, Gladys Dale, Joan Myer, and Joyce Cornish, among others.

Dec 12 In Dublin, at the Empire Theatre, John MacDonagh's play, *The Irish Jew*, opens. It's a four-act satire.

Dec 22 At London's Apollo Theatre, the holiday season is ushered in with a revival of *Where the Rainbow Ends*. *Peter Pan* has begun performances at the St. James's Theatre already, as has *Charley's Aunt* at the Duke of York's. At the London Hippodrome, *Jack and the Beanstalk* opens today for 137 performances. On Boxing Day, *Cinderella* begins a run of 96 performances at the Lyceum.

1921 BIRTHS/DEATHS/DEBUTS

Feb 9 American drama critic James Gibbons Huneker (b. 1859) dies in Brooklyn. Huneker became music and drama critic of the *Morning Advertiser* and the New York *Recorder* in 1890, later joining the *Sun* and the *NY Times*. Among his books on criticism are *Iconoclasts*, *Egoists*, and *Ivory, Apes, and Peacocks*. He also published a two-volume autobiography, *Steeplejack*, in 1919.

March 7 English playwright Paul M. Potter (b. 1853) dies in New York. Potter was the author and adapter of numerous plays, including the notable *Trilby*.

March 21 Ira Gershwin, under the pseudonym of Arthur Francis, contributes lyrics to the pre-Broadway tryout of *A Dangerous Maid*, opening tonight in Atlantic City, New Jersey.

April 8 Actress Julie Opp (b. 1871) dies in New York. After a successful career as a journalist, Opp was engaged by George Alexander for her first stage appearance at London's St. James's Theatre as Hymen in *As You Like It* in 1896. Her Broadway debut was made a year later, as Princess Pannonia in Pinero's *The Princess and the Butterfly*.

May 22 English actress Marie Effie Wilton Bancroft (b. 1839) is dead at Folkestone, Dover, England. Lady Bancroft made her London debut at the Lyceum Theatre in 1856. She later achieved success in burlesque at the Strand. In 1867, she married Squire Bancroft, and in 1880 the pair began management of the Haymarket Theatre.

June 11 American actor Frank Mills dies in Michigan Sanitarium. Born in 1870, Mills was a leading man for actresses Olga

Nethersole, Mrs. Fiske, and Grace George.

June 22 American stage director Edward P. Temple dies in New York at age 60. Temple was general stage director for the Shubert Brothers.

Sep 3 Gwen Ffrangcon-Davies makes her debut with the Birmingham Repertory Theatre in J. M. Barrie's *Quality Street*, the opening play of the tenth season.

Sep 15 American producer-manager William G. Smythe dies in New York at age 66. Smythe was a David Belasco executive for 20 years. He was also producer of *My Friend From India* and *The Man From Mexico*.

Oct 4 Victor Jacobi dies at 37, shortly after the brief four-week run of *The Love Letter* at the New York's Globe Theatre. It is said that the show's failure was the cause of his death.

Nov 11 American actress Claire Nagel is dead at age 25 in Reno, Nevada. She was married to producer Arthur Hammerstein.

Dec 28 Actor-producer Sir John Hare (b. 1844) is dead in Yorkshire, England. After an apprenticeship with the Bancrofts, Hare became manager of the Court Theatre in 1875. The Garrick Theatre came under his management in 1889, where he produced many of Pinero's plays. Equally popular in England and the United States, Hare was knighted in 1917.

1921 THEATERS/PRODUCTIONS

In Britain, patents are granted for: S. P. Thompson's device for simulating an airplane's flight, suspending the plane from a mast by cables; Schwabe & Company's lightning effect, produced by flash-lamps behind screens with a series of jagged openings.

Langdon McCormick receives a U.S. patent for a projection system in which shadows of objects are projected on a screen from the rear, with their details projected from the front.

In Dublin, the British government has imposed a curfew, forcing places of entertainment to close. Faced with an economic crisis, the Abbey Theatre's manager, Lennox Robinson, regretfully has to dismiss the professional company. Augusta, Lady Gregory, a founder with W. B. Yeats of the Irish National Theatre Society, insists on keeping the theatre open with part-time actors and student players.

Feb 11 The Ambassador Theatre, on West 49 Street in New York, the first of six theatres the Shuberts will build on 48 and 49 Streets, opens with the musical *The Rose Girl*, by William C. Duncan, with music by Anselm Goetzl. To maximize the use of the land on which the theatre is built, the architect Herbert J. Krapp designs the stage to run diagonally across the site.

March 2 The Klaw Theatre, on West 45 Street in New York, owned by producer Marc Klaw and designed by Eugene DeRosa, opens its doors with a star-studded production of Rachel Crother's *Nice People*. In 1929, the theatre is renamed the Avon. It is taken over by Columbia Broadcasting System to be used as a radio studio. It is razed in 1954.

March 9 In England, the Sheffield Repertory Company has its first official and recorded meeting.

March 24 In Norwich, Nugent Monck purchases an old Roman Catholic chapel, dating from 1794, to be the new home of the Norwich Players. It costs £1,700, but it will take the group several years to pay off debts incurred in converting it to a modified Elizabethan stage, called the Maddermarket Theatre.

May 30 Holabird and Roche are the architects for the new Apollo Theatre in Chicago, opening today at 45 West Randolph. It seats 1,707 people. Six years later, in May 1927, it will become a cinema, the United Artists.

June 15 Tonight, with a total of 1,291 performances, *Lightnin'* closes its record-breaking Broadway run.

June 15 For his annual ten *Best Plays*, Burns Mantle chooses the following: Guitry's *Deburau*, Archer's *The Green Goddess*, O'Neill's *The Emperor Jones*, Molnar's *Liliom*, Barrie's *Mary Rose*, Craven's *The First Year*, Crother's *Nice People*, Varesi/Byrne's *Enter Madame*, Galsworthy's *The Skin Game*, and Browne's *The Bad Man*. At the close of the Broadway season, Mantle notes a total of 157 productions. Sorting productions into genre-categories, one finds 40 dramas, 62 comedies, 39 musicals, and 16 revues. Some 68 productions seem successes, with 89 failures. Mantle calls this season a comedy year. This may be explained as a natural reaction in the aftermath of war. He says the success of the greatest comedy hits of the season owed more to their truthful writing and honesty in portraying native characters and characteristics. Between August and June in the season, there were 157 plays produced, averaging 98 performances each. Not counting Sundays, this also averages a new play every other day.

Sep 1 The National Theatre (1,200 seats) opens on West 41st Street in New York City. The theatre is built by Walter C. Jordan, at a cost of $1.95 million. The 86 ft. wide stage has a 40 foot opening and a 100 foot fly gallery. In 1959, the name will be changed to the Billy Rose Theatre, the first of several changes, including the Trafalgar and the Nederlander.

Sep 22 The Music Box Theatre opens on West 45th Street in New York City. The theatre is owned by Sam H. Harris and Irving Berlin. Berlin's *Music Box Revue* opens the theatre. The house is said to cost $1 million, including $187,000 for the premiere production. $5.50 is the top ticket price.

Sep 26 William Butler Yeats speaks during the interval at the opening of Norwich's new Maddermarket Theatre. Shakespeare's *As You Like It* is the inauguaral production. Director Nugent Monck has at one time managed the Abbey Theatre in Dublin. The Maddermarket Theatre has a modified Elizabethan theatre, converted from a former chapel. It seats 270 in a space 40 feet by 46 feet, including that part used by the stage. Seating will be reduced to 240 shortly, followed by 230 seats in 1930. In 1954, the house is enlarged to accomodate 326. In 1966, the building is extended to provide rehearsal space, a bar, and a foyer.

Oct Keene Summer, writing in the *American Magazine*, notes that the Shuberts now have 25 theatres in New York City, about 100 in other major U.S. cities, and at least 1,000 in lesser cities and towns across the country. These figures include theatres owned outright, as well as those leased or controlled by exclusive booking contracts. In the 1920—21 season, Summer reports, the Shuberts have been involved in no less than 50 productions, with an initial outlay of $5 million. They have employed 3,500 performers and musicians, in addition to hundreds of "below-the-line" theatre workers.

Nov The phrase "painting with light" is first used in print in the U.S. in *Arts and Decoration*, reprinted from the *Manchester Guardian*. It appears in an article written by Edward Gordon Craig. This article inspires a new era in stage-lighting, moving from basic stage illumination to an artistic statement through light.

Nov 27 Tonight is the Golden Jubilee of the Gaiety Theatre in Dublin. Because of the upheavals in Dublin occasioned by the War of Independence from Britain and by the Curfew, the night passes with no special festivity.

Dec 26 The 49th Street Theatre in New York opens with *Face Value*, by Laurence Grass. Its owners, the Shuberts, lose possession of the building during the Depression. In the late 1930's, it is leased briefly by the Federal Theatre Project, but is converted into a motion picture house in 1938. The theatre is razed in the 1940's.

Dec 31 At the close of this year, the "Third War" between the Shuberts and the Theatrical Syndicate is judged to have ended. There is said to be a "peace treaty" covering booking arrangements for all the American theatres playing legitimate productions, with the exception of those located in metropolitan New York.

He Who Gets Slapped

Jan 2 *Lawful Larceny* (NY—Republic—Comedy). More melodrama than comedy, Samuel Shipman's play features Margaret Lawrence as a wife whose husband is seduced by another woman and subsequently robbed in a gambling salon. This show runs beyond the season. It is loved by audiences and disparaged by reviewers.

Jan 9 *He Who Gets Slapped* (NY—Garrick—Drama). Leonid Andreyev's tragedy of the nobleman who has become a clown enjoys a long run beyond the season. The Theatre Guild produces, Gregory Zilboorg translates and Robert Milton stages. Richard Bennett and Margalo Gillmore play leads.

Jan 23 *The National Anthem* (NY—Henry Miller—Drama). J. Hartley Manners attacks the twin curses of jazz and drink in the play. His wife, Laurette Taylor, is featured with Ralph Morgan. It runs 114 performances.

Jan 31 *The Czarina* (NY—Empire—Comedy). Catherine the Great (Doris Keane) as seen by her lover Count Czerny (Basil Rathbone) is worth 136 performances in this translation from the Hungarian original by Edward Sheldon.

Feb 4 *Chauve-Souris* (NY—49th Street—Revue). This "Bat Theatre of Moscow" will move in summer to the Century Theatre Roof, where the exorbitant price of $5 per seat is charged for the 500 seats. By June, Nikita Balieff's Russian vaudeville will make a profit of $150,000 for producers Morris Gest and R. Ray Comstock. The performers are mainly former members of Stanislavsky's Moscow Art Theatre. The show lasts over 500 performances.

Feb 7 *The Cat and the Canary* (NY—National—Drama). John Willard's mystery melodrama features Florence Eldridge as a woman who must keep her sanity in order to inherit the wealth of an eccentric uncle. Henry Hull is also in the cast. It runs beyond the season. On Oct 31, it premieres at London's Shaftesbury with Mary Glynne. It plays 182 times.

Feb 20 *To the Ladies* (NY—Liberty—Comedy). Otto Kruger plays the visionary young Leonard Beebe, whose child-wife Elsie (Helen Hayes) takes matters in hand to ensure his success in business. Howard Lindsay stages. This George S. Kaufman and Marc Connelly amusement runs through the season.

Feb 21 *The Rubicon* (NY—Hudson—Comedy). From the French of Edouard Bourdet, this play features Violet Heming as a wife who has married only to punish the man she really loves. There are calls for censorship as a result of the theme, but the show runs through and beyond the season.

Feb 27 *Back To Methuselah,* (NY—Garrick—Drama) George Bernard Shaw's five-part epic of mankind, opens on Broadway in a Theatre Guild production. This is the first of three divisions of the play, each to play a week initially and later be performed in series by a large cast including Dennis King, Margaret Wycherly, Walter Abels, Ernita Lascelles, and Albert Bruning. Direction is divided among Alice Lewisohn, Agnes Morgan, Frank Reichler, and Philip Moeller. Woolcott of the NY Times says, ". . . he inspects man and finds him comically, pathetically sophomoric . . ." In Birmingham, England, the play opens, produced by Barry Jackson's Birmingham Repertory, on Oct 9, 1923, with remaining parts presented on the 10th, 11th, and 12th. Edith Evans is the Serpent. Adam and Eve are Colin Keith-Johnston and Gwen Ffrangcon-Davies. Others include Raymond Huntley, Cedric Hardwicke, Evelyn Hope, Margaret Chatwin, Phyllis Shand, and Melville Cooper. On Feb 18, 1924, the Birmingham production begins 20 performances in London at the Royal Court.

March 4 *The First Man* (NY—Neighborhood Playhouse—Drama). Eugene O'Neill's play lasts only 27 performances. Its plot involves a childless scientist cursing the fetus in his wife's womb. The wife dies in childbirth, and the child thrives. Augustin Duncan directs and plays the scientist. Critics judge it poorly cast in some respects and rather melodramatic.

March 7 *The Rose of Stamboul* (NY—Century—Musical). This Leo Fall score is not enhanced by Sigmund Romberg interpolations, say some critics, and the book, credited to Harold Atteridge, is also no novelty. Tessa Kosta is a Turkish princess who loves a poet who turns out to be the man she's been promised to in marriage. The show runs 111 performances.

March 9 *The Hairy Ape* (NY—Provincetown—Drama). Eugene O'Neill describes his play as a "comedy of ancient and modern life." Yank (Louis Wolheim), a steamship stoker, taunted by a rich girl (Mary Blair) for being a beast, seeks revenge on society. He is crushed to death by an ape he releases from the zoo. O'Neill says he wants to show that Yank's brute force is necessary for building the modern world, but it's dangerous when it gets out of control. The production's opening scene in a steamship stoke-hole, with multi-lingual profanity suggested, impresses audiences. The show runs through and beyond the season.

March 14 *The Truth About Blayds.* See L premiere, 1921.

April 26 *The Bronx Express* (NY—As-tor—Comedy). The Charles Coburns produce and play in this Owen Davis adaptation of a Russian comic fantasy. Coburn is a button-maker who falls asleep in a subway car and dreams of attending a party peopled by the characters in the subway ads. The show runs beyond the season.

May 1 *Partners Again* (NY—Selwyn—Comedy). Potash and Perlmutter return. Barney Bernard and Alexander Carr play the dialect comedians. The show runs beyond the season. On Feb 28, 1923, it comes to the Garrick in London with Robert Leonard and Philip White featured. Here it has 166 performances.

May 15 *Kempy* (NY—Belmont—Comedy). Elliott Nugent and his father, J. C. Nugent, collaborate on the script of this tale of mixed-up young lovers. They also play major roles, with Ruth Nugent as the ingenue. Augustin Duncan stages the show, which runs beyond the season.

May 23 *Abie's Irish Rose* (NY—Fulton—Comedy). Playwright Anne Nichols's decision to bring a young Jewish boy and a pretty Irish girl together in holy wedlock, letting their less liberated parents rage, provides the propulsion for this long-lasting comedy, which runs for 2,327 performances plus revivals. Robert B. Williams and Marie Carroll are the first Abie and Rosie. The show premieres at London's Apollo on April 11, 1927, with Russell Swann and Katherine Revner featured. It lasts only 16 weeks.

May 29 *Red Pepper* (NY—Shubert—Musical). James McIntyre and Thomas Heath star. Critics object to the lack of "real music" in the show, noting that the score is full of jazz. Despite efforts of these two black-face comedians, the show doesn't have a long run.

June 5 *From Morn Till Midnight* (NY—Garrick—Drama). Georg Kaiser's German tale of an embezzling bank cashier who explores the depths and shallows of humanity on a day-long debauch features Frank Reicher. The Theatre Guild production lasts only three weeks.

June 5 *The Ziegfeld Follies of 1922* (NY—New Amsterdam—Revue). Gilda Gray shimmies; Will Rogers philosophizes; Fokine choreographs; Gallagher (Ed) and Shean (Al) introduce themselves with "Mr. Gallagher and Mr. Shean." Ring Lardner writes the sketches. Music is by Victor

Herbert, Dave Stamper, and Louis Hirsch.

June 15 *Raymond Hitchcock's Pinwheel Revel* (NY—Earl Carroll—Revue). The 17th revue this season, this one is distinguished by its emphasis on dance, but not ballroom. Instead, the Japanese choreographer, Michio Ito, brings dances of India, Spain, Greece, and the Orient to the stage, with music by Brahms, Debussy, and other masters. Among the dancers are Michio and Yuji Ito, Agna Enters, Ragina Devi, and Maria Montero. Hitchcock and Frank Fay provide the comedy.

June 19 *Strut Miss Lizzie* (NY—Times Square—Revue). The Minsky Brothers produce this "colored vaudeville," featuring Henry Creamer and Turner Layton. It lasts only four weeks. Its dancing is praised as being "raucous."

July 17 *Plantation Revue* (NY—48th Street—Revue). This black musical show, with cake-walks, taps, and buck-and-wings, has only a five-week run. In the ensemble are Shelton Brooks, Will Vodery, and Florence Mills.

Aug 7 *Whispering Wires* (NY—49th Street—Drama). Kate McLaurin's mystery play, centering on telephoned death threats, achieves 352 performances. Olive Tell and Paul Kelly play leads.

Aug 22 *The Old Soak* (NY—Plymouth—Comedy). Don Marquis' drama, produced and staged by Arthur Hopkins, achieves a run of 423 performances. Harry Beresford is featured with Minnie Dupree. With the Volstead Act in full force, the public is especially amused by the clever way the alcoholic hero deals with family problems. The Old Soak has become known to readers of Marquis' column in the *Tribune*.

Aug 28 *George White's Scandals of 1922* (NY—Globe—Revue). Paul Whiteman's orchestra plays for the 11-week run, but George Gershwin's *Blue Monday Blues*, a 25-minute serious jazz opera, is cut from the show after the opening. "I'll Build a Stairway to Paradise" features girls in black patent leather ascending a white staircase. White produces, directs, and performs, joined by W. C. Fields and others.

Aug 28 *The Gingham Girl* (NY—Earl Carroll—Musical). A small-town boy comes to Greenwich Village to savor life in the city, but his sweetheart wins him back. With an Albert Von Tilzer score, this musical manages 422 performances.

Aug 29 *The Torchbearers* (NY—48th Street—Comedy). George Kelly has a hit with this parody of Little Theatre amateur playmaking. It runs for 135 performances and becomes a favorite for amateur players. Mary Boland and Allison Skipworth are prominent in the cast. It runs for 135 performances. It premieres in London at the Ambassadors' on April 20, 1925, with W. Graham Browne and Muriel Alexander. There are only 55 performances.

Sep 2 *Better Times* (NY—Hippodrome—Musical). The annual extravaganza at the Hippodrome, playing two-a-day, tallies 409 performances. R. H. Burnside devises the content, with Raymond Hubbell's music and Charles Dillingham's skill as a producer. 20 horses perform an equestrian ballet. This is Dillingham's last spectacle here.

Sep 4 *Sally, Irene and Mary* (NY—Casino—Musical). With an obvious reference to the hit musicals *Sally* and *Irene*, this expanded Eddie Dowling vaudeville sketch pleases audiences for 312 performances. Dowling stars. J. Fred Coots creates the score.

Sep 12 *The Greenwich Village Follies* (NY—Shubert—Revue). Director John Murray Anderson joins forces with George V. Hobart and Irving Caesar to create sketches and lyrics for this edition, which runs 27 weeks. Ted Lewis and his band play the Louis Hirsch score.

Sep 18 *The Awful Truth* (NY—Henry Miller—Comedy). Later to become a popular film, Arthur Richman's play wins 144 performances. Ina Claire is Lucy Warriner, who asks her ex-husband to give a good character reference to her new fiance from the West.

Sep 20 *The Passing Show of 1922* (NY—Winter Garden—Revue). Another Shubert revue, staged by J. C. Huffman, this edition runs just over ten weeks. Fred Allen describes the "Old Joke Cemetery." Ethel Shutta parodies O'Neill's *The Hairy Ape*. Willie and Eugene Howard sing "My Coal Black Mammy" and "Carolina in the Morning."

Sep 25 *La Tendresse* (NY—Empire—Drama). Henry Miller and Ruth Chatterton star in Henry Bataille's play. Miller, who also stages, plays an actor who traps his mistress in her infidelity. This runs two months.

Sep 27 *Loyalties.* See L premiere, 1922.

Oct 2 *Malvaloca* (NY—48th Street—Drama). Jane Cowl and Rollo Peters are the lovers, she reformed by his passion, in this Equity Players production of the Serafin and Joaquin Quintero play. It has only a six-week run in Manhattan.

Oct 2 *The Yankee Princess* (NY—Knickerbocker—Musical). This is Emmerich Kalman's *Bayadere (Die Bajadere)*, with English lyrics by B. G. DeSylva. Vivienne Segal plays the American girl, but the show runs only ten weeks.

Oct 9 *R. U. R.* (NY—Garrick—Drama). Karel Capek's Czech fable of life in the future with robots wins a 23-week run for this Theatre Guild production. In the cast are Louis Calvert, Basil Sydney, and Helen Westley. Opening in London at St. Martin's Theatre on May 5, 1923, the play has a cast including Basil Rathbone, Charles France, Beatrix Thomson, and Ian Hunter. It earns 126 performances.

Oct 23 *The Music Box Revue* (NY—Music Box—Revue). Irving Berlin's second edition features Bobby Clark and Paul McCullough. Charlotte Greenwood and William Gaxton are also on hand. Hassard Short stages this show which runs beyond the season. On May 15, 1923, the revue opens at London's Palace. The cast is primarily the same as in America. It has 118 performances.

Oct 23 *The Fool* (NY—Times Square—Drama). Channing Pollock's play is described as a "sermon drama," in which the hero tries to live as Christ might live in modern times. It runs beyond the season. On Sep 18, 1924, the show opens at London's Apollo with Henry Ainley in the lead. There are 138 performances.

Oct 24 *The Last Warning* (NY—Klaw—Drama). Thomas Fallon's mystery drama earns 238 performances. William Courtleigh plays a showman turned detective who opens up a supposedly haunted theatre and revives a fatal play to discover who murdered the theatre's former manager.

Oct 30 *Seventh Heaven* (NY—Booth—Drama). Helen Menken is featured in Austin Strong's play about a woman of the streets who is reformed by a sewerman she marries. The production runs beyond the season. On Sep 2, 1927, it opens in London at the Strand, where it has only 42 performances.

Oct 30 *Six Characters in Search of an Author* (NY—Princess—Drama). Luigi Pirandello's fable of real characters trying to get artificial actors to re-enact their story runs for 17 weeks in this Brock Pemberton production. Moffat Johnston, Margaret Wycherly, and Florence Eldridge play three of the characters.

Oct 31 *The World We Live In* (NY—Jolson—Comedy). This Czech play by Josef and Karel Capek has 111 performances. It is translated by Owen Davis and produced by William A. Brady. Robert Edeson plays a vagrant who dreams that in-

Merton of the Movies

sect life parallels the worst of human vices. Produced in London as *The Insect Play* on May 5, 1923, at the Regent Theatre, it has a run of 41 performances, adapted by Nigel Playfair and Clifford Bax. John Gielgud, Elsa Lanchester, and Claude Rains are in the cast.

Nov 6 *Up She Goes* (NY—Playhouse—Musical). Frank Craven's play, *Too Many Cooks*, is the basis for Craven's book, with lyrics by Joseph McCarthy and score by Harry Tierney. The Cooks are Alice Cook's (Gloria Foy) relatives, interfering with her romance with Albert Bennett (Donald Brian). The title refers to their dream-house, built on stage, act by act. The show runs eight months.

Nov 7 *Rain* (NY—Maxine Elliott—Drama). John Colton and Clemence Randolph adapt W. Somerset Maugham's story for the stage. Jeanne Eagle plays Sadie Thompson, the "bad" woman the missionary Reverend Davidson tries to reform. It runs beyond the season. The *NY Times* terms the play "strikingly original in drama and richly colored with the magic of the South Seas." On May 12, 1925, it opens at the Garrick in London with Olga Lindo as Sadie. There are 150 performances.

Nov 13 *Little Nellie Kelly* (NY—Liberty—Musical). Julian Mitchell helps George M. Cohan stage this Cohan-written and produced show which spoofs the popularity of mystery plays. It runs beyond the season. Of Feb 16, 1923, it opens at London's New Oxford where it has 255 performances.

Nov 13 *Merton of the Movies* (NY—Cort—Comedy). George S. Kaufman and Marc Connelly adapt Harry Leon Wilson's story of a small-town boy who dreams of a film career and through a fluke becomes a star. Glenn Hunter has the title role. The show runs beyond the season. On April 17, 1923, it premieres at London's Shaftesbury with Tom Douglas as Merton. It lasts just 38 performances.

Nov 14 *The Romantic Age.* See L premiere, 1920.

Nov 14 *The Love Child* (NY—Cohan—Drama). Martin Brown adapts Henri Bataille's melodrama in which Laura Thorne's illegitimate son pressures his mother's current lover to marry her lest the son debauch the lover's daughter. Sidney Blackmer is featured. The production runs for 21 weeks.

Nov 20 *The Lucky One* (NY—Garrick—Comedy). Theodore Komisarjevsky stages A. A. Milne's play for the Theatre Guild. Although the cast includes Dennis King, Romney Brent, Helen Westley, Percy Waram, and Violet Heming, the production lasts only five weeks. It's a tale of two brothers, the younger being "lucky," but the older finally getting the girl.

Nov 27 *Liza* (NY—Daly's—Musical). This all-black show runs for 21 weeks. The score is by Maceo Pinkard. Irvin Miller's

plot concerns the swindles of some con men. Margaret Simms stars with Will A. Cook, Billy Mills, and Quintard Miller in the cast. The dancing wins the critics' raves.

Nov 29 *It Is the Law* (NY—Ritz—Drama). Elmer Rice's melodrama shows two life-long pals contending for the same woman (Alma Tell). One frames the other on a murder charge when he is not chosen by her. Gloating proves his undoing. The show runs nearly four months.

Dec 20 *The God of Vengeance* (NY—Provincetown—Drama). Sholom Asch tells a bitter story of a Polish brothel keeper

who tries to arrange a respectable marriage for his daughter by one of his women. Unfortunately, she is procured before he can save her. Rudolph Schildkraut directs and plays the man. Also in the cast are Sam Jaffe, Morris Carnovsky, and Lillian Taiz. The production runs almost 17 weeks.

Dec 25 *Why Not?* (NY—48th Street—Comedy). Jesse Lynch Williams provides an answer to his Pulitzer prize-winning comedy, *Why Marry?* The show, an Equity Players production, runs for 15 weeks. The play deals with problems of modern divorce and divorce law.

1922   BRITISH PREMIERES

Jan 23 *The Bat.* See NY premiere, 1920.

Feb 1 *The Wheel* (L—Apollo—Drama). J. B. Fagan's play, seen in America as *The Wheel of Life,* has 137 performances, with Phyllis Nielson-Terry as Ruth, wife of a British colonel (Robert Horton) in India, who falls in love with a captain (Philip Merivale), only to realize honor and trust demand she stay with her husband. Also in the cast are some Indian actors and Edith Evans.

Feb 21 *The Lady of the Rose* (L—Daly's—Musical). Frederick Lonsdale adapts the Schanzer and Welisch original text, with Harry Graham creating English lyrics for Jean Gilbert's score. Phyllis Dare plays a countess whose virtue is threatened by a colonel who plans to execute her husband. The play's title refers to an old family portrait that comes to life whenever the house is in danger. There are 507 showings. On Oct 2, it comes to New York's Ambassador as *The Lady in Ermine.* Wilda Bennett is the countess. The show runs 232 performances.

Feb 25 *Rockets* (L—Palladium—Revue). There are 491 two-a-day showings of this Charles Henry spectacle, with Lorna and Toots Pounds, Charles Austin, Freddie Forbes, and others in the ensemble. Ernest Melvin provides lyrics for the tunes of Herman Darewski and J. A. Turnbridge.

March 1 *The Enchanted Cottage* (L—Duke of York's—Drama). Arthur Wing Pinero's play deals with a battered war veteran who marries the plainest girl in the village only to find that in their home they are beautiful to each other. Owen Nares and Laura Cowie are featured. It has only 64 performances. The show opens in New York at the Ritz on March 31, 1923, with Noel Tearle and Katharine Cornell featured. It lasts two months.

March 8 *Loyalties* (L—St. Martin's—Drama). John Galsworthy's play about British class attitudes features Eric Maturin and Ernest Milton. There are 405 performances. On Sep 27, it comes to New York's Gaiety with Felix Aylmer and

Charles Quartermaine in the cast. Here it has only 220 showings.

March 16 *Round in Fifty* (L—Hippodrome—Musical). Instead of 80 days, Phineas Fogg (Eddie Jaye) is asked to girdle the globe in only 50 days in this "musical adventure," with book by Sax Rohmer and Julian and Lauri Wylie. Music is by James Tate and Herman Finck, with lyrics by Clifford Harris and others. In the cast are Renee Reel, George Robey, Phil Lester, Marie Cazeneau, and Barry and Wallace Lupino. The show is played 471 times.

March 22 *The Man in Dress Clothes* (L—Garrick—Drama). Seymour Hicks plays Lucien, the title-role, who dissipates his fortune, after making a marriage of convenience with a poor girl. Seeing his despair and realizing his real love for her, she comes to his rescue. Hicks adapts the French text of Picard and Mirande. There are 232 performances. Also in the cast are Barbara Hoffe, Stanley Logan, and Joan Vivian-Rees.

April 13 *Tons of Money* (L—Shaftesbury—Comedy). The script, by Will Evans and Valentine, was rejected by many managers until Leslie Henson and Tom Walls decide to give it an expensive mounting and an "idiotic comedian" in the person of Ralph Lynn. The farce runs for 733 performances, with Willie Warde, George Barrett, Mary Brough, Madge Saunders, and the lovely leading lady, Yvonne Arnaud.

April 20 *Decameron Nights* (L—Drury Lane—Musical). Based on Boccaccio's tales—adapted by Robert McLaughlin and Boyle Lawrence—this show opens the newly outfitted Drury Lane, with producer-director Arthur Colins exceeding the visual mastery of Max Reinhardt, in the opinion of some critics. Herman Finck provides the music. In the cast are H. A. Saintsbury, Arthur Lewis, Wilette Kershaw, Ellis Jeffreys, Cowley Wright, and others. The elaborate show lasts for 370 performances.

May 18 *Whirled into Happiness* (L—Lyric—Musical). Robert Stolz's Viennese score gets a British libretto from Harry Graham. Billy Merson plays a music hall attendant who mistakes a hairdresser's assistant (Austin Melford) for a young lord, introducing him to an eligible young lady (Lily St. John), whose father is interested in the star of the show, Delphine de Lavalliere (Mai Bacon). Songs include "Once in a While." Fred Blackman directs, with A. J. Majilton setting the dances. There are 246 performances.

June 7 *The Dover Road.* See NY premiere, 1921.

Aug 11 *Snap* (L—Vaudeville—Revue). This show runs for 230 performances, the cast includes Cicely Debenham, Clarice Mayne, Roy Royston, and Denis Cowles. The music is by Kenneth Duffield, the text by Ronald Jeans and Dion Titheradge.

Aug 16 *Phi-Phi* (L—Pavilion—Musical). The title refers not to a fraternity but to a sculptor (Clifton Webb) in Athens in 400 B. C. The score by Christine is enhanced by songs from Cole Porter, Herman Darewski, and Chantrier. The Dolly Sisters and Edward Dolly devise the dances, with Frank Collins staging. There are 133 performances of this C. B. Cochran show, with a book by Fred Thompson and Clifford Grey.

Aug 22 *Dippers* (L—Criterion—Comedy). Ben Travers' farce runs for 175 performances. Binnie Hale, Jack Raine, and Hermione Gingold are featured. Ernest Trimmingham is the "Leader of the Coon Band."

Aug 26 *Bluebeard's Eighth Wife.* See NY premiere, 1921.

Sep 2 *East of Suez* (L—His Majesty's—Drama). W. Somerset Maugham's play revolves around a Eurasian who marries an Englishman who doesn't know that his school-friend has been her lover. Meggie Albanesi, Malcolm Keen, and Basil Rathbone have major roles. Basil Dean stages, using Chinese actors and ancient Chinese music for some street-scenes in modern Peking. Other music is composed by Eugene Goosens. There are 214 showings of the visually impressive production.

Sep 7 *Secrets* (L—Comedy—Drama). The secrets in Rudolf Besier and May Edginton's play are those locked in the heart of Lady Carlton (Fay Compton). An old woman in 1922, she relives the past. This tale of suffering and sentiment wins 374 performances.

Sep 19 *The Cabaret Girl* (L—Winter Garden—Musical). Jerome Kern provides the score, with a book by P. G. Wodehouse and George Grossmith, who also directs, plays a lead, and is a co-producer. There are 462 performances. In the ensemble are Dorothy Dickson, Heather Thatcher, Norman Griffin, Enid Taylor, Peter Haddon, Molly Ramsden, and others. Songs include Kern's "Looking All Over for You," "First Rose of Summer," and "Shimmy With Me."

Oct 11 *Angel Face* (L—Strand—Musical). From America, with a Victor Herbert score and a libretto by Harry B. and Robert B. Smith, this show has just 13 performances, even with a cast headed by Eric Blore.

Oct 25 *The Nine O'Clock Revue* (L—Little—Revue). There are 385 performance of this show which features such talents as Beatrice Lillie, Joan Emney, Morris Harvey, Irene Browne, and Bobby Blythe. Muriel Lillie devises the music, with the book by Harvey and Harold Simpson.

Oct 31 *The Cat and the Canary.* See NY premiere, 1922.

Dec 8 *Battling Butler* (L—New Oxford—Musical). This "musical farce" tells of a man who lies to his wife that he is a boxing champion. Jack Buchanan has the title-role. The story is by Austin Melford and Stanley Brightman, with songs by Douglas Furber (lyrics) and Philip Braham (music). There are 238 showings. On Oct 8, 1923, it opens at New York's Selwyn with Charles Ruggles in the lead. It runs beyond the season.

1922 REVIVALS/REPERTORIES

Jan 10 At the Abbey Theatre in Dublin, among the new plays this season are T. C. Murray's *Aftermath*, opening tonight; M. M. Brennan's *The Young Man from Rathmines* (April 6); R. J. Ray's *The Moral Law* (Aug 29); George Shiel's *Paul Twyning* (Oct 3), and Padraic Colum and E. W. Freund's *Grasshopper*, adapted from a German play.

Jan 23 In Hampstead at its own theatre, London's Everyman troupe opens its season with St. John Ervine's *Mixed Marriage*. Other productions include Shaw's *Fanny's First Play* (Feb 6), *Getting Married* (March 27), and *Misalliance* (April 8); O'Neill's *Ile* (April 17), Ibsen's *Hedda Gabler* (May 20), Drinkwater's *Mary Stuart* (Sep 25), and Shakespeare's *Twelfth Night* (Dec 20).

Jan 25 At London's Little Theatre, the Grand Guignol troupe is winding down with a series of one-act plays: *Amends, Changing Guard, De Mortuis, The Regiment, Cupboard Love.* There are 72 performances, with Sybil Thorndike, Lewis Casson, Ian Fleming, Brember Wills, and others in the company.

Feb 7 At London's Royal Court Theatre, a season of John Galsworthy revivals opens with *Justice* (3 weeks), followed by *The Pigeon* (3 weeks) on Feb 27. On March 20, *The Silver Box* (5 weeks) is presented, with *Windows* (five weeks) on April 25.

Feb 21 Arthur Wing Pinero offers his short play, *A Seat in the Park*, at a London matinee in aid of the League of Nations. Dion Boucicault, Irene Vanbrugh, and R. Lichfield Owen perform it.

Feb 26 At London's Kingsway Theatre, Luigi Pirandello's *Six Characters in Search of an Author* has a special production by the Stage Society. Franklin Dyall plays the Father. The play cannot be performed for the public, because it lacks the Lord Chamberlain's permission.

March 6 At London's Royal Victoria Hall—the "Old Vic"—Ibsen's *Peer Gynt* is revived. In February, OUDS, the Oxford Union Dramatic Society, has presented Ibsen's *The Pretenders* at Oxford's New Theatre.

March 19 Dedicated to the revival of old, forgotten plays, the Phoenix Society—an offshoot of the Stage Society—presents Dryden's tragedy *All for Love* in the West End at the Shaftesbury Theatre. On May 28, they produce Dryden's comedy, *Amphytrion*, at Daly's Theatre. At the same house, on Nov 5, they offer Marlowe's *The Jew of Malta*. On Nov 20, they are at the Old Vic with a production of Massinger's *A New Way to Pay Old Debts*.

April 3 At London's Little Theatre, the actors are largely those who have offered the horrors and comedies of the Grand Guignol Theatre for several seasons. A new series of one-act plays is opened for a run of 63 showings. The plays include *Amelia's Suitors, At the Telephone, Colombine, The Nutcracker Suite,* and *Progress.* Sybil Thorndike and Lewis Casson are leading performers.

April 17 *The Taming of the Shrew* opens the Shakespeare Festival in Stratford-upon-Avon, under W. Bridges Adams' direction. *All's Well That Ends Well* is the "birthday play." James K. Hackett, the American actor who has retired on this side of the Atlantic, plays the title-role in *Othello*. Other plays include *Twelfth Night, Julius Caesar, Much Ado About Nothing,* and a special production of *The Taming of the Shrew*, performed by the boys of All Saints Choir School, London. Katherine is played by a youngster named Laurence Olivier.

May 6 J. M. Barrie's *Dear Brutus* earns 258 performances in this revival at London's Wyndham's Theatre. It is produced by Gerald DuMaurier.

May 8 *Timon of Athens* opens in London's Old Vic Theatre, where Lilian Baylis began a cycle of Shakespeare's canon of plays in 1914. *Antony and Cleopatra* follows on Dec 4.

May 21 At London's Court Theatre, the Stage Society presents a matinee of Knut Hamsun's *At the Gates of the Kingdom*.

May 28 Moliere's *L'Avare* is presented at London's His Majesty's Theatre as part of the Theatre Française's visiting repertorie.

May 31 At London's Little Theatre, Sybil Thorndike and others offer their third program of one-act plays this season. Noel Coward's *The Better Half* is played by Ian Fleming, Auriol Lee, and Ivy Williams. Other plays include *A Happy New Year*, *To Be Continued*, *The Hand of Death*, and *The Sisters' Tragedy*.

June 5 Members of The Players founded by Edwin Booth on New York's Gramercy Park, move uptown to the Empire Theatre where they revive Sheridan's *The Rivals* for a week with an all-star cast, including Tyrone Power, Francis Wilson, Robert Warwick, Patricia Collinge, Violet Heming, Mary Shaw, James T. Powers, Henry E. Dixey, John Craig, and Pedro de Cordoba.

June 12 At London's Prince's Theatre, Sacha Guitry opens his four-week season of French plays. His drama *Pasteur*, is the premiere. Other productions include his *Jacqueline* and *Le Grand Duc*. He is supported by Lucien Guitry and Yvonne Printemps, among others.

June 30 At London's Playhouse Theatre Gladys Cooper plays the title-role in this revival of Arthur Wing Pinero's *The Second Mrs. Tanqueray*, with Dennis Eadie as her husband. The production draws for 222 performances.

July 24 The summer season at the Shakespeare Memorial Theatre in Stratford-upon-Avon features three productions which have just been seen at the Norwegian National Theatre in Oslo: *Much Ado About Nothing*, *Twelfth Night*, and *The Taming of The Shrew*. Dorothy Green is admired as Katherine, some critics insisting she is one of Britain's finest Shakespearean actresses. Also offered are *All's Well That Ends Well*, *Othello*, *Julius Caesar*, *Cymbeline*, and *Hamlet*. At the close of the season, the Birmingham Repertory Company visits the theatre with Wilde's *The Importance of Being Earnest*, Shaw's *Getting Married*, and Chapin's *The New Morality*.

July 25 Sybil Thorndike revives St. John Ervine's *Jane Clegg* at London's New Theatre for a run of 63 performances. Leslie Faber plays Henry to her Jane. On Sep 19, Thorndike opens a production of *The Scandal*, adapted from Henri Bataille's play. There are 77 showings, followed by a two-week revival of Shelley's *The Cenci*, with Thorndike as the doomed heroine.

Sep 2 The Birmingham Repertory Theatre opens its 11th season with J. M. Barrie's *The Admirable Crichton* in revival.

Sep 25 In Bristol at the Prince's Theatre, Noel Coward's three-act comedy, *The Young Idea*, is produced. It comes to the Savoy Theatre in London on Feb 1, 1923, for 60 performances.

Sep 26 Ethel Barrymore plays the title-role in Gerhart Hauptmann's German drama *Rose Bernd* at the Longacre Theatre in New York. The play concerns a peasant girl used and abused by scheming men. Arthur Hopkins produces and directs the show, which runs for 87 performances.

Oct 7 Despite the British aversion to Austro-German operettas during the late war, *The Last Waltz*, with a score by Oscar Strauss and an English libretto by Robert Evett and Reginald Arkell, achieves a run of 280 performances. Jose Collins, Bertram Wallis, Billy Leonard, and Amy Augarde are in the cast.

Oct 12 *The Co-Optimists* have their second London revue season; this time they perform at the Prince of Wales's Theatre for 29 weeks.

Oct 13 In London at the Regent Theatre, the Birmingham Repertory Company offers its production of Rutland Broughton's music-drama, *The Immortal Hour*. The show has 216 performances, with a cast including Gwen Ffrangcon-Davies, Dorothy D'Orsay, Margaret Chatwin, and Herbert Simmonds.

Oct 14 Previously banned by the censor, Eden Phillpott's *The Secret Woman* is given its first public performance by the Birmingham Repertory Theatre.

Nov 13 The Comedie Francaise appears in Manhattan at the 39th Street Theatre with Emile Augier's *L'Aventuriere*.

Nov 16 John Barrymore has a run of 101 performances in the Arthur Hopkins produced and directed production of *Hamlet*. Robert Edmond Jones designs for the Sam H. Harris Theatre in New York. The NY Times praises Barrymore, saying, "Vocally the performance was keyed low. Deep tones prevailed, tones of brooding, half-conscious melancholy. The 'reading' of the lines was flawless—an art that is said to have been lost. The manner, for the most part, was that of conversation, almost colloquial, but the beauty of rhythm was never lost, the varied flexible harmonies of Shakespeare's crowning period in metric mastery."

Dec 21 Just in time for Christmas, David Belasco produces and directs David Warfield as Shylock in a revival of *The Merchant of Venice*. Staged at New York's Lyceum Theatre, the production also uses the talents of Philip Merivale, Ian MacLaren, Julia Adler, Mary Servoss, and Albert Bruning. It runs nearly three months.

Dec 26 It's Boxing Day, so some leading West End theatres open traditional Christmas pantomimes and shows. At the Duke of York's, the show is Maeterlinck's *The Bluebird*. At the Lyceum Theatre, *Robinson Crusoe* comes to life. *Peter Pan* flies again at the St. James's. *Treasure Island* has already opened before Christmas at the Strand Theatre, as has *Cinderella* at the Hippodrome, and *Charley's Aunt* at the Royalty, where the revival lasts for ten weeks. The Empire offers *Arlequin*, while the Holborn Empire presents a revival of *Where the Rainbow Ends*. At the Regent, the show is *The Christmas Party*; at the Victoria Palace, *The Windmill Man*.

Dec 27 Ethel Barrymore is Juliet in Arthur Hopkin's production of Shakespeare's *Romeo and Juliet*, which has a brief run of 29 performances at New York's Longacre Theatre.

Dec 30 At London's Kingsway Theatre, Nigel Playfair revives John Gay's *Polly*, the sequel to *The Beggar's Opera*, which Playfair has recently revived with great success at the Lyric, Hammersmith. Clifford Bax adapts the playtext, with musical arrangements by Frederic Austin. There are 324 performances. Pitt Chatham and Lillian Davies are featured.

1922 BIRTHS/DEATHS/DEBUTS

Jan 30 British star Marie Lohr makes a belated New York debut in *The Voice from the Minaret* at the Hudson Theatre. The production runs only 13 performances. Other plays in her repertoire do not fare better. After a month, she departs.

March 4 Comedian and song writer Bert Williams is dead at age 46 in New York. Williams and George Walker formed a popular vaudeville team in 1895. In 1902, Williams wrote and produced an all-Negro musical, *In Dahomey*. After the death of Walker, Williams joined the *Ziegfeld Follies*, for which he wrote his own songs and other material.

March 12 Director-playwright-actor Reginald Denham directs his first London production, Edward Percy's *If Four Walls Told* at the Comedy Theatre.

May 1 Future playwright Tad Mosel is born George Ault Mosel, Jr. in Steubenville, Ohio.

May 26 American manager Charles Osgood dies in New York at age 63. Osgood was an executive in the Klaw & Erlanger offices for 30 years.

June 5 American actress and singer Lillian Russell (b. 1861) dies in Pittsburgh, Pa. Born Nellie Leonard, Russell was widely know on the American stage, first in comic opera, and later as a member of Weber and Fields' stock company.

Sep 11 A new singing talent is introduced: Jeanette MacDonald makes her debut in *A Fantastic Fricasee* at the Greenwich Village Theatre in a New York.

Sep 19 Victor Herbert's last show, *Orange Blossom*, is presented at New York's Fulton Theatre. "A Kiss in the Dark" becomes a hit.

Sep 20 Stage and screen actress Frances Heflin is born in Oklahoma City, Okla.

Oct 5 Russian actress and dramatic coach Eugenie Leontovich makes her New York debut in the vaudeville production, *Revue Russe*, at the Booth Theatre. Born in 1900 in Moscow, Leontovich is a grauduate of the Moscow Art Theatre.

Oct 7 English music hall performer Marie Lloyd (b. 1870) dies in London. Lloyd made her first appearance at the Royal Eagle Music Hall in 1885. Two years ago, on her 50th birthday, she was honored by a special performance at the Bedford Music Hall.

Oct 31 Noted actress-director-instructor Stella Adler makes her Broadway debut as Apatura Clythia in Josef and Karl Capek's *The World We Live In (The Insect Comedy)* at the Jolson Theatre under the name of Lola Adler.

Oct 31 Future stage and screen actress Barbara Bel Geddes is born to designer-producer-architect Norman Bel and Helen Belle (Sneider) Geddes in New York.

Nov 12 Future stage and screen actress Kim Hunter is born Janet Cole in Detroit, Michigan.

Nov 27 American actress Kate Ryan is dead at 65 in Trumbull Hospital in Brookline, Massachusetts. Ryan was once a member of the old Boston Museum Stock Company. Her book, *Old Boston Museum Days*, was published in 1915.

Dec 1 American press agent and drama editor William Raymond Sill dies in Flushing, New York at age 53. Sill left news reporting to become press agent for Weber and Fields. He was the first publicity agent for Keith's Palace in New York.

Dec 4 American poet and playwright Josephine Preston Peabody (b. 1874) dies in New York. Peabody's best-known works are *The Wolf of Gubbio*, *The Chameleon*, and *Portrait of Mrs. W.*, a prose play about the love affair of Mary Wollstonecraft and William Godwin.

Dec 20 Actor Morris Carnovsky makes his New York debut as Reb Aaron in Sholom Asch's *The God of Vengeance* at the Provincetown Playhouse.

Dec 25 Producer, actress, and writer Armina Marshall makes her debut as an actress appearing as a nun in Paul Claudel's *The Tidings Brought to Mary* at New York's Garrick Theatre.

also account for the large number of productions. Mantle notes more rapid failures this season, with $3.30 as the top ticket-price. Divided by genres, there have been 83 dramas, 69 comedies, 24 musicals, and 20 revues. There are 145 apparent failures (73%), with 51 plays seeming successes (27%).

June 15 Burns Mantle's selection of annual ten *Best Plays* are: O'Neill's *Anna Christie*, Dane's *A Bill of Divorcement*, Kaufman and Connelly's *Dulcy*, Andreyev's *He Who Gets Slapped*, McGuire's *Six-Cylinder Love*, Emery's *The Hero*, Milne's *The Dover Road*, Richman's *Ambush*, Maugham's *The Circle*, and Geraldy's *The Nest*. At season's close, twelve productions, past and present, boast of breaking the 500-performance mark. They are: *Lightnin'* (1,291), *The Bat* (867), *The First Year* (760), *Peg O' My Heart* (692), *East is West* (680), *Irene* (670), *A Trip to Chinatown* (657), *Adonis* (603), *Sally* (570), *The Music Master* (540), *The Boomerang* (522), and *Shuffle Along* (504).

Sep 11 San Francisco's new Curran Theatre opens tonight on Geary Street, next door to the Geary Theatre (1910). It's named for the West Coast producer-manager Homer Curran. The theatre seats 1,768 and for many years serves as the city's premiere house for touring Broadway musicals and productions of the Civic Light Opera, which serves both San Francisco and Los Angeles.

Sep 18 Today, Sam H. Harris and the Selwyns open their new Selwyn Theatre in Chicago, on Dearborn at Lake Street. The Selwyn is a twin to the Harris Theatre which will open on Oct 9. Both houses are designs of architects C. Howard Crane and H. Kenneth Franzheim.

Nov 20 In New Orleans, Louisiana, the Petit Theatre du Vieux Carre has its formal opening as the newly completed home of the former Drawing Room Players, an amateur group founded in 1916, which in 1919 adopted the name it now gives to its 410-seat playhouse. There are three plays on the opening-night bill: Calderon's *Little Stone House*, Sutro's *Man in the Stalls*, and Penney's *The Falcon and the Lady*. The dedication of this theatre encourages other American little theatre groups to build their own playhouses. Still functioning in the 1970's, the theatre group will claim the honor of being the oldest major non-professional group in the United States.

Dec Sholem Asch's *The God of Vengeance* arouses the protests of reformers, angered at its depiction of a Polish brothel-keeper and the dangers posed for his innocent daughter by this fact. It has 133 performances at the Provicetown Theatre before the police close the show. Standing trial, the producer and the leading players are convicted of presenting an immoral play.

1922   THEATERS/PRODUCTIONS

In Britain, patents are granted for: A. E. and R. Blackburn's rotary stage with sets joined bottom-to-bottom on a horizontal axis, with rotation in a vertical plane to change sets; C. Parolini's scrimlike projection-screen which permits cross-fades from film to live action.

U.S. patents granted this year include: Stephen Horn's for his rotary stage with its revolving ceiling-piece to provide an appropriate ceiling for each setting on the revolve; playwright George Kelly has devised an improved stage-brace.

This year Lord Cromer assumes the post of Lord Chamberlain, a position he will hold until 1938. He seeks to give up the powers of censor on the grounds that recent events have shown that it is increasingly difficult "for one individual to control the tide of modern thought, even were it advisable to do so." The Home Secretary rejects his proposal. The Lord Chamberlain denies a permit for public performance to *The Queen's Minister* because it proposes to show Queen Victoria and Lord Melbourne on stage. There is nothing in the play that has not already been found in the Queen's diaries or published in such biographies as Lytton Strachey's *Queen Victoria*, but the censor is firm. Only this year is Percy Bysschu Shelley's poetic drama, *The Cenci*, finally licensed for public performance.

Feb 27 The Earl Carroll Theatre (1,026 seats) opens in New York City. Earl Carroll, the successful director, producer, and song-writer, opens his own theatre where

he will present the *Earl Carroll Vanities* for the next two decades. The stage is equipped with an elevator forestage that can be used as a orchestra pit. The dimming equipment, which is permanently installed, unlike most Broadway theatres, has a pilot wheel for better mastering.

March 9 Alice Delysia is the star of this C. B. Cochran show, *Mayfair and Montmartre*, drafted by J. H. Turner. The critical response isn't pleasing to Cochran, so he threatens to stop inviting the critics to his shows. Later, he closes the production on the grounds that Delysia is having vocal trouble and cannot be replaced with a comparable British star. There are, nonetheless 77 performances at London's New Oxford Theatre. Frank Collins stages; Edward Dolly choreographs.

April 20 After interior reconstruction, the Theatre Royal, Drury Lane, London reopens with *Decameron Nights*. The capacity is now 2,283. The designers, J. Emblin-Walker and F. Edward Jones, have preserved the outer walls, famous portico, the colonnades, rotunda and Royal Staircase.

June Fifty-four Broadway theatres have been in operation this past 1921–22 season, offering a total of 196 attractions, 40 more than the previous season and 20 more than in any previous recorded season. In the past few years, at least a dozen new theatres have been opened and managers want them booked. Quick failures

Jan 15 *Give and Take* (NY—49th Street—Comedy). A factory-owner's son, back from college and filled with communistic ideas, insists the workers must take over the faltering concern. They almost destroy the business until a millionaire, just released from an asylum, comes up with a scheme to save the company. Aaron Hoffman's farce runs beyond the season, Vivian Tobin, Louis Mann, and Robert Craig are included in the cast.

Jan 22 *Polly Preferred* (NY—Little—Comedy). Guy Bolton's heroine, Polly (Genevieve Tobin), is a chorus girl who is helped by an unemployed salesman to become a star. This entertaining fluff runs beyond the season, produced by F. Ray Comstock and Morris Gest, the same team which is sponsoring the Moscow Art Theatre.

Jan 22 *Lady Butterfly* (NY—Globe—Musical). Werner Janssen, later to be conductor of his own symphony orchestra in Los Angeles, creates the score for this show, with its complications based on some mixed-up luggage. In the company are Edward Lester, later to head the Civic Light Opera of Los Angeles; Mabel Withee, Florenz Ames, and Marjorie Gateson. It runs four months and is admired for its ballroom, tap, and soft shoe dancing, rather than the plot. Ned Wayburn directs.

Jan 24 *The Dancing Girl* (NY—Winter Garden—Musical). J. C. Huffman stages this revue with a plot, under the supervision of J. J. Shubert. Bored socialites on an ocean liner go slumming in the steerage for thrills where a tempestuous Spanish dancer is discovered. Marie Dressler offers a parody of *Rain*. Others on hand include Jack Pearl, Bennie Leonard, Sally Fields, Tom Burke and Cyril Scott. The show runs nearly 16 weeks.

Jan 31 *Caroline* (NY—Ambassador—Musical). This is really the Central European operetta, *Der Vetter aus Dingsda*, removed to the American South just after the Civil War. Tessa Kosta, as Caroline, is in love with the memory of an old sweetheart. J. Harold Murray plays the hero who impersonates him and wins Caroline. This show runs beyond the season.

Feb 5 *Mary the 3rd* (NY—39th Street—Comedy). Rachel Crothers writes and stages this popular play, which runs beyond the season and is chosen as a *Best Play*. Louise Huff plays all three Marys, showing how they chose their husbands in 1870, 1897, and 1923.

Feb 7 *Wildflower* (NY—Casino—Musical). Otto Harbach and Oscar Hammerstein II devise a plot in which a peasant girl has to keep her temper for six months to win an inheritance. Edith Day plays the girl. The music is by Herbert Stothart

Polly Preferred

and Vincent Youmans, whose "Bambalina" becomes a hit. Oscar Eagle stages. The show runs beyond the season. It opens at London's Shaftesbury on Feb 17, 1926, with Evelyn Drewe featured. There are 114 performances.

Feb 10 *Icebound* (NY—Sam H. Harris—Drama). Owen Davis wins the Pulitzer Prize with this tale of the hard-bitten people of Northern Maine. Phyllis Povah and Robert Ames are featured. The show runs beyond the season. On Jan 29, 1928, the Sunday Play Society gives a special performance of the play with Gertrude Lawrence in the lead at London's His Majesty's.

Feb 12 *The Laughing Lady* (NY—Longacre—Comedy). Arthur Hopkins produces and directs Alfred Sutro's British play. Ethel Barrymore is Lady Marjorie, who comes to love the divorce lawyer (Cyril Keightley). The show has a three-month run.

Feb 19 *You and I* (NY—Belmont—Comedy). Philip Barry's play, with a cast including Frieda Inescourt, Geoffrey Kerr, Lucille Watson, and H. B. Warner, runs beyond the season. Robert Milton stages this Harvard Prize Play (1922) which shows a father who has sacrificed a career as a painter for love of his wife and son.

March 12 *Pasteur* (NY—Empire—Drama). Charles Frohman produces; Arthur Hornblow, Jr., adapts Sach Guitry's Parisian success; Henry Miller is Pasteur. Unfortunately, this production runs only two weeks. Its failure is laid to lack of knowledge of, or interest in, the French scientist who made milk safe to drink.

March 12 *Barnum Was Right* (NY—Frazee—Comedy). John Meehan stages the farce he and Philip Bartholomae have

written about an estate on Long Island that might contain gold. Donald Brian stars with Enid Markey, Lilyan Tashman, and William Morris. The show runs 11 weeks.

March 19 *The Adding Machine* (NY—Garrick—Drama). The Theatre Guild produces Elmer Rice's expressionistic play in which office workers are reduced to the character of ciphers. Dudley Digges, Helen Westley and Edward G. Robinson are in the cast. It runs nine weeks. The Stage Society presents it at London's Strand Theatre on March 16, 1924.

March 31 *The Enchanted Cottage*. See L premiere, 1922.

April 2 *Uptown West* (NY—Bijou—Drama). Lincoln Osborn's play focuses on a character whom critic Burns Mantle describes as an "Anglicized Jap," Sakamoto (Henry Herbert). His American wife turns from him to her own race; their child is killed. He strangles a drug addict, thinking it is his wife; and cuts his throat. Because the American girl (Florence Mason) escapes, Mantle labels the story "a happy one." The play runs beyond the season.

April 23 *The Devil's Disciple* (NY—Garrick—Comedy). George Bernard Shaw's fable of the American Revolution runs through and beyond the season in this Theatre Guild production. Basil Sydney is Dick Dudgeon.

May 21 *Aren't We All?* See L premiere, 1923.

May 24 *Sun Up* (NY—Provincetown—Drama). Lulu Vollmer's folk play features Lucille La Verne as a widow who has lost many of her family in wars and skirmishes with revenuers. The play runs beyond the season and is awarded a Pulitzer Prize. It comes to London's

Vaudeville on May 4, 1925, where it runs for 234 performances. La Verne repeats her role.

June 14 *The Passing Show* (NY—Winter Garden—Revue). Walter Woolf provides a powerful singing voice and handsome presence. George Jessel is the master of the revels, which have music by Sigmund Romberg and Jean Schwartz. J. C. Huffman stages, with J. J. Shubert supervising.

June 18 *George White's Scandals* (NY—Globe—Revue). This edition runs for 21 weeks, but its George Gershwin score has no hits.

June 19 *Helen of Troy, New York* (NY—Selwyn—Musical). George S. Kaufman and Marc Connelly create a poor Irish heroine, who wins the day, after being fired from a collar factory, by inventing a new soft collar. The show runs half a year. Helen Ford stars.

July 5 *Vanities of 1923* (NY—Earl Carroll—Revue). Peggy Hopkins Joyce wears a chinchilla coat; Joe Cook provides the humor, and the show runs over 25 weeks.

Aug 15 *Little Jessie James* (NY—Longacre—Musical). Harlan Thompson's book shows Jessie Jamieson pursuing her man, Paul Revere, in a Central Park West apartment. With a Harry Archer score and a Paul Whiteman band in the pit, not conducted by Whiteman, the show runs through and beyond the season. Jay Velie, Miriam Hopkins, and Allen Kearns are on hand. The production uses only eight chorus girls, a great saving on costs.

Aug 17 *Children of the Moon* (NY—Comedy—Drama). Martin Flavin's play features Henrietta Crosman as a neurotic matriarch who forbids her daughter to marry an aviator who has crashed into their garden. This appeals to audiences for 117 performances.

Aug 20 *Artists and Models* (NY—Shubert—Revue). This Shubert show enjoys a run of 39 weeks. Devised as competition to Earl Carroll's scantily clad lovelies, it uses Frank Fay to good effect as master of ceremonies.

Aug 20 *The Whole Town's Talking* (NY—Bijou—Comedy). Anita Loos teams with John Emerson to tell this tale of Chester Binney (Grant Mitchell), who has to invent a romantic past in Hollywood to impress the girl he loves (June Bradley). Audiences keep the show open for 173 performances.

Aug 28 *Little Miss Bluebeard* (NY—Lyceum—Comedy). Avery Hopwood's romantic comedy runs almost 22 weeks. Irene Bordoni plays Colette, a seeming victim of bigamy, who captures the love of a sympathetic composer (Bruce McRae).

Sep 3 *Poppy* (NY—Apollo—Musical). Madge Kennedy plays the title role in this show with book and lyrics by Dorothy Donnelly and score by Stephen Jones and Arthur Samuels. W. C. Fields plays a circus drifter and guardian of the orphaned

Poppy who proves to be an heiress. The show runs beyond the season. On Sep 4, 1924, it premieres at Gaiety in the West End, with Annie Croft in the lead. The show has 188 performances.

Sep 17 *The Changelings* (NY—Henry Miller—Comedy). Playwright Lee Wilson Dodd shows the anxieties of two middle aged married couples, longtime friends, whose interests have been joined by the marriage of their respective son and daughter. The follies of 1920's youths are sensibly resolved for a four-months' run. In the cast are Henry Miller, Laura Hope Crews, Ruth Chatterton, Blanche Bates, and Geoffrey Kerr.

Sep 20 *The Greenwich Village Follies* (NY—Winter Garden—Revue). John Murray Anderson stages such talents as Martha Graham, the dancing Cansinos, comic Tom Howard, and female impersonator Karyl Norman. The show runs for over 17 weeks. Reginald Marsh paints a show curtain, and James Reynolds designs a Spanish fiesta scene in the style of Velasquez. Graham and the Cansinos recreate Spanish dances.

Sep 22 *The Music Box Revue* (NY—Music Box—Revue). Irving Berlin provides music and lyrics, interpolating "What'll I Do?" sung by Grace Moore. Robert Benchley gives his "Treasurer's Report." George S. Kaufman's *If Men Played Cards as Women Do* is a hit. Hassard Short stages an ensemble including Florence O'Denishawn, Frank Tinney, Joseph Santley, and Phil Baker. The show runs 34 weeks.

Sep 24 *Chicken Feed* (NY—Little—Comedy). Guy Bolton's play is later renamed *Wages for Wives*, running 144 performances. Roberta Arnold plays Nell Bailey, who teaches village men something about sharing income and business matters with their wives and sweethearts.

Oct 1 *Tarnish* (NY—Belmont—Drama). Gilbert Emery's play is staged by John Cromwell. Ann Harding plays the brave young Tish Tevis, whose fiance (Tom Powers) proves to be a bit tarnished.

Oct 8 *Battling Butler.* See L premiere, 1922.

Oct 9 *The Nervous Wreck* (NY—Sam H. Harris—Comedy). Owen Davis's farce about a clerk who finds adventure in the West features Otto Kruger. The cast also includes William Holden and Edward Arnold. There are 279 performances. On Sep 17, 1924, it premieres at London's St. James's with a cast including William Farrell, May Duncan and Curtis Cooksey. It earns only 93 showings.

Oct 15 *For All of Us* (NY—49th Street—Drama). William Hodge writes, directs, and takes the lead. Critic Burns Mantle calls this a Christian Science theme, for the hero, formerly a drunken Irishman, cures a paralyzed businessman by restoring his mind to health so that the body may be healed. The play runs 27 weeks.

Oct 16 *The Shame Woman* (NY—Green-

wich Village—Drama). Playwright Lulu Vollmer, with *Sun-Up* a hit, has a kind of instant fame as this folk-drama of the North Carolina hills is praised. It runs 35 weeks. Florence Rittenhouse plays Lise Burns, a hill woman who has sinned and who murders her debaucher years later after he seduces her adopted daughter.

Oct 17 *The Dancers.* See L premiere, 1923.

Oct 20 *The Ziegfeld Follies of 1923* (NY—New Amsterdam—Revue). This edition runs nearly 42 weeks. The music is by Rudolf Friml, Victor Herbert, and Dave Stamper. The numbers are accompanied by Paul Whiteman's orchestra and feature such talents as Fannie Brice, Bert Wheeler, and Brooke Johns. James Reynolds designs the inventive settings, with costumes by Paris's Erte.

Oct 23 *The Swan* (NY—Cort—Comedy). Ferenc Molnar's Hungarian comedy, after several false tries, is successfully adapted by Melville Baker, a Charles Frohman playreader. Staged by Gilbert Miller, with a cast including Basil Rathbone, Eva LeGallienne, Philip Merivale, Hilda Spong, and Alison Skipworth, it runs for 32 weeks. The Equity strike closes it. Molnar's tale is of briefly frustrated royal romance—with some needed satire.

Oct 24 *Scaramouche* (NY—Morosco—Drama). Rafael Sabatini's romantic melodrama shows an orphan becoming a revolutionary and disguising himself as Scaramouche, a strolling *Commedia* player. About to avenge the murder of a revolutionary friend, he discovers his enemy is his long-lost father. The large cast includes Dorothy Tierney, Sidney Blackmer, Margalo Gillmore, Allyn Joslyn, and Sheldon Stanwood. The production has only 61 performances.

Oct 29 *Runnin' Wild* (NY—Colonial—Musical). A song from this show is to set the tone of the frantic 1920's: "The Charleston." Essentially a black vaudeville, the show is held together with the antics of Sam Peck and Steve Jenkins, who pass themselves off in Jimtown as mediums. They are played by the show's creators, Flournoy Miller and Aubrey Lyles. Music and lyrics are by James Johnson and Cecil Mack. Produced by George White, the show runs for 213 performances. Next to its comedians, 'Runnin' Wild' excels in eccentric dancing—some of the most exciting steps of the season, says the *NY Times*.

Nov 5 *White Cargo* (NY—Greenwich Village—Drama). Leon Gordon's picture of Englishmen on a West African rubber plantation features Richard Stevenson and Annette Margules. It runs beyond the season. On May 15, 1924, it opens in London's Playhouse with Mary Clare and Brian Aherne. There are 821 showings.

Nov 9 *Spring Cleaning* (NY—Eltinge—Comedy). Frederick Lonsdale's play focuses on a husband who brings home a prostitute to shame his wife, who surrounds herself with social reprobates. Estelle Winwood, Violet Heming, and Arthur Byron are featured. It runs beyond the season. On Jan 29, 1925, it opens at London's St. Martin's with Edna Best, Cathleen Nesbitt, and Ronald Squire in the cast. There are 262 performances.

Nov 15 *Queen Victoria* (NY—48th Street—Drama). Beryl Mercer plays the title role, with Clarence Derwent as Disraeli. By Walter Pritchard Eaton and David Carb, it is an Equity Players production, running less than six weeks.

Nov 19 *The Failures* (NY—Garrick—Drama). The Theatre Guild finds its production of H. R. Lenormand's play is also a failure, with only 40 performances. Jacob Ben-Ami plays He, a struggling playwright; Winifred Lenihan plays She, who takes to prostitution to support He.

Nov 20 *Robert E. Lee.* See L premiere, 1923.

Nov 27 *In the Next Room* (NY—Vanderbilt—Drama). Mrs. August Belmont (Eleanor Robson) joins Harriet Ford to write this mystery melodrama of a sinister Boule cabinet which leads to the deaths of two people. Guthrie McClintic stages the show, which has 159 performances. On June 6, 1924, the play begins a run of 202 performances in London at St. Martin's Theatre. Nora Swinburne and Francis Lister play major roles.

Nov 28 *Laugh, Clown, Laugh* (NY—Belasco—Drama). David Belasco, with Tom Cushing, adapts Faurto Martini's *Ridi, Pagliaccio* for the American stage. Lionel Barrymore is the unfortunate clown, in love with his ward, played by Irene Fenwick. The show runs nearly 17 weeks.

Dec 8 *The Potters* (NY—Plymouth—Comedy). J. P. McEvoy's play runs beyond the season, giving audiences a stage-version of the humorist's short-story characters, Ma, Pa, Bill, and Mamie Potter. Pa invests in oil stocks, and Mamie elopes. Donald Meek plays Pa Potter.

Dec 25 *Mary Jane McKane* (NY—Imperial—Musical). The music is by Vincent Youmans and Herbert Stothart. The book, by William Cary Duncan and Oscar Hammerstein II, is another rags-to-riches tale, featuring a poor Irish secretary (Mary Hay). The show has 151 performances.

Dec 28 *Saint Joan* (NY—Garrick—Drama). The Theatre Guild produces George Bernard Shaw's version of the St. Joan story with Winifred Lenihan in the title role. It runs beyond the season. On March 26, 1924, it premieres at the New Theatre in London with Sybil Thorndike as the Maid. It earns 244 performances.

Dec 29 *Roseanne* (NY—Greenwich Village—Drama). Chrystal Herne (in blackface) plays a black laundress whose trust in a black pastor is betrayed. This folkdrama of black life in Georgia is by Nan Bagby Stephens. It runs just over five weeks.

Dec 31 *Kid Boots* (NY—Earl Carroll—Musical). Golf and bootlegging are the comic themes in this show by W. A. McGuire and Otto Harbach, with music by Harry Tierney and lyrics by Joseph McCarthy. Eddie Cantor is starred. He interpolates the hit "Dinah." Florenz Ziegfeld produces. The show runs beyond the season. It comes to London's Winter Garden on Feb 2, 1926, with Leslie Henson in the title role. There are 163 performances.

Dec 31 *The Song and Dance Man* (NY—Hudson—Comedy). George M. Cohan stars as the man of the title in his own play, which he also produces. Down on his luck, the entertainer tries robbery, but is redeemed. This plot is rewarded with a three-month run.

1923 BRITISH PREMIERES

Jan 16 *A Roof and Four Walls* (L—Apollo—Comedy). There are 132 performances of E. Temple Thurston's four-act comedy, with a cast including Phyllis Neilson-Terry, Laura Smithson, Nicholas Hannen, and Lauderdale Maitland.

Jan 17 *Plus Fours* (L—Haymarket—Comedy). With the resumption of its run after a transfer to the St. James's, this play by Horace A. Vachell and Harold Simpson, earns a total of 150 performances. In the company are Una O'Connor, Clare Greet, C. Aubrey Smith, and Athene Seyler.

Feb 15 *The Dancers* (L—Wyndham's—Drama). Hubert Parson's romance tells the story of a dance hall proprietor who inherits an English title and fortune but never forgets his true love. Gerald du Maurier and Tallulah Bankhead are featured. The show runs for 346 performances. On Oct 17, it opens at New York's Broadhurst with Richard Bennett and Jean Oliver featured. The show can be seen 133 times.

Feb 16 *Little Nellie Kelly* (L—New Oxford—Musical). See NY premiere, 1922.

Feb 21 *Rats!* (L—Vaudeville—Revue). Gertrude Lawrence is in the cast of this Ronald Jeans-Philip Braham show, aided by the talents of Norah Blaney, Gwen Farrar, Alfred Lester, Rex O'Malley, and others. There are 285 performances.

Feb 24 *The Cousin from Nowhere* (L—Prince's—Musical). This show, about mistaken identity between lovers, is set in Holland. Helen Gilliland, Cicely Debenham, and Walter William play leads. Critics find the music more interesting than the plot. Edward Kunneke has created the score, with lyrics by Adrian Ross, R.C. Tharp, and Douglas Furber. Songs include "Magical Moon," Batavia," and "Two's Company, Three's None." The show runs for 105 performances.

Feb 28 *Partners Again.* See NY premiere, 1922.

March 3 *The Bad Man.* See NY premiere, 1920.

March 6 Produced first in America, A. A. Milne's comedy, *The Great Broxopp*, has only 37 performances in London at St. Martin's Theatre, despite a cast including Ian Hunger, Edmund Gwenn, Beatrix Thomson, Faith Celli, and others.

The Cousin from Nowhere

March 29 *Brighter London* (L—Hippodróme—Revue). With a cast including Annie Croft, Billy Merson, Elsie Prince, and Lupino Lane, this revue wins a run of 591 performances, playing two-a-day.

April 2 *At Mrs. Beam's* (L—Royalty—Comedy). C.K. Munro's play about a boardinghouse keeper who suspects a guest of being a killer runs 280 performances. It opens on April 26, 1926, at New York's Guild with Alfred Lunt and Lynn Fontanne. The show has 222 performances.

April 3 *The Rainbow* (L—Empire—Revue). George Gershwin provides the music for this show, with lyrics by Clifford Grey and book by Albert de Courville, Edgar Wallace, and Noel Scott. It wins 113 showings. The cast includes Lola Raine, Alec Kellaway, Grace Hayes, the American vaudeville team of Willie, West, and McGinty, and the Sixteen Empire Girls.

April 10 *Anna Christie.* See NY premiere. 1921.

April 10 *Aren't We All?* (L—Globe—Comedy). Frederick Lonsdale's comedy about a couple patching up their marriage after brief dalliances features Marie Löhr and Herbert Marshall. It earns a run of 110 performances. On May 21, it premieres at Broadway's Gaiety with Cyril Maude and Mabel Terry-Lewis. It runs beyond the season.

April 11 *So This Is London!* (L—Prince of Wales's—Comedy). Arthur Goodrich's "Anglo-American Comedy" wins 278 performances, with Raymond Hackett as the American boy (Hiram Draper, Jr.) and Dorothy Tetley as the English girl (Elinor Worthing) whose romance causes some fussing and fuming from strong-minded fathers on both sides of the Atlantic. Fred Kerr and Edward Robins play the fathers. John Meehan stages.

April 16 *You'd Be Surprised* (L—Covent Garden—Musical). This is called a "Jazzaganza." William K. Wells provides the music and some of the lyrics, with Melville Morris contributing the rest of the verses and the book. George Robey heads a cast including Lydia Lopokova, Leonid Massine, Ninette de Valois, Jack Edwards, and the Savoy Havana Band. It runs 270 performances.

April 17 *Merton of the Movies.* See NY premiere, 1922.

May 5 *The Insect Play; R. U. R.* See NY premieres, 1922.

May 9 *Ned Kean of Old Drury* (L—Drury Lane—Drama). Even though Arthur Shirley's play is staged elaborately in the theatre of the title itself, this historical drama about Edmund Kean (H.A. Saintsbury) can muster only 61 showings.

May 15 *The Music Box Revue.* See NY premiere, 1922.

May 29 John Drinkwater does not have as much success with the Protector as he has had with Abraham Lincoln. *Oliver Cromwell* runs only nine weeks at London's His Majesty's Theatre, and some critics find only one of its eight scences really dramatic. Henry Ainley is praised for his portrayal of Cromwell. Others include Irene Rooke, Milton Rosmer, and William Rea, as Charles I.

May 30 *Stop Flirting* (L—Shaftesbury—Musical). Fred Jackson provides the book and George Gershwin, William Daly, and Paul Lannin the songs for this show, which features Fred and Adele Astaire. There are 129 performances. Revived at the Strand Theatre in London on March 29, 1924, there are 194 further showings.

May 31 *Dover Street to Dixie* (L—Pavilion—Revue). There are 108 performances of this "most novel entertainment in town." Florence Mills and the "Plantation Company" create a sensation in the Dixie portion of the show, by Morris Harvey, Harold Simpson, and Lauri Wylie, with music by Herman Darewski and others. Stanley Lupino clowns; Odette Myrtil sings, dances, and fiddles. Other talents include Madge Compton, Mabel Green, Marjorie Brooks, and Lloyd Garrett.

June 5 *The Lilies of the Field* (L—Ambassador's—Comedy). J.H. Turner's play about two different sisters, who use their special wiles to lure beaus, earns 273 performances. The cast includes Gertrude Kingston, Hilda Bruce-Potter, Meggie Albanesi, Edna Best, Ruth Taylor, Margaret Carter, Gwynn Whitby, and Nancie Par-

sons. *The Times* describes the dialogue as witty.

June 30 *Robert E. Lee* (L—Regent—Drama). John Drinkwater's portrait of the Confederate general features Felix Aylmer. It earns 109 performances. It comes to New York's Ritz on Nov 20, with Berton Churchill as Lee. There are only 15 showings.

July 16 Benjamin Disraeli's novel, *Tancred*, is dramatized by Edith Millbank for a two-week run in London at the Kingsway Theatre.

Aug 2 *Enter Kiki.* See NY *Kiki* premiere, 1921.

Sep 4 *London Calling* (L—Duke of York's—Revue). Noel Coward and Ronald Jeans collaborate on the book, with songs by Coward, plus some by Philip Braham and Noble Sissle and Eubie Blake. The cast includes Coward, Gertrude Lawrence, Maisie Gay, and Eileen Molyneux. There are 317 performances.

Sep 5 *The Beauty Prize* (L—Winter Garden—Musical). Jerome Kern's score, with a book by P. G. Wodehouse and George Grossmith, wins 214 performances. Grossmith, Dorothy Dickson, and Leslie Henson star. Grossmith stages, with dances by Fred Leslie. Comelli creates the costumes; the Harker brothers, the settings. Songs include "Moon Love," "It's a Long, Long Day," and "Meet Me Down on Main Street."

Sep 6 *The Green Goddess.* See NY premiere, 1921.

Sep 8 *Head Over Heels* (L—Adelphi—Musical). There are 113 performances of Seymour Hicks's comedy, with songs by Adrian Ross, Harry Graham, and Harold Fraser-Simson. W. H. Berry, Helen Ferren, and Laurence Caird play leads.

Sep 17 *Outward Bound* is performed in Hampstead at the Everyman Theatre. Sutton Vane treats death as an ocean voyage. The play runs 124 performances after it transfers to the West End. On Jan 7, 1924, the show premieres at Broadway's Ritz, with Alfred Lunt and Dudley Digges. It runs 18 weeks.

Sep 20 *Hassan* (L—His Majesty's—Drama). James Elroy Flecker's Bagdad

Hassan

spectacle features Henry Ainley as Hassan, the poor candymaker who aspires to riches, power, and love of a beautiful woman. Michael Fokine choreographs to Frederick Delius's music. There are 281 showings. The show opens in New York at the Knickerbocker on Sep 22, 1924, with Randal Ayrton in the title role. It runs only two weeks.

Sep 22 *Catherine* (L—Gaiety—Musical). Jose Collins plays the princess who becomes Empress of All the Russias, to music by Tchaikovsky, chosen by Evett and Klein. The British book and lyrics are by Reginald Arkell and Fred de Gresac. The show earns 217 performances. Bertram Wallis, Robert Michaelis, Mark Lester, and Billy Leonard are also in major roles.

Sep 27 *Good Luck* (L—Drury Lane—Drama). Producer Arthur Collins has returned to the Drury's long-time policy of autumn melodrama, in this case one by Seymour Hicks and Ian Hay. It runs for 159 performances. The complicated plot includes a yacht wreck and motorboat rescue. Ellis Jeffreys, Edmund Gwenn, Gordon Harker, Claude Rains, C. W. Somerset, Arthur Treacher and Joyce Carey are in the cast.

Oct 2 In London at the Little Theatre, *The Little Revue* achieves a run of 196 performances.

Oct 9 *Back To Methuselah.* See NY premiere, 1922.

Oct 9 *The Return of Sherlock Holmes* (L—Prince's—Drama). Arthur Conan Doyle's character and his stories are worth 130 showings in this adaptation by J. E. Harold Terry and Arthur Rose, with Eile Norwood as Holmes and H. G. Stoker as Dr. Watson.

Oct 11 Returning to London's Prince of Wales's Theatre, *The Co-Optimists* revue enjoys its third successful season. This time there are 210 performances.

Nov 9 *Gold.* See NY premiere, 1921.

Nov 20 *Dulcy.* See NY premiere, 1921.

Dec 3 *The Rising Generation* (L—Shaftesbury—Comedy). Wyn Weaver and Laura Leycester's play suggests what would happen if children governed their schools and homes. The ensemble includes Sybil

Carlisle, Lawrence Hanray, E. Holman Clark, and Joan Barry. It runs for 237 performances.

Dec 20 *Madame Pompadour* (L—Daly's—Musical). Leo Fall's music is given British lyrics by Harry Graham, who collaborates with Frederick Lonsdale on an English book. Bertram Wallis plays Louis XV, with Evelyn Laye as Pompadour. Fred J. Blackman directs; settings are by Joseph and Phil Harker and Alfred Terraine. There are 467 performances.

1923 REVIVALS/REPERTORIES

Jan 8 The Moscow Art Theatre opens a January–February season of repertory at New York's 59th Street Theatre. They play Chekhov's *The Three Sisters* and *The Cherry Orchard*, Gorky's *The Lower Depths*, Tolstoi's *Czar Fyodor Ivanovitch*, and Turgenyev's *The Lady from the Provinces*. In the large ensemble are the troupe's founder, Constantin Stanislavsky, Olga Knipper-Tchekhova, Leonid Leonidoff, Olga Tarasova, Maria Ouspenskaya, Akim Tamiroff, and Nikolai Podgorny. The *NY Times* praises Stanislavsky's handling of *The Lower Depths*. "Students of ensemble acting will do well to give their attention, as coldly as they may, to the small riot of the third act, the climax and the dissolution of the dramatic action—the single scene that takes place out of doors. The thronged assembly in the court of Tsar Fyodor is a primer lesson in comparison. Stanislavsky's handling of the climax would well reward separate hearings for detached observations on its varying tempo, its groupings, its facial expressions and, above all, its vocal colorings."

Jan 9 In Dublin at the Abbey Theatre, the Dublin Drama League premieres J. B. McCarthy's *The Long Road to Garranbraher*. On Oct 1, Sean O'Casey's *Cathleen Listens In* opens, followed on Oct 21, by a translation of Martinez Sierra's *The Kingdom of God*.

Jan 24 Jane Cowl and Rollo Peters, as Romeo and Juliet, enjoy 157 performances, in Shakespeare's tragedy at New York's Henry Miller Theatre. This far outdistances Ethel Barrymore's 29 performances.

Jan 28 In London, the Phoenix Society revives John Ford's Jacobean tragedy, *'Tis Pity She's a Whore* at the Shaftesbury Theatre. On June 29, at the Regent Theatre, the play is Ben Jonson's *Volpone*. On Nov 18, also at the Regent, the Phoenix revives Christopher Marlowe's *Edward II*.

Jan 29 Robert Atkins stages *Henry VI, Part 1* at London's Old Vic Theatre for Lilian Baylis. Tonight, the first half of *Henry VI, Part 2* is also played. On Feb 12, *Henry VI, Part 2*—second half—and *Henry VI, Part 3* are staged by Atkins. *Titus Andronicus* is premiered on Oct 8, followed by *Troilus and Cressida* on Nov 5. With this production, the Old Vic Shakespeare Canon Cycle is complete.

Feb 5 At London's Garrick Theatre, Hugo von Hofmannsthal's *Jedermann*—adapted into English—has 21 performances, with John Martin-Harvey in the leading role. His wife, Nina de Silva, plays Good Deeds in this production, titled *Via Crucis*.

Feb 5 Henrik Ibsen's dramatic poem, *Peer Gynt* with the music composed for it by Edvard Greig, is presented by the adventurous Theatre Guild at the Garrick in New York. Theodore Komisarjevsky stages a large cast, including Selena Royle, Joseph Schildkraut, Dudley Digges, Helen Westley, Armina Marshall, Edward G. Robinson, and Rommey Brent. The production runs 15 weeks. "Komisarjevsky reduces the material portion of his investiture to a minimum . . . .But there is no parsimony practiced in the matter of atmospheric beauty in lighting, of varied richness in costume, and of skill in the acting and stage management," reports the *NY Times*.

Feb 12 *The Rolling Stones of 1924*, a revue, opens in Brixton at the Empress Theatre.

Feb 18 At the Lyric, Hammersmith, the Incorporated Stage Society presents Georges Duhamel's French comedy, *The Mental Athletes*.

March 12 At London's Old Vic, the poetic drama, *Arthur*, is presented. It's the work of Lawrence Binyon, in association with John Martin-Harvey, with music by Edward Elgar. Wilfrid Walter plays King Arthur, to Florence Buckton's Gwenevere.

March 12 Charles Rann Kennedy calls *The Chastening* a "modern miracle play," but it is clearly a reworking of the tale of Jesus disputing in the temple as a lad, to the amazement of Mary and Joseph. Presented by the Equity Players at New York's 48th Street Theatre, the production has only 19 performances. It features Kennedy, his wife Edith Wynne Matthison, and Margaret Gage as the thinly disguised Jesus.

March 24 Gladys Cooper revives Hermann Sudermann's German drama *Heimath* in Louis N. Parker's British version, *Magda*, for 128 performances.

April 8 Dickens' novel, *Nicholas Nickleby*, is dramatized for the Kinema Club and presented by Clive Currie at the King's Hall, Covent Garden.

April 10 At New York's 48th Street Theatre, Maurice Schwartz, star of the Yiddish theatre, produces *Anathema*, Leonid Andreyev's Russian fantasy and plays David Leizer, the man whom, Satan-Anathema (Ernest Glendinning) uses to turn people against God. It is followed by Gogol's *The Inspector General*, with Schwartz as the clerk who is mistaken for the official.

April 12 Sean O'Casey's *Shadow of a Gunman* has its world premiere in Dublin at the Abbey Theatre.

April 23 *Measure for Measure* is the "birthday play" in the four-week spring season at the Shakespeare Memorial Theatre in Stratford-upon-Avon. The other plays are *Richard III*, *The Merry Wives of Windsor*, *A Midsummer Night's Dream*, *Macbeth*, and Goldsmith's *She Stoops to Conquer*. W. Bridges Adams directs the festival and the productions, usually designing them as well.

April 23 Augustus Thomas and the Producing Manager's Association of New York, founding an American National Theatre ensemble, present a revival of *As You Like It*. Robert Milton directs an impressive cast, including Ian Keith, Marjorie Rambeau, Margalo Gillmore, Walter Abel, and Mercedes de Cordoba. The production lasts a week.

May 7 Determined to attract audiences, the Equity Players revive Sheridan's *The Rivals* at New York's 48th Street Theatre. The production runs three weeks. Eva LeGallienne, Vivian Tobin, James T. Powers, Mary Shaw, Violet Heming, Francis Wilson, Maclyn Arbuckle, McKay Morris, J. M. Kerrigan, John Craig, and Sidney Blackmer are in the company.

May 7 At New York's Nora Bayes Theatre, Walter Hartwig launches a week-long Little Theatre Tournament, with groups from New York, New Jersey, and Connecticut offering one-act plays. There are three $100 prizes and a David Belasco Trophy, which is won by the East-West Players of Manhattan.

May 7 The Ethiopian Art Theatre from Chicago presents a double bill in New York at the Frazee Theatre for eight performances. The plays are Oscar Wilde's *Salome* and a black folk-comedy, *The Chip Woman's Fortune*.

May 18 The Equity Players' production of Paul Kester's play *Sweet Nell of Old Drury* at the 48th Street Theatre runs beyond the season. Alfred Lunt is Charles II of England, with Laurette Taylor as his mistress, Nell Gwynne. Taylor's husband, J. Hartley Manners stages. Lynn Fontanne is Lady Castlemaine. Howard Lindsay is also in the ensemble.

May 19 Franz Lehar's *The Merry Widow* is revived in London at Daly's Theatre, with Evelyn Laye and Carl Brisson starring. The impressive sets are by the Harkers and Alfred Terraine. There are 222 performances.

May 24 This revival of J. M. Barrie's *What Every Woman Knows*, staged at London's

Apollo Theatre, has a run of 269 performances. Hilda Trevelyan and Godfrey Tearle play the leads.

June 4 The Players revive Sheridan's *The School for Scandal* for a week at New York's Lyceum Theatre. Ethel Barrymore is Lady Teazle. The all star cast includes John Drew, Francis Wilson, Henry E. Dixey, Etienne Girardot, Walter Hampden, and Caroll McComas.

June 4 Sacha Guitry opens his London season at the New Oxford Theatre with *Un Sujet de Roman* and *Comment on Ecrit l'Histoire*, supported by Lucien Guitry and Yvonne Printemps. On June 11, the play is *Le Veilleur de Nuit*, and on June 18, *Nono*, which is padded out with songs by Printemps and some stories told by Sacha Guitry. There are also some special matinees of Ibsen's *The Lady from the Sea (La Donna del Mare)* and *Ghosts (Spettri)*, starring Eleanora Duse, during the Guitry run. June 7 is the first of these.

June 6 At London's Lyceum Theatre, Dickens' *David Copperfield*, adapted by Walter Evelyn, has 30 performances.

July 10 John Masefield's play, *Melloney Holtspur; Or, The Pangs of Love*, opens the "Playbox matinees" in London at St. Martin's Theatre. The cast includes such favorites as Meggie Albanesi, Mary Jerrold, Malcolm Keen, Laura Cowie, and Ian Hunter.

July 21 The Birmingham Repertory Theatre opens its 12 season with J. M. Barrie's *The Professor's Love Story*.

The five-week summer season at the Shakespeare Memorial Theatre in Stratford-upon-Avon includes *Measure for Measure, Macbeth, Richard III, The Merry Wives of Windsor, A Midsummer Night's Dream*, and *She Stoops to Conquer*, all revived from the spring season. Also offered are *The Taming of the Shrew, Henry VI, Part 1*, and *Much Ado About Nothing*. These are followed by the Birmingham Repertory's productions of Drinkwater's *Mary Stuart* and Shaw's *Getting Married* and *Heartbreak House*.

Aug 15 J. M. Barrie's *The Will* is revived in London at St. Martin's Theatre, paired with *The Likes of Her*, for a run of 226 performances.

Sep 1 The Birmingham Repertory Theatre presents the English premiere of Lenonid Andreyev's *The Dear Departing*.

Sep 29 At London's New Theatre, Sybil Thorndike and Lewis Casson revive Shakespeare's *Cymbeline*. George Foss is Cymbeline. The production lasts three weeks.

Oct 2 E. H. Sothern and Julia Marlowe revive Shakespeare's *Cymbeline* in New York at the Jolson Theatre, with Sothern as Posthumous and Marlowe as Imogen. It runs less than two weeks, but is followed by other productions from their repertory such as *Hamlet, Twelfth Night, The Taming of the Shrew, Romeo and Juliet*, and *The Merchant of Venice*.

Oct 8 At London's Old Vic, Shakespeare's *Titus Andronicus* is revived by the resident company.

Oct 8 The Theatre Guild production of John Galsworthy's *Windows* runs only six weeks at New York's Garrick Theatre. In the cast are Henry Travers, Phyllis Povah, George Baxter, Frieda Inescourt, and Helen Westley.

Oct 15 From their own Paris playhouse the actors of the Grand Guignol Theatre come to New York with a mixed repertory of humor and horror. Their seven-week run is less than they had planned. For one week of the run, they are joined by Alla Nazimova. She has been banned from the Keith Vaudeville Circuit because her sketch, *The Unknown*, has been judged too bold.

Oct 16 W. B. Yeats's "poetic farce," *The Player Queen*, has 49 performances. It is paired with George Bernard Shaw's *The Shewing-Up of Blanco Posnet*. Part of a tenth subscription season, the bill is presented by the Neighborhood Players, including Esther Mitchell, Aline MacMahon, and Joanna Roos in New York.

Oct 25 Martin Harvey opens his brief New York season at the Century Theatre with the Gilbert Murray translation of Sophocles' *Oedipus Rex*, with incidental music by W. H. Hudson. He also offers *Hamlet, Via Crucis*, and *The Burgomaster of Stilemonde*.

Nov 1 Walter Hampden appears as Cyrano de Bergerac at the National Theatre in New York. Edmond Rostand's "poetic comedy" has been translated by Brian C. Hooker. The production, staged by the star, runs through and beyond the season. It uses Walter Damrosch's score for his opera *Cyrano* as incidental music. Carroll McComas is Roxanne.

Nov 5 At London's Kingsway Theatre, Shakespeare's *Twelfth Night* is revived by Donald Calthrop for 54 performances. On Nov 13, *A Midsummer Night's Dream* is offered at matinees, for 21 performances.

Nov 19 The Moscow Art Theatre returns for a second season in New York, opening with *The Brothers Karamazoff*. They return to Jolson's 59th Street Theatre in Jan 1924, and to the Imperial Theatre in May 1924. With a repertory of Chekhov, Ibsen, Tolstoi, Dostoievsky, Goldoni, Ostrovsky, Gorki, Schedrin, and Hamsun, they have 97 performances.

Nov 24 The Birmingham Repertory Company presents George Kaiser's German drama, *Gas*, translated by Hermann Scheffauer.

Nov 26 For two weeks, Arthur Hopkins revives his recent production of *Hamlet*, starring John Barrymore, this time shown in New York's Manhattan Opera House. $30,000 is taken in in one week.

Dec 3 *Andre Charlot's London Revue of 1924* opens at the Hippodrome in Golder's Green.

Dec 19 At Wyndham's Theatre in London, William Makepeace Thackeray's *The Rose and the Ring*, a "pantomime for great and small children," opens for a holiday run of 42 performances. In the cast are such actors as Raymond Massey, Hugh Sinclair, Johnny Danvers, Miles Malleson, and Evadne Price, as Princess Angelica.

Dec 22 Nigel Playfair revives *The Merry Wives of Windsor* at the Lyric, Hammersmith, for the holiday season.

Dec 26 With *This Fine-Pretty World* Percy MacKaye attempts a folk-drama of rural Kentucky. A husband (Gilly Maggot) is eager to be rid of his wife, but the wife (Aline MacMahon) outsmarts him in a court trial. The Neighborhood Players have a 33-performance run with this show at the Neighborhood Playhouse.

Dec 26 Boxing Day comes round, and London's Aldwych Theatre revives *Bluebell in Fairyland* for 32 performances. At the Lyceum, the Christmas panto is *Jack and the Beanstalk*. *The Windmill Man* returns to the Victoria Palace. Before Christmas, the Comedy has revived *Charley's Aunt*; the Adelphi, *Peter Pan*; the Garrick, *The Bluebird*; the Palladium, *Dick Whittington*; the Strand, *Treasure Island*, and the Holborn Empire, *Where the Rainbow Ends*.

1923 BIRTHS/DEATHS/DEBUTS

Jan 7 Future actor Vincent Gardenia is born Vincenzio Scognamiglio in Naples, Italy.

Jan 29 Playwright-director-producer Paddy Chayefsky is born in New York City.

Feb 27 Luther Adler, born Lutha Adler, makes his Broadway debut as the mature Leon Kantor in Fannie Hurst's comedy-drama, *Humoresque*, at the Vanderbilt Theatre. He had previously appeared with the Provincetown Players as Lutha Adler.

March 22 Marcel Marceau is born in Strasbourg, France, to Charles and Anne Mangel.

March 26 French actress Sarah Bernhardt (b. 1844) dies in Paris. Bernhardt began her training for the stage at age thirteen. Her double triumph as Cordelia in a French version of *King Lear* and the queen in *Ruy Blas* at the *Comedie-Francaise* in 1872 brought her to the head of her profession. Her American and European tours were many and successful. She was also an accomplished painter and sculptor.

Sarah Bernhardt

May 5 American actor Frank Finley Mackay dies in Coytesville, New Jersey at age 92. Mackay, a teacher of elocution, appeared with Mrs. John Drew's company and later managed Philadelphia's Chestnut Street Theatre. He also appeared with De Wolf Hopper and William H. Crane. Mackay founded the National Congress of Dramatic Art.

May 7 American actress and singer Sadie Martinot (b. 1861) dies in Ogdensburg, New York. Martinot began her stage career in 1876 as Cupid in a revival of *Ixion*. She was the original American Hebe in *H. M. S. Pinafore*.

June 15 On the traditional day marking the end of the current 1922–23 Broadway season, critic Burns Mantle selects his *Best Plays*. During the season, 180 new plays and revivals have been produced. Mantle's list includes: *Rain*, by John Colton and Clemence Randolph; *Loyalities*, by John Galsworthy; *You and I*, by Philip Barry; *Icebound*, by Owen Davis; *The Fool*, by Channing Pollock; *Mary the 3rd*, by Rachel Crothers; *R. U. R.*, by Karel Capek; *The Old Soak*, by Don Marquis; *Merton of the Movies*, by George S. Kaufmann and Marc Connelly, and *Why Not?*, by Jesse Lynch Williams. Mantle says of the season just concluded that if it "does not recommend itself to future historians of the theatre as the most notable of a generation, it should at least be given credit for being the first theatrical season in a generation that has not been described as "the worst in years." Of the 180 productions, 70 were dramas, 69 comedies, 31 musicals, and 10 revues. Failure seems to have been the lot of 135 shows (75%), with only 45 (25%) successful.

June 26 American comedian Bert Savoy is killed by lightning in Long Beach, New York. Savoy toured the United States and Alaska as a female impersonator. He also appeared in the *Ziegfeld Follies* and the *Greenwich Village Follies*. His age was

35.

July 30 British actor-manager Sir Charles Hawtrey (b. 1858) dies in London. Hawtrey made his first stage appearance under the name of Banks. In 1884, he produced *The Private Secretary*, in which he played Douglas Cattermole. Sir Charles was knighted in 1922.

Aug 27 English actress and dancer Letty Lind (b. 1862) is dead. Lind first appeared on stage at the Theatre Royal in Birmingham in 1867, as Eva in *Uncle Tom's Cabin*. In 1887, she joined the Gaiety Company to play in *Monte Cristo, Jr.*, and subsequently toured in America and Australia.

Aug 29 American producer and educator Franklyn H. Sargent is dead in Plattsburgh, New York. Sargent was head of the Sargent School of Dramatic Art in New York.

Sep 17 Florence Reed plays an aged Parisian harlot in *The Lullaby*, a British play by Edward Knoblock. She also impersonates the woman years before, showing how she was dragged down into her present state. The production attracts for 18 weeks at the Knickerbocker Theatre in New York.

Sep 26 Australian actor of stage and screen, Jerome Patrick, is dead in New York at age 40. Patrick was leading man to actresses Frances Starr and Emily Stevens. He last appeared with Alice Brady in *Zander the Great*.

Sep 26 Katherine Cornell plays the great love of the Great Lover's life in *Casanova*. Sidney Howard adapts the original play of Lorenzo de Azertis, but it runs only slightly over nine weeks at the Empire in New York.

Oct 9 Edith Evans debuts with the Birmingham Repertory Theatre in the English premiere of Shaw's *Back to Methuselah*.

Oct 29 Mae Barnes makes her Broadway debut as a singer-dancer in the musical comedy, *Running Wild*, at the Colonial Theatre.

Nov 8 American actor James O'Neill, Jr. dies in Trenton, New Jersey at age 43. He was the son of the late James O'Neill and brother of playwright Eugene O'Neill.

Nov 13 In *The Camel's Back*, W. Somerset Maugham creates a house-tyrant (Charles Cherry) who is subdued by a clever wife (Violet Kemble Cooper). This British import lasts only 15 performances in New York.

Nov 28 English comedian Tom McNaughton (b. 1867) dies in London. McNaugton played mostly in America after 1909, notably in *The Spring Maid*. He was the brother of comedians Fred and Gus McNaughton.

Nov 29 Eleanora Duse, the celebrated Italian actress, makes a farewell appearance on the stage of the Metropolitan Opera House, in Ibsen's *The Lady from the Sea*. She completes the week at the Century Theatre, with D'Annunzio's *La Citta Morta*, Ibsen's *Ghosts*, Gallarati-Scotti's *Cosi Sia*, and Praga's *La Porta Chiusa*. (She dies in Pittsburgh, near the scheduled close of her farewell tour.)

Dec 5 English actor Herbert Standing (b. 1846) dies in Los Angeles. Standing played in *Katherine and Petruchio* with Henry Irving and Ellen Terry. He was the father of Wyndham, Sir Guy, Percy, and Aubrey Standing.

1923 THEATERS/PRODUCTIONS

In Britain, patents are granted for: J. R. Robertson's apparatus for producing sound from photographic film, which in turn activates illumination in gas-tubes; B. Dean's cylindrical slides, illuminated from within, to produce a moving effect when rotated.

Max Hasait receives a U.S. patent for his system of moveable scenic panels which can alter the shape and size of a proscenium opening.

April 21 The Hedgerow Repertory Theatre, headed by Jaspar Deeter, opens its first season with *Candida*, by Bernard Shaw. Working in Moylan Rose Valley, Pennsylvania, Deeter and his permanent acting company of 25 intend to present modern classics in repertory.

July 5 The Earl Carroll Theatre, on the Southeast corner of 7 Avenue and 15 Street in New York, opens with the musical revue, *Earl Carroll's Vanities of 1923*. The owner, song-writer Earl Carroll, is forced to give-up the theatre during the Depression. In the 1930's, the theatre is converted into a theatre-restaurant called the Casa Manana.

Aug The Dunbar Theatre in Philadelphia, a black playhouse, is in financial trouble. Application for a receiver is filed.

Sep 12 In the published version of W. Somerset Maugham's play, *Our Betters*, an American girl accidentally encounters her married sister with a lover, ambiguously amorous in a summer house. It was played that way in America. Before the play could be licensed for public performance in London, however, the Lord Chamberlain has required Maugham to alter the playtext so an unrelated gentleman can make this unpleasant discovery.

Dec 24 The Shuberts open the Imperial Theatre (1,650 seats) on West 46th Street, with an entrance on West 45th Street in New York City. Herbert J. Krapp is the architect of this theatre, designed for musical attractions.

I'll Say She Is

Jan 4 *Hell-Bent for Heaven* (NY—Klaw—Drama). Hatcher Hughes sets his Pulitzer Prize-winning play about feuding clans in the Blue Ridge Mountains. The cast includes George Abbott; Glenn Anders, Clara Blandick, and John F. Hamilton. The production runs over 15 weeks.

Jan 9 *Andre Charlot's Revue of 1924* (NY—Time Square—Revue). Selected from the best of several London editions, the revue features three performers, Jack Buchanan, Gertrude Lawrence, and Beatrice Lillie—who are immediate hits with the public. Lawrence sings "Limehouse Blues." Lillie delights with comic routines. The show runs beyond the season, setting a pattern for more intimate, more witty, less lavish revues. The *NY Times* praises Lillie saying: "There is no one in New York quite comparable to [her] . . ."

Jan 15 *The Miracle* (NY—Century—Drama). This Max Reinhardt spectacle has enjoyed several European productions. It is presented in a theatre turned into the appearance of a gothic cathedral by designer Norman Bel Geddes. Performed in pantomime, the Karl Vollmoeller script tells the tale of a nun who flees into the sinful world. The image of the Madonna takes her place. Lady Diana Manners and Rosamund Pinchot star. It runs beyond the season.

Jan 21 *Lollipop* (NY—Knickerbocker—Musical). Vincent Youmans writes his first full show score, to a Zelda Sears book in which Laura Lamb (Ada May), an orphan, finds happiness. It runs 19 weeks.

Jan 21 *Sweet Little Devil* (NY—Astor—Musical). With a George Gershwin score, this show wins a 15-week run. The book, by Frank Mandel and Laurence Schwab, sets up Tom Nesbitt, a mining engineer in Peru, as the dupe of a money-hungry Follies girl. He opts for her sweet little roommate (Constance Binney) who has actually been writing her love-letters.

Jan 22 *Mr. Pitt* (NY—39th Street—Drama) Zona Gale's play is about Marshall Pitt, a small-town salesman, whose wife thinks him a fool and deserts him for a jazz trombonist. He goes to the Klondike and comes back richer, but his wife never returns. His son, now in college, is also embarrassed by him. Walter Huston plays Pitt; his son is played by Borden Harriman. Others in the cast include Antoinette Perry and Parker Fennelly. The play runs 11 weeks.

Jan 29 *The Goose Hangs High* (NY—Bijou—Drama). Lewis Beach's play runs beyond the season. It deals with a midwestern family whose children prove, when family problems threaten the parents, that they are resourceful and thoughtful despite first appearances.

Feb 5 *The Show-Off* (NY—Playhouse—Comedy). Author George Kelly's boastful Aubrey Piper (Louis John Bartels) becomes a classic American stereotype.

Feb 12 *Beggar on Horseback* (NY—Broadhurst—Comedy). George S. Kaufman and Marc Connelly's comedy about the dream of a harried young composer features Osgood Perkins and Spring Byington. The show runs beyond the season's close. On May 7, 1925, it opens at London's Queen's with A.E. Matthews and Dorothy Tetley. It has 80 performances.

March 3 *Fata Morgana* (NY—Garrick—Drama). The Theatre Guild presents Ernest Vajda's tale of youthful seduction and almost immediate disillusion at the hands of an older, married woman. Emily Stevens and Morgan Farley are featured. The production runs beyond the season. On Sep 15, 1924, the play opens at London's Ambassadors' with a cast including Roger Livesey and Flora Robson. There are 243 performances.

March 3 *The Outsider* (NY—49th Street—Drama). Katherine Cornell plays the crippled daughter of a surgeon. Her cure on a special stretching rack silences opposition to its effectiveness. She falls in love with its untrained inventor (Lionel Atwill). This production has a 13-week run. Dorothy Brandon is the playwright.

March 17 *Welded* (NY—39th Street—Drama). In Eugene O'Neill's drama, a couple find their marriage stronger than they thought. Doris Keane and Jacob Ben-Ami star. The play lasts three weeks. On Feb 16, 1928, it is given at London's Playroom Six.

March 27 *Vogues of 1924* (NY—Shubert—Revue). *Rain* is parodied, and Fred Allen and Jimmy Savo clown. This Shubert entertainment runs almost three months.

May 19 *I'll Say She Is* (NY—Casino—Revue). The zany stars of this show, with book by Will B. Johnstone and music by Tom Johnstone, are billed as Herbert, Leonard, Julius, and Arthur Marx, but they are better known as Zeppo, Chico, Groucho, and Harpo. Beginning with a reference to the act of their Uncle Al Shean, of Gallagher and Shean, they move on to murder, courtroom mayhem, and Napoleon and Josephine. The show is a hit, continuing beyond the season.

May 22 *Keep Kool* (NY—Morosco—Revue). Taking a cue from Calvin Coolidge's campaign slogan, this revue features the talents of Hazel Dawn and Charles King. One skit shows how O'Neill, Cohan, and Hopwood would variously dramatize the same story.

June 16 *So This Is Politics* (NY—Henry Miller—Comedy). Barry Connors' tale of a woman running for mayor of a small midwestern town is also known by a more suggestive title: *Strange Bedfellows*. The ambitious woman provokes a scandal, both at home and in the community, when she gets the support of a political boss of some notoriety. With Glenn Anders, Marjorie Gateson, and William Courtleigh, the show has 144 performances, despite the hot weather.

June 24 *The Ziegfeld Follies* (NY—New Amsterdam—Revue). Julian Mitchell stages this edition, which runs for 401 performances. It opens with Will Rogers, the Tiller Girls, Lupino Lane, Vivienne Segal, Glora Dawn, Brandon Tynan, and Ann Pennington. In the fall, the Russian Lilliputians are added. In the spring, Ray Dooley and W. C. Fields join the ensemble.

June 30 *George White's Scandals of 1924* (NY—Apollo—Revue). *Abie's Irish Rose* provides fit matter for parody. George Gershwin's "Somebody Loves Me," introduced by Winnie Lightner, proves popular. The show has 192 performances.

Aug 11 *Dancing Mothers* (NY—Booth—Comedy). Edgar Selwyn and Edmund Goulding write this comedy about a young woman whose mother has gone off to satisfy her urge for fun. Helen Hayes stars. It runs for 39 weeks. On March 17, 1924, it opens at London's Queen's with Jean Forbes-Robertson. The play earns 110 performances.

Aug 20 *The Dream Girl* (NY—Ambassador—Musical). Featuring Victor Herbert's last score, this show is produced posthumously and runs less than 15 weeks. Fay Bainter plays Elspeth, who becomes fascinated with the idea of reincarnation and dreams herself back in the 15th century. Walter Woolf plays her lover in both past and present. Rida Johnson Young and Harold Atteridge provide the libretto.

Sep 1 *Pigs* (NY—Little—Comedy). Anne Morrison and Paterson McNutt's play runs for 39 weeks. It features Wallace Ford as a young man who buys sick pigs cheap and sells them for a good profit when he has cured them.

Sep 1 *The Chocolate Dandies* (NY—Colonial—Musical). Noble Sissle and Lew Payton devise the book, with music and lyrics by Eubie Blake and Sissle. Payton dreams his race-horse, Dumb Luck, has won the race—shown on stage with three horses on a treadmill—but, on waking, he finds a rival has won. Expensively mounted, the show irritates some critics who expect a black show to be more simple and naive in its presentation. The production runs only three months. Josephine Baker is in the cast.

Sep 2 *Rose-Marie* (NY—Imperial—Musical). The book, by Otto Harbach and Oscar Hammerstein II, has Rose-Marie save her Mountie from a false charge of murder. Rudolf Friml provides the score which includes "Indian Love Call" and "The Song of the Mounties." Mary Ellis and Dennis King are featured. The show has 557 performances. On March 20, 1925, it opens at London's Drury Lane with Edith Day and Derek Oldham. The production earns a long run of 851 performances.

Sep 3 *Be Yourself* (NY—Sam H. Harris—Musical). George S. Kaufman and Marc Connelly turn an unproduced play, *Miss Moonshine*, into a musical, with music by Lewis Gensler and Milton Schwarzwald. The authors reduce a hillbilly feud to the level of college athletics, with letters awarded for shootings. Queenie Smith plays the heroine with verve, but the show runs only 93 performances.

Sep 3 *What Price Glory?* (NY—Plymouth—Drama). With the Great War now receeding into memory, playwrights Maxwell Anderson and Lawrence Stallings enjoy a success (299 performances) with their portraits of Sgt. Quirt (William Boyd) and Captain Flagg (Louis Wolheim) in action, both as lovers and fighters. With its unusually rough language and direct treatment of Americans in combat, the play shocks some and wins the admiration of others for not romanticizing war. Also in the ensemble are Brian Donlevy, George Tobias, and Leyla Georgie: Stark Young of the *NY Times* extols the play. "The fundamental quality of 'What Price Glory?' is irony. Irony about life and about the war, but irony so incontrovertible in its aspect of truth and so blazing with vitality as to cram itself down the most spreadeagle of throats. The chaos, the irrelevance, the crass and foolish and disjointed relation of these men's lives and affairs to the war shows everywhere, and the relation of the war to their real interests and affairs. This is a war play without puerilities and retorts at God and society, and not febrile and pitying, but virile, fertile, poetic and Rabelaisian all at once, and seen with the imagination of the flesh and mind together."

Sep 3 *The Passing Show of 1924* (NY—Winter Garden—Revue). Earning only 93 performances, this edition marks the end of the series. James Barton and Lulu McConnell provide most of the comedy, which deals with flappers, Coolidge, Prohibition, and gangsters. J. C. Huffman

stages, with the customary supervision of J. J. Shubert.

Sep 10 *Earl Carroll's Vanities* (NY—Music Box—Revue). This show runs nearly 17 weeks, with Joe Cook providing comedy and Sophie Tucker belting out some songs with off-color lyrics. Carroll produces and stages the material; he also is responsible for the music and lyrics. One number features a nude girl riding on a pendulum, thus circumventing the rule that nudes cannot move on stage.

Sep 16 *The Greenwich Village Follies of 1924* (NY—Shubert—Revue). "The Two Black Crows," (George) Moran and (Charles) Mack, offer blackface comedy, while the Dolly Sisters (Rosie and Jennie) provide glamour, including a number in which they and some collies move in harmony. Oscar Wilde's *The Happy Prince* becomes this edition's "Ballet Ballad." Vincent Lopez and his orchestra play the Cole Porter score. John Murray Anderson stages the show, which runs four months.

Sep 17 *Hassard Short's Ritz Revue* (NY—Ritz—Revue). Raymond Hitchcock acts as master of ceremonies, while Charlotte Greenwood sparks the comedy and offers some eccentric, long-legged dancing. Short stages some elegant show numbers, one of which has notorious women of the past, such as Salome and Camille, saunter across the stage, dressed in scarlet. The production runs nearly 14 weeks.

Sep 22 *Hassan*. See L premiere, 1923.

Sep 23 *Grounds for Divorce* (NY—Empire—Comedy). Guy Bolton adapts Ernest Vajda's Hungarian play about a woman, married to a divorce lawyer, who threatens divorce to save her marriage. It runs for 127 performances. On Jan 21, 1925 the play opens at the St. James's in London with Madge Titheradge as the woman. There are 118 showings.

Sep 24 *Minick* (NY—Booth—Comedy). Writers George S. Kaufman and Edna Ferber collaborate for a run of 141 performances. O. P. Heggie plays Old Man Minick, who comes to live with his married son, upsetting the family routine and introducing some new problems. Phyllis Povah and Antoinette Perry are also in the cast.

Oct 6 *The Fake*. See L premiere, 1924.

Rose Marie

Oct 6 *The Grab Bag* (NY—Globe—Revue). Ed Wynn assembles and stars in this show, featuring his customary grotesque costumes and crazy inventions, including a typewriter carriage for eating corn-on-the-cob.

Oct 9 *The Farmer's Wife*. See L premiere, 1924.

Oct 13 *The Guardsman* (NY—Garrick—Comedy). Ferenc Molnar's play tells of a jealous actor-husband who disguises himself as a Russian guardsman to test his wife's supposed fragile fidelity. Alfred Lunt and Lynn Fontanne star. The show runs 31 weeks. On June 20, 1925, it premieres at London's St. James's with Seymour Hicks and Madge Titheradge. On this side of the Atlantic there are only 17 performances.

Oct 15 *Artists and Models* (NY—Astor—Revue). Nude models in frozen poses attract audiences for 261 performances. Trini performs vivid Spanish dances, and there are Charlestons and other jazz numbers as well. J. J. Shubert takes credit for the staging.

Oct 15 *The Firebrand* (NY—Morosco—Comedy). Selected by Burns Mantle as one of the season's *Best Plays*, Edwin Justus Mayer's drama wins 261 performances, with Joseph Schildkraut playing Benvenuto Cellini. It opens at London's Wyndham's on Feb 8, 1926, with Ivor Novello featured. The production lasts 10 weeks.

Oct 21 *Tiger Cats*. See L premiere, 1924.

Oct 29 *Dixie to Broadway* (NY—Broadhurst—Revue). Florence Mills delights audiences with her singing, dancing, and gyrations in "Jungle Nights in Dixieland." U. S. Thompson, Hamtree Harrington, and Maud Russell are also in this all-black revue. It runs for 77 performances.

Nov 4 *Annie Dear* (NY—Times Square—Musical). Florenz Ziegfeld produces this musical version of Clare Kummer's comedy, *Good Gracious, Annabelle*, with his wife Billie Burke as Annie, a free-spirited wife who has deserted her husband. Kummer has added the music and lyrics herself, with some help from Sigmund Romberg. In the cast are John Byam, May Vokes, Ernest Truex and Bobby Watson,

and others. The show runs for 103 performances.

Nov 11 *Desire Under the Elms* (NY—Greenwich Village—Drama). Eugene O'Neill's New England setting of the Hippolytus legend transfers to Broadway and wins 208 performances. Walter Huston, Charles Ellis and Mary Morris are featured. The *NY Times* describes one scene as "written with such poetry and terrible beauty as we rarely see in the theatre." On Feb 24, 1931, the play is given at London's Gate Theatre with Flora Robson and Eric Portman.

Nov 24 *They Knew What They Wanted* (NY—Garrick—Comedy). Sidney Howard's tale of life in the California wine country features Pauline Lord and Glenn Anders. It runs 24 weeks. On May 18, 1926, it opens at the West End at St. Martin's with Tallulah Bankhead and Anders. It has 110 showings.

Nov 24 *My Girl* (NY—Vanderbilt—Musical). Attempting to win social acceptance, the Bob Whites of Omaha, removed to the East, hold a non-alcoholic party. A bootlegger, trying to hide his stock, enlivens proceedings, making the Whites a success. The book and lyrics are the work of Harlan Thompson, the score is by Harry Archer. This show runs half a year.

Dec 1 *Lady, Be Good* (NY—Liberty—Musical). With lyrics by Ira and music by George Gershwin, the Guy Bolton-Fred Thompson book is a series of cliché complications for Fred and Adele Astaire as a brother and sister thrown out of their house and now awaiting better times. Among the songs are "Fascinating Rhythm." The show runs for 330 performances. It opens in London at the Empire on April 14, 1926, with the Astaires again in the lead. There are 326 showings.

Dec 1 *The Music Box Revue* (NY—Music Box—Revue). This Irving Berlin revue has 184 performances, but it lacks fresh musical material. James Reynolds designs; John Murray Anderson stages. The ensemble includes comics Fanny Brice and Bobby Clark. Helen Tamiris dances. Oscar Shaw and Grace Moore perform Berlin ballads. Claire Luce is also on hand.

Dec 2 *The Student Prince* (NY—Jolson—Musical). Based on the play *Old Heidelberg*, this show's book and lyrics are by Dorothy Donnelly, with a Sigmund Romberg score which includes the "Drinking Song." The story involves a prince who falls in love with a waitress. Howard Marsh and Ilse Marvenga are featured. There are 608 performances. On Feb 3, 1926, it premieres at His Majesty's in London with Marvenga and Allan Prior. There are only 96 showings.

Dec 2 *The Harem* (NY—Belasco—Comedy). David Belasco produces and directs this Hungarian play by Ernest Vajda, adapted by Avery Hopwood. Lenore Ulric plays Carla, who disguises herself as a harem favorite to test her husband's fidelity, which proves non-existant. This show runs for 183 performances.

Dec 22 *The Youngest* (NY—Gaiety—Comedy). Philip Barry's play has a 13-week run and is designated one of Burns Mantle's seasonal *Best Plays*. Once called *Poor Richard*, the play focuses on the revolt of the young son of the Winslow family, secure in their social position and assumptions. Henry Hull plays young Richard.

Dec 23 *Topsy and Eva* (NY—Sam H. Harris—Musical). After 43 weeks in Chicago, the Duncan Sisters arrive in Manhattan with this musical version of *Uncle Tom's Cabin*. Rosetta Duncan wears blackface to play Topsy; Vivian Duncan, as Eva, has golden curls. The show, with music and lyrics credited to the sisters, runs almost 20 weeks. The book is by Catherine Chisolm Cushing.

Dec 23 *Ladies of the Evening* (NY—Lyceum—Drama). David Belasco, as producer-director, salutes the holiday season with Milton Gropper's plot about a man (James Kirkwood) who bets he can turn a street-walker into a good woman in a year. Beth Merrill plays Kay Beatty, who proves his point. This runs nearly five months.

Dec 23 *Old English* (NY—Ritz—Drama). See L premiere, 1924.

Dec 29 *Seeniaya Ptitza* (NY—Frolic—Revue). Impressario Sol Hurok imports this Russian revue, called *The Blue Bird*, in hopes of rivaling the success of *Chauve Souris*. It runs only ten weeks.

1924   BRITISH PREMIERES

Jan 2 *Puppets* (L—Vaudeville—Revue). Ivor Novello provides the music for Dion Titheradge's book and lyrics. The cast includes Binnie Hale, Stanley Lupino, Arthur Chesney, and Paul England. The revue earns 254 showings.

Jan 16 *Havoc* (L—Haymarket—Drama). Despite fears that a war play will not attract audiences, Harry Wall's tale of female betrayal and soldierly conduct at the front in 1918 earns 171 performances. Frances Carson, Leslie Faber, and Henry Kendall play leads. Ethel Griffies, Norah Robinson, and Richard Bird are also in the cast. Faber directs for the Daniel Mayer Company. The play was shown in November by the Repertory Players at the Regent Theatre.

Jan 26 *The Three Graces* (L—Empire—Musical). Ben Travers adapts the original Lombardo and Willner book and lyrics for this Franz Lehar show, staged by Tom Reynolds. Thorpe Bates is the Duke of Nancy, eager to reclaim his castle from Countess Helene (Winifred Barnes), who believes she owns it. In the process, he is mistaken for a Parisian actor, to play Adonis in a castle fete, with Helene as Venus. Costumes are by Comelli and settings by the Harkers and H. Humphries. W. H. Berry plays the comic Bousquet, singing "Bambolina," with Morris Harvey as a Dutch comic. The show runs 121 performances.

Feb 1 *It Pays To Advertise* (L—Aldwych—Comedy). Roi Cooper Megrue and Walter Hackett's American farce (1914) earns a run of 598 performances, with Doris Kendal as Mary Grayson. Others in the cast include Ralph Lynn, Tom Walls, Will Deming, and J. Robertson Hare.

Feb 2 *The Way Things Happen*, (L—Ambassadors'—Drama). Clemence Dane's play seen first in America in Newark, has only 65 showings. In the ensemble are Haidee Wright, Hilda Bayley, Walter Hudd, Olga Lindo, Leslie J. Banks, and Robert Harris, among others.

March 11 *The Farmer's Wife* (L—Royal Court—Comedy). Eden Phillpotts's amusing tale of rural Devon is produced by Barry Jackson from the Birmingham Repertory—where it was premiered in 1916. Melville Cooper and Evelyn Hope are featured. There is a long run—1,324 performances. It comes to New York's Comedy on Oct 9, where it runs only 15 weeks.

March 13 *The Fake* (L—Apollo—Drama). Frederick Lonsdale's play about a man who poisons a despicable aristocrat rather than let him ruin the life of a woman runs 210 performances. The cast includes Hesketh Pearson, Allan Jeayes, Godfrey Tearle, and Franklyn Bellamy. It arrives at New York's Hudson on Oct 6, with Godfrey Tearle, Frieda Inescourt, and Orlando Daly. There is an 11-week run.

March 14 *The Whirl of the World* (L—Palladium—Revue). This show has music by Frederick Chappelle and lyrics by Donovan Parson. Albert de Courville, Edgar Wallace, and William Wells devise the sketches. In the company are Billy Merson, Nellie Wallace, Hilda Denton, Walter Williams, Nervo and Knox, and Nattavo and Myrrio. It runs 627 performances.

March 17 *Dancing Mothers.* See NY premiere, 1924.

March 20 *Leap Year* (L—Hippodrome—Revue). There are 471 showings for this revue, tried out in Liverpool at the Olympia. George Robey heads the cast, with such entertainers as Betty Chester, Laddie Cliff, Bernard Dudley, Noel Leyland, and Maud Fane. Laurie Wylie provides the book for Clifford Harris' score.

March 26 *Saint Joan.* See NY premiere, 1923.

April 16 *Our Nell* (L—Gaiety—Musical).

Jose Collins stars as Charles II's mistress. This show has a book by Louis N. Parker and Reginald Arkell and score by Harold Fraser-Simson and Ivor Novello. There are 140 performances, with sets by Harker and Terraine, and direction by Arthur Bourchier. In the company are Arthur Wontner, Robert Michaelis, Walter Passmore, Miles Malleson, Reginald Bach, Amy Augarde, Muriel Pope, and Espinosa, as an Irish Dancer. She also choreographs.

April 22 *To Have the Honour* (L—Wyndham's—Comedy). A. A. Milne's light entertainment runs for 207 performances. Gerald Du Maurier plays Prince Michael, while various ladies are played by Faith Celli, Madge Titheradge, Doris Cooper, Una Venning, Grace Lane, and Joan Clement Scott.

May 12 *Toni* (L—Shaftesbury—Musical). Jack Buchanan choreographs and Herbert Bryan directs this show, in which Buchanan is Toni, proprietor of a millinery salon. He falls in love with a princess, played by June. Harry Graham and Douglas Furber concoct the book, with lyrics by Furber and music by Hugo Hirsch. The show is played 248 times.

May 15 *White Cargo*. See NY premiere, 1923.

June 6 *In the Next Room*. See NY premiere, 1923.

June 9 *The Rat* (L—Prince of Wales'—Drama). Ivor Novello stars in the title-role of an apache dancer who kills the man seeking to seduce his beloved partner Odile (Dorothy Batley). But she is charged with the murder and acquitted, returning to the arms of the anguished apache. The play is advertised as written by "David L'Estrange," but Novello and Constance Collier—who stages—are its real authors. Ads advise: "Gentlemen (and Ladies), you may smoke." There are 283 performances.

June 11 *Yoicks* (L—Kingsway—Revue). This show, "edited" by John Hastings Turner, wins 271 performances. In the ensemble are Donald Calthrop, Marjorie Gordon, Mark Lester, Mary Leigh, and Sunday Wilshin.

June 27 *The Street Singer* (L—Lyric—Musical). Frederick Lonsdale's play has music by H. Fraser-Simson and lyrics by Percy Greenbank. Ivy St. Helier provides extra numbers. Phyllis Dare plays Yvette, the little street singer who is in love with the untalented, starving painter Bonni (Harry Welchman). She is really the Duchess of Versailles, so all ends well. E. Lyall Swete stages, with choreography by Fred Leslie and sets by Joseph and Phil Harker. There are 360 performances.

July 3 *Midsummer Madness* (L—Lyric, Hammersmith—Comedy). Clifford Bax's play, with music by Armstrong Gibbs, enjoys a run of 123 performances. Marie Tempest, Frederick Ranalow, Marjorie Dixon, and Hubert Eisdell are in the cast.

July 22 *The Creaking Chair* (L—Comedy—Drama). Tallulah Bankhead is Anita Latter in Allan Tupper Wilkes' "formula whodunit" first known as *The Man in the Wheel Chair*. Also in the cast are Nigel Bruce, Fabia Drake, C. Aubrey Smith, Eric Maturin, and Rita John, among others. This play wins 235 showings. *The Times* reports that ". . . Miss Tallulah Bankhead has a part so enigmatic as to be a perpetual irritation."

Aug 13 *Storm* (L—Ambassadors'—Comedy). C. K. Munro writes this comedy which wins 116 performances. Elissa Landi is Storm. Jean Cadell, Alan Napier, Hugh Wakefield, and Joyce Kennedy are among the cast.

Sep 4 *Poppy*. See NY premiere, 1923.

Sep 9 *The Sport of Kings* (L—Savoy—Comedy). Ian Hay's domestic comedy is good for a run of 319 performances. The cast includes Mary Jerrold, Basil Foster, Minnie Rayner, E. Holman Clark, and Ena Grossmith.

Sep 11 *Primrose* (L—Winter Garden—Musical). With a George Gershwin score, Desmond Carter lyrics, and a book by George Grossmith and Guy Bolton, this show has 255 performances. Some extra lyrics are by Ira Gershwin. Among the popular songs are "Boy Wanted," "Wait a Bit, Susie," and "Naughty Baby." Margery Hicklin and Percy Heming are featured in this story about a novelist writing the serial, *Primrose*.

Sep 15 *Fata Morgana*. See NY premiere, 1924.

Sep 17 *The Nervous Wreck*. See NY premiere, 1923.

Sep 18 *The Fool*. See NY premiere, 1922.

Sep 23 *Charlot's Revue* (L—Prince of Wales's—Revue). Ronald Jeans contributes the book to Andre Charlot's show; lyrics are by Noel Coward and Irving Caesar, among others, with Coward, Vincent Youmans, Dave Stamper, and others providing music. The revue runs for 518 performances. The cast includes Phyllis Monkman, Maisie Gay, Morris Harvey, Queenie Thomas, Peter Haddon, Juliette Compton, Dorothy Dolman, and Sybil Wise.

Oct 20 *The Pelican* (L—Ambassadors'—Drama). Herbert Marshall, Rosina Filippi, Josephine Victor, Fred Kerr, Charles Cherry, and Mabel Terry Lewis are in the

(Desire Under the Elms) Eugene O'Neill

ensemble of this play by F. Tennyson Jesse and H. M. Harwood. It is seen 244 times.

Oct 21 *Old English* (L—Haymarket—Drama). John Galsworthy's portrait of a rugged individualist opens with a cast including Irene Rooke, Joan Maude, Lawrence Hanray, Norman McKinnel and Louise Hampton. It premieres in New York at the Ritz on Dec 23, with George Arliss featured. It runs for 23 weeks.

Oct 31 *Patricia* (L—His Majesty's—Musical). Geoffrey Gwyther provides the music for this "Comedy with Music," by Denis Mackail, Arthur Stanley, and Austin Melford. Dorothy Dickson and Philip Simmons appear in this story about a woman who marries a poor inventor. Max Rivers, Cicely Debenham, Willie Warde, and Fay Martin are also in the cast. Dion Titheradge stages. There are 160 performances.

Nov 25 Noel Coward plays the lead, Nicky Lancaster, in *The Vortex*, which he's also written. It's produced in Hampstead at the Everyman Theatre, with Lilian Braithwaite as Nicky's mother, in love with the young former fiance of the girl Nicky hopes to marry, despite his drug problem. There are 12 performances. On Dec 16, the play opens in the West End at the Royalty Theatre for a run of 224 performances. On Sep 16, 1925, it opens at New York's Henry Miller Theatre with Coward and Braithwaite again in the leads. There are 157 performances.

Dec 15 *Just Married* (L—Comedy—Comedy). Ann Nichols and Adelaide Matthews collaborate on this farce about people in the wrong staterooms. It runs 421 performances. Leonard Thompson and Leila Langley are in the cast.

1924 REVIVALS/REPERTORIES

Feb 4 At London's Prince's Theatre, the D'Oyly Carte Opera season opens for a run of 200 performances.

Feb 5 The Everyman Theatre in Hampstead stages *The Mask and the Face*, the Italian comedy of Luigi Chiarelli, translated by C. B. Fernald. It's revived at the Criterion on May 27, and then moved to the Comedy for a total of 230 performances.

Feb 7 Nigel Playfair revives Congreve's *The Way of the World* at the Lyric, Hammersmith, for a run of 150 performances.

Feb 19 At New York's Lyceum Theatre, *Antony and Cleopatra* is revived for 31 performances, with Rollo Peters and Jane

Cowl in the title roles.

March 3 Sean O'Casey's *Juno and the Paycock* has its world premiere in Dublin at the Abbey Theatre.

March 8 Sardou's *Dora* is revived in its English version, *Diplomacy*, in London at the Adelphi Theatre. Co-manager Gladys Cooper plays Dora, supported by Owen Nares, Dawson Milward, and Norman Forbes. The production runs for 365 performances.

April 21 *The Merry Wives of Windsor* opens the annual spring season of Shakespeare's plays in Stratford-upon-Avon at the Memorial Theatre. *King Lear* is the "birthday play," with Arthur Phillips as Lear. This tragedy has not been performed at Stratford since 1906. Other plays presented are *Othello, The Merchant of Venice, The Taming of the Shrew, Hamlet, A Midsummer Night's Dream,* and Sheridan's *The School for Scandal*. W. Bridges Adams is the director of the festival and the plays.

May 5 For one week, Walter Hartwig conducts the second annual Little Theatre Tournament at New York's Belasco Theatre. Again, troupes from New York, New Jersey, and Connecticut are the main competitors, but the Belasco Trophy goes to the Little Theatre Company of Dallas, Texas.

May 18 In London at the New Theatre, Ernst Toller's *Man and the Masses*, translated by Louis Untermeyer, is presented by the Incorporated Stage Society.

May 20 At New York's Neighborhood Playhouse, the Neighborhood Players stage *The Grand Street Follies*. Albert Carroll burlesques John Barrymore, Elsie Janis, and Jeanne Eagels. Agnes Morgan devises book and lyrics, with music by Lily Hyland. Neighborhood Players, resting from more serious dramas during the season, include Aline MacMahon and Joanna Roos.

May 28 Tonight's revival of Lehar's *The Merry Widow*, staged in London at the Lyceum Theatre, earns a run of 223 performances.

June 9 The Players revive Goldsmith's *She Stoops to Conquer* for one week at New York's Empire Theatre. In the distinguished cast are Helen Hayes, Selena Royle, Pauline Lord, Elsie Ferguson, and Effie Shannon.

June 25 Karen Bramson has adapted *Tiger Cats* from *Les Felines*, by Michael Orme. It deals with a sensuous woman who is rejected by her scientist husband. The show, given a matinee today at London's Savoy, eventually has 121 performances. Edith Evans and Robert Loraine are featured. On Oct 21, it comes to the Belasco on Broadway with Katharine Cornell as the wife. The production runs six weeks.

July 14 In Stratford-upon-Avon, the six-week summer season at the Shakespeare Memorial Theatre opens with *The Taming of the Shrew*. Also revived from the spring season are *King Lear, The Merry Wives of Windsor, The Merchant of Venice, Hamlet, A Midsummer Night's Dream,* and Sheridan's *The School for Scandal*. There are new productions of *Richard II* and *Antony and Cleopatra*.

July 16 *Sweeney Todd* opens in New York at the Frazee. This British melodrama, dating back at least to 1842, and credited to George Dibdin Pitt, is revived for 67 performances. Robert Vivian plays the Demon Barber of Fleet Street. Mrs. Lovett, the maker of meat pies, is played by Raphaella Ottiano.

Sep 2 For their fourth successful season, *The Co-Optimists* move to London's Palace Theatre for a 26-week run.

Sep 8 At the Abbey Theatre in Dublin, T. C. Murray's drama of Irish rural life, *Autumn Fire*, opens. On Sep 29, the new play is Sean O'Casey's one-act comedy of Dublin low-life, *Nannie's Night Out*.

Oct 5 Rudyard Kipling's one-act play, *Gow's Watch*, with Victor Lewisohn as Gow, is presented in London by the First Studio Theatre in Belgrave Square.

Oct 23 At the Lyric, Hammersmith, Nigel Playfair revives Sheridan's comic opera, *The Duenna*, with Linley's music arranged by Alfred Reynolds. In the company are Elsa Lanchester, Angela Baddeley, Elsie French (the Duenna), and Playfair, as Don Jerome. There are 141 performances.

Oct 27 Arthur Hopkins revives Arthur Wing Pinero's *The Second Mrs. Tanqueray* at the Cort Theatre in New York, providing a vehicle for Ethel Barrymore as Paula, the second wife whose "past" prevents her from being accepted socially or by her step-daughter. Henry Daniell plays her devoted husband. The production runs only nine weeks.

Oct 27 At the Everyman Theatre in Hampstead, George Bernard Shaw's *Misalliance* is revived. On Dec 26, Shaw's *The Philanderer* is produced.

Nov 3 Four sea-plays by Eugene O'Neill are linked by a narrative thread. They are *Moon of the Caribbees, The Long Voyage Home, In the Zone,* and *Bound East for Cardiff*. The plays, staged at New York's Provincetown Playhouse under the title *S.S. Glencairn*, have 105 performances.

Nov 23 *Judas Iscariot*, E. Temple Thurston's seven-scene play, has Campbell Gullan as its Judas at London's Scala Theatre. The Repertory Players include Raymond Massey, Joyce Kennedy, Roger Livesey, and Nigel Bruce.

Dec 6 In Birmingham, Barry Jackson's Repertory Company premieres Eden Phillpotts' comedy, *Devonshire Cream*.

Dec 16 The holiday season is underway; tonight at London's Shaftesbury Theatre the first children's treat opens: *Charley's Aunt*. Other which soon follow are *The Windmill Man* (Victoria Palace), *Treasure Island* (Strand), *Pollyanna* (St. James's), *Alf's Button* (Prince's), *Dick Whittington* (Oxford), *The Forty Thieves* (Lyceum), *Mother Goose* (London Hippodrome), *Where the Rainbow Ends* (Holborn Empire), *A Kiss for Cinderella* (Haymarket), and *Peter Pan* (Adelphi).

1924 BIRTHS/DEATHS/DEBUTS

Feb 18 American performer John J. Murray is dead in St. Petersburg, Florida. Murray was a member of the old theatrical team of Murray and Mack. He began his career as a circus clown and later became manager of two theatres in Warren, Ohio.

March 9 American actress and author May Tully dies in New York at age 40. Tully first played in stock companies and made her New York debut in *The Christian*. She wrote and produced *Mary's Ankle*.

March 15 American theatre manager Leonard P. Phelps dies in New York at age 72. Phelps first appeared in minstrel shows. He later became a long-time associate of playwright Charles Hoyt and Frank McKee.

March 17 Theatrical designer Eldon Elder is born in Atkinson, Kansas.

March 19 Tallulah Bankhead plays the title role in *Conchita*, Edward Knoblock's romantic comedy, premiering at London's Queens Theatre. There are just nine performances.

March 30 American librettist Glen MacDonough dies in Stamford, Connecticut, at age 57. MacDonough started as a reporter on the New York *World*. With Victor Herbert, he wrote *Babes in Toyland*. MacDonough also wrote a number of sketches for actress May Irwin.

April 20 Actress Nina Foch is born Nina Consuelo Maud Fock in Leyden, Netherlands.

April 24 Actress Eleanora Duse (b. 1858) dies in Pittsburgh at age 65. Born on a train between Venice and Vigevano, Italy, Duse was one of the great tragediennes of the international stage. Lauded for her emotional parts (Tosca, Fedora, and Camille), she was also outstanding in Henrik Ibsen's works, notably as Hedda Gabler, Nora, Rebecca West, and Ellida. She was an ardent champion of the plays of D'Annunzio.

April 26 Russel Nype is born in Zion, Illinois.

April 30 Composer-lyricist Sheldon Harnick is born in Chicago, Illinois.

Primrose

May 7 Tallulah Bankhead is in another failure in London. This time it is *This Marriage*, a drama by Eliot C. Williams. Cathleen Nesbitt, Herbert Marshall and Auriol Lee also act. The play runs only 20 performances.

May 13 American composer Louis Hirsch (b. 1887) dies in New York City. Hirsch composed music for *The Ziegfeld Follies of 1915, 1916*, and *1918; Going-Up*, and *The Honeymoon Express*, among others.

May 20 French star Mistinguette makes her American debut in *Innocent Eyes*, a revue at New York's Winter Garden Theatre. Both the show and the star misfire.

May 26 American composer and conductor Victor Herbert (b. 1959) dies in New York. Herbert is best known in the theatrical world for his operettas, which include *Babes in Toyland, Mlle. Modiste, Little Nemo, Naughty Marietta*, and *Princess Pat*.

June 2 Walter Verne Pidgeon, later to be a leading man in Hollywood, appears in *Elsie Janis at Home*, a revue premiering at London's Queens Theatre.

June 24 American actor Milton Nobles (b. 1847) dies in Brooklyn, New York. Nobles started as a juvenile in an Omaha stock company. He rose to stardom in *The Phoenix* and *Jim Bludsoe*, and co-starred with his wife Dolly in numerous plays. Two seasons before his death he played with Frank Bacon in *Lightnin'*.

June 24 American stage and screen actress Dennie Moore makes her stage debut in the *Ziegfeld Follies* at the New Amsterdam Theatre in New York.

Jun 29 In St. Paul's Church, Covent Garden, Charles Rann Kennedy and his wife, Edith Wynne Matthison, perform his play, *The Chastening*.

Sep 25 American actress Carlotta Crabtree (b. 1847) is dead. Crabtree, who was taught to dance by Lola Montez, was a popular child actress in the mining camps of California. Lotta, as she was known on stage, scored a success as Little Nell in *The Old Curiosity Shop* in New York in 1867. She retired in 1891, having amassed a large fortune, which she subsequently left to charity.

Sep 30 Author-playwright Truman Capote is born in New Orleans, Louisiana, to Julian and Nina Persons and is christened Truman Streckfus Persons.

Oct 5 John Gielgud appears in the cast of John Van Druten's *The Return Half*. It is performed by the RADA Ex-Students' Club in the Academy's theatre.

Oct 11 Maria Ouspenskaya, recently of the Moscow Art Theatre, decides to make America her home. Tonight she stars as Paris Pigeons in Stark Young's drama, *The Saint*. The show runs just over two weeks.

Oct 12 Edmund Wilson's drama of a streetgirl, *The Crime in the Whistler Room*, opens at the Provincetown Playhouse in New York. It has just 25 performances.

Nov 6 Charles Dillingham revives J. M. Barrie's *Peter Pan* at the Knickerbocker Theatre in New York, with Marilyn Miller as Peter. The production runs three months.

Nov 7 Wolf Mankewitz is born in London, England.

Nov 10 Lee Shubert gives the French actor, Firmin Gemier, of the Odeon in Paris, his American debut in New York's Jolson Theatre. For three weeks, Gemier plays a repertory including *L'Homme qui Assassina, L'Homme et ses Fantômes, Le Bourgeoise Gentilhomme*, and *The Taming of the Shrew*.

Nov 16 American manager, playwright, and composer Edward Everett Rice (b. 1848) dies in New York. Rice was composer of the successful burlesque, *Evangeline*, produced at Niblo's Garden in 1874. In 1900 he was the recipient of a testimonial benefit at the Metropolitan Opera House in celebration of 25 years of theatrical management.

Nov 30 Laurence Olivier has a very small role in *Byron*, by Alice Law. The Lyceum Club Stage Society presents it at the Century Theatre in Bayswater. Henry Oscar and Esme Biddle are Lord and Lady Byron.

Dec 12 Katharine Cornell, in the fourth New York production of George Bernard Shaw's *Candida*, at the 48th Street Theatre, has a run of 143 performances. She follows the Candidas of Dorothy Donnelly, Chrystal Herne, and Hilda Spong.

Dec 24 English drama critic W. A. Darlington's first play, a dramatization of his novel, *Alf's Button*, opens at London's Prince's Theatre.

Dec 26 Basil Dean retires from the directorship of the Drury Lane Theatre in London.

Dec 27 London dramatic critic-playwright William Archer (b. 1856) is dead. Archer settled in London in 1878, where he became critic successively to *Figaro*, the *World*, the *Tribune*, and the *Nation*. His translations of the plays of Henrik Ibsen were instrumental in the launching of the "new drama" of the 1890's. In 1923 Archer's melodrama, *The Green Goddess*, was produced at St. James's Theatre.

1924 THEATERS/PRODUCTIONS

In Britain, patents are granted for: W. J. Nash's process for producing imitation grass matting; T. Kay's siren-like device for producing wind effects.

U.S. patents granted this year include Max Hasait's for a rotary-stage which is really drum-like, containing an elevator, and moving on rails below the stage. In the 1970's, a similar concept of a drum-revolve containing an elevator will be a central feature of the new Olivier Theatre stage in London's National Theatre complex.

The Shubert Theatre Corporation begins the American theatre year, as usual, with its own scenery studio, its own scenery workshop, its own property workshop, and, of course, its own electrical shop. In addition, it also has a large "reservoir of stage equipment." This includes 40 sets of stage-hangings, 14,000 individual costumes, 50 complete sets of electrical stage-equipment, and 2,000 trunks and crates for transporting equipment on the road.

The government of the Irish Free State makes a £850 grant to Dublin's internationally famed Abbey Theatre. This subsidy will be annually renewable. At this time, no theatre in Britain—or anywhere in the English-speaking world—receives direct state subsidy, W. B. Yeats, one of the Abbey's founders, notes with pride.

Pasadena Playhouse director Gilmor Brown begins experiments with his new "Playbox Theatre," first working in his own living room and later in a building not part of the Playhouse complex. What is notable about these theatre adventures is Brown's early attempts at central and flexible staging, years before Margo Jones earns attention for her similar experiments in Dallas.

Jan Eugene O'Neill, Kenneth McGowan, and Robert Edmond Jones, having formed a producing triumvirate from their Provincetown Players association, present Strindberg's *The Spook Sonata* for a three-week run in New York.

Feb 9 The Birmingham Repertory Theatre gives what is stated to be its final performance. The Lord Mayor is in attendance and schemes are outlined to guarantee audiences if Barry Jackson will consent to re-open the theatre.

April 15 Harry Robert Law patents an American scenic apparatus to be used for modifying the size of the proscenium opening. The apparatus consists of a group of parallel panels suspended immediately upstage and onstage of the proscenium opening.

April 15 The Jewish Theatrical Guild of America is formed. Among the prominent members are William Morris, Eddy Cantor, and George Jessel. Loney Haskell is Recording Secretary.

May This month, Chicago's Powers Theatre is demolished. Opening in 1872 as Hooley's Theatre, it became the Powers in 1898, when architects Wilson and Marshall remodeled it. It seated 1,500. The last performance on its boards is Otis Skinner's appearance on May 4 in *Sancho Panza*.

May The British dramatist-critic, St. John Irvine, noting the relative failure of the citizens of Birmingham to support Barry Jackson's Repertory Theatre, proposes establishment of a provincial repertory circuit. If six cities, such as Glasgow, Edinburgh, Birmingham, Leeds, Manchester, and Liverpool, were to each have its own repertory company, then they could play a month in each city, with half-year contracts for the actors.

May 17 *Earl Carroll's Vanities* is today the last show to use the stage of Chicago's Colonial Theatre. It will be torn down. The Colonial was formerly the unlucky Iroquois Theatre which, in 1903, was the scene of a tragic fire in which over 600 perished.

May 31 The employment agreement signed between Actors' Equity Association and the Producing Managers' Association after the first actors' strike five years ago expires. The Shuberts and some allied independents such as the Selwyns and A. H. Woods have already signed a new agreement, so their shows remain open. An Erlanger group, including producers such as Charles Dillingham, Gilbert Miller, Arthur Hopkins, Sam H. Harris, John Golden, and Henry W. Savage, resist Equity demands. Seven of their shows are closed. By late summer, after compromises, a ten-year Equity shop contract is approved. 80% of actors employed must belong the the union; 20% can be independent but must pay a sum equal to dues.

June Writing in *Play Pictorial*, the editor, B. W. Findon, deplores the current boycotts by the Actors' Association of such companies as those managed by John

Martin Harvey and Eva Moore. The actors' actions, says Findon, are bringing the stage down to the level of Thames-side dockers. Martin Harvey, he notes, graduated from the (Henry) Irving school, "which knew nothing of trade unionism, but which was well versed in the art of the drama." Union contracts are, in fact, causing managers to engage fewer "extra ladies and gentlemen." Similarly, "the theatre orchestra is becoming a thing of the past."

June 15 At the Broadway season's close, critic Burns Mantle notes that he and his fellow critics found it "more productive of good drama than any previous season within their memories." Of the 196 productions surveyed, less than 40 were musicals. Mantle designates ten *Best Plays*: Ferenc Molnar's *The Swan*, Sutton Vane's *Outward Bound*, George Kelly's *The Show-Off*, Hatcher Hughes' *Hell-Bent for Heaven*, George S. Kaufman and Marc Connelly's *Beggar on Horseback*, Lulu Vollmer's *Sun-Up*, Lewis Beach's *The Goose Hangs High*, Lee Wilson Dodd's *The Changelings*, Guy Bolton's *Chicken Feed*, and Gilbert Emery's *Tarnish*. Of the total productions, 88 were dramas, 67 comedies, 26 musicals, and 15 revues. Seeming success is the reward of 53 shows, (27%), with failure the lot of 143 (73%).

June 23 The Sheffield Repertory Company moves from the Shipton Street Little Theatre to its new home in a South Street schoolroom. The opening production is G. Martinez Sierra's *The Romantic Young Lady*.

June 24 On this date, The Shubert Theatre Corporation officially takes over the various business enterprises previously conducted by the Shubert Theatrical Company, Sam S. and Lee Shubert, Inc., Shubert Consolidated Enterprises, Inc., and other affiliated interests.

July 19 The Organizing Committee for the Re-opening of the Birmingham Repertory Theatre reaches its goal of 4,000 subscriptions for a series of six plays.

Sep In *Play Pictorial*, editor B. W. Findon reports on the controversy surrounding the decision to broadcast some plays and musicals. Some provincial theatre managers have threatened not booking broadcast plays, fearing no one will buy tickets. Findon notes that were he living outside London and could hear a play on the wireless, he'd go home to do so and not stay in town. He says of suburban and country friends, "they are well satisfied with their evening's entertainment at home, which costs them so little, and so satisfactorily fills in the time between dinner and bed."

Sep 27 After a seven-month closing, the Birmingham Repertory Theatre re-opens with *The Seal Woman*, by Mrs. Kennedy Fraser and Harley Granville Barker, directed by Barry Jackson, with music conducted by Adrian Boult.

Oct In Philadelphia, the Broad Street Theatre comes under the management of the Stanley Company, which converts it to cinema use. Opened in 1876 as Kiralfy's Alhambra Palace, the playhouse has been also known as the Lyceum, the South Broad, Haverly's and McCaull's Opera House. The theatre seats 1,373, with a proscenium opening of 33 feet wide by 36 feet high. The first complete version of *Faust* in America was presented on this stage, which also supported Julia Marlowe, Sarah Bernhardt, Maud Adams, John Drew, Mrs. Fiske, Otis Skinner, Fritzi Scheff, the Barrymores, and Jeanne Eagles.

Nov 2 New York's Governor Alfred E. Smith lays the cornerstone for the Theatre Guild's new home, the Guild Theatre.

Nov 8 The Fortune Theatre, off Covent Garden, opens with Laurence Cowen's *Sinners*. The theatre, designed by Ernest Schaufelberg, is the first theatre to be built in London after World War I and has a capacity of 440. It perpetuates the name of the 17th century playhouse in Golden Lane, Cripplegate, burned down in 1613.

Nov 11 The Martin Beck Theatre (1,200 seats) opens on West 45 Street in New York City. The only American theatre in the Byzantine style, it was designed by the San Francisco architect, G. Albert Lansburgh, to Martin Beck's specifications.

Dec 18 Tonight, San Francisco's old Columbia Theatre re-opens as the Geary Theatre. Designed by Bliss and Favel, it seats 1,496 and has a proscenium opening 36 feet wide by 32 feet high. It is used primarily for legitimate plays, having a stage 86 feet wide by 46 feet deep.

Dec 24 Chanin's 46th Street Theatre in New York, owned by the Chanin brothers and designed by Herbert J. Krapp, opens with *The Greenwich Village Follies*. When the Chanins lose control of the theatre in 1932, their name is dropped from the marquee. Built to house musicals, it presents, among others; *DuBarry Was A Lady*, *Finian's Rainbow*, *Guys and Dolls*, *Damn Yankees*, *How to Succeed in Business Without Really Trying*, *1776*, and *The Best Little Whorehouse in Texas*.

Dec 26 At London's Drury Lane Theatre, Alfred Butt and Basil Dean present a revival of Shakespeare's *A Midsummer Night's Dream*, which costs the large sum of £8,000. Despite a cast including Edith Evans, Athene Seyler, Mary Clare, Gwen Ffrangcon-Davies, and Leon Quartermaine, the production is not well received. B. W. Findon, editor of *Play Pictorial*, seeing Basil Dean's *Dream* at the Drury Lane, guesses that the concept was to provide "a roaring farce for the benefit of Bottom and Company." All the show needs, he says, is a comedian like the late Dan Leno to make it a typical Drury Lane pantomime.

Jan 5 *Is Zat So?* (NY—39th Street—Comedy). James Gleason and Richard Taber write this play about a down-and-out manager and a fighter who disguise themselves as servants in order to help a wealthy young man unmask his crooked brother-in-law. Gleason plays the manager. The show has an extremely long run of 618 performances. It opens in London at the Apollo on Feb 15, 1926 with Gleason repeating his role. On this side of the Atlantic, the show has only 234 performances.

Jan 5 *Mrs. Partridge Presents* (NY—Belmont—Comedy). Guthrie McClintic produces and stages Mary Kennedy and Ruth Hawthorne's play, which runs 18 weeks. Blanche Bates plays a loving but bossy modern mother who tries to run her children's lives. They have their own ideas about what they should be doing. Ruth Gordon plays a "Dumb Dora" chum of Mrs. Partridge's stage-struck daughter.

Jan 7 *Big Boy* (NY—Winter Garden—Musical). Al Jolson stars as a jockey who wins a race despite efforts to displace him. Harold Atteridge invents the story, with lyrics by B.G. DeSylva and music by James Hanley and Joseph Meyer. The show runs only six weeks because Jolson is unwell. It returns in August for 15 more weeks.

Jan 12 *Processional* (NY—Garrick—Drama). John Howard Lawson's "jazz symphony of American life" is set against the background of a strike in a West Virginia coal mine, featuring characters representing agitators, capitalists, Klansmen, and other American types. The show runs three months. The cast includes Ben Grauer, Philip Loeb, Will Hays, William Canfield, George Abbot, Lee Strasberg, Sanford Meisner, Alvah Bessie, and June Walker.

Jan 26 *Beyond* (NY—Provincetown Playhouse—Drama). Walter Hasenclever's Expressionist drama runs for two weeks, interpreted by Helen Gahagan and Walter Abel. Rita Matthias has translated this fable of burning passion, expunged through murder.

Feb 10 *The Dark Angel* (NY—Longacre—Drama). Patricia Collinge plays an English girl who falls in love after the Great War, thinking her first love dead in combat. He's not dead, but blind, and he releases her from her promise. This British import draws audiences for 63 performances.

Feb 19 *Exiles* (NY—Neighborhood Playhouse—Drama). James Joyce's tale of an Irish triangle, with the jealousy of an expatriate husband returned to Ireland as the driving force, has 41 performances. Ian Maclaren plays the husband.

Feb 23 *Ariadne* (NY—Garrick—Comedy). Laura Hope Crews has the title-role

Processional

in A.A. Milne's play about a wife who flirts with her husband's client to teach her husband a lesson. This Theatre Guild production runs only six weeks. On April 22, the play premieres in London at the Haymarket with Fay Compton in the lead. It lasts only 53 performances.

March 10 *The Fall Guy* (NY—Eltinge—Comedy). This play by James Gleason and George Abbott runs almost three months. Ernest Truex plays decent but poor Johnnie Quinlan who is set up as "fall guy" for some dope-peddlers.

April 9 *Wild Birds* (NY—Cherry Lane—Drama). Dan Totheroh's folk tragedy is set in the Middle West. It has won the University of California's contest for new plays, judged by Eugene O'Neill, Susan Glaspell, and George Jean Nathan. Although it has only 44 performances, Burns Mantle admires it enough to list it as a *Best Play*.

April 13 *Tell Me More* (NY—Gaiety—Musical). George Gershwin provides the score for the book by Fred Thompson and William Wells. Lyrics are by Ira Gershwin, Desmond Carter, and B.G. De Syilva. The story concerns a man who falls in love with a girl at a masked ball. Alexander Gray and Phyllis Cleveland are featured. On May 26, it opens at London's Winter Garden with Elsa MacFarlane and Arthur Margetson as the lovers. It runs 263 performances.

April 15 *O, Nightingale* (NY—49th Street—Comedy). Sophie Treadwell's account of an aspiring young actress' adventures in trying to carve out a career for herself attracts only for 29 performances. Martha Bryan Allen plays the actress, Appolonia Lee.

May 12 *A Bit of Love* (NY—48th Street—

Drama). This British import by John Galsworthy lasts only four performances. O. P. Heggie plays a minister who remains married to his wife to protect her true love's reputation.

June 8 *The Garrick Gaieties* (NY—Garrick—Revue). With songs by Lorenz Hart and Richard Rodgers, this show is presented by "junior members of the Theatre Guild." Talents such as Sterling Holloway, Sanford Meisner, Philip Loeb, and Romney Brent mock some recent Guild productions. It is Rogers and Hart's debut.

June 18 *The Grand Street Follies* (NY—Neighborhood Playhouse—Revue). Agnes Morgan provides book and lyrics for this edition, which runs 148 performances. Broadway shows are spoofed in "They Knew What They Wanted Under the Elms," with a parody of Robert Edmond Jones' setting for *Desire Under the Elms*. Albert Carroll, Helen Arthur, Irene Lewisohn, Ian Maclaren, Blanche Talmud, and Whitford Kane are in the large ensemble.

June 22 *George White's Scandals* (NY—Apollo—Revue). The Albertina Rasch Girls offer graceful, balletic dances, contrasting to the livelier choreography given the chorus girls. Harry Fox and Helen Morgan are in the show, which runs for 171 performances. The score is by Ray Henderson. B. G. DeSylva and Lew Brown create the lyrics.

June 24 *Artists and Models* (NY—Winter Garden—Revue). The Shuberts give audiences 411 performances of nudes (not moving) and lavish dance numbers. The Gertrude Hoffman Girls provide precision dancing; the chorus does the Charleston and the Hula. Phil Baker jokes and plays his concertina. Also on hand are Lulu McConnell, Billy B. Van, and Walter Woolf.

July 6 *The Earl Carroll Vanities* (NY—Earl Carroll—Revue). Ted Healy is the comic spark of this show, which runs for 440 performances. With sketches by many hands, including Arthur (Bugs) Baer, Blanche Merrill, Julius Tannen, Jimmy Duffy, and Jay Gorney, the show is still in progress at midnight of its opening.

Aug 18 *Gay Paree* (NY—Shubert—Revue). Paris is hardly mentioned in Harold Atteridge's sketches or Clifford Grey's lyrics. With comedian Chic Sale doing monologues about the homely folks in Hickville, plus pretty chorus girls and lavish spectacles, the show runs nearly half a year.

Sep •7 *Outside Looking In* (NY—Greenwich Village—Drama). In Maxwell Anderson's play of hobo-life, James Cagney plays Little Red, protector of a prostitute (Blythe Daly) who has murdered her seducer-step-father. The production, produced by Kenneth Macgowan, Robert Edmond Jones, and Eugene O'Neill, has 113 performances.

Sep 7 *Cradle Snatchers* (NY—Music Box—Comedy). Mary Boland, Edna May Oliver, and Margaret Dale play three young wives who think their husbands may be cheating on them with flappers. They invite some college boys (one played by Humphrey Bogart) to a party to get even with their spouses. Russell Medcraft and Norma Mitchell's play runs for 478 performances.

Sep 8 *Captain Jinks* (NY—Martin Beck—Musical). Clyde Fitch's 1901 play is adapted by Frank Mandel and Laurence Schwab as a musical, with a score by Lewis Gensler and Stephen Jones. B. G. DeSylva provides the lyrics. J. Harold Murray is Jinks, with comedian Joe E. Brown as a cab-driver. The show runs 167 performances.

Sep 14 *The Jazz Singer* (NY—Fulton—Drama). George Jessel plays Jack Robin, son of Cantor Rabinowitz, who runs away to become a jazz singer. By Samson Raphaelson, this show runs 303 performances. Later, with Al Jolson instead of Jessel, it becomes the first sound motion-picture.

Sep 15 *The Green Hat.* See L premiere, 1925.

Sep 16 *No, No, Nanette!* See L premiere, 1925.

Sep 16 *The Vortex.* See L premiere, 1924.

Sep 17 *First Flight* (NY—Plymouth—Drama). Collaborators Maxwell Anderson and Laurence Stallings get only 12 performances from this play. Arthur Hopkins stages and produces this tale of a young Andrew Jackson (1788) taking leave of a pretty girl he's met on a trip through North Carolina, where he has also had to fight some duels.

Sep 18 *Dearest Enemy* (NY—Knickerbocker—Musical). Flavia Arcaro and Helen Ford play the women who entertained the British in order to enable Gen. Putnam's troops to join Washington's. Herbert Fields writes the book, with lyrics by Lorenz Hart and music by Richard Rodgers. "Here in My Arms" is a popular song from the show, which runs for 286 performances.

Sep 21 *The Vagabond King* (NY—Casino—Musical). Brian Hooker and W. H. Post adapt Justin McCarthy's *If I Were King*, with a score by Rudolf Friml which includes "Only a Rose" and "Love Me Tonight." Dennis King and Max Figman are in the cast. The show has 511 performances. It premieres in London at the Winter Garden on April 19, 1927, with Derek Oldham and H.A. Saintsbury. There are 480 showings.

Sep 22 *Sunny* (NY—New Amsterdam—Musical). This show features Marilyn Miller as a circus performer who stows away on an ocean liner to follow her lover (Paul Frawley) back to America. Otto Harbach and Oscar Hammerstein II devise the book and lyrics for a Jerome Kern score which includes "Who?" The show runs for 517 performances. On Oct 7, 1926, the musical opens at the Londons Hippodrome with Binnie Hale as Sunny. There are 363 showings.

Sep 23 *The Butter and Egg Man* (NY—Longacre—Comedy). George S. Kaufman's play enjoys a run of 243 performances. Supposedly coined by night club hostess Texas Guinan, the title jokingly refers to theatre "angels" who back plays with very little knowledge of show-business. On Aug 30, 1927, the play opens at the Garrick in London, where it lasts only four weeks.

Sep 29 *Accused* (NY—Belasco—Drama). Eugene Brieux's French play is adapted by George Middleton, with E. H. Sothern as the lawyer who defends a former sweetheart against a charge of murder. She's guilty, he discovers, but he gets her acquitted. Later, he learns she killed her husband to protect him. This runs three months, keeping Sothern busy but permitting his wife, Julia Marlowe, to take a rest from their regular Shakesperean repertory. As usual, David Belasco both stages and produces.

Oct 5 *Hay Fever.* See L premiere, 1925.

Oct 6 *These Charming People* (NY—Gaiety—Comedy). The success of Michael Arlen's *The Green Hat* helps this Arlen script to get an American production. It runs for 107 performances, outlining a father's efforts to keep one of his daughter's marriage to a British publisher intact. Otherwise, the son-in-law will demand payment of a $50,000 debt. Alma Tell is the skittish daughter; Cyril Maude, her father, and Edna Best, her sister. Herbert Marshall is in the cast.

Oct 9 *The Call of Life* (NY—Comedy—Drama). Arthur Schnitzler's tale of a girl

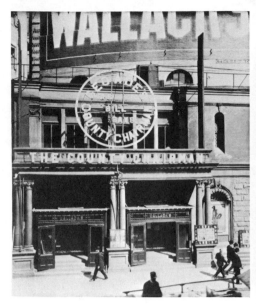
Wallacks Theater

tied to a slowly dying father has only 19 performances, despite the presence of Eva LeGallienne as the girl. She gives her father sleeping drops so she can spend a last night with her beloved who's going off to die in battle. Father dies; the doctor protects her, and she thinks of being a nurse at the front.

Oct 12 *Craig's Wife* (NY—Morosco—Drama). Not only is this George Kelly play one of the season's 10 *Best Plays*, it also wins the Pulitzer Prize. Chrystal Herne plays Harriet Craig, a house-proud woman who destroys her marriage because her possessions are more important to her than people. Kelly stages. There are 360 performances. On Jan 31, 1929, the play opens at London's Fortune, with Phyllis Nielson-Terry in the lead. It has a short run.

Oct 13 *Appearances* (NY—Frolic—Drama). The author, Garland Anderson, writes of a black bellboy—which he was in San Francisco when he wrote the play—who is falsely accused of rape and clears himself because of his faith. The play has 23 performances.

Oct 19 *The Glass Slipper* (NY—Guild—Drama). The Theatre Guild mounts Ferenc Molnar's fable about the infatuated young maid Irene (June Walker) who is desperate when Lajos (Lee Baker) decides to marry the woman (Helen Westley) who owns the boarding-house. She gets her man, but the show gets only 65 performances.

Oct 20 *The Enemy* (NY—Times Square—Drama). Channing Pollock's play, set against the background of the Great War as it affects Vienna, shows that hatred, leading to war, is the greatest enemy. Walter Abel, Fay Bainter, and Lyonel Watts play leads. The production has 203 performances.

Oct 21 *Lucky Sam McCarver* (NY—Playhouse—Drama). In Sidney Howard's play, John Cromwell takes the role of an upwardly mobile barkeeper who marries a society girl on her way down (Clare Eames). The show has only 29 performances, but is admired by some critics.

Oct 26 *Easy Come, Easy Go* (NY—Cohan—Comedy). Otto Kruger and Victor Moore play two men who rob a midwestern bank and hide out at a Health Farm. Edward Arnold is also on hand. Owen Davis's farce runs only 23 weeks.

Nov 2 *Laff That Off* (NY—Wallack's—Comedy). Don Mullally writes about a woman down on her luck and taken in by three bachelor pals. It takes two years for one of them to realize that he loves her; in the meantime, she's run off with their bank account. Shirley Booth stars. The show runs 390 performances.

Nov 2 *Princess Flavia* (NY—Century—Musical). *The Prisoner of Zenda* is set to music by Sigmund Romberg. It runs 19 weeks, with Evelyn Herbert as Flavia.

Nov 2 *Young Woodley* (NY—Belmont—Drama). John Van Druten, a teacher in Wales, writes of adolescent love and agony in such a frank manner that the play is refused performance permission in London. George Tyler and Basil Dean present it first in Boston, and its reception in both Boston and New York is enthusiastic. The play has 260 performances. Glenn Hunter and Helen Gahagan play leads.

Nov 9 *The Last of Mrs. Cheyney.* See L premiere, 1925.

Nov 9 *The Last Night of Don Juan* (NY—Greenwich Village—Drama). The production team of O'Niell, Macgowan, and Jones offers Edmond Rostand's play, translated by Sidney Howard. Stanley Logan and Henry O'Neill are Don Juan and the Statue of the Commander. The production plays only two weeks.

Nov 9 *Naughty Cinderella* (NY—Lyceum—Comedy). Avery Hopwood adapts this French farce which runs 15 weeks. Irene Bordoni plays a secretary who lands her man, though he's using her only to fool a husband about his intentions toward his wife.

Nov 10 *Charlot's Revue of 1926* (NY—Selwyn—Revue). Over 17 weeks of performances are the reward of this new edition, which returns Jack Buchanan, Beatrice Lillie, and Gertrude Lawrence to Broadway. Buchanan stages.

Nov 16 *Twelve Miles Out* (NY—Playhouse—Drama). Mildred Florence has the lead in William McGuire's melodrama about rum-runners who invade a home, followed closely by a gang of hi-jackers. The show runs nearly six months. However, in London, where it opens on Jan 26, 1927, at the Strand, it lasts only 53 performances.

Nov 16 *In a Garden* (NY—Plymouth—Comedy). Philip Barry's play features Laurette Taylor as a playwright's wife who leaves both him and her would-be lover

when she finds they have been manipulating her. Frank Conroy and Louis Calhern also play. Arthur Hopkins produces and directs. The production has only 73 performances.

Nov 23 *A Lady's Virtue* (NY—Bijou—Drama). As is her custom, Rachel Crothers stages her own play. Florence Nash is cast as Sally, bored with marriage and impressed during a visit to New York City with the sexual freedom of the smart set. She even pairs her husband (Robert Warwick) with a French opera singer, but discovers at last that the security of marriage is best. This runs 17 weeks.

Nov 24 *Alias the Deacon* (NY—Sam H. Harris—Comedy). Berton Churchill plays the Deacon, a card-sharper who fleeces club-ladies of their spare change and saves the mortgage on Widow Clark's hotel. This show runs for nearly 35 weeks.

Dec 7 *Easy Virtue* (NY—Empire—Drama). Jane Cowl is featured in this Noel Coward play about a woman of supposed easy virtue who marries into an austere family. The show runs 147 performances. On June 9, 1926, it opens at London's Duke of York's with a cast including Jane Cowl and Mable Terry-Lewis. Here, it earns 124 performances.

Dec 8 *The Cocoanuts* (NY—Lyric—Musical). George S. Kaufman with some help from Morrie Ryskind, outlines a vehicle for the Marx Brothers, which has Groucho as a Florida real-estate developer. Irving Berlin provides the score. The show runs for 377 performances. It opens at London's Garrick on March 20, 1928, without the Marx Brothers. Minus the stars, it has a short run.

Dec 10 *The Fountain* (NY—Greenwich Village—Drama). Robert Edmond Jones stages Eugene O'Neill's play about Ponce de Leon (Walter Huston) and the Fountain of Youth. Macklin Morrow designs the settings. Produced by Macgowan, Jones, and O'Neill, it has only 28 performances.

Dec 14 *Merchants of Glory* (NY—Guild—Drama). The Theatre Guild earns only 42 performances with this staging of the sardonic Marcel Pagnol/Paul Nivoix play. When the supposedly dead hero, Sgt. Bachelet, returns to Paris a shattered amnesiac, his presence proves an embar-

rassment to those who trade on his fame. He has to disappear again.

Dec 15 *The Dybbuk* (NY—Neighborhood Playhouse—Drama). David Vardi, assisted by Alice Lewisohn, stages this English version of S. Ansky's tale of a wronged spirit possessing the body of his beloved, basing it on the Habimah production. It enjoys a 15-week run.

Dec 21 *One of the Family* (NY—49th Street—Comedy). Grant Mitchell and Kay Johnson star as a married couple who turn on their abusive, meddling family. This pleases audiences for 238 performances.

Dec 22 *The Patsy* (NY—Booth—Comedy). Barry Connors's play has Claiborne Foster as the irritating Patricia Harrington, who buys a book on personality and learns to charm the man she loves. The show has 245 performances. On Dec 19, 1928, it opens at the Apollo in London, with American actress Helen Ford in the role of Patricia. The show runs 17 weeks.

Dec 24 *The Greenwich Village Follies* (NY—46th Street—Revue). This edition, staged by Hassard Short, runs nearly 23 weeks, but it has few outstanding numbers. It is the last Follies in the regular series; a separate edition appears in 1928.

Dec 28 *By the Way.* See L premiere, 1925.

Dec 28 *Tip-Toes* (NY—Liberty—Musical). The book is by Guy Bolton and Fred Thompson; the music and lyrics by George and Ira Gershwin. Queenie Smith plays the title-role of a hoofer, a member of a vaudeville team down on its luck in Florida and hoping to find Tip-Toes a wealthy match. "Sweet and Low Down" and "That Certain Feeling" become hits. The show runs for 192 performances. On Aug 31, 1926, it comes to London's Winter Garden with Dorothy Dickson in the title-role. Here it earns 182 showings.

Dec 30 *Song of the Flame* (NY—44th Street—Musical). George Gershwin provides the title song but most of this operetta-like score is by Herbert Stothart. The Flame (Tessa Kosta) is an aristocrat rousing Russian peasants against oppression. The book is the work of Otto Harbach and Oscar Hammerstein II. Given a lavish staging with many rich costumes, Russian chorus, and augmented orchestra, the production lasts for nearly 28 weeks. Arthur Hammerstein produces.

1925   BRITISH PREMIERES

Jan 22 *By the Way* (L—Apollo—Revue). This show has sketches by Ronald Jeans and Harold Simpson, music by Vivian Ellis, and lyrics by Graham John. The cast includes Cicely Courtneidge and Jack Hulbert. There are 341 showings. It opens at New York's Gaiety on Dec 28, 1925, with Courtneidge and Hulbert. Here it runs 22 weeks.

Jan 29 *Spring Cleaning.* See NY premiere, 1923.

Feb 21 *Katja, the Dancer* (L—Gaiety—Musical). With a score by Jean Gilbert, this show has a run of 505 performances. Lilian Davies (dressed by Idare) is Katja, a dispossessed princess seeking vengeance on Prince Carl of Koruja (Gregory Stroud), who has, she wrongly thinks, seized her titles and lands. The book is by Frederick Lonsdale and Harry Graham. It is based on the Jacobson and Oesterreicher original. Fred Blackman stages, with sets by Alfred Terraine and the Harkers.

March 11 *No, No, Nanette!* (L—Palace—Musical). This American show, with a score by Vincent Youmans and book and lyrics by Frank Mandel, Otto Harbach, and Irving Caesar features George Grossmith as a Bible publisher who is severe with daughter Nanette (Binnie Hale). Irene Brown is also in the cast. There are 665 performances. On Sep 16, the show opens on Broadway at the Globe, after a year's run in Chicago, with road companies already performing. Louise Groody is in the title-role. "Tea for Two" and "I Want To Be Happy" are instant hits. The production wins 321 performances. It's revived in 1971.

March 18 *The Tyrant* (L—New—Drama). Rafael Sabatini's four-act play about Borgia tyranny has a run of 124 performances. The large cast, includes Isobel Elsom, Nona Wynne, Frank Vosper, Hugh Williams, Donald Wolfit, Alec Clunes, and Matheson Lang.

March 19 *Better Days* (L—Hippodrome—Revue). This is a Laurie Wylie set of sketches, with lyrics by Clifford Harris and music by Herman Finck. R. P. Weston and Bert Lee also contribute. Maisie Gay and Stanley Lupino are leading talents. There are 135 performances.

March 20 *Rose Marie*. See NY premiere, 1924.

March 30 *Sky High* (L—Palladium—Revue). George Robey heads the cast in this show of 32 scenes, devised by Albert de Courville, Harold Simpson, and Paul G. Smith. Lyrics are by Adrian Ross, with music from Harry Rosenthal, Frederick Chappelle, Tom Johnstone, and Marc Antony. Nellie Wallace, Marie Blanche, Toots and Lorna Pounds, and others are in the cast. The show runs for 134 performances.

April 20 *The Torchbearers*. See NY premiere, 1922.

April 21 *Fallen Angels* (L—Globe—Comedy). Noel Coward's play, with Tallulah Bankhead as Julia and Edna Best as Jane, two wives who get tipsy while trying to get even with their husbands for indifference, wins 158 performances. On Dec 1, 1927, it premieres at New York's 49th Street Theatre with Fay Bainter and Estelle Winwood as the wives. Guthrie McClintic stages. The show runs just over four weeks.

April 22 *Ariadne*. See NY premiere, 1925.

April 30 *On With the Dance* (L—Pavilion—Revue). Noel Coward has written the book and lyrics. Philip Braham has helped him on the music. The cast includes Alice Delysia, Nigel Bruce, Terri Storri, Hermione Baddeley, Leonide Massine,

No, No Nanette

Douglas Byng, Max Rivers, Lance Lister and Amelia Allen. The show runs for 229 times.

May 4 *Sun Up*. See NY premiere, 1923.

May 7 *Beggar on Horseback*. See NY premiere, 1924.

May 12 *Rain*. See NY premiere, 1922.

May 26 *Tell Me More*. See NY premiere, 1925.

June 2 *Cleopatra* (L—Daly's—Musical). Oscar Straus's score gets some added numbers by Arthur Wood, who also conducts. The original German text of Brammer and Gruenwald is adapted by J. H. Turner, with lyrics by Harry Graham. Evelyn Laye plays the title-role, with Shayle Gardner as her Antony. Oscar Asche stages; Espinosa choreographs, and the Harkers and Alfred Terraine create the historical settings. Comelli designs the many Egyptian costumes, which are much admired. Carl and Tilly Brisson dance some specialties. There are 110 performances.

June 8 *Hay Fever* (L—Ambassadors'—Comedy). Noel Coward's comedy, supposedly based on a weekend in the country with J. Hartley Manners and Laurette Taylor, has Marie Tempest and W. Graham Browne as the egocentric theatre couple who neglect their invited guests to posture and pose. Helen Spencer and Robert Andrews are also in the cast. The show wins 837 performances. *The Times* praises Tempest as: "altogether at her brightest and best . . ." On Oct 5, 1925, it premieres at New York's Maxine Elliott with Laura Hope Crews, Harry Davenport, Gavin Muir, and Frieda Inescourt, among others. It lasts only 49 performances but eventually becomes popular with amateur groups.

June 9 *Mixed Doubles* (L—Criterion—Comedy). On its provincial tryout tour,

Frank Stayton's farce has been called *Jazz Marriage*. With its current name, it earns a London tenure of 102 performances. C. Aubrey Smith, Yvonne Arnaud, George Tully and Faith Celli play the leads. Ian Fleming and Ernest Mainwaring are also in the cast.

June 11 After a Stage Society performance, Ashley Dukes' comedy, *The Man With a Load of Mischief*, opens in London's West End, at the Theatre Royal, Haymarket. The title is the name of an inn where the action unfolds, involving Fay Compton as a Lady, accompanied by her maid (Joyce Kennedy), confronting a Nobleman (Frank Cellier), assisted by his man (Leon Quartermaine). Alfred Clark and Clare Greet, as the innkeepers, complete the cast. E. Lyall Swete stages, with atmospheric setting and handsome costumes by Aubrey Hammond. There are 261 performances, with the Lady escaping from her master, the Prince, to fly with her lover, the former valet.

June 20 *The Guardsman*. See NY premiere, 1924.

June 30 *The Gorilla* (L—Oxford—Drama). Ralph Spence's American mystery play opens for a run of 134 performances, with Mimi Crawford as Alice Denby and Henry Wolston as Cyrus Stevens.

July 7 *We Moderns* (L—New—Comedy). Israel Zangwill's play has already been produced in America; at the New, it has 38 performances. Re-opened at the Fortune on Sep 12, it has a further 98 repetitions.

July 22 *A Cuckoo in the Nest* (L—Aldwych—Comedy). Ben Travers writes an Aldwych farce, with Yvonne Arnaud, Roger Livesey, Rene Vivian, Madge Saunders, and Ralph Lynn in leads. The show runs 876 performances.

July 29 *Lavendar Ladies* (L—Comedy—Comedy). Louise Hampton and Mary Jerrold play Anne and Rose Lavendar, in Daisey Fisher's play. Elissa Landi and Herbert Marshall are April and Hayward Clear. The production has 156 performances.

Aug 12 *No. 17* (L—New—Drama). Leon M. Lion directs J.J. Farjeon's melodrama about a comical vagrant, who helps a man solve the mystery of the corpse in No. 17 and the disappearance of wanted criminals through this seemingly deserted house. Lion and Nicholas Hannen play leads. The show runs 210 performances.

Sep 2 *The Green Hat* (L—Adelphi—Drama). Tallulah Bankhead is featured in Michael Arlen's romance about a woman who protects the "purity" of her husband's reputation, ruining hers after he commits suicide. The play was produced last season in Chicago and Detroit. In Britain there are 128 showings. On Sep 15, it opens in New York with Katharine Cornell in the lead. Here it wins 231 performances.

Sep 9 *The Unfair Sex* (L—Savoy—Comedy). Author Eric Hudson has a posthumous success with this farce, which achieves a run of 262 performances. Athene Seyler and Basil Foster play Diana and Geoffrey Trevor.

Sep 10 *The Emperor Jones.* See NY premiere, 1920.

Sep 22 *The Last of Mrs. Cheyney* (L—St. James's—Comedy). Gladys Cooper plays the title-role in Frederick Lonsdale's play about a former shop-girl who has taken up theft. She is tutored by a man (Ronald Squire) who poses as her butler. Gerald Du Maurier directs and is featured as her love interest. There are 514 performances. On Nov 9, 1925, it opens at New York's Fulton with Ina Claire, A.E. Matthews, and Roland Young. On this side of the Atlantic there are 385 showings.

Sep 24 *The Moon and Sixpence* (L—New—Drama). W. Somerset Maugham's tale, based on the life of Paul Gauguin, is dramatized by Edith Ellis. Henry Ainley is Strickland; Leslie Banks is Faraday. Grace Lane plays Amy Strickland; Viola Tree, Rose Waterford; and Esme Hubbard, Charlotte Jay.

Sep 30 *Folies Bergere Revue* (L—Palladium—Revue). This show opens for a run of 121 performances. It is, however, an English revue, with only a sprinkling of French performers.

Oct 2 *Chauve-Souris* (L—Strand—Revue). Nikita Balieff's Moscow cabaret opens its London season.

Oct 7 *Mercenary Mary* (L—London Hippodrome—Musical). There are 446 showings of this musical, with book by Fred Jackson and score by William Friedlander and Con Conrad. Peggy O'Neil plays Mary, with Sonnie Hale as Jerry, who proposes to solve some financial woes by posing as a co-respondent in a divorce suit between Mary and her newly acquired husband, Chris (A. W. Bascomb). All ends well, staged by William Mollison and choreographed by Larry Ceballos.

Nov 11 *Betty in Mayfair* (L—Adelphi—Musical). There are 182 showings of this musical, based on *The Lilies of the Field.* The score is by Harold Fraser-Simson, book by J. H. Turner and lyrics by Harry Graham. Evelyn Laye and Mary Leigh play Betty and Kitty. Joseph and Phil Harker design and execute the settings.

Nov 23 *The Ghost Train* (L—St. Martin's—Drama). Arnold Ridley's thriller has some train passengers who've missed their connection trapped overnight in a mysterious, haunted Cornish railroad station. In the company, among others, are Mary Clarke Edith Saville, Neville Brook, Vincent Holman, Basil Howes, and Edna Davies. The show runs 665 performances.

sity Drama Society in London at the Oxford Theatre.

Feb 11 Paul Robeson is featured as Jones in this revival of Eugene O'Neill's *Emperor Jones,* which is paired with O'Neill's *The Dreamy Kid.* The double-bill runs for 28 performances at New York's 52nd Street Theatre.

Feb 16 Max Reinhardt's *Sumurun,* a wordless play outlined by Friedrich Freska, with music by Victor Hollaender, opens at the London Coliseum.

Feb 19 In London at the Haymarket Theatre, John Barrymore plays the title-role in *Hamlet* for 67 performances. Fay Compton, Constance Collier and Malcome Keen play leads.

Feb 24 In this revival of Henrik Ibsen's *The Wild Duck,* at New York's 48th Street Theatre, Blanche Yurka plays Gina Ekdahl, with Helen Chandler as her daughter Hedwig. Warburton Gamble is Hjalmar Ekdahl, the husband. The production is played 103 times.

Feb 24 In Dublin at the Abbey Theatre, Dorothy Macardle's new play, *The Old Woman.* is premiered. On March 17, F. J. H. O'Donnell's *Anti-Christ* is unveiled, with a cast including Tony Quinn, May Craig, Arthur Shields, and Barry Fitzgerald. On March 31, the play is Lennox Robinson's *The Portrait.* On Oct 12, it's another Robinson drama, *The White Blackbird.*

March 5 At the Lyric, Hammersmith, Sheridan's *The Rivals* is revived for 91 performances by Nigel Playfair. On June 23, Playfair brings back his successful *Beggar's Opera* production for 61 repetitions. This is followed by *And That's the Truth,* on Sep 17, adapted from Pirandello's *Cosi e se vi Pare.* On Oct 28, Bickerstaff's comic opera, *Lionel and Clarissa,* is revived.

March 6 In a series of 14 special matinees, *Pierrot the Prodigal,* a mime by Michel Carre, *fils,* is presented at New York's 48th Street Theatre. Laurette Taylor and Clarence Derwent are in this stylized tale of love and loss.

March 9 At Wimbledon, Hamilton Deane offers his stage adaptation of Bram Stoker's vampire-thriller, *Dracula.*

March 30 *Charlot's Revue,* as played in America, returns to London with a cast including Beatrice Lillie, Gertrude Lawrence, and Herbert Mundin. It appears at the Prince of Wales's Theatre, where it opened in 1924.

April 3 In Manchester at the Opera House, Gustav Holst's *At the Boar's Head* is presented by the British National Opera Company. It's based on Shakespeare's *Henry IV* and old English melodies. Tudor Davies sings Prince Hal.

April 8 Lord Byron's dramatic poem, *Cain,* is given 14 performances by the Manhattan Little Theatre Club at the Lenox

1925   REVIVALS/REPERTORIES

Jan 10 Walter Hampden revives Shakespeare's *Othello* for 57 performances at the Shubert Theatre in New York. Jeannette Sherwin and Mabel Moore take turns playing Desdemona. Balliol Holloway is the Iago.

Jan 14 Nikita Balieff returns to New York with his *Chauve-Souris* Russian revue. It plays 61 performances at the 49th Street Theatre.

Jan 14 Sybil Thorndike, after her recent success in the title-role, revives George Bernard Shaw's *Saint Joan* at London's Regent Theatre for a further run of 134 performances.

Jan 25 John Dryden's *The Assignation; Or, Love in a Nunnery* is revived by the Phoenix at the Aldwych Theatre. At the Regent, on July 5, they offer *The Rehearsal,* by George Villiers, On Oct 25, their production is Marlowe's *Doctor Faustus,* staged at the Oxford Theatre, followed by a Nov 22 opening of their revival of Congreve's tragedy, *The Mourning Bride,* at the Scala Theatre.

Jan 26 George Bernard Shaw's translation of Siegfried Trebitsch's drama, *Jitta's Atonement,* has a London showing at the Grand in Putney Bridge. Violet Vanbrugh plays the title-role of Jitta.

Feb 2 At the Lyric Theatre, Henrik Ibsen's *The Lady from the Sea* is played as a matinee benefit for the Norwegian Sailors' Church in London.

Feb 10 Henrik Ibsen's *Peer Gynt* is revived by members of the Oxford Univer-

No. 17

Little Theatre. Charles Gibney and Alberta Gallatin play Adam and Eve, Cain's unfortunate parents.

April 11 The Shuberts revive Gilbert and Sullivan's *The Mikado* in New York at the 44th Street Theatre, with Tom Burke as Nanki-Poo, for 33 performances. Two days later, a revival of *Princess Ida* opens at the Shubert Theatre, but not produced by the brothers. With Tessa Kosta as Ida, this runs for five weeks.

April 11 At Hampstead's Everyman Theatre, Sutton Vane's *Overture* is presented. On May 16, G. K. Chesterton's *Magic* is played. On June 12, Eugene O'Neill's *The Long Voyage Home* is produced. On July 15, shortly after it's been played in Italian by an Italian company, Pirandello's *Henry IV* is offered in English. On Aug 17, Goldoni's *Mirandolina* is produced, among other plays presented this year.

April 13 *The Winter's Tale* opens the annual spring Shakespeare season in Stratford-upon-Avon at the Memorial Theatre. Festival director W. Bridges Adams stages and designs the production, in which he casts Randle Ayrton as King Leontes. *King John* is the "birthday play." Other plays include *As You Like It*, *The Two Gentlemen of Verona*, *Twelfth Night*, *Much Ado About Nothing*, *Macbeth*, and Sheridan's *The Critic*.

April 13 *Casear and Cleopatra*, George Bernard Shaw's play is revived by the Theatre Guild, with Helen Hayes as the youthful Egyptian queen and Lionel Atwill as the aging Caesar. The production runs only six weeks, staged by Philip Moeller, at New York's Guild Theatre.

April 21 George Bernard Shaw's *Casear and Cleopatra* earns 78 performances in this revival at London's Kingsway Theatre. The production is by the Birmingham Repertory Players, Barry Jackson's

troupe. This is followed on June 29, by Harold Chapin's *The New Morality*, for 40 performances. On Aug 25, Jackson offers his modern-dress production of *Hamlet*. There are 86 performances. On Nov 17, the ensemble offers *The Old Adam*, by Cicely Hamilton, formerly called *The Human Factor*, when performed in Birmingham.

May 5 For the first time since 1907–08 season, Ibsen's *Rosmersholm* is revived on Broadway. This time Margaret Wycherly is Rebecca West. Others in the cast include Josephine Hull and J. M. Kerrigan. The production plays 30 times.

May 11 Samuel Eliot, Jr.'s adaptation of *The Loves of Lulu* opens at the 49th Street Theatre in New York, with Margot Kelly as Lulu, Frank Wedekind's seductress-destroyer. It lasts only two weeks.

May 11 In Glasgow, at the Royal Theatre, Robert Bane's historical play, *James the First of Scotland* is premiered. William Rea plays the king.

May 17 At London's Scala Theatre, the Renaissance Theatre stages *The Maid's Tragedy*, by Beaumont and Fletcher. On June 28, they offer *Rule a Wife and Have a Wife*, by the same authors. On Oct 11, the revival is John Webster's *The White Devil*. On Dec 6, the group presents *Arden of Faversham*.

May 24 Godfrey Tearle is Hamlet, presented by the Fellowship of Players at the Prince of Wales's Theatre. The Fellowship offers Sunday performances—not a regular playing-day for these employed professionals so they have the opportunity to play Shakespeare.

June 1 New York's actors' club, the Players, revives Pinero's *Trelawny of the "Wells"* for a week at the Knickerbocker Theatre. The large, star-studded cast includes Charles Coburn, Laurette Taylor,

Ernest Lawford, Violet Heming, Amelia Bingham, and John Drew. It is revived the same day in London at the Old Vic.

June 10 *The Fantasticks*, Edmond Rostand's play, is revived at Wadham College, Oxford, by the Oxford Union Drama Society (OUDS). On June 19, the group revives Rostand's *The Two Pierrots*.

June 12 At Hampstead's Everyman Theatre, Eugene O'Neill's play, *Diff'rent*, is produced. On June 30, Ibsen's *The Wild Duck* is revived.

June 15 At London's Oxford Theatre, a two-week Pirandello season begins. Gino Cervi, Marta Abba, and Lamberto Picasso are among the players, who present such dramas as *Henry IV*, *Naked*, *Six Characters in Search of an Author*, and *Right You Are If You Think You Are*.

June 16 St. John Ervine's *Mary, Mary, Quite Contrary*, premiered in 1923 at the Abbey Theatre in Dublin, opens in London at the Savoy Theatre, but it runs only six weeks.

June 22 At the Lyric, Hammersmith, the Oxford Players revive Chekhov's *The Cherry Orchard*, transferring it to the Royalty Theatre for a trial run of 136 performances. John Gielgud, Alan Napier and Mary Gray are cast.

July 5 J. R. Ackerly's play *Prisoners of War*, about the emotional stresses, experienced by British prisoners detained in Switzerland in World War I is presented at London's Royal Court for the Three Hundred Club. On Aug 31, it opens at the Playhouse for a three-week run. Raymond Massey plays Captain Hickman.

July 12 Lytton Strachey's "tragic melodrama," *The Son of Heaven*, is performed at a benefit for the London Society for Women's Service at the Scala Theatre. J. S. Strachey is the second Eunuch, with Geoffrey Webb as Wang Fu. The Dowager Empress of China and her son the Emperor are played by Gertrude Kingston and Dennis Arundell.

July 13 Randle Ayrton is King John in the opening revival at the Shakespeare Memorial Theatre in Stratford-upon-Avon. The current summer season of Shakespeare's plays includes other revivals from the spring: *As You Like It*, *The Winter's Tale*, *The Two Gentlemen of Verona*, *Twelfth Night*, *Much Ado About Nothing*, *Macbeth*, and Sheridan's *The Critic*. Also in the repertory are new productions of *Love's Labour's Lost* and *Julius Ceasar*.

Aug 26 In London at His Majesty's Theatre, the Co-Optimists, outfitted in Pierrot costumes, begin their current revue season. There are 203 performances of this fifth edition.

Sep 14 Kenneth Macgowan, Robert Edmond Jones, and Eugene O'Neill offer a two-week run in New York at Daly's Theatre of their revival of William Congreve's Restoration comedy, *Love for Love*. Earlier, in March, it has had a six-week run downtown at the Greenwich Village Theatre.

Sep 14 George Bernard Shaw's *Arms and the Man* is revived by the Theatre Guild for 180 performances, with Lynn Fontanne and Alfred Lunt. Philip Moeller stages.

Sep 25 At the Playhouse in Liverpool, the Liverpool Repertory Theatre Company premieres Susan Glaspell's play, *The Inheritors*, produced at the Provincetown Playhouse in New York in 1921. The production moves to London to the Everyman Theatre in Hampstead. Two other Glaspell works, *The Verge* and *Bernice* are seen in London this season, as well.

Oct 10 Walter Hampden revives *Hamlet* for 68 performances at the Hampden Theatre in New York. Ethel Barrymore is his Ophelia.

Oct 10 *Polly*, John Gay's sequel to *The Beggar's Opera*, focuses on Macheath's adventures in the New World. It has 43 revival performances at the Cherry Lane Theatre in New York.

Oct 12 At London's Royalty Theatre, Synge's *The Playboy of the Western World* is revived for a five-week run by Dennis Eadie and James B. Fagan. On Nov 16 at the same theatre, O'Casey's *Juno and the Paycock* is played.

Nov 1 At London's Scala Theatre, the Jewish Drama League presents Israel Zangwill's "historical farce," *The King of Schnorrers.*

Nov 2 Thomas Hardy's own adaptation of *Tess of the D'Urbervilles*—titled *In Barnes*—opens at the Garrick Theatre in London for a run of 50 performances.

Nov 9 A modern *Hamlet* bows at New York's Booth Theatre. Basil Sydney stars with Helen Chandler. The production runs 11 weeks.

Nov 10 Henrik Ibsen's *The Master Builder* is staged in New York at the Maxine Elliott Theatre, with Eva LeGallienne as Hilda. It runs nearly ten weeks.

Nov 23 The Theatre Guild continues its George Bernard Shaw productions with *Androcles and the Lion* and *The Man of Destiny* at the Klaw Theatre in New York. Romney Brent plays the Lion's part, with Henry Travers as Androcles. This double-bill runs over two months.

Nov 30 Harley Granville Barker's 1910 comedy, *The Madras House*, has a revival run of 103 performances in London at the Ambassadors' Theatre.

Dec 6 At a special performance in London at the Duke of York's Theatre, the Incorporated Stage Society presents Anton Chekhov's *Ivanoff*, with Robert Farquharson in the title-role.

Dec 6 For one evening only at New York's Knickerbocker Theatre, George C. Tyler shows theatre colleagues the attractive production of Sheridan's *The School for Scandal* he has mounted for national touring.

Dec 14 Players from Constantin Stanislavsky's Moscow Art Theatre Musical Studio pay a brief visit to New York at the Jolson Theatre, with a repertory which includes Aristophanes' *Lysistrata* (with music by Gliere), Offenbach's *La Perichole* (adapted by Nemirovitch-Dantchenko and Galperin), a Bizet-adaptation called *Carmencita and the Soldier*, Pushkin's *Love and Death*, Rachmaninoff's *Aleko*, Arensky's *The Fountain*, and Gliere's *Cleopatra.*

Dec 17 At London's Shaftesbury Theatre, the Christmas season is ushered in with the revival of J. M. Barrie's *Peter Pan*. Other theatres soon follow with traditional pantomimes or musicals: *Bluebell in Fairyland* (Chelsea Palace), *Baby Mine* (Apollo), *The Blue Kitten* (Gaiety), *The Blue Bird* (Garrick), *Where the Rainbow Ends* (Holborn Empire), *Dick Whittington* (Lyceum), *Alf's Button* (Oxford), *Cinderella* (Palladium), *A Message from Mars* (Playhouse), *Treasure Island* (Strand), and *The Windmill Man* (Victoria Palace).

Dec 23 At London's Empire Theatre, Sybil Thorndike, Lewis Casson, and Bronson Albery undertake production of Shakespeare's plays, opening with a revival of *Henry VIII*, played by Norman V. Norman. Casson is Prologue and Griffith. Thorndike plays Queen Katharine, with Angela Baddeley as Anne Bullen. Laurence Olivier plays the First Serving-Man.

Dec 26 Walter Hampden and Ethel Barrymore revive *The Merchant of Venice* at Hampden's Theatre in New York, but it runs less than seven weeks.

1925 BIRTHS/DEATHS/DEBUTS

Jan 8 Future lighting designer Tharon Musser is born in Roanoke, Virginia.

Feb 18 American playwright Martha Morton dies in New York at age 60. Morton was author of the successful *A Bachelor's Romance*, *The Merchant*, *The Fool of Fortune*, *Her Lord and Master*, and *The Three Hearts.*

Feb 21 American playwright and composer Alfred Baldwin Sloane (b. 1872) dies in Red Bank, New Jersey. Sloane wrote a number of musical comedy successes, including *Excelsior, Jr.*, *Liberty Belles*, and *Jubilee*. He also wrote the first two *Greenwich Village Follies.*

Feb 28 Vaudeville comedian Joseph M. Norcross dies in Springfield, Massachusetts at age 84. Norcross and his wife were billed "the oldest couple in vaudeville" until a few years before his death.

March 10 Stage and screen actor Frank McHugh understudies Ernest Truex as Johnnie Quinan in *The Fall Guy* at the Eltinge Theatre. McHugh comes to the New York stage after 15 years apprenticeship as actor and stage manager in stock repertory, vaudeville, and minstrels shows throughout the country.

March 21 Future director-theorist Peter Brook is born in London.

March 25 French-born actor and director Louis F. Massen dies in Morsemere, New Jersey at age 67. Massen served as general stage manager for David Belasco for 12 years. He was married to Marie Burroughs, who was E. S. Willard's leading lady.

April 28 English-born Sydney Mather dies in New York at age 49. Mather played in support of Julia Marlowe for many years. He was a member of John Barrymore's first *Hamlet* company.

May 3 American comedian John Russell dies in Glendale, California, at age 69. Russell and his brother James played in vaudeville as *The Irish Servant Girls*. Later he starred in *The Female Detectives* and *Sweet Marie.*

June 3 American actor Walter E. Perkins dies in Brooklyn, New York at age 55. Perkins toured for many years in *My Friend From India* and *The Man From Mexico.*

June 3 Barry Vincent Jackson, the artistic director of the Birmingham Repertory Theatre, is knighted by King George V.

June 19 English actor-manager Leonard Rayne (b. 1869) is dead. Rayne was identified mainly with the stage in South Africa, which he visited in 1895 playing Hamlet, Richard III, Shylock, and Virginius. Apart from his Shakespearean roles he appeared as Rip Van Winkle, Sherlock Holmes, Napoleon, and other historical and literary characters.

June 25 Actress June Lockhart is born in New York City to actors Gene and Kathleen (Arthur) Lockhart.

July 1 Stage and screen actor Farley Granger is born in San Jose, California.

July 24 American actor John J. Morrisey is dead in New York at age 70. Morrissey was instrumental in establishing the first Orpheum vaudeville circuit. He was a member of the Haverly Minstrels.

Aug 3 American actress Kate Meek is dead in New York at age 87. Meek played in support of Edwin Forrest, Edwin Booth, Charlotte Cushman, and Joseph Jefferson. She later joined the Frohman Company supporting John Drew, Maude Adams, and Otis Skinner. Her last engagement was with Nazimova in *Marionettes.*

Sep 2 Actress-dancer Marge Champion, christened Marjorie Celeste Belcher, is born in Hollywood, California, to ballet teacher Ernest Belcher and his wife.

Sep 20 Future director Albert Marre is born in New York City.

Oct 5 Actress Imogene Coca appears as a chorus girl in Tom Johnstone's musical comedy, *When You Smile*, at the National Theatre in New York. She made her stage debut as a tap dancer in vaudeville at the age of nine.

Oct 3 Playwright-actor-director John Cecil Holm makes his first professional appearance as Detective Dempsey in Charles Horan's *The Devil Within*, with the James G. Carroll Players in Pittsfield, Massachusetts.

Oct 14 Vaudeville performer Eugene Sandow is dead at age 58 in London. Born in Germany, Sandow became a British subject and toured in America, first for Abbey, Shoeffel and Grau, and later under the management of Florenz Ziegfeld.

Oct 16 Stage and screen actress Angela Lansbury is born in London to actress Moyna Macgill.

Oct 22 English dancing master, director, and designer John Tiller is dead in New York at age 73. Tiller was head of the famous Tiller dancing schools in England. His "Tiller Girls" were popular in West End revues.

Nov 10 Future star Richard Burton is born in Pontrhydyfen, South Wales. Son of a coal miner, he is christened Richard Walter Jenkins, Jr.

Nov 20 American actress and writer Clara Morris (b. 1846) dies in New Canaan, Connecticut. Morris began her career in Cleveland, Ohio, when she was 13. She played in many famous stock companies and later became a star under the management of Augustin Daly. Morris was the author of *Life on the Stage* (1901), *Stage Confidences* (1902), and *The Life of a Star* (1906).

Nov 24 Playwright, critic, and historian Percy Hetherington Fitzgerald is dead at age 91. Fitzgerald was the author of *Life of David Garrick*, *The Kembles*, *Henry Irving*, and *The Romance of the English Stage*, among others. He was drama critic of *The Observer* and of *The Whitehall Review*.

Dec 2 Julie Harris is born in Grosse Point, Michigan.

Dec 21 Buelah Bondi makes her New York City debut as Maggie in Kenneth Webb's comedy, *One of the Family*. Born Beulah Bondy on May 3, 1892, in Chicago, Bondi has been appearing with stock companies in the midwest since 1919.

Dec 24 Producer and composer Richard Myers composes "Whistle Away Your Blues" for the *Greenwich Village Follies* at the 46th Street Theatre in New York. This is his first theatrical assignment.

Dec 31 American playwright Lillian Hellman is wed to writer Arthur Kober.

1925 THEATERS/PRODUCTIONS

In Britain this year, patents are granted for: H. F. Maynes' apparatus to give the effect of a train travelling past scenery; A. Jullet's stage constructed with a rear wall that is a projection screen on one side and a stage setting on the other.

Max Hasait receives a U.S. patent for his moveable stage device which can rotate, as well as move laterally, vertically, and upstage-downstage.

Le Cercle Moliere is founded by C. De Lalonde, Louis Philippe Gagnon, and Raymond Bernier in St. Boniface, Manitoba, Canada. Arthur Boutal will become director in 1928, and his wife Pauline will succeed him in 1941, serving as director until 1968. It is the only French language company west of Quebec.

In Dublin, the famed Abbey Theatre creates a second stage, the Peacock Theatre, which is intended to be an experimental annex to the parent-playhouse. The intimate house has just 102 seats.

The British Puppet and Model Theatre Guild (BPMTG) is founded to improve the standard of puppetry in all its forms, to promote interest in puppets and model theatre and to provide a means of communication between its members, the amateur and professional puppeteers of Britain. H. W. Whanslaw is the founder and the first president.

Feb 19 Application is made for a Royal Charter for the Shakespeare Memorial Theatre in Stratford-upon-Avon. It is soon granted by King George V.

March 31 *Sooner or Later* opens at the Neighborhood Playhouse in New York. The production is designed by Donald Oenslager who uses—for the first time in a theatrical production—Thomas Wilfred's clavilux. The clavilux is a color-organ, and Oenslager uses it to project "mobile rhythms of crystalline life."

Spring During considerations for the Pulitzer Prize for Drama, jurors Jesse Lynch Williams and Clayton Hamilton favor *What Price Glory?* by Maxwell Anderson and Laurence Stallings. The frank and salty language of this World War I drama offends novelist Hamlin Garland, the senior juror. Williams and Hamilton compromise, joining Garland in choosing Sidney Howard's *They Knew What They Wanted* for the prize.

April 13 The Guild Theatre, on West 52 Street in New York, designed by Howard Crane and founded by members of the Theatre Guild, opens with a production of George Bernard Shaw's *Caesar and Cleopatra*. From 1943–50, the theatre is used as a radio playhouse, but returns to presenting dramas when the American National Theatre and Academy buys the Guild on March 31, 1950, and renames it the A.N.T.A. Theatre. It is sold for $627,000.

April 20 The Theatre Royal Bury St. Edmunds closes as a theatre venue. It is to be used in future as storage for brewery barrels.

May The Lord Chamberlain has denied Basil Dean a license to stage Eugene O'Neill's *Desire Under the Elms*.

May 4 Walter Hartwig again conducts the annual Little Theatre Tournament at Wallack's Theatre in New York. For the second year, the Little Theatre of Dallas wins the Belasco Trophy, with a production of Paul Green's *The No 'Count Boy*. Troupes from Ohio, Pennsylvania, and Michigan compete for the first time with those from the New York area. There are eight performances.

May 18 Under the direction of Gilmore Brown, tonight the Pasadena Playhouse opens, new home of the Community Players, which have been performing for almost nine years in a former burlesque house. Designed in the California style, with a welcoming patio and walls suggesting whitewashed adobe, topped with red tile roofs, the comfortable theatre seats 820, 212 of them in a balcony. The proscenium opening is 31 feet 6 inches wide by 20 feet high. The stage is 80 feet wide and 31 feet deep. The grid is 67 feet above the stage, equipped with 45 sets of lines. There is also a 300-seat recital hall and other amenities, with a total property value of $400,000, making this one of Americans most impressive community or little theatres. At the end of its first 25 years, the Playhouse will have produced 1,348 plays, 483 of them premieres, a record in its time.

June At the end of the 1924–25 Broadway season, Burns Mantle notes the production of over a score of revivals. There has been an increase of 34 productions over last season, with a total of 230 shows offered. Sorted into categories, they are: 106 dramas, 80 comedies, 31 musicals, and 13 revues. Only 58 shows seem successes (25%), with 172 failing (75%).

June 15 *Best Plays* this season are *What Price Glory?* (Anderson/Stallings), *They Knew What They Wanted* (Howard), *Desire Under the Elms* (O'Neill), *The Firebrand* (Mayer), *Dancing Mothers* (Selwyn/Goulding), *Mrs. Partridge Presents* (Kennedy/Hawthorne), *The Fall Guy* (Gleason/Abbott), *The Youngest* (Barry), *Minnick* (Ferber/Kaufman), and *Wild Birds* (Totheroh).

June 30 For this fiscal year, The Shubert Theatre Corporation reports net income of $1,075,831. With 154,040 shares out-

John Barrymore as Hamlet

standing, the earning per share is $7.17. No dividend is declared.

July Before Ben Travers' Aldwych farce, *Cuckoo in the Nest*, could be licensed for public performance, the Lord Chamberlain's Office has demanded a special rehearsal of a bedroom scene which has worried the Examiner of Plays. Later, Travers is to recall that, thanks to the fine performance of Yvonne Arnaud in the scene, the play has been passed.

Fall At the beginning of a new theatre season, there are only 634 American theatres outside the metropolitan centers such as New York, Boston, Philadelphia, St. Louis, and Chicago which are available for booking touring legitimate productions. 886 theatres are now unavailable, owing to conversion to films or other uses, or they have been closed entirely. This contrasts with 1,520 theatres available in 1910.

Sep The first formalized training for stage-designers begins at the Yale School of Drama in New Haven, Connecticut. Stanley McCandless teaches lighting design.

Sep 1 Writing in the *Fortnightly Review*, the Lord Chamberlain's Examiner of Plays, G. S. Street, notes that he has become convinced that censorship of plays before production is indispensible "... in the interests of the theatre." He reasons that his own work in helping authors and managers prepare acceptable scripts for the London stage has protected them from attacks by the large and varied group of puritanical British who value their immunity from shock more than they honor the art of the dramatist.

Oct 22 "To restore the Old Visions and to win the New": these words are carved over the entrance to Chicago's Kenneth Sawyer Goodman Memorial Theatre, opening tonight beneath the Chicago Art Institute. John Galsworthy's *The Forest* has its American premiere, chistening the stage, which has the latest technical equipment, including a plaster sky-dome, instead of a cyclorama. Howard Van Doren Shaw has designed the theatre to seat about 700 spectators, appropriate for little theatre productions, but the stage is as large as most Chicago commercial theatres. Thomas Wood Stevens, formerly of Carnegie Institute of Technology, will direct the repertory theatre company and the theatre school associated with it. The playhouse is a memorial to a young playwright who died while in military train-

ing during the Great War.

Oct 30 London's first club theatre, The Gate Theatre Salon, opens in Floral Street, Covent Garden. The initial play is Susan Glaspell's *Berenice*, directed by Peter Godfrey. He also manages the theatre with Molly Veness.

Nov 10 In Boston, The Repertory Theatre opens on Huntington Avenue, with a 1,000-seat main theatre and a 450-seat smaller auditorium. This theatre has grown out of Henry Jewett's 12-week season of Shakespeare in Boston in 1915. Reorganized after internal disruptions, the theatre produces and also trains actors in its workshop. In its first 11 years of life, it is to claim production of 194 plays, 56 of them American premieres, and 90 of them new to Boston.

Nov 24 The Forrest Theatre, on West 49th Street in New York, owned by the Shuberts and named for the great 19th Century actor Edwin Forrest, opens with *Mayflowers* by A. Richman and G. Grey. From 1945–59, it is known as the Coronet Theatre, but under new ownership it is renamed the Eugene O'Neill Theatre. Playwright Neil Simon is the current owner of the theatre.

Nov 25 The Carolina Playmakers move into their permanent home on the campus of the University of North Carolina. Named the Tarheel Theatre, the building is a Grecian structure, built over a century ago and used as a ballroom, a library, and for other functions over the years. As a tribute to their new home, The Playmakers present *Out of The Past*, by Francis Gray Patten. As the curtain rises, the audience sees that the setting is the moonlit portico of the structure itself.

Dec There are 67 legitimate theatre productions on tour in America as of the first week of this month. In 1900, there were 392.

Dec 7 The Biltmore Theatre, on West 47th Street in New York, opens with the production *Easy Come, Easy Go*. The Chanin brothers lose possession of the theatre in the 1930's, and it is sold to Warner Brothers, and subsequently leased to the Columbia Broadcasting System. In 1962, the theatre returns to presenting plays, and houses such hits as *Barefoot in the Park* and the rock musical *Hair*.

Jan 5 *A Night in Paris* (NY—Casino de Paris—Revue). Jack Pearl does German dialect comedy; Norma Terris sings some of J. Fred Coots' songs, and the Gertrude Hoffman Girls appear as Africans, cosmetics, and flowers. With J. C. Huffman's staging, the show lasts 335 performances.

Jan 13 *The House of Usher* (NY—5th Avenue—Drama). Thirteen proves an unlucky number for this production of Henry Esmond's British play about the daughter (Rosalinde Fuller) of a wealthy English Jew (Clarence Derwent), who defies him when he forbids her to love his poor and gentile secretary. After three weeks, the show is burned out and has to move to the Mansfield Theatre. Later it moves to the Mayfair, completing 198 performances.

Jan 21 *The Makropoulos Secret* (NY—Charles Hopkins—Drama). Helen Menken plays Emilia Marty, the opera star who must recover the secret by which she has already lived 300 years if she is to live on another 300. Adapted from Karel Capek's *Komedie*, staged by Charles Hopkins, the play draws for 11 weeks.

Jan 23 *The Great God Brown* (NY—Greenwich Village—Drama). Eugene O'Neill experiments with masks, with which four major characters are able to reveal exterior and interior personalities. Designer Robert Edmond Jones stages. He also produces, with O'Neill and Kenneth Macgowan. The production attracts for 271 performances. "Obscure or clear, 'The Great God Brown' is packed with memorable substance," says the *NY Times*. On June 19, 1927, the Stage Society presents it at London's Strand.

Feb 1 *Shanghai Gesture* (NY—Martin Beck—Drama). Florence Reed plays Mother Goddam, once a Chinese princess but now a brothel-keeper waiting to revenge herself on Charteris (McKay Morris), the Briton who sold her into slavery. This show runs for 206 performances.

Feb 2 *The Great Gatsby* (NY—Ambassador—Drama). Owen Davis adapts F. Scott Fitzgerald's popular novel, with James Rennie as Jay Gatsby, the jilted ex-soldier who gets rich bootlegging to have money enough to win back Daisy (Florence Eldridge), who has married rich Tom Buchanan (Elliot Cabot) while he was at war. Staged by George Cukor, the production runs 14 weeks.

Feb 9 *Lulu Belle* (NY—Belasco—Drama). Edward Sheldon and Charles MacArthur collaborate on this steamy tale of a Harlem harlot (Lenore Ulric, in blackface makeup) who lures a White Plains barber (Henry Hull) away from his wife and family. Produced and staged by David Belasco, this show runs for 461 performances. In the next season, the play is

listed as objectionable by moral reformers, but is not raided. "... plot and story. ... are quite lost in the jumble of exact detail," complains the *NY Times*.

Feb 16 *Bunk of 1926* (NY—Heckscher—Revue). Gene Lockhart is the lead in this show for which he's also created songs and sketches. In April, it moves to Broadway and the Broadhurst for a total run of 104 performances despite charges of immorality.

March 12 *The Moon Is a Gong* (NY—Cherry Lane—Drama). Novelist John Dos Passos investigates the influence of jazz on modern life, includes a funeral with mourners doing the Charleston around the corpse. It runs only 18 performances.

March 15 *Juno and the Paycock* (NY—Mayfair—Drama). Sean O'Casey's tale of Dublin during the "troubles" runs over nine weeks. Augustin Duncan directs and stars with Louise Randolph.

March 17 *The Girl Friend* (NY—Vanderbilt—Musical). The title song, with its Charleston rhythms, and "The Blue Room" become rapid hits in this show, which has Lorenz Hart lyrics and Richard Rodgers score. The book, by Herbert Fields, tells of a man training to win a bicycle race by linking his cycle to a churn. Produced by Lew Fields, the show runs for 409 performances.

March 22 *Ashes*. See L premiere, 1926.

April 26 *Sex* (NY—Daly's—Comedy). Mae West plays Margie LaMont, a Montreal woman with a fondness for the British Navy. This spicy tale draws audiences through the season, finally tallying 375 performances. The following season, it is raided as an immoral production; the cast is arrested. Mae West, as the show's co-producer and star, is fined $500 and sent to jail for 10 days. "A crude, inept play, cheaply produced and poorly acted—that, in substance is 'Sex' ..." reports the *NY Times*.

May 10 *The Garrick Gaieties of 1926* (NY—Garrick—Revue). With music and lyrics by Rodgers and Hart, this edition features a burlesque of musicals called *Rose of Arizona*, a forerunner of *Little Mary Sunshine*. Sterling Holloway and Bobbie Perkins introduce the song hit, "Mountain Greenery." The show has 174 performances.

May 18 *Great Temptations* (NY—Winter Garden—Revue). Getting ready for the summer revue trade, the Shuberts engage Hazel Dawn, J. C. Flippen, Jack Benny, and Billy Van, among others, for this collage of show-parodies, comic monologues, and chorus routines. Maurice Rubens provides the score. This revue runs over six months.

June 14 *George White's Scandals* (NY—Apollo—Revue). This, the eighth edition, runs the longest of all, 424 performances. White and William Wells devise the sketches, Ray Henderson creates the music, and lyrics are from B. G. DeSylva and Lew Brown. Among the personalities are Ann Pennington, Willie and Eugene Howard, and Harry Richman and Frances Williams.

June 15 *The Grand Street Follies* (NY—Neighborhood Playhouse—Revue). This, the fourth edition, is the second in the same season. Agnes Morgan, who stages, provides book and lyrics. The music is composed by Arthur Schwartz, Lily Hyland, and Randall Thompson.

July 14 *The Blonde Sinner* (NY—Cort—Musical). Leon DeCosta's play, with musical specialties in it, runs nearly 22 weeks. Enid Markey is mistaken for a divorce co-respondent as she takes in comic boarders in a Long Island manor she and her husband have rented for the summer. Charlestons are among the dance treats.

July 26 *Americana* (NY—Belmont—Re-

Shanghai Gesture

vue). J. P. McEvoy's sketches, with music by Con Conrad and Henry Souvaine, and special songs by the Gershwins and others, run for 28 weeks. The company includes Lew Brice, Helen Morgan, Charles Butterworth, and Betty Compton.

Aug 24 *Earl Carroll's Vanities* (NY—Earl Carroll—Revue). Opening night seats cost $100 for this edition of Carroll's scantily-clad chorines. Comedy is in the hands of Julius Tannen, Moran and Mack, and Smith and Dale. The show runs 303 performances.

April 26 *At Mrs. Beam's* See L premiere, 1923.

Aug 30 *The Donovan Affair* (NY—Fulton—Drama). Owen Davis's play involves the murder of a man whose ring is alleged to have given him power over women. It runs four months. On Feb 15, 1927, it opens at London's Duke of York's where it runs two months.

Sep 6 *Castles in the Air* (NY—Selwyn—Musical). This show, from Chicago, is a variation on the girl and prince theme. J. Harold Murray and Vivienne Segal play leads. With book and lyrics by Raymond Peck and score by Percy Wenrich, the show runs for five months.

Sep 8 *Queen High* (NY—Ambassador—Musical). A hit in Philadelphia, this show which is based on the farce *A Pair of Sixes*, tells a tale of partners who fall out and play poker to see who will run the business. The loser must become the winner's butler. Charles Ruggles is featured. Lewis Gensler provides the score, B.G. DeSylva the lyrics, and Lawrence Schwab and De Sylva the book. There are 378 performances. On Nov 2, 1926, it comes to Queen's at the West End with Hermione Baddeley, Joseph Coyne, and Anita Elsom. It runs 198 performances.

Sep 9 *Two Girls Wanted* (NY—Little—Comedy). Nydia Westerman and Charlotte Denniston play two struggling working-girls who decide to leave Manhattan offices for domestic work. It just happens to be in the home of the fiance of the man one of them loves. Gladys Unger's script, Winchell Smith's staging, and the cast's playing win the show nearly 400 performances.

Sep 16 *Broadway* (NY—Broadhurst—Drama). Philip Dunning and George Abbott's tale is set in a cabaret where a song-and-dance man is in love with a woman whose affections are also sought by a gangster. Lee Tracy, Sylvia Field, and Robert Bleckler are in the cast. The show tallies 603 performances. Mantle picks it as a *Best Play*. On Dec 22, 1926, it opens at the Strand in London. It has 252 performances.

Sep 18 *Countess Maritza* (NY—Shubert—Musical). Emmerich Kalman's operetta, adapted by Harry B. Smith, with some Romberg and Goodman interpolations, runs for nearly ten months. Yvonne D'Arle is the countess, in love with—but

Broadway

suspicious of—her estate's overseer. He is really a count (Walter Woolf) who loves her, too, but doesn't want to be thought a fortune-hunter. "Play Gypsies—Dance Gypies" rapidly becomes a popular favorite from this score. J. J. Shubert takes credit for the staging.

Sep 20 *The Ramblers* (NY—Lyric—Musical). Bert Kalmar and Harry Ruby, with help on the book from Guy Bolton, devise the music and lyrics for this romp. Bobby Clark stars with Paul McCullough. The show earns 289 performances.

Sep 20 *Honeymoon Lane* (NY—Knickerbocker—Musical). Eddie Dowling and James Hanley write the book, lyrics, and music. Dowling plays an Irish lad who pursues his beloved (Pauline Mason) to Broadway, where she seeks—unsuccessfully, as it turns out—a career. The show enjoys 364 performances.

Sep 21 *Fanny* (NY—Lyceum—Comedy). Fanny Brice graduates from revues to plays, but only for 63 performances. She plays a companion to a rich lady philanthropist. She beats a gang of robbers in Arizona, using her Yiddish wiles to vamp the leader. Willard Mack's plot has been improved by David Belasco, who also directs and produces.

Sep 28 *Gentlemen Prefer Blondes* (NY—Times Square—Comedy). Anita Loos and John Emerson collaborate on the saga of Lorelei Lee, the girl from Little Rock who collects wealthy gentlemen and costly gifts. June Walker, Frank Morgan, and Edna Hibbard are featured. The show runs 199 performances. On April 2, 1928, it opens at London's Prince of Wales's with Joan Bourdelle playing Lorelei.

Sep 29 *The Captive* (NY—Empire—Drama). Edouard Bourdet's *La Prisonniere*, adapted by Arthur Hornblow, Jr., treats a hitherto taboo subject on Broadway: lesbianism, though the theme is not clearly stated. Irene (Helen Menken) is under the influence of a woman friend.

Gilbert Miller stages. There are only 160 performances. Raided by order of the District Attorney, the production is withdrawn, to win the release of the cast, which has been arrested. The production has been grossing $20,000 per week.

Oct 4 *Deep River* (NY—Imperial—Musical). Styled a "native opera," the book and lyrics are Laurence Stallings, with a score by Frank Harling. Arthur Hopkins produces and directs, with Lottice Howell as Muguette the quadroon beauty over whom two men lose their lives. Admired by critics, the show has only a four-week run.

Oct 6 *Black Boy* (NY—Comedy—Drama). Paul Robeson plays the title role, a roustabout who wins a boxing championship. Surrounded by parasites and a mistress, Irene (Edith Warren), he's done in by dissipation and loses the title. Defeated, he also discovers Irene is really black, passing as white. Jim Tully and Frank Dazey's drama has only 37 performances.

Oct 6 *Berkeley Square*. See L premiere, 1926.

Oct 11 *An American Tragedy* (NY—Longacre—Drama). Patrick Kearney dramatizes Theodore Dreiser's novel. The show wins 216 performances. Morgan Farley stars with Katherine Wilson and Miriam Hopkins. The theme offends some would-be theatre reformers, so the play is put on the District Attorney's list of objectionable plays.

Oct 12 *Criss Cross* (NY—Globe—Musical). Jerome Kern's score and Fred Stone's fantasy earns 206 performances. Stone and daughter Dorothy take the leads.

Oct 12 The Harris Theatre in New York presents *We Americans*. The story is about a Jewish girl, Beth Levine, who reproaches her kindly parents for not keeping pace with American life and becoming good citizens. She leaves home, and they go to night-school to improve. All ends well for 118 performances. In the cast are Luther Adler and Muni Weisenfrend, later to be known as Paul Muni.

Oct 18 *On Approval* (NY—Gaiety—Comedy). Frederick Lonsdale's British play about a couple testing their compatability before marriage features Violet Kemble Cooper and Wallace Eddinger. It earns a 12-week run. On April 19, 1927, it premieres at London's Fortune with Valarie Taylor and Edmond Breon as the pair. On this side of the Atlantic there are 469 showings.

Oct 20 *The Noose* (NY—Hudson—Drama). A young man is sentenced to be hanged after he murders a gangster in order to keep his parentage a secret and protect his mother's name. This melodrama lasts for 197 performances, with a cast including Lester Lonergan, Jack Daley, Mae Clark, and Barbara Stanwyck.

Oct 22 *The Ladder* (NY—Mansfield—Drama). The 789 performances of this tale

Oh, Kay

of reincarnation—revealed in a dream—says nothing about its popularity, since it is kept running by its patron, Edgar B. Davis, determined that the public shall profit from its message. J. Frank Davis is the author; Brock Pemberton is the producer and director. Antoinette Perry plays the lead.

Oct 25 *Daisy Mayme* (NY—Playhouse—Comedy). George Kelly's play with Jessie Busley as Daisy, runs for 14 weeks. Burns Mantle selects it as a *Best Play* of the season. Carlton Brickert plays Cliff, the 40-year-old bachelor surrounded by women who finally gets the one he deserves. Kelly directs.

Oct 26 *Caponsacchi* (NY—Hampden's—Drama). The title role, in this adaptation of Robert Browning's *The Ring and the Book*, goes to Walter Hampden, who produces and directs and in whose theatre it is presented for 269 performances.

Nov 3 *The Play's the Thing* (NY—Henry Miller—Comedy). Ferenc Molnar's Hungarian love-charade with theatre people is adapted by P.G. Wodehouse. Holbrook Blinn, Catherine Dale Owen, Edward Crandall and Reginald Owen are featured. It achieves 326 showings. On Dec 4, 1928, it opens at London's St. James's with Gerald Du Maurier, Henry Daniell, and Ursula Jeans.

Nov 8 *Oh, Kay* (NY—Imperial—Musical). This P.G. Wodehouse and Guy Bolton tale of rum-runners and Long Island romance has music and lyrics by the Gershwins, with help from Howard Dietz. Among the memorable songs are "Someone to Watch Over Me," "Do-Do-Do," "Clap Yo' Hands" and "Maybe." Gertrude Lawrence, Oscar Shaw, and Victor Moore are featured. There is an eight-month run. On Sep 21, 1927, it opens at London's His Majesty's with Lawrence and Harold French. It runs 214 performances.

Nov 9 *Gay Paree* (NY—Winter Garden—Revue). With some new material, including a muckraking parody of muckraker Ida Tarbell, this second edition is also the final one. J. J. Shubert stages, with help from J. C. Huffman and Felix Seymour. The show runs for 175 performances.

Nov 11 *The Squall* (NY—48th Street—Drama). Nubi, a gypsy girl, takes refuge from her chief with a family, whose male members she seduces. In the cast are Romney Brent, Dorothy Stickney, Blanche Yurka, and Suzanne Caubet. This show runs for 444 performances.

Nov 15 *Pygmalion* (NY—Guild—Comedy). The Theatre Guild offers Lynn Fontanne as Eliza Doolittle, in Bernard Shaw's saga of her rise from Covent Garden Market to smart salons. Henry Travers plays her father, and Reginald Mason is the phonetician Henry Higgins.

Nov 23 *This Was a Man* (NY—Klaw—Comedy). Noel Coward wins only a four-week stay for this play. Nigel Bruce plays a major who tries to expose his best friend's wife (Francine Larrimore) in her infidilities. He also errs, but the husband (A. E. Matthews) can no longer ignore her conduct.

Nov 29 *The Constant Wife* (NY—Maxine Elliott—Comedy). W. Somerset Maugham's fiction of the clever Constance (Ethel Barrymore) who takes her husband's infidelity in stride, using it as reason enough to go on a holiday with a former suitor, and yet remain constant, runs 29 weeks. C. Aubrey Smith plays her husband. Gilbert Miller stages. The play opens in London at the Strand on April 6, 1927, with Fay Compton and Leon Quartermaine in the leads. It has 70 showings.

Nov 30 *The Desert Song* (NY—Casino—Musical). Sigmund Romberg provides the score, and Otto Harbach, Oscar Hammerstein II, and Frank Mandel the book and lyrics for this show about a French lieutenant secretly helping native rebels. "Riff Song" and "One Alone" are among the memorable songs. Robert Halliday is featured with Vivienne Segal. There are 471 performances. On April 7, 1927, the show opens at London's Drury Lane with Harry Welchman and Edith Day. It achieves 432 performances.

Dec 9 *The Constant Nymph*. See L premiere, 1926.

Dec 10 *The Trumpet Shall Sound* (NY—American Laboratory—Drama). Thornton Wilder's play is about a man who finds the servants have turned his house, in his absence, into a rooming house full of unfortunates. Staged by Richard Boleslavsky, it receives 30 performances.

Dec 27 *Peggy-Ann* (NY—Vanderbilt—Musical). Lew Fields produces this show, with book by son Herbert and music and lyrics by Rodgers and Hart. Helen Ford plays Peggy-Ann, a working girl who dreams of a more elegant life in New York City. It is a reworking of the Marie Dressler vehicle *Tillie's Nightmare*. There are 333 showings. On July 27, 1927, it opens at London's Daly's with Dorothy Dickson in the title-role. The show has 132 performances.

Dec 28 *Betsy* (NY—New Amsterdam—Musical). This show has Rodgers and Hart music and lyrics, but more memorable is an Irving Berlin interpolation, "Blue Skies." Borrah Minnevitch and his Harmonica Orchestra win applause for a version of Gershwin's "Rhapsody in Blue." The show closes after 39 performances.

Dec 29 *Devil in the Cheese* (NY—Charles Hopkins—Comedy). Tom Cushing creates a plot in which an archaeologist (Robert McWade) eats some ancient cheese which helps him see what's going on inside his lovesick daughter's head. Bela Lugosi plays a Greek priest. This runs nearly five months.

Dec 30 *In Abraham's Bosom* (NY—Provincetown—Drama). Paul Green's folk tragedy, staged by Jasper Deeter, wins the Pulitzer Prize. After closing in Greenwich Village, it later opens briefly uptown at the Garrick Theatre, and has a further six weeks back in the Village after the award is announced, for a total of 116 performances. In the cast are Frank Wilson, Rose McClendon, Jules Bledsoe, and others who recreate black life in North Carolina's eastern section in 1885. Bledsoe plays Abraham, striving to improve his people's lot, scoffed at, and finally killed by avengers of his murder of his white half-brother.

Dec 30 *Chicago* (NY—Music Box—Comedy). Maurine Watkins' tale of a fast-living woman who shoots her husband features George Abbott and Francine Larrimore. It runs nearly 22 weeks and is chosen as a "Best Play." It has a brief showing at London's Gate Theatre beginning March 13, 1935. Molly Johnson and Vincent Price are in the cast.

1926 BRITISH PREMIERES

Jan 26 *Scotch Mist* (L—St. Martin's—Comedy). Tallulah Bankhead is Mary Denvers, in a cast which includes Beatrix Lehmann, Edmond Breon, Brember Wills, Robert Horton, and Godfrey Tearle. The play runs for 114 performances.

Feb 2 *Kid Boots* See NY premiere, 1923.

Feb 3 *The Student Prince* See NY premiere, 1924.

Feb 8 *The Firebrand* See NY premiere, 1924.

Feb 15 *Is Zat So?* See NY premiere, 1925.

Feb 17 *Wildflower* See NY premiere, 1923.

Feb 23 *R. S. V. P.* Joyce Barbour sings "Gentlemen Prefer Blondes" in this show, primarily by Archibald de Bear, with music by Norman O'Neill. Cyril Ritchard is in the troupe, which earns a runs of 295 performances.

Feb 24 *Palladium Pleasures* (L—Palladium—Revue). There are 309 performances for this show with a book by Laurie Wylie, Greatrex Newman, Gilbert Lofthouse, and Ronald Jeans. Vivian Ellis provides the score. Lorna and Toots Pounds, Billy Merson, George Clarke, Tiny Mite, and Pearl Dawn are among the entertainers, with Anton Dolin and Iris Rowe as a dancing duo.

March 15 *Ashes* (L—Prince of Wales's—Drama). Vera, Countess of Cathcart, bases her play on a personal scandal. There are only eight performances and considerable critical disapproval of the tastelessnes of dramatizing the affair. On March 22, it opens at New York's National with the Countess featured. It runs for a week of what Burns Mantle describes as "polite booing."

March 16 *The Best People* (L—Lyric—Comedy). Avery Hopwood and David Gray's play achieves a very long run of 809 performances, with Nora Swinburne and Hugh Williams as the children of the "best people," who won't marry their parents' choices. She wants the family chauffeur (Ian Hunter) and he loves a chorus girl (Maisie Darrell). Olga Lindo, as another chorus girl, adds innuendo and comedy to the affairs. Henrietta Watson and C. V. France are the suffering parents. William Mollison stages. "She is, indeed, the quintessence of vulgarity; but vulgarity, treated by an artist, has its own distinction, and there is not a ha'porth of offence, rather a real fineness and exquisiteness in the superficial commonness of Miss Olga Lindo. She makes a new language, you might say, of her American slang, a kind of elegant *argot* in its very inelegance, its fantastic incongruity with the persons addressed." *The Times*, reports.

April 10 *Riverside Nights* (L—Lyric, Hammersmith—Revue). The river is the Thames, near the Lyric, where Nigel Playfair and A. P. Herbert have concocted this show, with music by Frederick Austin and Alfred Reynolds. The show is praised and moves to the West End's Ambassadors' Theatre, returning to the Lyric for a total of 229 performances. In the company are Playfair, Elsa Lanchester, Miles Malleson, Marie Dainton and Kathlyn Hilliard.

April 14 *Lady, Be Good.* See NY premiere, 1924.

April 15 *This Woman Business* (L—Haymarket—Comedy). Benn W. Levy's play earns 187 performances. Fay Compton and Frank Cellier play leads.

April 29 *Cochran's Revue, 1926* (L—Pavilion—Revue). Black Americans Noble Sissle and Eubie Blake are among the songsmiths contributing to this show, which has 148 performances. Hermione Baddeley, Annie Croft, Ernest Thesiger, Leonide Massine, Vera Nemtchinova, Billy Bradford, Douglas Byng, Basil Howes, Lance Lister, Florence Desmond, and Joan Clarkson are in the cast.

May 1 *The Ringer* (L—Wyndham's—Drama). Who is the Ringer, that criminal master of disguise, and how has he managed to kill Maurice Meister (Franklin Dyall), the fence and corrupt solicitor, under the noses of Scotland Yard? This mystery by Edgar Wallace has 410 performances. Gerald Du Maurier directs.

May 21 *Aloma* (L—Adelphi—Drama). This "tale of the South Seas," by John Hymer and Le Roy Clemens, is a variation on the theme of lovers temporarily associated with wrong partners. It uses Vivienne Osborne, Clay Clement, Francis Lister, and W. Cronin Wilson. A.H. Van Buren stages, with sets by the Harkers. There are 138 showings.

June 9 *Easy Virtue.* See NY premiere, 1925.

June 16 *Granite* (L—Ambassadors'—Drama). Clemence Dane's uncompromising play about a woman on a granite island in the care of the man who killed her husband features Sybil Thorndike, Lewis Casson, and Nicholas Hannen. The play is admired, but it does not last longer than 62 performances. It comes to New York's American Laboratory on Feb 11, 1927, with Blanche Tancock as the woman.

June 30 *Rookery Nook* (L—Aldwych—Comedy). This is another of Ben Travers' Aldwych farces, with a cast including Ethel Coleridge, Mary Brough, J. Robertson Hare, Tom Walls, Ralph Lynn, and Winifred Shotter. It wins a run of 409 showings.

July 20 *Ask Beccles* (L—Globe—Drama). This mystery, by Cyril Campion and Edward Dignon, has been first seen in suburban London at the Q, in Kew Bridge, where a number of successful new scripts are being tried out. Moving to the West End, it has a run of 150 performances, followed by a revival at the Comedy Theatre. Basil Foster plays Beccles, with a cast including Barbara Hoffe, Eric Maturin, and Victor Lewison, among others.

Aug 12 *Escape* (L—Ambassadors'—Drama). John Galsworthy's episodic drama tells the story of a man sent to prison for manslaughter, his escape, and final surrender. Nicholas Hannen is featured. The production has 248 showings. It comes to New York's Booth on Oct 26, 1927, with Leslie Howard featured. It wins 173 performances.

Aug 24 *The Queen Was in the Parlour* (L—St. Martin's—Drama). Noel Coward's romance has 136 performances. Herbert Marshall, Madge Titheradge, and Lady Tree are featured.

Aug 31 *Tip Toes.* See NY premiere, 1925.

Sep 6 *And So To Bed* (L—Queen's—Comedy). J.B. Fagen produces his own play, based on some presumed adventures of Samuel Pepys. Edmund Gwenn is featured. There are 331 performances. On Nov 9, 1927, it opens at New York's Shubert with Wallace Eddinger and Yvonne Arnaud. There are 189 showings.

Sep 7 *The Whole Town's Talking* (L—Strand—Comedy). Anita Loos and her husband John Emerson earn 119 showings of their play, already produced in 1922 in Hempstead, Long Island. In the cast are such players as Mona Harrison, Jack Melford, John Deverell, Sylvia Hawkes, Ethel Baird, and Catherine Dale Owen.

Sep 11 *Blackbirds.* (L—Pavilion—Revue). Lew Leslie conceives and stages this black revue, written by George W. Meyer. The show has a run of 279 performances. *The Times* reports, " . . . there is little that is beautiful, according to English ideas, in the matter, the music, or the setting of *Blackbirds*, but the dancing is certainly wonderful in its vigour, and occasionally comic. . . ."

Sep 14 *The Constant Nymph* (L—New—Drama). Basil Dean and Margaret Kenny adapt her popular novel about a man who marries a woman while in love with another. He eventually leaves his wife and elopes with the girl, who dies before they are married. Noel Coward, Edna Best, and Cathleen Nesbitt are featured. There are 382 performances. On Dec 9, it opens at New York's Selwyn with Glenn Anders and Beatrix Thomson. It runs over 18 weeks.

Oct 6 *Berkeley Square* (L—St. Martin's—Drama). John Balderston, assisted by J. C. Squire, creates this play based on Henry James's *The Sense of the Past*. In it an American is able to travel back to the era of his family's founding in the 18th century. The cast includes Brian Gilmour, Beatrice Wilson, Lawrence Anderson, and Jean Forbes-Robertson. It runs for 181 performances. On Nov 4, 1929, it opens at New York's Lyceum with Leslie Howard featured.

Oct 7 *Sunny.* See NY premiere, 1925.

Oct 21 *Princess Charming* (L—Palace—Musical). There are 362 performances of this Hungarian tale, with an English book by Arthur Wimperis and Laurie Wylie and a score by Albert Szirmai. Robert Russell and Jack Waller also contribute songs. Alice Delysia, George Grossmith, Winnie Melville, John Clarke, and W.H. Berry play leads. The show is staged by William Mollison and choreographed by the Espinosas.

Nov 2 *Queen High.* See NY premiere, 1926.

Nov 3 *Yellow Sands* (L—Haymarket—Comedy). Barry Jackson brings his production of the Eden and Adelaide Phillpotts play to the West End for a run of 610 performances. H.K. Ayliff stages, with sets by Paul Shelving. Cedric Hardwicke, Ralph Richardson, and Frank Vosper play in this comedy about heirs to a valuable inheritance.

Nov 17 *My Son John* (L—Shaftesbury—Musical). Oscar Straus provides the score, with a libretto by Graham John. Added songs are by Desmond Carter, Harry Graham, Billy Thompson, Jr., and Vivian Ellis. There are 255 performances. Among the ensemble are Betty Chester, Billy Merson, Annie Croft, Vera Pearce, Margery Aldington, and Charles Stone.

Nov 29 *The First Year.* See NY premiere, 1920.

Dec 1 *Lido Lady* (L—Gaiety—Musical). The songs are by Rodgers and Hart, but Ronald Jeans reworks the original book by Bolton, Kalmar, and Ruby for British audiences. There are 259 performances. The cast includes Jack Hulbert, Phyllis Dare, Cicely Courtneidge, and Bobby Comber.

Dec 22 *Broadway.* See NY premiere, 1926.

1926 REVIVALS/REPERTORIES

Jan 16 Tonight, Chekhov's *Uncle Vanya* is produced at the Barnes Theatre, after which it transfers to the West End and the Duke of York's for 36 performances. On Feb 16, Chekhov's *The Three Sisters* is revived, with a cast including Mary Sheridan, John Gielgud, Beatrix Thomson, and Ion Swinley. On April 18, Gogol's *The Government Inspector* is revived and later moved to the Gaiety Theatre for four weeks, with a cast including Charles Laughton and Claude Rains as the servant and the bogus official.

Jan 25 Franz Werfel's *Goat Song* is a tale of peasant rebellion and hereditary taint in 18th century Serbia. It lasts only 58 performances. Jacob Ben-Ami stages for the Theatre Guild at the Guild Theatre in New York. The large cast includes Judith Lowry, Lynn Fontanne, Blanche Yurka, Helen Westley, Dwight Fry, Edward G. Robinson, and Alfred Lunt.

Jan 26 Hermman Sudermann's German drama, *Magda*, runs for three weeks in Lawrence Anhalt's revival at New York's 49th Street Theatre. Bertha Kalich stars.

Jan 30 At London's Kingsway Theatre, Barry Jackson, of the Birmingham Repertory Company, revives Rutland Broughton's *The Immortal Hour* for 65 showings, followed by his Birmingham production of *The Marvellous History of Saint Bernard*, by Henry Gheon. This earns 69 repetitions, with Laurence Olivier as a minstrel and Gwen Ffrangcon-Davies as Marguerite.

Jan 31 The Repertory Players try out Eugene O'Neill's *Beyond the Horizon* in London at the Regent Theatre. Raymond Massey, Leslie Banks, Aubrey Mather, and Marie Ney are cast. In March, the production is revived for a two-week run at the Everyman Theatre in Hampstead.

Feb 7 At London's Regent Theatre, the Fellowship of Players presents Shakespeare's *Richard II*, with Leslie Faber as the king and Edmund Willard as Bolingbroke. Eric Portman plays Lord Ross. It revives *Pericles*, played by Philip Desborough, in London at the Scala Theatre on March 14. At the Apollo, the group revives *The Taming of the Shrew* on Sep 26. On Dec 12, the Fellowship offers *Romeo and Juliet* at the Strand Theatre.

Feb 8 *The Plough and the Stars*, by Sean O'Casey, has its world premiere in Dublin at the Abbey Theatre tonight. On Feb 11, the word has got round to some Irish patriots who decide O'Casey has maligned those who fought for Ireland's freedom against the British. They provoke a riot during the performance which is comparable to that which greeted the premiere of J. M. Synge's *The Playboy of the Western World* in 1907.

Feb 16 Charles Gilpin returns to the role of Jones in this 35-performance revival of O'Neill's *The Emperor Jones*, at New York's Provincetown Playhouse. On Nov 10, there are 61 additional performances at the Mayfair Theatre.

Feb 20 Leonid Andreyev's *He Who Gets Slapped* is produced in Birmingham by Barry Jackson's Repertory Company, with Muriel Hewitt and Stanley Lathbury. On March 30, in Barnes, Andreyev's play, *Katerina*, is given a premiere, with John Gielgud, Frances Carson, Clare Greet, and Jean Forbes-Robertson among the cast members. On Nov 22, Andreyev's *The Life of Man* is revived at the Gate Theatre Salon in London.

March 3 George Bernard Shaw's *Mrs. Warren's Profession* wins 68 showings in this revival at London's Strand Theatre. Edyth Goodall plays Mrs. Warren.

April 5 The Shuberts revive the old melodrama, *The Two Orphans*, for a month at New York's Cosmopolitan Theatre. The large cast includes many major talents such as Robert Loraine, Wilton Lakaye, Henry E. Dixey, Robert Warwick, Jose Ruben, Fay Bainter, May Robson, Henrietta Crosman, Florence Nash, and Mrs. Thomas Whiffen.

April 12 At Stratford-upon-Avon, the spring season of Shakespeare's plays opens with *Henry IV, Part 2*. Randle Ayrton plays Falstaff, with Sebastian Shaw as Prince Hal. Owing to the recent disastrous fire which has destroyed all of the old Memorial Theatre except its library-museum wing, the plays are produced in the "Picture House," under the direction of W. Bridges Adams. The "birthday play" is *Coriolanus*. The other plays in the four-week season are *A Midsummer Night's Dream*, *The Merchant of Venice*, *Richard II*, *Romeo and Juliet*, and *The Merry Wives of Windsor.*

April 13 Earlier premiered at Dublin's Abbey Theatre, T.C. Murray's *Autumn Fire*, a play of rural Ireland has Una O'Connor as Ellen Keegan. The production, at London's Little Theatre, plays eight weeks. Later in the year, the play will be seen in New York at the Klaw Theatre.

April 19 Winthrop Ames' revival of Gilbert & Sullivan's *Iolanthe* runs through the New York season at the Plymouth Theatre, for a total of 299 performances.

May 3 Walter Hartwig again conducts the annual Little Theatre Tournament at the Nora Bayes Theatre in New York. Among the plays are Djuna Barnes' *The Dove*, James Branch Cabell's *Simon's Hour*, and Martin Flavin's *Brains*. The Belasco Trophy again goes to Texas' Dallas Players. Britain's Huddersfield Thespians win a prize, too.

May 14 Tonight at London's Globe Theatre, Louis Verneuil opens a French season of plays. The first play is his own comedy, *Ma Cousine de Varsovie*, in which he stars. On May 24, he offers his *Le Fauteuil 47*, in which he plays Paul.

May 17 The Princess Theatre of Madrid, headed by the "Bernhardt of Spain," Maria Guerrero, and Fernando Diaz de Mendoza, makes its American debut in a week's engagement at the Manhattan Opera House. The Spanish repertoire includes modern plays by Benevente and Quintero.

June 10 Mrs. Patrick Campbell returns to the London stage as Countess Strong-i'-th'-Arm, in H. F. Maltby's *What Might Happen*. In the cast at the Savoy Theatre are such players as Edmund Gwenn, Lilian Braithwaite, and Fred Kerr. There are only 52 performances.

June 12 At Barry Jackson's Birmingham Repertory Theatre, the play is *The Barber and the Cow*, by D. T. Davies. This Welsh comedy is animated by Ralph Richardson, Cedric Hardwicke, and Dorothy Black, among others.

June 12 W. Somerset Maugham's comedy, *Caroline*, is revived for 153 performances in London at the Playhouse, with Edith Evans, C. Aubrey Smith, Henry Daniell, Marie Lohr, and Irene Vanbrugh as Caroline.

June 19 At London's Strand Theatre, the Stage Society offers a performance of Eugene O'Neill's *The Great God Brown*, with Hugh Williams and John Gielgud. On July 14, O'Neill's monologue, *Before Breakfast*, is presented by the Etlinger Theatre School at its auditorium. On October 27, at the Arts Theatre Club, O'Neill's *Where the Cross is Made* opens.

June 21 From Paris Sacha Guitry and Yvonne Printemps come to London to offer a limited run of *Mozart*, Guitry's popular play about the composer, with music by Reynaldo Hahn. Printemps plays Mozart, to Guitry's Grimm.

July 5 The nine-week summer season of Shakespeare's plays at Stratford-upon-Avon opens with *The Merry Wives of Windsor*, revived from the spring season and produced in the "Picture House," owing to the destruction of the old Shakespeare Memorial Theatre by fire in March. Also offered are *Coriolanus, Henry IV, Part 2, A Midsummer Night's Dream, The Merchant of Venice, Richard II, Romeo and Juliet*, and a new production of *The Tempest*.

Aug 25 The sixth season of *The Co-Optimists* revue ensemble wins a run of 27 weeks in London at His Majesty's Theatre.

Sep 4 The Liverpool Repertory Company in London at the Playhouse offer A. A. Milne's *Portrait of a Gentleman in Slippers*. Herbert Lomas plays Henry XXIV.

Sep 6 In Dublin, at the Abbey Theatre, *The Big House*, a play by Lennox Robinson, is presented. On Dec 6, the new play is *The Farm*, by Sean Ogain. The following day, W. B. Yeats' version of Sophocles *Oedipus The King* is produced, with F. S. McCormick as Oedipus, Eileen Crowe as Jocasta, and Barry Fitzgerald as Creon.

Sep 30 At London's Kingsway Theatre, Henrik Ibsen's *Rosmersholm* is revived, with Edith Evans as Rebecca West and Charles Carson as John Rosmer. It is seen 52 times.

Oct 11 In New York the Theatre Guild produces Franz Werfel's *Juarez and Maximilian* a chronicle of events in Mexico City and the field between 1865–67, leading to the overthrow of the puppet-emperor Maximilian. Initially it has six weeks of performances before being played in repertory. Alfred Lunt and Clare Eames play the Emperor and his Carlotta. Also in the distinguished company are Harold Clurman, Sanford Meisner, Edward G. Robinson, Morris Carnovsky, Albert Bruning, Cheryl Crawford, Earle Larimore, Dudley Digges, Arnold Daly, Philip Loeb, and Margalo Gillmore.

Oct 25 Eva LeGallienne settles her Civic Repertory Theatre in the refurbished 14th Street Theatre, with Jacinto Benevente's *Saturday Night*. Even with LeGallienne's staging, the production manages only 13 performances. Anton Chekhov's *The Three Sisters*, opening on Nov 8, fares better with 39 performances. Beatrice Terry, Rose Hobart, and LeGallienne play. Henrik Ibsen's *The Master Builder*, is added to the repertory for 29 performances. John Gabriel Borkman receives 15 performances in repertory.

Oct 27 Edward Sheldon's American play, *Romance*, earns 131 performances in this revival at London's Playhouse Theatre.

Nov 8 At London's Gate Theatre Salon, Eugene O'Neill's play about an inter-racial love, *All God's Chillun Got Wings*, has its British premiere. Harold Young plays Jim Harris, with Molly Veness as Ella Downey. On March 13, 1933, it is revived at the Embassy Theatre in London, with Paul Robson as Jim Harris, the black man who loves the white girl, Ella Downey, played by Flora Robson. Andre van Gyseghem directs.

Nov 15 Among other revivals this season at the Lyric, Hammersmith, Nigel Playfair offers Moliere's *The Would-Be Gentleman*, newly translated by F. Anstey. Playfair and Sydney Fairbrother play M. Jourdain and his wife. James Whale, Miles Malleson, and Florence McHugh are also in the company. Much earlier in the year, on Jan 4, the Irish Players at the Abbey Theatre in Dublin have offered Lady Gregory's translation of the play, with Barry Fitzgerald as M. Jourdain and Maureen Delaney as Mme. Jourdain.

Nov 22 Producer E. Ray Goetz rushes an English version of Sacha Guitry's *Mozart* on stage at New York's Music Box Theatre, with his wife, Irene Bordoni, in a breeches role as the young composer, charming the ladies of Paris. This runs four weeks. It's followed by a five-week engagement of Guitry's own Paris production, with Yvonne Printemps as Mozart. Guitry stages and is also in the company. This show opens on Dec 27. Both productions use the music Reynaldo Hahn has composed for Guitry.

Nov 29 Previously seen in Britain as *The Daisy*, Ferenc Molnar's *Liliom* opens in a new version—by the same translators, Shillingford and Ellis—at the King's Theatre, Southsea, later moving to the Duke of York's in the West End. Ivor Novello plays Liliom, with Fay Compton, Charles Laughton, Violet Farebrother, and Ben Webster in the cast.

Nov 29 The Theatre Guild presents Sidney Howard's *Ned McCobb's Daughter*, the story of the resourceful Carrie McCobb Callahan (Clare Eames), who outsmarts her thieving husband's bootlegger brother, played by Alfred Lunt. Others on hand are Margalo Gillmore, Morris Carnovsky, Edward G. Robinson, and Earle Larimore. The show runs for 156 performances, joined in repertory by Howard's *The Silver Cord* on Dec 20, with Laura Hope Crews as the son-devouring Mrs. Phelps. Staged by John Cromwell, this has 112 performances.

Nov 30 The Actors Theatre Company revives Eugene O'Neill's *Beyond the Horizon* for ten weeks at New York's Mansfield Theatre. Judith Lowry, Robert Keith, and Aline MacMahon are in the ensemble.

Dec 6 Continuing their program of classics in repertory, Eva LeGallienne and her Civic Repertory Theatre colleagues offer Carlo Goldoni's *La Locandiera*, or *The Mistress of the Inn*. It receives 31 performances, with LeGallienne as Mirandolina, the mistress. *Twelfth Night* joins the repertory on Dec 20, for 26 performances.

Aloma

Dec 6 Producer Winthrop Ames has his second successful Manhattan Gilbert & Sullivan revival, following last season's *Iolanthe*. This time it's *The Pirates of Penzance* which runs 16 weeks.

Dec 12 Two London groups devoted to special performances of challenging new plays and classics, the Stage Society and the Three Hundred Club, join to present D. H. Lawrence's *The Widowing of Mrs. Holroyd*. Marda Vanne plays the title-role.

Dec 13 From Moscow, the Habimah troupe comes to New York's Mansfield Theatre to present S. Ansky's *The Dybbuk*. Alternating with *The Eternal Jew* and *The Deluge*, the productions total 111 performances. Eugene Vakhtangov directs. Three days later, the Neighborhood Playhouse *Dybbuk* production is revived for 41 performances, but it's in English.

Dec 21 The holidays are on the way, and with them the annual entertainments for children. Today, the show is the perennially popular *Charley's Aunt* at London's St. James's Theatre. This of course is not a traditional fairytale pantomime, but is judged suitable for children. In recent years, light comedies, musicals, even mysteries have all been offered as holiday shows. Among this season's fare: *Peter Pan* (Adelphi), *Puss in Boots* (Apollo), *Where the Rainbow Ends* (Holborn Empire), *Sleeping Beauty* (Lyceum), *Alladin* (Palladium), *When Knights Were Bold* (Scala), *Treasure Island* (Strand), *The Windmill Man* (Victoria Palace), and *A Midsummer Night's Dream* (Winter Garden).

Dec 24 Although it's the Christmas season, the revival of *Macbeth* in London at the Prince's Theatre is not in the nature of a holiday pantomime. Henry Ainley and Sybil Thorndike are Macbeth and his lady, with Lewis Casson as Banquo and Master Jack Hawkins as Fleance. Margaret Webster and Alan Webb appear in smaller roles.

Jan 20 Future actress Patricia Neal is born in Packard, Kentucky.

Feb 7 English drama critic and historian Thomas McDonald Rendle (b. 1856) is dead. Rendle succeeded Clement Scott as drama critic for the *Daily Telegraph*. He also served as reviewer for the *Daily Mail*.

Feb 14 American manager George Middleton is dead in South Pasadena, California, at age 81. Middleton was one of the founders of the Kohl-Middleton films and the Orpheum circuit of vaudeville theatres.

March 18 Mrs. John Barrymore (Michael Strange) plays Eleanora, who brings the healing message of Easter to her strife-torn family, in Strindberg's *Easter*. With *One Day More*, the production runs 28 times at New York's Princess Theatre.

April 1 Actor Jacob P. Adler the noted exponent of the Yiddish drama (b. 1855) dies at age 71 in New York City. Born in Odessa, Russia, he was, for a time in the Russian Civil Service. He was manager of the Grand Theatre in New York for a number of years.

April 9 American actor-manager Henry Miller (b. 1860) dies in New York. Miller played in support of Helena Modjeska, Adelaide Nielson, Mme. Janauschek, and Clara Morris. He became leading man of the Empire Theatre Stock Company. Miller's plays include *The Great Divide*, *The Famous Mrs. Fair*, *Pasteur*, *The Changelines*, and *Embers*.

April 13 Helen Hayes is hailed as a worthy successor to Maude Adams in the role of Maggie Shand, in J. M. Barrie's *What Every Woman Knows*. This revival runs beyond the season's end, closing after 268 performances.

April 14 Senorita Raquel Meller opens on Broadway at the Empire Theatre in a month-long engagement, sharing her repertoire of Spanish songs, accompanied by members of the Philharmonic Society of New York. Orchestra seats are an unheard-of $25. She is a success, not only in New York, but also in Boston, Philadelphia, Pittsburgh, Cleveland, and Chicago, where the top is only $10. (Robert Benchley promptly burlesques her songs and program-notes.)

April 19 Actor-manager Sir Squire Bancroft (b. 1841) dies. Bancroft, with his actress-wife Marie Wilton, introduced a number of reforms on the British stage, both with regards to acting and to the type of play produced. To them is attributal the vogue of the drawing-room comedy and drama with their typical stage settings and decor.

June 24 American stage director and producer Julian Mitchell dies in Long Branch, New Jersey at age 72. Mitchell, originally a dancer at Niblo's Gardens, began directing when he was 20. He staged 13 of the 19 *Ziegfeld Follies* produced during his lifetime. Mitchell was the husband of dancer Bessie Clayton.

June 24 An unknown, Paulette Goddard, appears in the chorus of *No Foolin'*, which opens today at the Globe Theatre in New York.

Aug 20 American stage and screen actor William Owens is dead in Chicago at age 63. Owens played in support of many stars including Julia Marlowe, Ada Rehan, and Lewis Morrison.

Sep 13 American stage and screen actor Frank Norcross dies in Glendale, California, at age 70. Norcross supported many stars during his career, being at one time Fanny Davenport's leading man.

Sep 20 Kate Smith makes her Broadway debut as Tiny Little in *Honeymoon Lane*. She is described as a "coonshouting blues singer."

Sep 21 In *Yellow*, Chester Morris plays the yellow Val Parker, who deserts his pregnant girl-friend (Shirley Warde) to marry a society girl (Selena Royle). Refusing his money, the spurned girl takes to the streets to support the child. She shoots him when he tries to renew their relationship, but he doesn't die, and she doesn't improve. Margaret Vernon's play runs for 17 weeks at the National Theatre in New York.

Sep 24 Midget comedian Tom Thumb is dead in Los Angeles at age 84. Thumb, whose family name was Darius Adner Alden, was a famed attraction of circuses and museums for 60 years.

Sep 25 American actor Joseph Jefferson Holland is dead at age 65 in New York. Named after his famous godfather, Holland made his adult debut playing in Daly's company from 1886–89, and touring with his elder brother, Edmund Milton. His father was the English actor, George Holland.

Oct 11 Actor Roger DeKoven makes his first New York appearance as a walk-on in Franz Werfel's *Juarez and Maximilian* at the Guild Theatre. He is a student at the Theatre Guild School.

Oct 25 Actress-director Eva Le Gallienne launches the Civic Repertory Theatre with the opening of Jacinto Benevente's *Saturday Night*, in which she plays Imperia under her own direction. The actress made her stage debut in London as a Page in Alfred Sutro's adaptation of Maeterlinck's *Monna Vanna* at the Queen's Theatre in 1914.

Nov 8 American actor-producer James K. Hackett (b. 1869) is dead in Paris. Hackett joined Daniel Frohman's company in 1895, where he appeared in *The Prisoner of Zenda* and similar plays. With the profits of his production of *The Walls of Jericho*, he opened his own theatre in New York.

1926 THEATERS/PRODUCTIONS

In Britain, patents are granted for: A. B. Hector's Color Music device, which arranges light sources in a logarithmic spiral; J. G. Walker's projection screen, which permits the insertion of set elements such as windows or doors below the portion used for scenic projection.

Joseph A. Cunningham receives a U.S. patent for his treadmill and back screen with scenic view, in which the movement of the view is coordinated with the speed of the treadmill.

The Public Morality Council—formerly called the London Council for the Promotion of Morality—informs the Lord Chamberlain, official censor of plays in Great Britain, of its objections to "offensive language in plays and improper reference to the Deity." The Council also makes the Prime Minister aware of its anxieties about "the atmosphere and general tone of certain plays."

Jan The Lord Chamberlain's Office issues some revisions in the regulations for licensing all plays, pantomimes, musicals, and revues. One of these is that a copy of every new play and of every new act, scene, or addition or alteration must be sent to the office by the theatre licensee *at least seven days before* the first acting of presentation. The copy remains with the office for purposes of record. Licenses are issued only to theatre managers, not to authors or owners of plays. All alterations or additions to plays must be submitted *before* they are produced, or the play may be closed. The office fee for reading a three-act play is £2-2s.

Feb 15 The Mansfield Theatre opens in New York City. The theatre is named for Richard Mansfield, the American actor who died in 1907. The theatre will be rechristened the Brooks Atkinson Theatre in 1960.

Feb 22 After a performance of his popular revue, *Vanities*, Earl Carroll stages a party in the theatre. A highlight is provided when a Carroll showgirl steps into an on-stage bathtub filled with champagne. After an investigation, Carroll is charged with violating the Volstead Act. He insists the liquid was ginger ale and sherry. Convicted of perjury, Carroll is fined and sentenced to 366 days in the federal peni-

Princess Charming

tentiary in Atlanta. He's released shortly after four months, and the show thrives.

Feb 23 The Vaudeville Theatre opens on the Strand after its third re-construction. Robert Atkinson has designed this 659-seat theatre, changing the previous horse-shoe shaped auditorium into an oblong, but leaving the 1899 facade unaltered. J.M. and R. Gatti are the managers and the opening show is an Archie de Bear revue, *R.S.V.P.*

March It is only 33 years since George Bernard Shaw has written his controversial play, *Mrs. Warren's Profession.* Now at last, the Lord Chamberlain's office gives permission for its first public performance in London.

March 8 Work begins on an extension to the "Picture House"—actually the Greenhill Street Cinema in Stratford-upon-Avon—to make a temporary theatre-home for the annual spring festival season of Shakespeare's plays. On March 6, the 47-year-old Shakespeare Memorial Theatre has been gutted by fire.

April Stanley McCandless uses the Linnebach projector (a type of shadow box) for projections designed for a production of Henrik Ibsen's *Brand* at the Yale Theatre. Donald Oenslager designs.

April 14 The Dramatists' Guild's Basic Agreement with theatre managers in the U. S. and Canada goes into effect on this date. The agreement requires managers to produce only works by Guild members, with some limited foreign exceptions. There are also effective protections for playwrights in the agreement.

April 18 John Drinkwater, playwright and theatre-man, broadcasts his poem, written as an appeal for the *Daily Telegraph* Fund to construct a new Shakespeare Memorial Theatre in Stratford-upon-Avon. This evening the poem is also read aloud in 60 theatres throughout England as well.

May Writing in *Play Pictorial*, editor B. W. Findon comments on the disappearance from the London theatre-scene of the actor-manager, Gerald Du Maurier being the last.

Summer District Attorney Banton asks a jury of New Yorkers to see *Bunk of 1926*, charged with immorality. As a result, the show is ordered closed, but an injuction stays this.

June The Lord Chamberlain notifies licensees of those theatres licensed by him that Sunday play performances shall only be permitted—unless he makes a specific exception—to those societies which are "bona fide established for the private performance of stage plays." Tickets shall only be available to members of the society, who may bring a reasonable number of guests. No tickets are to be sold at the theatres. No payment to performers may be made, beyond an honorarium for expenses. No intoxicants may be sold or supplied. No performances at all are to be permitted on Christmas Day or Good Friday.

June 15 Surveying production activity on Broadway for the season, Burns Mantle cites 263 new plays and revivals. Of these, 220 are new plays, with only two or three dozen judged successful with the public. Less than a half-dozen, however, meet Mantle's standards of fulfilling author-promise or establishing new artistic standards. Of the new works, 170 are legitimate plays; the rest are musicals and revues. Only 33 plays have more than 100 performances, now regarded as a successful run and 20 musicals win 100 or more performances. The ten *Best Plays* for the 1925–26 Broadway season are: Kelly's *Craig's Wife*—which has also won the Pulitzer Prize, O'Neill's *The Great God Brown*, Ansky's *The Dybbuk*, Pollock's *The Enemy*, Lonsdale's *The Last of Mrs. Cheyney*, Hurlbut's *The Bride of the Lamb*, Van Druten's *Young Woodley*, Kaufman's *The Butter and Egg Man*, Connelly's *The Wisdom Tooth*, and Arlen's *The Green Hat.*

June 30 This fiscal year, the net income of the Shubert Theatre Corporation totals $2,320,867. There is no dividend, although the 154,040 shares have each earned $15.06.

Oct John Mason Brown, writing in *Theatre Arts Monthly*, notes that this season the most notable of foreign plays are not to be seen on Broadway, but instead at the so-called "art theatres," particularly the four experimental playhouses, the Neighborhood, the Guild, the Laboratory, and Eva LeGallienne's new Civic Repertory. "Certainly the prices . . . fifty cents to $1.50 evenings and Saturday matinées are no more unusual than the plays she has announced."

Oct 11 Foes of vice succeed in getting the dramatization of Dreiser's *An American Tragedy* included on the Manhattan District Attorney's list of plays to be investigated for alleged immorality.

Oct 26 Eva LeGallienne opens her Civic Repertory Theatre at the old 14th Street Theatre in New York.

Nov 1 The 58th Street Theatre, between 6th and 7th Avenues in New York, presents *Two Girls Wanted.* Producer-owner John Golden sells the theatre in 1933. Subsequently, it is used as a legitimate theatre, a motion-picture house, and a church. It is currently owned by the American Broadcasting Company and used as a TV studio.

Nov 9 A special matinee of Shakespearian scenes is presented in London at the Theatre Royal, Drury Lane. King George V and Queen Mary attend this benefit performance which raises £ 2,600 for the building of a new Shakespeare Memorial Theatre in Stratford-upon-Avon.

Dec 10 In New Haven, the new Yale University Theatre opens with a production of *The Patriarch.* The 700 seats are filled with academic dignitaries, such as Yale's president, James Rowland Angell, and Broadway celebrities. Eyes are on Edward S. Harkness, who has given $2 million two years ago for the establishment at Yale of a Department of Drama and a theatre to complement it. The head of the program is none other than Professor George Pierce Baker, who now sees the dream he nourished at Harvard University—always unfriendly to the drama as an academic pursuit—in his "47 Workshop" become a handsome reality. Architects Blackall, Clapp & Whittemore have created a theatre which is neo-Gothic inside and out, a fitting accessory to much of the surrounding campus. Settings for Boyd Smith's rustic drama are the work of Donald Oenslager, a recent graduate of Baker's Harvard Workshop.

Dec 26 The Mayor of New York, James Walker, tells Broadway theatre owners and producers they must reform the moral quality of some productions. Under pressure from Governor Alfred E. Smith, a committee of nine is formed (actors, authors, producers). Surveying current shows, they find objectionable *The Captive, New York Exchange, Sex, An American Tragedy, Lulu Belle, The Virgin Man,* and *Night Hawk.*

Dec 30 Peter Glenny's play, *New York Exchange*, about a promising young tenor who allows himself to be kept by a rich and aging woman (Alison Skipworth) is deemed objectionable enough to be put on the NY District Attorney's list of morally questionable plays. Nonetheless, it runs over ten weeks.

Jan 18 *The Barker* (NY—Biltmore—Drama). Claudette Colbert plays Lou, a carnival snake-charmer, who charms the barker's college-boy son. Walter Huston plays the father who insists his son must be a lawyer, not a carnival worker. Kenyon Nicholson's play runs for 29 weeks.

Jan 26 *Saturday's Children* (NY—Booth—Comedy). The Actors' Theatre produces Maxwell Anderson's wry picture of a young couple who separate because the man is not really committed to the match. Ruth Hammond and Richard Barbee are the couple. Ruth Gordon and Beulah Bondi are also in the cast. There are 310 performances. On Jan 23, 1934, the comedy, "revised" by Cecil Madden, opens at London's Westminster with Roger Maxwell and Joyce Barbour. It does not have a long run.

Jan 31 *The Road to Rome* (NY—Playhouse—Comedy). Robert E. Sherwood's vision of Hannibal's march on Rome has moments verging on satire, mingled with historical romance. Jane Cowl and Philip Merivale have the leading roles. It runs 440 performances. On May 16, 1928, the show premieres at London's Strand with a cast including J.M. Kerrigan, Isabel Jeans, Natalie Moya, and Merivale as Hannibal.

Feb 2 *Rio Rita* (NY—Ziegfeld—Musical). Opening America's most splendid musical theatre, this show with its striking Joseph Urban settings—complementing the playhouse which he has also designed—runs for 494 performances. In Guy Bolton and Fred Thompson's book, Jim (J. Harold Murray) loves Rita (Ethelind Terry), but his rival (Vincent Serrano) tells her Jim and his Texas Rangers are looking for her brother. Harry Tierney and Joe McCarthy provide the score. Bert Wheeler and Robert Woolsey spark the comedy. ". . . *Rio Rita* breaks no fresh trail into the hinterland of musical comedy; the book is commonplace enough and the humor will never hold both its sides with laughter. But for sheer extravagance of beauty, animated and rhythmic, *Rio Rita* has no rival among its contemporaries," reports the *NY Times*.

Feb 22 *Crime* (NY—Eltinge—Drama). Samuel Shipman and John B. Hymer write this melodrama of a couple forced into crime by a master crook. Douglass Montgomery and Sylvia Sidney are featured. It runs over 23 weeks. On Oct 18, the play comes to London at the Queen's with Miriam Seegar and Albert Hayes as the couple. There are 163 performances.

March 2 *Right You Are If You Think You Are* (NY—Guild—Drama). Luigi Pirandello's paradoxical story leaves small-town meddlers still baffled when they try to find out why Ponza (Edward G. Robinson) has his mother (Beryl Mercer) live apart from him and his wife (Armina Marshall). The Theatre Guild production has 48 performances.

March 21 *Her Cardboard Lover* (NY—Empire—Comedy). Jeanne Eagels plays Simone, who hires Andre (Leslie Howard) to make love to her so she won't be tempted to rejoin her husband. Gilbert Miller stages Jacques Deval's French froth for a 19 week run. On Aug 21, 1928, it opens in London at the Lyric, with Howard again as Andre and American actress Tallulah Bankhead as Simone. There are 173 performances.

March 22 *The Spider* (NY—46th Street—Drama). Fulton Oursler and Lowell Brentano craft this mystery melodrama which features John Halliday and Roy Hargrave. It runs for 40 weeks. The show opens at London's Winter Garden on March 1, 1928, in an adaptation by Roland Pertwee. The cast includes Lennox Pawle, Basil Loder, and Betty Schuster.

April 11 *The Second Man* (NY—Guild—Comedy). The Theatre Guild produces S.N. Behrman's play about a luxury-loving writer, interested in the wealth of one woman but attracted to the person of another. Alfred Lunt, Lynn Fontanne, and Margalo Gillmore are in the cast. The production runs 22 weeks. On Jan 24, 1928, the play opens on the West End at the Playhouse with Noel Coward, Zena Dare, Raymond Massey, and Ursula Jeans. There are 109 performances.

April 21 *The Field God* (NY—Greenwich Village—Drama). Fritz Leiber plays Hardy Gilchrist, a hard-working, honest farmer who denies the God his neighbors worship. In Paul Green's folk-play of eastern North Carolina, he suffers misfortune and shunning until he conforms. The production has 45 performances.

April 25 *Hit the Deck* (NY—Belasco—Musical). Vincent Youmans provides the score and Herbert Fields adapts the play *Shore Leave* for the book about a girl who pursues her sailor-love around the world. Louise Groody and Charles King are featured. The show has 352 performances. On Nov 3, it opens at the London Hippodrome with a story adapted by R.P. Weston and Bert Lee. The cast includes Sydney Howard, Stanley Holloway, and Ellen Pollock. The show runs nearly 35 weeks.

April 25 *The Circus Princess* (NY—Winter Garden—Musical). Emmerich Kalman's operetta is adapted by Harry B. Smith, running half a year. Guy Robertson plays a disinherited prince who joins a circus as a masked marvel. Despite complications, he wins a princess (Desiree Tabor) who is his rich uncle's widow.

May 3 *A Night In Spain* (NY—44th Street—Revue). The Shuberts use an Iberian theme, Spanish plays and players being in vogue. This runs nearly seven months, with Jean Schwartz's music and a cast including Phil Baker, Ted and Betty Healy, Helen Kane, and Grace Hayes.

May 19 *The Grand Street Follies* NY—Neighborhood—Revue). This edition runs nearly 19 weeks, with Dorothy Sands, Aline Bernstein, Albert Carroll, and others spoofing Broadway shows and personalities. Max Ewing composes the score for Agnes Morgan's book and lyrics.

May 31 *Merry-Go-Round* (NY—Klaw—Revue). Libby Holman sings "Hogan's Alley." Another new face in the cast is Leonard Sillman. Older favorites are Marie Cahill, William Collier, and Etienne Girardot. Allan Dinehart stages, and artist Walt Kuhn devises the pantomimes and dances. The show, with a score by Henry Souvaine and Jay Gorney and lyrics by Howard Dietz and Morrie Ryskind, runs for 17 weeks.

July 5 *Padlocks of 1927* (NY—Shubert—Revue). The title of this Shubert show is a back-handed salute to the Wales Padlock Law, designed to discourage production of immoral dramas. Billy Rose contributes the lyrics, and Texas Guinan, famed for her "Hello, suckers!" greeting as a nightclub hostess, is the star. Others in the troupe are Lillian Roth, George Raft, and J. C. Flippen. The show runs three months.

July 11 *Africana* (NY—Daly's—Revue). Ethel Waters' singing and dancing win praise in this black show, written and composed by Donald Heywood. It runs nine weeks.

July 12 *Rang Tang* (NY—Royale—Revue). Miller and Lyles, of *Shuffle Along*, help stage this black show and head the cast as well. "In Monkeyland" is admired for its choreography. Also in the ensemble are Daniel Haynes, Zaidee Jackson, Josephine Jackson, Lavinia Mack, and Lillian Westmoreland. The show achieves 119 performances.

Aug 16 *The Ziegfeld Follies of 1927* (NY—New Amsterdam—Revue). His right to use the title cleared, Florenz Ziegfeld spends $289,000 on this edition. Joseph Urban designs lavish settings, including a jungle with cobras, flamingos, and tigers. Claire Luce rides through this on a live ostrich. Irving Berlin provides music and lyrics. Eddie Cantor, in blackface, is the show's star; he stops it after 167 performances, claiming exhaustion and wanting more pay. Equity sides with Ziegfeld. Also on stage are Ruth Etting, Harry McNaughton, Helen Brown, the Brox Sisters, and the Albertina Rasch Girls.

Sep 1 *Burlesque* (NY—Plymouth—Comedy). Arthur Hopkins produces and stages this play about stage life which he's also

Circus Princess

worked on with author George Watters. Barbara Stanwyck, Hal Skelly, and Oscar Levant are in the cast. The show's fidelity to the life and talk backstage at a burlesque house is a shock to some. The production runs nearly 47 weeks. The comedy opens at London's Queen's on Dec 3, 1928, with Claire Luce and Nelson Keys. On this side of the Atlantic, it runs for 18 weeks.

Sep 6 *Good News* (NY—46th Street—Musical). John Price Jones and Mary Lawlor are featured in this story of college and football mania. The book is by Laurence Schwab and B. G. DeSylva. DeSylva and Lew Brown devise the lyrics for Ray Henderson's music. Among the hits are "The Varsity Drag" and "The Best Things in Life Are Free." The show runs 551 performances. On Aug 15, 1928, it opens at London's Carlton with George Murphy and Julie Johnston. It attracts audiences for over four months.

Sep 12 *My Maryland* (NY—Jolson—Musical). Clyde Fitch's *Barbara Frietchie* now has the music of Sigmund Romberg. Dorothy Donnelly adapts the play and provides the lyrics for this long-running show (312 performances). Evelyn Herbert plays Barbara, who prefers a Yankee captain to a Confederate swain.

Sep 12 *Baby Cyclone* (NY—Henry Miller—Comedy). In George M. Cohan's farce, Spencer Tracy plays a husband who sells his wife's Pekinese with predictable domestic complications. The show runs 23 weeks. On April 10, 1928, it opens at London's Lyric with a cast including Helen Haye, Sebastian Smith, Frederick Volpe, Kathleen O'Regan, and Joseph Coyne. It does not have a long run.

Sep 19 *The Trial of Mary Dugan* (NY—National—Drama). Bayard Veiller's melodrama tells of a Follies girl accused of murdering her lover. Ann Harding has the title role. There are 437 performances. On March 6, 1928, the play comes to the Queen's in London with Genevieve Tobin as Mary. The production lasts 39 weeks.

Sep 19 *Four Walls* (NY—John Golden—Drama). Muni Weisenfrend (Paul Muni) plays Benny Horowitz, a crook who goes straight after a term in Sing Sing. An accidental killing puts him again in the hands of the law. George Abbott stages the play which he and Dana Burnet have crafted. Also in the cast are Lee Strasberg, Sanford Meisner, and William Pawley. The *NY Times* praises Weisenfrend's acting. ". . . Mr. Wisenfrend, who, playing his second English-speaking part, contributes a sensitive, understanding and full-rounded portrayal . . ."

Sep 26 *The Letter.* See L premiere, 1927.

Sep 26 *The Merry Malones* (NY—Erlanger—Musical). To open A. L. Erlanger's new theatre, George M. Cohan invents this tale of Molly Malone who won't marry Joe Westcott if he inherits money. Joe's father solves that problem by giving the money to Molly. Cohan produces and provides music and lyrics; Edward Royce stages. The show runs six months.

Sep 26 *Manhattan Mary* (NY—Apollo—Musical). Ed Wynn, as Crickets, a waiter in a failed Village restaurant, helps the owner's daughter Mary (Ona Munson) get a job in *George White's Scandals*. George White is in the cast and makes sure that she does; he also stages and dances while Wynn conducts the pit orchestra. Music and lyrics are by the team of B. G. DeSylva, Lew Brown, and Ray Henderson. The show runs 33 weeks.

Sep 29 *Murray Hill* (NY—Bijou—Comedy). Leslie Howard writes this vehicle for himself. He plays Wrigley, who bribes his way into the house of a beautiful stranger (Genevieve Tobin) he's seen in a Manhattan traffic-jam.

Oct 3 *Yes, Yes, Yvette* (NY—Sam H. Harris—Musical). Even with lyrics by Irving Caesar, who provided them for *No! No! Nannette!*, this show is no answer or sequel. In 40 performances, it is a fast failure, despite the talents of Jeannette MacDonald as Yvette. The chorus is admired for its dancing of the Black Bottom.

Oct 3 *Sidewalks of New York* (NY—Knickerbocker—Musical). Eddie Dowling and James Hanley take credit for book, lyrics, and music, but this show has only 112 performances. Ruby is played by Ruby Keeler, who leads the chorus. Also in the cast are Smith and Dale, Jim Thornton, Josephine Sabel, and Barney Fagan. The plot concerns Mickey O'Brien, loved by Gertie, who's in an orphan asylum. He wins a prize and is adopted by a millionaire. She thinks she's lost him, but she hasn't.

Oct 5 *Dracula.* See L premiere, 1927.

Oct 10 *The 5 O'Clock Girl* (NY—44th Street—Musical). Guy Bolton and Fred Thompson write this fable about a shopgirl who phones a handsome rich young man every day at five—eventually meeting and winning him. Bert Kalmar and Harry Ruby provide the music and lyrics. Mary Eaton and Oscar Shaw are featured. It runs 280 performances. On March 21, 1929, the play opens at the London Hippodrome with Jean Colin and Ernest Truex. Here it runs just over 15 weeks.

Oct 10 *Porgy* (NY—Guild—Drama). The Theatre Guild produces Dorothy and Du Bose Heyward's tale of Porgy and Bess on Catfish Row in Charleston. Frank Wilson and Evelyn Ellis have the leads. The production has 367 performances. On April 10, 1929, the play opens at His Majesty's in London with the same leads.

Oct 18 *The Ivory Door* (NY—Charles Hopkins—Drama). A.A. Milne's fantasy about a king who dares to go through the Ivory Door, whence no man has ever returned alive features Henry Hull. Linda Watkins is also in the cast. The production runs nearly 39 weeks. The drama opens on April 17, 1929, at London's Haymarket where it does not have a long run.

Oct 18 *Interference.* See L premiere, 1927.

Oct 26 *Escape.* See L premiere, 1926.

Nov 2 *John* (NY—Klaw—Drama). Philip Barry's play portrays John the Baptist. Jacob Ben-Ami and Constance Collier play leads. Guthrie McClintic stages; the production closes after 11 performances.

Nov 3 *A Connecticut Yankee* (NY—Vanderbilt—Musical). Mark Twain's comic novel is adapted by Herbert Fields with music and lyrics by Richard Rodgers and Lorenz Hart. William Gaxton is the Yankee, dreaming he is back in Camelot. Constance Carpenter and Nana Bryant are featured. Songs include "Thou Swell" and "My Heart Stood Still." Busby Berkeley invents the dances. There are 418 performances. It opens in London at Daly's on Oct 10, 1929, under the title *A Yankee*

Porgy

at the Court of King Arthur.

Nov 4 *The Wicked Age* (NY—Daly's—Comedy). Mae West, unrepentant after her brush with the forces of decency and law, returns to the stage briefly—19 performances—as Babe Carson, a plump flapper who is thrown out by her father for holding a wild party in their home.

Nov 8 *Coquette* (NY—Maxine Elliott—Drama). Helen Hayes is featured in this play about unrequited love, by Ann Preston Bridges and George Abbott. Abbott also directs. It runs nearly 46 weeks and is selected as a "Best Play" by Burns Mantle. On June 3, 1929, it opens at London's Apollo with Helen Ford, Walter Abel, and Elisha Cook, Jr.

Nov 9 *And So To Bed*. See L premiere, 1926.

Nov 14 *The Marquise*. See L premiere, 1927.

Nov 15 *Artists and Models* (NY—Winter Garden—Revue). This edition runs 19 weeks, with 100 chorus girls, the music being provided by Ted Lewis and his orchestra. Comedy is the forte of Jack Pearl.

Nov 21 *The Doctor's Dilemma* (NY—Guild—Drama). The Theatre Guild presents George Bernard Shaw's fable of the surgeon who decides against using his skill to help a morally flawed but brilliant artist for 115 performances. Alfred Lunt, Lynn Fontanne and Baliol Holloway play the leads.

Nov 22 *Funny Face* (NY—Alvin—Musical). Fred and Adele Astaire are featured in this George and Ira Gershwin show. Victor Moore and William Kent play comic thieves, looking for some pearls Astaire has locked up for his ward. "'S Wonderful," "He Loves And She Loves," and "My One And Only" are hits. The pro-

duction runs over 30 weeks. The musical opens at London's Princes's on Nov 8, 1928, with the Astaires again in the leads. Here it runs 33 weeks.

Nov 30 *Golden Dawn* (NY—Hammerstein's—Musical). This curious tale, by Otto Harbach and Oscar Hammerstein II, opens the new Hammerstein's Theatre, named for Oscar I. Arthur Hammerstein produces; Reginald Hammerstein and Dave Bennett direct. With an operetta score by Emmerich Kalman, Robert Stolz, and Herbert Stothart, the action is laid in Africa, where a cruel black overseer (Robert Chisholm) pursues the blonde Dawn (Louise Hunter). The blacks are whites in blackface. Archie Leach (later Cary Grant) plays Anzac. The show runs 23 weeks.

Dec 1 *Fallen Angels*. See L premiere, 1925.

Dec 26 *Behold the Bridegroom* (NY—Cort—Drama). George Kelly stages his own play, which runs 11 weeks. Judith Anderson plays Antoinette Lyle.

Dec 27 *Show Boat* (NY—Ziegfeld—Musical). Oscar Hammerstein II adapts Edna Ferber's popular novel of riverboat showpeople and their romances and disappointments. The music is composed by Jerome Kern. His score becomes a classic with such hits as "Ol' Man River" and "Make Believe." Helen Morgan, Norma Terris, Charles Winninger, Howard Marsh, and Jules Bledsoe are among the large cast. The show achieves 572 performances in its first two seasons. "Showboat is . . . just about the best musical piece ever to arrive under Mr. Ziegfeld's silken gonfalon," reports the *NY Times*. The musical opens in London at the Drury Lane on May 3, 1928, with Cedric Hardwicke, Alberta Hunter, Marie Burke, Howett Worster, Edith May, and Paul Robeson in the cast. It runs 11 months.

Dec 27 *Paris Bound* (NY—Music Box—Comedy). Philip Barry's comedy of infidelity and modern manners, produced and directed by Arthur Hopkins, features Madge Kennedy and Donn Cook. It runs nearly 30 weeks. On April 30, 1929, it opens at the Lyric in London with Edna Best and Herbert Marshall. Laurence Olivier is also in the cast.

Dec 28 *The Royal Family* (NY—Selwyn—Comedy). The famous Barrymores are reputed the model for George S. Kaufman and Edna Ferber's romping satire on the characters and aspirations of a talented and thoroughly theatrical family. Haidee Wright, Ann Andrews, and Otto Kruger are featured. The show runs 43 weeks. It opens at London's Lyric on Oct 23, 1934, where it is called *Theatre Royal*. Marie Tempest and Laurence Olivier play major roles. It runs nearly 22 weeks, in Noel Coward's staging.

1927   BRITISH PREMIERES

Jan 26 *Twelve Miles Out*. See NY premiere, 1925.

Jan 29 *Interference* (L—St. James's—Drama). Roland Pertwee and Harold Dearden's "whodunit" has a run of 412 showings. It is directed by Gerald Du Maurier, who also produces with Gilbert Miller and Frank Curzon. Du Maurier, Hilda Moore, Herbert Marshall, and Moyna MacGill play leads. On Oct 18, it comes to Broadway at the Empire where it runs 28 weeks.

Feb 14 *Dracula* (L—Little—Drama). Hamilton Deane adapts Bram Stoker's vampire novel. Raymond Huntley is in the title role, with Deane and Dora May Patrick. The show, which transfers to the Duke of York's, runs 49 weeks. On Oct 5, 1927, it opens at New York's Fulton with Bela Lugosi as the Count. Dorothy Peterson and Nedda Harrigan are in the cast. The thriller runs for 261 performances.

Feb 15 *The Donovan Affair*. See NY premiere, 1926.

Feb 15 *The Apache* (L—Palladium—Musical). Ralph Benatzky's score survives, with a book by Dion Titheradge, based on the Benatzky-Welleminsky original. Dorothy Ward plays Lalage, with Shaun Glenville as Theophile, and Carl

Brisson as Romain. The show runs nearly five months.

Feb 16 *The Marquise* (L—Criterion—Comedy). Noel Coward's tale of the marquise who saves her daughter from marrying her half-brother features Marie Tempest in the title role. It runs four months. On Nov 14, 1927, the play opens at the Biltmore in New York with Billie Burke in the lead. Madge Evans is her daughter. It runs 10 weeks.

Feb 19 *The Blue Mazurka* (L—Daly's—Musical). Franz Lehar's score acquires a British book, based by Monckton Hoffe on the Leo Stein and Bela Jenback original. Harry Graham provides lyrics. Bertram Wallis is Baron von Reiger, with Billie Hill as Gretl Unger. There are 139 performances.

Feb 24 *The Letter* (L—Playhouse—Drama). W. Somerset Maugham's play about a woman accused of murdering her lover features Gladys Cooper, Leslie Faber, and Nigel Bruce. There are 338 performances. On Sep 26, 1927, the show opens in New York at the Morosco with Katharine Cornell as the woman. It runs 13 weeks.

March 15 *The Fanatics* (L—Ambassadors'—Drama). In Miles Malleson's play, young couples discuss promiscuity in "experimental marriages." In the cast are

Ursula Jeans, Marie Ault, Paul Gill, Alison Leggatt, and Nicholas Hannen, among others. The production runs for 39 weeks.

April 6 *The Constant Wife.* See NY premiere, 1926.

April 7 *The Desert Song.* See NY premiere, 1926.

April 11 *Abie's Irish Rose.* See NY premiere, 1922.

April 19 *On Approval.* See NY premiere, 1926.

April 19 *The Vagabond King.* See NY premiere, 1925.

April 21 *Marigold* (L—Kingsway—Comedy). Young Marigold (Angela Baddelley) runs away to Edinburgh Castle to see young Queen Victoria's visit, leaving behind an elderly fiance and flying to the loving arms of a young lieutenant, Archie (Deering Wells). L. Allen Harker and F. R. Pryor's "arcadian comedy" earns a run of 649 performances and a 1936 revival.

April 27 *Lady Luck* (L—Carlton—Musical). Rodgers and Hart contribute songs to this show by Firth Shephard, with music by H. B. Hedley and Jack Strachey, and lyrics by Desmond Carter. It wins a run of 324 performances. Among the cast members are Laddie Cliff, Cyril Ritchard, Leslie Henson, Madge Elliott, and Phyllis Monkman.

May 10 *The Blue Train* (L—Prince of Wales's—Musical). Robert Stolz provides the score, with additional numbers by Ivy St. Helier. Reginald Arkell and Dion Titheradge adapt the original Gruenwald and Stein book. Lily Elsie, darling of the Edwardians, returns to the stage as Eileen Mayne, eager to win back her lost love, Lord Antony Stowe (Arthur Margetson). She's aided by the comical Freddy (Bobby Howes) and Josephine (Cicely Debenham). Jack Hulburt stages. There are 116 showings.

May 11 *The Terror* (L—Lyceum—Drama). Edgar Wallace's thriller holds audiences for a run of nearly 31 weeks. In the cast are Carol Reed, Felix Aylmer, Gwen Wyndham, Lena Maitland, and Dennis Neilson-Terry, among others.

May 19 *One Dam Thing After Another* (L— Pavilion—Revue). Ronald Jeans devises the sketches, with songs by Rodgers and Hart. There are 236 performances: with artistes including Jessie Matthews, Sonnie Hale, Douglas Byng, Max Wall, Mimi Crawford, and Lance Lister.

May 30 *The Garden of Eden* (L—Lyric—Drama). Tallulah Bankhead titillates and shocks in the role of Toni Lebrun, which requires her at one point to be seen in underthings—much to the astonishment of the President of France, when he visits the production. Avery Hopwood's adaptation of the Bernauer-Oesterreicher play earns a run of 29 weeks. Also in the cast are Eva Moore, George Bellamy, Annie Esmond, Hugh Williams, and Eric Maturin, among others.

June 8 *The Silent House* (L—Comedy-Drama). John Brandon and George Pickett's menacing mystery thriller runs over a year. Pickett and Franklin Dyall play leads.

June 27 *Blue Skies* (L—Vaudeville—Revue). This revue does well with 190 showings. J. W. Jackson arranges the musical numbers, with Josephine Trix, Max and Harry Nesbitt, Jack Smith, and Elsa Macfarlane among the performers.

June 28 *The Spot on the Sun* (L—Ambassadors'—Drama). Marie Tempest plays Mrs. Patrick in J. H. Turner's play. Also in the cast are Frank Cellier, Fabia Drake, and Lady Tree, among others. The play runs nearly four months.

July 4 *Thark* (L—Aldwych—Comedy). Another Ben Travers Aldwych farce about hunting for ghosts, this lively show wins a run of 401 performances, with a cast including Ena Mason, Ralph Lynn, Mary Brough, Tom Walls, Winifred Shotter, and J. Robertson Hare. "As it is, it is full of entertaining fragments. . . . But stories and chatter in detachment do not quite make a good farce," reports *The Times.*

July 20 *Shake Your Feet* (L—Hippodrome—Revue). Music credits go to George Gershwin, Fred Astaire, and Jack Strachey, among others. Noel Scott, Greatrex Newman, and Clifford Grey concoct the sketches. Jack Hylton's Band plays for a company including Billy Merson, Joyce Barbour, Gwen Farrar, Milton Hayes, Max Rivers, and the Five Hoffman Girls. The show has a 25-week run.

July 27 *Peggy-Ann.* See NY Premiere, 1926.

Aug 30 *The Butter and Egg Man.* See NY premiere, 1925.

Sep 2 *Seventh Heaven.* See NY premiere, 1922.

Sep 7 *The High Road* (L—Shaftesbury—Comedy). Frederick Lonsdale's play runs nearly 30 weeks, with a cast including such players as Gertrude Kingston, Ian Hunter, Marjorie Brooks, Fred Kerr, Colin Keith-Johnstone, Allan Aynesworth, and Mary Jerrold.

Sep 8 *The Girl Friend* (L—Palace—Musical). With songs by Rodgers and Hart, Con Conrad, and Gus Kahn, this musical is adapted from the book *Kitty's Kisses,* written by Harbach and Bartholomae, by the team of R. P. Weston and Bert Lee. Popular songs are "Blue Room" and "Mountain Greenery." It earns 421 performances. William Mollison stages, with dances by Max Scheck. Hal Willis and Hazel MacFarlane perform dance specialties; the Ramblers Quartet is also on hand. Louise Brown plays Kitty, discovered in the Dennison's hotel-suite by an irate Mrs. Dennison (Evelyn Hope). The lawyer (Roy Royston) she engages to take action against her seemingly errant husband (Bernard Clifton) loves Kitty, and all is well. George Gee, Sara Allgood,

Emma Haig, and Sebastian Smith are also in the cast.

Sep 13 *The Silver Cord* (L—St. Martin's—Drama). Sidney Howard's play about a possessive, destructive mother, Mrs. Phelps (Lilian Braithwaite), earns a six-month run. Her sons are played by Brian Aherne (David) and Denys Blakelock (Robert). The young women who love them, Hester and Christina, are acted by Marjorie Mars and Clare Eames, the playwright's wife.

Sep 21 *Oh, Kay.* See NY premiere, 1926.

Oct 18 *Crime.* See NY premiere, 1927.

Nov 3 *Hit the Deck.* See NY premiere, 1927.

Royal Family

Nov 24 *Home Chat* (L—Duke of York's—Comedy). Noel Coward's play nearly achieves a five-week run, with a cast including Nina Boucicault, George Relph, Marda Vanne, Henrietta Watson, and Madge Titheradge.

Dec 1 *Clowns in Clover* (L—Adelphi—Revue). Jack Hulburt directs and stars in this show, with June, Cicely Courtneidge, Irene Russell, Bobbie Comber, and others. Ronald Jeans devises the revue, with songs by a number of composers and lyricists. There are 508 showings.

Dec 6 *The Wrecker* (L—New—Drama). This is "Another Train Mystery," by Arnold Ridley and Bernard Merivale. Staged by Sewell Collins, it has a run of 165 performances. G.H. Mulcaster and Owen Roughwood play leads, with Edna Davies, Keneth Kent, and Fabia Drake also in the ensemble.

Dec 17 *Sirocco* (L—Daly's—Drama). This proves to be an ill wind for playwright Noel Coward; the production has only 28 showings. Ivor Novello plays Sirio Marson, with George Coulouris, Ada King,

Blyth Daly, and Aubrey Mather.

Dec 23 *Bits and Pieces* (L—Prince's—Revue). George Robey is the star of this show by H. E. Petley. Such is Robey's popularity that the production remains on view for 21 weeks.

a *Gunman*, set amidst the "troubles" in Ireland, has an eight-week run at London's Royal Court. The Irish performers include Arthur Sinclair, Maire O'Neill, Sara Allgood, Tony Quinn, Harry Hutchinson, and Eileen Carey. In January, O'Casey's *Juno and the Paycock* has been revived at the Criterion and then transferred to the Vaudeville for a run of two months.

1927   REVIVALS/REPERTORIES

Jan 3 The Theatre Guild produces an adaptation of Dostoevsky's *The Brothers Karamazov*, by Jacques Copeau and Jean Croue. It has 56 performances at New York's Guild Theatre, with the brothers played by Dudley Digges, Alfred Lunt, George Gaul, and Morris Carnovsky. Lynn Fontanne, Clare Eames, and Edward G. Robinson are also in the cast. Philip Moeller stages.

Jan 10 Mrs. Fiske plays Mrs. Alving in this modern-dress revival of Henrik Ibsen's *Ghosts*. It lasts three weeks, staged by Harrison Grey Fiske.

Jan 19 At London's Kingsway Theatre, George Bernard Shaw's *Pygmalion* is revived for 25 performances, with Gwen Ffrangcon-Davies as Eliza Doolittle and Esme Percy as Henry Higgins. On Feb 10, *Man and Superman* is produced, for a run of 44 showings. On Dec 5, at the Little Theatre, *Getting Married* is revived for three weeks, followed on Dec 26, by *You Never Can Tell*.

Jan 20 At the Lyric, Hammersmith, Nigel Playfair revives Farquhar's Restoration comedy, *The Beaux' Strategem*, for a run of 18 weeks, with Edith Evans and Winifred Evans. On June 2, *When Crummles Played* opens for a run of 115 performances, with Hermione Baddeley, Miriam Lewes, and Ernest Thesiger.

Jan 24 Eva LeGallienne's Civic Repertory Theatre on 14th Street continues its season with 57 performances of the Martinez Sierra drama, *The Cradle Song*, with LeGallienne in the lead. This is chosen as a "Best Play." Susan Glaspell's *Inheritors* is revived for 17 performances on March 15, with Josephine Hutchinson and LeGallienne.

March 14 At the Abbey Theatre in Dublin, Augusta, Lady Gregory, unveils her version of Cervantes' *Don Quixote*. It's called *Sancho's Master*, with Barry Fitzgerald as Sancho and F. J. McCormick as Quixote. On May 9, the premiere is Lady Gregory's *Dave*. On May 16, John Guinan's *Black Oliver* is presented. W. B. Yeats' version of Sophocles' *Oedipus at Colonus* is produced on Sep 12, with McCormick in the title-role and Fitzgerald as Creon. On Nov 29, the play is George Shiels' *Cartney and Kevney*.

April 18 The Theatre Guild revives A. A. Milne's *Mr. Pim Passes By* at New York's Garrick Theatre for 9 weeks.

April 18 *The Taming of the Shrew* opens

the spring Shakespeare season at Stratford-upon-Avon, currently housed in the cinema on Greenhill Street because of the destruction of the Shakespeare Memorial Theatre in 1926. *Henry V* is the "birthday play." Other productions presented by the company's director, W. Bridges Adams, include *Macbeth*, *Twelfth Night*, *Much Ado About Nothing*, *Hamlet*, and Sheridan's *The Rivals*.

May 2 Directed by the playwright Martinez Sierra, the Spanish Art Theatre, returning to Spain from a South American tour, offers New York a two-week repertory, including *The Cradle Song*, *Angela Maria*, *The Road to Happiness*, *The Romantic Young Lady*, *The Girl and the Cat*, *The Blind Heart*, and *The Royal Peacock*. Catalina Barcena is the leading performer.

May 2 Walter Hartwig is back with his Little Theatre Tournament. In seven performances, 17 troupes compete, with the Belasco Trophy going to Britain's Welwyn Garden City Theatre Society. Prizes are also won by the Krigwa Players Little Negro Theatre of Harlem and the Memphis Little Theatre, among others.

May 22 *David*, a play by D. H. Lawrence, is presented by the Three Hundred Club, in association with the Stage Society, at the Regent Theatre in London. Robert Harris plays the title-role.

May 27 Sean O'Casey's play, *Shadow of*

July 11 The eight-week summer season of Shakespeare productions in Stratford-upon-Avon opens with *Antony and Cleopatra*, a new staging. The festival is held in the Greenhill Street cinema, owing to the 1926 burning of the Shakespeare Memorial Theatre. Other plays offered are *Henry V*, *The Taming of the Shrew*, *Macbeth*, *Twelfth Night*, *Much Ado About Nothing*, *Hamlet*, and Sheridan's *The Rivals*. A new production of *As You Like It* is also programmed.

Sep 3 At the Repertory Theatre in Birmingham, Barry Jackson's company offers John Drinkwater's comedy, *Bird in Hand*. Peggy Ashcroft and Laurence Olivier are in the cast.

Sep 12 In Hammersmith, at the Lyric Theatre, a series of Shakespeare revivals opens with *The Taming of the Shrew*, presented by the Old Vic Company. Petruchio and Katherine are Lewis Casson and Sybil Thorndike. Torin Thatcher, Eric Portman, Andrew Leigh, and others are in the ensemble. *The Merchant of Venice* follows, with Casson and Thorndike as Shylock and Portia. *Much Ado About Nothing* has them cast as Benedick and Beatrice. In December, *Shrew* is returned to the bill.

Oct 3 Walter Hampden plays Dr. Stockmann at his own New York theatre, in this revival of Henrik Ibsen's *An Enemy of the People*. It runs for four months.

Oct 18 Eva LeGallienne's Civic Repertory

The Desert Song

Theatre brings Herman Heijermans' Dutch drama, *The Good Hope*, to Manhattan for 49 performances. The title is the name of a fishing ship with a rotten hull, sent to sea by a dishonest owner who knows the danger the crew faces. On Nov 28, Gustav Weid's futuristic Danish drama, *2 × 2 = 5*, is premiered for 16 performances.

Nov 14 Ruth Draper, the monologist, opens her show of character sketches for a matinee run, adding evening performances on the 21, for a total of 36 times in London at the Criterion Theatre. In July, she has played for two weeks at the Garrick Theatre.

Nov 17 Max Reinhardt brings a repertory of his productions from Germany, opening with *A Midsummer Night's Dream* in New York's Century Theatre. The cast includes Paul Hartman, Dagny Servaes, Hans and Hermann Thimig, Rosamond Pinchot, Eduard Von Winterstein, Hans Moser, Tilly Losch, Harald Kreutzberg, Alexander Moissi, and Lili Darvas. Reinhardt also presents the Von Hofmannstahl version of *Everyman*, with Moissi as Everyman; Buechner's *Danton's Tod*, with Paul Hartman as Danton; Langer's *Peripherie*, Goldoni's *Servant of Two Masters*, and Tolstoi's *He Is To Blame for Everything*.

Nov 27 *First-Class Passengers Only* has three leading characters, called Edith, Osbert, and Sacheverell Sitwell. They are very well cast in the persons of the Sitwells themselves, Osbert and Sacheverell being the play's authors. The comedy is about retaliation for a social climber. Val Gielgud, Sybil Arundale, Phyllis Dean, and Esme Percy are among the players in this production at the Arts Theatre in London. *The Times* writes "We cannot help thinking that it would have been more amusing and less cruel if it had been performed in the privacy of a country-house where every one knew every one else. It has an air of whispering in corners, and depends for a great part of its entertainment on one's knowledge of a code. . . . Altogether a strange and erratic evening—something between a *revue* without music and a venomous charade."

Nov 28 Sean O'Casey's *The Plough and the Stars*, a drama of Dublin life during the 1915–16 abortive Irish rebellion plays four weeks at New York's Hudson Theatre, with the Irish Players directed by Arthur Sinclair, who also plays the boastful Fluther Good. Among the others are Maire O'Neill, Shelah Richards, Sara Allgood, Michael Scott, and E.J. Kennedy. Moving to the Gallo Theatre, on Dec 19, they open O'Casey's *Juno and the Paycock* for five weeks.

Dec 19 At London's Garrick Theatre, the Christmas season and young audiences are saluted with a revival of *Robinson Crusoe*. In the days immediately following, other holiday shows will be *Peter Pan* (Gaiety), *Where the Rainbow Ends* (Holborn Empire), *Cinderella* (Palladium), *Alice in Wonderland* (Savoy), *Bluebell in Fairyland* (Scala), *The Windmill Man* (Victoria Palace), and *Dr. Dolittle's Play* (Rudolf Steiner Hall).

1927 BIRTHS/DEATHS/DEBUTS

Jan 11 At London's Savoy Theatre in a special matinee, J. M. Barrie's *Quality Street* is presented by a cast of children of theatre people, with names such as Casson, Fagan, McLeod, Carson, Grant, Hyson, Gee, and Truex.

Feb 1 At London's Rudolf Steiner Hall, Prince Nicholas Galitzine plays a servant in Jose Echegaray's drama, *The Great Galeoto*, with Josephine Wilson as Feodora.

Feb 24 At London's Victoria Palace, King George V and Queen Mary, with the Princess Royal, attend the Royal Variety performance, in aid of the Variety Artists' Benevolent Fund.

Feb 27 American playwright Roi Cooper Megrue (b. 1883) is dead in New York. Megrue is the author of *Tea for Three*, *It Pays to Advertise* (with Walter Hackett), *Under Cover*, *Under Fire*, *Her Own Way*, and *Among the Girls*.

March 18 Composer-arranger John Kander is born in Kansas City, Missouri.

April 20 Actor Sam Levene makes his Broadway debut as William Thompson in James Rosenberg's romantic melodrama, *Wall Street*, at the Hudson Theatre. Born in Russia in 1905, Levene studies acting at the American Academy of Dramatic Art in New York.

April 25 American actress Kitty Morton is dead in New York at age 65. Morton was second of the Four Mortons who appeared in vaudeville. She was the mother of Clara and Paul Morton.

May 3 Russian-born director and producer Rouben Mamoulian stages a matinee series of George M. Cohan's *Seven Keys to Baldpate* at London's Garrick Theatre. From 1923–25 Mamoulian directed and produced a repertory of operas, operettas, and musicals at the Eastman Theatre in Rochester, New York.

May 7 American actor Bruce McRae (b. 1867) dies in New York. McRae became prominent as a leading man playing in support of prominent stars, notably Ethel Barrymore. His last engagement was with Grace George in *The Legend of Leonora*.

May 22 American comedian Denman Maley is dead in Collingswood, New Jersey at age 50. Maley played in a number of Charles Hoyt comedies starting with *A Black Sheep*. His last engagement was in *The Butter-and-Egg Man*.

May 23 At the Drury Lane Theatre, the King and Queen attend the annual matinee in aid of King George's Pension Fund for Actors and Actresses. Matheson Lang appears in E. Temple Thurston's *The Wandering Jew*.

May 26 American drama critic James S. Metcalfe (b. 1858) dies in New York. Metcalfe was dramatic editor for *Life* for 31 years. He later became associated with the *Wall Street Journal*. Metcalfe was married to actress Elizabeth Tyree.

May 30 American actress Florence Eldridge is wed to actor Fredric March.

June 14 English playwright and novelist Jerome K. Jerome (b. 1859) is dead. Jerome's theatrical fame rests mainly on his *The Passing of the Third Floor Back*, in which Forbes-Robertson scored triumphantly. He also wrote *On the Stage and Off* and *Stageland: Curious Habits and Customs of Its Inhabitants*.

June 17 Micheal macLiammoir and Hilton Edwards, both young actors of proven talent, meet in Enniscorthy. MacLiammoir, a gifted artist and designer, does a gouache later of Edwards as Mephistopheles. They are now touring in *Faust* with the Anew McMaster ensemble. In 1928, they will found the Dublin Gate Theatre. In later years, macLiammoir is to recall of the early days that they didn't lose any money—as they had none to lose. Dublin, he is to remember, was chosen for the theatre, rather than London, where Edwards has been an Old Vic actor, because, says macLiammoir, "Dublin has next to nothing. What's growing must be fed."

July 9 Actor John Drew (b. 1853) dies in San Francisco. Author of *My Years on the Stage* (1922), Drew was the son of Louisa Lane Drew, manager of Philadelphia's Arch Street Theatre. Drew's early successes occurred during his engagement with Augustin Daly, and in later years, under the management of the Frohmans. He was last seen on tour in Pinero's *Trelawney of the 'Wells'*.

July 17 American stage and screen actress Florence Roberts (b. 1871) dies in Los Angeles. Roberts appeared with great success as Ophelia, Juliet, Portia, Rosalind, Camille, and La Tosca. In 1907 she made an impression by her acting the part of the Body in the morality play, *The Struggle Everlasting*.

July 26 American actress and scenario writer June Mathis dies in the 48th Street Theatre during a performance of *The Squall*. She was 35. Mathis had played in vaudeville and in several comedies before turning to writing. Her achievements included the writing of *The Four Horsemen of the Apocalypse* and the engagement of Rudolph Valentino to play the lead.

Aug 13 American actress Elita Proctor Otis is dead in Pelham, New York at age 76. Otis starred for many years in such plays as *Oliver Twist*, *The Sporting Duchess*, and *The Two Orphans*. She later appeared in vaudeville.

Aug 17 American Pulitzer Prize playwright George Kelly tries his hand at writing and staging a revue, *A La Carte*. It manages only 45 performances.

Oct 31 American novelist, playwright, and librettist John Luther Long (b. 1861) is dead at age 66. Long collaborated with David Belasco on *Madame Butterfly*, *The Darling of the Gods*, and *Adrea*, in which Mrs. Leslie Carter played the title role.

Nov 1 American comedienne-singer Florence Mills (b. 1895) dies in New York.

Mills was one of the first and most popular black comediennes. Her credits include *Shuffle Along*, *From Dixie to Broadway*, and *The Blackbirds*.

Nov 8 Tyrone Guthrie, one day to become a noted stage-director, is now a playwright. At Glasgow's Lyric Theatre, his "charade in one act," *Victorian Nights*, opens.

Nov 12 The Queen of Spain attends *Lady Luck* at London's Carlton Theatre.

Nov 16 At the Royal Court in London, Charles Laughton plays the title-role in Arnold Bennett and Edward Knoblock's *Mr. Prohack*, with Hilda Sims as Mrs. Prohack. Elsa Lanchester is Mimi Winstock.

Nov 22 Jessie Tandy and Roland Culver are in *The Manderson Girls*, presented at Playroom Six in London.

says that *The Chocolate Soldier* and *Arms and the Man* are two distinct plays. . . . If *The Chocolate Soldier* is filmed, care must be taken that nothing is quoted from the letterpress of Mr. Shaw's play, *Arms and the Man*, nor must his name appear in connection with it, as he would immediately prosecute should there be any suggestion that he had had anything to do with the writing of *The Chocolate Soldier*."

March 20 *What Price Glory* opens the new Philadelphia cinema, the Fox-Locust. Although it begins life as a film theatre, it is to be converted to legitimate theatre performances, taking the name of the Locust Street Theatre in 1930. It is to become one of the city's leading playhouses, with 1,418 seats. In the 1950's, the William Goldman management will take it over, calling it the New Locust, but continuing the legitimate policy. In the 1970's, it is infrequently used and often threatened with demolition.

March 28 The Majestic Theatre, on West 44 Street in New York, designed by Herbert J. Krapp and built as part of the Chanin brother's theatre chain, opens with *Rufus LeMaire's Affairs*. Built as a musical house, the Majestic has been the home for *Carousel*, *South Pacific*, *The Music Man*, *A Little Night Music* and *The Wiz*. The theatre is currently under Shubert management.

April 8 Abe Erlanger, once a dominant force in American theatre management and production, with former partner Marc Klaw, today reveals in an advertisement in the *NY Times* that his net worth is still "in excess of $5,000,000." This, despite the obvious triumph of the Shuberts in their fight against Klaw and Erlanger and the once-feared Theatrical Syndicate.

April 9 The Cleveland Play House troupe has been so successful in its theatre in a former church that it now moves to larger quarters in the renovated Drury Lane Theatre on East 86 Street in this Ohio City. Sem Benelli's *The Jest* opens the new theatre. In 1938, the first theatre grant to be given by the Humanities Division of the Rockefeller Foundation will be given to help pay off costs of this renovation.

April 20 The Arts Theatre opens in the Arts Theatre Club in London. Because of its status as a private club, productions will not have to undergo censorship by the Lord Chamberlain. The 339-seat theatre has been designed by P. Morley Horder, and the managing directors, Bernard Isaac and Lionel Barton, open with *Picnic*, an intimate revue.

April 27 The Carlton Theatre in London opens on the Haymarket with the musical play, *Lady Luck*. Frank T. Verity and S. Beverley are the designers of this 1,150-seat theatre. In April 1929, it will be converted into a cinema.

May 14 Chicago's Apollo Theatre, de-

1927 THEATERS/PRODUCTIONS

In Britain this year, patents are granted for: N. H. Martinez's method of dividing the stage into zones of different colored light, so that costumes and set elements moving from zone to zone appear to change color; A. Heinz' scenic tower-element with rotatable tiers, fountains, foliage, lighting, and other ornaments.

Approximately 48 theatres are currently involved in the Abe Erlanger chain. Erlanger and his associates own, operate, control, or book these playhouses on exclusive long-term lease agreements.

Jan 11 The Royale Theatre opens on West 45 Street in New York City. The theatre is the sixth built by the Chanin Corporation.

Jan 18 New York's District Attorney raids *The Virgin Man*, halting it at 63 performances. The cast is arrested, but gets suspended sentences. Jail sentences and fines of $250 are given the producer and the author, William Francis Dugan, who also has directed the play.

Jan 29 The Public Theatre, at 66 2nd Avenue in New York, owned by Schulman-Goldberg, opens with *Parisian Love*. On Nov 5, 1957, the theatre reopens as the Anderson Theatre, with *The Girl of the Golden West*. On Oct 18, 1958, once again the theatre reopens with a new name, the Anderson Yiddish Theatre, presenting *A Family Mishmash*.

Feb 1 From this date for a minimum of five years, American theatre managers who wish to produce the plays written by members of the Dramatists' Guild are obligated, by the terms of the Guild agreement they have signed, not to produce plays by non-Guild members, with certain exceptions, such as the one play per year allowed for production by non-Guild members writing in Britain. Canada is treated as America, not an extension of

Britain. This creates effectually a closed-shop.

Feb 2 The Ziegfeld Theatre opens on 6 Avenue and West 54 Street in New York City. The theatre, designed by Joseph Urban, is to house the musical comedies and revues of Florenz Ziegfeld. The stage has a gilt cyclorama 59 feet high.

Feb 9 Mae West is arrested for presenting a play which is seen likely to corrupt the morals of youth. The drama is *Sex*, which she has written, with a starring role for herself.

Feb 24 The Theatre Masque, on West 45 Street in New York, owned by the Chanin brothers and designed by Herbert J. Krapp, opens with *Puppets of Passion*, an adaptation from the Italian *Rossodi San Secondo*. In 1937, the Chanins lose control. Under new management, it is called the John Golden Theatre. Subsequently, it returns to live drama and presents such notable shows as *Angel Street*, which runs for 1,293 performances.

Feb 26 *Collette* is the last show on the stage of Philadelphia's Forrest Theatre, marked for destruction in the months following. Its cornerstone was laid by Fritzi Scheff in 1906 and it has been host to many major productions.

March 18 George Bernard Shaw is the defendant in a suit brought by an American film producer, Jesse A. Levinson, who is seeking a declaration that the operetta, *The Chocolate Soldier*, does not reproduce a substantial part of Shaw's *Arms and the Man*; he also wants it established that he can produce a film of the first work without Shaw's consent. The action, it is judged, is not maintainable in English courts, nor has a case been made, even though Levinson introduces a letter from Blanche Patch, Shaw's secretary, which says in part: "Mr. Bernard Shaw

signed in 1921 by Holabird and Roche, today becomes the United Artists Theatre, dedicated to cinema.

June 8 Lee Shubert writes J. & W. Seligman and Company, bankers for the Shubert Theatre Corporation, that the firm is at the time "interested" in 95 first-class theatres.

June 15 At the close of the 1926–27 Broadway season, Burns Mantle points out that statistics are a problem, since there are different systems of classification for productions. He opts for 264 new productions and revivals, 123 of which were dramas, 78 comedies, 38 musicals of various kinds, and the rest revivals. For Mantle, 70% of the productions have

The Blue Train

been failures at the box-office, though some showed artistic merit. In his annual survey of the Broadway season, Mantle chooses ten *"Best Plays"*. The choices, with some advice from Mantle's fellow critics, are: Dunning and Abbott's *Broadway*, Anderson's *Saturday's Children*, Watkins' *Chicago*, Maugham's *The Constant Wife*, Sherwood's *The Road to Rome*, Molnar's *The Play's the Thing*, Howard's *The Silver Cord*, Martinez Sierra's *The Cradle Song*, Kelly's *Daisy Mayme*, and Green's *In Abraham's Bosom*—which also wins the Pulitzer Prize. The New York critics who vote the season's best plays are: John Anderson, *NY Evening Post*; Brooks Atkinson, *NY Times*; Robert Benchley, *Life*; Gilbert Gabriel, *NY Evening Sun*; Percy Hammond, *NY Herald Tribune*; George Jean Nathan, *American Mercury*; E. W. Osborne, *NY Evening World*; Frank Vreeland, *NY Evening Telegram*; Alexander Woollcott, *NY Morning World*.

June 30 Shubert Theatre Corporation earnings are down at the close of the fiscal year. The net income is $1,633,577. With 160,670 shares outstanding, the earning for each is $10.16. A $5 dividend

per share is declared.

July 4 The Cape Playhouse opens today in Dennis, Massachusetts. Theatre architect and stage-designer Cleon Throckmorton has converted the old 1790 Nobscusset Meeting House into this handsome playhouse, one day to be known as "America's Most Famous Summer Theatre." Basil Rathbone and Violet Kemble Cooper inaugurate the house with Molnar's *The Guardsman*.

Sep 26 The Erlanger Theatre opens on West 44 Street in New York City. The theatre is named for Abraham Erlanger, a leading member of the theatre syndicate which was formed in 1896. The opening production is George M. Cohan's *The Merry Malones*. The cost of the theatre is in excess of $1.5 million. In 1932, the name will be changed to the St. James. It will house the hits *Oklahoma! The King and I* and *Hello, Dolly!*, among others.

Oct 3 The Erlanger Theatre opens in Philadelphia with the musical, *Criss Cross*, starring Dorothy and Fred Stone. Costing $2.5 million, it is designed by the firm of Hoffman and Henon, with 1,864 seats. Both spacious and lavish, the theatre is to alternate between films and stage shows, such as *My Fair Lady* and *Funny Girl*, which are to try out here prior to Broadway. Its proscenium is 40 feet wide by 28 feet high, with a stage 66 feet wide by 40 feet deep. It will be demolished in Sep 1978.

Oct 7 The *New Statesman* reports that the adjudicators in the competition to design a new home for Shakespeare's plays in Stratford-upon-Avon are having a difficult time in reaching a decision. None of the designs is worth having, it seems.

Nov 2 In New York, Mrs. August Belmont gives a dinner in honor of Clarence Mackay, former Comstock Lode "King"

and head of AT&T, to raise funds for the reconstruction of the Shakespeare Memorial Theatre in Stratford-upon-Avon. Charles Evans Hughes and others attend. John D. Rockefeller pledges a gift of £100,000. As the campaign for building funds continues, Edward Harkness gives £20,000. When the drive is completed, half the money raised will have come from American donors, many of them people of limited means but admirers of the works of Shakespeare.

Nov 22 The Gate Theatre opens in London at its new location on Villiers Street with Simon Gantillon's *Maya*. Gwen Ffrangcon-Davies is in the lead. Velona Pilcher has replaced Molly Veness as Peter Godfrey's partner in management.

Nov 22 The Alvin Theatre, on West 52 Street in New York, designed by Herbert J. Krapp and named by combining the first several letters in producers' Alex Aarons' and Vinton Freedley's names, opens with the Astaires dancing in *Funny Face*, written by Fred Thompson and Paul Gerard Smith, with music by George Gershwin and lyrics by Ira Gershwin. Built to showcase Broadway musicals, in the 1930's and 1940's it is a site of radio broadcasts but returns to housing musicals and legitimate dramas.

Nov 30 Hammerstein's Theatre, at 1697 Broadway in New York, designed by Herbert J. Krapp and built by Arthur Hammerstein in honor of his father, Oscar Hammerstein, opens with *Golden Dawn*. In 1931, under new ownership, the theatre is renamed the Billy Rose Music Hall. It briefly reverts to presenting legitimate theatre, but in 1936, the Columbia Broadcasting System buys the theatre and uses it as a radio-television playhouse. In 1967, it is renamed the Ed Sullivan Theatre.

Dec 5 In a statement submitted today to the New York Stock Exchange, the Shubert Theatre Corporation notes that it now has 104 first-class theatres in its circuit. In addition, the Shubert theatres now house more than 60% of all the first-class legitimate theatre productions in the entire United States.

Dec 26 Eleven new plays open tonight on Broadway. During this Christmas Week, a total of 17 new plays will be premiered.

Jan 3 *She's My Baby* (NY—Globe—Musical). Bert Kalmar and Harry Ruby's book, about a hero who has to pretend to be married and a father in order to borrow $200,000, is staged with Rodgers and Hart providing music and lyrics. Beatrice Lillie and Clifton Webb are in the cast. The show runs only nine weeks.

Jan 9 *Marco Millions* (NY—Guild—Drama). Eugene O'Neill's oriental epic features Alfred Lunt, Baliol Holloway, and Margalo Gillmore. The Theatre Guild production runs nearly three months. On Dec 26, 1938, the drama comes to London's Westminster with Griffith Jones as Marco and Robert Harris as Kublai Khan.

Jan 10 *Rosalie* (NY—New Amsterdam—Musical). Marilyn Miller is the princess of Romanza, who falls in love with a West Point officer (Oliver McLennan). He flies the Atlantic, imitating Lindbergh, to be near her. The George Gershwin-Sigmund Romberg score has lyrics by P. G. Wodehouse and Ira Gershwin. The book is by Guy Bolton and William A. McGuire, who also helps Florenz Ziegfeld stage the show. It runs for 335 performances.

Jan 12 *Cock Robin* (NY—48th Street—Comedy). Philip Barry and Elmer Rice collaborate on this "whodunit," which is described as a "comedy-drama." Beulah Bondi, Muriel Kirkland, and Henry D. Southard are in the cast. The show has 100 performances. It opens in London at the Little on Feb 24, 1933, with V. C. Clinton-Baddeley, Jack Livesey, Kim Peacock, Nancy Price and Winifred Evans performing. It has a short run.

Jan 25 *The Queen's Husband* (NY—Playhouse—Drama). Robert E. Sherwood writes this story about the husband of a queen who takes over when she is away. Roland Young is featured. The show runs for 125 performances. On Oct 6, 1931, it opens at London's Ambassadors' with Barry Jones as the husband. It earns a run of 138 performances.

Jan 30 *Strange Interlude* (NY—John Golden—Drama). Eugene O'Neill's nine-act play is the saga of Nina Leeds and the men in her life. In it O'Neill uses the device of having characters speak their inner thoughts aloud while the stage action freezes. Lynn Fontanne is featured by the Theatre Guild. The drama is an immediate success, winning the Pulitzer Prize and running for 426 performances. Brooks Atkinson of the *NY Times* pans it saying: "When the aside merely elaborates the spoken thought it deadens the action until 'Strange Interlude' looks like a slow-motion picture. And one irreverently suspects that there may be an even deeper thought unexpressed than the nickel-weekly jargon that Mr. O'Neill offers as thinking." On Feb 3, 1931, the play opens

Strange Interlude

at London's Lyric with Mary Ellis in the lead. It does not have a long run.

Feb 9 *Rain or Shine* (NY—George M. Cohan—Musical). Vaudeville's Joe Cook plays Smiley Johnson, who saves the Wheeler circus for Mary Wheeler (Nancy Welford) from a rascal (Joe Lyons). The book is by James Gleason and Maurice Marks, with Jack Yellen's lyrics and a score by Milton Ager and Owen Murphy. The show attracts patrons for over 11 months.

Feb 20 *Whispering Friends* (NY—Hudson—Comedy). George M. Cohan's farce runs 14 weeks, with Joe and Emily Sanford (William Harrigan and Anne Shoemaker) defending their marriage against the gossip of friends (Chester Morris and Elsie Lawson).

Feb 27 *Keep Shufflin'* (NY—Daly's—Musical). With Clarence Todd's aid, Fats Waller and Jimmy Johnson compose the score for this sequel to *Shuffle Along*. Flournoy Miller and Aubrey Lyles's book has Steve Jenkins and Sam Peck (played by the authors) trying to redistribute the wealth by blowing up some banks. The show runs 104 performances.

March 13 *The Three Musketeers* (NY—Lyric—Musical). William A. McGuire writes the book, based on the Dumas novel. He also directs. Rudolf Friml provides the score, with lyrics by P.G. Wodehouse and Clifford Grey. Dennis King, Vivienne Segal, and John Clarke are in the cast. The show runs nearly 10 months. It opens on March 28, 1930, at London's Drury Lane for 240 performances.

April The world premiere of Eugene O'Neill's *Lazarus Laughed* occurs this month at Gilmore Brown's Pasadena Playhouse in Southern California. The production is sumptuous.

April 9 *Diamond Lil* (NY—Royale—Drama). Mae West, as Lil, unwittingly helps a Salvation Army Captain (Curtis Cooksey) crush white slavery in which a former lover is involved. The salvationist turns out to be a police captain. West also stages. The play runs 22 weeks. The *NY Times* writes, "[Mae West] is a good actress . . . even though her playwriting is a bit thick. . . . If you can stay in the theatre you are likely to enjoy it."

April 26 *Present Arms* (NY—Mansfield—Musical). Rodgers and Hart create the score and lyrics for Herbert Fields' book. Charles King plays a tough Marine who pretends to be an officer to impress Lady Delphine (Flora LeBreton). He's exposed and punished but later rewarded for heroism. "You Took Advantage of Me" is sung by Joyce Barber and Busby Berkeley—who also choreographs the dances. Alexander Leftwich stages the rest of the production, which runs just over 19 weeks.

May 9 *Blackbirds of 1928* (NY—Liberty—Revue). Lew Leslie offers a revue with an all-black cast. Dorothy Fields and Jimmy McHugh team to create the lyrics and music. "Diga Diga Do" and "I Can't Give You Anything But Love" are two successful songs. The ensemble includes Bill Robinson (Bojangles), Mantan Moreland, Elizabeth Welch, Eloise Uggams, Adelaide Hall, Aida Ward, and Ruth Johnson. The show runs 518 performances.

May 28 *The Grand Street Follies* (NY—Booth—Revue). Staged by Agnes Morgan, this edition has the customary spoofs of Broadway plays, including *Strange Interlude* as "Strange Inner Feud." Dorothy Sands burlesques Mae West playing Juliet in a Max Reinhardt production on the steps of the New York Public Library. Al-

1928   BIRTHS/DEATHS/DEBUTS

Jan 1 American actress and dancer Loie Fuller (b. 1863) dies in Paris at age 65. Fuller toured with Buffalo Bill and W. J. Florence. She introduced her famous serpentine dance for the first time at the Columbus Theatre in New York in 1891. Fuller published two volumes of reminiscences: *Fifteen Years of My Life* in 1908 and *Fifteen Years of a Dancer's Life* in 1913.

Jan 11 American actor Tim Murphy is dead in New York at age 67. Murphy began his early days in vaudeville as an imitator of actors. His first stage successes were scored in the Charles Hoyt comedies, notably *A Texas Steer*, in which he starred for many years.

Jan 20 Actor Peter Donat is born in Kentville, Nova Scotia, Canada.

Jan 23 American actor Guy Nichols is dead in Hempstead, New York at age 65. Nichols played in support of leading stars for 50 years. His last engagement was in *The Shannons of Broadway*.

Feb 10 Music hall comedian Little Tich dies in London at age 59. Tich, whose real name was Harry Relph, began his career as a child singer and performer. He was popular in Paris and was a friend of Toulouse-Lautrec.

Feb 16 Comedian and vaudevillian Eddie Foy (b. 1856) dies in Kansas City, Missouri. Foy, an entertainer from childhood, was performing in Chicago's Iroquois Theatre in 1903 when fire broke out. He played in musical comedy until 1913, when he went into vaudeville, accompanied by his seven children. His autobiography, *Clowning Through Life*, was published this year.

March 5 American actress Bessie Love makes her first stage appearance as Bonny in a West Coast tour of *Burlesque* opening at the Geary Theatre in San Francisco. Born Juanita Horton in Midland, Texas, Love has been an extra in films.

March 20 American actor William Norris (b. 1870) dies in New York. Norris played prominently in *Children of the Ghetto*, *Babes in Toyland*, *Madame Sherry*, *Francesco di Rimini*, and *A Connecticut Yankee*.

March 28 American actress Florence Rittenhouse is dead in New York at age 35. Rittenhouse achieved professional success in *The Shame Woman*. She was president of the Twelfth Night Club at the time of her death.

March 30 Director, producer, and writer Worthington Miner marries actress Frances Fuller.

April 1 Future actor George Grizzard is born in Roanoke Rapids, North Carolina.

May 5 Loring Mandel is born in Chicago, Illinois.

May 9 Benn W. Levy's play has Tallulah Bankhead star in *Mud and Treacle* as Polly Andrews at London's Globe Theatre. Basil Dean directs. The comedy does not have a long run.

May 28 James Cagney is a hoofer in *The Grand Street Follies*.

June 18 Leslie Howard writes "a bit of tomfoolery," called *Tell Me the Truth*, but he doesn't appear in the London production at the Ambassadors' Theatre. Among those who do, however, are Iris Hoey, Clare Greet, and Edna Davies.

June 27 American actor and producer Robert Bruce Mantell (b. 1854) dies in Atlantic Highlands, New Jersey. Mantell made his first appearance with Boucicault in England in 1876. In 1878 he played opposite Modjeska in America. Mantell won a reputation both in England and America as a romantic interpreter of Shakespearean tragedies.

July 1 Ohio-born playwright Avery Hopwood (b. 1882) dies in Juan-les-Pines, France. Hopwood had his first play, *Clothes*, written with Channing Pollock, produced in 1906. Other works include *The Gold Diggers*, *The Bat*, (co-authored with Mary Roberts Rinehart), and *Getting Gertie's Garter*, with Wilson Collison.

July 2 American actor Charles A. Stevenson is dead in New York at age 77. Stevenson was Mrs. Leslie Carter's leading man for many years, later supporting Jane Cowl and Henrietta Crosman. He retired in 1918 after an engagement in *East is West*.

Aug 17 Stage and screen actress Helen Hayes marries playwright Charles G. MacArthur.

Aug 18 English-born actor and playwright Grant Stewart is dead in Woodstock, New Jersey at age 63. Stewart played many years in support of the Coghlans, Olga Nethersole, Ethel Barrymore, and Annie Russell. His plays include *Caught in the Rain* and *Arms and the Girl*.

Sep 7 Clark Gable plays the role of A Man in Sophie Treadwell's controversial drama, *Machinal*.

Sep 17 Roddy McDowall is born in London, England.

Nov 26 Actress Claire Luce makes her London debut as Bonny in George Manker Watters and Arthur Hopkins' *Burlesque* at Golder's Green. Born in Syracuse, New York, Luce studied dance at Denishawn School and first appeared as a ballet dancer in Sol Hurok's Russian Opera Company in 1921.

Nov 27 American producer Gertrude Macy begins her theatrical career as assistant stage manager for Margaret Ayer Barnes' dramatization of Edith Wharton's *The Age of Innocence* at the Empire Theatre in New York. She is also secretary to actress Katharine Cornell.

Dec 14 American actor Theodore Roberts (b. 1861) dies in Hollywood. Roberts joined Fanny Davenport's company in 1888 as a leading man. In 1906 he supported Bertha Kalich in *The Kreutzer Sonata*. Roberts' major roles included Falstaff, Tabywana in *The Squaw Man*, and John Gale in *The Barrier*.

Dec 17 Future actress Julia Meade is born in Boston, Massachusetts.

Dec 19 English-born playwright J. Hartley Manners (b. 1870) dies in New York City. Manners had a successful career as actor and playwright in London before arriving with Mrs. Langtry in America. Of his more than 30 plays, the best known is *Peg O' My Heart*, which he wrote for his actress wife, Laurette Taylor.

1928   THEATERS/PRODUCTIONS

In Britain this year, patents are granted for: W. E. Kimber's apparatus for opening and closing a theatre curtain; British Thomson-Houston Company's flickering flame effect made by reflecting light from a body of mercury agitated by a magnet.

Jan 5 Elizabeth Scott, 29 years old and the only woman entrant, wins the architectural competition for the design of a new Shakespeare Memorial Theatre in Stratford-upon-Avon. Her design breaks with the Victorian tradition of the burnt theatre but incorporates some of its remains, notably the library-museum portion. Her design is Art Deco in warm red brick. There are intimations in the newspapers that the judging panel has had a difficult time in choosing because none of the plans submitted has been outstanding.

Feb 6 The theatre which was rebuilt after the great fire in 1906 in San Francisco, with a history of name-changes—the *Columbia*, the *Wilkes*—re-opens as the *Geary*.

Feb 14 After major reconstruction, London's Old Vic re-opens with *Romeo and Juliet*.

Feb 21 Simon Gantillon's play *Maya* is closed after 15 performances. Acting on a complaint, the New York District Attorney sends an assistant to see the play, about a Marseilles prostitute who is all things to all men. Rather than have the theatre closed for a year under the Wales Padlock Law, the producers withdraw the drama.

Feb Although John Van Druten's play, *Young Woodley*, has already been a hit in the United States, Lord Cromer, the Lord Chamberlain has refused it a license for public London performances. Longing to produce it, Basil Dean has been in discussions with the Lord Chamberlain for some 18 months. He has refused it a license, having read it three times. But, after seeing a performance at the Arts Theatre Club, he is impressed by the sincerity of Dean and his players and the delicacy of their treatment of the story. He permits performances, but the play can go on tour only if the actors are sincere.

Spring The Theatre Guild, despite its dedication to production of classics and important new drama, arouses the ire of moral reformers with two of its offerings: Eugene O'Neill's *Strange Interlude* and Ben Jonson's *Volpone*. O'Neill's play has been banned in Boston. In New York, *Volpone* offends with the immorality it presents on stage. In both cases, the District Attorney declines to proceed against the plays, considering them to have artistic merit.

rooms across a small street are reached via tunnel. The theatre has a large pipe-organ which is later removed.

May 7 Again it's time for Walter Hartwig's Little Theatre Tournament, with the David Belasco Trophy being given to the Androssan Saltcoats Players of Androssan, Scotland. Other troupes have come from Alabama, Georgia, and Tennessee to compete with ensembles from the New York area during the week-long event.

May 22 Jack A. Partington obtains a United States patent for a stage tracking system which enables scenery bearing wagons to move laterally, upstage and downstage, as well as change from one set of tracks to another.

June 4 Eva LeGallienne and her company inaugurate the Berkshire Playhouse in Stockbridge, Massachusetts, with *The Cradle Song*. The theatre is actually the Old Stockbridge Casino, designed by Stanford White in 1887 and purchased for $1 in 1927 to preserve this example

Hopkins' *Burlesque*, Abbott and Bridgers' *Coquette*, Kelly's *Behold the Bridegroom*, the Heywards' *Porgy*, Barry's *Paris Bound*, Galsworthy's *Escape*, Cormack's *The Racket*, and O'Casey's *The Plough and the Stars*.

June 30 Net income for the Shubert Theatre Corporation at the end of this fiscal year is $1,256,436. With 180,020 shares outstanding, there is a per-share earning of $7.53, with a $5 dividend declared. These figures do not include the 50% of the income of the Shuberts' London company which belongs to the American firm.

Sep 3 The Sheffield Repertory Company opens its season at its new Townhead Street Theatre in Great Britain with *The Dover Road*.

Sep 24 Philadelphia's Dunbar Theatre, home of "colored musical comedy and road shows," embarks on a new policy of feature films and tab shows with a new name, Gibson's Dunbar.

Oct 1 Mae West's new play, *Pleasure Man*, opens and is closed by the New York police. Alan Brooks plays Rodney Terrill, an actor who has taken advantage of women once too often. The brother of one of them, trying to make him inoperable sexually, causes his death. This occurs at a party attended by theatre folk and some transvestites.

Nov This month in Dublin, Hilton Edwards and Micheal macLiammoir establish their own performance ensemble, moving into the Peacock Theatre, an offspring of the Abbey Theatre.

Nov 19 Edward Gordon Craig's first design asignment for the American theatre, given him by producer George C. Tyler, is a revival of *Macbeth*, staged by Douglas Ross at the Knickerbocker Theatre.

Nov 26 A stage-play is broadcast for the first time on BBG. It is the Sheffield Repertory Company's production of *Clogs to Clogs*, by John Walton.

Dec There are 86 legitimate theatre productions on tour in America as of the first week of this month. In 1900 there were 392.

Dec 20 The Ethel Barrymore Theatre on West 47 Street in New York, designed by Herbert J. Krapp and owned by the Shuberts, opens with a production of G. Martizez Sierra's *The Kingdom of God*. The theatre is named for actress Ethel Barrymore, who came under Shubert management that year.

Dec 24 The Craig Theatre at 152 West 54 Street in New York opens on the eve of the stock market crash with a production of *Potiphar's Wife*. Built by the architectural firm of R. E. Hall and Company, the theatre has a short, unsuccessful history.

Blue Eyes

April 20 The directors of Dublin's Abbey Theatre reject Sean O'Casey's new play, *The Silver Tassie*, which deals with the meaninglessness of war.

April 27 With the premiere of Jerome Kern's *Blue Eyes*, Edward Laurillard opens his new theatre, the Piccadilly. The theatre was designed by Bertie Crewe and Edward A. Stone, interiors by Marc-Henri. The decorative scheme is green and gold, the wood-paneling in the playhouse is fine walnut. There are some 1,400 seats in the stalls, grand circle and upper circle.

May 1 Philadelphia has a new Forrest Theatre to replace the one torn down last year. This playhouse is on a different site, however, located at 11 and Walnut Streets. The stage has 70 lines and is 96 feet wide by 44 feet deep. Its proscenium opening is 46 feet wide by 29 feet high. Dressing-

of the "architectural genius of America" as a home for performance and exhibition of the various arts. Daniel Chester French, the sculptor, donates land for the reconstruction of the dismantled Casino.

June 15 At the close of the Broadway season, some 270 productions have opened. Forty of them have been revivals. Of the 200 plays which could be called new, however, 136 are box-office failures, with only 28 real financial successes. The customary seasonal average, says Burns Mantle, is three failures to every success. Of the 270 productions, 173 were dramas, 60 comedies, 30 musicals, and 7 revues. Some 71% of the shows were apparent failures, with only 29% of the productions successful. Mantle's annual ten *Best Plays* are: Kaufman and Ferber's *The Royal Family*, O'Neill's *Strange Interlude* (which also wins the Pulitzer Prize), Watters and

1929   AMERICAN PREMIERES

Jan 9 *Follow Thru* (NY—46th Street—Musical). Golf and country-club life in New Jersey are the main motifs of the B.G. DeSylva and Laurence Schwab book, with music and lyrics by DeSylva, Brown and Henderson. "My Lucky Star" and "Button Up Your Overcoat" are among the songs. Irene Delroy, Madeline Cameron, and Eleanor Powell are in the cast. There are 403 performances. Londoners first see the musical on Oct 3, 1929 at the Dominion where it earns a run of 148 performances. Leslie Henson plays a lead and co-directs.

Jan 10 *Street Scene* (NY—Playhouse—Drama). Elmer Rice stages his stark play about tenement life with Mary Servoss, Russell Griffin, and Erin O'Brien-Moore among the cast. A Pulitzer Prize-winner, the drama runs for 601 performances. It opens at London's Globe on Sep 9, 1930, with a cast including Servoss and O'Brien-Moore. The show runs nearly 19 weeks.

Jan 14 *Gypsy* (NY—Klaw—Drama). Torn between two men, unable to fix her affections, Maxwell Anderson's heroine ends in suicide. The production, staged by George Cukor, runs only two months, but Burns Mantle singles it out as a "Best Play." Claiborne Foster, Lester Vail, and Louis Calhern are in the cast. In Anderson's script, though not during the Broadway run, Ellen saves herself from death by asphyxiation at the last minute.

Jan 23 *Serena Blandish* (NY—Morosco—Comedy). S. N. Behrman bases his play on Enid Bagnold's novel, with Ruth Gordon as Serena who is launched in London society by a jeweler (Clarence Derwent) who uses her to show off his wares. Constance Collier and Hugh Sinclair are also in the cast. The play runs for nearly three months.

Jan 25 *The Subway* (NY—Cherry Lane—Drama). Elmer Rice's story of a pathetic office-worker who seeks fulfillment in drab surroundings runs four weeks. It is given a special performance by the Stage Society at London's Garrick on July 14.

Feb 11 *Dynamo* (NY—Martin Beck—Drama). In Eugene O'Neill's symbolic drama, Glenn Anders plays Reuben, who sees the god-force in electricity. He sacrifices himself on the altar of his god, a dynamo. The Theatre Guild earns only 50 performances, despite a cast including Claudette Colbert and Dudley Digges.

Feb 12 *My Gal Friday* (NY—Republic—Drama). In William Grew's play, three chorus girls are ordered by their stage-manager to entertain male guests at a party given by the show's backer. They dope the wine and leave undergarments in the men's beds. The next day, they claim they've been attacked. With wives and sweethearts suddenly on hand, the men

settle out of court. This entertainment runs for nearly eight months.

Feb 18 *Pleasure Bound* (NY—Majestic—Revue). Busby Berkeley stages the dances; Lew Morton does the sketches. Phil Baker and his accordion and German-dialect comedian Jack Pearl amuse the patrons for 136 performances. The Shuberts have intended this as a musical version of *Potash and Perlmutter*, but that plot vanishes before the Broadway opening.

Feb 19 *Let Us Be Gay* (NY—Little—Comedy). Rachel Crothers' latest effort runs just over four months. She stages this social comedy about a divorced wife (Francine Larrimore), who finds divorce isn't the answer. Crothers' portrait of the redoubtable Mrs. Boucicault (Charlotte Granville) is admired. Producer John Golden, eager to be relaxing in Florida, has left most of the production details to Crothers.

Feb 20 *Harlem* (NY—Apollo—Drama). The lively dancing at a Harlem rent-party causes a mild sensation in Broadway audiences. Burns Mantle calls it "orgiastic." The Williams family has come to Harlem from South Carolina; they find survival in New York difficult. Cordelia (Isabell Washington), a wild daughter, leaves a West Indian lover for a Harlem gambler who is then killed. W. J. Rapp and Wallace Thurman's play requires a large cast of Harlemites. It runs for 93 performances.

Feb 25 *Meet the Prince* (NY—Lyceum—Comedy). A. A. Milne's play allows Basil Sydney to pretend he is a Balkan prince. Mary Ellis is cast as his wife, Jennifer, who pretends to be a general's widow. Meeting at a house-party, they patch up their differences. Eric Blore is also in the cast. The show runs three months.

March 11 *Spring Is Here* (NY—Alvin—Musical). Librettist Owen Davis has the right season but for his collaborators, Rodgers and Hart (music and lyrics), there's been a terrible miscalculation. Glenn Hunter, the talented leading man, cannot sing. So the best songs have to go to John Hundley, who loses the girl. One of them, "With A Song In My Heart," becomes a classic. The show runs for 104 performances.

March 22 *Journey's End*. See L premiere, 1929.

April 1 *Mrs. Bumpstead-Leigh* (NY—Klaw—Comedy). Harry James Smith's play about social aspirations earns a nine-week run. Stella Mayhew, Mrs. Fiske, and Eleanor Griffith play main roles.

April 4 *Bird in Hand*. See L premiere, 1928.

April 10 *The Vegetable* (NY—Cherry Lane—Comedy). F. Scott Fitzgerald's

Camel Through the Needle's Eye

fantasy has Jerry Frost dream he's President. Life in the White House convinces him he'd rather be a mailman. Lee Strasberg directs. The show runs for only 13 performances.

April 15 *Camel Through the Needle's Eye* (NY—Martin Beck—Drama). Miriam Hopkins plays Susi Pesta, daughter of a poor woman who seeks unmarried happiness with the son of a rich man. This show runs over six months.

April 15 *The Love Duel* (NY—Barrymore—Drama). Zoe Akins adapts this Central European play for Ethel Barrymore, who plays She, a woman of the world who has met her match in He (Louis Calhern). The duel is a draw, ending in marriage. The show runs 11 weeks.

April 22 *Messin' Around* (NY—Hudson—Revue). Another black show, this one has a lively African dance by Cora La Redd and a boxing match between two girls who aren't faking. Jimmy Johnson provides the music. The show runs just short of four weeks. Critics have been accused of having a double-standard for white and black revues. Richard Watts, Jr., of the *Herald-Tribune*, notes this production would have been "inexcusable" if white, and says it's no better because it's black.

April 30 *The Little Show* (NY—Music Box—Revue). Dwight Deere Wiman stages this popular show which runs ten months. Howard Dietz and Arthur Schwarz are responsible for the lively lyrics and score. In the bright company are Clifton Webb, Libby Holman, Fred Allen and his sidekick Portland Hoffa, Romney Brent, and

Peggy Conklin. "Moanin' Low" is a hit, with music by Ralph Rainger.

May 1 *The Grand Street Follies* (NY—Booth—Revue). The last edition of these Follies, the sketches are the usual parodies of Broadway shows and historical events. Albert Carroll and Dorothy Sands mimic with spirit and James Cagney dances. The show survives only 93 performances.

May 14 *Pansy* (NY—Belmont—Revue). An all-black musical, this show has only three preformances, even with Bessie Smith in the cast. Brooks Atkinson calls it the worst show of all time. The score is by Maceo Pinkard.

May 21 *A Night in Venice* (NY—Shubert—Revue). This title has nothing to do with the operetta of the same name. Instead it is a Shubert show, part of the "Night in . . ." series; the last, in fact. It runs 22 weeks, with comedian Ted Healy wrestling a bear, among other treats. Busby Berkeley choreographs.

June 20 *Hot Chocolates* (NY—Hudson—Revue). Music is by Thomas "Fats" Waller and Harry Brooks. "Ain't Misbehavin'" is a hit. Louis Armstrong, an orchestra member, offers a trumpet solo. Andy Razaf's sketches deal with life in Harlem and other topics of the day. Also in the company are Jazzlips Richardson, Jimmie Baskette, and Thelma Meers. The show runs for 219 performances. ". . . fast-moving show, produced with more slickness and competence than any of its immediate predecessors," says the *NY Times*.

July 1 *Earl Carroll's Sketch Book* (NY—Earl Carroll—Revue). To some, this is just Carroll's *Vanities* in another guise. Music and lyrics are credited to Jay Gorney and E. Y. Harburg, but Billy Rose and others have also contributed. With Will Mahoney, William Demarest, and Patsy Kelly as comedians, the show runs for 400 performances.

Aug 6 *It's A Wise Child* (NY—Belasco—Comedy). Mildred McCoy plays Joyce, who tells an unwanted middle-aged suitor she's going to have another man's child. This puts him off, as intended, but it also has the same effect on the man she thinks she loves, Roger Baldwin (Humphrey Bogart). Produced and staged by David Belasco, the show runs for 45 weeks.

Sep 3 *Sweet Adeline* (NY—Hammerstein's—Musical). Helen Morgan sings "Why Was I Born?," "Here Am I," and "Don't Ever Leave Me." As the heroine she begins her singing career in her father's Hoboken beer-garden and goes on the New York stage when her sweetheart chooses her sister. Oscar Hammerstein II fashions book and lyrics for Jerome Kern's score. Arthur and Reginald Hammerstein produce and direct, respectively. The show is an immediate success, but runs only 234 performances because of the stock-market crash's effects on audiences.

Sep 17 *The Street Singer* (NY—Shubert—Musical). Busby Berkeley stages and co-produces with the Shuberts. Cyrus Wood and Edgar Smith's book shows Suzette (Queenie Smith) rising from a street vendor to a star of the *Folies Bergere*. Caesar Romero and Guy Roberston are also on hand. The show lasts 191 performances.

Sep 18 *Strictly Dishonorable* (NY—Avon—Comedy). Preston Sturges' light comedy of a young woman finding herself in the milieu of a mid-Manhattan speakeasy is an instant success. It runs beyond the season for a total of 557 performances. Muriel Kirkland plays the girl.

Sep 19 *Rope's End.* See L premiere (*Rope*), 1929.

Sep 23 *George White's Scandals* (NY—Apollo—Revue). This edition has 161 performances, with Willie and Eugene Howard providing most of the comedy. George White performs and stages, with Florence Wilson choreographing the Abbott Dancers.

Strictly Dishonorable

Sep 24 *See Naples and Die* (NY—Vanderbilt—Comedy). Elmer Rice's "extravagant comedy" about a woman who breaks with her fiance to marry a Russian features Claudette Colbert. It runs nearly eight weeks. On March 22, 1932, it comes to London's Little after January performances at the Embassy. Here it earns 101 showings.

Sep 30 *By Candle Light.* See L premiere, 1928.

Oct 2 *The Criminal Code* (NY—National—Drama). Martin Flavin shows life and problems in prisons, from both the prisoner and the guards' viewpoints, complete with a prison mutiny. The social issues raised create lively discussion among critics and audiences alike. The

production runs nearly 22 weeks.

Oct 9 *June Moon* (NY—Broadhurst—Comedy). Ring Lardner and George S. Kaufman take their audiences inside the mysteries of writing popular songs to make a living. Staged by Kaufman, the show runs 34 weeks.

Oct 21 *Maggie the Magnificent* (NY—Cort—Comedy). George Kelly writes and directs this play about a young woman (Shirley Warde) who has higher aspirations than her mother and her people. Joan Blondell and James Cagney are in the cast, but the show runs just four weeks.

Oct 24 *The Silver Tassie.* See L premiere, 1929.

Nov 5 *Bitter Sweet.* See L premiere, 1929.

Nov 5 *Broken Dishes* (NY—Ritz—Comedy). Bette Davis is the rebellious Elaine, who gets her meek father (Donald Meek) to help her stand up to her domineering mother (Ede Heinemann). Martin Flavin's play runs over 22 weeks.

Nov 11 *Heads Up* (NY—Alvin—Musical). Little does Martha (Janet Velie) know about her yacht, which is being used for rum-running. The Rodgers and Hart score and lyrics and the book by John McGowan and Paul Gerard Smith draw for 18 weeks. Victor Moore and Ray Bolger add a light touch.

Nov 26 *Sons O'Guns* (NY—Imperial—Musical). Fred Thompson and Jack Donahue provide the book and J. Fred Coots the score for this story of a man who finds his valet is now his top-sergeant. Jack Donahue and Lily Damita are in the cast. The adapted show opens at the London Hippodrome on June 26, 1930, with Bobby Howes heading the company. There are 211 performances.

Nov 27 *Fifty Million Frenchmen* (NY—Lyric—Musical). Cole Porter creates music and lyrics for Herbert Fields' book. "You've Got That Thing" and "You Do Something To Me" are hits. William Gaxton plays an American playboy who gets Looloo Caroll (Genevieve Tobin) by pretending to be an impoverished tourist guide. The show runs nearly eight months.

Dec 13 *Michael and Mary* (NY—Charles Hopkins—Drama). A.A. Milne's play about a couple facing blackmail features Henry Hull and Edith Barrett. There are 246 performances in the 299-seat playhouse. It comes to London's St. James's on Feb 1, 1930, with Edna Best and Herbert Marshall. The play earns 159 performances.

Dec 25 *Top Speed* (NY—46th Street—Musical). The dance routines zip along, with Ginger Rogers as Babs, pursued by a broker's clerk pretending to be a millionaire. Guy Bolton's pre-crash book is several months out of date, but with the Kalmar and Ruby lyrics and score, the show achieves 102 performances.

Dec 26 *Death Takes a Holiday* (NY—Ethel Barrymore—Drama). Walter Ferris adapts

Alberto Casella's Italian play in which Death takes a few days off to find out what life is like. Philip Merivale plays Prince Sirki (Death). The production lasts nearly 23 weeks. It opens at London's Savoy on June 18, 1931, with Ernest Milton (Sirki) and Celia Johnson.

Dec 28 *The First Mrs. Fraser*. See L premiere, 1929.

Dec 30 *Wake Up and Dream*. See L premiere, 1929.

1929   BRITISH PREMIERES

Jan 21 *Journey's End* (L—Savoy—Drama). R. C. Sherriff's potent drama of courage among doomed British soldiers at the front in World War I earns a run of 594 performances. James Whale directs. The play has been given a special production on Dec 10, 1928, at the Apollo Theatre, with Laurence Olivier in that cast. On March 22, 1929, Whale stages the play for New Yorkers at the Henry Miller Theatre for 485 performances. Jack Hawkins and Colin Keith-Johnston are in the company.

Jan 24 *The Lady With a Lamp* (L—Garrick—Drama). Reginald Berkeley's play about Florence Nightingale comes to the West End after first being seen at the Arts Theatre. Edith Evans is in the lead. At the Garrick, the production runs for 22 weeks. The drama opens at New York's Maxine Elliott on Nov 19, 1931, with Evans repeating her role. Although the production wins critical admiration, there are only 12 performances.

Jan 30 *Beau Geste* (L—His Majesty's—Drama). Basil Dean stages this romantic drama he's adapted, aided by Charlton Mann, from P. C. Wren's novel. Laurence Olivier is Beau Geste. Also in the large cast are Madeleine Carroll, Jack Hawkins, Marie Lohr, and Joan Henley.

Jan 31 *Craig's Wife*. See NY premiere, 1925.

Feb 8 *The Sacred Flame*. See NY premiere, 1928.

Feb 11 *Mr. Cinders* (L—Adelphi—Musical). Binnie Hale is Jill, an heiress who falls in love with a poor orphan, Jim (Bobby Howes). This Cinderella plot is the idea of Clifford Grey and Greatrex Newman. The music is the work of Vivian Ellis and Richard Myers. Leo Robin provides added lyrics. George D. Parker stages; Fred Leslie and Max Rivers choreograph. 528 performances reward the expenditures for a number of lavish sets and special effects—including a high-speed express train, a coupe, and an 18th century costume ball.

Feb 28 *Merry, Merry* (L—Carlton—Musical). This show, by Bert Lee and R. P. Weston, based on a Thompson-Archer original, earns a run of nearly 23 weeks. W. H. Berry plays the comic Jimmie Diggs. William Mollison stages. The music is by Jack Waller, Harris Weston, and J. A. Tunbridge.

March 20 *Love Lies* (L—Gaiety—Musical). Stanley Lupino stages and collaborates with Arthur Rigby on book and lyrics. The score is by Hal Brody. Lupino is in the cast, as are Cyril Ritchard, Madge Elliott, Gilly Flower, Laddie Cliff, and Bubbles Brown. This production earns a run of nearly 11 months.

March 21 *The 5 O'Clock Girl*. See NY premiere, 1927.

March 27 *Wake Up and Dream* (L—Pavilion—Revue). Cole Porter writes the music and J.H. Turner devises the material. Jessie Matthews, Tilly Losch, Douglas Byng, and Moya Nugent are among the company. The show runs 33 weeks. The revue comes to New York's Selwyn on Dec 30, with Jack Buchanan, Tilly Losch, and Jessie Matthews. There are only 136 showings.

April 3 *Little Accident*. See NY premiere, 1928.

April 4 *The New Moon*. See NY premiere, 1928.

April 10 *Porgy*. See NY premiere, 1927.

April 17 *The Ivory Door*. See NY premiere, 1927.

April 25 *Rope*. (L—Ambassadors'—Drama). Patrick Hamilton's drama has two Oxford roommates killing a boy for thrills, after which they hide his body in a chest and serve tea on it to the boy's father. Reginald Denham directs Brian Aherne and Anthony Ireland, among others. On Sep 19, the play opens at the Masque Theatre in New York as *Rope's End*, again staged by Denham, for 100 performances. Sebastian Shaw and Ivan Brandt play the youthful killers. Years later, the script is the basis for Alfred Hitchcock's film thriller, *Rope*.

April 30 *Paris Bound*. See NY premiere, 1927.

May 7 *A Cup of Kindness* (L—Aldwych—Comedy). Ben Travers writes another of his popular "Aldwych farces," staged by Tom Walls, who's also in the cast, with Winifred Shotter, Ralph Lynn, Mary Brough, and J. Robertson Hare, among others. The production earns a run of nine months.

May 8 *The Matriarch* (L—Royalty—Drama). G. B. Stern adapts her novel, *The Tents of Israel*, for the stage. Mrs. Patrick Campbell plays the matriarch. Directed by Frank Vernon, the production runs nearly seven months.

June 3 *Coquette*. See NY premiere, 1927.

June 3 *Mariette* (L—His Majesty's—Musical). The score is by Oscar Straus, with a book by Sacha Guitry, who plays the leading role of Prince Louis-Napoleon. Yvonne Printemps plays opposite him as Mariette Fleury.

June 4 *The Devil in the Cheese* (L—Comedy—Comedy). Tom Cushing's fantasy features Dennis Hoey, Sydney Fairbrother and Bramwell Fletcher.

June 12 *Hold Everything*. See NY premiere, 1928.

June 19 *Exiled* (L—Wyndham's—Comedy). John Galsworthy calls this an "Evolutionary Comedy," but it's closer to a dramatized tract about class confrontation.

July 2 *The First Mrs. Fraser* (L—Haymarket—Comedy). St. John Ervine's story of an aging lawyer who divorces his devoted wife and marries a selfish girl features Marie Tempest and Ursula Jeans as the women in the lawyer's life. It runs 632 performances. The play opens at New York's Playhouse on Dec 28, with Grace George as the first wife. It runs 11 months in George's own staging.

July 18 *Bitter Sweet* (L—His Majesty's—Musical). Noel Coward writes and composes this operetta about a woman who becomes an opera star and eventually a titled lady. Peggy Wood is featured. There are 697 performances. The play opens on Broadway at the Ziegfeld on Nov 5, with Evelyn Laye as the heroine. On this side of the Atlantic, the show runs five months. Coward stages in London and New York.

Aug 12 *The Middle Watch* (L—Shaftesbury—Drama). This runs over 48 weeks. It is staged by Frank Cellier, with Reginald Gardiner, Ann Todd, Clive Currie, Jane Baxter, and Aubrey Mather. Ian Hay and Stephen King-Hall are the authors.

Sep 17 *The Apple Cart* (L—Queen's—Comedy). George Bernard Shaw's new play he calls a "Political Extravaganza." It has an 8-month run. It is staged by H. K. Ayliff, and produced by Barry Jackson of the Birmingham Repertory Company. Thirty years from now, King Magnus of England (Cedric Hardwicke) confronts his strident Labour cabinet, which insists he resign. A corrupt business syndicate, Breakages, Ltd., is behind all this. Magnus seems ready to quit his hereditary throne but, discovering the Americans wish to return to British rule, he conceives a scheme to retain power. Barbara Everest is his queen, Jemima; Edith Evans is his intellectual mistress, Orinthia. The play has premiered in Warsaw, followed by Jackson's productions at the Malvern Festival and in Birmingham.

Sep 18 *The Calendar* (L—Wyndham's—Drama). Edgar Wallace's "Racing Play" earns a run of over 26 weeks. Owen Nares, Cathleen Nesbitt, and Gordon Harkes are in the cast.

Sep 19 *Jew Suss* (L—Duke of York's—Drama). Ashley Dukes describes this adaptation he's made of Lion Feuchtwanger's historical romance as a tragi-comedy. It runs more than 26 weeks. Matheson Lang has the title-role. Lang and Reginald Denham direct. Others in the large cast include Felix Aylmer, Peggy Ashcroft, A. Bromley Davenport, and Veronica Turleigh.

Sep 24 *Sorry You've Been Troubled* (L—St. Martin's—Comedy). Marion Lorne is Phoebe Selsey, operator of the switchboard at Grand Hotel. She is link in a number of interlocking plots involving guests and hotel staff, such as the mysterious dead body in Room 503, which disappears after it's reported, or the vanishing diamond bracelet. Walter Hackett's action-packed play runs nearly five months, staged by the author. Alick Johnstone designs.

Sep 30 *The Bachelor Father* (L—Globe—Comedy). The play by Edward C. Carpenter is about an old codger who summons three of his illegitimate children from various parts of the world and makes them at home in the ancestral Surrey mansion. Miriam Hopkins, C. Aubrey Smith, Francis Lister, and Rex O'Malley are in the cast.

Oct 3 *Follow Through*. See NY premiere, 1929.

Oct 10 *A Yankee at the Court of King Arthur*. See NY premiere (*A Connecticut Yankee*), 1927.

Oct 11 *The Silver Tassie* (L—Apollo—Drama). Sean O'Casey calls this anti-war play a tragi-comedy. The title refers to the trophy of an athletic contest. Beatrix Lehmann, Barry Fitzgerald, Ian Hunter, Charles Laughton, and Emlyn Williams are among the players. The drama comes to New York's Irish Theatre on Oct 24, 1929, where it receives 51 performances. Sterling Oliver and Allyn Gillen are in the cast.

Oct 14 *Symphony in Two Flats* (L—New—Comedy). Ivor Novello stars in his new play which runs 19 weeks. The comedy is about rejected love. Raymond Massey directs.

Nov 8 *The House That Jack Built* (L—Adelphi—Revue). This show lasts nearly 34 weeks. It is staged by Jack Hulbert, who also performs with such talents as Cicely Courtneidge, Irene Russell, and Bobby Comber, Ronald Jeans and Douglas Furber provide the book, with songs by Ivor Novello and Donovan Parsons. Vivian Ellis and Arthur Schwartz also contribute some songs.

Nov 12 *Art and Mrs. Bottle* (L—Criterion—Comedy). Benn W. Levy's play, staged by the author, has Irene Vanbrugh, Betty Stockfield, Esmond Knight, and Frederick Lloyd as the Bottles.

Nov 14 *Dear Love* (L—Palace—Musical). This show is staged by William Mollison, with music by Haydn Wood, Joseph Tunbridge, and Jack Waller, and book by Dion Titheradge, Lauri Wylie, and Herbert Clayton. It lasts four months.

1929 REVIVALS/REPERTORIES

Jan 2 The Dublin Gate Theatre, with Hilton Edwards directing and Micheal macLiammoir designing, continues its initial season at the Peacock Theatre—attached to the Abbey Theatre—with Greensfelder's *Six Stokers Who Own the Bloomin' Earth*, followed by O'Neill's *Anna Christie*. This is the last play of the first season.

Jan 14 At the Civic Repertory Theatre in New York, Eva LeGallienne stages a Spanish drama, *The Lady from Alfaqueque*, translated by the Granville Barkers. It has 17 performances. 19 performances are won by Leonid Andreyev's *Katerina*, with Alla Nazimova as the woman whose husband's mistaken mistrust drives her to be the thing he thinks she is.

Jan 21 A real Mississippi River showboat troupe, the Thom Company, offer two melodramas, *The Parson's Bride* and *Shadow of the Rockies*, during a brief engagement at New York's Belmont Theatre.

Jan 28 In Hampstead at the Everyman Theatre, St. John Ervine's *The Ship* opens, with Hugh Williams and Katie Johnson, among others. On Feb 18, the play is Mordaunt Shairp's *The Offence*. *The Pleasure Garden*, by Beatrice Mayor, is seen on March 8. Molly Kerr's *Requital* is played on April 23. On May 13, there is a revue, *Morning, Noon, and Night*. Kitty Willoughby's *Smoke Persian* opens on May 28. On June 11, *Suburbia Comes to Paradise*, by Bergere and Fergusson, premieres. Wilfred Eyre's *Speed Limit* is the play on June 24. July 3, it's Bjornson's Norwegian drama, *The Gauntlet*, with Strindberg's *The Father* on July 22.

Feb 4 At London's Old Vic Theatre, Tom Robertson's *Caste* is revived, staged by Andrew Leigh.

Feb 18 Anna Cora Mowatt's mid-19th century American comedy of New York *nouveaux riches* manners, *Fashion*, moves to the Kingsway Theatre after opening at London's Gate Theatre in January. Marie Dainton plays the social-climbing Mrs. Tiffany, with director Peter Godfrey as the bogus French count she wants to marry her daughter.

Feb 19 Ernst Toller's German drama, *Hoppla, Wir Leben*, opens at London's Gate Theatre, translated by Herman Ould as *Hoppla*. Peter Godfrey directs a cast including Beatrix Lehmann and Robert Newton.

March 1 The Dublin Gate Theatre opens its second season with Tolstoi's *The Power of Darkness*. Playing in a temporary home, the Peacock Theatre, the troupe next offers Sears' *Juggernaut*, followed by Rice's *The Adding Machine*, Capek's *R. U. R.*, Raynal's *The Unknown Warrior*, a triple-bill of *Tristram and Iseult*, *The Little Man*, and *A Merry Death*, closing the season with Tocher's *The Old Lady Says "No!"*, which opens on June 19.

March 5 Eugene O'Neill's *Before Breakfast*, with Mary Blair as the complaining wife whose monologue prompts the suicide of her unseen husband, opens at New York's Provincetown Playhouse, on a double-bill with Vergil Geddes' *The Earth Between*.

March 14 James Laver adapts Klabund's adaptation of an old Chinese play, *The Circle of Chalk*—much later to be adapted again by Bertolt Brecht—for London's New Theatre. Anna May Wong and Laurence Olivier play leads. *The Times* reports that the play "has become a vast, trundling cartload of gilded and painted bricks, dragging its way for three hours on what journey we hardly know. . . ."

March 30 At the Q Theatre, in Kew Bridge, Lennox Robinson's Irish comedy, *The Far-Off Hills*—which always seem greener than those close at hand—opens with a cast including the Irish players Sara Allgood, Una O'Connor, J. A. O'Rourke, and Fred O'Donovan.

April 15 Shakespeare's *Twelfth Night* opens the annual spring season of productions of his works at Stratford-upon-Avon in the festival's temporary quarters in a local cinema. *Much Ado About Nothing* is the "birthday play." Other plays are *The Taming of the Shrew*, *Richard II*, *The Merchant of Venice*, *Macbeth*, *Hamlet*, and Sheridan's *The School for Scandal*. W. Bridges Adams is in charge of the season, directing and designing.

April 29 Clemence Dane's play, *Mariners*, has Lewis Casson and Sybil Thorndike as the Rev. Benjamin and Lily Cobb. Casson directs this production at Wyndham's Theatre in London. On May 29, Casson and Thorndike present a double-bill: St. John Ervine's *Jane Clegg* and Gilbert Murray's translation of Euripides' *Medea*. Thorndike takes the title-roles, playing opposite Casson.

April 29 Morris Guest imports the Freiburg Passion Play from Germany where it has been performed every three years since 1760. The handsome production is mounted in the huge Hippodrome Theatre in New York. Leading roles are played by the Fassnacht Family; Adolph Fassnacht is the Christ. Unfortunately, the production runs only six weeks.

May 6 Again Little Theatre takes the stage

for a week in New York, with Walter Hartwig's annual Tournament. At the Waldorf Theatre, local troupes compete with ensembles from Long Island, Rhode Island, Washington, D.C., Ohio, Alabama, Maryland, and Colorado. The Belasco Trophy goes to the Gardens Players of Forest Hills.

July 1 In its temporary playhouse in the Greenhill Street Cinema, the Shakespeare Memorial Theatre opens its summer season in Stratford-upon-Avon with *Hamlet.* During the nine-week season, the plays include *Much Ado About Nothing, The Taming of the Shrew, Richard II, The Merchant of Venice, Macbeth, Hamlet, Twelfth Night,* and Sheridan's *The School for Scandal.* A new production of *Romeo and Juliet* joins these revivals from the spring season.

July 8 In this edition of the annual revue of *The Co-Optimists* at London's Vaudeville Theatre, the "Pierrotic Entertainment" is headed by Stanley Holloway, Davy Burnaby, Elsa Macfarlane, Phyllis Monkman, Betty Chester, Sydney Howard, and Peggy Petronella. Laddie Cliff stages, with sketches by Greatrex Newman, Archibald De Bear, and Burnaby. Melville Gideon composes the music. The show runs nearly 17 weeks.

July 15 William Poel provides a shortened version of George Chapman's play titled *The Conspiracy and Tragedy of Charles, Duke of Byron.* He stages it for the Elizabethan Stage Circle, in London at the Royalty Theatre. Robert Speaight plays the Duke, supported by such players as playwright Emlyn Williams, Winifred Evans, Stringer Davis, and George Ellis.

July 27 In London, at the Apollo Theatre, Oscar Asche stages Shakespeare's *The Merry Wives of Windsor* in modern dress. He himself is Falstaff, with Robert Atkins as the jealous Mr. Ford and Evelyn Hope as his clever wife. Marie Ault is Mistress Quickly.

Sep 9 Today marks the opening of the third season of the Dublin Gate Theatre Studio in its temporary home at the Peacock Theatre. It has already been a busy year, for the first season ended in January; the second began in March and ended in June, and now another is launched by the theatre's co-founding talents's Hilton Edwards—who directs and acts, and Micheal macLiammoir, who designs and acts. The premiere tonight is macLiammoir's *The Ford of the Hurdles.* His *Diarmuid and Grainne* follows in revival, staged at the Mansion House.

Sep 16 Eva LeGallienne's Civic Repertory Theatre opens its New York season with Chekhov's *The Sea Gull,* with LeGallienne as Masha and Josephine Hutchinson as Nina. Merle Maddern plays Arkadina. The production is played 63 times; successes from last season are also brought back. The repertoire includes *The*

Cherry Orchard, The Master Builder, The Cradle Song, and *The Would-Be Gentleman.* On Dec 6, Tolstoi's *The Living Corpse (Redemption)* opens, staged by Jacob Ben-Ami, who plays the failed Fedya. Josephine Hutchinson is Lisa, the woman he leaves but fails to divorce. The production has 33 performances.

Sep 21 The Shuberts begin a series of revivals of musicals at the Jolson Theatre in New York, with Victor Herbert's *Sweethearts.* During the season they revive *Mlle. Modiste*—with Fritzi Scheff, *Naughty Marietta, The Fortune Teller, Babes in Toyland, Robin Hood, The Chocolate Soldier, The Merry Widow, The Prince of Pilsen, Serenade,* and *The Count of Luxembourg.* Ilse Marvenga, Tessa Kosta, Al Shean, and other stars are brought back in these shows.

Oct 7 In Toronto, Ontario, the Shakespeare Memorial Theatre Company of Stratford-upon-Avon opens its second North American tour.

Oct 7 Ruth Langner translates *Karl and Anna,* Leonhard Frank's story of two German prisoners in a Russian camp. Richard (Frank Conroy) tells Karl (Otto Kruger) all about his wife (Alice Brady). Karl escapes, goes to Berlin, passes himself off as Richard; Anna, knowing he's not, accepts him, bears his child, and goes off with him when Richard finally returns. The Theatre Guild can get only 49 performances from this fare at the Guild Theatre in New York.

Oct 21 At London's Savoy Theatre, a season of Gilbert & Sullivan is opened with the D'Oyly Carte's production of *The Gondoliers,* Henry Lytton is the Duke of Plaza-Toro. On Nov 4, *Ruddigore* is revived, with Winnie Melville as Rose Maybud. *Patience* is opened on Nov 11. Darrell Fancourt and Martyn Green are Col. Calverly and Major Murgatroyd. On Nov 18, it's *The Yeoman of the Guard,* with Derek Oldham as Col. Fairfax. On Dec. 2, *Princess Ida* features Winifred Lawson in the title-role. *Pinafore* bows on the 9; Bertha Lewis is Little Buttercup. On Dec 16, *The Mikado* is sung. On Dec 30, the musical treat is *Iolanthe.*

Oct 28 At London's Old Vic Theatre, Moliere's *The Imaginary Invalid,* as adapted by F. Anstey, opens. Harcourt Williams stages. Brember Wills is Argan; Donald Wolfit, Dr. Purgon; Martita Hunt, Beline; John Gielgud, Cleante; and Margaret Webster, Toinette.

Oct 31 The Shuberts revive Johann Strauss's *Die Fledermaus* as *A Wonderful Night,* with Archie Leach (Cary Grant) as Max, the husband who goes to a ball instead of to jail. The show runs nearly four months.

Nov 7 At the Everyman Theatre in Hampstead, George Bernard Shaw's *Captain Brassbound's Conversion* is revived, with Malcolm Morley in the title-role. On Dec 3, Alexander Ostrovsky's *The Storm*

Mr. Cinders

opens, staged by Morley. Jerome K. Jerome's *The Passing of the Third Floor Back* is revived on Dec 23, with Henry Hallat directing and playing the Stranger.

Nov 25 The Theatre Guild in New York gets only a six-week run from *The Game of Love and Death,* Romain Rolland's tale of courage and sacrifice during the French Revolution. Claude Rains plays Jerome de Courvoisier, who gets passports for both his wife (Alice Brady) and her lover (Otto Kruger). She decides to join Jerome at the guillotine, sending her lover to freedom. Rouben Mamoulian directs. On Dec 17, the Guild opens *Red Rust,* by Krichon and Ouspensky, a Russian play about the corruption and punishment of a Soviet cell-leader. It has 65 performances, with the director, Herbert J. Biberman, playing the villain. Lionel Stander, George Tobias, and Lee Strasberg are also in the cast.

Nov 28 At London's Kingsway Theatre, Sheridan's 18th century comedy, *The School for Scandal,* is revived, staged by Frank Cellier.

Dec 19 London is again in the grip of the holiday season, and *Peter Pan* returns for audiences of all ages. It's at the St. James's Theatre, with Jean Forbes-Robertson in the title-role. On Dec 23, a number of holiday shows open: *Charley's Aunt* (Daly's), *Arms and the Man* (Royal Court), *The Private Secretary* (Criterion), *Where the Rainbow Ends* (Holborn Empire), and *When Knights Were Bold* (Playhouse). Later entries include *The Sleeping Beauty* (Drury Lane), *Puss in Boots* (Lyceum), *The Ghost Train* (Comedy), *The Rose and the Ring* (Lyric, Hammersmith), *Treasure Island* (Strand), *Babes in the Wood* (Scala), *Shock-Headed Peter* (Wimbledon), *The Windmill Man* (Victoria Palace), and *The Shepherdess Without a Heart* (King's Hammersmith).

Dec 23 To greet the holiday season, the New York Theatre Guild unveils S. N. Behrman's *Meteor*, a story about Raphael Lord (Alfred Lunt), whose intelligence makes him rich but not always happy. Lynn Fontanne is the wife who leaves him. The production runs nearly 3 months.

1929 BIRTHS/DEATHS/DEBUTS

Jan 7 English dramatist Henry Arthur Jones (b. 1851) is dead. Jones' first play, *Only Round the Corner*, was produced in 1878. Others include *The Crusaders*, *The Triumph of the Philistines*, *The Liars*, *Cock o' the Walk*, and *Mrs. Dane's Defense*. Jones also wrote *The Renascence of the English Drama*, *Foundations of a National Drama*, and *Theatre of Ideas*.

Jan 9 Actress Audrey Christie makes her New York City stage debut as Olive in Laurence Schwab and B. G. DeSylva's *Follow Thru* at the 46th Street Theatre. She first appeared as a dancer in vaudeville on the Keith-Orpheum Circuit three years ago.

Jan 15 Ned Wayburn, the man credited with inventing tap-dancing and a longtime Broadway musical and revue director, stages *Ned Wayburn's Gambols*, a failure. Despite a wide variety of dance numbers—Oriental, Gypsy—and the singing of Libby Holman, the show, at New York's Knickerbocker Theatre, has only 31 performances.

Jan 24 Authors Basil Rathbone and Walter Ferris write *Judas*, a biblical drama. Rathbone plays Judas. Richard Boleslavsky directs; William A. Brady, Jr., and Dwight Deere Wiman produce. At New York's Longacre Theatre the show runs for 12 performances.

Feb 12 English actress Lily Langtry (b. 1852) dies in Monaco. Langtry made her stage debut with the Bancrofts at the Haymarket Theatre as Kate Hardcastle in 1881. She organized her own company and played in London and the provinces, as well as touring the United States.

March 5 Screen actress Bette Davis makes her New York City stage debut in the role of Floy Jennings in Vergil Geddes' *The Earth Between* at the Provincetown Playhouse.

March 31 American theatre historian and playwright Brander Matthews (b. 1852) is dead at age 77. Matthews was the first American professor of dramatic literature, a post he held from 1900–24 at Columbia University. Among his writings are *The Development of the Drama*, *Shakespeare as a Playwright*, and his autobiography, *These Many Years*. Matthews was also an incorporator of The Players.

May 18 American actress Mary Shaw dies in New York City. Born in 1854, Shaw began her career with the Boston Museum, later supporting Helena Modjeska, Julia Marlowe, and Mrs. Fiske. Her later years were devoted principally to the plays of George Bernard Shaw and Henrik Ibsen. She played on tour in the Civic Repertory's production of *The Cradle Song*.

June 4 Alfred Lunt and Lynn Fontanne are Albert and Ilse in *Caprice*, translated by Philip Moeller from the original of G. Sil-Vara. Moeller stages the play for London's St. James's Theatre.

Jun 22 The Ranee of Sarawak has written a play—*Heels of Pleasure*. Today, it's on view in London at the Arts Theatre. Margot St. Leger and Kate Cutler are among those in the cast.

July 29 In London, at the Golder's Green Theatre, the play is *Magic Slippers*. It's the work of W. A. Darlington, who is to achieve note as a drama critic, rather than as a playwright. Reginald Bach directs.

Sep 11 Laurence Olivier makes his New York debut today at the Eltinge Theatre on 42nd Street. The play is *Murder on the Second Floor*.

Sep 21 Director, actor, producer, and writer Robert Lewis makes his first New York appearance as an actor with the Civic Repertory Theatre. He attended the Juilliard School of Music.

Oct 3 American actress Jeanne Eagels (b. 1894) dies in New York. Eagels made her first appearance as Puck in *A Midsummer Night's Dream* at age seven. Her most successful role was a Sadie Thompson in *Rain* which opened on Broadway in 1922 and ran for two years. She then toured in the play for another season.

Nov 5 English actress Evelyn Laye makes her New York debut as the Marchioness of Shayne in Noel Coward's *Bitter Sweet* at the Ziegfeld Theatre. Laye made her debut as Nang-Ping in *Mr. Wu* at the Theatre Royal in Brighton in 1915.

Nov 5 Madeleine Carroll and Eric Portman play a Young Woman and a Young Man in John Galsworthy's drama, *The Roof*, staged by Basil Dean at London's Vaudeville Theatre.

Nov 13 Val Gielgud's new play, *Chinese White*, opens in London at the Arts Theatre, staged by Owen Nares.

Nov 23 Barry Jackson, founder of the Birmingham Repertory Theatre in England, speaks to a meeting of theatre enthusiasts in Montreal, Canada. As a result, a committee is formed to organize the Montreal Repertory Theatre. Under director-manager Martha Allan, the first production, A.A. Milne's *The Perfect Alibi*, is presented the following March at Moyse Hall of McGill University. By 1932, Montreal Repertory Theatre will have its own house and a large audience among English-speaking Montrealers.

Nov 24 American actor Raymond Hitchcock (b. 1865) dies in Beverly Hills. Hitchcock made his first appearance as a "star" at the Tremont Theatre in Boston in 1903 in *The Yankee Consul*. Among his many successes were *Hitchy-Koo*, *The Sap*, *The Old Soak*, and *Raymond Hitchcock's Pinwheel*.

Nov 25 Stage and screen actor Henry Fonda makes his Broadway debut as a walk-on in Romain Rolland's *The Game of Love and Death*, starring Alice Brady and Otto Kruger, at the Guild Theatre.

Dec 9 English actor George Coulouris makes his Broadway deubt as Friar Peter in Olga Katzin's *The Novice and the Duke*, a modern dress version of *Measure for Measure*.

1929 THEATERS/PRODUCTIONS

The two theatrical patents granted in Britain this year both relate to control of curtains. F. E. Weidhaas has devised a system of independent cables, permitting a curtain to be opened in a number of configurations, or "drapes."

The Lord Chamberlain bans production of Hubert Griffith's drama, *Red Sunday*, not only because of its concern with Lenin and the Russian Revolution, but also because the King's brother-in-law, the executed Tsar Nicholas, is also in the cast

of characters. Britons are to be defended against Communist ideas presented in other works as well. Tretyakov's *Roar China* is banned. Pudovkin's film *Mother* is banned by the film censors in 1930.

Peter Godfrey's staging of Oscar Wilde's banned drama, *Salome*, at the Gate Theatre so impresses the Lord Chamberlain's Office that the ban on public performance is at last lifted, with a license offered for a production by the Cambridge Festival Theatre, who are not now in a position

Symphony in Two Flats

to produce it.

Jan 25 Chicago's impressive new Civic Opera House opens with a production of *Aida*. Located at 20 North Wacker Drive, the huge house seats 3,714. Architects are Graham, Anderson, Probst, and White. In November, the smaller Civic Theatre will open in the same building.

April 19 As the drive for donations to construct a new Shakespeare Memorial Theatre in Stratford-upon-Avon continue, American supporters report a total of £165,750 collected thus far in the United States.

May 15 A. L. Erlanger acquires ownership of the Klaw Theatre, on West 45 Street in New York, and renames it the Avon. After *Tight Breeches* is presented here in 1934, it becomes a broadcasting studio and is torn down in 1954.

Summer This is the first season of the Malvern Festival, with George Bernard Shaw as its patron, promising to write plays specially for the event. Barry Jackson and Roy Limbert are the Festival's founders. The Festival will run until temporarily stopped by war in 1939, after which it will have a brief revival in 1949, when the response is not encouraging, leading to termination. During its life, nearly 70 plays by nearly 40 playwrights will be presented. 21 of them are by Shaw, who gives the Malvern Festival the world premieres of *Geneva, In Good King Charles' Golden Days*, and *On the Rocks*. The first English performances of The

Apple Cart, Bouyant Billions, Too True To Be Good, and *The Simpleton of the Unexpected Isles* are given at the Festival. Rudolf Besier's *The Barretts of Wimpole Street* has its world premiere here.

June 15 Looking back on its tenth Broadway season, the Theatre Guild can take pride in these statistics: 70 plays produced; 9,000 performances given; 32,000 subscribers in New York alone. Activities are now extended to Guild subscribers in a number of American cities: Chicago, Philadelphia, Boston, Cleveland, Pittsburgh, Baltimore, Detroit, Cincinnati, St. Louis, and Washington, D.C.

Critic Burns Mantle's ten *Best Plays* for the Broadway season include: Nichols and Brown's *Wings Over Europe*, Anderson's *Gypsy*, Rice's *Street Scene*—which also wins the Pulitzer Prize, Sherriff's *Journey's End*, Barry's *Holiday*, Crothers' *Let Us Be Gay*, Hecht and MacArthur's *The Front Page*, Dell and Mitchell's *Little Accident*, Sierra's *The Kingdom of God*, and Treadwell's *Machinal*. Mantle says this is the worst season in memory of living playgoers, a statement which has been in print a hundred times in the past six months. The rapid encroachments on the theatre audience by "Talkies," a glut of bad plays, high ticket prices, speculators' gouging on tickets, bad management, and other causes are blamed for the poor season. There have been 224 Broadway productions, 30 less than in the previous season. Approximately 150 of them have been plays, not musicals, but few have enjoyed

success. Only 44 shows are seen as successful (20%). There have been 133 dramas, 58 comedies, 27 musicals, and 6 revues.

July 2 The foundation stone is laid for the new Shakespeare Memorial Theatre in Stratford-upon-Avon. Elizabeth Scott, the theatre's architect, participates in the Masonic rituals and is the first woman ever to do so. In the evening, *Richard II* is played.

Aug 10 Century Lighting, Inc., is founded by Edward Kook and Joseph Levy, with offices and a small factory at 351 West 52nd Street, New York. Century Lighting is to become one of the leading manufacturers and innovators of stage lighting equipment.

Sep 30 Because Eugene O'Neill's *Strange Interlude* has been banned in Boston, Massachusetts, it is performed instead in nearby Quincy.

Oct 21 The second Savoy Theatre opens on the Strand with *The Gondoliers*. This 1,122 seat theatre has been designed by Frank Tugwell, with interiors by Basil Ionides and is under the management of Rupert D'Oyly Carte. The original theatre seated 986 and opened on Oct 10, 1881, closing for the current renovation on June 3, 1929.

Oct 23 The Dominion Theatre opens on Tottenham Court Road in London with the musical comedy, *Follow Through*. Leslie Henson and Firth Shephard are the producers and managers of this 2,000-seat theatre, later to be converted into a 1,712-seat cinema.

Nov 11 Chicago celebrates Armistice Day in a special way, by inaugurating a new theatre: the Civic Theatre. It's in the same building as the Civic Opera House, at 20 North Wacker Drive. Designed by Graham, Anderson, Probst, and White, it seats 970 people. The opening attraction is *Hamlet*, starring Fritz Leiber.

Nov 25 The Duchess Theatre opens on Catherine Street, just off London's Strand. The first production is *Tunnel Trench*. The architect, Ewen Barr, has created a "modern Tudor Gothic facade," and the interior design is by Marc-Henri and Laverdat. The capacity is 474.

Dec 1 In London, a mass meeting of actors and actresses, seeking more effective protection in their work and a strong bargaining agent to represent them, vote unanimously to form the British Actors Equity Association. Rules and constitution will be adopted in May of next year. Eventually, one role of Equity will be to regulate and restrict appearances of American actors on British stages, just as American Actors' Equity will do for the United States with regard to British performers.

Jan 6 *Waterloo Bridge* (NY—Fulton—Drama). Robert E. Sherwood's story of a brief encounter between an American soldier on leave and a chorus-girl runs for 64 performances, with Glenn Hunter and June Walker in the leading roles. Winchell Smith stages.

Jan 14 *Strike Up the Band* (NY—Times Square—Musical). George and Ira Gershwin provide music and lyrics for this satire. Morrie Ryskind softens the hard edges of George S. Kaufman's irony, with an American war against Switzerland—to protect American chocolate products—turned into a dream. Dudley Clements, Bobby Clark and Paul McCullough are featured. The show runs six months.

Feb 12 *Topaze* (NY—Music Box—Comedy). Benn W. Levy's adaption of Marcel Pagnol's tale of the innocent Topaze who rapidly masters the arts of graft achieves 159 performances. Frank Morgan plays the title role. On Oct 8, it opens at London's New Theatre with Raymond Massey in the lead.

Feb 13 *The Last Mile* (NY—Sam H. Harris—Drama). John Wexley's play about a condemned murderer setting down the events and emotions leading to his execution is directed by Chester Erskin. James Bell plays the young killer; Spencer Tracy is also in the cast. The production runs nine months.

Feb 18 *Simple Simon* (NY—Ziegfeld—Musical). Ed Wynn and Guy Bolton sketch out the book for this fantasy in which Wynn dreams of being among his favorite fairy-tale characters. Florenz Ziegfeld produces, with luxuriant Joseph Urban settings and music and lyrics by Rodgers and Hart. Ruth Etting has a success singing "Ten Cents a Dance." The show runs 17 weeks.

Feb 24 *The Apple Cart* (NY—Martin Beck—Comedy). George Bernard Shaw's political fantasy, with Tom Powers as King Magnus, who threatens to abdicate England's throne and stand for parliament, runs for 11 weeks in the Theatre Guild production. Philip Moeller stages, with a cast of ministers and officials including Claude Rains, Morris Carnovsky, and Helen Westley. On March 17, the Guild Theatre is the scene of the Guild's production of Turgenev's *A Month in the Country*. With Alla Nazimova as the amorous, restless Natalia Petrovna, the staging lasts 71 performances.

Feb 26 *The Green Pastures* (NY—Mansfield—Comedy). Marc Connelly's dramatization of Roark Bradford's black folktale of biblical characters and events enjoys a run of 640 performances. Richard Harrison plays The Lord in this all-black cast. "Mr. Connelly has made the transition from Negro comedy to universal drama . . ." says the *NY Times*.

March 3 *Flying High* (NY—Apollo—Musical). Bert Lahr plays a mechanic who breaks a flying record because he doesn't know how to land the plane. Kate Smith, as his love interest, sings "Red Hot Chicago." George White engages the team of DeSylva, Brown, and Henderson to provide lyrics and score for this show, which runs for nearly 45 weeks. *The NY Times* reports "It is obstreperous buffoonery. . . . Kate Smith bellows in such volume that the orchestra swoons in despair."

April 14 *Hotel Universe* (NY—Martin Beck—Drama). Philip Barry's play brings together some Americans who become metaphysically introspective. It plays ten weeks, with such Theatre Guild stalwarts as Morris Carnovsky, Glenn Anders, Franchot Tone and Ruth Gordon.

April 22 *Stepping Sisters* (NY—Belmont—Comedy). Coming to rehearse for a benefit, three society matrons discover they knew each other working in burlesque. They are horrified that their pasts may become known. This Howard Comstock farce lasts for 333 performances.

Simple Simon

June 4 *Garrick Gaieties* (NY—Guild—Revue). This Theatre Guild revue runs nearly five months, with music by Marc Blitzstein, Aaron Copland, Vernon Duke, and Kay Swift; lyrics by Johnny Mercer, E. Y. Harburg, and Ira Gershwin, among others. Talents include Imogene Coca, Hildegarde Halliday, and Sterling Holloway.

June 10 *Artists and Models* (NY—Majestic—Revue). Despite its customary complement of beautiful girls and lovely costumes—or lack of them—the growing Depression seems to be discouraging audiences for such theatrical fare. This Shubert show has only 55 performances.

July 1 *Earl Carroll's Vanities* (NY—New Amsterdam—Revue). Carroll's new revue includes one scene in which a man pursues some underwater nymphs, catching one just as the lights go out. Patsy Kelly, Faith Bacon, and Jack Benny are

in the cast. It runs 215 performances.

Sep 11 *That's Gratitude* (NY—John Golden—Comedy). Frank Craven writes and stars in the play about a man who aids a homely woman. The show runs 197 performances.

Sep 22 *A Farewell To Arms* (NY—National—Drama). Laurence Stallings dramatizes Ernest Hemingway's popular novel of two lovers on the Italian front in World War I. Elissa Landi and Glenn Anders play leads. Rouben Mamoulian directs. The show runs only three weeks.

Sep 23 *Fine and Dandy* (NY—Erlanger—Musical). This show, with music by Kay Swift and book by Donald Ogden Stewart deals with a man who becomes the general manager of a tool-factory by romancing the widowed heiress. Joe Cook is the comic lead. Eleanor Powell dances. It runs eight months.

Sep 24 *Once in a Lifetime* (NY—Music Box—Comedy). George S. Kaufman and Moss Hart have a hit with this satire on Hollywood moviemaking. Spring Byington is the influential movie critic and Kaufman the playwright. It runs nearly 51 weeks. The *NY Times* terms it a "rough-and-tumble burlesque." On Feb 23, 1933 it opens at London's Queen's but doesn't win a long run. Its success comes much later in a Royal Shakespeare Company production in 1979.

Sep 25 *The Greeks Had a Word for It* (NY—Sam H. Harris—Comedy). Zoe Akins imagines the lively loves of three Follies girls (Dorothy Hall, Verree Teasdale, and Muriel Kirkland). It runs 253 performances.

Sep 29 *Mrs. Moonlight* (NY—Charles Hopkins—Drama). Benn W. Levy's British import wins 321 performances. Edith Barrett plays Sarah Moonlight who cannot age, as a result of a magic wish. Leo G. Carroll is in the cast, directed by Charles Hopkins.

Oct 7 *Brown Buddies* (NY—Liberty—Musical). Carl Rickman invents the tale of black doughboys, with a score by Joe Jordan and Millard Thomas. Bill "Bojangles" Robinson and Adelaide Hall are featured. The show runs 111 performances.

Oct 14 *Girl Crazy* (NY—Alvin—Musical). George Gershwin's score, with brother Ira's lyrics, includes such hits as "Bidin' My Time," "Embraceable You," "But Not for Me," and "I Got Rhythm," which is belted out by Ethel Merman. In Guy Bolton and John McGowan's book, playboy Danny Churchill is sent to Arizona to get away from booze, girls, and gambling, all of which he manages to find or import. Best of all the girls for him is Molly Gray (Ginger Rogers). Willie Howard clowns as a New York cabbie. In the orchestra are some unknowns: Glenn Miller, Benny

Goodman, and Gene Krupa. The show runs for 34 weeks. The *NY Times* reports, "The dancing combines intricacy and speed in the manner of the day, and it is definitely one of the assets. Another is Ethel Merman, whose peculiar song style was brought from the night clubs to the stage to the vast delight last evening of the people who go places and watch things being done.... The ingenue, Miss Rogers, is an oncoming young person of the type whom, at her first appearance, half of the audience immediately classifies as 'cute.' "

Oct 15 *Three's a Crowd* (NY—Selwyn—Revue). "Body and Soul" and "Something To Remember You By" are introduced by Libby Holman. Fred Allen, Clifton Webb, Tamara Geva, and Fred MacMurray provide humor in sketches by Howard Dietz and others. Arthur Schwartz provides most of the music for the show, which runs for 272 performances.

Oct 22 *Lew Leslie's Blackbirds* (NY—Royale—Revue). Eubie Black provides the music, Andy Razaf devises the lyrics, and Flournoy Miller sets the sketches for this all-black show. Ethel Waters, Minto Cato, and Jazzlips Richardson are in the cast. It runs 57 performances.

Oct 27 *Roar China* (NY—Martin Beck—Drama). In S. Tretyakov's play a native rebellion is sparked by intransigence of a British warship's captain, seeking to punish the murder of an American exporter (William Gargan). A large number of Chinese performers are cast in Chinese roles in this Theatre Guild production. It runs nine weeks, staged by Herbert Biberman.

Oct 29 *On the Spot.* See L premiere, 1930.

Nov 3 *Elizabeth the Queen* (NY—Guild—Drama). Maxwell Anderson's verse play centers on the betrayed love of Elizabeth for Essex, with Lynn Fontanne and Alfred Lunt as the lovers. This Theatre Guild production runs for 147 performances.

Nov 13 *Grand Hotel* (NY—National—Drama). Vicki Baum's tale of 36 hours and curious characters in Berlin's Grand Hotel runs for 459 performances. The cast includes Eugenie Leontovich, Henry Hull, and Sam Jaffe. The play, adapted by Edward Knoblock, premieres on Sep 3, 1931, at London's Adelphi with Elena Miramova, Ursula Jeans, Lyn Harding, and Ernest Milton, among the cast. It runs just short of 19 weeks.

Nov 17 *Sweet and Low* (NY—46th Street—Revue). Billy Rose produces and composes this show, with his wife, Fanny Brice, as its main attraction. It runs 23 weeks. Arthur Treacher, George Jessel, and James Barton are in the cast.

Nov 18 *Tonight or Never* (NY—Belasco—Comedy). This is David Belasco's last production before his death. Helen Gahagan plays the prima donna in Lili Hatvany's play. Melvyn Douglas is a scout

Three's a Crowd

for the Metropolitan Opera who is anxious to marry her. It runs almost seven months.

Nov 18 *Smiles* (NY—Ziegfeld—Musical). Vincent Youmans composes the score, which includes "Time On My Hands." The book is based on a Noel Coward story about a French waif, brought to America, who tries high society. This Ziegfeld production has a cast including Marilyn Miller, Fred and Adele Astaire, and Eddie Foy, Jr. It runs only 63 performances.

Nov 19 *The Vinegar Tree* (NY—Playhouse—Comedy). Winchell Smith stages Paul Osborn's comedy about a woman anxious to relive a day in her past. Mary Boland is featured. The show has 229 performances. Osborn's play opens in London on June 8, 1932, at the St. James's with a cast including Henry Daniell, Barbara Hoffe, Marie Tempest, Celia Johnson, Louis Hayward and W. Graham Browne, who also directs. It does not have

a long run.

Dec 5 *Overture* (NY—Longacre—Drama). Although it has only 41 performances, William Bolitho's play is chosen as one of the season's "Best Plays" by Burns Mantle. It tells the tale of post-war citizens' rebellion in Germany, led to miserable defeat by a pathetically sincere idealist. In the cast are Pat O'Brien, William Foran, and Barbara Robbins.

Dec 8 *The New Yorkers* (NY—Broadway—Musical). Herbert Fields' book is about a girl's dream of falling in love with a bootlegger. Cole Porter provides the score, which includes "I Happen To Like New York," sung by Rags Ragland. Others in the cast include Jimmy Durante, Ann Pennington, Hope Williams, and Marie Cahill and Richard Carle making their farewell to Broadway. The show runs 21 weeks.

Dec 15 *Petticoat Influence.* See L premiere, 1930.

1930   BRITISH PREMIERES

Jan 22 *Darling! I Love You* (L—Gaiety—Musical). Desmond Carter, H.B. Hedley, Harry Acres, Billy Mayerl and Frank Eyton provide the songs and Stanley Brightman and Arthur Rigby the book for this musical about a man with a wife who has the odd fixation of hugging attractive men. They can only be released by saying the show's title phrase. Ella Logan, George

Clarke, and Wyn Richmond are in the cast. There are 147 performances.

Jan 29 *Nine Till Six* (L—Apollo—Drama). Kay Hammond is Beatrice in Aimee and Philip Stuart's play, which runs nearly 15 weeks.

Feb 1 *Michael and Mary.* See NY premiere, 1929.

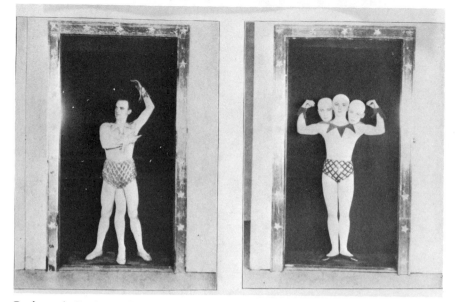

Cochoran's Review (The Three-Headed Man)

Feb 4 *Almost a Honeymoon* (L—Garrick—Comedy). Walter Ellis's farce about a young woman in a bedroom with a strange man who got there by mistake runs 49 weeks.

Feb 7 *Honours Easy* (L—St. Martin's—Comedy). Roland Pertwee's play runs four months, with a cast including Ann Todd, Diana Wynyard, Allan Aynesworth, and Norman McKinnel.

Feb 14 *Silver Wings* (L—Dominion—Musical). Ralph Richardson is Gilbert in this Dion Titheradge and Douglas Furber adaptation of the play, *The Broken Wing*. Songs are by Jack Waller and Joseph Tunbridge. The show runs for over 21 weeks.

Feb 18 *A Night Like This* (L—Aldwych—Comedy). Ben Travers writes another of his popular "Aldwych farces." This one runs nearly 34 weeks. Tom Walls stages and is in the cast, which includes Mary Brough, Winifred Shotter, Ralph Lynn, and J. Robertson Hare.

Feb 20 *Here Comes the Bride* (L—Piccadilly—Musical). Based on the play by MacGregor and Harback, the Weston and Lee book, with a score by Arthur Schwartz, earns a run of 22 weeks. Vera Bryer, Jean Colin, Edmund Gwenn are in the cast.

Feb 23 *Once in a Lifetime*. See NY premiere, 1930.

March 27 *Charles B. Cochran's 1930 Revue* (L—Pavilion—Revue). This show, with sketches and lyrics by Beverly Nichols and music by Vivian Ellis is notable for the choreography of H. George Balanchine and Serge Lifar. The show has 243 performances.

March 28 *The Three Musketeers*. See NY premiere, 1928.

April 2 *On the Spot* (L—Wyndham's—Drama). Charles Laughton is featured in Edgar Wallace's thriller about a Chicago gangster. Gillian Lind and W. Cronin-Wilson are also in the cast. There are 342 performances. On Oct 29, the play begins a 21 week run in New York at the Forrest Theatre, with Anna May Wong, Glenda Farrell, and Crane Wilbur, among others.

June 3 *Petticoat Influence* (L—St. Martin's—Comedy). Frank Allenby and Diana Wynyard are featured in Niel Grant's play about a woman who tries to help her husband get a high government post. There are 283 showings. On Dec 15, the play comes to New York's Empire with Helen Hayes featured. It runs three months.

June 11 *The Way To Treat a Woman* (L—Duke of York's—Drama). Walter Hackett's mystery of an international group of detectives trying to solve a murder has C. Aubrey Smith, Boris Ranevsky, Dorothy Lane, Cathleen Nesbitt, and Marion Lorne in the cast. It runs 53 weeks.

June 25 *The Love Race* (L—Gaiety—Musical). Stanley Lupino stages this show he's written, with many songs by Jack Clarke (music) and Desmond Carter (lyrics). It runs nearly 30 weeks, with a large cast that includes Laddie Cliff, Gilly Flower, Arty Ash, Wyn Weaver, Cyril Ritchard, and Lupino himself.

June 26 *Sons O'Guns*. See NY premiere, 1929.

June 26 *Cynara* (L—Playhouse—Drama). Gladys Cooper and Jim Warlock are featured in H. M. Harwood and R. Gore Brown's story of a man whose infidelity leads his wife to suicide. It runs 41 weeks. On Nov 2, 1931, the drama comes to New York at the Morosco with Philip Merivale and Adrianne Allen in the cast. The production runs over 26 weeks.

June 30 *The Swan* (L—St. James's—Comedy). Frenenc Molnar's Hungarian romance wins him 140 performances. The title refers to the beautiful but over-stately young Princess Alexandra (Edna Best) who fails to arouse the wooing instincts of the diffident Prince Albert (Herbert Marshall). Both their mothers are determined that the match shall work. Arousing Albert's jealousy by allowing a court tutor, Dr. Agi (Colin Clive), to reveal his ardor for the princess only complicates matters when she responds. Gilbert Miller is producer-director. Also in the cast are Charles France, Basil Loder, Henrietta Watson, and Irene Vanbrugh, among others.

Sep 4 *Charlot's Masquerade* (L—Cambridge—Revue). The new Cambridge Theatre opens with Beatrice Lillie in this revue. Ronald Jeans and Rowland Leigh take major credit for book and lyrics, respectively, with tunes by Ivor Novello, Kenneth Tod, William Walter and Jack Strachey. In one sketch Lillie lampoons Tallulah Bankhead.

Sep 9 *Street Scene*. See NY premiere, 1929.

Sep 23 *The Barretts of Wimpole Street* (L—Queen's—Comedy). Rudolph Besier's romantic account of the courtship of Elizabeth Barrett by poet Robert Browning comes to the West End after premiering at the Malvern Festival on Aug 20. Gwen Ffrangcon-Davies and Scott Sunderland are the two lovers. There are 529 performances. "The play is splendid story-telling . . . it has humour and deep poignancy and is delightful to the eye; above all, it does no dishonour to a great love story." . . . , reports *The Times*. On Feb 9, 1931, the play opens at New York's Empire, with Katharine Cornell and Brian Aherne in the leads. The production runs almost 47 weeks and then tours.

Sep 24 *Private Lives* (L—Phoenix—Comedy). The new Phoenix Theatre opens with Noel Coward's sophisticated comedy of marital rupture and repair, with Coward, Gertrude Lawrence, Laurence Olivier, and Jill Esmond in major roles. There are only 101 performances, but 716 in a 1944 revival. This becomes a favorite of both professional and amateur theatre groups. "Mr. Coward has an unsurpassed gift for combining entertainment with nothingness. . . ." reports *The Times*. The play comes to New York at the Times Square on Jan 27, 1931, with the same cast. Otto Kruger and Madge Kennedy replace Coward and Lawrence on May 11. There is a total run of 32 weeks.

Sep 29 *Leave It To Psmith* (L—Shaftesbury—Comedy). P.G. Wodehouse and Ian Hay write this farce which has Basil Foster in the title role. It runs nearly 19 weeks.

Sep 30 *The Breadwinner* (L—Vaudeville—Comedy). W. Somerset Maugham's comedy features Jack Hawkins and Peggy Ashcroft. It runs nearly five months.

Oct 8 *Topaze*. See NY premiere, 1930.

Nov 24 *Marry the Girl* (L—Aldwych—Comedy). Arthur Miller and George Arthurs write another farce; this one wins a run of six months. In the cast are Winifred Shotter, Ralph Lynn, Doreen Bendix, and Mary Brough.

Nov 27 *Oh, Daddy!* (L—Prince's—Comedy). This farce, by Austin Melford, is really based on a German original by Franz Arnold and Ernst Bach. Transferred to the West End from its first production in Streatham Hill, it has 195 performances.

Dec 3 *Ever Green* (L—Adelphi—Musical). Rodgers and Hart provide the music and lyrics and Benn W. Levy the book for this story of a women who pretends to be 60 years old, the product of rejuvenation, in order to break into show-business. Jessie Matthews plays the lead.

The scenes, by Ernest Stern, astonish the audience. In "Dancing on the Ceiling" Matthews and Sonnie Hale seem to be doing just that. There are 254 performances.

Dec 17 *The Chelsea Follies* (L—Victoria Palace—Revue). Archibald de Bear and Reginald Arkell devise the sketches and lyrics for this "neighborhood revue." Jimmy Nervo, Teddy Knox, and Eddie Grey are in the company. This intimate show runs nearly 27 weeks.

1930 REVIVALS/REPERTORIES

Jan 6 At London's Savoy Theatre, the D'Oyly Carte company offers a revival of Gilbert & Sullivan's *Trial by Jury* and *The Pirates of Penzance*. On Feb 13, the troupe presents *The Sorcerer*.

Jan 6 George Bernard Shaw's *Man and Superman* is revived at London's Royal Court Theatre. On Jan 13, the revival is *The Doctor's Dilemma*. *Misalliance* is played on March 17.

Jan 9 Leo Bulgakov presents a new version of Gorki's *The Lower Depths*, titled *At the Bottom*. It has 72 performances in New York. On Feb 25, a revival of Chekhov's *The Sea Gull* runs only five performances.

Jan 27 At the Civic Repertory Theatre, Serafin and Joaquin Quintero's *The*

Woman Have Their Way, translated by the Granville Barkers, has 25 performances. Eva LeGallienne stars. On April 21, *Romeo and Juliet* joins the repertory for 16 performances.

Feb 12 Tonight, the first signs of a rash of *Hamlet* revivals are seen in London with this production at the Royal Court, with Esme Percy as the prince. On April 22, Henry Ainley appears as Hamlet at the Haymarket Theatre. On April 28, at the Old Vic, John Gielgud offers his Hamlet interpretation. On June 2, August Schlegel's German version of *Hamlet* is on view at the Globe, with Alexander Moissi as the Dane. On June 24, at the Embassy Theatre Gerald Lawrence appears as Hamlet.

Charlot's Masquerade

Feb 17 The Dublin Gate Theatre, presents Goethe's *Faust* to baptise the new theatre. This is a continuation of the third Gate season, begun in September. Other plays include the Balderston/Squire *Berkeley Square*, Sierra's *The Wife to a Famous Man*, Rann-Kennedy's *The Terrible Meek*, Kaiser's *Gas*, Sears' *Juggernaut* (revival), macLiammoir's *Easter 1916*, Strindberg's *Simoom*, Pratt's *Ten Nights in a Bar-Room*, and Jensen's *The Witch*, followed by the last play of the season, Ould's *The Light Comedian*, opening on June 12.

Feb 24 At London's Old Vic Theatre, George Bernard Shaw's *Androcles and the Lion* is revived, with Brember Wills and Richard Riddle in the respective roles.

March 5 At the Garrick Theatre, in London's West End, Nigel Playfair revives Dumas' 19th century romance, *The Lady of the Camellias*. Tallulah Bankhead is Marguerite Gauthier, with Glen Byam Shaw, her Armand.

March 20 Ibsen's *A Doll's House* is revived in London at the Arts Theatre. Gwen Ffrangcon-Davies plays Nora. On April 19, the Everyman Theatre produces *Ghosts*, with Sybil Thorndike as Mrs. Alving. Later in the year, on Oct 9, the Everyman offers Ibsen's *The Wild Duck*, with Sybil Arundale as Gina. On Oct 15, the Arts presents Ibsen's *Little Eyolf*, with Jean Forbes-Robertson as Rita Allmers.

March 24 The Chicago Civic Shakespeare Society, lead by Fritz Leiber, present a repertory of *Hamlet*, *Macbeth*, and *Twelfth Night*, at New York's Shubert Theatre, for 11 performances.

April 21 In Stratford-upon-Avon, *The Merry Wives of Windsor* opens the season in the cinema in Greenhill Street. *Othello* is the "birthday play" in this five-week season, produced by W. Bridges Adams. Other plays include *A Midsummer Night's Dream*, *Much Ado About Nothing*, *Romeo and Juliet*, *Twelfth Night*, *Richard II*, *Hamlet*, *Macbeth*, and *The Tempest*.

May 19 Paul Robeson appears as Othello in London at the Savoy Theatre.

June 5 The Philadelphia Theatre Association brings Aristophanes' *Lysistrata* to Broadway with Violet Kemble Cooper in the title role. Doris Humphrey and Charles Weidman choreograph. Jose Limon is in the cast.

July 7 The Shakespeare Memorial Theatre of Stratford-upon-Avon opens its nine-week summer season with *Othello*. Other spring season reprises include *A Midsummer Night's Dream*, *The Merry Wives of Windsor*, *Much Ado About Nothing*, *Romeo and Juliet*, *Twelfth Night*, *Richard II*, *Hamlet*, *Macbeth*, and *The Tempest*. *As You Like It*, not seen in the spring, is also on the bill.

Aug 4 Micheal macLiammoir revives his play, *Diarmuid and Grainne*, to open the fourth season of the Dublin Gate Theatre. A revival of *Ten Nights in a Bar-Room* follows. Director Hilton Edwards next stages Farquhar's *The Beaux' Strategem*. Other plays are Bramson's *Tiger Cats*, Clarke's *The Hunger Demon*, Bernard Shaw's *Back to Methuselah*, Murray's *A Flutter of Wings*, Shakespeare's *The Merchant of Venice*, St. John Ervine's *The Lady of Belmont*, and *Christmas Pie*.

Sep 2 John Martin Harvey returns to London at the Savoy Theatre with a revival of George Bernard Shaw's *The Devil's Disciple*. On Oct 17, Martin Harvey revives Charles Reade's old play, *The Lyons Mail*. On Nov 7, the revival is *The Only Way*, based on Dickens' *A Tale of Two Cities*.

Oct 6 Eva LeGallienne opens the current season of her Civic Repertory Company on 14th Street in New York with a revival of *Romeo and Juliet*, followed by other productions already in repertory. This is to be the last season. On Oct 20, Jean Giraudoux's *Siegfried* opens for 23 performances, with Jacob Ben-Ami.

Dec 1 New York's Civic Repertory Theatre presents Susan Glaspell's *Alison's House*, based on incidents in the life of Emily Dickinson. In repertory there are 41 performances. The play later wins a Pulitzer Prize.

Dec 17 The holiday season has arrived with this day's production of A. A. Milne's *Toad of Toad Hall*, based on Kenneth Grahame's *The Wind in the Willows*, shown at London's Lyric Theatre. Other holiday offerings include *The Maid of the Mountains* (London Hippodrome), *The Toymaker of Nuremburg* (Kingsway), *Cinderella* (Grafton), *Where the Rainbow Ends* (Holborn Empire), *Peter Pan* (Palladium), *The Private Secretary* (Apollo), *Charley's Aunt* (New), *Alice in Wonderland* (Savoy), *Land of the Christmas Stocking* (Everyman), *A Pair of Trousers* (Criterion), *Jack and the Beanstalk* (Children's) *Carpet Slippers* (Embassy), *Aladdin* (Dominion), *Robinson Crusoe* (Lyceum), *Treasure Island* (Prince of Wales's), *The Windmill Man* (Scala), *No. 17* (Royalty), and *A Christmas Carol* (Fortune).

1930 BIRTHS/DEATHS/DEBUTS

Jan 12 Producer-scenic designer Edgar Lansbury is born in London to actress Moyna Macgill.

Feb 17 China's great actor, Mei Lan-Fang appears in New York at the 49th Street Theatre for a five-week engagement. He plays female roles in scenes from major plays of the classical Chinese repertory.

March 2 Actor-singer John Cullum is born in Knoxville, Tennessee.

March 10 English actress Marie Studholm (b. 1875) dies in London. Studholm was a popular star of the London musical stage. She was well known in America through her appearances in *An Artist's Model*, *San Toy*, and *Lady Madcap*.

March 11 Vaudeville producer and theatre executive Edward Franklin Albee dies in Palm Beach, Florida, at age 72. Albee joined B. F. Keith in 1885 in the presentation of variety shows, and by 1920 had a vaudeville circuit of some 70 houses and an interest in about 300 others.

April 24 American actress and singer Adele Ritchie (b. 1874) is dead in Laguna Beach, California. Ritchie made her first appearance on the New York stage in 1893 in *The Isle of Champagne*. In 1902 she played Mrs. Pineapple in *A Chinese Honeymoon*, after which she appeared in vaudeville before returning to a series of stage roles.

May 2 Playwright Bernard Slade is born in St. Catharines, Ontario, Canada.

June 4 Actor-singer Ray Heatherton makes his Broadway debut in the revue, *The Garrick Gaieties*, at the Guild Theatre.

June 11 Shakespearean authority, lawyer, and oil magnate Henry Clay Folger dies at age 73. His death occurs just two weeks after the laying of the cornerstone for the Shakespeare Library in Washington, D.C., which is to house his great collection of Shakespeareana. He leaves the institution an endowment of seven million dollars.

June 13 English actor-manager Arthur Lewis (b. 1846) is dead. Lewis was a member of Mary Anderson's company at the Lyceum Theatre from 1883 to 1889, and later toured with her in America. Lewis represented actresses Rejane and Bernhardt and actors Coquelin and Antoine in their London engagements.

June 28 American actor and singer Joe Schenck is dead in Detroit, Michigan at age 39. Schenck was the partner of Gus Van in the popular team of Van and Schenck. Later they were a featured pair in the *Ziegfeld Follies* and part owners in cabaret ventures.

July 15 Actor Rudolph Schildkraut is dead in Los Angeles at age 65. Born in Constantinople, Schildkraut achieved prominence in the New York theatre after having gained a reputation in the Jewish theatre both in Europe and America. He was engaged in directing motion pictures in Hollywood at the time of his death.

July 26 American actress Emma Marble is dead in New York at age 88. Marble was the granddaughter of William Warren, Sr., who came to America in 1796 with the second company of English actors. She was the niece of William Warren, comedian of the Boston Museum Company. Marble acted with Edwin Booth and Lawrence Barrett.

Sep 15 American stage and screen actor Milton Sills (b. 1882) dies in Los Angeles. Sills was a member of Donald Robertson's New Theatre Company in Chicago. He was one of the organizers of the Academy of Motion Picture Arts and Sciences.

Oct 1 American dancer and comedian Jack Donahue is dead at age 38 in New York. Donahue was well known in vaudeville before appearing in *The Ziegfeld Follies of 1920*. He is part author, with Phil Dunning, of the play, *The Understudy*.

Oct 6 American actress Dolly Nobles is dead in Brooklyn, New York, at age 67. Nobles was the wife of the late actor Milton Nobles. Their joint successes on stage included *The Phoenix* and *Love and Law*.

Nov 8 American actress Clare Eames (b. 1896) is dead in London. Eames attracted considerable attention in New York when she appeared as Mary Stuart in John Drinkwater's play of that name. Among her notable roles were Lady Macbeth, Hedda Tesman, and Empress Carlotta.

Nov 25 American minstrel Willis Sweatnam is dead in New York at age 76. Sweatnam was a featured singer and dancer with all the famous minstrels starting with Frank Clark's Lilliputians and ending with Jack Haverly and in troupes of his own.

Nov 26 Actor Rex Harrison makes his London debut as the Hon. Fred Thrippleton in Florence Kilpatrick's *Getting George Married* at the Everyman Theatre.

Dec 5 Producer Frederick Brisson accepts his first theatrical assignment in a managerial capacity for the London production of the continental cabaret drama, *The Wonder Bar*, at the Savoy.

1930 THEATERS/PRODUCTIONS

Conrad and Howard Maurer received U.S. patents for a theatrical waterfall effect, in which a downward moving belt is made to look like water coursing down the rough cliff scenic element in which it is mounted. British Actors Equity Association is formed this year.

The Lord Chamberlain bans Marion Norris' play *Alone*, a dramatization of Radcliffe Hall's novel of Lesbianism, *The Well of Loneliness*.

This year, Arthur Hopkins, Brock Pemberton, and Gilbert Miller, all responsible producers, rally other Broadway producers to form the League of New York Theatres. A major function of the League is the prevention of ticket-selling abuses by brokers. Legitimate brokers are made members of the group. The new system breaks down, to be taken over by a Postal Telegraph operation in which a theatre patron can order tickets by phone or telegraph for only 50 cents more than list price, the tickets to be delivered by messenger.

Feb 15 After two years of temporary residence at Dublin's Peacock Theatre, the Dublin Gate Theatre opens its permanent home at the historic Assembly Rooms built in 1785.

Feb 21 The McCarter Theatre (1,077 seats) opens in Princeton, New Jersey. McCarter premieres include *Our Town* in 1938, and *Bus Stop* in 1955.

April 3 The Prince Edward Theatre, known as the London Casino after 1936, opens with the romantic musical comedy, *Rio Rita*. Edward A. Stone is the designer with interior decorations by Marc-Henri and Laverdat. The theatre has a capacity of 1,800 and is managed by Lee Ephraim.

May 12 The New Yorker Theatre, on West 54th Street in New York, opens with Ibsen's *The Vikings*, which is the only time to date this work is presented in New York. From 1933–36, the space is used as a theatre-restaurant named Casino de Paree. For a brief time, the Federal Theatre Project uses it to showcase musicals. In 1943, the Columbia Broadcasting Company leases it for use as a radio and television studio. It later becomes a popular discotheque, Studio 54.

May 21 Charter members of British Actors Equity Association adopt the rules and constitution of the new organization for protecting the rights and persons of actors and actresses. In December of this year, the association will be registered as a trade union. It is to be affiliated with the TUC and STUC and incorporate the Variety Artistes' Federation.

June At the close of the 1929–30 Broadway season, there were 240 productions of which 13 were dramas, 61 comedies, 38 musicals, and 10 revues. Of the 240 productions 196 (82%) of them were failures, with only 44 (18%) successes. Burns Mantle selects the ten *Best Plays* of this economically wounded Broadway season of 1929–30. They are Connelly's *The Green Pastures*—also the Pulitzer Prize play, Flavin's *The Criminal Code*, Balderston's *Berkeley Square*, Sturges' *Strictly Dishonorable*, Wexley's *The Last Mile*, Ervine's *The First Mrs. Fraser*, Lardner and Kaufman's *June Moon*, Milne's *Michael and Mary*, Ferris' *Death Takes a Holiday*, and Stewart's *Rebound*. Mantle notes that the financial crisis has forced the closing of some theatres; rentals and wages have been reduced because box-office profits have been curtailed. In the past season, there have been some 240 new stage works, of which 154 are nonmusical. With the close of the decade of the 1920's, it is worth noting that Man-

Green Pastures

tle's annual survey of the Broadway season is supplemented only by summaries of theatre production in Chicago, San Francisco, and Southern California. No other American city is considered important enough to include in the record.

July 1 Earl Carroll includes one number of his new *Vanities* which presents Faith Bacon, a Carroll dancer, clothed in nothing but a small fan. The Manhattan police close the show for this and other indecenies. When Carroll gives Bacon a larger fan and makes some other changes, the revue resumes its run, none the worse for the publicity.

Sep 4 The Cambridge Theatre, at Cambridge Circus in London, opens with *Charlotte's Masquerade*. The capacity of the theatre is 1,275, and the manager is B.H. Meyer. The theatre has been designed by Wimperis, Simpson, and Guthrie with interior decoration by Serge Chermayeff. The interior will be re-decorated in 1950 and the theatre will be used as a cinema between Sep 1967 and Feb 1968, later returning to legitimate use.

Sep 23 Rudolf Besier's play about the courtship of Elizabeth Barrett by Robert Browning, *The Barretts of Wimpole Street*, provokes a protest by the descendants of Edward Moulton Barrett, shown in the drama as something of a tyrant over his daughter. As censor and licensor of plays for public performance, the Lord Chamberlain is sensitive to such complaints and later responds that no play dealing with recent events will be licensed before it has been "submitted for approval to the existing relatives of the personages depicted in the play."

Sep 24 The Phoenix Theatre, off Charing Cross Road in London, opens with *Private Lives*. Charles B. Cochran is the manager of this 1,028 seat theatre designed by Sir Giles Gilbert Scott, Bertie Crewe, and Cecil Masey, with Theodor Komisarjevsky as art director.

Sep 29 London's Whitehall Theatre opens with *The Way To Treat A Woman*, transferred from the Duke of York's. Edward A. Stone has designed the 628 seat theatre, with interiors by Marc-Henri and Laverdat, and Walter Hackett is the manager.

Oct 10 Cardinal Hayes denounces the New York stage as indecent, in his capacity as Archbishop of New York City. The *NY Herald-Tribune* chronicles his objections.

Oct 15 Director and lighting expert Hassard Short innovates in staging *Three's A Crowd* at New York's Selwyn. General Electric will give him an award for such changes as omitting footlights and hanging lighting instruments on a balcony rail.

Nov 13 The first preset control dimmerboard is developed for the Broadway production of *Grand Hotel*, produced by Herman Shumlin and designed by Aline Bernstein at the National Theatre. This lighting-board has a master control for a number of dimmers, which enables the action and the illumination of the play to flow from area to area.

Dec 8 The Broadway Theatre, on Broadway and 53rd Streets in New York, originally designed by Eugene DeRosa in 1924 as a vaudeville-motion-picture house, opens its doors to theatre by presenting *The New Yorkers*, written by Herbert Fields, with music and lyrics by Cole Porter. Until 1954, the theatre lives a schizophrenic life, alternating between theatre and films. Since then, the theatre houses some outstanding musicals, including *Gypsy*, *Purlie*, and *Evita*.

Dec 19 The Leicester Square Theatre in London opens with the film *Viennese Nights* and a staged dance production. The 2,000-seat theatre has been designed by Andrew Mather, and after repeated efforts with film and variety will become a cinema. April 1968 reconstruction will reduce the capacity to 1,763.

Jan 13 *Tomorrow and Tomorrow* (NY—Henry Miller—Drama). Zita Johann stars in Philip Barry's play about a woman whose child is not her husband's although he believes it is. The show runs nearly 26 weeks.

Jan 19 *You Said It* (NY—46th Street—Musical). Harold Arlen contributes his first full Broadway score to this college comedy by Jack Yellen and Sid Silvers. The show runs six months.

Jan 26 New York's Theatre Guild produces Lynn Riggs' *Green Grow the Lilacs* for a modest run of eight weeks. Franchot Tone and June Walker play leads. The play becomes the basis for *Oklahoma!*

Jan 27 *Private Lives.* See L premiere, 1930.

Feb 9 *The Barretts of Wimpole Street.* See L premiere, 1930.

Feb 15 *There's Always Juliet* (NY—Empire—Comedy). John Van Druten's tale of love at first sight between an American architect (Herbert Marshall) and a British woman (Edna Best) could run longer than 108 times, but Hollywood producers buy out the run to bring Marshall to the sound studios.

March 15 *As Husbands Go* (NY—John Golden—Comedy). Jay Fassett and Lily Cahill are the leads in Rachel Crother's play about a husband who is more concerned about his wife's welfare than is her lover. It runs 148 performances.

April 23 *Brass Ankle* (NY—Masque—Drama). Alice Brady and Ben Smith appear in DuBose Heyward's drama about a women married to a white supremacist, who discovers she is racially mixed. The show manages only 44 performances.

June 1 *The Third Little Show* (NY—Music Box—Revue). Beatrice Lillie spoofs Ruth Draper, the monologist. She also sings "There Are Fairies At the Bottom Of My Garden" and Noel Coward's "Mad Dogs and Englishman." The show runs 17 weeks.

June 1 *Unexpected Husband* (NY—48th Street—Comedy). Barry Connors's play about an unmarried couple who find themselves in the same bed runs for four months.

June 3 *The Band Wagon* (NY—New Amsterdam—Revue). Arthur Schwartz provides the score and Howard Deitz the lyrics for such songs as "High and Low" and "I Love Louisa." Fred and Adele Astaire are in the cast. Tilly Losch dances on sloped, mirrored floors as "Dancing in the Dark" is sung. The show runs for 260 performances. The *NY Times* reports, ". . . Tilly Losch raises musical show dancing to the level of a fine art. . . . the satire is adroit, informed and intelligent. You need not check your brains with your hat."

There's Always Juliet

July 1 *The Ziegfeld Follies of 1931* (NY—Ziegfeld—Revue). Having halted the Follies several seasons before, Florenz Ziegfeld returns for his last edition, complete with Joseph Urban's customary lavish settings. There is the salute to the opening of the Empire State Building. Ruth Etting, Helen Morgan and Harry Richman are among the principals. There are 165 performances.

Aug 27 *Earl Carroll's Vanities* (NY—Earl Carroll—Revue). Carroll opens his new theatre with a lavish revue staring William Demarest, Lillian Roth and Will Mahoney. It runs nearly 35 weeks.

Sep 14 *George White's Scandals* (NY—Apollo—Revue). Music and lyrics are by Ray Henderson and Lew Brown. Rudy Vallee sings; so does Ethel Merman: "Life Is Just a Bowl of Cherries." Ray Bolger dances. The production has 202 performances.

Sep 16 *Singin' the Blues* (NY—Liberty—Drama). Frank Wilson stars in John McGowan's "Negro melodrama" about a black who accidently shot a policeman. Mantan Moreland and Jack Carter are also in the cast.

Oct 5 *The Left Bank* (NY—Little—Drama). Elmer Rice's drama of American expatriates in Paris includes Cledge Roberts, Katherine Alexander, and Merle Maddern in the cast. It runs just over 30 weeks. On Sep 26, 1932, the show opens at London's Ambassadors' with a cast including Natalie Moya, Sunday Wilshin, and Margaret Moffat. It does not have a long run.

Oct 13 *Everybody's Welcome* (NY—Shubert—Musical). Based on *Up Pops the Devil*, this show has music by Sammy Fain with book by Harold Atteridge. Oscar Shaw and Harriett Lake (Ann Sothern) sing the leads. A hit song, interpolated into the Fain score, is "As Time Goes By." The show has 139 performances.

Oct 15 *The Cat and the Fiddle* (NY—Globe—Musical). Jerome Kern provides the score for Otto Harbach's book about a young composer whose operatic score needs livelier rhythms—supplied by the American girl who loves him. The score includes "The Night Was Made For Love" and "The Love Parade." George Metaxa and Bettina Hall are featured. The show has 395 performances. On March 4, 1932, the show comes to London's Palace with a cast including Peggy Wood, Francis Lederer, Alice Delysia, and Austin Trevor. It runs over 27 weeks.

Oct 26 *Mourning Becomes Electra* (NY—Guild—Drama). The Theatre Guild produces Eugene O'Neill's New England trilogy based on Aeschylus's *Oresteia*. The three plays are shown in six hours, with a dinner-break, six days a week. Alla Nazimova, Lee Barker, Thomas Chalmers, Alice Brady, and Earle Larimore are featured. Philip Moeller stages. It wins 150 performances.

Nov 2 *Cynara.* See L premiere, 1930.

Nov 2 *The Laugh Parade* (NY—Imperial—Revue). Ed Wynn stars in this revue with music by Harry Warren. "You're My Everything" becomes a hit. It runs for 321 performances.

Nov 6 *Counsellor-At-Law* (NY—Plymouth—Drama). Elmer Rice produces and directs his play about the professional and private tensions of a successful lawyer (Paul Muni). The show runs 292 performances. On April 10, 1934, it opens at London's Piccadilly where it runs for four months.

Nov 9 *Brief Moment* (NY—Belasco—Comedy). Drama critic Alexander Woollcott takes to the stage in S. N. Behrman's sophisticated story about a rich boy who marries a musical comedy actress (Francine Larrimore). Woollcott's role is written for him. The show runs for four months.

Nov 9 *The Social Register* (NY—Fulton—Comedy). Anita Loos and John Emerson create this comedy about a showgirl who takes the starch out of her rich boyfriend's society mother. Lenore Ulric and Sidney Blackmer are featured. It runs three months.

Nov 16 *Reunion in Vienna* (NY—Martin Beck—Comedy). The Theatre Guild produces Robert E. Sherwood's comedy about a psychiatrist's wife urged to cure an infatuation by seeing her aristocratic old flame. Lynn Fontanne and Alfred Lunt star. The play lasts 33 weeks. It opens in London at the Lyric on Jan 3, 1934, with the same leads. On this side of the Atlantic it earns a run of six months.

Nov 24 *The Good Fairy* (NY—Henry Miller—Comedy). Helen Hayes stars in Ferenc Molnar's play about a cinema usherette who wants to help others. It runs 151 performances.

Dec 9 *Springtime for Henry* (NY—Bijou—Comedy). Benn W. Levy's farce about a man and his intriguing new secretary features Leslie Banks, Helen Chandler, and Nigel Bruce. The play enjoys 199 performances. On Nov 8, 1932, it opens at London's Apollo with Ronald Squire, Joan Barry, and Bruce. It earns 104 showings.

Dec 26 *Of Thee I Sing* (NY—Music Box—Musical). George S. Kaufman and Morrie Ryskind create an affectionate, Pulitzer Prize-winning satire on American politics with William Gaxton as Wintergreen, the presidential candidate running on a platform of love. Grace Brinkley, Lois Moran, and Victor Moore are in the cast. The music and lyrics are by George and Ira Gershwin. "Love Is Sweeping the Country" becomes a hit. The show has 441 performances.

1931   BRITISH PREMIERES

Jan 8 *Folly To Be Wise* (L—Piccadilly—Revue). Jack Hulburt devises and directs this revue with a score by Vivian Ellis and book and lyrics by Dion Titheradge. The cast includes Cicely Courtneidge and Nelson Keys. It runs eight months.

Jan 9 *The Song of the Drum* (L—Drury Lane—Musical). Vivian Ellis and Herman Finck provide the score and Desmond Carter the lyrics for this musical. Fred Thompson and Guy Bolton devise a story of intrigue in a mythical Eastern kingdom. Derek Oldham, Marie Burke, and Helen Gilliland are in the cast. It runs 131 performances.

Jan 17 *Colonel Satan* (L—Haymarket—Comedy). This is Booth Tarkington's American play about a French adventure of Colonel Aaron Burr (Frank Vosper). In the cast are such players as Nigel Bruce, Jeanne de Casalis, Lilian Cavanagh, Jack Livesey, and Esme Percy. The production doesn't win a long run.

Jan 22 *The Improper Duchess* (L—Globe—Comedy). Yvonne Arnaud and Frank Cellier appear in this story of a king and duchess caught in a compromising situation. There are 349 performances.

Feb 2 *After All* (L—Criterion—Drama). John Van Druten's play has been previewed by the Stage Society in March 1930. Now it earns a run of 33 weeks, staged by Auriol Lee and with a cast including Lilian Braithwaite, Aubrey Mather, and Madeleine Carroll.

Feb 3 *Strange Interlude.* See NY premiere, 1928.

Feb 16 *Good Losers* (L—Whitehall—Comedy). Michael Arlen and Walter Hackett write this popular play which includes Cathleen Nesbitt and Marion Lorne in the cast. There are 134 performances.

Feb 24 *Desire Under the Elms.* See NY premiere, 1924.

March 5 *Stand Up and Sing* (L—Hippodrome—Musical). Jack Buchanan stars in his new musical—written with Douglas Furber, who provides the lyrics for the Philip Charig and Vivian Ellis score. He portrays a man who solves a robbery and thus wins the girl. There are 325 performances.

March 19 *Cochran's 1931 Revue* (L—Pavilion—Revue). Noel Coward conceives both book and music for this show, produced by Charles Cochran. Frank Collins directs the company, which includes Bob Clark, Melville Cooper and Ada May.

April 6, *Autumn Crocus* (L—Lyric—Drama). Francis Lederer plays Andreas Steiner in C. L. Anthony's romance. Basil Dean's direction involves a cast including Frederick Ranalow, Martita Hunt, Jack Hawkins, George Zucco, Fay Compton, and Jessica Tandy. The show runs over 46 weeks.

April 8 Hans Muller's adaptation of *Zum weissen Rossl* by Blumental and Kadelburg is revived at London's Coliseum. Ralph Benatsky and Clifford Stolz provide the score for this story of an emperor's visit to an inn. Lea Aeidl, Clifford Mollison, and Frederick Leister are in the cast. There are 651 performances.

May 7 *Lean Harvest* (L—St. Martin's—Drama). Ronald Jeans' play runs four months. Raymond Massey directs.

May 14 *The Good Companions* (L—His Majesty's—Musical). Edward Knoblock and J.B. Priestley adapt Priestley's novel for the stage. Richard Addinsell composes the score; Harry Graham and Frank Eyton the lyrics. The large cast includes John Gielgud.

May 15 *The Old Man* (L—Wyndham's—Drama). Edgar Wallace directs his own play about illicit love-affairs, blackmail, and attempted murder.

May 26 *Turkey Time* (L—Aldwych—Comedy). This is another Ben Travers "Aldwych farce," with an eventual record of 263 performances. Tom Walls directs and is featured. Also on hand are Winifred Shotter and other Aldwych farce regulars.

June 2 *The Sign of the Seven Dials* (L—Cambridge—Revue). This Archibald de Bear revue takes its name from the district in which the theatre has been built. In the ensemble are Billy Leonard, Tessa Deane and Seymour Hicks, among others.

June 18 *Death Takes a Holiday.* See NY premiere, 1929.

June 25 *Late Night Final* (L—Phoenix—Drama). Raymond Massey directs and is featured in Louis Weitzenkorn's melodrama. Francis Sullivan, Beatrix Lehmann, and Louise Hampton are also in the cast. It runs 132 performances.

July 7 *Nina Rosa* (L—Lyceum—Musical). Sigmund Romberg writes the score, Irving Caesar the lyrics and Otto Harbach the book for this show about a girl who inherits a goldmine. Ethelind Terry is in the title role. It runs 111 performances.

Aug 3 *The Life Machine.* See NY premiere *(Machinal)*, 1928.

Aug 10 *The Midshipmaid* (L—Shaftesbury—Comedy). Ian Hay and Stephen King-Hall write about a girl who disguises herself as a midshipman to be near her lover. Jane Baxter and Basil Foster are featured. The show runs 227 performances.

Aug 17 *Waltzes from Vienna* (L—Alhambra—Musical). Hassard Short and Desmond Carter outline the scenario from a German original by Willmer, Reichert, and Marischka. The story deals with young Johann Strauss's successful attempt to win his father's approval for his career as a composer. The score is made up of melodies by the Strausses. Robert Halliday and Charles France play the Strausses. The show has 607 showings.

Sep 3 *Grand Hotel.* See NY premiere, 1930.

Sep 17 *Viktoria and Her Hussar* (L—Palace—Musical). Paul Abraham writes the score and Harry Graham the British book for this musical based on the German of

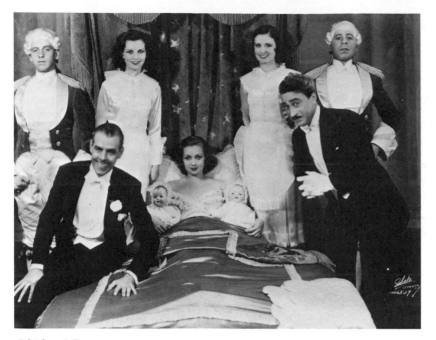

Of Thee I Sing

Grunwald and Lohner-Beda. Margaret Carlisle has the title role. There are 100 performances.

Sep 19 *The Painted Veil* (L—Playhouse—Drama). Bartlett Cormack adapts W. Somerset Maugham's novel. The cast includes Gladys Cooper, Lewis Casson, and Arthur Margetson. The show runs four months.

Sep 30 *Elizabeth of England* (L—Cambridge—Drama). There are 123 performances of this "legend" by Ferdinand Bruckner, adapted by Ashley Dukes. Phyllis Nielson-Terry plays the queen, with Leslie Perrins, her Essex.

Oct 6 *The Queen's Husband.* See NY premiere, 1928.

Oct 7 *The Anatomist* (L—Westminster—Drama). James Bridie's play about Scottish grave robbers features Flora Robson and Henry Ainley. Tyrone Guthrie stages. There are 127 performances.

Oct 8 *Vile Bodies* (L—Arts—Comedy). Nigel Playfair stages Evelyn Waugh's play.

Oct 8 *For the Love of Mike* (L—Saville—Musical). Jack Waller and Joseph Tunbridge write the music, Clifford Grey the lyrics, and H.F. Maltby the book for this "play with tunes." Featuring Peggy Cart-

wright, with Viola Tree and Alfred Drayton, the show runs 30 weeks.

Oct 13 *Cavalcade* (L—Drury Lane—Drama). Noel Coward directs his play, a saga of two families from 1899 to the present. Mary Clare, Edward Sinclair, Una O'Connor and Fred Groves are among the cast. Coward composes "Mirabelle" and "Twentieth Century Blues" for the production.

Dec 15 *Can the Leopard?* (L—Haymarket—Comedy). Gertrude Lawrence, Kay Hammond, and Ian Hunter appear in Ronald Jeans' play, which runs 165 performances.

Dec 17 *Walk This Way* (L—Winter Garden—Revue). Gracie Fields sings "The Doll and the Golliwog" in this show, conceived by Archie Pitt. Gordon Courtney devises the songs, with dances by Freddie Lord. There are 149 performances.

Dec 23 *Hold My Hand* (L—Gaiety—Musical). Stanley Lupino writes and directs this show which has songs by Noel Gay and Desmond Carter. It deals with a guardian, his young ward, and their romantic entanglements. Lupino, Jessie Matthews, Sonnie Hale, and Harry Milton are featured. There are 212 performances.

1931   REVIVALS/REPERTORIES

Jan 6 Sadler's Wells Theatre offers *Twelfth Night*, with John Gielgud, Ralph Richardson and Dorothy Green.

Jan 12 The fourth season continues at the Dublin Gate Theatre, with Burke's *Bride*, followed by a revival of Tocher's *The Old Lady Says "No!"*. The next production is *Sweeney Todd*. Other plays in the season are Merijkowsi's *Tzar Paul*, *The Dublin Revue*, Duke's *The Man with a Load of*

Mischief, and a double-bill to end the season in May: O'Neill's *Where the Cross Is Made* and Davies' *The Mollusc*.

Jan 26 Eva LeGallienne and Morgan Farley star in the Civic Repertory Theatre's production of *Camille*. It wins 57 performances at New York's 14th Street Playhouse.

Feb 16 The Old Vic Theatre in London revives Shaw's *Arms and the Man* with

Marie Ney, John Gielgud, and Ralph Richardson in the cast.

Feb 26 Raymond Massey stages this revival of W. Somerset Maugham's *The Circle* at London's Vaudeville Theatre. Celia Johnston, Allan Aynesworth, Athene Seyler, and Nigel Playfair are in the cast.

March 6 The Theatre Guild mounts Hans Chlumverg's *Miracle at Verdun* at New York's Martin Beck. It runs only 49 performances. Shaw's *Getting Married* opens on March 30, with Romney Brent and Dorothy Gish in the cast. It has 48 performances.

March 20 Nikita Balieff's *Chauve Souris* presents Pushkin's *The Queen of Spades* at London's Cambridge Theatre. Lydia Sherwood and Marie Ault are featured.

March 22 The Stage Society revives George Bernard Shaw's *Widowers' Houses*, for a speical London performance at the Prince of Wales's Theatre. In the cast are Cedric Hardwicke, Phyllis Shand, and Marjorie Mars. At the Royal Court on March 30, Shaw's *Mrs. Warren's Profession* is produced, with Miriam Lewes. On April 6, *Saint Joan* opens at His Majesty's with Sybil Thorndike. *Pygmalion* is revived on May 4 at the Kingsway Theatre. On May 18 at that theatre, the play is Shaw's *Man and Superman*.

April 2 Tonight begins a series of revivals of musicals at Daly's Theatre in London. *The Belle of New York* is given, followed on June 1, by *The Geisha*. *Florodora* is revived on July 29, and *A Country Girl* on Sep 29. *Monsieur Beaucaire* begins on Nov 16. *La Poupee* opens on Dec 24.

April 7 A group of Irish Players present George Shiels's *The New Gossoon* at London's Apollo Theatre. The name is changed to *The Girl of the Pillow* during the short run.

April 13 The annual Shakespeare festival in Stratford-upon-Avon opens with Randle Ayrton as the king in *King Lear*. Other plays in the five-week season are *Macbeth*, *The Taming of the Shrew*, *Measure for Measure*, *Antony and Cleopatra*, and *The Winter's Tale*, chosen as the "birthday play." W. Bridges Adams heads the company as director and designer.

April 14 I.J. Golden's *Precedent* is apparently based on the trial of Tom Mooney, a labor organizer framed for a bombing. It runs 184 performances at New York's Provincetown Theatre.

May 27 Constant Lambert's adaption of Oscar Wilde's *Salome* opens at London's Gate Theatre with Margaret Rawlings in the title role. On Oct 5, it is given at the Savoy Theatre with Joan Maude as Salome.

June 29 *Antony and Cleopatra* opens the ten-week summer season of Shakespeare's plays at Stratford-upon-Avon. From the spring season, other revivals include *The Winter's Tale*, *King Lear*, *Macbeth*, *The Taming of the Shrew*, and *Mea-*

sure for Measure. Added to these are *A Midsummer Night's Dream* and *The Merry Wives of Windsor*.

Aug 3 To open the fifth season of the Dublin Gate Theatre, Hilton Edwards (directing and acting) and Micheal mac-Liammoir (designing and acting) revive their production of *Tsar Paul*. Other plays include Wilde's *Lady Windermere's Fan*, Gogol's *The Government Inspector*, the Earl of Longford's *The Melians*, Capek's *R. U. R.* (revival), Dukes' *Jew Suss*, Sears' *The Dead Ride Fast*, Robinson and Paisley's *The Archdupe*, Manning's *Youth's the Season—?*, and *Mogu of the Desert*, by Padraic Column, opening on the day after Christmas.

Sep 14 At London's St. James's *A Trip to Scarborough*, by Vanbrugh and Sheridan, is revived with Ernest Thesiger, Robert Donat, Frances Carson, and Gillian Lind. On Sept 19, Nigel Playfair revives Congreve's *The Old Bachelor* at the Lyric. The cast includes Edith Evans and Diana Wynyard.

Sep 21 The Theatre Guild produces Alfred Savoir's *He*, about a man who presents himself as God to an atheist convention. Tom Powers leads. It runs only five weeks. On Oct 6, Lawrence Langer produces *The Streets of New York, or Poverty Is No Crime*, for the Guild. It has 87 performances. Ibsen's *The Pillars of Society* opens on Oct 14, for two showings. On Dec 26, Will Cotton's *The Bride the Sun Shines On* opens. It runs nearly 10 weeks.

Sep 23 Maurice Schwartz, a leader of the Yiddish theatre, brings Sholem Aleichem's *If I Were You* to New York's Ambassador Theatre where it runs nearly 10 weeks.

Sep 28 New York's Group Theatre presents Paul Green's *The House of Connelly*, about the decline of a Southern plantation family. Staged by Lee Strasberg and Cheryl Crawford, and with Clifford Odets, Franchot Tone, and Stella Adler in the cast, it runs over 11 weeks at the Martin Beck. According to J. Brooke Atkinson of the *NY Times*: " . . . their group performance is too beautifully imagined and modulated to concentrate on personal achievements. There is not a gaudy, brittle or facile stroke in their acting. For once a group performance is tremulous and pellucid, the expression of an ideal. Between Mr. Green's prose poem and the Group Theatre's performance it is not too much to hope that something fine and true has been started in the American Theatre." On Dec 10 the Group Theatre presents Paul and Clair Sifton's *1931-* , about a man and woman reduced to misery by the Depression who turn to socialism. Lee Strasberg directs the cast including Franchot Tone, Clifford Odets and Stella Adler. There are only 12 performances.

Nov 4 Edmund Willard plays *Othello* at London's Arts Theatre. On Nov 16, Theo-

dore Komisarjevsky directs Ronald Mackenzie's *Musical Chairs*. The cast includes John Gielgud, Margaret Webster, and Jessica Tandy.

Nov 5 Raymond Massey stars in *Hamlet* in this New York revival.

Nov 10 Ethel Barrymore comes to Broadway with Sheridan's *The School for Scandal* at the theatre named for her. It runs three weeks.

Nov 15 Cornelia Otis Skinner presents her six character sketches, *The Wives of Henry VIII*, at New York's Avon Theatre for 69 performances. Eight of her earlier monologues are also on the program, including *In a Gondola*, *A Lady Explorer*, and *A Southern Girl in the Sistine Chapel*.

Nov 16 Fritz Leiber brings the Chicago

Civic Shakespeare Society to Broadway's Royale Theatre with himself spotlighted as Shylock, in *The Merchant of Venice*. *Hamlet* and *Julius Caesar* are added treats in this brief engagement.

Dec 21 Four holiday entertainments open today: *Peter Pan* (Palladium), *Where the Rainbow Ends* (Holborn Empire), *When Kinghts Were Bold* (Duke of York's), and *A Pair of Spectacles* (Westminister). They are rapidly followed by *Aladdin* (Lyric, Hammersmith), *Toad of Toad Hall* (Savoy), *Buckie's Bears* (Royalty), *Alf's Button* (Scala), *The Windmill Man* (Victoria Palace), *Dick Whittington* (Garrick), *Treasure Island* (New), *Peg O' My Heart* (Prince's), *Cinderella* (Lyceum), and *Robin Hood* (Q Theatre).

1931 BIRTHS/DEATHS/DEBUTS

Feb 9 Stage and screen actor Brian Aherne makes his New York debut as Robert Browning in Rudolf Besier's *The Barretts of Wimpole Street* at the Empire Theatre.

March 11 American theatre owner Fred G. Nixon-Nirdlinger is shot and killed in Nice, France, by his third wife, Charlotte Nash. Age 54, he was owner of the Nixon-Nirdlinger theatres in Philadelphia.

March 15 American actor James Neill is dead in Glendale, California, at age 70. Neill's first stage success was in *The Senator* with William H. Crane in New York in 1883. He later established stock companies in Denver, Cincinnati, St. Paul, Minneapolis, and Winnipeg. He was also a member of the original Lasky-Famous Players Stock Company. Neill was married to actress Edyth Chapman.

March 20 Stage and screen actor Hal Linden is born Harold Lipshitz in New York City.

March 25 American drama critic and playwright John J. McNally is dead in Brooklyn, New York at age 76. McNally was drama editor of the Charleston *Chronicle*, Boston *Times*, and Boston *Herald*. He wrote a series of comedies for German comedians, the Rogers Brothers—*Rogers Bros. in a Reign of Terror*, *In Wall Street*, and *In Harvard*, among others.

May 14 American actor-manager and playwright David Belasco (b. 1859) dies in New York. Belasco was a child actor in his home state of California. In his twenties he began his playwriting career. Success came with collaborations of *The Girl I Left Behind Me* (1893), *Madame Butterfly* (1900) and *The Girl of the Golden West* (1905). In 1906 he built the Stuyvesant Theatre in New York. It was renamed the Belasco in 1910.

May 18 Actor Robert Morse is born in Newton, Massachusetts.

July 30 American theatre manager Hor-

ace McVicker is dead in Sea Bright, New Jersey, at age 75. McVicker was the son of J. H. McVicker, manager of Chicago's McVicker Theatre. Edwin Booth and Ethel Barrymore were two of the stars Horace McVicker managed. He was also manager of the Abbey and Knickerbocker Theatres in New York.

Aug 27 American composer Burton Lane writes the music for the 9th edition of *Earl Carroll's Vanities*. Born Burton Levy, Lane launched his musical career by composing high school marches. He later became a staff composer for a music publishing house.

Cavalcade

Sep 9 American actor and dramatist Eugene Wyley Presbrey (b. 1853) dies in Hollywood. Presbrey first appeared on stage in 1874 in the Boston Theatre. His plays include *The Courtship of Miles Standish*, *A Ward of France*, *A Virginia Courtship*, *Raffles*, and *Mary, Mary, Quite Contrary*.

Sep 23 American playwright and author Meyer Levin plays the role of Katz in Sholem Aleichem's *If I Were You* at the Ambassador Theatre on Broadway. Levin was creator and director of the Relic House Marionette Theatre in Chicago in 1927.

Sep 24 Anthony Newley is born in London, England.

Sep 30 Charles Laughton and Elsa Lanchester are introduced to Broadway at the Lyceum in *Payment Deferred*, adapted from C. S. Forester's novel. Laughton plays the murderous William Marble for 70 performances. Lanchester and Laughton married in 1918, the year she founded the Children's Theatre in Soho, London.

Oct 3 Composer Sammy Fain makes his Broadway debut as composer of the music for Harold Atteridge's musical comedy, *Everybody's Welcome*, at the Shubert Theatre.

Oct 23 Actor, director, producer, and writer Arnold Moss makes his Broadway debut as the Page Boy in Chodorov and Barton's *Wonder Boy* at the Alvin Theatre.

Nov 6 Future director Mike Nichols is born Michael Igor Peschkowsky in Berlin, Germany.

Nov 12 American actor Fritz Tiden is dead in Liberty, New York at age 54. Tiden appeared in *When We Were Twenty-One* with Nat Goodwin and Maxine Elliott, *Sherlock Holmes* with William Gillette, *The Bad Man* with Holbrook Blinn, and *100 Years Old* with Otis Skinner.

Dec 1 American actor Thomas MacLarnie is dead in Brighton, Massachusetts, at age 60. MacLarnie began his career with James O'Neill in *The Count of Monte Cristo* and *Virginius*. He was well known in both Eastern and Western stock companies. MacLarnie played the Judge in *Lightnin'* from 1918-21.

David Belasco

Dec 30 London-born Tyrone Power (b. 1869) dies in Hollywood. Power's grandfather was the famous 19th-century actor of Irish characters. His stage career began in St. Augustine, Florida, in 1884. Power later became a member of the Augustin Daly Comedy Company. He appeared in support of William Faversham, Mrs. Fiske, Julia Marlowe, Mrs. Leslie Carter, and others.

total number of performances of all productions, tallied in terms of eight performances per week.

June 1 With the current season at an end, Eva LeGallienne has already decided against a subsequent season at her Civic Repertory Theatre in New York on 14 Street. She cites a need to pause and rethink the operation. Despite houses filled to 94% of capacity in some seasons, the annual operating deficit has been as high as $100,000. There will be only one more season for LeGallienne's theatre, that of 1932-33, with its costly and very successful *Alice in Wonderland* production. After that, sponsors cannot guarantee another season.

June 15 With unemployment endemic and bread-lines in the streets, the 1930-31 Broadway season has 50 fewer new shows than the previous season. With 190 new productions, there are also no less than 20 revivals of older plays, with seven return engagements of productions which have been on tour or waiting in the warehouse.

June 15 Burns Mantle's list of ten *Best Plays* for the Broadway season are: Anderson's *Elizabeth the Queen*, Barry's *Tomorrow and Tomorrow*, Kaufman and Hart's *Once in a Lifetime*, Riggs' *Green Grow the Lilacs*, Crothers' *As Husbands Go*, Glaspell's *Alison's House*, Weitzenkorn's *Five Star Final*, Bolitho's *Overture*, Besier's *The Barretts of Wimpole Street*, and Baum's *Grand Hotel*.

June 22 The Windmill Theatre in London opens with *Inquest*. The 322-seat theatre has been designed by Howard Jones who has converted it from a former cinema, the Palais de Luxe, which opened in 1910.

Aug 18 A method of construction for a revolving stage on a central pivot is patented with the U.S. by Charles E. Pressly. The method includes the use of radially arranged stringer-members and castors and is to become a standard method of construction, as explained in stagecraft textbooks.

Aug 19 Otis Skinner today dedicates the John Drew Theatre of Guild Hall, East Hampton, Long Island.

Oct 7 Today the main ensemble of Dublin's Abbey Theatre departs for an American tour. A second company remains in Dublin to continue regular performances.

Oct 7 The Westminister Theatre in London on Buckingham Palace Road opens with *The Anatomist*. Anmer Hall is the manager and he has converted the former St. James Picture Theatre (opened 1924) into a 603-seat theatre, designed by Arnold Dunbar Smith.

Oct 8 The Saville Theatre opens on Shaftesbury Avenue in London with *For The Love of Mike*. Jack Walker is the manager of this 1,200-seat theatre, designed by T.P. Bennett & Sons, with Bertie Crewe as consultant.

1931 THEATERS/PRODUCTIONS

Jan 6 The Sadler's Wells Theatre opens in London, with *Twelfth Night*. The 1,499-seat theatre has been designed by F.G.M. Chancellor and is managed by Lilian Baylis. The original theatre, The Sadler's Musick House, had opened on June 3, 1683. In the early 19th century, it had been the home of Aquatic Drama and, after 1843, of Phelp's Shakespeare productions. That theatre was demolished in 1927.

March 6 Burlesque comes to the Eltinge Theatre on West 42 Street in New York. Rising production costs and economic difficulties involved with the theatres on this block have forced legitimate productions to find playhouses farther up Broadway.

April 14 Harrison J. L. Frank receives an American patent for Automatic Light Control. This invention seeks to eliminate the human element from lighting control and to operate the various dimmers and switches automatically. This is achieved by using a player-piano roll-type recording system to actuate relays which, in turn, control motors which control dimmers.

May 27 At long last, Britain's Lord Chamberlain permits public performance of Oscar Wilde's *Salome*, banned in the British Isles, but publicly performed in Paris as long ago as 1896.

June At the opening of this decade, there are 64 theatres available for Broadway shows, but bankruptcies and other hazards of the Depression—including the growing popularity of sound films—will reduce that number to 32 in the following decade. This season just past, there have been a total of 190 productions. There have also been 1,685 theatre-weeks, the

Green Grow the Lilacs

Jan 4 *The Devil Passes* (NY—Selwyn—Comedy). In Benn W. Levy's play, Basil Rathbone plays a young curate who is actually the Devil in disguise. The show runs three months.

Jan 12 *The Animal Kingdom* (NY—Broadhurst—Comedy). Leslie Howard and Gilbert Miller produce Philip Barry's play with Samson-and-Delilah overtones. Howard plays the man whose wife has sapped his vitality. The production runs 23 weeks. On April 2, 1947, the play opens in London at the Playhouse where it does not have a long run.

Jan 18 *Distant Drums* (NY—Belasco—Drama). Dan Totheroh's saga of pioneers on the Oregon Trail in 1848 features Pauline Lord. It has only a five-week run.

Jan 19 *Whistling in the Dark* (NY—Ethel Barrymore—Comedy). Ernest Truex and Claire Trevor are featured in this melodramatic farce by Laurence Gross and Edward Childs Carpenter. It deals with a novelist who is held captive by some crooks so he can work out a perfect murder scenario for them. There are 143 performances.

Feb 17 *Face the Music* (NY—New Amsterdam—Musical). Irving Berlin's score, coupled with Moss Hart's book, proves a delight, with Depression-pressed sophisticates breakfasting at the Automat and singing "Let's Have Another Cup of Coffee." The show runs nearly 21 weeks.

March 8 *Hot-Cha!* (NY—Ziegfeld—Musical). Brown and Henderson provide the lyrics and music, collaborating on the book with Mark Hellinger. Bert Lahr is featured as a speakeasy waiter in Mexico City, transformed into a bullfighter. The show, produced by Florenz Ziegfeld, has 119 performances.

March 9 *Night Over Taos* (NY—48th Street—Drama). The Group Theatre mounts Maxwell Anderson's play about Spanish feudalists resisting American encroachments in New Mexico. J. Edward Bromberg, Stella and Luther Adler, Clifford Odets, and Franchot Tone are in the cast. There are just 13 performances.

April 25 *Another Language* (NY—Booth—Drama). Rose Franken's play about a sensitive young man who falls in love with an understanding aunt features Glenn Anders, Dorothy Stickney, John Beal, and Margaret Wycherly. It runs 43 weeks. The show opens at London's Lyric on Dec 1, with Mary Jerrold, Louis Hayward, Herbert Marshall, and Edna Best.

Sep 14 *Clear All Wires* (NY—Times Square—Comedy). Herman Shumlin produces and directs Sam and Bella Spewack's play about a foreign correspondent in Moscow. Thomas Mitchell is the reporter. The show runs nearly three months. On June 6, 1933, it comes to London's Garrick where it does not have a long run.

Sep 15 *Flying Colors* (NY—Imperial—Revue). Howard Dietz and Arthur Schwartz create the lyrics and music for this costly show. The cast includes Clifton Webb, Buddy and Vilma Ebsen, Imogene Coca, and Tamara Geva. "Louisiana Hayride" is a hit.

Sep 27 *Earl Carroll's Vanities* (NY—Broadway—Revue). Vincente Minnelli stages this show with a score by Harold Arlen and Ted Koehler. The company includes Milton Berle, Max Wall, and Helen Broderick. "I Gotta Right to Sing the Blues" is a hit. The show runs only 11 weeks.

Oct 5 *Americana* (NY—Shubert—Revue). J.P. McEvoy devises the sketches and E.Y. Harburg the lyrics. Harburg and Jay Gorney create "Brother, Can You Spare a Dime?" The show doesn't quite make a ten-week run.

Oct 6 *When Ladies Meet* (NY—Royale—Comedy). In Rachel Crothers' play, the ladies are the wife and the mistress of the same man, discussing him without knowing they are talking about the same person. Selena Royle and Frieda Inescourt are featured. It runs for nearly 22 weeks. On April 26, 1933, the play opens at London's Lyric with Ann Todd and Marie Tempest. It wins 108 performances.

Oct 10 *Criminal at Large* (NY—Belasco—Drama). Scotland Yard is baffled in the late Edgar Wallace's murder mystery, but Emlyn Williams, as an unbalanced peer, provides a clue. Guthrie McClintic stages, with Cleon Throckmorton's settings. The show attracts for five months.

Oct 11 *I Loved Your Wednesday* (NY—Harris—Drama). Molly Ricardel and William Du Bois's play about a love triangle has Humphrey Bogart, Frances Fuller, and Henry Fonda in the cast. It runs two months.

Oct 22 *Dinner at Eight* (NY—Music Box—Drama). George S. Kaufman stages this play he's devised with Edna Ferber. Several plot threads are interwoven, tragedy being counterpoised with brittle sophistication. The cast includes Conway Tearle, Sam Levene, Constance Collier, and Cesar Romero. The production runs 29 weeks. On Jan 6, 1933, it opens at London's Palace with Irene Vanbrugh, Tristan Rawson, Mabel Terry-Lewis, Laura Cowie, Lyn Harding, and Carol Goodner among the cast. It runs 27 weeks.

Oct 27 *Dangerous Corner.* See L premiere, 1932.

Oct 31 *The Late Christopher Bean* (NY—Henry Miller—Comedy). Sidney Howard adapts Rene Fauchois' play about a famed artist who was a forger. Beulah Bondi, Pauline Lord, Clarence Derwent, and George Couclouris are in the cast. On May 16, 1933, adapted by Emlyn Williams, the play comes to London's St. James's with Cedric Hardwicke, Edith Evans, and Clarence Derwent. There are 488 performances.

Nov 8 *Music in the Air* (NY—Alvin—Musical). This show by Oscar Hammerstein II, with a score by Jerome Kern, tells of two Bavarian villagers' (Al Shean and Walter Slezak) adventures in Munich. Joseph Urban designs the sets, each scene having been conceived by Kern and Hammerstein with a different musical form as its theme. "I've Told Every Little Star" is a hit. It runs 18 weeks initially, with a return engagement of 91 performances. The show opens at London's His Majesty's on May 19, 1933, with Eve Lister, Bruce Carfax, Marie Minto, and Charles V. France among the cast. There are 275 performances.

Nov 19 *Autumn Crocus* (NY—Morosco—Drama). Dody Smith's play runs for over 26 weeks, introducing American audiences to the Czech actor, Francis Lederer. A British drama, it shows Patricia Collinge as a spinster who has a chance for an affair with a handsome, married Tyrolean inn-keeper.

Face the Music

Nov 26 *Take a Chance* (NY—Apollo—Musical). Nacio Herb Brown, Richard Whiting, and Vincent Youmans provide the music for this revue satirizing American history. Jack Haley and Sid Silvers are featured. Ethel Merman is a hit in a minor role, singing "Eadie Was a Lady" and "Rise 'n Shine." The show runs eight months.

Nov 29 *Gay Divorce* (NY—Ethel Barrymore—Musical). Cole Porter provides the music and lyrics for this Dwight Taylor book about a man trying to help a woman divorce her husband. Fred Astaire and Claire Luce are featured. "Night and Day" is a hit. The show runs 31 weeks. On Nov 2,, 1933, the show opens at London's Palace with Astaire and Luce repeating their roles. The show runs nearly 23 weeks.

Dec 7 *Walk a Little Faster* (NY—St. James—Revue). Vernon Duke creates the score, with lyrics by E. Y. Harburg; one memorable song is "April in Paris." Beatrice Lillie clowns in skits by S. J. Perelman. The show runs 15 weeks.

Dec 12 *Biography* (NY—Guild—Comedy). Ina Claire stars in S.N. Behrman's tale of an amorous artist who is having her life-story recorded. This Theatre Guild production runs 283 performances. It opens on April 25, 1934, at London's Globe with Claire again in the lead. Laurence Olivier is also in the cast. It does not have a long run.

Dec 20 *Lucrece* (NY—Belasco—Drama). Katharine Cornell produces Andre Obey's French version of the Rape of Lucrece, translated by Thornton Wilder, with

Twentieth Century

music by Deems Taylor. She plays Lucrece to Brian Aherne's Tarquin. There are only 31 performances.

Dec 26 *Shuffle Along of 1933* (NY—Mansfield—Musical). Even with music and lyrics by Eubie Blake and Noble Sissle, this ghost of former treats musters only 17 performances.

Dec 29 *Twentieth Century* (NY—Broadhurst—Comedy). Ben Hecht and Charles MacArthur rework Charles Milholland's play about a Broadway producer who needs to make up with a cinema star. Moffat Johnston and Eugenie Leontovich are featured. It runs 19 weeks.

premiere, 1929.

March 23 *I Lived With You* (L—Prince of Wales's—Comedy). Ivor Novello writes and is featured in this play about the unfortunate consequences of sudden wealth. Ursula Jeans and Cicely Oates are in the cast. There are 120 performances.

April 26 *Pleasure Cruise* (L—Apollo—Comedy). Owen Nares and Madeleine Carroll play leads in Austen Allen's variation on the theme of *Die Fledermaus*. There are 126 performances.

May 17 *Dangerous Corner* (L—Lyric—Drama). J.B. Priestley's play about the results of a remark at a dinner party, features Flora Robson, Marie Ney, and Esme Church, among others. Tyrone Guthrie directs. It has 151 performances. On Oct 27, it premieres at New York's Empire where it runs nearly 26 weeks.

May 23 *Party* (L—Strand—Comedy). This new Ivor Novello play earns a run of five months, staged by Athole Stewart. Among the players are Benita Hume, Sebastian Shaw, Douglas Byng, Agnes Imlay, Joan Swinstead, and Lilian Braithwaite. On Aug 23, 1933, the play opens in New York at the Playhouse, with Mrs. Patrick Campbell in the central role of a star of former times who can still hold her own with a currently popular actress. The show runs nearly six weeks.

May 24 *Casanova* (L—Coliseum—Musical). The British book and lyrics are by Harry Graham, the music by Johann Strauss, for this extremely grand and elaborate production based on the great lover's life. Arthur Fear plays the title role. There are 429 performances.

June 8 *The Vinegar Tree*. See NY premiere, 1930.

June 11 *Out of the Bottle* (L—Hippodrome—Musical). Vivian Ellis and Oscar Levant create the score for this show, based on F. Anstey's play, *The Brass Bottle*. Fred Thompson and Clifford Grey have manufactured the libretto. As staged by Julian

1932   BRITISH PREMIERES

Jan 3 *1066 And All That* (L—Arts—Revue). Michael Watts's "historical entertainment is adapted from the successful parody history of the same name by W.C. Sellar and R.J. Yeastman. The cast includes Walter Hudd and Jean Cadell.

Jan 4 *Bow Bells* (L—Hippodrome—Revue). Dion Titheradge and Ronald Jeans provide the book and Desmond Carter and Henry Sullivan the songs for this show which runs 29 weeks. The cast includes Binnie and Robert Hale, Andre Randall, and Max Wall, among others.

Jan 19 *While Parents Sleep* (L—Royalty—Comedy). Nigel Playfair, Hugh Williams, Jack Hawkins, and Frances Doble are featured in this comedy about a young man being seduced while his parents are asleep upstairs. The show runs 826 performances.

Jan 30 *Helen!* (L—Adelphi—Musical). Eric Wolfgang Korngold arranges the Jacques Offenbach score of *La Belle Helene* to fit A.P. Herbert's reworking of the original Meilhac and Halevy text. Evelyn Laye has the title role. The show, produced by Max Reinhardt, runs six months.

Feb 9 *The Green Back* (L—Wyndham's—Drama). This is another Edgar Wallace thriller, featuring Gerald Du Maurier. It earns 157 showings.

Feb 10 *The Rose Without a Thorn* (L—Duchess—Drama). Clifford Bax's play about Henry VIII and Catherine Howard features Frank Vosper and Angela Baddeley. It runs 113 performances.

Feb 24 *Derby Day* (L—Lyric, Hammersmith—Musical). This comic opera by A. P. Herbert (libretto) and Alfred Reynolds (score), runs almost 23 weeks.

March 4 *The Cat and the Fiddle*. See NY premiere, 1931.

March 7 *Dirty Work* (L—Aldwych—Comedy). Ben Travers' farce about an attempt to trap a thief features Constance Carpenter and Archibald Batty, among others. It runs 195 performances.

March 9 *Tobias and the Angel* (L—Westminster—Comedy). James Bridie dramatizes the apocryphal tale of the Book of Tobit, with Frederick Piper, and Henry Ainley in the title-roles.

March 22 *See Naples and Die*. See NY

Wylie, the show earns 109 performances. In the cast are such entertainers as Audrey Pointing, Frances Day, Polly Walker, Sebastian Smith, Cecil Humphreys, and Clifford Mollison.

June 26 *Richard of Bordeaux* (L—New—Drama). John Gielgud plays Richard in this chronicle by Gordon Daviot. On Feb 14, 1934, the show opens on Broadway at the Empire with Dennis King in the lead. It runs 38 performances.

June 30 *Evensong* (L—Queen's—Drama). Edward Knoblock and Beverly Nichols adapt the novel Nichols has written. With a cast including Edith Evans, Ethel Glendinning, and Violet Vanbrugh, the production runs nearly 27 weeks.

Aug 9 *Orders Are Orders* (L—Shaftesbury—Comedy). Ian May and Anthony Armstrong's farce about a cinema company invading a military barracks features Ernest Jay, Marjorie Corbett, and Basil Foster, among others. It runs 193 times.

Aug 16 *Behold, We Live!* (L—St. James's—Drama). Gertrude Lawrence appears in John van Druten's modern tragedy about a woman, in an unhappy marriage, who loses the man she loves. There are 158 performances.

Aug 31 *Night of the Garter* (L—Strand—Comedy). Angela Baddeley is featured in this Austin Melford adaptation of a farce by Avery Hopwood and Wilson Collison. The show earns 245 performances.

Sep 5 *Fifty-Fifty* (L—Aldwych—Comedy). Winifred Shotter is featured in H.F. Maltby's adaptation of a French farce by Louis Verneuil and Georges Berr. There are 161 performances.

Sep 16 *Words and Music* (L—Adelphi—Revue). Noel Coward writes and stages his revue which includes such songs as "Mad Dogs and Englishmen" and "Mad About the Boy." Among the company are Romney Brent, Moya Nugent, and Doris Hare. The show runs 164 performances.

Sep 26 *The Left Bank*. See NY premiere, 1931.

Sep 27 *Strange Orchestra* (L—St. Martin's—Drama). John Gielgud stages Rodney Ackland's drama with Jean Forbes-Robertson, Robert Harris, and Laura Cowie among the players. It runs 17 weeks.

Oct 6 *Road House* (L—Whitehall—Drama). Walter Hackett's play earns a run of nearly 43 weeks, staged by Thomas Reynolds. Among the cast are Ronald Shiner, Marion Lorne, Godfrey Tearle, Charles Quartermaine, and the buskers, Dan and Van. Kitty, recently returned from South Africa, has loaned her car. Unfortunately, it was borrowed by a gang of thieves, and the police arrest her as an accomplice in their robbery of a jewelry store. Incriminating evidence has been planted on her as well. Her innocence is proved at the close. "Miss Marion Lorne's guileless jaw falls at the base attack; her

innocence is a thousand times assured in her impassioned breathlessness, her protestant gasps, her smile of a robin accused of pilfering an eagle's nest. . . . Miss Lorne is gloriously coy and deliciously aghast . . . ," reports *The Times.*

Oct 7 *Children in Uniform* (L—Duchess—Drama). Cathleen Nesbitt plays the headmistress of a strict girls school in Christa Winsloe's controversial drama *Maedchen in Uniform*, about the special friendships that develop. Barbara Burnham has done the translation. It runs 33 weeks. On Dec 30, 1932, it opens at New York's Booth Theatre where it has only 12 performances.

Oct 12 *Service* (L—Wyndham's—Drama). Leslie Banks, Jack Hawkins, Ann Todd, and Joyce Kennedy appear in C.L. Anthony's play which runs 25 weeks.

Oct 31 *Wild Violets* (L—Drury Lane—

Musical). This reminiscence of love in the 1890s has a score by Robert Stolz and a book by Hassard Short, Desmond Carter, and Reginald Purdell. Charlotte Greenwood and Jerry Verno are featured. There are 291 performances.

Nov 1 *For Services Rendered* (L—Globe—Drama). W. Somerset Maugham's bitter play about veterans of World War I features a cast including Cedric Hardwicke, Flora Robson, Charles France, and Ralph Richardson. On April 12, 1933, it comes to the Booth in New York with a cast including Leo G. Carroll, Lillian Kemble Cooper, and Fay Bainter. It lasts only 21 showings.

Nov 8 *Springtime for Henry*. See NY premiere, 1931.

Dec 1 *Another Language*. See NY premiere, 1932.

1932   REVIVALS/REPERTORIES

Jan 4 At London's Old Vic Theatre, Beaumont and Fletcher's comedy, *The Knight of the Burning Pestle*, is revived, staged by Theodore Komisarjevsky. Anthony Quayle and Margaret Halstan are featured.

Jan 12 The Dublin Gate Theatre continues its fifth season with Cassella's *Death Takes a Holiday*, followed by Shakespeare's *Hamlet*, Pagnol's *Topaze*, Goddard's *Obsession in India*, Christine, Countess of Longford's *Queens and Emperors*, Pearse's *The Singer*, France's *The Man Who Married a Dumb Wife*, macLiammoir's *Easter 1916* (revival), the Balderston/Squire *Berkeley Square* (revival), and Le Fanu's *Carmilla*, adapted by the Earl of Longford, a patron of the theatre. Opening May 3, this is the last production of the current season.

Jan 25 At London's Q Theatre, *Julius Caesar* is revived, with George Skillan in the title-role. On Feb 8, at the Haymarket Theatre, Lyn Harding appears as Caesar. On Feb 10, the Shakespeare revivals continue, with *Romeo and Juliet* at London's Embassy Theatre. Sebastian Shaw and Joyce Bland are the star-crossed lovers. On Feb 22, at the Q Theatre at Kew Bridge, *Hamlet* is brought back, with Victor Lewisohn as the Dane. On April 4, at the St. James's Theatre, Ernest Milton in the title-role in *Othello*.

Feb 15 John Drinkwater's *Abraham Lincoln* is revived at London's Old Vic Theatre. Harcourt Williams plays the title-role.

Feb 18 Pirandello's *Six Characters in Search of an Author* is revived at London's Westminster Theatre, staged by Tyrone Guthrie. Flora Robson plays the Stepdaughter.

Feb 22 At Daly's Theatre in London, the practice of reviving old operettas and

musicals continues with this production of *San Toy*. On March 24, *Miss Hook of Holland* is exhumed. At the Shaftesbury Theatre, on March 31, *The Chocolate Soldier* returns to the stage. On April 14, the musical revival is Millocker's *The Dubarry*, staged at His Majesty's. On April 26, Daly's revives *The Duchess of Dantzig*. At the Dominion Theatre on May 31, *The Land of Smiles* is revived.

Feb 29 Denis Johnston's *The Moon in the Yellow River* provides the Theatre Guild with a compelling picture of rebellious Irishmen. It runs five weeks in New York. On April 4, the Guild produces George Bernard Shaw's chatty fantasy, *Too True To Be Good*, with Beatrice Lillie, Claude Rains, and Leo G. Carroll. It has only 57 performances.

April 18 Shakespeare continues popular in major West End and smaller London theatres. Tonight, at the Kingsway Theatre, Russell and Eileen Thorndike play the Macbeths. On April 19, they are in *The Merchant of Venice*. On the 20th, they appear in *The Taming of the Shrew*. The next night sees them in *Twelfth Night*, followed on the 23rd, by *Romeo and Juliet*, with only Russell Thorndike (Mercutio) in the cast, the leads being played by the director of this ensemble, Peter Dearing and Mary Casson. Also on that day, *Hamlet* is offered, with the Thorndikes as Hamlet and Gertrude. On April 28, at the St. James's Theatre, *The Merchant of Venice* has Ernest Milton for its Shylock. On May 24, *Twelfth Night* opens at the New Theatre, with director Robert Atkins as Sir Toby.

April 23 The new Shakespeare Memorial Theatre in Stratford-upon-Avon opens with *Henry IV, Part 1*, directed and designed by W. Bridges Adams. Other plays in the five-week spring season include

Casanova

Henry IV, Part 2, Twelfth Night, Julius Caesar, As You Like It, A Midsummer Night's Dream, and *King Lear.*

April 25 H.K. Ayliff revives George Bernard Shaws's *Heartbreak House* at London's Queen's Theatre, with Cedric Hardwicke and Edith Evans.

May 9 Florenz Ziegfeld revives *Show Boat* for over 22 weeks at the Casino Theatre in New York. Paul Robeson sings "Old Man River."

June 27 The summer season in the new Shakespeare Memorial Theatre in Stratford-upon-Avon opens with *Twelfth Night.* Productions from the spring season are revived; among them are *Henry IV. Parts 1 & 2, Julius Caesar, As You Like It, A Midsummer Night's Dream,* and *King Lear.* New for the summer visitors is Theodore Komisarjevsky's production of *The Merchant of Venice.*

July 6 Tyrone Guthrie stages *Love's Labour's Lost* at London's Westminster Theatre, with Anthony Quayle and Vera Poliakoff.

July 19 At London's Garrick Theatre, Leon M. Lion revives John Galsworthy's *Escape,* followed, on Aug 22, with his *Loyalties.* On Sep 29, Lion revives *Justice.*

Aug 1 Chekhov's *The Cherry Orchard* opens the sixth season at the Dublin Gate Theatre, with staging by Hilton Edwards, and designs by Micheal macLiammoir. Other plays include Congreve's *The Way of the World,* Zola's *Therese Raquin,* MacArdle's *Dark Waters,* Ibsen's *Peer Gynt,* Wilde's *An Ideal Husband,* Shakespeare's *Romeo and Juliet,* Chekhov's *The Seagull,* Manning's *Youth's the Season—?,* and Rostand's *Cyrano de Bergerac.*

Sep 13 H.K. Ayliff stages George Bernard Shaw's *Too True To Be Good,* at the New Theatre in London. In the cast are Cedric Hardwicke and Ralph Richardson among others. On Sep 18, the Old Vic Theatre revives Shaw's *Caesar and Cleopatra,* with Malcolm Keen and Peggy Ashcroft in the title-roles. On Nov 25, Shaw's *Getting Married* is revived at the Little Theatre.

Sep 26 At the Savoy Theatre, the D'Oyly Carte Opera Company opens a season of Gilbert & Sullivan with *Trial by Jury* and *The Pirates of Penzance.* On Oct 3, *The Gondoliers* opens. On the 10, *Ruddigore;* on the 17, *Iolanthe,* and on the 24, *The Mikado,* followed by *H. M. S. Pinafore* and *Cox and Box* on Oct 31. On Nov 7, *Patience* is produced, followed by *Princess Ida* on the 14; *The Yeomen of the Guard,* on the 21, and, on Dec 12, *The Sorcerer.*

Sep 26 The Group Theatre in New York presents John Howard Lawson's *Success Story,* about the strivings of a Jew, who resents capitalism, working in a gentile firm. Luther and Stella Adler are featured. It runs 15 weeks.

Oct 17 Owen and Donald Davis adapt Pearl S. Buck's best-selling novel, *The Good Earth,* for New York's Theatre Guild. Claude Rains is featured. The show runs seven weeks.

Oct 17 At New York's Martin Beck Theatre, the Abbey Theatre Irish Players offer a repertory including Paul Vincent Carroll's *Things That are Caesar's,* Lennox Robinson's *The Far-Off Hills,* and George Shiel's *The New Gossoon.* The engagement is five weeks.

Oct 26 Returning from a "sabbatical" sojourn in Europe, Eva LeGallienne re-opens her Civic Repertory Theatre in New York on 14 Street. Her first offering is a revival of Molnar's *Liliom.* The production is played 35 times. On Nov 14, a play about the romantic inclinations of Jane Austen, *Dear Jane,* opens for 11 performances. On Dec 12, LeGallienne and Florida Friebus adapt Lewis Carroll's *Alice in Wonderland* and *Through the Looking-Glass.* Josephine Hutchinson is Alice. It later moves uptown to the New Amsterdam. The Civic Repertory show runs four months.

Nov 17 The Shakespeare Theatre Company begins a season of low-priced (25 cents to $1) performances in the re-named Jolson Theatre, now the Shakespeare. Managed by Julius Hopp and Percial Vivian, the company offers 15 productions for a total of 249 performances, possibly a Broadway season's record for the Bard in repertory. *A Midsummer Night's Dream* opens; other plays include *King Lear, Romeo and Juliet, The Tempest, Julius Caesar, Othello, Macbeth, The Merchant of Venice, Twelfth Night, As You Like It,* and *Much Ado About Nothing.*

Nov 27 At London's Arts Theatre, Robert Atkins stages *All's Well That Ends Well,* with Martita Hunt, Walter Hudd, and Iris Baker, among others.

December 19 *Buckie's Bears* is the first of the Christmas season's shows to open this year, with Leo Genn in the cast at the Garrick Theatre. On the 20th, two more open: *The Streets of London* (Ambassadors') and *Alice and Thomas and Jane* (Westminster). Other popular shows are *Where the Rainbow Ends* (Holborn Empire), *Alice in Wonderland* (Little), *Jack and the Beanstalk* (Embassy), *Peter Pan* (Palladium), *Toad of Toad Hall* (Royalty), *Puss in Boots* (Brixton), *Aladdin* (Grand, Croydon), *Mother Goose* (Daly's), *When Knights Were Bold* (Fortune), *Lilac Time* (Globe), *The Babes in the Woods* (King's, Hammersmith), *Dick Whittington* (London Hippodrome), *The Sleeping Beauty* (Lyceum), *Robinson Crusoe* (Scala), and *Monsieur Beaucaire* (Queen's) Oscar Asche also revives *The Merry Wives of Windsor* at the Winter Garden.

Dec 26 Walter Hampden revives Rostand's *Cyrano de Bergerac* for two weeks at New York's New Amsterdam Theatre.

Dec 26 At London's Kingsway Theatre, the holiday season is to be celebrated in bloody fashion. The play is *Sweeney Todd, The Demon Barber of Fleet Street: Or, A String of Pearls.* Tod Slaughter and Jenny Lynn are featured.

1932 BIRTHS/DEATHS/DEBUTS

Jan 29 American actor Geroge W. Monroe is dead in Atlantic City at age 75. Monroe appeared with John C. Rice on the variety stage in *My Aunt Bridget* and similar plays for 12 years. He retired in 1923.

Jan 30 American actor and playwright William T. Hodge (b. 1874) dies in Greenwich, Connecticut. Hodge had his first success in *Sag Harbour* in 1900. He made a personal hit as the Indiana lawyer, Pike, in *The Man From Home,* and based all his future parts on this character, writing his plays himself.

Feb 15 Actress and director-producer Minnie Maddern Fiske (b. 1865) dies in Hollis, Long Island. On her marriage to producer-playwright Harrison Grey Fiske, the actress retired for a period of four years. Her return to the stage was as the heroine in her husband's play, *Hester Crewe.* Nora in *A Doll's House* and Mrs. Alving in *Ghosts* are two of her memorable roles. She also wrote a number of plays.

March 31 Future producer-director Michael Murray is born in Washington, D.C.

April 13 Jean Arthur makes her New York stage debut as Anna in *Foreign Affairs,* by Paul Hervey Fox and George Tilton, at the Avon Theatre.

May 23 Playwright-director Augusta Lady Gregory (b. 1852) dies on her estate at Coole in Galway, Ireland. Gregory, an ardent supporter of the Irish Dramatic Movement, wrote numerous plays for the

Abbey Theatre among which are *The Rising of the Moon* and *The Gaol Gate*. She co-authored (with Yeats) *The Pot of Broth* and *Cathleen ni Houlihan*. She also translated a version of Moliere's plays titled *The Kiltartan Moliere*.

July 22 Florenz Ziegfeld (b. 1867) dies in Santa Monica California. Ziegfeld originated and perfected the American musical revue in a series of productions called the *Ziegfeld Follies*, which began in 1907 and ran for 24 consecutive editions under the caption *An American Institution*. His first wife was actress Anna Held. The second was Billie Burke.

Aug 22 American actor Wilton Lackaye (b. 1862) dies in New York City. Lackaye appeared many times with Fanny Davenport, and in 1887 had a success in *She*.

He also played Jean Valjean in his own dramatization of *Les Miserables*. Lackaye's greatest role was Svengali.

Oct 14 American actress Jesse Bonstelle dies in Detroit. Bonstelle began her career in a road company of *Bertha, the Beautiful Sewing Machine Girl*. Among the prominent actors she taught are Katharine Cornell, Ann Harding, Melvyn Douglas, and Kenneth McKenna.

Nov 27 English actor William J. Rea (b. 1884) is dead. Rea toured in the provinces for some years in melodrama, later joining the Birmingham Repertory Theatre. Among his notable performances were Sir Paddy Cullen in *The Doctor's Dilemma*, Petruchio in *The Taming of the Shrew*, Sir Epicure Mammon in *The Alchemist*, and Abraham Lincoln.

1932   THEATERS/PRODUCTIONS

Among patents granted in Britain this year is one to W. and R. L. Burrows for a method of producing designs by placing loose pieces of fabric between a rear-lit screen and its light source.

U.S. patents granted this year include: Jack Norworth's system of scenic screens on endless belts which produce the illusion of motion by moving from the downstage legs of the proscenium arch upstage on a diagonal, converging behind an object or scenic element at center stage; Arthur J. Moulton's central rotating bank of seating, surrounded by annular stages, a concept already patented.

The playwright-director Rachel Crothers this year organizes the Stage Relief Fund, raising eventually $58,000 to aid some 6,000 out-of-work theatre people in America.

Feb 3 London's Windmill Theatre adopts a policy of non-stop variety shows.

April 22 Finishing touches are being put on London's new Shakespeare Memorial Theatre in Stratford-upon-Avon, replacing the 1879 Memorial Theatre which has burned in 1926. The design, chosen in competition, is the work of Elizabeth Scott; the finished theatre has been designed in detail by the architects Scott, Sheperd, and Breakwell. The auditorium is 76 feet by 86 feet and seats 1,000 in stalls and balcony. The proscenium opening is 30 feet wide, but the actual stage is 55 feet wide and it is 45 feet deep. From stage floor to the grid, the height is 70 feet. There is an apron stage and proscenium doors. The center stage can sink, and there are two wagon-stages in the wings at each side for rapid scene-changes. There is even a domed sky-piece which moves in on rails. The Art Deco theatre has cost £175,000, leaving £90,000 over from the total pledged to build the new playhouse. This is to be an endowment for production and maintenance.

June With the close of the 1931–32 Broadway season, despite the inroads of the Depression, there have been 195 productions, but a number have been failures. There have been a total of 1,496 theatre-weeks, down almost 200 weeks from last season, reckoned in terms of 8 performances per week. There have been 134 new plays in a total of 195 productions, including revivals. Burns Mantle notes four failures for every box-office success, the new low average caused by the effect of the Depression on lowering rentals, wages, and other production costs, encouraging the mounting of scripts which otherwise wouldn't be seen on Broadway. Financially, this has been the worst season in recent memory. Both the Shubert and Erlanger producing organizations, faced with bankruptcy, have had to bury old rivalries, with national touring to benefit from the results. The annual ten Broadway *Best Plays* chosen by Mantle are: O'Neill's *Mourning Becomes Electra*, Sherwood's *Reunion in Vienna*, Green's *The House of Connelly*, Rice's *The Left Bank*, Barry's *The Animal Kingdom*, Behrman's *Brief Moment*, Franken's *Another Language*, Levy's *The Devil Passes*, Harwood and Gore-Browne's *Cynara*, and the Pulitzer Prize-winner, *Of Thee I Sing*, compounded from the talents of Kaufman, Ryskind, and the Gershwins.

July 16 In Central City, Colorado, the old Central City Opera House re-opens after remodelling designed to preserve its historic character but also to make it adaptable to the needs of modern production. Lillian Gish stars in *Camille*.

Sep 15 *Flying Colors* opens at New York's Imperial Theatre. Producer Max Gordon and designer Norman Bel Geddes incorporate motion-pictures in the "Louisiana Hayride" number.

Oct 9 Today is the official opening of the Palais Montcalm, Quebec City, Canada. Until 1970, this will be the most important theatrical hall (along with the Capitol building) in the city of Quebec.

Oct 12 Burlesque performances are back on West 42 Street's once famed Theatre Block in New York. Both the Republic and the Eltinge are allowed to resume performances, recently halted owing to public protests about the offensiveness of large posters illustrating the attractions inside and the raucous and aggressive manner in which street barkers have tried to lure or coerce people into their shows. From this day, there are to be no barkers and only modest, inoffensive street advertisment. Nor will either playhouse be able to call itself a burlesque theatre. Instead, the official titles of the respective shows will be "The Republic Frolics" and "The Eltinge Follies."

Nov 11 The San Francisco War Memorial Opera House opens tonight. The huge and handsome Beaux Arts building is part of an integrated Beaux Arts Civic Center, including an impressive domed City Hall, a Civic Auditorium (built in 1915 for the Panama-Pacific Exposition), and the Veterans Building, which also opens this year, complete with a 1,100-seat theatre. The Opera House seats 3,285, with a proscenium opening of 52 feet wide by 51 feet high and a stage 131 feet wide by 83 feet deep. The height to the gridiron is 140 feet, accomodating opera scenery on a grand scale. G. Albert Lansburgh and Arthur Brown, Jr., are the architects of both this and the Veterans Building. (The latter theatre is notable for the 1915 Exposition murals of Frank Brangwyn.) The Opera House will serve as the home of the San Francisco Opera, Ballet, and Symphony, until the Louise Davies Symphony Hall is opened in 1980 for orchestral concerts. Large-scale touring musicals also play the Opera House over the years.

Alice in Wonderland

Jan 16 *Pigeons and People* (NY—Harris—Comedy). Played without an intermission, by its author, this *tour-de-force* permits George M. Cohan, as an apparently unbalanced man, to say a great many shrewd and amusing things. It has 70 performances.

Jan 20 *Pardon My English* (NY—Majestic—Musical). Herbert Fields tells this tale of two innocent dancing Americans, arrested as crooks in Dresden. George and Ira Gershwin provide the score and lyrics. Yet the show has only 46 performances.

Jan 21 *We, the People* (NY—Empire—Drama). Elmer Rice produces and stages his play, an indictment of the failure of the American economic system and the promises of the American dream. The production lasts only 49 performances.

Jan 24 *Design for Living* (NY—Ethel Barrymore—Comedy). Noel Coward writes and stars in this play about two men who are in love with the same woman and want to share her. Alfred Lunt and Lynn Fontanne are featured. The show runs 17 weeks. On Jan 25, 1939, the play opens at London's Haymarket with Diana Wynyard, Anton Wallbrook and Rex Harrison. The comedy runs over 25 weeks.

Feb 15 *One Sunday Afternoon* (NY—Little—Drama). James Hagan's play of the troubles of plain people in hard times

Design for Living

features Lloyd Nolan and Francesca Bruning. It has 143 performances.

Feb 20 *Alien Corn* (NY—Belasco—Drama). Katharine Cornell produces and stars in Sidney Howard's play about a sensitive musician trapped in a small women's college in the Midwest. Siegfried Rumann, Luther Adler, and James Rennie are also featured. It runs for three months. On July 5, 1939, it opens in London at Wyndham's with Margaretta Scott and John Clements.

March 1 *Run, Little Chillun'* (NY—Lyric—Drama). Hall Johnson's play is about the conflict between the Hope Baptists and the pagan New Day Pilgrims. Harry Bolden and Fredi Washington are featured in this all-black drama, rich with music and dance. It runs nearly four months.

March 6 *Both Your Houses* (NY—Royale—Drama). Maxwell Anderson's satire indicts the power-brokers of both political parties as they trick an earnest reformer. Morris Carnovsky, J. Edward Bromberg, and Shepperd Strudwick are featured in this Theatre Guild production, which runs 120 performances. The play later wins a Pulitzer Prize.

March 10 *Lone Valley* (NY—Plymouth—Drama). Sophie Treadwell's play about a prostitute who inherits a ranch in the Southwest has only three performances.

March 16 *Three-Cornered Moon* (NY—Cort—Comedy). Alfred de Liagre, Jr., and Richard Aldrich produce Gertrude Tonkonogy's play about a family which loses its money and does not know how to work. The cast includes Ruth Gordon and Brian Donlevy. It runs nearly 10 weeks. On Nov 26, 1934, it comes to London's Westminster with Kay Hammond. It does not have a long run.

Sep 8 *Murder at the Vanities* (NY—New Amsterdam—Musical). The murder of a showgirl is an excuse for Earl Carroll getting something like a *Vanities* revue on stage. Bela Lugosi, Jean Adair and Robert Cummings are in the company. The show runs 26 weeks.

Sep 21 *Double Door* (NY—Ritz—Drama). Elizabeth McFadden's melodrama about a woman who locks another in the family burial vault to prevent her from marrying her brother runs 18 weeks. Mary Morris, Aleta Freel, and Richard Kendrick appear. The play opens on March 21, 1934, at London's Globe with Sybil Thorndike in the lead.

Sep 26 *Men in White* (NY—Broadhurst—Drama). Sidney Kingsley's play deals with a doctor who must decide between love and duty. The cast includes Luther Adler, J. Edward Bromberg and Ruth Nelson. This Group Theatre production runs 11 months. On June 28, 1934, the play comes to the

Lyric Theatre in an "Anglicized" version by Merton Hodge. Jill Esmond, Robert Douglas, and Lewis Casson are in the cast. The play runs four months.

Sep 28 *Sailor, Beware!* (NY—Lyceum—Comedy). Bruce Macfarlane plays the sailor who can overcome any woman, until he meets "Stonewall" Billie Jackson (Audrey Christie). Kenyon Nicholson directs the play he's written with Charles Robinson. There are 500 performances.

Sep 30 *As Thousands Cheer* (NY—Music Box—Revue). Moss Hart and Irving Berlin's show parodies current events. Marilyn Miller, Clifton Webb, Helen Broderick, and Ethel Waters are featured. Waters sings "Heat Wave." The show runs 400 performances.

Oct 2 *Ah, Wilderness* (NY—Guild—Comedy). The Theatre Guild produces Eugene O'Neill's only comedy, an idealized nostalgic picture of the American family. George M. Cohan, Elisha Cook, Jr., and Gene Lockhart are featured. It runs nine months. The *NY Times* reports that it is "one of his best works . . . Now it is possible to sit down informally with Mr. O'Neill and to like the people of whom he speaks and the gentle, kindly tolerance of his memories." On May 4, 1936, the show premieres in London's Westminster, with Cyril Cusak and Fred Johnson in the cast.

Oct 9 *The Pursuit of Happiness* (NY—Avon—Comedy). Armina Marshall and Lawrence Langner's play about a runaway Hessian soldier who wins his Revolutionary love features Tonio Selwart and Peggy Conklin. On May 30, 1934, the show opens in London's Vaudeville Theatre with Conklin repeating her role. It has a short run.

Oct 20 *The Green Bay Tree* (NY—Cort—Drama). Laurence Olivier plays Julian Dulcimer, who gives up the girl who loves him (Jill Esmond—Mrs. Olivier) for the sybaritic life offered him by an older man (James Dale). Leo G. Carroll plays the butler, Trump. Jed Harris produces and stages, with sets by Robert Edmond Jones. Mordaunt Shairp's British drama runs nearly 21 weeks, admired as a brilliant production but criticized for showing a way of life which could be a bad moral influence on some viewers as well as offending the sensibilities of other spectators. Homosexuality is not mentioned by name. "The relationship is abnormal, since Mr. Dulcimer, with all his petty sensuousness, is an abnormal person, but there is nothing in the play to indicate that the relationship is more than passively degenerate. . . . Laurence Olivier's Julian is an extraordinary study in the decomposition of a character. Mr. Olivier's ability to carry a character through from casual begin-

Tobacco Road

nings to a defeated conclusion, catching all the shades of meaning as he goes, is acting of the highest quality," reports Brooks Atkinson of the *NY Times*.

Oct 21 *Let Em Eat Cake* (NY—Imperial—Musical). The Gershwins, Morrie Ryskind, and George S. Kaufman try for a sequel to *Of Thee I Sing*, but this lasts only 90 performances.

Oct 23 *Her Master's Voice* (NY—Plymouth—Comedy). Clare Kummer's story of a young married man whose domestic problems are solved when he becomes a radio crooner features Roland Young and Laura Hope Crews. It has 224 performances.

Nov 18 *Roberta* (NY—New Amsterdam—Musical). Otto Harbach writes the libretto and Jerome Kern the score for Alice Duer Miller's story about an American football player who inherits a Paris dress shop. It runs 37 weeks. This is Kern's last major Broadway score.

Nov 20 *She Loves Me Not* (NY—46th Street—Comedy). Howard Lindsay adapts Edward Hope's novel about a showgirl (Polly Walters) who, having witnessed a gangland killing, flees to a Princeton dorm. The show runs 45 weeks. On May 1, 1934, it opens at London's Adelphi where it is not successful.

Nov 21 *Birthright* (NY—49th Street—Drama). There are only seven performances for Richard Maibaum's play about the sufferings of a German-Jewish family under Hitler's Nazis.

Nov 29 *Peace on Earth* (NY—Civic Repertory—Drama). The Theatre Union stages George Sklar and Albert Maltz's anti-war play. Robert Keith is featured. The show has an initial run of four months. On Dec 9, 1934, it comes to London's Phoenix, presented by the Left Theatre.

Dec 2 *Blackbirds of 1933* (NY—Apollo—Revue). Lew Leslie tries again but even the snappy black tap-dancing doesn't help. The show has only 25 performances.

Dec 4 *Tobacco Road* (NY—Masque—Drama). Despite critical expressions of shock at the blatant vulgarity of Jack Kirkland's dramatization of the Erskine Caldwell novel about poor white Georgia sharecroppers, this show becomes a sensational long-run hit with 3,182 performances. Henry Hull heads the cast. The *NY Times* reports that the play has "moments of merciless power." The play is staged at London's Gate Theatre on May 19, 1937, with Hedley Briggs, Nigel Stock, and Kay Lewis.

1933   BRITISH PREMIERES

Jan 5 *Fresh Fields* (L—Criterion—Comedy). Ivor Novello's play features Ellis Jeffreys and Lilian Braithwaite as two impoverished gentlewomen who take Australian boarders into their London mansion. There are 464 performances. On Feb 10, 1936, it opens at New York's Empire featuring Margaret Anglin and Mary Sargent. It runs 10 weeks.

Jan 6 *Dinner at Eight*. See NY premiere, 1932.

Jan 24 *The Beggar's Bowl* (L—Duke of York's—Drama). Richard Wagner's various love-affairs are chronicled in this play by Hugh Marleyn. Frank Hervey plays Wagner.

Jan 27 *Mother of Pearl* (L—Gaiety—Musical). Oscar Straus's music combines with A.P. Herbert's story of a woman who thinks she has a rival for the love of an officer, only to find out that the rival is his mother. Alice Delysia, Sepha Treble, and Richard Dolman are featured. The show wins 181 performances.

Jan 30 *A Bit of A Test* (L—Aldwych—Comedy). Ben Travers presents another "Aldwych farce." This one runs 18 weeks, with a cast including J. Robertson Hare, Renee Gadd, and Joan Brierley.

Feb 8 *Ten Minute Alibi* (L—Haymarket—Drama). Anthony Armstrong's play deals with a man who protects his love by murdering the man who is trying to seduce her. Anthony Ireland, Celia Johnson, and Robert Douglas are featured. There are 878 performances.

Feb 21 *It's You I Want* (L—Daly's—Comedy). Maurice Braddell's farce features Sholto Delaney and Viola Tree, among others. It runs 33 weeks.

Feb 24 *Cock Robin*. See NY premiere, 1928.

March 1 *Jolly Roger* (L—Savoy—Musical). This burlesque about romance and daring in 17th century Jamaica has music by Walter Leigh, book by Scobie MacKenzie and V.C. Clinton-Baddeley. The latter is also responsible for the lyrics. Sara Allgood and Victor Orsini are featured. There are nearly 200 performances.

March 28 *He Wanted Adventure* (L—Saville—Musical). R.P. Weston and Bert Lee adapt Walter Hackett's play, *Ambrose Applejohn's Adventure*. Music is by Jack Waller and Joseph Tunbridge. Judy Gunn and Bobby Howes are featured. There are 153 performances.

April 6 *The Rats of Norway* (L—Playhouse—Drama). Raymond Massey directs Keith Winter's play and also takes the part of Hugh Sebastian. In the cast as well are Laurence Olivier, Cecil Parker, Gladys Cooper, and others.

April 25 *How D'You Do?* (L—Comedy—Revue). This revue has a score by Ord Hamilton and a book by Arthur Macrae. There are 244 performances.

April 26 *When Ladies Meet*. See NY premiere, 1932.

May 16 *The Late Christopher Bean*. See NY premiere, 1932.

May 19 *Music in the Air*. See NY premiere, 1932.

May 26 *Wild Decembers* (L—Apollo—Drama). Clemence Dane's life of the Brontes features Emlyn Williams, Diana Wynyard, Thea Hold, and Ralph Richardson.

June 6 *Clear All Wires*. See NY premiere, 1932.

June 13 *Eight Bells*. (L—Duchess—Drama). Percy Mandley's nautical tale features Kathleen O'Regan. The show runs six months.

June 14 *Proscenium* (L—Globe—Drama). Ivor Novello writes and is featured in this play with a cast including Joan Barry and Fay Compton. The show runs seven months.

July 11 *Other People's Lives* (L—Wyndham's—Drama). *A.A.* Milne's play has Maurice Evans as Arnold Waite. Leonora Corbett, Lawrence Hanray, and Kathleen Harrison are in the company, which is directed by Maxwell Wray.

Sep 5 *The Distaff Side* (L—Apollo—Drama). John Van Druten's play is about five different kinds of women and the problems the new sexual and social freedoms have brought them. Sybil Thorndike, Martita Hunt, and Dorothy Holmes-Gore are featured. It runs 102 performances. On Sep 25, 1934, the show opens at New York's Booth with Thorndike, and Mildred Natwick among the cast. It runs 19 weeks.

Sep 14 *Sheppy* (L—Wyndham's—Drama). W. Somerset Maugham's play about a barber who wins the sweepstakes and tries to share the money with the poor features Angela Baddeley, Ralph Richardson, and Eric Portman. On April 19, 1944, it opens at New York's Playhouse with Edmund Gwenn. It runs just three weeks.

Sep 19 *A Sleeping Clergyman* (L—Piccadilly—Drama). Godfrey Baxter plays the title-role in James Bridie's play, which features Phyllis Shand, Ernest Thesiger, and Robert Donat. The production runs 29 weeks.

Oct 6 *Nymph Errant* (L—Adelphi—Musical). Cole Porter's music and lyrics are combined with a book by Romney Brent to produce this show that runs for five months. Gertrude Lawrence, Betty Hare, and May Agate are in the large cast.

Oct 18 *The Wind and the Rain* (L—St. Martin's—Comedy). Merton Hodge's play about a medical student who must choose between two women features Celia Johnson, Judy Gunn, Margaret Moffat, and Robert Harris. The show wins 1,001 performances.

Nov 2 *Gay Divorce.* See NY premiere, 1932.

Nov 16 *Please* (L—Savoy—Revue). Dion Titheradge and Robert MacGunigle provide book and lyrics and Vivian Ellis and Austin Groom-Johnson the music for this revue with Beatrice Lillie. It runs 108 performances.

Nov 25 *On the Rocks* (L—Winter Garden—Comedy). George Bernard Shaw's play features Lewis Casson, Walter Hudd, and Fay Davis, among others. It does not have a long run, with only 41 showings.

Nov 28 *Laburnum Grove* (L—Duchess—Comedy). J.B. Priestley's play reveals a man who, tired of his family's complaints, confesses that he is a counterfeiter. The production runs 42 weeks. On Jan 14, 1935, it opens at New York's Booth with Edmund Gwenn in the lead. There are 131 performances.

Dec 8 *Escape Me Never* (L—Apollo—Drama). Margaret Kennedy's play, about a woman totally devoted to her lover, features Elizabeth Bergner and Hugh Sinclair. It has 320 performances.

Dec 21 *The Old Folks at Home* (L—Queen's—Drama). H.M. Harwood's play features W. Graham-Browne and Marie Tempest. The production wins 204 performances.

the scene of Bertolt Brecht's adaptation of John Gay's *The Beggar's Opera,* called *The Threepenny Opera,* with Kurt Weill's score. Robert Chisholm and Steffi Duna are featured. The show runs for 12 performances. The *News* calls the show "sugar-coated communism" while the *Evening Post* says it is "appallingly stupid."

April 17 This spring is the first time the Shakespeare Memorial Theatre in Stratford-upon-Avon has had a continuous season, running through the summer until Sep 9. *Much Ado About Nothing* opens the festival, with Rachel Kempson as Hero. She also appears as Ophelia in *Hamlet.* Theodore Komisarjevsky stages *Macbeth* and *The Merchant of Venice.* Tyrone Guthrie stages *Richard II, Coriolanus, As You Like It, Romeo and Juliet,* and *The Taming of the Shrew* are given.

May 8 New York's Theatre Guild presents W. Somerset Maugham's adaptation of Luigi Chiarelli's Italian drama *The Mask and the Face.* Leo G. Carroll, Shirley Booth, Humphrey Bogart and Judith Anderson are in the cast. It runs five weeks.

May 27 Gerald Du Maurier stars in a revival of Victorien Sardou's French drama, *Diplomacy,* at London's Prince's Theatre.

June 21 Nigel Playfair, Angela Baddeley, and Glen Byam Shaw are featured in this revival of Edmond Rostand's *The Fantasticks* at London's Lyric.

July 6 *The Drunkard,* a 19th century temperance melodrama, opens in Los Angeles at the Theatre Mart, revived by Galt Bell and James and Mildred Ilse. The production becomes a local institution, joined in 1953 by *The Wayward Way,* a musical version. The show runs for 26 years and 9,477 performances before closing on Oct 17, 1959.

Sep 3 The Dublin Gate Theatre launches its seventh season with Sears' *Grania of the Ships.* Other plays include *Yahoo,* by the Earl of Longford, Wilde's *The Importance of Being Earnest*—with Micheal macLiammoir and Cyril Cusak in the male leads, Shakespeare's *Richard III,* Ibanez' *Blood and Sand,* Le Fanu's *Carmilla* (revival), and on Dec 26, Shakespeare's *A Midsummer Night's Dream.*

Sep 18 At the Old Vic Theatre in London, Tyrone Guthrie stages *Twelfth Night,* with Lydia Lopokova, Ursula Jeans, and Athene Seyler. On Oct 9, Chekhov's *The Cherry Orchard,* translated by Herbert Butler and staged by Guthrie, is animated by Charles Laughton, Flora Robson and Elsa Lanchester. On Dec 4, *Measure for Measure* is revived in a Guthrie staging, with Laughton, and Flora Robson.

Oct 4 John Martin Harvey stars in this revival of *The Bells* at London's Savoy Theatre.

Oct 16 Lawrence Langner's verse version of Moliere's comic classic, *The School for Husbands* premieres at New York's Em-

---

1933   REVIVALS/REPERTORIES

Jan 8 At London's Arts Theatre John Fernald stages three one-act plays, two of them American: Susan Glaspell's *Suppressed Desires* and Thornton Wilder's *The Long Christmas Dinner.* On Jan 11, Lennox Robinson stages Paul Vincent Carroll's *Things That Are Caesar's.* On Jan 26, the Welsh National Theatre produces Richard Hughes's *The Comedy of Good and Evil.*

Jan 17 At the Dublin Gate Theatre, the sixth season continues with Flecker's *Don Juan,* followed by a revival of Cassella's *Death Takes a Holiday.* Other plays include Aeschylus' *Agamemnon,* Bernard Shaw's *Heartbreak House,* Su Ting Po's *Princely Fortune,* Mannings's *Storm Over Wicklow,* Sheridan's *St. Patrick's Day,* Christine, Countess of Longford's *Mr. Jiggins of Jigginstown,* macLiammoir's *The Ford of the Hurdles* (revival), Tocher's *A Bride for the Unicorn* (Tocher-Johnston), and Shairp's *The Crime at Blossoms,* which is the final production of the season, opening on May 23. As usual, Hilton Edwards stages and Micheal mac-

Liammoir designs.

Feb 13 Peggy Ashcroft appears in John Drinkwater's *Mary Stuart,* revived at London's Old Vic.

Feb 21 New York's Theatre Guild produces George O'Neil's *American Dream,* about the American promise gone sour. Gale Sondergaard, Claude Rains, and Helen Westley are in the cast.

Feb 27 The Negro Theatre Guild in New York produces J. Augustus Smith's *Louisiana,* showing the conflict between Christianity and voodoo.

March 6 Eva LeGallienne revives Chekhov's *The Cherry Orchard* at Broadway's New Amsterdam. It receives 30 performances.

March 27 Sheridan's *The School for Scandal* is revived at London's Old Vic with Alaistair Sim, Anthony Quayle, and Peggy Ashcroft in the cast. On May 1, Sheridan's *The Rivals* is given at London's Embassy Theatre.

April 13 New York's Empire Theatre is

pire Theatre. Osgood Perkins and June Walker are featured. This Theatre Guild production runs nearly 15 weeks.

Nov 6 At London's Phoenix Theatre, Fabia Drake and Joyce Carey are Rosalind and Celia in this revival of Shakespeare's *As You Like It*. The following evening, at Sadler's Wells, *Henry VIII* is revived, staged by Tyrone Guthrie, with Charles Laughton.

Nov 17 Noel Coward revives his *Hay Fever* at London's Shaftesbury Theatre.

Nov 27 Maxwell Anderson's new historical play *Mary of Scotland*, wins the Pulitzer Prize, with Helen Hayes as the queen. Philip Merivale is her Bothwell. In its initial engagement for the Theatre Guild, the play enjoys a 31-week run at New York's Alvin Theatre.

Dec 20 At London's Westminster Theatre, *Alice and Thomas and Jane* opens, beginning the season of holiday shows for children of various ages. The next day, Wyndham's Theatre opens *What Happened to George*. Other plays on succeeding days include *Alice in Wonderland* (Duke of York's), *Beau Brummell* (Saville), *Where the Rainbow Ends* (Holborn Empire), *Lilac Time* (Alhambra), *When Knights Were Bold* (Fortune), *Charley's Aunt* (Gaiety), *Alf's Button* (Kingsway), *Peter Pan* (Palladium), *Toad of Toad Hall* (Royalty), *Hansel and Gretel* (Cambridge), *Treasure Island* (Comedy), *Queen of Hearts* (Lyceum), *Buckies' Bears* (Playhouse), *Daddy Long-Legs* (Victoria Palace), *Aladdin* (Embassy), *The Three Musketeers* (Q), and *Uncle Tom's Cabin* (Gate).

the Ziegfeld Theatre.

Sep 11 At London's Queen's Theatre, *First Episode* is tried out, the work of a new young playwright from whom much will later be heard: Terence Rattigan, who's collaborated with Philip Heimann on the script. Later, the play is shown in the West End.

Sep 24 American publisher and producer Horace Liveright (b. 1886) dies in New York City. Liveright was one of the first producers to take an interest in the plays of Eugene O'Neill. Among his productions were *An American Tragedy*, *Dracula*, and *The Dagger and the Rose*. In 1930 Liveright became an adviser to Paramount Studios.

Oct 10 Daniel Massey is born in London, England, to actors Raymond and Adrianne (Allen) Massey.

Dec 7 American producer Adolph Klauber (b. 1879) dies in Louisville, Kentucky. Klauber held the post of drama critic of the *NY Times* from 1906–18, after which he devoted himself to theatrical production. Eugene O'Neill's *The Emperor Jones* and *Diff'rent* were among his contributions. He was also associated with his wife, actress Jane Cowl, in her productions.

1933   BIRTHS/DEATHS/DEBUTS

Jan 20 Stage and screen actress Lee Grant makes her stage debut in Franco Leoni's one-act opera, *L'Oracolo*, at the Metropolitan Opera House in New York.

Jan 22 American theatrical agent Elizabeth Marbury (b. 1856) dies in New York at age 76. Marbury handled the American productions of the plays of Sardou, Shaw, Wilde, Barrie, and others. In 1914 she incorporated her business as the American Play Company. Marbury published her autobiography, *My Crystal Ball*, in 1923.

Jan 31 English dramatist-novelist John Galsworthy (b. 1867) dies in Hampstead, England. Galsworthy entered the theatre in 1906, when George Bernard Shaw's play of social discussion were attracting attention. His first play, *The Silver Box*, was produced in 1906. It was Galsworthy's succeeding dramas, *Joy*, *Strife*, and *Justice*, however, that established him as a serious playwright.

Feb 27 English actor and music hall performer Arthur Roberts (b. 1852) is dead. After a distinguished career as a music hall singer, Roberts devoted himself to the playing of numerous sketches in variety theatres from 1914 to the 1920s. He published his reminiscences in 1895 and another volume, *Fifty Years of Spoof* in 1927.

April 8 English actress Cicely Richards is dead at age 83. Richards was a member of London's Vaudeville Company from 1874 to 1882. She played in nearly all the leading West End theatres and toured America with Olga Nethersole. In 1904–05 she toured with Beerbohm Tree's Shakespearean Company playing Mistress Page in *The Merry Wives of Windsor* and Maria in *Twelfth Night*.

May 25 Future actress Sarah Marshall is born to actors Herbert Marshall and Edna Best.

July 10 Architect and scene designer Joseph Urban dies at age 61 in New York. Born in Vienna, Urban emigrated to the United States in 1911 and was naturalized in 1917. He served as scene designer for the Metropolitan Opera and for the *Ziegfeld Follies*, as well as architect of

1933   THEATERS/PRODUCTIONS

April 23 Ottawa, Canada hosts the first Dominion Drama Festival, under the patronage of Governor General Lord Bessborough. Funded through donations, including $2,500 from the Massey Foundation, the Festival brings together outstanding local productions from across Canada.

Summer In Canada, the town of Banff—in the heart of a great national park and on the shores of Lake Louise—is host to a "Summer School in the Arts Related to the Theatre." The program is to develop into The Banff Centre for Continuing Education as well as the Banff Festival of the Arts, held each summer.

June 5 The Open Air Theatre in London's Regents Park opens with *Twelfth Night*. Sydney W. Carroll and Lewis Schauerein are managing this 1,200-seat theatre.

June 10 In the depths of the Great Depression, the Barter Theatre opens in Abingdon, Virginia. Founder Robert Porterfield, a native son, has assembled a company of unemployed actors to present John Golden's *After Tomorrow* as the premiere production. Audience members barter such things as country hams, eggs, pickles, a rooster, and a devils' food cake for admission. Tickets cost 35 cents or the equivalent. In 1946, the Barter will become the official theatre of the State of Virginia, a solidly established institution in a country town.

June 15 Despite the rigors of the Depression, the 1932–33 Broadway season claims 180 new productions, 110 of them dramatic. Burns Mantle notes this is 15 or 16 less than last season and 50 to 60 less than in the booming Twenties. There are more failures this season, attributable to many causes, with cash shortages, producer's inexperience, and good playwrights being lured to Hollywood cited as main reasons. Half Broadway's theatres have been empty all season; only half the actors are working. Of the 50 revivals, most are returns of successful shows from the past few seasons, priced at $1 top in many cases. Audiences who hadn't been able to afford Broadway shows in recent years return to the theatres. Mantle's choice of annual ten *Best Plays* for the Broadway season are: Anderson's *Both Your Houses*, Kaufman and Ferber's *Dinner at Eight*, Crothers' *When Ladies Meet*, Coward's *Design for Living*, Behrman's *Biography*, Howard's *Alien Corn* and his *The Late Christopher Bean*, Rice's *We, the People*, Cohan's *Pigeons and People*, and Hagan's *One Sunday Afternoon*. *Both Your Houses* also wins the Pulitzer Prize.

Sep 9 At Stratford-upon-Avon, the first continuous spring and summer season in the new Shakespeare Memorial Theatre closes after having entertained a record 133,705 spectators.

Jan 4 *The Ziegfeld Follies* (NY—Winter Garden—Revue). This edition is Florenz Ziegfeld in name only, thanks to Billie Burke Zeigfeld who has some posthumous debts to pay. The Shuberts are behind this, with Fannie Brice introducing the character of Baby Snooks. Most of the music by by Vernon Duke. The show runs for 23 weeks.

Jan 8 *Days Without End* (NY—Henry Miller—Drama). The Theatre Guild produces what is described as a "modern miracle play" by Eugene O'Neill. Using devices from *The Great God Brown* and *Strange Interlude*, he has his hero, John, played by two actors. Earle Larimore is the real man, an embittered atheist. Stanley Ridge plays John's baser self, concerned only with physical love and indulgence. This character uses a mask and speaks the silent thoughts of John's lower nature. When his wife learns of his infidelity, she sickens unto death, recovering only when John rediscovers his lost faith and his baser self dies. Seven weeks are all this show can muster. Catholic critics praise it. On Feb 3, 1935, the Stage Society presents this play at London's Grafton Theatre. Lewis Casson directs a cast including Henry Daniell, Harcourt Williams, Iris Baker, and Marjorie Clayton.

Jan 16 *Wednesday's Child* (NY—Longacre—Drama). Frank Thomas, Jr. plays the child in Leopold Atlas's play about a boy torn between his divorced parents. Although Burns Mantle calls this one of his *Best Plays*, the show lasts only 95 performances.

Jan 23 *No More Ladies* (NY—Booth—Comedy). A.E. Thomas's play, examining the question is marriage worth the effort, features Melvyn Douglas, Ruth Watson, Sheridan Warren, and Marcia Townsend. The show runs five months.

Jan 30 *All the King's Horses* (NY—Shubert—Musical). Edward Horan writes the score for this musical about a man who trades places with a king. Guy Robertson is featured. The show runs 15 weeks.

Feb 13 *The Shining Hour* (NY—Booth—Drama). Keith Winter's story of a love triangle features Gladys Cooper, Adrianne Allen, and Raymond Massey. It has 121 performances. On Sep 4, 1934, it opens at London's St. James's with the same cast. Here it wins 213 performances.

Feb 14 *Richard of Bordeaux.* See L premiere, 1932.

Feb 24 *Dodsworth* (NY—Shubert—Comedy). Disney Howard adapts Sinclair Lewis's novel. Walter Huston is the title role, with Fay Bainter and Nan Sunderland. There are 131 performances.

March 6 *Yellow Jack* (NY—Martin Beck—Drama). Sidney Howard's adaptation of the chapter in Paul DeKruif's *Microbe*

Dodsworth

Hunters, dealing with Walter Reed's work on Yellow Fever, has John Miltern as Reed. Although the play is admired, it runs only 10 weeks.

March 10 *The Drunkard* (NY—American Music Hall—Drama). This venerable melodrama, supposedly first staged by P. T. Barnum in 1843 in his American Museum in New York, has been found in 1926 in some old manuscripts in Berkeley, California. It runs a total of 277 performances. On Nov 26, the old play is revived in London at the Garrick Theatre, with Robert Lang as the villain.

March 15 *New Faces* (NY—Fulton—Revue). Charles Dillingham produces Leonard Sillman's show, designed to show off new talent. The cast includes Henry Fonda, Imogene Coca, Nancy Hamilton, and Sillman. The show, which has been premiered at the Pasadena Playhouse as *Low and Behold*, runs 149 performances.

April 18 *Stevedore* (NY—Civic Repertory—Drama). George Sklar and Paul Peters win 111 performances for their play about the ugliness of racism among the poor. Millicent Green and Jack Carter are featured. It runs for 110 performances. On May 6, 1935, it opens at London's Embassy Theatre. The production is notable for the presence of Paul Robeson, who plays Lonnie Thompson.

April 19 *Are You Decent?* (NY—Ambassador—Comedy). Playwright Crane Wilbur imagines a liberated young woman who wants to have a baby without marriage. The show runs 188 performances.

Aug 27 *Life Begins at 8:40* (NY—Winter Garden—Revue). The title parodies the best-seller, *Life Begins at Forty*, and the comics include Bert Lahr and Luella Gear. Ray Bolger's dancing is a feature as well. This Shubert show, which began as another edition of the *Follies*, enjoys a run of 237 performances. Harold Arlen provides the score, with lyrics by Ira Gershwin and E. Y. Harburg.

Sep 8 *Kill That Story* (NY—Booth—Comedy). James Bell plays Duke Devlin, a tough newspaperman who exposes his crooked publisher as the cause of a poor stenographer's suicide, to convince his own ex-wife of his innocence. Harry Madden and Philip Dunning's melodrama, staged by George Abbott, wins 117 performances.

Sep 12 *Judgment Day* (NY—Belasco—Drama). Elmer Rice produces and stages his play about a conspiracy trial in Southeastern Europe. Josephine Victor and Walter Greaza play the revolutionaries who are being framed. The production—designed by Aline Bernstein—lasts almost 12 weeks.

Sep 17 *First Episode.* See L premiere, 1934.

Sep 22 *The Great Waltz* (NY—Center—Musical). Hassard Short's staging of this operetta, based on the music and some incidents from the lives of Johann Strauss, father and son, plays over 37 weeks. Guy Robertson and Marion Claire play Johann, Jr., and his love. Adapted by Moss Hart, the show costs $250,000 using the Cener's modern machinery to effect transformations of Albert Johnson's scenes in full view of the audience.

Sep 25 *The Distaff Side.* See L premiere, 1933.

Sep 26 *Small Miracle* (NY—Golden—Drama). Norman Krasna's melodrama, with Ilka Chase, Myron McCormick, and Lucille Strudwick, runs for 117 performances.

Sep 29 *Merrily We Roll Along* (NY—Music Box—Drama). George S. Kaufman and Moss Hart collaborate on this story of a playwright who is an artistic rut at 40. Kenneth MacKenna leads the cast. The show runs over 19 weeks.

Oct 1 *The First Legion* (NY—46th Street—Drama). Emmet Lavery's story of a crisis of faith among several Jesuit fathers features Whitford Kane, Pedro de Cordoba, Bert Lytell, and Charles Coburn. It runs for 112 performances. On July 28, 1937, the show premieres at London's Daly's Theatre with Kim Peacock, Charles V. France, Franklin Dyall and Colin Keith-Johnston. It earns 102 showings.

Oct 5 *Lost Horizons* (NY—St. James—Drama). Harry Seall's script about a woman who, having committed suicide, discovers how she could have helped the lives of others, features Jane Wyatt. Burns Mantle selects it as a *Best Play*, although it runs only seven weeks.

Oct 17 *Personal Appearance* (NY—Henry Miller—Comedy). Lawrence Rile's play tells of a film star who nearly runs off with a local garage-man. Gladys George and Philip Ober are featured. There are over 500 performances.

Oct 22 *Within the Gates* (NY—National—Drama). Sean O'Casey's symbolic drama of various hurt humans expounding their problems in a visionary Hyde Park baffles some critics and audiences. In two engagements, separated by a brief tour, it wins only 141 performances. Melvyn Douglas stages.

Oct 23 *Conversation Piece.* See L premiere, 1934.

Oct 25 *Between Two Worlds* (NY—Belasco—Drama). Elmer Rice's indictment of the parisitism of the capitalist class features Rachel Hartzel and Joseph Schildkraut. It runs for four weeks.

Oct 30 *The Farmer Takes a Wife* (NY—46th Street—Comedy). Marc Connelly and Frank Elser have written this comedy about a farmer who wants to marry a cook who won't leave Eire Canal. Henry Fonda is featured. The show runs only 104 performances, but is chosen as a *Best Play*.

Nov 7 *Dark Victory* (NY—Plymouth—Drama). Tallulah Bankhead appears in George Brewer and Bertram Boch's story of a woman with only six months to live. The show has just over six weeks to live.

Nov 20 *The Children's Hour* (NY—Maxine Elliott—Drama). Lillian Hellman's vital play about the results of lying and character assassination features Katherine Emery, Anne Revere, and Florence McGee. It is a contender for the Pulitzer Prize but is passed over because of the muted issue of lesbianism. The play is a sensation, running for 691 performances. Beginning Nov 12, 1936 it is seen briefly at London's Gate Theatre with Ursula Jeans and Valerie Taylor.

Nov 21 *Anything Goes* (NY—Alvin—Musical). Cole Porter provides the music and lyrics for a book by Bolton, Wodehouse, Lindsay, and Crouse. Songs include "Blow, Gabriel, Blow," "You're the Top," "All Through the Night" and "I Get a Kick Out of You." The show runs over a year with Ethel Merman, William Gaxton, and Victor Moore featured. In later decades it will be seen as the essence of the '30s musical. On June 14, 1935, it opens in London with Jeanne Aubert, Richard Clarke, and Jack Whiting. It has 261 showings.

Nov 28 *Revenge With Music* (NY—New Amsterdam—Musical). Charles Winninger, Libby Holman, George Metaxa, and Ilka Chase are featured in this story of a groom who takes revenge on a Spanish provincial governor, trying to seduce his bride, by wooing the governor's lady. Howard Dietz and Arthur Schwartz provide the score, which includes "You And The Night And The Music." The show runs nearly five months.

Dec 4 *Post Road* (NY—Masque—Comedy). Wilbur Daniel Steele and Norma Mitchell's play tells of a rooming-house operator who realizes that some guests are kidnappers. Lucile Watson is featured. There are 212 performances.

Dec 10 *Sailors of Cattaro.* See L premiere, 1934.

Dec 21 *Ode to Liberty* (NY—Lyceum—Comedy). Ina Claire plays a woman who tries to help a Communist who has shot at Hitler. Walter Slezak is featured. The show runs nine weeks.

Dec 25 *Accent on Youth* (NY—Plymouth—Comedy). Nicholas Hannen and Constance Cummings are featured in Samson Raphaelson's story of an older man who loves a young woman. It runs nearly 29 weeks.

Dec 27 *Thumbs Up* (NY—St. James—Revue). "Autumn in New York" and "Zing Went the Strings of My Heart" are two hits from this show, produced by Eddie Dowling, with an ensemble including Dowling, Ray Dooley, Bobby Clark, Jack Cole, and Eunice Healy. The show runs nearly five months.

1934 BRITISH PREMIERES

Jan 3 *Reunion in Vienna.* See NY premiere, 1931.

Jan 23 *Saturday's Children.* See NY premiere, 1927.

Jan 26 *First Episode* (L—Comedy—Comedy). Terence Rattigan and Philip Heimann write this story of a young student and his brief affair with an actress. Max Adrian and Merial Forbes are in the cast. On Sep 17, the show opens at New York's Ritz Theatre with John Halloran and Leona Maricle. It runs five weeks.

Feb 1 *Mr. Whittington* (L—London Hippodrome—Musical). Jack Buchanan stages and plays the title-role of the fabled Lord Mayor of London. The book is the work of Clifford Grey, Greatrex Newman, and Douglas Furber, with music by John Green, Jack Waller, and Joseph Tunbridge. The show runs 37 weeks.

Feb 16 *Conversation Piece* (L—His Majesty's—Comedy). Noel Coward's comedy about a French duke who hopes to marry off a cabaret singer to a rich Englishman so they can both live well wins 177 performances. Coward heads the cast. On Oct 23, it opens at New York's 44th Street Theatre, again with Coward in the lead. There are only 55 performances.

Feb 28 *The Golden Toy* (L—Coliseum—Musical). Dion Titheradge writes the book and lyrics for this show, which is based on Carl Zuckmayer's romantic German play. The music is by Robert Schumann. Peggy Ashcroft, Ernest Thesiger and Wendy Toye are in the cast. It runs 23 weeks.

March 7 *Nurse Cavell* (L—Vaudeville—Drama). C. S. Forester and C.E.B. Roberts write this story of the martyr World War I nurse. Nancy Price plays the title-role.

March 21 *Double Door.* See NY premiere, 1933.

March 31 *Sporting Love* (L—Gaiety—Musical). This Stanley Lupino-written show wins 302 performances, with Lupino both in the company and directing.

April 2 *Libel!* (L—Playhouse—Drama). Produced by Leon M. Lion, this script credited to Ward Dorane has a 33 week run, with a cast including Nigel Playfair, Aubrey Mather, Frances Doble, and Malcolm Keen. On Dec 20, 1935, Otto Ludwig Preminger stages *Libel* for producer Gilbert Miller at his father's theatre, the Henry Miller, in New York for a five-month run. Colin Clive plays Sir Mark Loddon, shell-shocked in the Great War and accused of being an imposter.

April 4 *Sixteen* (L—Criterion—Drama). Aimee and Philip Stuart's play, first seen in March at the Embassy Theatre, earns a run of nearly six months. Antoinette Cellier and Godfrey Tearle are featured.

April 8 *Sailors of Cattaro* (L—Phoenix—Drama). The Left Theatre presents Friedrich Wolfe's anti-war play. Among the cast are Ben Weldon, Alfred Atkins and Aubrey Menon. On Dec 10, it comes to New York's Civic Repertory with George

Tobias, Howard da Silva, and Tom Powers are in the cast. This Theatre Union production runs three months.

April 10 *Counsellor-at-Law.* See NY premiere, 1931.

April 24 *Why Not Tonight? L—Palace—Revue).* Ord Hamilton writes most of the music for this revue with Florence Desmond, Polly Luce, Nelson Keys, and Betty Hare among the cast. There are 136 performances.

April 25 *Biography.* See NY premiere. 1932.

May 16 *Touch Wood (L—Haymarket—Comedy).* Flora Robson, Ian Hunter, and Marie Ney are featured in C.L. Anthony's play, which earns 213 performances.

May 29 *Vintage Wine (L—Daly's—Drama).* Ashley Dukes and director Seymour Hicks adapt Alexander Engel's original version for a run of 215 performances.

June 7 *Living Dangerously (L—Strand—Drama).* Godfrey Tearle, Carol Goodner, and Allen Aynesworth are featured in this play by Reginald Simpson and Frank Gregory. It runs for 25 weeks.

June 8 *Queen of Scots (L—New—Drama).* Gordon Daviot writes this historical play, which earns a run of 106 performances. Gwen Ffrangcon-Davies plays the proud queen, with Felix Aylmer as her half-brother James Stuart and Margaret Webster as Mary Beaton. Laurence Olivier is her Bothwell.

June 28 *Men in White.* See NY premiere, 1933.

July 4 *The Maitlands (L—Wyndham's—Drama).* Theodore Komisarjevsky directs Ronald Mackenzie's play, featuring John Gielgud. The production runs 141 performances.

Aug 6 *Admirals All (L—Shaftesbury—Comedy).* Clive Currie, Laura La Plante, and Diana Beaumont are featured in this play by Ian Hay and Stephen King-Hall. It runs 192 performances.

Aug 22 *Family Affairs (L—Ambassadors'—Drama).* Gertrude Jenning's play features Lilian Braithwaite. It runs 349 performances.

Aug 25 *Blackbirds of 1934 (L—Coliseum—Revue).* Lew Leslie's show has such talents as Bessie Dudley, Blue McAllister, the Famous Blackbird Choir, and the Blackbird Beauty Chorus. The show has 193 performances. *The Times* is not pleased with the singing but praises the dancing which it calls "an abundant rattle of the first quality." On Dec 20, *Blackbirds of 1935* opens at the Coliseum.

Sep 5 *Murder in Mayfair (L—Globe—Drama).* Ivor Novello's play is adorned by Novello in the role of Jacques Clavel. The production runs five months.

Sep 10 *Young England (L—Victoria Palace—Drama).* Walter Reynold's modern patriotic melodrama involving a cross-section of older Britons and decent young Englishmen wins a cult-following of those amused by the play's wholesome earnestness. The show has 278 performances.

Sep 13 *Eden End (L—Duchess—Drama).* J.B. Priestley's story of a woman who tries to give up the theatre and live in an English village features Ralph Richardson, Alison Leggatt, and Beatrix Lehmann, among others. On Oct 21, 1935, the play comes to New York's Masque with Estelle Winwood in the lead. The production runs three weeks.

Sep 27 *Yes, Madam? (L—Hippodrome—Musical).* Waller and Tunbridge write the music and Weston and Lee the lyrics for this show based on a novel by K.R.G. Browne. Binnie Hale, Bobby Howes, and Billy Leonard are featured. The production has 302 performances.

Sep 28 *Streamline (L—Palace—Revue).* Vivian Ellis provides the score and A.P. Herbert the lyrics for this story by Ronald Jeans. Florence Desmond, Tilly Losch, and Kyra Nijinsky are in the cast. The show runs 22 weeks.

Oct 3 *Hi-Diddle-Diddle (L—Comedy—Revue).* William Walker and Robert Nesbitt provide the sketches and songs for this show which runs nearly 25 weeks.

Oct 5 *Hyde Park Corner (L—Apollo—Drama).* Walter Hackett's play earns a run of almost 31 weeks. In the company are Godfrey Tearle, Gordon Harker, Marion Lorne, and Mervyn Johns.

Oct 23 *Theatre Royal.* See NY premiere (*The Royal Family*) 1927.

Oct 31 *Sweet Aloes (L—Wyndham's—Drama).* Tyrone Guthrie directs Jay Mallory's play about a woman whose illegitimate child is raised by others. Margaret Webster, Diana Wynyard and Joyce Carey are featured. There are 476 performances.

Nov 20 *Flowers of the Forest (L—Whitehall—Drama).* John Van Druten's play about the effects of World War I on a woman features Gwen Ffrangeon-Davies, Lewis Casson, and Marda Vanne. It opens at the Martin Beck in New York on April 8, 1935, with Katharine Cornell starring. The show runs five weeks.

Nov 22 *The Greeks Had a Word for It (L—Duke of York's—Comedy).* Zoe Akins' American play wins a six-month run, staged by A. R. Whatmore. Hermione and Angela Baddeley are Polaire and Schatze. Robert Newton plays Boris Feldman.

Dec 19 *Jill Darling! (L—Saville—Musical).* Mariott Edgar and Desmond Carter provide the book and Vivian Ellis the score for this show which earns 242 performances. Frances Day is in the title-role.

1934   REVIVALS/REPERTORIES

Jan 16 *Wuthering Heights* opens the new year at the Dublin Gate Theatre, but it is only a continuance of the current seventh season. Hilton Edwards directs, and Micheal macLiammoir designs. Other plays include *Storm Song*, by E. W. Tocher, later describes this failure as "more of a burp than a song"; Molnar's *Liliom*, Shaw's *Dark Lady of the Sonnets*, Christine, Countess of Longford's *The New Girl*, O'Neill's *Before Breakfast*, Rowley's *Apollo in Mourne*, Shakespeare's *Hamlet*, Winsloe's *Children in Uniform*, Manning's *Happy Family*, with season's end revivals in May of Johnston's *The Old Lady Says "No!"* and *Happy Family*.

Jan 27 At London's Alhambra Theatre, Shakespeare's *Henry V* has Godfrey Tearle as the heroic young king and Yvonne Arnaud as Princess Katharine of France. On Feb 20, Tearle plays Marc Antony in *Julius Caesar*, with Basil Gill as Brutus. On March 14, Gill is Antonio in *The Merchant of Venice*, with Franklin Dyall as Shylock and Marie Ney as Portia.

Feb 5 At London's Old Vic Theatre, Oscar Wilde's *The Importance of Being Earnest*, is staged by Tyrone Guthrie. On March 6 Congreve's *Love for Love* is revived, staged by Guthrie also. Charles Laughton plays Tattle, with Flora Robson as Mrs. Foresight. This duo impersonate the ambitious Scots in *Macbeth* on April 2.

Feb 7 O'Casey's symbolic drama, *Within the Gates*, is shown in London at the Royalty Theatre. At the Little Theatre on March 1, O'Casey's *Juno and the Paycock* is revived.

Feb 21 The Theatre Guild produces John Wexley's *They Shall Not Die*, a drama about the plight of the Scottsboro Boys. Some critics term it a propaganda play.

Feb 26 From Paris and their Théâtre du Vieux-Colombier, come Jacques Copeau's Compagnie des Quinze to London's New Theatre, to play Andre Obey's *Don Juan*. Pierre Fresnay has the title-role.

March 8 At London's Prince's Theatre, Paul Kester's historical romance, *Sweet Nell of Old Drury*, is revived. Phyllis Neilson-Terry plays Nell.

April 15 Donald Wolfit appears in Henrik Ibsen's *The Master Builder* in this revival at London's Westminister Theatre. On May 13 a revival of Dryden's *Aureng-Zebe* takes the stage with Hubert Langley in the title role.

April 16 *The Tempest* opens this year's season of Shakespearean productions in Stratford-upon-Avon at the Shakespeare Memorial Theatre. In this last season under the direction of W. Bridges Adams, *A Midsummer Night's Dream* is the "birthday play." Other plays presented include *Twelfth Night, Much Ado About Nothing, Julius Caesar, Henry V, Romeo and Juliet*, and *Love's Labour's Lost*.

May 3 At London's Sadler's Wells Theatre, Harley Granville Barker's *The Voysey Inheritance* is revived, staged by the author and Harcourt Williams, who plays Trenchard Voysey, K.C.

May The summer season of plays in the Open Air Theatre in London's Regent's Park begins with Shakespeare's *As You Like It*, staged by Robert Atkins, with John Drinkwater as the wicked duke and Anna Neagle as Rosalind, May 28 sees a revival of *Twelfth Night*, with Neagle as Olivia and Drinkwater as Malvolio. Jack Hawkins is Orsino. *The Tempest* is shown on June 5; Drinkwater is Prospero; a young actress named Greer Garson plays Iris. On June 12, *The Comedy of Errors* opens, with Philip Ben Greet as Aegeon. June 19 is the day of *A Midsummer Night's Dream's* opening, with Martita Hunt as Helena and Phyllis Neilson-Terry as Oberon. *Richard III* is played on June 26, with Peter Glenville in the title-role. George Bernard Shaw's *The Six of Calais*, staged by Maxwell Wray, opens on July 17, with Hubert Gregg as the Black Prince and Garson as a court lady. *Androcles and the Lion* is on the bill as well. *Romeo and Juliet* is played on August 7; Ben Greet is Friar Laurence.

June 19 At the Little Theatre, in London, George Bernard Shaw's *Village Wooing* is paired in premiere with John Galsworthy's *The Little Man*.

Sep 3 London's famed D'Oyly Carte Opera Company visits Broadway for 15 weeks at the Martin Beck Theatre, with such performers as Martyn Green, Sydney Granville, Derek Oldham, Leslie Rands, Muriel Dickson, Dorothy Gill, Kathleen Frances, and Marjorie Eyre. The Gilbert & Sullivan repertory is *The Gondoliers, Cox and Box, Iolanthe, The Pirates of Penzance, H. M. S. Pinafore, Trial by Jury, The Mikado, Princess Ida, Ruddigore, Patience*, and *The Yeoman of the Guard*.

Sep 4 *The Shining Hour.* See NY premiere, 1934.

Sep 17 At London's Old Vic Theatre, Shakespeare's *Antony and Cleopatra* is revived, staged by Henry Cass, with Wilfrid Lawson and Mary Newcombe in the title-roles. On Oct 15, Maurice Evans plays Richard II. On Nov 5, Cass stages *Much Ado About Nothing*, with Evans and Newcombe as Benedick and Beatrice. Shaw's *Saint Joan* opens on Nov 26, with Newcombe as the Maid and Evans as the Dauphin.

Sep 18 Max Reinhardt's Greek Theatre production of Shakespeare's *A Midsummer Night's Dream* in Los Angeles is described in the *Los Angeles Times* as using 4,000 arc lights, myriad flaming torches, and a 350-foot bridge along which Puck— played by 13-year-old Mickey Rooney—

makes his "quicksilver" moves. 150,000 people see the seven performances. The entire Los Angeles Philharmonic plays the Mendelssohn score. Later, Reinhardt will make his only Hollywood film of this play, based on this production.

Sep 20 At London's Winter Garden, Robert Atkins stages a revival of George Bernard Shaw's *Androcles and the Lion*, paired with Moliere's *Love is the Best Doctor.*

Sep 24 Denis Johnston's Irish play, *The Moon in the Yellow River* staged by the playwright, earns 128 performances at London's Westminister Theatre.

Oct 1 Henrik Ibsen's *An Enemy of the People* opens at London's Embassy Theatre. Eileen Thorndike has staged this revival. John Fernald stages the revival of J. M. Barrie's *Dear Brutus* on Oct 15. On Nov 19, Thorndike directs C. K. Munro's *Ding and Co.* On Dec 3, Fernald mounts *The Dominant Sex*, which wins 642 performances after a West End transfer in 1935.

Oct 5 After months of planning, the American Children's Theatre opens its production of *The Chinese Nighingale*, adapted from the tale of Hans Christian Anderson, at its Columbus Circle Theatre of Young America. After one week, the venture closes.

Oct 8 The New York Theatre Guild produces this James Bridie drama, *A Sleeping Clergyman* told in flashbacks, of the odd influences of heredity on some Scots. With only a five-week run the play doesn't even reach all the Guild's subscribers.

Oct 22 The eighth season of the Dublin Gate Theatre begins with Shakespeare's *Julius Caesar*. Other productions include Vanbrugh's *The Provok'd Wife*, Smith's *The Drunkard*, and Hsiung's *Lady Precious Stream*, a Christmas treat.

Nov 3 Eva LeGallienne stages and plays Rostand's *L'Aiglon*, adapted by Clemence Dane, with Ethel Barrymore as the Duchess of Parma. The show runs 58 performances at New York's Broadhurst Theatre. LeGallienne also offers four performances each of her Civic Repertory productions of *Cradle Song* and *Hedda Gabler.*

Nov 12 Dublin's Abbey Theatre Players return to New York with a five-week-long program of repertory at the John Golden Theatre, including Robinson's *The Far-Off Hills, Drama at Inish*, and *Church Street*; Synge's *The Playboy of the Western World, The Well of the Saints*, and *The Shadow of the Glen*; O'Casey's *Juno and the Paycock* and *The Plough and the Stars*; Yeats' *Resurrection*, Duffy's *The Coiner*, Shiels' *The New Gossoon*, and MacNamara's *Look at the Heffernans.* Barry Fitzgerald and Arthur Shields are prominent in the casts.

Nov 14 At London's New Theatre, John Gielgud appears as Hamlet in his own staging. There are 155 performances.

Nov 28 The Group Theatre presents Melvin Levy's *Gold Eagle Guy*, the saga of a sailor who gets rich through exploitation. The cast is headed by Guy Button. The production runs two months.

Dec 10 New York's Theatre Guild presents Maxwell Anderson's *Valley Forge*, a versified view of the historical event. It runs just over seven weeks.

The Children's Hour

Dec 15 At London's Holborn Empire, Christmas is off to an early start with the revival of *Where the Rainbow Ends.* On the 18th, *The Bing Boys are Here* opens at the Alhambra, followed on the 19th, by *Alice in Wonderland* (Duke of York's). In rapid succession come *A Waltz Dream* (Winter Garden), *The Ghost Train* (Criterion), *Charley's Aunt* (Daly's), *What Happened to George* (Savoy), *The Belle of New York* (Garrick), *The Luck of the Navy* (Playhouse), *When Knights Were Bold* (Fortune), *Toad of Toad Hall* (Royalty), *Cinderella* (Drury Lane), *Peter Pan* (Palladium), *Sinbad the Sailor* (Embassy), *Dick Whittington* (Lyceum, Streatham Hill), *Aladdin* (Prince Edward, Golders Green Hippodrome), *Buckie's Bears* (Scala), *Jack and the Beanstalk* (Wimbledon), *Treasure Island* (Piccadilly), *Robin Hood and the Babes in the Wood* (Victoria Palace), and *If I Were King* (Queen's).

Dec 20 Katharine Cornell's production of *Romeo and Juliet* enjoys a Broadway run of 77 performances at New York's Martin

193

Beck Theatre. Her cast includes *Orson Wells* (Tybalt), *Edith Evans* (Nurse), *Basil Rathbone* (Romeo), *Brian Aherne* (Mercutio), and *John Emery* (Benvolio). Guthrie McClintic stages and *Martha Graham* choreographs.

Dec 24 The Theatre Guild produces S.N. Behrman's *Rain From Heaven*, a polemic against fascism in Germany. It runs for 99 showings.

1934   BIRTHS/DEATHS/DEBUTS

Feb 24 Actress-singer Joan Diener is born in Cleveland, Ohio.

March 11 American actress Margaret Illington (b. 1881) dies in Miami Beach. Engaged by Daniel Frohman, Illington first appears at the Criterion Theatre in New York in 1900. Three years later she married Frohman, whom she divorced in 1909. She later toured under the management of her second husband, Major Bowes, making her last appearance in 1919.

April 11 Actor-playwright-producer Gerald du Maurier (b. 1873) dies in London. Du Maurier made his first appearance at the Garrick Theatre in 1894. His great success came in 1906 as the gentleman crook in *Raffles*. An exponent of natural acting, he was knighted in 1922. A memoir, *Gerald, a Portrait*, was published in 1934 by his daughter Daphne.

April 25 American playwright and writer Archibald MacLeish writes the libretto of the ballet, *Union Square*, at the St. James Theatre in New York.

July 2 Black playwright-producer Ed Bullins is born in Philadelphia, Pennsylvania.

July 28 Stage and screen actress Marie Dressler (b. 1869) is dead in Santa Barbara, California. Although she served a long apprenticeship to the stage, Dressler is best remembered for her work in films. At 14 she joined a succession of light opera companies, later playing vaudeville. She also appeared with Lillian Russell and her company.

Aug 30 American producer Charles Dillingham (b. 1868) dies in New York. Dillingham introduced George Bernard Shaw's *Man and Superman* to America in 1905, followed by the comedies of Frederick Lonsdale. At the height of his prosperity he had as many as six plays running at once, and although he produced over 200 plays, his career ended in bankruptcy in 1933.

Sep 5 W. (Walter) Bridges Adams says farewell as the director of the Shakespeare Festivel productions at the Memorial Theatre in Stratford-upon-Avon.

Oct 6 Actress-singer Lena Horne makes her New York debut as a Quadroon Girl in Kenneth Perkins' three-act drama, *Dance with Your Gods*, at the Mansfield Theatre.

Nov 2 English actor Bassett Roe (b. 1860) is dead. Roe made a notable success in 1884 as Macari in *Called Back*. He played a variety of roles on the London stage including Athos in *The Three Musketeers*, Black Michael in *The Prisoner of Zenda*, and Charles, King of France in *King Henry V*. Roe was a director of the Royal General Theatrical Fund.

Nov 17 American actress and vocalist Phyllis Rankin (b. 1874) is dead in Canton, Pennsylvania. Rankin made her first New York appearance in 1890 as Felice in *Sara*, and subsequently appeared with Rose Coghlan and Mrs. John Drew. She later played vaudeville with her husband actor Harry Davenport. Her father was actor-manager Arthur McKee Rankin.

dience. The ten *Best Plays* from Mantle's annual list of Broadway hits are: Anderson's Pulitzer Prize-winning *Mary of Scotland*, Kingsley's *Men in White*, Howard's *Dodsworth*, O'Neill's *Ah, Wilderness!*, Wexley's *They Shall Not Die*, Kummer's *Her Master's Voice*, Thomas' *No More Ladies*, Atlas' *Wednesday's Child*, Winter's *The Shining Hour*, and Shairp's *The Green Bay Tree*.

June 22 In Norwich, the historic Theatre Royal, the second of that name, built in 1826 and enlarged in 1913, suffers a disastrous fire, which leaves only some walls standing.

Aug 18 Today the Cort Theatre in Chicago closes for the last time. It is marked for demolition.

Sep 22 The Center Theatre on 6th Avenue between 48th and 49th Streets in New York formerly known as the motion-picture house, RKO Center, opens its doors as a legitimate theatre with the musical extravaganza, *The Great Waltz*, conceived and directed by Hassard Short. Until 1950, the Center houses dramatic spectacles and ice shows, but is taken over by NBC Television and soon converted into an office building.

Nov 2 Depression economics have hit the Theatre Block on West 42nd Street very hard. Today, the once legitimate Apollo Theatre opens a new era with a policy of four-a-day burlesque shows, with Max Wilner as the manager.

Nov 6 U.S. patents granted this year include one to the noted director-choreographer Busby Berkeley for his system of concentric rotary stages which can also be raised and lowered. This has theatre applications, but will be most effectively used in Berkeley's cinema dance sequences.

Dec 13 Originally known as the Hollywood Theatre, located on West 51st Street in New York, and designed by Thomas W. Lamb to present Warner Brothers pictures, the theatre presents its first live production, the musical revue *Calling All Stars*, by Lew Brown. Two years later, it is renamed the 51st Street Theatre, and in 1949 it is renamed the Mark Hellinger in honor of the Broadway columnist. In 1956 *My Fair Lady* opens here and runs for six years.

1934   THEATERS/PRODUCTIONS

Because of its references to lesbianism, Edouard Bourdet's *La Prisonniere* is still under the Lord Chamberlain's ban, despite its successful stagings in America. It is only permitted private club performance at the Arts Theatre, although in 1933, Mordaunt Shairp's *The Green Bay Tree*, hinting at male homosexuality was licensed by the Lord Chamberlain's Office.

This year the Director of Public Prosecutions undertakes 17 proceedings against productions judged offensive. All prosecutions are successful; all are directed against shows played outside London. Most of the charges relate to nudity or near-nudity, not to offensive ideas.

April 7 Demolition begins on the London Pavilion which first housed music hall in 1884. It will be rebuilt as a 1,180-seat cinema, set to open in September.

June 15 Critic Burns Mantle writes that the 1933–34 Broadway season: "will be recorded as one of the outstanding years of the theatre's history." After five years of deep economic depression, the theatre is making a comeback, recovering optimism, energy. Only 23 of the season's 125 drama and musical productions have a run of more than 100 performances, making it a season of short runs. Banks who now control a number of theatres will not take a chance, unlike producers, on extending a run to help a show find its au-

Jan 7 *The Petrified Forest* (NY—Broadhurst—Drama). Humphrey Bogart is featured in Robert E. Sherwood's melodrama about a gangster, asked by a poet (Leslie Howard) to shoot him so he can leave his insurance money to a waitress (Peggy Conklin). The drama has 197 performances. On Dec 16, 1942, it comes to London's Globe with Hartley Power (Duke Mantee), Constance Cummings, Owen Nares, Joyce Kennedy and Douglas Jeffries. The production runs just over 17 weeks.

Jan 7 *The Old Maid* (NY—Empire—Drama). Zoe Akins wins a Pulitzer Prize for this play based on Edith Wharton's novel of an old maid who must watch her own daughter raised by another. Helen Menken and Judith Anderson play leads. The show runs 38 weeks.

Jan 14 *Laburnam Grove*. See L premiere, 1933.

Jan 16 *Point Valaine* (NY—Ethel Barrymore—Drama). Noel Coward's steamy drama of amour in the Hotel Valaine on the point of a tropical island features Lynn Fontanne as Linda, the hotel's proprietress. Louis Hayward plays a young aviator-guest who is drawn to Linda, only to learn from her Russian headwaiter Stefan (Alfred Lunt) that he is Linda's secret lover. Repentant, Stefan is rejected by Linda. He commits suicide. Even with Coward's staging, audiences support the production for only seven weeks.

Jan 28 *Prisoners of War* (NY—Ritz—Drama). Based on some actual experiences, J. R. Ackerly's play shows what happens to a group of British officers, interned in neutral Switzerland during the Great War. Captain Conrad becomes fond of Lt. Grayle, so much so that the other prisoners comment cruelly on it and Grayle fights with Conrad. He withdraws, transferring his affections to a potted plant. Frank Merlin stages; Cleon Throckmorton designs. The plays lasts only a week.

Jan 30 *Three Men on a Horse* (NY—Playhouse—Comedy). George Abbott and John Cecil Holm devise this story about a greeting-card writer who has a gift for picking winning race-horses. Shirley Booth, Garson Kanin, and Sam Levene are in the cast. There are 835 performances. On Feb 18, 1936, the play opens at London's Wyndham's Theatre where it has less than 100 performances.

Feb 19 *Awake and Sing* (NY—Belasco—Drama). Clifford Odets's stark drama of the effects of the Depression on a Jewish family in the Bronx runs 26 weeks, with Stella Adler in a lead. "He [Odets] may not be a master yet, but he has the ability to be one," reports the *NY Times*. On Feb 20, 1938, the Stage Society sponsors a London showing of the play at the Vaudeville Theatre.

Feb 20 *The Bishop Misbehaves* (NY—Cort—Comedy). Frederick Jackson's play imagines a Bishop of Broadminster who finds some stolen jewels in a London pub and through his knowledge of detective fiction is able to trap the thieves and set things right. Walter Connolly plays the cleric; Jane Wyatt the young lady to whom the jewels belong. The public allows 121 performances of this tale.

March 4 *Petticoat Fever* (NY—Ritz—Comedy). Mark Reed's farce about an isolated wireless operator starved for female companionship features Dennis King and Leo G. Carroll. It runs for 17 weeks. On Feb 20, 1936, the show opens at London's Daly's with King again featured.

March 26 *Till the Day I Die* (NY—Longacre—Drama). Clifford Odet's story of a proletarian underground leader, tortured by the Nazis to inform on his co-workers, features Alexander Kirkland. It runs for 17 weeks. Odet's *Waiting for Lefty* is also produced. In this drama union radicals demand a strike, but Lefty never comes to the meeting; he's been shot.

April 8 *Flowers of the Forest*. See L premiere, 1934.

April 23 *Kind Lady* (NY—Booth—Drama). Edward Chodorov adapts Hugh Walpole's novel of a kind, wealthy lady who finds herself made a prisoner by an unscrupulous young man she's befriended. Grace George and Henry Daniell are featured. It runs 102 performances. On June 11, 1936, the drama premieres at London's Lyric, where it is unsuccessful.

June 4 *Earl Carroll Sketch Book* (NY—Winter Garden—Revue). Carroll conceives this show as a showgirl's idea of American history. Ken Murray is the M. C., with a large company including Billy Revel and Charlotte Arren. It runs for 207 performances.

Sep 4 *Moon Over Mulberry Street* (NY—Lyceum—Comedy). Cornel Wilde plays a young man from Little Italy who falls in love with the daughter of the Park Avenue patron who's put him through law school. Nicholas Cosentino's play enjoys 303 performances.

Sep 16 *The Night of January 16* (NY—Ambassador—Drama). Ayn Rand's play depicts the trial of a woman charged with murdering a financial wizard. Members of the audience are the jury. There are alternative endings to suit either a guilty or an innocent verdict. Walter Pidgeon and Doris Nolan are in the cast. The show runs over 29 weeks. On Sep 29, 1936, it premieres at London's Phoenix.

Sep 19 *At Home Abroad* (NY—Winter Garden—Revue). Howard Dietz and Arthur Schwartz write the lyrics and music for this revue which features Beatrice Lillie, Eddie Foy, Jr., Ethel Waters, and

The Petrified Forest

Eleanor Powell. Vincente Minnelli stages and designs. It runs over six months.

Sep 23 *If This Be Treason* (NY—Music Box—Drama). Dr. John Haynes Holmes and Reginald Lawrence write this story of an effort by the Japanese and American people to outlaw war. McKay Morris is featured. The show runs only five weeks.

Sep 25 *Winterset* (NY—Martin Beck—Drama). Maxwell Anderson's verse tragedy based on the Sacco and Vanzetti case features Burgess Meredith and Margo. The show runs for 195 performances and wins the Drama Critics' Circle Award. "'Winterset' lives on a plane of high thinking, deep emotion and eloquent writing. . . ." reports the *NY Times*.

Sep 26 *Paths of Glory* (NY—Plymouth—Drama). Arthur Hopkins produces and directs Sidney Howard's stage version of this story about a French regiment ordered to assault an invincible German position in World War I. The show runs only three weeks.

Oct 3 *Squaring the Circle* (NY—Lyceum—Comedy). Valentine Katayev's story of two couples in Communist Russia who want to switch wives runs 108 performances.

Oct 10 *Porgy and Bess* (NY—Alvin—Musical). The Theatre Guild produces this "American folk-opera" by DuBose Heyward and Ira Gershwin—based on the Heywards' play *Porgy*—with the score of

George Gershwin. Todd Duncan sings the role of Porgy, a black cripple in Catfish Row who wins Bess (Anne Wiggens Brown) and kills her former lover Crown (Alexander Campbell). John W. Bubbles plays the pimp and dope-peddler Sportin' Life. The predominantly black cast has a run of nearly four months. "I Got Plenty O' Nuttin' " and "Summertime" are among the songs.

Oct 12 *Jubilee* (NY—Imperial—Musical). Cole Porter adds music and lyrics to Moss Hart's book, showing the Royal Family kicking up its heels incognito. Melville Cooper, Mary Boland, and Montgomery are featured. Songs include "Just One of Those Things" and "Begin the Beguine." The show runs 21 weeks.

Oct 15 *Bright Star* (NY—Empire—Drama). Philip Barry's play about a man who marries a rich woman he does not love features Lee Tracy and Julie Haydon. It has only seven performances.

Oct 21 *Eden End.* See L premiere, 1934.

Oct 24 *Mulatto* (NY—Vanderbilt—Drama). Langston Hughes's play about racial prejudice features Rose McClendon. It wins 373 performances.

Oct 28 *Dead End* (NY—Belasco—Drama). Sidney Kingsley's saga about the contrasts in wealth and poverty which lead to criminality features a large cast including Gabriel Dell, Huntz Hall and Leo Gorcey, later known as "Dead End Kids." The show runs 687 performances.

Nov 5 *Pride and Prejudice* (NY—Music Box—Comedy). Helen Jerome successfully adapts Jane Austen's novel for the stage. The cast includes Percy Waram, Lucile Watson, Brenda Forbes, and Colin Keith-Johnston. The show runs 27 weeks. On Feb 27, 1936, it opens at London's St. James's with Dorothy Hyson, Celia Johnson and Leueen MacGrath. It runs for nearly 10 months.

Nov 6 *Let Freedom Ring* (NY—Broadhurst—Drama). Albert Bein adapts Grace Lumpkin's novel, *To Make My Bread*, about labor unrest in the cotton mills. Will Geer, Tom Ewell, and Robert Porterfield are in the ensemble. The show has 108 performances.

Nov 16 *Jumbo* (NY—Hippodrome—Musical). Ben Hecht and Charles MacArthur have devised the book and Rodgers and Hart the music and lyrics for this show about a circus. Songs include "Little Girl Blue" and "My Romance." Jimmy Durante stars. Billy Rose spends $340,000 to make the Hippodrome look like a circus and to fill the stage with real circus acts. Its 233 performances pay back only half the investment.

Nov 26 *First Lady* (NY—Music Box—Comedy). George S. Kaufman stages this play he's written with Katharine Dayton. Jane Cowl plays an influential Washington lady, modeled on Alice Roosevelt Longworth. The show runs nearly 31 weeks.

Jumbo

Nov 27 *Boy Meets Girl* (NY—Cort—Comedy). Sam and Bella Spewack's lively farce about making pictures in Hollywood, complete with a pregnant innocent around whom the plot swirls, is an immediate hit. Allyn Joslyn, Jerome Cowan, Peggy Hart, and Garson Kanin are in the ensemble. It runs 669 performances. On May 27, 1936 it opens at London's Shaftesbury with Helen Chandler featured.

Dec 5 *May Wine* (NY—St. James—Musical). Sigmund Romberg provides the score and Oscar Hammerstein the lyrics for Frank Mandel's book about a woman who marries an absent-minded psychoanalyst to get his money. Nancy McCord and Walter Slezak are featured. The show runs 213 performances.

Dec 9 *Paradise Lost* (NY—Longacre—Drama). Clifford Odets offers this tale of contrasting conservative and radical philosophies. Morris Carnovsky and Luther Adler play leads. The production closes after nine weeks.

Dec 20 *Libel.* See L premiere, 1934.

Dec 25 *George White's Scandals* (NY—New Amsterdam—Revue). Bert Lahr, Rudy Vallee, and Willie and Eugene Howard are featured in this revue, with score by Ray Henderson and lyrics by Jack Yellen. There are 110 performances.

Dec 26 *Victoria Regina* (NY—Broadhurst—Drama). Helen Hayes scores a great personal success in Laurence Houseman's history of the Queen. It runs 517 performances. On June 21, 1937, it premieres at London's Lyric, with Pamela Stanley in the title role. The show runs 42 weeks.

1935 BRITISH PREMIERES

Jan 30 *Love on the Dole* (L—Garrick—Drama). Walter Greenwood, aided by Ronald Gow, adapts his novel about bad times in Britain and their effect on working-class lives. Wendy Hiller is featured. The production runs 49 weeks. On Feb 24, 1936, the show comes to Broadway at the Shubert with Hiller repeating her role. Here it runs 18 weeks.

Feb 25 *Jack O'Diamonds* (L—Gaiety—Musical). Noel Gay writes the score, Clifford Gray and H.F. Maltby the book for this musical featuring Viola Compton. The show runs almost four months.

March 20 *Cornelius* (L—Duchess—Drama). Ralph Richardson appears in J.B. Priestley's play.

April 19 *Charlot's Char-A-Bang* (L—Vaudeville—Revue). Andre Charlot's new show features Reginald Gardiner, Elsie Randolph, and Richard Murdoch. It has 101 performances.

April 24 *Tovarich* (L—Lyric—Comedy). Robert E. Sherwood adapts Jacques Deval's play about Russian nobels who must survive in Paris by working as servants. Cedric Hardwicke and Eugenie Leontovich play leads. The production runs a year. *The Times* calls it "entertaining nonsense." On Oct 15, 1936, it premieres at New York's Plymouth with John Halliday and Marta Abba. It runs nearly 45 weeks.

April 25 *1066 and All That* (L—Strand—Revue). Reginald Arkell earns a run of 387 performances with this revue, staged by Herbert Prentice and Archibald de Bear. In the company are Naunton Wayne, Millie Sim and Scott Sunderland. The title and the historical parodies have been successful in some past seasons as well.

May 2 *Glamorous Night* (L—Drury Lane—Musical). Ivor Novello creates both book and score for this show with lyrics by Christopher Hassall. Novello, Clifford Heatherley, and Barry Jones are in the cast. The musical runs over 30 weeks.

May 15 *The Mask of Virtue* (L—Ambassadors'—Comedy). Ashley Dukes adapts Carl Sternheim's German play, with Jeanne de Casalis, Vivian Leigh, and Lady Tree. It has 117 performances.

May 23 *Gay Deceivers* (L—Gaiety—Musical). Charlotte Greenwood, Wyn Weaver, Enid Lowe, and Claire Luce are featured in this show, based on a French original. The production lasts for 123 performances.

May 30 *Golden Arrow* (L—Whitehall—Drama). Laurence Olivier directs and stars in this new play by Sylvia Thompson and Victor Cunard. Greer Garson is featured.

May 31 *Night Must Fall* (L—Duchess—Drama). Emlyn Williams' thriller about a charming, boyish murderer, features May Whitty, Angela Baddeley, and Williams. It wins 435 performances. On Sep 28, 1936, it opens at New York's Ethel Barrymore with the same cast. It lasts only eight weeks, but becomes a favorite with little theatre groups.

June 12 *The Two Mrs. Carrolls* (L—St. Martin's—Drama). Martin Vale's play features Leslie Banks, Evelyn Moore, and Joan Maude. It runs more than 33 weeks.

June 14 *Anything Goes.* See NY premiere, 1934.

July 31 *The Unguarded Hour* (L—Daly's—Drama). Godfrey Tearle, Atholl Fleming, and Malcolm Keen animate Ladislaus Fodor's play.

Aug 14 *Tulip Time* (L—Alhambra—Musical). Colin Wark writes the score and Worton David and Alfred Parker the text for this show featuring Sydney Fairbrother, George Gee, and Wendy Toye. There are 427 performances.

Aug 21 *Full House* (L—Haymarket—Comedy). Isabel Jeans, Maidie Andrews, Lilian Braithwaite, and Heather Thatcher appear in Ivor Novello's show. It runs 23 weeks.

Oct 1 *Sweeney Agonistes* (L—Westminster—Drama). T. S. Eliot's poetic drama, with music by William Alwyn, has John Moody as Sweeney. Rupert Doone stages a cast including Stefan Schnabel, Isobel Scaife, and Ruth Wynn Owen. On the double-bill, staged by Tyrone Guthrie is W. H. Auden's *The Dance of Death*.

Oct 2 *Please, Teacher!* (L—Hippodrome—Musical). Jack Waller and Joseph Tunbridge create the score and R.P. Weston and Bert Lee the lyrics for this show which runs 300 performances. Bobby Howes and Sepha Treble play leads.

Oct 15 *Espionage* (L—Apollo—Drama). Walter Hackett's play earns a run of over 21 weeks. In the cast are Cyril Smith, Marion Lorne, Frank Cellier, Eric Maturin, and Jeanne Stuart.

Oct 30 *Call it a Day* (L—Globe—Drama). C.L. Anthony's play about a series of potential crises in the day of a middle-class family features Fay Compton and Owen Nares. There are 509 showings. On Jan 28, 1936, it comes to New York's Morosco with Gladys Cooper and Philip Merivale. Here it earns a six-month run.

Oct 31 *Seeing Stars* (L—Gaiety—Musical). Guy Bolton and Fred Thompson devise the book for the lyrics of Graham John and the music of Martin Broones. Leslie Henson, Rob Currie, and Naomi Waters are among the cast. There are 236 performances.

Nov 1 *Murder In the Cathedral* (L—Mercury—Drama). T.S. Eliot's poetic play about Thomas a Becket features Robert Speaight as the Archbishop. The production runs almost 23 weeks.

Nov 8 *Anthony and Anna* (L—Whitehall—Comedy). St. John Ervine's play features Jessica Tandy and Harold Warrender. It earns 739 showings.

Nov 12 *Twenty To One* (L—Coliseum—Musical). L. Arthur Rose writes this "musical sporting farce," with a score by Billy Mayerl and lyrics by Frank Eyton. The large cast includes Winnie Sloans, Doris Rogers, and Margaret Yarde. It has a 48-week run.

1935 REVIVALS/REPERTORIES

Jan 1 Maurice Evans and Cathleen Nesbitt play the leads in *The Taming of the Shrew* at London's Sadler's Wells.

Jan 14 Kataev's *Squaring the Circle* opens the new year for the Dublin Gate Theatre. Other plays include Earl of Longford's *Ascendancy*; Bronte's *Wuthering Heights*; Monson's *Three Leopards*, Chesterton's *Magic*, Shakespeare's *Othello*, Johnston's *A Bride for the Unicorn*, Longford's *Yahoo*, and a revival of Johnston's *The Old Lady Says "No!"*, ending the season in May. Following this, the troupe goes to London to present a bill of three productions from the Gate at the Westminster Theatre.

Jan 21 *Othello*, with Abraham Sofaer in the title-role, opens at London's Old Vic Theatre. On Feb 11, the Gilbert Murray translation of Euripides' *Hippolytus* is paired with *The Two Shepherds*, by Gregorio and Maria Martinez Sierra.

Feb 16 Sol Hurok brings the Moscow Art Theatre Players to Broadway's Majestic Theatre for 52 performances of Gogol's *Revisor* and *Marriage*, Chekhov's *I Forgot*, Lavrenoff's *Enemies*, Bulgakov's *The White Guard*, Ostrovsky's *Poverty Is No Crime*, and Berger's *The Deluge*. After a brief tour, the company returns for 28 more performances, this time at the Public Theatre.

Feb 18 New York's Theatre Guild presents George Bernard Shaw's *The Simpleton of the Unexpected Isles*. It runs only five weeks.

March 4 At the Q Theatre at Kew Bridge, George Bernard Shaw's *Misalliance* is revived. On this same evening, at the Old Vic Theatre, the revival is Shaw's *Major Barbara*. On March 11, at the Q Theatre, Shaw's *Caesar and Cleopatra* is revived. On May 13, it's Shaw's *Candida*.

March 27 From the Chester Mystery Play Cycle, *The Play of the Shepherds* is produced in London at the Ambassadors'

Theatre. This is followed by the medieval morality play, *Everyman*.

March 29 New York's Theatre Union produces Albert Maltz's *Black Pit*, about a poor striker forced to survive by becoming an informer on labor unrest. Alan Baxter is featured. The play runs nearly 11 weeks.

April 11 John Galsworthy's *Justice* is revived in London at the Playhouse Theatre, staged by Leon M. Lion, who plays Hector Frome. On May 2, Lion revives Galsworthy's *The Skin Game*. Galsworthy's *A Family Man* follows on May 30.

April 15 *Antony and Cleopatra* opens the season at the Shakespeare Memorial Theatre in Stratford-upon-Avon, newly under the directorship of B. Iden Payne. Other plays include *The Merchant of Venice*, *As You Like It*, *The Merry Wives of Windsor*—staged by the Russian director, Theodore Komisarjevsky; *The Taming of the Shrew*, *Henry IV, Part 1*, and *All's Well That Ends Well*, played to celebrate Shakespeare's birthday.

April 29 Maurice Evans stars in *Hamlet* at London's Old Vic.

May 19 At New York's Mecca Theatre, the Group Theatre, the Theatre of Action, and the new Dance League join forces to offer *Spring Varieties*, with Art Smith's strike play, *The Tide Rises*, and Clifford Odets's *I Can't Sleep*.

May 20 The Theatre Guild's leftist satirical revue, *Parade*, has a score by Jerome Moross. It is written by George Sklar, Kyle Crichton, and David Lesan. The show lasts only five weeks.

Summer *Zion Passion Play*, a dramatization of the life, death, and resurrection of Jesus Christ, is adapted by the Rev. Jabez Taylor. In 1969, a new 1,200-seat outdoor amphitheatre is opened in Zion, Illinois, for the production.

June 18 The summer drama season in Re-

Oregon Shakespeare Festival

gent's Park at the Open Air Theatre is launched with a revival of *Twelfth Night*. *As You Like It* follows on July 2, Ben Jonson's *Chloridia* is next, on July 16; it's a masque, as its partner on the double-bill is also: John Milton's *Comus*. On July 30, *A Midsummer Night's Dream* is staged. On Sep 3, *Love's Labour's Lost* is offered.

July 1 Sacha Guitry comes to London's Daly's presenting his staging of his own comedy, *Le Nouveau Testament*, played in French by a cast including Guitry, Jacqueline Delubac, and Betty Daussmond. On July 8, they present Guitry's *Mon Double et Ma Moitie*.

July 2 Today in Ashland, Oregon, Angus Bowmer presents what he optimistically calls 'The First Annual Oregon Shakespearean Festival." The first productions are *The Merchant of Venice* and *Twelfth Night*, staged by Bowmer.

July 15 George Bernard Shaw's *Arms and the Man* is presented at London's Embassy Theatre. On July 22, the Q Theatre revives *Mrs. Warren's Profession. Man and Superman* is produced at the Cambridge Theatre on Aug 12, *Pygmalion* on Sep 2, and *The Apple Cart* on Sep 25. On Nov 4, the Q offers *Major Barbara*.

July 30 Maurice Schwartz and his American Yiddish Art Theatre Company open in London at His Majesty's with Schwartz's *Yoshe Kalb*. On Aug 19, the troupe plays Jacob Gordin's *God, Man, and Devil*. Sholem Asch's *God of Vengeance* is produced on Sep 18.

Sep 20 Alfred Lunt and Lynn Fontanne present *The Taming of the Shrew* at New York's Guild Theatre. It runs more than four months.

Sep 30 At the Lyric, Hammersmith, director Arthur Phillips plays Shylock in his revival of *The Merchant Venice*. On Oct 17, *Romeo and Juliet* is revived at the New Theatre, staged by John Gielgud. Laurence Olivier is Romeo to Peggy Ashcroft's Juliet. On Oct 22, Henry Cass revives *Julius Caesar* at the Old Vic Theatre, with Cecil Trouncer in the title-role. On Nov 5, at the Lyric, Hammersmith, *Macbeth* returns. On Nov 19, at the Westminster Theatre, it's *Timon of Athens*, with Ernest Milton as Timon. Ion Swinley is Macbeth at the Old Vic on Dec 3.

Oct 8 The ninth season of the Dublin Gate Theatre opens with Gheon's *The Marriage of St. Francis*. Other plays include Shakespeare's *The Taming of the Shrew*, Baty's *Crime and Punishment*, Rice's *Not for Children*, and a Christmas revival of *Romeo and Juliet*.

Nov 12 Marie Ney, Vivienne Bennett, and Nancy Hornsby are featured in Chekhov's *The Three Sisters*, revived at London's Old Vic.

Nov 19 At New York's Civic Repertory, the Theatre Union presents Bertolt Brecht's adaptation of Gorki's *Mother*. It has 36 performances, with Brecht on hand.

Dec 12 Alla Nazimova brings her production of Henrik Ibsen's *Ghosts* to Broadway's Empire Theatre for a run of 81 performances.

Dec 14 The holidays are greeted at London's Vaudeville Theatre with *Sleeping Beauty: Or, What A Witch!* On Dec 18, *Where the Rainbow Ends* is again at the Holborn Empire. On Dec 21, at His Majesty's, *La Poupee* is revived. Other Christmas treats are: *Alice Through the Looking-Glass* (Little), *The Magic Marble* (Lyric, Hammersmith), *The Impresario from Smyrna* (Westminster), *Jack and the Beanstalk* (Drury Lane, Brixton, King's, Hammersmith), *Bluebell in Fairyland* (Scala), *When Knights Were Bold* (Fortune), *The Forty Thieves* (Lyceum), *Peter Pan* (Palladium), *Buckie's Bears* (Garrick), *Dick Whittington* (Embassy), and *Robinson Crusoe* (Wimbledon).

March 14 American Negro actor Richard Berry Harrison is dead at age 70. Son of slaves, Harrison was teaching dramatics and elocution when he was persuaded to play "De Lawd" in Connelly's *The Green Pastures*. He appeared in the part nearly 2,000 times, and in 1931 was awarded the Spingarn medal for his performance.

April 19 Dudley Moore is born in Dagenham, Essex, England.

May 8 Actress Salome Jens is born in Milwaukee, Wisconsin.

May 28 The Theatre Royal, Drury Lane,

Richard B. Harrison

is host to a testimonial matinee for Marie Tempest's Golden Jubilee.

Sep 11 Billed as Geoffrey Lind, actor Jeffrey Lynn makes his first stage appearance in New York as a walk-on and assistant stage manager in Damon Runyan and Howard Lindsay's *A Slight Case of Murder*.

Sep 14 Actress Dame Madge Kendal (b. 1849) dies in Hertfordshire. Kendal (Margaret Robertson) made her London debut as Ophelia in 1865. From 1879 to 1888, she appeared at the St. James' Theatre under the management of her husband and Sir John Hare. Kendal's greatest triumph in later years was in *The Elder Miss Blossom*. She received the D.B.E. in 1926.

Sep 23 American actor De Wolf Hopper (b. 1858) dies in Kansas City, Missouri.

1935   BIRTHS/DEATHS/DEBUTS

Jan Hugh Hunt is appointed Resident Producer of Dublin's Abbey Theatre.

Jan 6 Author-educator George Pierce Baker (b. 1866) dies in New York. Baker was the first Professor of Dramatic Literature at Harvard University, where he founded the 1947 Workshop. In 1925 he became director of the post-graduate Department of Drama at Yale University until his retirement in 1933.

Feb 11 American actor-director Paul Mann makes his first Broadway appearance under two names. He is billed as Paul Mann in the role of the Second Man and as Yisrol Libman in the role of a Woodcutter in the Neighborhood Playhouse production of Garcia Lorca's *Bitter Oleander*. Mann was born Yisrol Paul Mann Liebman.

Feb 21 Future playwright Leonard Melfi is born in Binghamton, New York.

After gaining prominence in New York in the 1880's, Hopper joined Weber and Fields, and later achieved fame in Gilbert and Sullivan roles. His recital of *Casey at the Bat* became a classic. A book of memoirs, *Once a Clown, Always a Clown*, was published in 1927.

Sep 26 American theatrical manager William A. Brady (b. 1863) dies in New York. Brady began his stage career in 1882 and last acted in 1928 in *A Free Soul*. His productions include *Gentleman Jack*, *Uncle Tom's Cabin*, *The Skin Game*, and *Street Scene*. The actress, Alice Brady, is his daughter.

Oct 7 Actor-playwright Francis Wilson (b. 1854) dies in New York. Wilson appeared in a succession of musical comedies from 1886 to 1904, when he turned to straight comedy. His own play, *The Bachelor's Baby*, was a financial success. In 1913 he was elected president of the newly formed Actors' Equity Association.

Nov 26 Marian Mercer is born in Akron, Ohio.

Dec 23 English actor-manager Robert Loraine (b. 1876) dies in London. Loraine made his first appearance on stage in 1889 playing with Herbert Beerbohm Tree and George Alexander, and subsequently made a hit as D'Artagnan in *The Three Musketeers*. Among his later roles were Cyrano de Bergerac, Adolph in Strindberg's *The Father*, Petruchio, and Mercutio.

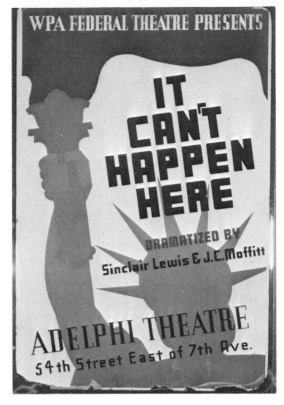

It Can't Happen Here

1935 THEATERS/PRODUCTIONS

Jan 18 *Battleship Gertie*, produced by Courtney Burr, opens at the Lyceum Theatre in New York. Designer Boris Aronson uses representational projections of architectural detail to suggest change in locale in his settings.

Feb 15 Today, the London Theatre Council is formed. It is representative of the Society of West End Theatre Managers and British Actor's Equity Association. The objects of the council are to regulate relations between managers and artists.

March 14 Jo Mielziner creates a "light curtain" for Archibald Macleish's *Panic*, which opens at the Imperial Theatre in New York.

May 2 The Old Globe Theatre opens in San Diego at the California Pacific International Exposition. It later becomes the home of the San Diego National Shakespeare Festival.

June 15 Although drama critic Burns Mantle closes his record on this date, the New York theatre season, in his opinion, has actually come to a full stop at the end of May. August is no longer a real beginning of the season either. In the season just completed, 1934–35, there have been 110 dramatic productions, with 28 that were musicals of one kind or another. Eleven of those have been Gilbert & Sullivan revivals, however. There have been 14 drama revivals, the most successful being Katharine Cornell's *Romeo and Juliet*. Eighteen plays have come from Britain, with nine others from European lands. For the first time in the American *Best Plays* annuals, Mantle appends an omnibus listing of productions under the heading: *Off Broadway*. Revivals of melodramas, classics, and Ibsen are among the productions, as well as experimental plays and stagings by workers' and political groups. The ten *Best Plays* on Mantle's annual list are: Hellman's *The Children's Hour*, Anderson's *Valley Forge*, Sherwood's *The Petrified Forest*, Akins' *The Old Maid*, Raphaelson's *Accent on Youth*, Kaufman and Hart's *Merrily We Roll Along*, Odets' *Awake and Sing*, Elser and Connelly's *The Farmer Takes a Wife*, Hayden's *Lost Horizons*, and Van Druten's *The Distaff Side*.

Aug 27 Today marks the official opening of the new Federal Theatre Project of the Works Progress Administrations (WPA) in Washington, D.C. Hallie Flanagan, formerly in charge of the theatre program at Vassar College, is installed as National Director of the project, designed to provide work for theatre people and free or low-cost entertainment around the nation in a time of economic depression.

Sep 17 A U.S. patent is given the Kleigl Brothers for the Kleiglight. The Kleiglight is a type of ellipsodial reflector spotlight, to become one of the most widely used types of lighting instruments in the 20th century.

Sep 23 Tonight, Clifford Bax's *The Rose Without a Thorn* marks the opening of a new era of theatre in Perth, Scotland, with the management of Marjorie Dence and David Steuart. The Theatre, rebuilt in 1924 after a fire, is modeled on a court theatre, with two balconies. Dence and Steuart offer repertory, with no less than 19 productions in the 1935–36 season. Despite initial disappointments, perserverance begins to pay off, with notable figures such as George Bernard Shaw and J. B. Priestley praising the Perth Theatre.

Sep 30 Just over a year after its destruction by fire, Britain's Norwich Theatre Royal, managed by Jack Gladwin, lives again, this time in an ultra-modern Art Deco playhouse on the traditional theatre site. *White Horse Inn* is the opening show, with such headliners during the inaugural season as Harry Lauder, Gracie Fields, and Mantovani and His Orchestra.

Oct 22 The New York Drama Critics' Circle (NYDCC) is officially formed to award a prize for the best new play by an American playwright produced in New York during the theatrical season.

Oct 28 Sidney Kingsley's *Dead End* opens at the Belasco Theatre in New York. Designer Norman Bel Geddes has created a realistic water ripple-effect, through the use of a pan of water, spotlights, and fans.

Nov This month, the first issue of *Federal Theatre*, the American magazine of the Federal Theatre Project, appears. It continues publication until 1937.

Jan 16 *Russet Mantle* (NY—Masque—Comedy) Lynn Riggs's comedy about a young poet who falls in love with a pregnant socialite features John Beal and Martha Sleeper. There are 117 performances.

Jan 21 *Ethan Frome* (NY—National—Drama). Owen and Donald Davis adapt Edith Wharton's novella for the stage. Raymond Massey, Pauline Lord, and Ruth Gordon are featured. The production runs 15 weeks. The *NY Times* writes ".... Ruth Gordon, Pauline Lord and Raymond Massey ... are hereby nominated for immortality ...."

Jan 28 *Call It a Day.* See L premiere, 1935.

Jan 30 *The Ziegfeld Follies* (NY—Winter Garden—Revue). The Shuberts produce this show with Fanny Brice, Bob Hope, Eve Arden, and Judy Canova. George Balanchine and Robert Alton choreograph. Because of Brice's illness, the show runs only 115 performances.

Feb 17 *End of Summer* (NY—Guild—Comedy). The Theatre Guild's production of S. N. Behrman's play runs 19 weeks, with Osgood Perkins as a bitter psychiatrist, whose attitudes about success illuminate the problems of characters at both ends of the social scale during a Maine summer.

Feb 24 *Love on the Dole.* See L premiere, 1935.

Feb 25 *The Postman Always Rings Twice* (NY—Lyceum—Drama). James M. Cain's novel becomes a play featuring Richard Barthlemess. He falls in love with the wife (Mary Philips) of a roadside-stand proprietor. They kill her husband, but are acquitted of murder. Later, when they are driving, she's accidentally killed, but he is hanged for her presumed murder on circumstantial evidence.

March 24 *Idiot's Delight* (NY—Schubert—Comedy). Robert E. Sherwood's comedy about a couple who find each other amid the growth of fascism and the outbreak of war runs for nearly 38 weeks in this Theatre Guild production. Alfred Lunt and Lynne Fontanne are starred. Sherwood's play wins the Pulitzer Prize. On March 22, 1938 it opens at London's Apollo with Raymond Massey in the leading role. There it runs 29 weeks.

April 11 *On Your Toes* (NY—Imperial—Musical). Rodgers and Hart provide the music and lyrics for this show about a man from a family of hoofers who gets his chance to produce a jazz ballet called "Slaughter on Tenth Avenue." George Balanchine choreographs the ballet, featuring Tamara Geva and Ray Bolger. The show runs nearly 10 months.

April 18 *Bury the Dead* (NY—Ethel Barrymore—Drama). Irwin Shaw's one-act protest against war runs three months. In Shaw's drama, six dead soldiers refuse to be buried. Not even their wives' pleading will deter them from carrying their message against war across the world. Robert Porterfield and Joseph Kramm are among the soldiers.

April 30 *Pre-Honeymoon* (NY—Lyceum—Comedy). Anne Nichols's play depicts a senator, engaged to be married, who decides to have a pre-marital fling with a bubble dancer. Jessie Royce Landis and Clyde Fillmore play leads. The show runs eight months.

May 19 *New Faces of 1936* (NY—Vanderbilt—Revue). Leonard Sillman's revue boasts Imogene Coca, Van Johnson, and Katherine Mayfield, among others. It runs six months.

Sep 14 *The Ziegfeld Follies of 1936–1937* (NY—Winter Garden—Revue). After a summer vacation, the January edition returns, but with some new principals. Fanny Brice is now paired with comedian Bobby Clark. Gypsy Rose Lee, formerly of burlesque, makes her *Follies* debut with an elegant strip-routine which critics find amusing rather than titillating. The show runs 112 performances.

Sep 21 *Reflected Glory* (NY—Morosco—Comedy). Tallulah Bankhead stars in George Kelly's play about an actress tempted to abandon the stage for matrimony. The production runs 16 weeks.

Sep 28 *Night Must Fall.* See L premiere, 1935.

Sep 29 *Love from a Stranger.* See L premiere, 1936.

Oct 6 *St. Helena* (NY—Lyceum—Drama). Napoleon's last years in exile are depicted by R. C. Sherriff and Jeanne de Casalis, with Maurice Evans as the deposed Emperor. Although there are only 63 performances, the play and production are admired by critics.

Oct 15 *Tovarich.* See L premiere, 1935.

Oct 22 *Stage Door* (NY—Music Box—Comedy). George S. Kaufman stages this play he's worked on with Edna Ferber. It features Margaret Sullavan as a young woman who must choose between a stage or a screen career. The show runs for 21 weeks. The comedy opens at London's Saville on Feb 21, 1946, where it has a short run.

Oct 26 *It Can't Happen Here* (NY—Adelphi—Drama). Around the United States, 18 producing units of the Federal Theatre simultaneously offer Sinclair Lewis's vision of what might happen to America and Americans if some native Fascists, using Nazi methods, were to be elected to high office. Most of the runs are long, New York's 95 performances being the record.

Oct 29 *Red, Hot, and Blue* (NY—Alvin—Musical). Cole Porter composes the score,

The Postman Always Rings Twice

including "It's De-Lovely." The book, by Howard Lindsey and Russel Crouse, tells of a rich lady running a charity lottery with the assistance of some convicts. Ethel Merman, Jimmy Durante and Bob Hope lead the cast. It runs for 23 weeks.

Nov 19 *Johnny Johnson* (NY—44th Street—Drama). Kurt Weill provides the music for Paul Green's saga of a simple young stone-cutter who is opposed to war but nonetheless gets caught up in it. Russell Collins plays the title role. This Group Theater show runs for 68 performances.

Nov 24 *Tonight at 8:30.* See L premieres, 1936.

Dec 14 *You Can't Take It With You* (NY—Booth—Comedy). George S. Kaufman and Moss Hart concoct this play about a zany household struggling through the Depression. Josephine Hull, Henry Travers, and Mitzi Hajos are among the cast. There are 837 performances. On Dec 22, 1937, the show premieres at London's St. James's with A.P. Kaye and Hilda Trevalyan.

Dec 16 *Brother Rat* (NY—Biltmore—Comedy). This light-hearted look at a military school by John Monks, Jr., and Fred Finklehoff features Eddie Albert, Jose Ferrer, and Robert Griffith. It runs for 577 performances.

Dec 23 *The Wingless Victory* (NY—Empire—Drama). Maxwell Anderson's drama of New England racial prejudices features Walter Abel and Katharine Cornell. The play opens in London at the Phoenix on Sep 8, 1943, with Rachel Kempson. It does not have a long run.

Dec 25 *The Show Is On* (NY—Winter Garden—Revue). Vincente Minnelli assembles, stages, and designs this attractive show, with the talents of Bert Lahr, Beatrice Lillie, Mitzi Mayfair, and Reginald

Gardiner. The score is largely by Vernon Duke, but there are interpolations by Rodgers and Hart, and a Hoagey Carmichael/Stanley Adams hit, "Little Old Lady." The show lasts nearly 30 weeks.

Dec 26 *The Women* (NY—Ethel Barrymore—Comedy). Claire Booth's tart portraits of some New York society women and the intrigues they plan features Margalo Gillmore, Arlene Francis, Marjorie Main, and Ilka Chase among others. The show settles in for a long run. On April 20, 1939, it opens at London's Lyric where Karen Peterson has the central role. It runs for 155 performances.

1936   BRITISH PREMIERES

Jan 9 *Tonight at 8:30* (L—Phoenix—Comedy). Noel Coward presents his first program of three one-act plays under this title. Others follow through May. The plays include *Family Album, We Were Dancing, The Astonished Heart, Red Peppers, Hands Across the Sea, Fumed Oak, Shadow Play, Ways and Means* and *Still Life.* Coward, Gertrude Lawrence, Alan Webb, Moyna Nugent, and Edward Underdown are among the cast. On Nov 24, the show opens at New York's National where it runs nearly 15 weeks.

Jan 30 *The Dog Beneath the Skin* (L—Westminster—Comedy). W. H. Auden and Christopher Isherwood write this satire featuring Geoffrey Wincott.

Feb 4 *Follow the Sun* (L—Adelphi—Revue). Ronald Jeans and J. H. Turner assemble this revue, with Arthur Schwartz's music and lyrics by Howard Dietz and Desmond Carter. It wins 204 showings, with a cast including Claire Luce, Ada Reeve and Vic Oliver.

Feb 18 *Three Men on a Horse.* See NY premiere, 1935.

Feb 20 *Petticoat Fever.* See NY premiere, 1935.

Feb 26 *Promise* (L—Shaftesbury—Drama). J. M. Harwood translates Henri Bernstein's French play. Edna Best, Ann Todd, Madge Titheradge and Ralph Richardson appear. It earns 100 performances.

Feb 27 *Pride and Prejudice.* See NY premiere, 1935.

March 6 *Dusty Ermine* (L—Comedy—Drama). Ian Fleming plays Inspector Helmsley in Neil Grant's play, staged by A. R. Whatmore. The production earns a run of seven months.

Mar 31 *Love From a Stranger* (L—New—Drama). Frank Vosper adapts Agatha Christie's tale and is featured. Vosper plays a psychopathic murderer, plotting the death of his new wife. On Sep 29, Vosper again plays the lead in his play when it opens at New York's Fulton Theatre for a brief run of 31 performances. Even more sinister than the plot, however, is Vosper's mysterious death during his return to England after the play closes. He disappears from the ship; his bruised body washes up on the French coast weeks later.

April 1 *Spread It Abroad* (L—Saville—Revue). With William Walker's music and Herbert Farjeon's book, this revue wins a run of 26 weeks. In the company are Michael Wilding, Hermione Gingold, Dorothy Dickson, and Nelson Keys.

April 11 *The Frog* (L—Prince's—Drama). Ian Hay adapts Edgar Wallace's mystery novel, involving an attempt to overthrow the Prime Minister. Jack Hawkins, Christine Barry, and Dorothy Tetley are in the cast. The show wins 483 performances.

April 14 *Whiteoaks* (L—Little—Drama). Mazo de la Roche adapts her *Whiteoaks of Jalna* for the stage. Jane Savile is featured. The show runs for 827 performances. On March 23, 1938, the play opens at New York's Hudson with Ethel Barrymore. It runs 14 weeks.

April 16 *After October* (L—Criterion—Drama). Rodney Ackland's play wins a run of 39 weeks. In the company are Diana Beaumont, Griffith Jones and Iris Baker.

May 4 *Ah, Wilderness.* See NY premiere, 1933.

May 13 *Aren't Men Beasts* (L—Strand—Comedy). Robertson Hare is featured in Vernon Syvlaine's farce. It runs over 35 weeks.

May 27 *Boy Meets Girl.* See NY premiere, 1935.

May 28 *The Fugitives* (L—Apollo—Drama). Walter Hackett's drama features Godfrey Tearle, Marion Lorne, and Phyllis Dare. It runs 171 performances.

July 9 *Blackbirds of 1936* (L—Gaiety—Revue). Johnny Mercer provides the lyrics and Rube Bloom the music for this new edition of Lew Leslie's black revue. The company includes Jules Bledsoe, Una Carlisle, and Katie Hall. The production runs nearly four months. On Nov 9, the second edition opens at the Adelphi with Batie and Foster, Tim Moore, and Fela Sowande.

Aug 6 *The Amazing Dr. Clitterhouse* (L—Haymarket—Drama). Ralph Richardson plays the title role in Barre Lyndon's play about a doctor who dabbles in crime to study the reactions of criminals 'at work. The production runs 492 performances. On March 2, 1937, it opens at New York's Hudson Theatre where it plays only 10 weeks.

Aug 31 *The Two Bouquets* (L—Ambassadors'—Comedy). Eleanor and Herbert Farjeon create this "Victorian comedy with music." It wins a run of almost 38 weeks, with an ensemble including Bruce Carfax, Edith Lee, Joyce Barbour, and Gertrude Musgrove.

Sep 11 *Careless Rapture* (L—Drury Lane—Musical). Christopher Hassell provides the lyrics for composer Ivor Novello's book. The cast includes Ivan Samson, Dorothy Dickson, and Novello. The production runs 37 weeks.

Sep 15 *This'll Make You Whistle* (L—Palace—Musical). Guy Bolton and Fred Thompson concoct the book, with songs by Sigler, Goodhart, and Hoffman. Jack Buchanan stages and plays the leading role. The production wins 190 performances.

Sep 15 *Mademoiselle* (L—Wyndham's—Comedy). Noel Coward stages this Jacques Deval play, adapted by Audrey and Waveney Carten. Greer Garson, Nigel Patrick, Isabel Jeans, and Cecil Parker appear. There are 147 performances.

Oct 13 *Jane Eyre* (L—Queen's—Drama). There are 300 performances of Helen Jer-

You Can't Take it With You

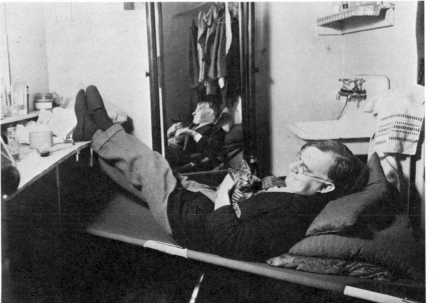

ome's adaptation of Charlotte Bronte's novel. Curigwen Lewis plays the title role, with Reginald Tate as Mr. Rochester.

Nov 6 *French Without Tears* (L—Criterion—Comedy). Terence Rattigan's comedy about Britons in France at a "crammer" where they are trying to master French features Trevor Howard, Guy Middleton, Rex Harrison, and Jessica Tandy. It runs for 1,039 performances. On Sep 28, 1937, the show opens at New York's Henry Miller where it has only 111 performances.

Nov 12 *Housemaster* (L—Apollo—Drama). Ian Hay adapts his novel about a headmaster who tries to reform a housemaster of the Old Guard at a British boy's school. Frederick Leister, Hilda Trevelyan, and Robert Craven are featured. There are 662 performances.

Dec 3 *O Mistress Mine* (L—St. James's—Comedy). Yvonne Printemps and Pierre

Fresney animate Ben Travers's comedy.

Dec 14 *The Boy David* (L—His Majesty's—Drama). Theodore Komisarjevsky stages J. M. Barrie's biblical drama, with the refugee German actress Elizabeth Bergner as David.

Dec 16 *Busman's Honeymoon* (L—Comedy—Comedy). Mystery novelist Dorothy L. Sayers—who's collaborated on this play with M. St. Clare Byrne—calls it a "detective comedy." It is a great success, running for a year.

Dec 22 *Balalaika* (L—Adelphi—Musical). This pre-Revolutionary vision of Russia in song and dance—with a score by George Posford and Bernard Gruen—earns a run of 570 performances. Leontine Sagan stages the book by Eric Maschwitz, with the aid of a large cast, including Eric Marshall, Anna Brunton, and Clifford Mollison.

Youmans' score, this Frank Mandel, Otto Harbach and Irving Caesar London revival of *No, No, Nannette!* is not the success it once was. Barbara Vernon is Nanette, with Clifford Mollison as Billy Early.

July 14 The Federal Theatre produces Paul Vulpius's Viennese farce, *Help Yourself*. It runs 10 weeks.

July 28 The Oregon Shakespearean Festival opens its second season in Ashland. The program of three plays consists of *The Merchant of Venice* and *Twelfth Night*, both revived from last summer, and a new staging of *Romeo and Juliet*, all directed by the festival's founder, Angus Bowmer.

Aug 3 At the Dublin Gate Theatre, Don Marquis' *Master of the Revels* opens the tenth season. Other plays this season include Robinson's *When Lovely Women*, Somin's *Close Quarters*, Gheon's *The Marvellous History of St. Bernard*, Ellis' *Portrait in Marble*, Housman's *Victoria Regina*, Shakespeare's *Twelfth Night*, Priestley's *Laburnam Grove*, Ibsen's *Brand*, and Sheridan's *The School for Scandal*.

Aug 20 The D'Oyly Carte Opera Company returns to Broadway with its repertory of authorized Gilbert & Sullivan productions for an engagement of nearly five months at the Martin Beck Theatre. The works presented are virtually the same as in its previous visit.

Sep 14 Tyrone Guthrie revives Shakespeare's *Love's Labour's Lost* at London's Old Vic Theatre, with Michael Redgrave and Rachel Kempson. Guthrie revives Wycherley's Restoration comedy, *The Country Wife*, on Oct 6; Redgrave, Edith Evans and Ruth Gordon are featured. On Nov 10, the revival is *As You Like It*, with Redgrave, Evans and Alec Guinness. Thomas Dekker's Jacobean tragi-comedy, *The Witch of Edmonton*, is revived on Dec 8, with Guinness, Redgrave, Evans, and Beatrix Lehmann.

Sep 28 At London's Covent Garden, W. Bridges Adams stages Sophocles' *Oedipus Rex*, in the Gilbert Murray translation. John Martin Harvey and Miriam Lewes play Oedipus and Jocasta.

Sep 29 Norman Marshall stages *Oscar Wilde*, by Leslie and Sewell Stokes, at London's Gate Theatre. Robert Morley plays Wilde. On Oct 10, 1938, it opens at New York's Fulton with Morley repeating his role.

Oct 1 The *White Horse Inn* is revived at New York's Center Theatre. With Ralph Benatsky's score and lyrics from Irving Caesar, David Freedman adapts the German libretto of Hans Mueller. This Viennese operetta is lavishly staged by Erik Charell, with sets by Ernst Stern and some costumes by Irene Sharaff. Max Rivers devises the dances. Leading roles in this sentimental romance are played by William Gaxton, Kitty Carlisle, and Robert

1936   REVIVALS/REPERTORIES

Jan 12 The Theatre Union begins a series of Sunday performances at the Civic Repertory Theatre in New York. Among the productions are Paul Green's *Hymn To the Rising Sun* and *Unto Such Glory*, Albert Maltz's *Private Hicks*, John Wexley's *Running Dogs*, George Sklar and Paul Peters' *A Letter to the President*, Irwin Shaw's *Bury the Dead* (New Theatre League auspices), and *Picket Line*, as Shakespeare, Coward, and Shaw might have written it.

Jan 14 At the Dublin Gate Theatre, Hilton Edwards stages Dell's *Payment Deferred*, followed by a revival of the Balderston/Squire *Berkeley Square*.

Jan 14 At London's Old Vic Theatre, the new year is launched with a revival of Shakespeare's *Richard III*. On Feb 4, the play is *St. Helena*, by R. C. Sherriff and Jeanne de Casalis. *The Winter's Tale* opens on March 17. *King Lear* follows on April 7. *St. Helena* moves to Daly's Theatre on March 19.

Jan 27 Moris Gest produces the classical Chinese play *Lady Precious Stream* at New York's Booth Theatre. It runs 13 weeks.

Feb 2 Supervised by John Houseman, the Negro Theatre Unit of the WPA's Federal Theatre Project presents Frank Wilson's *Walk Together Children*, a plea for racial unity. On March 11, it offers Rudolph Fisher's *Conjur Man Dies*. Orson Welles stages *Macbeth* for the group in April. It premieres on the ninth.

Feb 21 The Federal Theatre produces Edwin and Albert Barker's *American Holiday* at New York's Manhattan theatre. On March 2, it offers Samuel Warshawsky's *A Woman of Destiny* at the Willis. T.S. Eliot's *Murder in the Cathedral*, based on the martyrdom of St. Thomas a Becket, is given at the Manhattan on March 20.

Six days later *In Heaven and Earth*, by Arthur Goodman and Washington Pezet, is offered at the Willis. Victor Wolfson's *Bitter Stream* is given at the Civic Repertory on March 30. On May 15, the Federal Theatre offers Orie Lashin and Milo Hastings's *Class of '29*. Michael Gold and Michael Blankfort's dramatization of the story of John Brown, *Battle Hymn*, is given on May 22.

March 1 The Theatre of Action in New York offers Michael Blankfort's *The Crime* and Paul Peters' *The Green Bundle*. On March 21, the Theatre Collective takes over the Provincetown Playhouse to perform three one-act plays, including Albert Maltz's *Private Hicks*.

March 9 Katharine Cornell revives Shaw's *Saint Joan* at New York's Martin Beck Theatre.

March 14 *The Living Newspaper: Triple-A Plowed Under*, written by New York reporters, premieres at New York's Biltmore. This drama, depicting recent news stories runs 85 performances. Other editions are offered in May and July.

April 13 *The Taming of the Shrew* opens the season at the Shakespeare Memorial Theatre in Stratford-upon-Avon. The other plays are *Julius Caesar*, staged by John Wyse; *King Lear*, directed by Theodore Komisarjevsky; *The Merchant of Venice*, *Romeo and Juliet*, *Much Ado About Nothing*, and *Troilus and Cressida*, the "birthday play." Donald Wolfit plays the Danish Prince in *Hamlet*.

May 20 Theodore Komisarjevsky stages Chekhov's *The Seagull* at London's New Theatre, with Edith Evans leading the cast, which includes John Gielgud and Alec Guinness.

July 8 Even with the rousing Vincent

Oscar Wilde

Halliday. Billy House and Oscar Ragland provide comic relief, and there are some "Native Tyroleans" on hand for folk-dances and local color. The production runs seven months in the Rockefeller Center Theatre.

Oct 8 John Gielgud, directed by Guthrie McClintic, appears as Hamlet in a very successful production, designed by Jo Mielziner. With 132 performances, this is a new record for *Hamlet* or any play by Shakespeare on Broadway.

Oct 14 At London's New Theatre, Theodore Komisarjevsky stages a revival of Shakespeare's *Antony and Cleopatra*, with Donald Wolfit and Eugenie Leontovich in the title-roles.

Oct 14 At New York's 44th Street Theatre, *Daughters of Atreus* opens. This adaptation of the Orestiean legend by Robert Turner, has only 13 performances.

Nov 10 Leslie Howard offers his subtle, modern interpretation of *Hamlet* at Broadway's Imperial Theatre. It runs only five weeks.

Nov 16 Alla Nazimova plays Ibsen's *Hedda Gabler* at New York's Longacre Theatre for four weeks.

Nov 30 The Theatre Guild produces William McNally's *Prelude to Exile*, about

Richard Wagner's interlude in Zurich. It runs six weeks.

Dec 1 Harley Granville Barker revives his *Waste* at London's Westminster Theatre.

Dec 16 The Holborn Empire opens the Christmas season of pantomimes, musical revivals, and adventure thrillers, with its production of *Where the Rainbow Ends*. On the 17th, the Vaudeville offers *Sleeping Beauty: Or, What a Witch*, while *The Astonished Ostrich* opens at the Duke of York's Theatre. Other holiday productions include *Alice Through the Looking-Glass* and *Curse It, Foiled Again!* (both at the Little), *What's Become of the Fairies?* (Piccadilly), *The Boy Who Lost His Temper* (Cambridge), *Mother Goose* (Hippodrome), *Cinderella* (Coliseum, Embassy), *Adventure* (Victoria Palace), *The Melody That Got Lost* (Embassy), *Puss in Boots* (Lyceum), *Buckie's Bears* (Kingsway), *The Soul of Nicholas Snyders* (Arts), *When Knights Were Bold* (Fortune), *The Scarlet Pimpernel* (Queen's), *Aladdin* (Golder's Green Hippodrome), *Jack and Jill* (Wimbledon), *Treasure Island* (Aldwych), and *Bluebell in Fairyland* (Scala). *Peter Pan*, a Palladium special, features Charles Laughton as Captain Hook and Elsa Lanchester as Peter Pan. This show opens on Dec 26, with Jenny Wren as Tinker Bell.

1936 BIRTHS/DEATHS/DEBUTS

Jan 11 English actor-producer Ian Robertson (b.1858) is dead. Robertson spent ten years in America where he played with Modjeska, Edwin Booth, Lawrence Barrett, A. M. Palmer, the Frohmans, and others. He was stage manager at the Bos-ton Museum Theatre where he produced a number of Shakespearean plays. Robertson wrote several plays, some of which were produced by his brother, Sir Johnston Forbes-Robertson.

Feb 7 English-born actor O. P. Heggie (b.1879) dies in Hollywood. Heggie made his first appearance on the London stage in 1906 after a six-year engagement in Australia. His many roles include Androcles in *Androcles and the Lion*, Sir Peter Teazle in *The School for Scandal*, and Diggory in *She Stoops to Conquer*. Heggie has been active in films since 1927.

April 25 American drama critic Percy Hammond (b.1873) dies in New York City. Hammond spent the last 15 years of his life on the staff of *The NY Tribune* (later *The Herald-Tribune*), where his predecessors had been Heywood Broun and William Winter. He first served as drama editor of *The Chicago Evening Post*, and then, in 1909, became critic of *The Chicago Tribune*.

May 4 Actor-producer-playwright Cyril Cusack makes his London debut as Richard in Eugene O'Neill's *Ah, Wilderness!* at the Westminster Theatre.

May 17 English actor Ernest Glendinning (b. 1884) dies in South Coventry, Connecticut.

May 17 Actor-manager Sir Philip (Ben) Greet dies in London. Greet first appeared on stage at Southampton in 1879. In 1886 he gave the first of his many open-air productions of Shakespearean plays and formed the company with which he toured the United Kingdom and America in the 1920s and 1930s. He was knighted in 1929.

June 14 American producer Marc Klaw (b.1858) dies in Sussex, England. In 1896 Klaw founded the Theatrical Syndicate, an association of American businessmen, which controlled the principal theatres in the United States for nearly 16 years. He became an independent producer in 1920, when he severed his partnership with Abraham Erlanger.

Aug 15 Actor Sir Henry Alfred Lytton (b.1867) dies in London. Sir Henry spent most of his theatrical career interpreting the comic roles in Gilbert and Sullivan. He wrote two autobiographical works, *Secrets of a Savoyard*, in 1922 and *A Wandering Minstrel*, in 1933. Lytton received his knighthood in 1930.

Aug 16 Actress-singer Anita Gillette is born Anita Lee Luebben in Baltimore, Maryland.

Sep 17 Anne Baxter makes her Broadway debut as Elizabeth Winthrop in Marie Baumer and Martin Berkeley's *Seen but Not Heard* at the Henry Miller Theatre.

Sep 27 Leon Ames makes his New York debut as Gordon Reese in Henry Misrock's comedy, *Bright Honor*, at the 48th Street Theatre.

Oct 23 Actress Meg Mundy plays the secretary in Sidney Kingsley's *Ten Million Ghosts* at the St. James Theatre in New York. Mundy began her stage career as a concert singer, appearing as a soloist with the New York Philharmonic Orchestra.

The Dramatists Guild and the League of New York Theatres sign a five-year agreement this year on the division of income from the sale of a play to the cinema industry. 60% is the author's; 40% will go to the producer or producers. Even if a play has been financed on Broadway by a film company, cinema rights to it must be offered in the open market. This will prove to discourage Hollywood investments on Broadway.

Jan 23 Elmer Rice resigns his post as director of New York City Federal Theatre, in protest against censorship from Washington of the proposed first *Living Newspaper* production, *Ethiopia*.

April 2 The London Casino, formerly the Prince Edward Theatre, opens with *Folies Parisiennes*. The former theatre has been converted to a cabaret restaurant at a cost of £25,000.

June There have been 135 productions on Broadway this season just closed. Counting theatre-weeks at 8 performances a week, the performance total is 1,299 theatre-weeks.

June 4 Today marks the first performance of the play *CCC Murder Mystery* in New York State. The drama has been written and adapted for production by youths working in each of the 259 Civilian Conservation Corps camps around the United States.

June 15 For Burns Mantle and a number of fellow critics, this past Broadway season "has been the most exciting and the most satisfying of any New York has enjoyed since the year that preceded the crash of '29." For some, the backing of play-production by motion-picture companies which are looking for film subjects is in part responsible. The inauguration of the Federal Theatre Project is cause for hope. For all its excellence and excitement, however, the season has had only 102 productions, a great decrease from the years before the Depression, and 30 less than in the previous season. Mantle again chooses the annual *Best Plays*. They are: Anderson's *Winterset*, Sherwood's *Idiot's Delight*, Behrman's *End of Summer*, Dayton and Kaufman's *First Lady*, Housman's *Victoria Regina*, the Spewacks' *Boy Meets Girl*, Kingsley's *Dead End*, Smith's *Call It a Day*, the Davis's *Ethan Frome*, and Jerome's *Pride and Prejudice*. *Idiot's Delight* wins the Pulitzer Prize, but this season, for the first time, the New York Drama Critics' Circle also gives a prize for the best play. Their choice is *Winterset*. Mantle also provides a summary of theatre activity Off Broadway in his *Best Plays*. It includes productions by labor and Socialist-oriented groups, foreign-language theatre stagings in French, Italian, and Yiddish by New York groups, Irish and other ethnic theatre works in English, monodramas, children's theatre shows, and marionette and puppet theatre attractions. Nearly 2,600 free performances in schools, hospitals, and other public venues have been given by units of the Federal Theatre in New York as well.

July The second oldest surviving playhouse in America ceases to exist. Philadelphia's Arch Street Theatre, 609–615 Arch Street, is demolished. Designed by the distinguished American architect, William Strickland, it was constructed from 1826–28.

Aug Philadelphia's Garrick Theatre is razed. Designed to be both spacious and intimate by architect Willis Hale, it opened in 1901, with Richard Mansfield starring.

Sep 1 The Alhambra Theatre Royal, in London's Leicester Square, gives its closing performance prior to demolition: a production of *Sim-Sala-Bim*, a "great Mystery spectacle by Dante, the Danish magician."

Sep 17 In Seattle, the Negro Unit opens its production of Aristophanes' classic Greek comedy, *Lysistrata*. It will be closed tomorrow by the WPA, owing to "complaints about the play."

Sep 26 At the close of the season, with eight plays in rotating repertory, the Shakespeare Memorial Theatre in Stratford-upon-Avon is able to announce a record attendance of 193,362 spectators.

Nov 30 The Crystal Palace in London, which was the pride of the Victorian era, is totally destroyed by fire. The fire can be seen almost as far as the English Channel.

Dec 3 In Houston, Texas, the Houston Community Players offer their first production, Oscar Wilde's *The Importance of Being Earnest*, directed by the group's founder, Margaret Jones, later to become internationally known as Margo Jones, famed for her dedication to theatre-in-the-round and encouraging new American playwrights. Admission to the production costs just 25 cents.

Love From a Stranger

Jan 7 *The Eternal Road* (NY—Manhattan Opera House—Drama). Max Reinhardt mounts Franz Werfel's pageant of great biblical tales of courage, set in a framework of Eastern European Jews threatened with extinction. Norman Bel Geddes designs the elaborate production which includes a cast of hundreds. The music is by Kurt Weill. Sam Jaffee, Lotte Lenya, and Olive Deering are among the cast. This epic costs half a million dollars. With only 153 performances, it is a financial failure.

Jan 9 *High Tor* (NY—Martin Beck—Comedy). Maxwell Anderson mixes reality and fantasy with verse as he revives the spirits of those who died on Henry Hudson's ship the *Onrust* to help confound the development schemes of greedy moderns on the banks of the Hudson River. Burgess Meredith, Peggy Ashcroft and Hume Cronyn are also in the cast. The production runs almost 22 weeks.

Jan 13 *Behind Red Lights* (NY—Mansfield—Drama). Samuel Shipman and Beth Brown write this expose of Park Avenue vice. Dorothy Hall is featured. The show has 177 performances.

Feb 8 *The Masque of Kings* (NY—Shubert—Drama). Maxwell Anderson writes this tragedy based on the suicides of Crown Prince Rudolph and his mistress, Maria Vetsera, at the hunting lodge at Mayerling. Henry Hull and Margo are featured in the Theatre Guild production. The show lasts 11 weeks. The play has a brief run at London's Gate Theatre beginning April 20, 1938. Eric Portman and Jill Furse head the cast.

Feb 8 *Yes, My Darling Daughter* (NY—Playhouse—Comedy). Mark Reed's story of a liberated woman features Lucile Watson and Peggy Conklin. The comedy enjoys 405 performances.

Feb 20 *Having a Wonderful Time* (NY—Lyceum—Comedy). Marc Connelly stages Arthur Kober's tale of Teddy Stern's search for romance at Camp Kare-Free in the Berkshires. Katherine Locke and Jules Garfield are featured for 372 performances.

March 2 *The Amazing Dr. Clitterhouse.* See L premiere, 1936.

April 9 *Excursion* (NY—Vanderbilt—Comedy). Victor Wolfson, hitherto known as a radical playwright, creates a social comedy. It runs nearly 15 weeks.

April 14 *Babes In Arms* (NY—Shubert—Musical). This show, with book and lyrics by Lorenz Hart and score by Richard Rodgers, centers on some lively youngsters who will be sent to the county farm unless they can raise money. So they put on a show. Among the hits are "My Funny Valentine," "Where Or When" and "The Lady Is a Tramp." Mitzi Green, Dan Dailey,

The Eternal Road

Robert Rounseville, and Alfred Drake are in the cast. George Balanchine choreographs. The show, which costs only $55,000, runs for nine months.

May 19 *Room Service* (NY—Cort—Comedy). George Abbott produces and directs John Murray and Allen Boretz's brash comedy about an impoverished but resourceful producer desperately trying to hold his team together in a hotel room he can't pay for. Sam Levene, Teddy Hart, Eddie Albert, and Betty Field are in the cast of this hit. On Dec 15, it premieres at London's Strand, with Helen Gillette and Boris Ranevsky in the cast, but it does not have a long run.

Sep 22 *George and Margaret.* See L premiere, 1937.

Sep 28 *French Without Tears.* See L premiere, 1936.

Sep 29 *The Star-Wagon* (NY—Empire—Comedy). Maxwell Anderson devises a dramatic vehicle for Burgess Meredith who plays a man permitted to see into the future. Lillian Gish is also featured.

Oct 7 *Susan and God* (NY—Plymouth—Comedy). Rachel Crothers writes this story of a woman, converted to a religious cult, who gains perspective thanks to a previously alcoholic but now repentant husband. Gertrude Lawrence and Paul McGrath are featured. The show runs nine months.

Oct 9 *The Fireman's Flame* (NY—American Music Hall—Musical). This Victorian melodrama, with music and lyrics by Richard Lewine and Ted Fetter, is produced in 19th century style. Ben Cutler plays Harry Howard, a brave fireman who saves a Wall Street millionaire and his ward from incendiary death. It runs for 204 performances.

Oct 27 *Many Mansions* (NY—Biltmore—Drama). Jules Eckert Goodman and his

son Eckert write this story of a young minister who is dismissed for his Christian acts. Alexander Kirkland is featured. The production runs nearly five months.

Nov 2 *I'd Rather Be Right* (NY—Alvin—Musical). In Moss Hart and George S. Kaufman's book, the President must balance the budget for two young lovers to have enough money to marry. The music is by Rodgers and Hart. George M. Cohan plays a President very much like Franklin Roosevelt. The show runs nine months.

Nov 4 *Golden Boy* (NY—Belasco—Drama). Luther Adler stars in Clifford Odets' story of a man who gives up a possible career as a violinist to become a prize-fighter. This Group Theatre production runs over 31 weeks. On June 21, 1938, it premieres at the St. James's in London with Adler again featured. Here it has 109 performances.

Nov 15 *Too Many Heroes* (NY—Hudson—Drama). Dore Schary, to wield great power as a film-studio executive in Hollywood, now offers a play of social consciousness, a concern which will remain with him as a man and a dramatist. There are only 16 performances, however, of this story of a peaceable millworker who is goaded into joining a mob and accidentally killing a man.

Nov 17 *Father Malachy's Miracle* (NY—St. James—Comedy). Brian Doherty adapts this play from a novel by Bruce Marshall. Al Shean plays the good father who prays for a modern miracle, which is granted. The comedy runs 125 performances. It opens in London at the Embassy on March 28, 1945 with W.G. Fay as the priest.

Nov 23 *Of Mice and Men* (NY—Music Box—Drama). John Steinbeck's starkly realistic, plainspoken story of the dispossessed and their dreams features Wallace Ford and Broderick Crawford. It wins 207 performances. On April 12, 1939, the show opens at London's Gate Theatre. John Mills and Niall MacGinnis have the leads.

Nov 27 *Pins and Needles* (NY—Labor Stage—Revue). Cast from members of the International Ladies' Garment Workers' Union, this show is such a success off Broadway that it soon moves to Broadway for an extended run, with a company also on tour. Harold Rome provides music and lyrics. "Sing Me a Song of Social Significance" is popular, as are political parodies. Material is provided by Arthur Arent, Marc Blitzstein, Emanual Eisengerg, and Charles Friedman, who also directs in the renamed Princess Theatre. Its total run is 1,108 performances.

Dec 1 *Hooray for What!* (NY—Winter Garden—Musical). Howard Lindsay and Russel Crouse write the book, E.Y. Harburg the lyrics and Harold Arlen the score for this Ed Wynn vehicle. The plot deals with a man who invents a gas that kills humans as well as bugs, a weapon eagerly sought by war-minded nations. The show runs for 200 performances.

Dec 8 *Siege* (NY—Longacre—Drama). Irwin Shaw's play shows the internal strife and courage among a group of Spanish Loyalists preparing for their last assault. There are only six performances.

Dec 22 *Between the Devil* (NY—Imperial—Musical). Jack Buchanan, Evelyn Laye, and Adele Dixon come from London for this Howard Dietz story. It deals with a man who finds his first wife isn't

Of Mice and Men

as dead as he thought and thereafter has to divide his time between Paris and London to keep his two wives apart. Arthur Schwartz contributes the score, which is conducted by Donald Voorhees. It runs for 93 performances.

Dec 25 *Three Waltzes* (NY—Majestic—Musical). Clare Kummer and Rowland Leigh adapt this Viennese operetta about three generations of Hiller girls and their loves. Kitty Carlisle and Michael Bartlett are featured. There are 122 performances.

1937 BRITISH PREMIERES

Feb 2 *Home and Beauty* (L—Adelphi—Revue). This is styled as a Coronation Revue, with a book by A. P. Herbert and music by Nikolaus Brodszky and Henry Sullivan. The headliners are Binnie Hale and Nelson Keys.

Feb 5 *On Your Toes* (L—Palace—Musical). George Abbott, Lorenz Hart, and Richard Rodgers have devised this show, staged by Leslie Henson in the West End. Vera Zorina plays Vera Barnova; others in the cast include Jack Whiting (Phil Dolan), Gina Malo (Frankie Frayne), Eddie Pola (Sidney Cohn), and Vernon Kelso (Sergei). April 19, the production moves to the Coliseum.

Feb 18 *Big Business* (L—Hippodrome—Musical). Among the funny folk in this lively show are Bertha Belmore, Vera Pearce, Bobby Howes, and David Burns. Jack Waller and Joseph Tunbridge compose the music, with lyrics by Bert Lee and Desmond Carter. Lee, Carter, and K. R. G. Browne concoct the book. Staged by Ralph Reader, the production has a run of almost four months.

Feb 25 *George and Margaret* (L—Wyndham's—Comedy). In Gerald Savory's

play, the title characters are awaited but do not appear. Nigel Patrick, Joyce Barbour, and Ann Casson play leads. There are 799 performances. On Sep 22, it opens at New York's Morosco with Alan Webb, Moya Nugent, and Irene Browne. It runs for nearly 11 weeks.

March 11 *Bats in the Belfry* (L—Ambassadors'—Comedy). Authors Diana Morgan and Robert MacDermot are served by a cast including Vivian Leigh, Charles Hawtry, and Lilian Braithwaite. This show runs over 22 weeks.

April 3 *The Ascent of F.6* (L—Little—Drama). This play by W.H. Auden and Christopher Isherwood features William Devlin, Raf de la Torre, Ruth Taylor, and Erik Chitty.

April 7 *London After Dark* (L—Apollo—Drama). Walter Hackett's play earns a five-month run. Among the cast are Cathleen Nesbitt, Leonard Upton, Marion Lorne, and Ethel Ramsay.

April 12 *Black Limelight* (L—St. James's—Drama). Gordon Sherry's play has a good run of 414 performances.

April 26 *Red Bright and Blue* (L—Vaudeville—Revue). Andre Charlot's show has music by Monte Crick, Dennis van Thal, and Nat Ayer, Jr. It is devised by Edgar Blatt, Dan Soutter, and Ronald Frankau. Myra Morton, Bert Brownbill, and Renee Roberts are in the cast. Described as a "non-stop revue," it has less than 100 performances.

May 19 Elmer Rice's American melodrama, *Judgement Day*, is staged by Murray MacDonald at London's Embassy Theatre. Glynis Johns plays Sonia; Catherine Lacey, Lydia. Also in the large cast are Alan Napier, Charles Quartermaine, Hubert Harben, and Eric Berry. On June 2, it opens at the Strand Theatre for a run of 116 performances.

May 26 *He Was Born Gay* (L—Queen's—Comedy). John Gielgud and Emlyn Williams co-direct Williams' play, with Gielgud and Williams in the leads.

June 3 *Yes, My Darling Daughter* (L—St. James's—Comedy). Rodney Ackland has to make Mark Reed's play more English, but director Alfred De Liagre, Jr., still manages to give it an American touch. Jessica Tandy is Ellen Murray. Evelyn Roberts, Margaret Bannerman, Ena Moon, Sybil Thorndike, Leon Quartermaine, and Alec Clunes are also in the cast.

June 21 *Victoria Regina.* See NY premiere, 1935.

July 16 *St. Moritz* (L—Coliseum—Revue). After operetta revivals, the Coliseum gets a real stage novelty: an ice revue. Max Rivers devises the skating numbers, with the entire production developed by Stanley Bell. Herbert Griffiths provides the musical score. There are 485 performances.

July 28 *The First Legion.* See NY premiere, 1934.

Aug 26 *Time and the Conways* (L—Duchess—Drama). J.B. Priestley's play about a woman who dreams of her family's future wins a seven-month-run. Among the players are Jean Forbes-Robertson, Barbara Everest and Rosemary Scott. The show opens at the Ritz in New York on Jan 3, 1938 with Jessica Tandy as the woman. The drama runs only four weeks.

Sep 1 *Crest of the Wave* (L—Drury Lane—Musical). Ivor Novello plays the leading role in this musical he's written. Lyrics are by Christopher Hassall. Leontine Sagan directs a cast including Marie Lohr, Dorothy Dickson, Minnie Rayner, and Finlay Currie. The show runs nearly 26 weeks.

Sep 8 *Bonnet Over the Windmill* (L—New—Comedy). Dodie Smith's play has 101 performances, with a cast including Ivy St. Helier, William Douglas Home, James Mason, and Gillian Maude. Murray MacDonald directs.

Sep 16 *Going Greek* (L—Gaiety—Musical). Guy Bolton, Fred Thompson and Douglas Furber write the book and Sammy Lerner, Al Goodhart and Al Hoffman the music for this musical featuring Gavin Gordon, Louise Browne, and Leslie Henson. It runs over 38 weeks.

Sep 22 *I Have Been Here Before* (L—Royalty—Drama). Lewis Casson directs and plays in J.B. Priestley's story of reincarnation. On Oct 13, 1938, the play opens on Broadway at the Guild, where it runs only 20 performances.

Oct 14 *Hide and Seek* (L—Hippodrome—Musical). Cicely Courtneidge and Bobby Howes star in this show by Guy Bolton, Fred Thompson and Douglas Furber. The

songs are by Vivian Ellis, Sammy Lerner, Al Goodhart, and Al Hoffman. It runs over 25 weeks.

Oct 15 *Autumn* (L—St. Martin's—Drama). Gregory Ratoff and Margaret Kennedy adapt Ilya Surguchev's play for the British stage. Flora Robson and Jack Hawkins play leads. The production runs five months.

Oct 26 *Yes and No* (L—Ambassadors'—Comedy). Kenneth Horne's light play earns the author a four-month run. The cast includes Diana Churchill, Denys Blakelock and Robert Eddison.

Nov 23 *Robert's Wife* (L—Globe—Drama). St. John Ervine's play concerns a married couple who have careers that clash with family life. Owen Nares and Edith Evans appear. The production runs for 606 showings.

Nov 30 *Thank You, Mr. Pepys!* (L—Shaftesbury—Comedy). W.P. Lipscomb's play is based on Arthur Bryant's biography of Pepys. Edmund Gwenn, Barry K. Barnes, and Marjorie Mars are in the cast. There are 126 performances.

Dec 15 *Room Service*. See NY premiere, 1937.

Dec 16 *Me and My Girl* (L—Victoria Palace—Musical). Noel Gay writes the music and L. Arthur Rose and Douglas Furber invent the book for this musical. Jean Capra, Doris Rogers, and Wallace Lupino are in the company. There are 1,646 performances.

Dec 22 *You Can't Take It With You*. See NY premiere, 1936.

side Players present *Much Ado About Nothing* with Margaretta Scott and Jack Hawkins. On March 14, *The Merry Wives of Windsor* opens with Ray Byford and Violet and Irene Vanbrugh.

Jan 31 Based on Emily Bronte's novel by playwright John Davison, *Wuthering Heights*, gets a showing from the New Shop Window in London's Little Theatre. Gabrielle Casartelli and Reginald Tate play Catherine Earnshaw and Heathcliff. On February 7, at the Strand Theatre, Mary Pakington and Olive Walters' *Wuthering Heights* is performed by the 1930 Players, with John Clements as Heathcliff.

Feb 5 Maurice Evans has a substantial success with his revial of Shakespeare's *King Richard II* on Broadway at the St. James Theatre. It wins 133 performances.

Feb 11 At London's New Theatre, Michael Redgrave and Edith Evans play leads in *As You Like It*. On March 23, Evans and Leslie·Banks are featured in *The Taming of the Shrew*.

Feb 17 The Theatre Union produces John Howard Lawson's *Marching Song*. This play, presented at New York's Nora Bayes, exposes the intrigues of factory-owners and strikebreakers. Grover Burgess is featured. It runs nearly eight weeks.

March 2 James Mason is featured in Robert E. Sherwood's *The Road to Rome*, which is revived at London's Embassy Theatre. The production moves to the Savoy on March 15.

March 8 The Theatre Guild produces Bruno Frank's *Storm Over Patsy* at New York's Guild Theatre. The story concerns an insensitive Scottish politician whose callous attitude about an Irish woman's dog costs him dearly. Ian McLean and Sara Allgood are featured. It runs six weeks.

March 29 *The Bat*, by Mary Roberts Rinehart and Avery Hopwood, is revived in London's Embassy Theatre. Michael Redgrave and Drusilla Wills are in the cast.

1937 REVIVALS/REPERTORIES

Jan 5 Tyrone Guthrie stages *Hamlet* at London's Old Vic with Laurence Olivier in the lead. On Feb 23, he produces *Twelfth Night* with Olivier, Jessica Tandy, and Alec Guinness. *Henry V* is offered on April 6 wilth Olivier and Tandy. Eliot's *Murder in the Cathedral* begins on June 8 with Robert Speaight featured.

Jan 5 The tenth season of the Dublin Gate Theatre continues with revivals of Wilde's *The Importance of Being Earnest* and Cassella's *Death Takes a Holiday*, following which these two and seven other Gate productions are taken to Cairo and Alexandria on the ensemble's second tour to Egypt.

Jan 6 Robert Edmond Jones's production of *Othello*, which he designed and staged for the Opera House in Central City, Colorado, comes to Broadway's New Amsterdam Theatre. Walter Huston plays the Moor.

Jan 8 John Houseman produces Christopher Marlowe's *Dr. Faustus* for the Federal Theatre's Project 891. The production is given at New York's Maxine

Elliott Theatre. Jack Carter and Orson Welles appear. Welles also produces and directs.

Jan 17 At the Ring, Blackfriars, the Bank-

Crest of the Wave

March 29 E. Martin Browne stages *A Midsummer Night's Dream* as the opening production of the new season at the Shakespeare Memorial Theatre in Stratford-upon-Avon. *The Winter's Tale* is the "birthday play," with *Henry V* chosen to celebrate the coronation of King George VI. Jonson's *Every Man in His Humour* observes the Jonson Tercentenary. Other plays in the repertory chosen by director B. Iden Payne are *King Lear*, *As You Like It*, *The Merry Wives of Windsor*, *Hamlet*, and *Cymbeline*.

April 7 Eugene O'Neill's *Anna Christie* is revived in London at the Westminster Theatre with Flora Robson in the title-role.

April 28 The Studio Theatre of the Federal Theatre Project revives James Bridie's *Tobias and the Angel* in New York at the Provincetown Playhouse for 22 performances. Ellen van Volkenburg directs.

May 9 Jules Eckert Goodman's play, *The Great Romancer*, is presented at London's Strand Theatre by the Repertory Players. Charles LeFeaux stages, with Robert Morley playing the title-role of Alexander Dumas. Eric Berry is Dumas *fils*, with Coral Browne as Adah Isaacs Menken and Anthony Quayle as Alfred de Vigny. On June 15, the production moves to the New Theatre.

June 7 The Federal Theatre's Negro Theatre Unit presents George MacEntee's *The Case of Philip Lawrence*. This is the story of a black college graduate who is framed for a murder. Maurice Ellis has the title role.

June 14 At the Open Air Theatre in Regent's Park, the summer season opens with *The Merry Wives of Windsor*, staged by Robert Atkins. Roy Byford is Falstaff. On June 21, *A Midsummer Night's Dream* is revived, with Pamela Brown as Hermia and Jean Forbes-Robertson as Puck. *Julius Caesar* opens on July 5, with Neil Porter as Caesar and Eric Portman as Brutus. Milton's *Comus* is revived on July 19, with *The Winter's Tale* following on Aug 2. Jack Hawkins is Leontes, with Phyllis Neilson-Terry as his queen. *Twelfth Night*, staged by Atkins, opens on Aug 16. *The Tempest*, on Aug 23, has Ion Swinley as Prospero and Janet Johnson as Miranda. On September 6, *The Comedy of Errors* opens, also staged by Atkins.

Aug 2 The third annual Oregon Shakespearean Festival opens in Ashland under the direction of Angus Bowmer. *The Taming of the Shrew*, *Twelfth Night* and *Romeo and Juliet* are presented.

Aug 2 Cocteau's *The Infernal Machine* opens the eleventh season of the Dublin Gate Theatre. Other plays in the program are Vanbrugh's *The Provok'd Wife*, Williams' *Night Must Fall*, Housman's *Victoria*, Shakespeare's *Macbeth*, Rice's

Judgement Day, Daviot's *Richard of Bordeaux*, Ganley's *Murder, Like Charity . . .*, *Hamlet*, and Smith's *The Drunkard*.

Aug 9 At London's Haymarket Theatre, a complement of Irish players revive O'Casey's *Juno and the Paycock*. Sara Allgood and Arthur Sinclair are featured.

Sep 6 John Gielgud plays the king in *Richard II* at London's Queen's Theatre. Michael Redgrave appears.

Sep 21 Tyrone Guthrie revives Shaw's *Pygmalion* at London's Old Vic. Diana Wynyard and Robert Morley are featured. On Oct 12, Emlyn Williams and Marie Ney have the leads in *Measure for Measure*. *Richard III* opens on Nov 2, with Williams in the title role. *Macbeth* returns to the Vic stage on Nov 26, with Laurence Olivier and Judith Anderson. On Dec 27, Guthrie stages *A Midsummer Night's Dream* with Ralph Richardson, Robert Helpmann, and Vivian Leigh.

Oct 1 The Federal Theatre Project produces Lehman Engel's *A Hero Is Born* at New York's Adelphi. This musical is based on a fairy-tale of a Queen who hides from her son the wonderful gifts the fairies have brought. The show has 50 performances.

Oct 2 Dublin's Abbey Theatre Players return to Broadway with a repertory of Irish plays at the Ambassador Theatre. They stay almost 11 weeks, with dramas by Synge, O'Casey, Robinson, and Deevy.

Oct 4 At London's King's Theatre, Hammersmith, John Martin Harvey plays Prof. Paul Gurdner in Hans Mueller's German drama, *Tuberin 5*, adapted for the British stage by Peter Gray. Martin Harvey's wife, Nina de Silva, is Nada.

Oct 6 The Theatre Guild produces Ben Hecht's *To Quito and Back*, the story of a man who deserts his wife to fight fascists in South America. Sylvia Sidney and Leslie Banks are featured. There are 46 performances of this drama, staged at New York's Guild Theatre.

Oct 29 At the Lafayette Theatre in Harlem, the Federal Theatre's Negro Unit revives Eugene O'Neill's sea plays—including *Moon of the Caribbees*, *In the Zone*, *Bound East for Cardiff*, and *The Long Voyage Home*—with Canada Lee as Yank. Staged by William Challee, they run more than two months.

Nov 1 Jean Giarudoux has used the story of Jupiter and Alkmena for the 38th time, hence the name of this play, *Amphitryon 38*. Alfred Lunt and Lynn Fontanne are featured in this Theatre Guild production which runs 19 weeks. On May 18, 1938 the show, adapted by S.N. Behrman, comes to London's Lyric with Lunt and Fontanne again in the lead.

Nov 11 Orson Welles stages *Julius Caesar* in a modern production stressing apt comparisons between power-struggles in ancient Rome and in modern Europe. Seen

at New York's Mercury Theatre, it runs nearly five months.

Nov 16 At the Embassy Theatre in London, Shakespeare's *Cymbeline* is revived, with a last act revised and rewritten by George Bernard Shaw. George Woodbridge plays the title-role.

Nov 16 The Theatre Guild produces Gaston Baty's adaption of Flaubert's *Madame Bovary* at New York's Broadhurst. It runs only 39 performances.

Nov 19 Michael MacOwan produces the revival of Eugene O'Neill's *Morning Becomes Electra* at London's Westminster Theatre. Beatrix Lehmann is featured. There are 106 showings.

Nov 22 The Theatre Guild produces a timely drama, Sidney Howard's *The Ghost of Yankee Doodle*. The play deals with a woman pacifist, whose industrialist family would profit from selling arms to Japan. Ethel Barrymore and Dudley Digges are featured. There are 48 performances.

Nov 25 Tyrone Guthrie revives Sheridan's comedy, *The School for Scandal*, at London's Queen's Theatre. John Gielgud and Michael Redgrave are Joseph and Charles Surface.

Dec 7 Lewis Casson stages Euripide's *The Trojan Women* at London's Adelphi Theatre with Sybil Thorndike in the lead.

Dec 16 As usual in recent years, the Holborn Empire starts the Christmas season off with its children's show, *Where the Rainbow Ends*. On Dec 22, the Playhouse opens its production of *Alice Through the Looking-Glass*. Other holiday treats are *A Kiss for Cinderella* (Phoenix), *Aladdin* (Adelphi), *Peter Pan* (Palladium—with Anna Neagle in the title-role), *Cinderella* (Prince's), *Beauty and the Beast* (Lyceum), *Jack and the Beanstalk* (Streatham Hill), *When Knights Were Bold*

George Gershwin

(Fortune), *Bluebell in Fairyland* (People's Palace), *Humpty Dumpty* (Golder's Green Hippodrome), *Treasure Island* (Savoy), *Sweet Nell of Old Drury* (Queen's), *The Boy Who Lost His Temper* (Garrick), and *The Sleeping Beauty* (Wimbledon).

Dec 27 Jed Harris as director-producer, offers Henrik Ibsen's *A Doll's House* at Broadway's Morosco. Ruth Gordon is featured. The production runs 18 weeks.

1937 BIRTHS/DEATHS/DEBUTS

Jan 7 German actress and singer Lotte Lenya makes her New York City debut as Miriam in Franz Werfel's Bibilcal spectacle, *The Eternal Road*, at the Manhattan Opera House.

March 25 English dramatist-poet and actor John Drinkwater (b. 1882) dies in London. Drinkwater was one of the founding members of Barry Jackson's Pilgrim Players, which gave rise to the Birmingham Repertory Theatre. Acclaimed for his verse plays, it was his prose play *Abraham Lincoln*, however, that brought him critical and popular success in both London and New York.

April 18 Actor-director-producer Robert Hooks is born Bobby Dean Hooks in Washington, D.C.

April 27 Actress Sandy Dennis is born in Hastings, Nebraska.

April 29 American playwright-actor William Gillette (b. 1855) is dead. Gillette was the author of a number of adaptations and dramatizations of novels in which he appeared himself, the most notable being *Sherlock Holmes* and *Esmeralda*. Of his original plays, the best known are *Held by the Enemy* and *Secret Service*.

April 29 American critic and playwright Norman Hapgood is dead at age 69. Hapgood was drama critic of the New York *Commercial Advertiser* and the *Bookman* in the early 1900's. His book, *The Stage in America*, published in 1901, became a standard work in theatre libraries.

May 13 Stage and screen actress Zohra Lampert is born in New York City.

June 14 Actor Barnard Hughes makes his Broadway debut in the revival of John Willard's mystery melodrama, *The Cat and the Canary*, at the Majestic Theatre.

June 19 Scottish dramatist and novelist Sir James Matthew Barrie (b. 1860) dies in London. Although his earliest plays were all successful, it was his *The Professor's Love Story* that established Barrie as a successful playwright. In 1897 the play *The Little Minister* established him as a wealthy man, and in 1904 *Peter Pan* took the stage. His last play, *The Boy David*, was written for Elisabeth Bergner.

July 11 American composer George Gershwin (b. 1898) dies in Hollywood. Gershwin's early successes include *George White's Scandals, Funny Face*, and in 1931 *Of Thee I Sing*—the first musical to win a Pulitzer Prize. His folk opera, *Porgy and Bess*, has become an American classic.

Aug 6 British theatrical producer Annie Elizabeth Fredericka Horniman (b. 1860) dies in London. Horniman was first connected with play production in 1894, and in 1903 established the Abbey Theatre in Dublin. Later in England, she produced over 200 plays including *Jane Clegg, Hindle Wakes, The Mob*, and *The Younger Generation*.

Aug 11 American author and playwright Edith Wharton (b. 1862) dies in Pavilion Colombes, France. Wharton's dramatization of her novel, *The House of Mirth*, in collaboration with Clyde Fitch, proved to be an unsuccessful venture in 1906. The adaptations of *Ethan Frome* by Owen Davis and *The Old Maid* by Zoe Akins were well received.

Oct 11 Stage and screen actor Ron Leibman is born in New York City.

Nov 3 Producer Winthrop Ames (b. 1870) dies in Boston. Ames was appointed managing director of the New Theatre in New York in 1908 where he attempted to establish a repertory theatre. He later built and managed the Little and the Booth Theatres, where he supervised several notable productions. He retired in 1932.

Nov 6 Actor-manager Sir Johnston Forbes-Robertson (b. 1853) dies at St. Margaret's Bay, Dover, England. Sir Johnston made his first stage appearance in 1874, and from then until his retirment in 1913, he had a long and varied career. He went into management in 1895. His performances as Hamlet and as the Stranger in *The Passing of the Third Floor Back* are considered memorable. His autobiographical *A Player Under Three Reigns* was published in 1925.

Nov 8 English actress, author, and producer Gertrude Kingston (b. 1866) dies in London. Kingston made her London debut in 1888. She appeared in a number of George Bernard Shaw's plays, including *Great Catherine* which was written specifically for her. Kingston also wrote and produced several plays. She also published a book of reminiscences.

Nov 25 English producer Lilian Baylis (b. 1874) dies. She was founder of the Old Vic and Sadler's Wells. Under her management, all Shakespeare's plays, from *The Taming of the Shrew* in 1914 to *Troilus and Cressida* in 1923, were produced at the Old Vic.

Dec 29 Author, humorist, and playwright Don Marquis (b. 1878) dies in Forest Hills, New York. Among Marquis' dramatic works are *Master of the Revels, The Dark Hours, Out of the Sea*, and his dramatization of his novel, *The Old Soak*.

1937 THEATERS/PRODUCTIONS

In Britain C.H.A. Camain is granted a patent for a planetarium-type device giving the visual impression of interstellar space. This year a U.S. patent is granted to Clyde Powell for his device to create the illusion that a target or surface has been hit by a projectile.

This year the Lord Chamberlain invokes a special conference on the problems of nudity on stage. Current regulations demand that producers submit photos of the poses to be shown on stage. The Lord Chamberlain must be satisfied that these exhibitions have "sufficient artistic merit," not merely being excuses to display nude female bodies. They may be "accurate representations of actual works of art, paintings, or sculptures." Producers and theatre managers who continue to offend the Lord Chamberlain's sense of propriety and of the artistic discover that the number of prosecutions increases as does the heaviness of the fines, following this conference.

Jan 22 London's Empire Theatre closes its doors after the final performance of *Lady Be Good*, with Fred and Adele Astaire. The Prince of Wales attends this last performance in the soon-to-be demolished theatre.

Feb 10 The fledgling and innovative young American director, Margo Jones, uses an actual Houston courtroom as the stage and auditorium for her production of Elmer Rice's *Judgment Day*.

March Only a month after Maxwell Anderson's *The Masque of Kings* opens, the playwright finds himself facing a $25,000 suit filed by a noblewoman who claims she has been unfavorably represented in this quasi-historical romance. The son of the Archduke of Tuscany also protests Anderson's depiction of his father as a villain. Author and producer—the Theatre Guild—settle out of court.

April 5 Ria Mooney is to be director of the Abbey Experimental Theatre, to produce in Dublin's Peacock Theatre, the second stage of the noted Abbey Theatre.

April 6 A U.S. patent is granted Joseph Levy, assignor to Century Lighting, Inc., for the Lekolight. The Lekolight is a type of ellipsoidal reflector spotlight.

April 16 Briton George Bernard Shaw gives permission to the American Federal

Theatre Project to produce his plays at the low royalty rate of only $50 a week.

April 26 Following the example of George Bernard Shaw, Eugene O'Neill gives the Federal Theatre Project permission to mount productions of his dramas for a $50 per week royalty.

April 30 New York City's Mayor Fiorello H. LaGuardia effectively kills burlesque today by denying licenses to theatres which have been specializing in that form of entertainment.

May 17 For the first time in modern theatre history, a cast and an audience stage a sit-down strike. The Federal Theatre Project's Dance Unit, currently producing *How Long Brethern* and *Candide* on a double-bill at the Nora Bayes Theatre, urge the audience to join them in protest against cuts in the Federal Theatre budget.

May 19 Elmer Rice's *Judgement Day* nearly does not open on the London stage. The Lord Chamberlain has considered banning it on the ground that it contains a thinly disguised presentation of the Reichstag Trial.

May 20 Governor Herbert Lehman, the *NY Times* reports, has vetoed the Dunnigan Bill, which would have set up a one-man censor for the stage.

June 10 Director Margo Jones uses theatre-in-the-round staging for the first time in Houston, Texas, when she produces Norman Krasna's *Louder, Please* in the Lamar Hotel.

June 15 In sharp contrast to production figures of a decade past, there are only 90 new plays produced in the Broadway season of 1936–37, according to drama critic Burns Mantle. This current figure is only a third of the number of productions in the boom years of the Twenties. The figures also represents a reduction from the previous season, although the economy is improving. One reason for this is the withdrawal of major film companies from backing Broadway shows, owing to an author production 60/40% royalty split on film rights. Last season, 20 shows had Hollywood funding; this season, only one had it. Mantle also notes a shortage of good new plays. Mantle's annual list of ten *Best Plays* includes the following dramas: Anderson's *High Tor*, Kaufman and Hart's *You Can't Take It With You*, Green's *Johnny Johnson*, Turney's *Daughters of Atreus*, Kaufman and Ferber's *Stage Door*, Boothe's *The Women*, Sherriff and Casalis' *St. Helena*, Reed's *Yes, My Darling Daughter*, Wolfson's *Excursio*, and Deval and Sherwood's *Torvarich*. Off Broadway, there have been numerous productions. Among the categories singled out by Mantle are Monodrama, Puppets, Children's Theatre, College Plays, Foreign Language Theatre, French, German, Italian, Spanish, and Yiddish, as well as the usual collection of revivals of classics and productions of experimental plays in theatres and au-

ditoriums around New York City. Summing up the past season's Federal Theatre activities in New York, Ma:ntle notes the large number of free performances of musicals, dramas, vaudevilles, and puppet shows. In the summer of 1936, each of New York's five boroughs had a Caravan Theatre touring neighborhoods. (Around the U.S., weekly Federal Theatre audeinces are estimated at 350,000.) Of the numerous metropolitan productions of new works and revivals, Mantle mentions the work of such Federal Theatre groups as the Negro Unit, the Children's Unit, the Teaching Theatre Technique Unit, the Experimental Theatre Unit, the Classic Theatre, the Irish Theatre, and the Theatre of Youth.

July 19 The Ogunquit Playhouse opens in Ogunquit, Maine. Theatre director Walter Hartwig has Alexander Wyckoff design the theatre in the New England style. For some years, in Ogunquit and before that in Peterboro, New Hampshire, and Bristol, Connecticut, Hartwig's Manhattan Theatre Colony has offered practical professional threatre training in summer.

Aug 20, Philadelphia's Broad Street Theatre is doomed, Today a demolition permit is granted for this 1876 playhouse, used for films during the 1920's, but returned to legitimate use in this decade. It has recently been Philadelphia's "class house."

Sep This month, Philadelphia's Adelphi Theatre is torn down.

Sep 24 In Cleveland, Ohio, a bomb blows up part of the roof of the Cleveland Play House's Drury Lane Theatre. Suspect is a local labor union, demanding salaries for stage-hands in this theatre, which survives with a great deal of volunteer work.

Sep 25 Daly's Theatre, Leicester Square in London closes after performances of *The First Legion*. The theatre is to be demolished.

Oct 27 The second Prince of Wales's Theatre in London opens with *Les Folies de Paris*. This 1,139 seat theatre is designed by Robert Cromie.

Nov 26 In Charleston, South Carolina, the newly reconstructed Dock Street Theatre, recreated in the Planter's Hotel building, itself on or near the site of the original Dock Street Theatre of 1735/6, formally opens with a production of Farquhar's *The Recruiting Officer*. This play was the premiere presentation at the Dock Street playhouse two centuries ago.

Dec 3 The Royal Adelphi Theatre on the Strand in London re-opens after its fourth major re-construction this time to the design of architect Ernest Schaufelberg. The capacity is now 1,481; the theatre is managed by Charles B. Cochran. The opening production is Rodgers and Hart's *Ever Green*. ("Royal" will be dropped from the theatre's name in 1940).

WPA audience

Jan 12 *Tortilla Flat* (NY—Henry Miller—Comedy). Jack Kirkland adapts John Steinbeck's novel of life among shack-dwellers in a California slum. The show has only five performances.

Jan 25 *Bachelor Born* (NY—Morosco—Comedy). Ian Hay's play about a British bachelor headmaster whose enemy is vanquished by some lively young ladies runs for 400 performances.

Jan 26 *Shadow and Substance* (NY—Golden—Drama). Paul Vincent Carroll's Irish play, contrasting the simple faith of a maid (Julie Haydon) with the learning of a priest (Cedric Hardwicke), runs over 34 weeks.

Feb 3 *On Borrowed Time* (NY—Longacre—Comedy). Paul Osborn adapts Lawrence Watkin's novel in which Gramps (Dudley Digges) keeps Death (Frank Conroy) up a tree until he can make sure his grandson (Peter Holden) is cared for. The show runs 10 months. On Oct 4, 1938, the play opens at the Haymarket in London in an adaptation by Ian Hay. On this side of the Atlantic, Frederick Leister plays Gramps.

Feb 4 *Our Town* (NY—Henry Miller—Drama). Thornton Wilder wins a Pulitzer Prize for his drama about small town people's lives and loves. Martha Scott (Emily) and Frank Craven (stage manager) are among the cast. The production last 42 weeks. The play coms to London's New Theatre on April 30, 1946, with Richard Hylton and Carolyn Wall as George and Emily.

Feb 15 *Once is Enough* (NY—Henry Miller—Comedy). With Raymond Sovey's setting, producer-director Gilbert Miller, brings Frederick Lonsdale's British play to life on Broadway. Ina Claire plays the sophisticated Duchess of Hampshire who would rather condone adultery than give up the Duke (Hugh Williams). There are 105 performances.

March 23 *Whiteoaks.* See L premiere, 1936.

April 13 *What a Life* (NY—Biltmore—Comedy). George Abbott produces and directs Clifford Goldsmith's play about Henry Aldrich (Ezra Stone) and his lively exploits at Central High School. Butterfly McQueen, Eddie Bracken, and Betty Field are also in the cast. The show settles in for a long run and soon becomes an even longer-running radio serial.

May 11 *I Married an Angel* (NY—Shubert—Musical). Richard Rodgers and Lorenz Hart fashion music and lyrics for this story about a banker who vows to marry an angel. Dennis King and Vera Zorina are featured. George Balanchine supplies the choreography. The show runs for 42 weeks.

What A Life

Sep 21 *You Never Know* (NY—Winter Garden—Musical). Cole Porter later describes this as his worst show. Songs include "At Long Last Love" and "What Shall I Do." The plot involves love mix-ups among servants and masters. Rex O'Malley, Clifton Webb, Libby Holman, and Lupe Velez are cast. It runs nearly 10 weeks.

Sep 22 *Hellzapoppin'* (NY—46th Street—Revue). Ole Olsen and Chic Johnson's high spirits, zaniness, and vulgarity give this show a long run of 1,404 performances. The music and lyrics are by Sammy Fain and Charles Tobias. On April 10, 1948, the revue opens at London's Prince's where it does not have a long run, even headed by Olsen and Johnson.

Sep 24 *Sing Out the News* (NY—Music Box—Revue). "Franklin D. Roosevelt Jones" is a big hit in Harold Rome's score for this satiric liberal revue, with sketch material by Kaufman and Hart. In the company are Jean Peters, June Allyson, and Will Geer. The show has 105 performances.

Sep 28 *Kiss the Boys Good-Bye* (NY—Henry Miller—Comedy). Clare Boothe's new comedy seems to be a satire on the nationwide search for an actress to play Scarlet O'Hara in *Gone With the Wind.* Boothe, however, sees it as an indictment of the implicit fascism of the manners

and morals of the American South. Helen Claire is featured. There are 286 performances.

Oct 8 *The Fabulous Invalid* (NY—Broadhurst—Drama). George S. Kaufman and Moss Hart's play about the decline of the historic Alexandria Theatre runs for only 65 performances.

Oct 13 *I Have Been Here Before.* See L premiere, 1937.

Oct 15 *Abe Lincoln in Illinois* (NY—Plymouth—Drama). Robert E. Sherwood's saga of Lincoln features Raymond Massey in the title role. The play wins the Pulitzer Prize and much critical and popular praise for Sherwood and Massey. It runs for 472 performances.

Oct 19 *Knickerbocker Holiday* (NY—Ethel Barrymore—Musical). Maxwell Anderson and Kurt Weill team up to create a vision of New Amsterdam in the days of Peter Stuyvesant. Walter Huston, as the aging governor, sings "September Song." The show is not really a critical or a financial success, running only 21 weeks.

Nov 9 *Leave It To Me* (NY—Imperial—Musical). Cole Porter provides music and lyrics for this show by Samuel and Bella Spewack. It details the comic adventures of a U.S. ambassador to Russia who tries to get himself recalled. Victor Moore, Gene Kelly, Sophie Tucker, and Mary Martin

Abe Lincoln in Illinois

are in the cast. Martin is an immediate hit with "My Heart Belongs to Daddy." The show has 307 performances.

Nov 23 *The Boys From Syracuse* (NY—Alvin—Musical). George Abbott, assisted by Rodgers and Hart (music and lyrics), adapts Shakespeare's *Comedy of Errors* with some Broadway flavor. Among the musical numbers are "This Can't Be Love" and "Falling in Love With Love." Eddie Albert, Ronnie Graham, Teddy Hart, Jimmy Savo, and Burl Ives are featured George Balanchine provides the choreography. It runs over 29 weeks.

Dec 7 *Here Comes the Clowns* (NY—Booth—Drama). Philip Barry's play about man's need to find meaning in life and resist harmful compromises features Madge Evans and Eddie Dowling. The

show, which mystifies some critics, runs 11 weeks.

Dec 8 *Spring Meeting.* See L premiere, 1938.

Dec 28 *The Merchant of Yonkers* (NY—Guild—Comedy). Thornton Wilder's story of matchmaker Dolly Levi features Percy Waram, Tom Ewell, Jane Cowl, and June Walker. Max Reinhardt directs. With only 39 performances it is a failure. Several decades later, however, as the musical *Hello, Dolly!* Wilder's book will become a long-running international success.

Dec 29 *Everywhere I Roam* (NY—National—Drama). Arnold Sundgaard celebrates the American farmer in this show featuring Dean Jagger, Katherine Emery, Robert Porterfield, Robert Breen and Anne Francis. It runs only two weeks.

1938 BRITISH PREMIERES

Jan 26 *Nine Sharp* (L—Little—Revue). Hermione Baddeley and Cyril Ritchard head the ensemble of this nine o'clock revue, devised by Herbert Farjeon, with music by Walter Leigh. It runs 405 performances.

Feb 10 *The Island* (L—Comedy—Drama). Merton Hodge's play features Godfrey Tearle, Anthony Shaw, and Margery Caldicott, among others. It runs over 25 weeks.

Feb 22 *Dodsworth* (L—Palace—Drama). The popular Sinclair Lewis novel, dramatized for the American stage by Sidney

Howard, now opens in the West End, staged by Edward Sobol. Philip Merivale plays the title-role, with Gladys Cooper as Fran Dodsworth.

March 16 *Operette* (L—His Majesty's—Musical). Noel Coward stages this show he's written and composed. The cast includes Phyllis Monkman, John Laurie, Edward Cooper, Pamela Randell, Peggy Wood and Irene Vanbrugh. It runs four months.

March 24 *Idiot's Delight.* See NY premiere, 1936.

April 9 *Poison Pen* (L—Shaftesbury—Drama). Richard Llewellyn's play has Peggy Primrose, Ethel Warwick, Ida Teather, and George Wray in its cast. It runs almost 22 weeks.

April 13 *Wild Oats* (L—Prince's—Musical). This "Song and Laugh" show, by Douglas Furber is based on a plot by Firth Shephard, with music by Noel Gay. Its company includes Vera Pearce, Barry O'Neill, and Sydney Howard. It has an eight-month run.

April 27 *Banana Ridge* (L—Strand—Comedy). Ben Travers's farce about a mother who entertains two suitors, each of which might be the father of her son, features Travers, Kathleen O'Regan, and Olga Lindo. It wins 291 performances.

May 5 *Pelissier's Follies of 1938* (L—Saville—Revue). In this lively company are Billie Hill, Doris Hare, Lyle Evans, and John Mills, among others.

May 11 *People of Our Class* (L—New—Comedy). St. John Ervine's play transfers from its earlier showings at the Streatham Hill Theatre. Among the cast members are Athene Seyler, Nicholas Hannen, Mary Jerrold, Ursula Jeans, and Bernard Lee.

May 19 *Happy Returns* (L—Adelphi—Revue). Beatrice Lillie heads this troupe, with Constance Carpenter, Bud Flanagan, and Charles Hawtrey also in the company.

May 26 *Glorious Morning* (L—Duchess—Drama). Jessica Tandy is featured in Norman MacOwan's play about a modern St. Joan who is determined to fight the forces of totalitarianism. The production achieves 324 performances. It survives barely a week in New York, opening at the Mansfield on Nov 26.

May 31 *Spring Meeting* (L—Ambassadors'—Comedy). John Gielgud directs this "light comedy" by M.J. Farrell and John Perry. This tale of an Irish baronet and his marriageable daughters features Zena Dare, W.G. Fay, and Margaret Rutherford. It runs 39 weeks. On Dec 8, it premieres at New York's Morosco with Gladys Cooper, Robert Flemyng, Arthur Shields and A.E. Matthews.

June 9 *The Sun Never Sets* (L—Drury Lane—Musical). With music by Cole Porter and Kenneth Leslie-Smith, the book is based on Edgar Wallace's West African stories by Pat Wallace and Guy Bolton. Some of the cast are Todd Duncan (Bosambo), Charles Farrell (Joe Hooling), Leslie Banks (Sanders), and Edna Best, as Dina Fergusson. Basil Dean and Richard Llewellyn collaborate on the direction.

June 16 *Comedienne* (L—Haymarket—Comedy). Ivor Novello earns 141 performances with his new play. In the cast are Kathleen Harrison, Lilian Braithwaite, Alan Webb and Fabia Drake, among others.

June 21 *Golden Boy.* See NY premiere, 1937.

Aug 17 *The Fleet's Lit Up* (L—Hippodrome—Musical). Ralph Reader, Stanley Lupino, and Adele Dixon are featured in this Guy Bolton, Fred Thompson, and Bert Lee show. Vivian Ellis contributes the songs. The show runs 25 weeks.

Aug 31 *Running Riot* (L—Gaiety—Musical). Louise Browne, Ann Coventry, and Arthur Ives are in a special ballet in this show by Douglas Furber, based on a Guy Bolton-Firth Shephard plot. Vivian Ellis provides the songs. The show has a run of 26 weeks.

Sep 6 *Room for Two* (L—Comedy—Comedy). Gilbert Wakefield's play has Hugh Wakefield, Joyce Heron, Margery Morris, and Elsie Randolph in the cast. It runs 33 weeks.

Sep 14 *Dear Octopus* (L—Queen's—Comedy). Dodie Smith's play offers glimpses of a family past as several generations celebrate a Golden Wedding anniversary. Marie Tempest, Leon Quartermaine, and John Gielgud are featured. It runs almost 47 weeks. On Jan 11, 1939, the show comes to New York's Broadhurst with Rose Hobart, Jack Hawkins, and Lillian Gish. It has only 53 performances.

Sep 20 *The Corn Is Green* (L—Duchess—Drama). Emlyn Williams' play about the a schoolteacher who inspires a Welsh boy to strive for an education instead of a life in the mines features Williams and Sybil Thorndike. It runs for 395 performances. On Nov 26, 1940, the play comes to the National Theatre in New York with Ethel Barrymore and Richard Waring. The play has 472 performances.

Sep 23 *Goodbye, Mr. Chips* (L—Shaftesbury—Drama). James Hilton and Barbara Burnham's adaptation of Hilton's novel earns 132 performances. Leslie Banks plays Mr. Chips.

Oct 4 *On Borrowed Time*. See NY premiere, 1938.

Oct 11 *When We Are Married* (L—St. Martin's—Comedy). J.B. Priestley's "farcical comedy" depicts three married couples who discover that they may not legally be married. Raymond Huntley, Ethel Coleridge, Mai Bacon, Patricia Hayes, and Muriel George are cast. On Dec 25, 1939, the comedy comes to New York's Lyceum with Estelle Winwood, J.C. Nugent, Tom Powers, and Alison Skipworth, among others. The show runs nearly 21 weeks.

Oct 14 *Quiet Wedding* (L—Wyndham's—Comedy). Esther McCracken's play features Glynis Johns, Marie Lohr, and Clive Morton. It draws audiences for 227 performances.

Oct 18 *Goodness, How Sad!* (L—Vaudeville—Comedy). Tyrone Guthrie stages Robert Morley's comedy featuring Arthur Hambling and Kathleen Boutall. It runs

for 229 performances.

Nov 22 *Geneva* (L—Saville—Comedy). George Bernard Shaw offers what he calls "a fancied page of History." In this satire on current European problems, Germany, Italy, and Russia are called to Geneva to answer charges of criminal activities. Alison Legatt is featured. The production runs nearly 30 weeks. On Jan 30, 1940, it opens at New York's Henry Miller Theatre with Jessica Tandy in the cast. There are only 15 showings.

Nov 24 *Under Your Hat* (L—Palace—Musical). Jack Hulbert stages and plays Jack Millet in this show he's written with Archie Menzies and Arthur Macrae. Vivian Ellis provides the songs. Others in the cast include Cicely Courtneidge, Leonora Corbett and Frank Cellier. The show has 512 performances.

Dec 26 *Marco Millions*. See NY premiere, 1928.

1938   REVIVALS/REPERTORIES

Jan 1 Orson Welles and John Houseman produce a series of revivals in New York this season. Today at the Mercury they open Thomas Dekker's *The Shoemaker's Holiday*, written in 1600. On Jan 3, they introduce Marc Blitzstein's music-drama *The Cradle Will Rock* at the Windsor. It deals with a corrupt industrialist who is eventually opposed by organized labor. On April 29, they revive George Bernard Shaw's *Heartbreak House* at the Mercury. They present Georg Buechner's *Danton's Death* at the Mercury on Nov 2.

Jan 11 Two revivals conclude the eleventh season of the Dublin Gate Theatre: Johnston's *The Old Lady Says "No!"* and the Balderstson/Squire *Berkeley Square*. Following these performances, the en-

semble tours its productions to the Opera House, Cork, and the Grand Opera House, Belfast. It then departs on its third international tour, visiting Egypt as before, and adding Greece and Malta.

Jan 17 At New York's Adelphi Theatre *The Living Newspaper: One-Third of a Nation* is presented. The text of this play is compiled by Arthur Arent for the Federal Theatre Project. Based on the researchers of the *Newspaper's* staff, the show deals with housing problems. It runs for 237 performances.

Jan 25 The Federal Theatre stages a number of revivals and new works this season. Tonight begins a series of repertory produced and directed by Charles Hopkins at New York's Maxine Elliott Theatre. The works includes are Shaw's *Pygmalion*, O'Neill's *Diff'rent*, Fitch's *Captain Jinks*, Toller's *No More Peace*, and Shakespeare's *Coriolanus*. On March 2 the Negro Theatre Unit stages William DuBois's *Haiti* at the Lafayette. It receives 168 performances. On March 18, the Federal Theatre offers E.P. Conkle's *Prologue to Glory*, the story of the young Lincoln, at the Maxine Elliott. The production has 167 performances. Shaw's *On the Rocks* opens at Daly's on June 15 for 54 performances.

Jan 28 Michel Saint-Denis' staging of Chekhov's *The Three Sisters* comes to the Queen's Theatre in London. The sisters are Gwen Ffrangcon-Davies, Carol Goodner, and Peggy Ashcroft.

Feb 8 At London's Old Vic Theatre, Tyrone Guthrie revives Shakespeare's *Othello*, with Ralph Richardson as the Moor and Laurence Olivier as Iago. On March 15, the play is James Bridie's *The King of Nowhere*, directed by Esme Church, with a cast including Vivienne Bennett, Laur-

Banana Ridge

ence Olivier, Alexander Knox, and Marda Vanne. *Coriolanus*, staged by Lewis Casson, follows on April 19, with Laurence Olivier in the title-role.

Feb 15 The Birmingham Repertory Theatre celebrates its 25th birthday and opens its production of *Bird in Hand*.

Feb 16 E. Martin Browne's staging of T. S. Eliot's *Murder in the Cathedral* is imported to Broadway by Gilbert Miller and Ashley Dukes. Robert Speight plays Thomas, the martyred archbishop of Canterbury. There are only 21 performances.

Feb 19 New York's Group Theatre produces Robert Ardrey's *Casey Jones* at the Fulton. Charles Bickford plays the title role of a crack railroad engineer. It runs only three weeks.

Feb 21 The Theatre Guild produces S.N. Behrman's *Wine of Choice*, a comedy about a young woman in love with a dedicated Marxist who has no time for love. Claudia Morgan, Theodore Newton and Alexander Woollcott are in the cast. It has 43 performances.

Feb 28 Keneth Kent stages O'Neill's *Beyond the Horizon* at London's Q Theatre.

March 28 The Theatre Guild revives Chekhov's *The Sea Gull* with Alfred Lunt and Lynn Fontanne. It lasts only 41 performances.

April 11 *Macbeth* opens the season of Shakespearean plays at the Memorial Theatre in Stratford-upon-Avon. *Henry VIII* is the "birthday play." Theodore Komisarjevsky stages *The Comedy of Errors*. Andrew Leigh directs *A Midsummer Night's Dream*. Other plays programed by festival director B. Iden Payne include *Twelfth Night*, *Two Gentlemen of Verona*, *Romeo and Juliet*, and *The Tempest*. The long season will close on Sep 24.

April 21 Co-directors John Gielgud and Glenn Byam Shaw revive *The Merchant of Venice* at London's Queen's Theatre. Gielgud plays Shylock with Shaw as Gratiano. Peggy Ashcroft is Portia.

April 29 In Chicago, the Federal Theatre opens *Spirochete*, a Living Newspaper documentary-drama by Arnold Sundgaard. It is about syphilis and the need to combat it.

June 14 At the Regent's Park Open-Air Theatre, the summer play season opens with a Robert Atkins mounting of *A Midsummer Night's Dream*. *The Tempest* opens on June 28. On July 12, *Twelfth Night* is revived. Aristophanes' *Lysistrata* offers an alternative to Shakespeare on July 19. *As You Like It* is given. James Bridie's *Tobias and the Angel* is revived on Aug 23. *Dream* returns on Sep 5.

June 15 Rollo Gamble stages Nikolai Gogol's *Marriage* at London's Westminister Theatre.

Aug This month the Dublin Gate Theatre opens its 12th season with Bernard Shaw's

One Third of a Nation

Don Juan in Hell and Shakespeare's *A Comedy of Errors*, followed by Achard's *Le Corsaire*, which Micheal macLiammoir has translated as *Hollywood Pirate*. Other plays this season are Bastian/Merivale's *the Underground Hour*, Lenormand's *Juliet in the Rain*, Williams' *Night Must Fall* (revival), O'Neill's *Mourning Becomes Electra*, Shakespeare's *Julius Casear*, Wilde's *The Importance of Being Earnest* (both revivals), and the holiday treat, Fagan's *And So To Bed*.

Aug 5 Opening its fourth season in Ashland, the Oregon Shakespearean Festival offers *Hamlet*, *Twelfth Night*, *The Merchant of Venice* and *The Taming of the Shrew*.

Aug 24 Alexander Teixeira de Mattos' play, *Thou Shalt Not—*, a translation of Emile Zola's *Therese Raquin*, opens at the Playhouse Theatre in London. Frank Birch directs; Cathleen Nesbitt plays Therese.

Sep 20 Tyrone Guthrie revives Arthur Wing Pinero's *Trelawny of the "Wells"* at London's Old Vic Theatre. On Oct 11, a moderndress *Hamlet* is presented uncut, with Alex Guinness as the Dane. Shaw's *Man and Superman* is staged on Nov 21. On Dec 6, Sheridan's *The Rivals* returns. On Dec 26, Guthrie revives *A Midsummer Night's Dream*.

Oct 1 The Federal Theatre produces Theodore Pratt's *The Big Blow* at New York's Maxine Elliott Theatre. This drama about the fight against bigotry enjoys 157 performances. On Dec 16, the Negro Theatre Unit presents George Bernard Shaw's *Androcles and the Lion* for a run of 13 weeks. It is given in Harlem at the Lafayette Theatre.

Oct 6 Michel Saint-Denis stages Bulgakov's *The White Guard* at London's Phoenix Theatre. The cast includes Michael Redgrave, Peggy Ashcroft, George Devine, and Glen Byam Shaw. On Dec 1, Saint-Denis revives *Twelfth Night* with Devine, Redgrave, and Ashcroft among the players.

Oct 12 Maurice Evans performs an uncut *Hamlet* at New York's St. James Theatre. It runs 12 weeks.

Oct 19 Michael MacOwan stages J.B. Priestley's *Dangerous Corner* at London's Westminister Theatre.

Dec 14 The Holborn Empire opens the holiday season by reviving its production of *Where the Rainbow Ends*. On Dec 21, the Playhouse revives *Alice Through the Looking-Glass*, which is seen on the 23 in a different version at the Queen's Theatre. Other holiday treats are *Babes in the Wood* (Drury Lane), *The Scarlet Pimpernel* (Embassy), *Jack and the Beanstalk* (Golder's Green Hippodrome), *Charley's Aunt* (Haymarket), *The Sleeping Beauty* (King's Hammersmith; Streatham Hill), *Peter Pan* (Palladium), *Red Riding Hood* (Covent Garden), *The Boy Who Lost His Temper* (Duke of York's), *Queen of Hearts* (Lyceum), *Let's Pretend—* (St. James's), *Treasure Island* (Savoy), *Hansel and Gretel* (Scala), and *Dick Whittington* (Wimbledon).

Dec 22 Sutton Vane's *Outward Bound* is revived on Broadway at the Playhouse for a run of 32 weeks. Laurette Taylor, Florence Reed, Bramwell Fletcher, and Vincent Price, among others are in the cast. Otto Preminger stages.

Dec 26 The Russian "Bat" cabaret, *La Chauve Souris*, returns to London for the holidays at the Fortune Theatre.

Jan 21 Esme Beringer has the title role in Hamlet, revived at London's Arts Theatre.

Jan 25 Donald Wolfit stars in Jonson's Volpone at the Westminster Theatre in London.

Jan 29 English actor Henry Reeves-Smith (b. 1862) is dead. Reeves-Smith played at the Park Theatre in New York in 1881 and supported Fanny Davenport at Toole's in Diane in 1-82. During the 1920s he appeared in Grounds for Divorce, The High Road, and Just Fancy among others.

Feb 9 Ballerina-actress Maria Karnilova makes her first Broadway appearance in the chorus of the Dorothy Fields-Arthur Schwartz musical comedy, Stars in Your Eyes at the Majestic Theatre.

April 29 Actress Geraldine Fitzgerald makes her Broadway debut in the role of Ellie Dunn in Geroge Bernard Shaw's Heartbreak House at the Mercury Theatre.

Sep 19 Actress Pauline Frederick (b. 1885) dies in Beverly Hills, California. Frederick made her first appearance on stage in New York's Knickerbocker Theatre in 1902 with the Rogers Brothers. From 1915–23, she devoted herself to movies. Her London debut was made in 1927 at the Lyceum Theatre as Jacqueline in Madame X.

Oct 22 Canadian-born actress May Irwin (b. 1862) dies in New York City. Irwin joined Tony Pastor's company at the old Metropolitan Theatre in New York in 1877. She made her first London appearance with the Daly Company in 1884. In 1922 she played in The '49ers at New York's Punch and Judy Theatre.

Nov 2 Producer-director Richard Barr begins his acting career with Orson Welles' Mercury Theatre Company as a "conven-

Pauline Fredericks

tion attendant" in Buchner's Danton's Death.

Dec 27 Wisconsin novelist and playwright Zona Gale (b. 1874) dies in Chicago. Gale won the 1921 Pulitzer Prize for her dramatization of her novel, Miss Lulu Bett. Her autobiographical narrative consists of two volumes, When I was a Little Girl (1913) and Portage, Wisconsin (1928).

Third of a Nation, closing tonight, has been seen since its opening in January by 217,458 people.

Nov 25 On the advice of the London County Council, the Lord Chamberlain has withdrawn the license of the Royalty Theatre, and the matinee performance of The Milkman's Round, by the Southern Cross Players, closes the theatre.

Dec 3 The Carolina Playmakers Theatre formally reopens today with a bill of experimental plays. The Tarheel Theatre, which had been the Playmakers home, was gutted by a fire last August and has now been restored.

Dec 6 Hallie Flanagan, National Director of the Federal Theatre Project, appears before the Dies Committee, a congressional panel investigating Un-American Activities (HUAC) in the United States. She defends the project against accusations that it has been infiltrated and taken over by Communists.

1938 THEATERS/PRODUCTIONS

March 22 In order for Robert E. Sherwood's Idiot's Delight to receive a license for London performances, the Lord Chamberlain's Office, requires that no direct references be made to Mussolini or Italy, nor can the soldiers be dressed in Italian uniforms. All this, in spite of the fact that the intended locale and governmental apparatus are quite clear.

June On Broadway this past season, productions have totalled 111. There have been 1,117 theatre-weeks, a total of all performances of all productions, counted at eight performances a week. Burns Mantles' list of annual ten Best Plays includes: Steinbeck's Of Mice and Men, Wilder's Pulitzer Prize-winning Our Town, Carroll's Shadow and Substance,

Osborn's On Borrowed Time, Anderson's The Star-Wagon, Crothers' Susan and God, Conkle's Prologue to Glory, Behrman's Amphitryon 38, Odets' Golden Boy, and Goldsmith's What a Life. The growth in amateur and semi-professional theatre activity Off Broadway in the past season is impressive. As in the previous season, Mantle reports on such categories as Children's Theatre, Puppets Foreign-language Theatre, Monodramas, and College Drama Clubs, which include Harvard's Hasty Pudding Club and Princeton's Triangle Club. Various labor groups, as well as ensembles dedicated to special kinds of plays, have offered numerous productions.

Oct 22 The New York production of One

Jan 3 *Mamba's Daughters* (NY—Empire—Drama). Dorothy and DuBose Heyward dramatize his novel about the problems of Southern Black women. Ethel Waters, Georgette Harvey, and Jose Ferrer are in the cast. The show runs five months.

Jan 5 *The Gentle People* (NY—Belasco—Drama). The Group Theatre produces Irwin Shaw's drama of two men who finally rebel against being shaken down by a gangster. Sam Jaffe, Roman Bohen, and Franchot Tone appear. There are 141 performances.

Jan 10 *The White Steed* (NY—Cort—Drama). Paul Vincent Carroll's Irish play pits the native good sense of Canon Lavelle (Barry Fitzgerald) against the fussy legalisms of Father Shaughnessy (George Coulouris) in an Irish village where tempers are easily aroused. The play runs 17 weeks.

Jan 11 *Dear Octopus*. See L premiere, 1938.

Jan 18 *Set To Music* (NY—Music Box—Revue). Noel Coward's show is built around the talents of Beatrice Lillie, with much of its material from his London revue *Words and Music*. "Mad About the Boy," "The Party's Over," and "The Stately Homes of England" are popular songs in the show. Gladys Calthrop designs. The show runs four months.

Jan 21 *The American Way* (NY—Center—Drama). This "spectacle play," by George S. Kaufman and Moss Hart celebrates and surveys the past 40 years of life in America as seen from the vantage point of the family. Fredric March and Florence Eldridge are featured.

Feb 4 *One for the Money* (NY—Booth—Revue). Gertrude Macy is one of the producers of Nancy Hamilton's conservative revue about society and the wellheeled. Alfred Drake, Gene Kelly, and Keenan Wynn are among the cast. The production runs for 132 showings.

Feb 7 *I Must Love Someone* (NY—Longacre—Drama). Jack Kirkland and Leyla Georgie tell the story of a group of kept women, one of which wants a stable life with a real husband. Martha Sleeper appears. The show has 191 performances.

Feb 9 *Stars in Your Eyes* (NY—Majestic—Musical). J.P. MacEvoy provides the book and Arthur Schwartz and Dorothy Fields the muisic and lyrics for this story of a Hollywood star pursuing a man who loves another. Ethel Merman, Richard Carlson, Tamara Toumanova, and Jimmy Durante head the cast. The show runs four months.

Feb 11 *Lew Leslie's Blackbirds of 1939* (NY—Husdon—Revue). Johnny Mercer provides some lyrics; Sammy Fain, Mitchell Parish, and Ferde Grofe (orchestration) also contribute. J. Rosamond

Johnson is here with his choir. Lena Horne, Ralph Brown, and others perform. It closes after nine performances.

Feb 15 *The Little Foxes* (NY—National—Drama). Lillian Hellman's story of the greed of a Southern family and the heartlessness of its most glamorous member features Tallulah Bankhead with Dan Duryea and Patricia Collinge. It runs 410 performances. " . . . ' The Little Foxes' is so cleverly contrived that it lacks spontaneity," reports the *NY Times*. On Oct 21, 1942, it opens at London's Piccadilly with Fay Compton in the lead. It doesn't reach the 100-performance mark.

March 8 *Family Portrait* (NY—Morosco—Drama). Judith Anderson plays the Virgin Mary in Lenora Coffee and William Joyce's picture of the Holy Family. The production runs 111 performances. On Feb 17, 1948, it is shown at London's Strand with Fay Compton as Mary.

March 14 *The First American Dictator* (NY—Bayes—Drama). Nathan Sherman and Jacob Weiser's biography of Huey Long of Lousisana runs for only nine performances.

March 28 *The Philadelphia Story* (NY—Shubert—Comedy). Katharine Hepburn scores a success as Tracy Lord in Philip Barry's popular comedy set among the socialites on the Main Line outside Philadelphia. Also in the cast are such talents as Lenore Lonergan, Vera Allen, Shirley Booth, Van Heflin, and Joseph Cotton. The Theatre Guild has the hit it has long desired. It runs a year. Robert Edmond Jones designs the sets and lighting for director Robert Sinclair. On Dec 1, 1949 it opens at London's Duchess with Margaret Leighton, Antony Forwood and Hugh Sinclair. Staged by Harold French and set by Anthony Holland, the production lasts for 85 performances.

April 17 *No Time for Comedy). (NY—Ethel Barrymore—Comedy). S.N. Behrman creates this play about a woman whose playwright husband, appalled at the world's current chaos, is having trouble writing for the theatre. Katharine Cornell and Laurence Olivier play the leads. It has 185 showings. On March 27, 1941, it opens at London's Haymarket with Rex Harrison and Lilli Palmer. The production runs nearly 11 months.*

June 19 *The Streets of Paris* (NY—Broadhurst—Revue). The Shuberts join Olsen and Johnson to present this revue with words and music predominantly by Harold Rome and Jimmy McHugh. Carmen Miranda is a hit singing "The South American Way." Others in the cast are Gower Champion, Bobby Clark, and Bud Abbott and Lou Costello. The show runs for 274 performances.

June 20 *From Vienna* (NY—Music Box—

The Straw Hat Review

Revue). Talents from Central Europe, calling themselves the Refugee Artists Group, offer a musical collage, with some of the adaptations done by John LaTouche. The company includes Illa Roden, Paul Lindenberg, Fred Lorenz, and Maria Pichler. The show runs ten weeks.

July 6 *Yokel Boy* (NY—Majestic—Musical). Lew Brown's musical about a young girl who comes to Hollywood, where her career doesn't blossom but her boyfriend's does features Lois January and Buddy Ebsen. There are 208 performances.

Aug 28 *George White's Scandals* (NY—Alvin—Revue). The *Scandals* return for the last time. Jack Yellen and Sammy Fain devise the words and music with sketches by White and others. Among the cast are Ann Miller, the Three Stooges, Ben Blue, and Ray Middleton. The show runs 15 weeks.

Sep 27 *See My Lawyer* (NY—Biltmore—Comedy). Milton Berle, Millard Mitchell, and Gary Merrill play three young lawyers (Jewish, Irish, and Italian, supposedly) who found their fortunes representing an eccentric playboy (Eddie Nugent) who's always getting into trouble. Richard Maibaum and Harry Clark's farce runs seven months.

Sep 29 *The Straw Hat Revue* (NY—Ambassador—Revue). Max Liebman assembles this show, with music and lyrics by James Shelton and Sylvia Fine. Originally organized for summer audiences at Camp Tamamint in Pennsylvania, the revue wins 75 performances on Broadway. Imogene Coca, Danny Kaye, Alfred Drake, Jerome Robbins, and Ruthanna Boris are in the cast. The show costs $8,000 to stage on Broadway.

Oct 11 *Skylark* (NY—Morosco—Comedy). Samson Raphaelson adapts one of his short stories for the stage. Gertrude Lawrence plays the restive wife of an advertising man (Donald Cook), who sacrifices his spouse and home-life to the convenience of his clients. The show runs eight months. On March 26, 1942, it comes to London's Duchess with Constance Cummings in the lead. There are 109 performances.

Oct 16 *The Man Who Came to Dinner* (NY—Music Box—Comedy). Monty Woolley plays the acerbic Sheridan Whiteside, the man who comes to dinner and then injures himself so that he has to remain in the home in a wheelchair until he recovers. George S. Kaufman and Moss Hart model the character on the person and foibles of critic Alexander Woollcott. The show has 739 performances. On Dec 4, 1941, it opens at London's Savoy with Robert Morley in the lead. A hit on this side of the Atlantic as well, it has 709 showings. *The Times* calls it: "A bright, light, genially American, slightly farcical and thoroughly enjoyable comedy. . . . It is at the wisecracks we laugh and it is their cutting edge that we admire."

Oct 18 *Too Many Girls* (NY—Imperial—Musical). Rodgers and Hart write the songs for this college romance which includes "I Didn't Know What Time It Was." Marcy Wescott, Richard Kollmar, Van Johnson, Eddie Bracken, Hal LeRoy, and Desi Arnez are in the cast. George Abbott produces and stages the show which runs 31 weeks.

Oct 25 *The Time of Your Life* (NY—Booth—Comedy). William Saroyan's sentimental slice-of-life in a San Francisco bar wins 186 performances and both the Pulitzer Prize and the Drama Critics' Circle Award. In the ensemble of this Theatre Guild production are Will Lee, Julie Haydon, Gene Kelly, Celeste Holm, Len Doyle, and Tom Tully. The show opens at the Lyric, Hammersmith, on Feb 14, 1946, with Margaret Johnston, Walter Crisham, Irene Worth, Miriam Karlin, and Eileen Herlie among the cast.

Nov 3 *Margin for Error* (NY—Plymouth—Drama). Clare Boothe sets her comedy-melodrama in the library of a Nazi German Consul in "an American City prior to 1939." This is the first play about the Nazi menace to have a big commercial and critical success on Broadway. It runs 33 weeks. Otto Preminger directs and acts, with Bramwell Fletcher, Sam Levene, El-

speth Eric, and Leif Ericson also in the cast. On Aug 1, 1940, it opens in London at the Apollo with Margaretta Scott and Dennis Arundell.

Nov 8 *Life With Father* (NY—Empire—Comedy). Howard Lindsay and Russel Crouse adapt Clarence Day's stories about his family to create this long-running hit with 3,224 performances. Lindsay, his wife Dorothy Stickney, John Drew Devereaux, and Teresa Wright are among the cast. The comedy comes to London's Savoy on June 5, 1947, where it earns 427 showings. Leslie Banks, Sophie Stewart and Roland Bartrop are in the cast.

Nov 17 *Very Warm For May* (NY—Alvin—Musical). Oscar Hammerstein II provides the book and Jerome Kern the score for this story of a girl who leaves school to join a summer theatre. Grace McDonald and Eve Arden are in the cast. Kern's "All the Things You Are" is an instant hit. The show has only 59 performances.

Nov 20 *The World We Make* (NY—Guild—Drama). Sidney Kingsley produces and directs this play he's made from Millen Brand's novel, *The Outward Room*, with sets by Harry Horner. Margo plays a woman released from a mental hospital and trying to make a life for herself. The show runs for ten weeks.

Nov 27 *Key Largo* (NY—Ethel Barrymore—Drama). Maxwell Anderson writes this story of a man who finally has a tragic recognition of past cowardice and dies with courage. Paul Muni is featured. Uta Hagen, Jose Ferrer, and Karl Malden are also in the cast. Staged for the Play-

wrights' Company, it has 105 performances.

Nov 29 *Swingin' the Dream* (NY—Center—Musical). Erik Charell stages his and Gilbert Seldes's swing version of Shakespeare's *Midsummer Night's Dream* with a largely black cast including Louis Armstrong, Jackie "Moms" Mabley and Butterfly McQueen. The show lasts only 13 performances.

Nov 30 *Morning's at Seven* (NY—Longacre—Comedy). Paul Osborn's tale of four sisters and their families and troubles in an American small-town earns only 44 performances, unlike the success it is to have in a 1980 revival. Nonetheless, it is admired by some critics, chosen by critic Burns Mantle as a *Best Play*, anthologized, and often produced by amateur theatres. The sisters are played by Effie Shannon, Jean Adair, Dorothy Gish, and Kate McComb.

Dec 6 *DuBarry Was a Lady* (NY—46th Street—Musical). Cole Porter creates the music and lyrics for the book by B.G. De Sylva and Herbert Fields. The story revolves around a nightclub men's room attendant who longs for the star of the show. Taking a Mickey Finn, he dreams he is Louis XIV and she DuBarry. Bert Lahr and Ethel Merman play the leads. "Katie Went To Haiti," "Do I Love You?" and "Friendship" are hits. The show runs 408 performances. On Oct 22, 1942, it opens at London's His Majesty's with Frances Day and Arthur Riscoe. On this side of the Atlantic it runs over 22 weeks.

Dec 25 *When We Are Married.* See L premiere, 1938.

1939 BRITISH PREMIERES

Jan 25 *Design for Living.* See NY premiere, 1933.

Jan 26 *Tony Draws a Horse* (L—Criterion—Comedy). Lesley Storm's entertainment wins a run of almost 46 weeks. In the cast are Nigel Patrick, Diana Churchill, Kay Astor, and Lilian Braithwaite, among others.

Jan 31 *Gas Light* (L—Apollo—Drama). Patrick Hamilton's thriller about a fiendish husband who is systematically driving his wife insane features Dennis Arundell, Gwen Ffrangcon-Davies, and Milton Rosmer. The show runs nearly 15 weeks. On Dec 5, 1941, it opens at New York's Golden under the title *Angel Street*. Vincent Price, Judith Evelyn, and Leo G. Carroll are the leads. In America the show has an extremely long run—1,295 performances.

Feb 12 *On the Frontier* (L—Globe—Drama). Benjamin Britten composes the music for W.H. Auden and Christopher Isherwood's anti-war play, presented by the Group Theatre. Tenor Peter Pears is

an Announcer, with Tristan Rawson, Mary Barton, Eric Berry, Everley Gregg, and Lydia Lopokova in the cast.

Feb 22 *Johnson Over Jordan* (L—New—Drama). Playwright J.B. Priestley calls his script a "modern morality play." Basil Dean stages, using a cast which includes Edna Best, Jill Johnson and Ralph Richardson as Robert Johnson. On March 21, the play moves to the Saville Theatre.

March 21 *The Family Reunion* (L—Westminster—Drama). E. Martin Browne stages T.S. Eliot's poetic drama which has its roots in the Oresteian trilogy of Aeschylus. Browne, Colin Keith-Johnston, Helen Haye, Michael Redgrave, and Catherine Lacey are in the cast.

March 22 *The Man in Half Moon Street* (L—New—Drama). Barre Lyndon's mystery melodrama features Leslie Banks, Ann Todd, and Malcolm Keen. It runs six months.

March 23 *The Dancing Years* (L—Drury Lane—Musical). Ivor Novello writes and composes this show, with lyrics by Chris-

Swingin' the Dream

topher Hassall. Novello also has the lead. In the ensemble are Minnie Rayner, Frances Clare, Marry Ellis, and Anthony Nichols, among others. There are 187 performances.

April 20 *The Women.* See NY premiere, 1936.

April 21 *The Little Revue* (L—Little—Revue). Herbert Farjeon (words) and Walter Leigh (music) provide the raw material, shaped by director Hedley Briggs and a cast including Cyril Ritchard, Hermione Baddeley, Charolotte Leigh, Ronald Waters, and Joyce Grenfell. The show earns a run of 415 performances.

June 21 *After the Dance* (L—St. James's—Drama). Terence Rattigan's play is directed by Michael MacOwan, with a cast including Hubert Gregg, Catherine Lacey, Viola Lyel, and Robert Harris.

July 5 *Alien Corn.* See NY premiere, 1933.

Aug 23 *Spotted Dick* (L—Strand—Comedy). Ben Travers' farce about some jewels that are mistakenly pawned features Joyce Barbour, Alfred Drayton, and Josephine Travers. It wins 260 performances.

Oct 11 *The Little Dog Laughed* (L—Palladium—Revue). This revue, by George Black, Peter Titheradge, and Gale Pedrick, earns 461 performances. Black and Robert Nesbitt stage a cast which includes Jimmy Nervo, Teddie Knox, Jimmy Gold, Charlie Naughton, and Bud Flanagan.

Oct 31 *The French for Love* (L—Criterion—Comedy). As staged by William Mollison, this production has a run of nearly 30 weeks. Alice Delysia plays Hortense; Carl Jaffe, Pierre; Cecil Parker, Victor and Athene Seyler, Amy. The play has been previewed at the Richmond Theatre on Oct 9. Margeurite Steen and Derek Patmore are the playwrights.

Nov 3 *Runaway Love* (L—Saville—Musical). Barry Lupino is featured in this show he has staged with co-author Frank Eyton. The score is by Billy Mayerl. Hilda Davies, Wyn Weaver, and Tony Lupino are also in the cast. It runs six months.

Nov 14 *Black Velvet* (L—Hippodrome—Revue). This is styled "an intimate rag" by its creators, George Black, Mary Dunn, and Douglas Furber. With Harry Parr-Davies's score and some Cole Porter songs, the show earns a long run of 620 performances. Among the company are Carole Lynne, Vic Oliver, Teddy Brown and Cyril Smith.

Nov 29 *Eve on Parade* (L—Garrick—Revue). "A Musical Crazy Show" is the description of this revue which enjoys a run of 7 months. Jack Taylor directs an ensemble including Ernie Gerrard, Claude and Harry Lester, Beatrix Richards and Tubby Turner.

Dec 12 *Ladies in Retirement* (L—St. James's—Drama). Reginald Denham directs this mystery thriller he has written with Edward Percy. Joan Kemp-Welch and Mary Merrall are in the cast. The production runs 22 weeks. On March 26, 1940, it opens at New York's Henry Miller with Flora Robson and Isobel Elsom. The show plays 151 times.

Dec 20 *All Clear* (L—Queen's—Revue). Taking its title from wartime air raid terminology, this show is written and staged by Harold French. The cast includes Bobby Howes, Fred Emny, Robert Eddison, and Beatrice Lillie. It runs five months.

Dec 21 *Shepherd's Pie* (L—Prince's—Revue). Douglas Furber dishes up "a menu of song, dance, and laughter" for 336 performances. He directs a troupe which includes Pat Taylor, Sydney Howard, Raymond Newell, Vera Pearce and Phyllis Robins.

1939   REVIVALS/REPERTORIES

Jan 5 Isadore Godfrey, the musical conductor of the D'Oyly Carte Opera Company, leads the ensemble back to Broadway to the Martin Beck Theatre for 77 performances of their Gilbert & Sullivan repertory.

Jan 10 *Wuthering Heights* is again revived by the Dublin Gate Theatre, continuing the 12th season. A revival of Cassella's *Death Takes a Holiday* brings the season to an early close, following which the company leaves Dublin on tour. The first stops are Cork and Belfast. After that, the international tour begins, with performances in Ljubljana, Zagreb, Belgrade, Sofia, Bucharest, and Salonika.

Jan 12 Estelle Winwood directs and plays Lady Bracknell in this revival of Oscar Wilde's *The Importance of Being Earnest*. With Clifton Webb as Jack Worthing, it runs for 61 performances at New York's Vanderbilt Theatre.

Jan 22 During this decade of prelude to World War II, there has been little notice taken on the London stage of the rise of Nazism in Germany or Fascism in Italy. Now at the Everyman Theatre in Hampstead, the play of the moment is *Anschluss*, described as a "chronicle play by an anonymous author."

Jan 24 At London's Old Vic Theatre, Tyrone Guthrie brings back *She Stoops to Conquer*, with Pamela Brown and John Mills. Ibsen's *An Enemy of the People*, also staged by Guthrie, follows on Feb 21, with Roger Livesey. On March 28, Guthrie and company present Shakesperare's *Taming of the Shrew*, with Livesey and Ursula Jeans. On June 27, Auden and Isherwood's *The Ascent of F.6* is revived, directed by Rupert Doone, with Alec Guinness.

Jan 27 Cyril Cusak plays Christy Mahon, the title-role, in this revival of John Millington Synge's *The Playboy of the West-*

ern World. London's Mercury Theatre is the venue.

Jan 30 Maurice Evans, after his success with a full-length *Hamlet*, revives Shakespeare's *Henry IV, Part 1* for 74 performances on Broadway at the St. James Theatre.

Jan 31 John Gielgud stages this revival of Oscar Wilde's *The Importance of Being Earnest* at London's Globe Theatre. He plays the lead, Joyce Carey, Edith Evans and Margaret Rutherford are among the cast.

Feb 3 The Theatre Guild offers Stefan Zweig's *Jeremiah*, a play about the biblical prophet who denounces war and evil but is rejected by his people. John Gassner, Worthington Miner, and Cornell Wilde are in the cast. Presented at New York's Guild Theatre, it has only 35 performances.

Feb 12 Lord Dunsany's *The Bureau de Change* opens at London's Playhouse Theatre. It's paired with Bernard Shaw's *The Shewing-Up of Blanco Posnet*. Catherine Lacey, Esme Percy and Margaret Pawling are in the ensemble. On Feb 17, Shaw's *The Doctor's Dilemma* returns to the London stage at the Westminster Theatre, Stephan Haggard is featured. On March 28, it moves to the Whitehall Theatre.

Feb 28 The Comedie Française comes to London for a repertory engagement at the Savoy Theatre. The troupe opens with Moliere's *L'Ecole des Maris* and Alfred de Musset's *Le Chandelier*. On March 3, they open de Musset's *A Quoi Revent les Jeunes Filles* and Jean-François Regnard's *Le Legataire Universel*.

March 1 The Federal Theatre premieres *The Swing Mikado*, its highly successful black version of Gilbert & Sullivan's comic tale at New York's New Yorker. It has already been seen in Chicago. The show has 62 performances before being bought by Broadway producers and opened, on May 1, at the 44th Street Theatre, where it lasts only three weeks. On March 23, producer Michael Todd brings his black version *The Hot Mikado* to Broadway at the Broadhurst. Bill Robinson heads the cast. It runs 85 performances and is then moved to the Hall of Music at the World's Fair.

March 19 The Stage Society offers Federico Garcia Lorca's Spanish drama, *Marriage of Blood (Blood Wedding)*, at London's Savoy Theatre. Vera Lindsay, David Markham and Martita Hunt are in the cast.

March 20 Bram Stoker's *Dracula* comes back to life at London's Winter Garden Theatre in the Hamilton Deane-John Balderston version, staged by Bernard Jukes. Deane and Jukes play Dracula and Renfield. Yona Wells is the unfortunate Lucy.

March 26 At London's Arts Theatre, Beatrix Thomson's play, *Sons of Adam*, dealing with the plight of Jewish refugees from European oppression, is presented by the Arts Theatre Club and the New Shop Window. Among the cast are Jose Collins, Arthur Wontner and Basil Summers.

April 3 Theodore Komisarjevsky's production of *The Taming of the Shrew* opens the season at Stratford-upon-Avon's Shakespeare Memorial Theatre. This is the Diamond Jubilee of the Festival; *Much Ado About Nothing* is the "birthday play." Irene Hentschel, the first woman director to work in the Memorial Theatre, stages *Twelfth Night*. Baliol Holloway directs *As You Like It*. Robert Atkins stages *Othello*. Komisarjevsky's production of *The Comedy of Errors* is also on view. Other plays are *Coriolanus* and *Richard III*.

April 20 The International Ladies' Garment Workers' Union revue, *Pins and Needles 1939*, with music by Harold Rome, is on Broadway with some new material, at the Windsor Theatre. Ultimately it will run more than 1,000 performances.

April 24 Geroge Bernard Shaw's *Candida*, with Catherine Lacey in the title-role, is revived in London at the Westminster Theatre. On May 29, Shaw's *Pygmalion* comes to life at the Embassy Theatre, with Margaret Rawlings as Elza.

April 24 The Federal Theatre produces *Sing for Your Supper* at New York's Adelphi. The revue has some barbed satire on foreign affairs such as the Nazi annexation of Austria. There is a more optimistic tone in sketches about American life. Paula Laurence, Israel Lansky, and Paul Jacchia are in the large cast. The show runs beyond the season.

May 18 Maurice Schwartz and his Yiddish Art Theatre of New York open in London's Garrick Thatre with *The Water Carrier*, a folk comedy by J. Prager, with music by I. Alshansky. Schwartz stages.

On June 5, the company plays H. Leivick's *Professor Schelling*.

May 18 Robert Edmond Jones, as Managing Director of the American Lyric Theatre, opens a repertory of music and dance-drama on Broadway at the Martin Beck Theatre. Among the productions are *The Devil and Daniel Webster*, by Stephen Vincent Benet (book) and Douglas Moore (score); *Filling Station*, by Lew Christiansen (choreography) and Virgil Thomson (score); *Susanna, Don't You Cry*, based on Stephen Foster's music, by Sarah Newmeyer and Clarence Loomis; and a program of ballets from Ballet Caravan (Lincoln Kirstein), including Eugene Loring's *Billy the Kid*, with Aaron Copland's score.

May 19 The Federal Theatre produces George Sklar's *The Life and Death of an American*, the saga of a man who climbs the coroprate ladder only to fall during the Depression. Arthur Kennedy is featured in the drama, presented at New York's Maxine Elliott. This is one of the last Federal Theatre productions before Congress ends funding.

Summer In Spearfish, South Dakota, the *Black Hills Passion Play* opens. Its performers are largely refugees from political oppresion in Europe—augmented by local citizens—and the play is like that performed in Oberammergau. This American version is so well received that it becomes an annual event.

June 3 The summer season of plays in Regent's Park at the Open-Air Theatre begins with *Much Ado About Nothing*, with Cathleen Nesbitt. *Pericles* opens on June 20, with Robert Eddison in the title-role. On July 4, *A Midsummer Night's Dream*, is presented with Romney Brent as Bottom. *Twelfth Night* is revived on July 31, with Jessica Tandy. On Aug 7, Bridie's *Tobias and the Angel* returns. On Aug 28, *Twelfth Night* comes back.

June 4 The Sunday Theatre offers Nesta Pain's *The Jews of York*, a tale of the terrible ordeal they suffered in the 13th century at the hands of debtor Christians. This drama is shown at the Duchess Theatre in London.

June 26 At London's Queen's Theatre, Sean O'Casey's *The Plough and the Stars* is revived, with some Irish players. Hugh Hunt directs a cast including Sara Allgood, Maire O'Neill, Liam Gaffney and Cyril Cusak.

June 28 John Gielgud plays *Hamlet* at the Lyric Theatre, London, with Fay Compton·and Jack Hawkins in the cast.

Aug 4 The fifth season of the Oregon Shakespearean Festival. There are four plays offered in repertory. Two are revivals from last summer: *Hamlet* and *The Taming of the Shrew*. *As You Like It* and *A Comedy of Errors* are newly mounted.

Aug 21 *Will Shakespeare*, by Clemence Dane, opens the 13th season of the Dub-

lin Gate Theatre. Other plays include Priestley's *I Have Been Here Before*, Bernard Shaw's *Pygmalion*, Collis' *Marrowbone Lane*, Lennox/Ashley's *Third Party Risk*, Auden/Isherwood's *The Ascent of F6*, the Quinteros' *A Hundred Years Old*, and Shakespeare's *The Merry Wives of Windsor*.

Sep 20 *Farjeon's Little Revue* re-opens at London's Little Theatre. On Sep 25, at the Victoria Palace, *Me and My Girl*, re-opens after its temporary closure. On Sep 27, *Tony Draws a Horse* re-opens at the Comdey Theatre. All have been closed immediately on the outbreak of war on the continent.

Oct 2 Adjusting to the state of war, the Old Vic Company opens its season, not at its historic home, but at the Streathem Hill Theatre, with a revival of *Romeo and Juliet*, directed by Murray MacDonald, with Robert Donat and Constance Cummings as the title-role lovers. On Oct 4, Bernard Shaw's *The Devil's Disciple*, staged by Esme Church, is revived, with Donat and Stewart Granger. On Oct 5, the revival is Goldsmith's *The Good-Natured Man*, directed by Tyrone Guthrie, with Andrew Cruikshank, Max Adrian, Cummings, and Donat. Shaw's *Saint Joan* is revived, in Esme Church's staging, on Oct 10, with Cummings and Granger.

All Clear

Oct 16 At London's Q Theatre, Beatrix Lehmann directs a triple-bill: O'Casey's *A Pound on Demand*, Strindberg's *Pariah*, and O'Casey's *The End of the Beginning*. Among her troupe are Irene Handl, Edgar K. Bruce, John Laurie, and Beatrix Fielden-Kaye.

Nov 14 The Group Theatre offers Robert Ardrey's *Thunder Rock* the tale of a man who becomes a lighthouse keeper because he is disgusted with the modern world. Luther Adler is featured. There are only 23 performances at New York's Mansfield Theatre.

Nov 20 At London's Embassy Theatre, Shakespeare's *Julius Caesar* is revived in modern-dress, staged by Henry Cass.

Walter Hudd, Eric Portman, Godfrey Kenton, Hugh Giffith and Ian Carmichael are in major roles.

Dec 7 Alec Guinness adapts Dickens' *Great Expectations* for the stage. He is also in the cast which includes Martita Hunt and Marius Goring. The production is presented at the Rudolf Steiner Hall in London.

Dec 18 At London's Arts Theatre, the holiday season in time of war opens with a Nativity play by Gwendolyn Downes, *The Unveiling*. On Dec 19, at the Piccadilly, Machiavelli's Rensaissaance comedy, *Mandragola*, is revived. On Dec 20, Shaw's *Major Barbara* is revived at the Westminster Theatre. Other holiday shows and revivals include *Where the Rainbow Ends* (Holborn Empire) *The Importance of Being Earnest* (Globe), *The Sleeping Beauty* (Golder's Green Hippodrome), *Aladdin* (Streatham Hill), and *Cinderella* (Coliseum).

The Philadelphia Story and *Here Come the Clowns*, Carroll's *The White Steed*, Coffee and Cowen's *Family Portrait*, and Boothe's *Kiss the Boys Good-Bye*.

June 30 Today, by Act of Congress, the Federal Theatre Project is brought to an official close, a demise vigorously fought by many theatre people, objected to by editorialists and commentators, and regretted by audiences who have enjoyed the free and low-cost productions.

July Scotland's Perth Theatre opens its first Scottish Theatre Festival. James Bridie is the Festival's patron. Bridie writes a new play for the occasion: *The Golden Legend of Shults*. Alec Guinness and Pamela Stanley star in *Romeo and Juliet*. Shaw's *Caesar and Cleopatra* and Chekhov's *The Seagull* are also produced. Unfortunately, World War II intervenes, so the second festival cannot be held until 1945.

1939   BIRTHS/DEATHS/DEBUTS

Jan 28 The Irish poet, patriot, and politician, William Butler Yeats, dies in Roquebrune, France. Yeats, a founder with Augusta, Lady Gregory, and others of the Irish National Theatre Society and of the famed Abbey Theatre, created much-admired poetic dramas for its stage, inspired by Irish legend and history. Yeats was awarded the Nobel Prize for Literature in 1923.

March 31 Playwright Israel Horovitz is born in Wakefield, Massachusetts.

April 8 American actress Bertha Kalich (b. 1874) dies in New York City. Kalich made her first New York appearance as a singer in 1895 in *La Belle Helene* and *The Gypsy Baron*. She subsequently made a reputation in her Yiddish performances in *A Doll's House*, *Fedora*, and others. Kalich's English-speaking debut was as *Fedora* in 1905.

Aug 23 American playwright Sidney Coe Howard (b. 1891) dies in Tyringham, Massachusetts. His first popular success was the Pulitzer Prize winning *They Knew What They Wanted*. Then followed *The Silver Cord*, *The Late Christopher Bean*, *Alien Corn*, and many adaptations.

Oct 24 American-born actor Hurd Hatfield makes his New York debut as Kirilov in George Shdanoff's drama, *The Possessed*, after his stage debut in Devonshire, England, last spring.

Nov 3 Future playwright Terence McNally is born in St. Petersburg, Flordia.

Nov 10 Stage and screen actor Etienne Girardot is dead in Hollywood at age 83.

Dec 18 American critic and columinst Heywood Campbell Broun (b. 1888) dies in New York. Journalist for the New York *Tribune* and *World* and the Scripps-Howard papers, Broun's book of theatre criticisms, *Seeing Things at Night*, was published in 1921.

Dec 31 Sir Frank Benson dies at the age of 81. He had been the major director and actor at the Shakespeare Memorial Theatre in Stratford-upon-Avon from 1886 to 1919. As actor-manager, he also took his company to London and on provincial tours. In 1913, he headed the Stratford troupe's first American tour. In 1916, he was knighted by King George V.

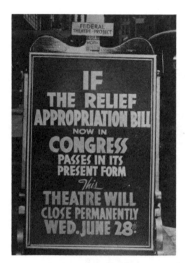

Federal Theatre Project poster

1939   THEATERS/PRODUCTIONS

Edward Gilbert is granted a U.S. patent for a scenic system for the stage using two or more turntables and a series of hinged, double-faced flats which can be turned like pages to reveal new settings.

Feb 18 On Treasure Island, in San Francisco Bay, the *Federal Theatre* opens as a part of the Golden Gate International Exposition.

Feb 25 *Running Riot* closes at the Gaiety Theatre on the Strand in London and is the last stage production at that theatre.

April 13 A fire today in Atlantic City, New Jersey destroy the Casino and Blaker's Theatre at a loss of $300,000.

April 24 With the opening of the revue *Sing for Your Supper* tonight at New York's Adelphi Theatre, audiences have the opportunity to see what can be accomplished with 18 months of rehearsals. This unheard of rehearsal period leads to accusations of boondoggling with Federal Theatre Project funds.

June 15 There have been about 80 new dramatic and musical productions on Broadway this past season, by critic Burns Mantle's count. As usual, the percentage of financial successes—which is not always linked to critical success—is one out of four. Broadway producers have been expecting the opening of the 1939 New York World's Fair to generate increased audiences for shows, but just the opposite is the case. Fair-goers prefer to linger at Flushing Meadows to enjoy the many amazing mechanized exhibits and visions of the future. Mantle's choices for the annual ten *Best Plays* include: Sherwood's *Abe Lincoln in Illinois*—the Pulitzer Prize play, Hellman's *The Little Foxes*, Odets' *Rocket to the Moon*, Kaufman and Hart's *The American Way*, Behrman's *No Time for Comedy*, Barry's

July 1 In New Hope, Pennsylvania, the Bucks County Playhouse opens for the first time with Edward Everett Horton in his perennial comic role in *Springtime for Henry*. The Playhouse will not only provide summer stock-theatre for fugitives from the Manhattan summer weather, but will also be the scene of some pre-Broadway try-outs.

Sep 4 All theatres in England are ordered closed because of the blitz. The closure will last 12 days. The Windmill Theatre is the only London theatre not to close in the war, other than for the compulsory period.

Sep 21 *The Era*, a weekly London journal reporting on theatre and variety performances since the mid-19th century, ceases publication.

Sep 25 Sheffield Repertory Company relocates to Southport because of the outbreak of war. The opening play is *Laburnum Grove*. Remaining here until 1946, the company will perform 240 plays in this location.

Jan 9 *The Male Animal* (NY—Cort—Comedy). Elliott Nugent and James Thurber write this comedy about a professor whose job and marriage are in danger. Nugent is featured. Gene Tierney, Ruth Matteson, and Don DeFore are also in the cast. There are 243 performances. The show opens in London at the New Theatre on June 27, 1949, with Arthur Hill as the professor. It wins a run of 120 performances, after an earlier showing at the Arts Theatre in May.

Jan 22 *Two on an Island* (NY—Broadhurst—Comedy). Elmer Rice's island is Manhattan where two small-town youngsters, played by Betty Field and John Craven, are trying to succeed as actress and author respectively. Produced by the Playwrights' Company, the show runs three months.

Jan 30 *Geneva.* See L premiere, 1938.

Jan 31 *My Dear Children* (NY—Belasco—Comedy). After 33 weeks in Chicago, this play by Catherine Turney and Jerry Horwin comes to New York for 117 performances. John Barrymore stars in this tale about a matinee idol and his family.

Feb 8 *Two for the Show* (NY—Booth—Revue). Nancy Hamilton's show, has Betty Hutton jitterbugging, Richard Haydn doing comic monologues, and the talents of Alfred Drake, Brenda Forbes, and Keenen Wynn. Morgan Lewis' "How High The Moon" becomes a popular song.

Feb 22 *Night Music* (NY—Broadhurst—comedy). Clifford Odets tells the story of Steve Takis (Elia Kazan), sent from Hollywood to bring some trained monkeys back from New York. The monkeys get him in trouble with the police and an actress, but all turns out well, and he decides to seek his fortune in Manhattan. Hanns Eisler, who will flee the country during the postwar Communist scares, provides the music. This Group Theatre production also used Jane Wyatt, Virginia Stevens, Tom Tully, Sanford Meisner, Morris Carnovsky, David Opatoshu, Ruth Nelson, Will Lee, and Art Smith. Harold Clurman stages; Mordecai Gorelik designs. The show dies after 20 performances.

March 6 *The Fifth Column* (NY—Alvin—Drama). Ernest Hemingway's play about Spain during the Civil War gets a reworking from Benjamin Glazer for the Theatre Guild. Featuring Franchot Tone and Katherine Locke, it runs 11 weeks.

March 23 *Separate Rooms* (NY—Maxine Elliott—Comedy). Glenda Farrell plays a frigid actress who likes her pet Chihuahua better than she does her playwright husband (Lyle Talbot). The play, by Alan Dinehart and Joseph Carole, runs through the season for 613 performances.

March 26 *Ladies in Retirement.* See L

Two for the Show

premiere, 1939.

April 12 *The Living Newspaper: Medicine Show* (NY—New Yorker—Drama). This edition is not produced by the Federal Theatre, which has gone out of business June 30, 1939. Instead Carly Wharton and Martin Gabel present Oscar Saul and H. R. Hays' survey of American medical care and the attendant indictment of the American Medical Association's restrictive practices. There is also a plea for Socialized Medicine and passage of a Public Health bill. The show runs four weeks, with a cast including Gabel, Dorothy McGuire, Olive Deering, John Randolph, and Alfred Ryder.

April 13 *My Heart's In the Highlands* (NY—Guild—Comedy). William Saroyan's special brand of poetic Armenian-American optimism and love of mankind puzzles some critics. Even with a Group Theatre cast, it runs for only 44 performances. This saga of Ben Alexander (Philip Loeb), a poverty-stricken poet who takes to the open road, is supported by Robert Lewis' direction, Paul Bowles' music, and Herbert Andrews' designs.

April 29 *There Shall Be No Night* (NY—Alvin—Drama). The Theatre Guild and the Playwrights Company join forces to present Robert E. Sherwood's drama of the courage of the Finns, recently overrun by Russian invaders. Alfred Lunt and Lynn Fontanne head the cast. It runs 181 performances. The play opens at London's Aldwych on Dec 15, 1943, with Lunt and Fontanne in the same roles. There are 220 showings.

May 28 *Louisiana Purchase* (NY—Imperial—Musical). Irving Berlin provides the score and Morrie Ryskind the book and lyrics for this story of a senator sent to investigate corruption in Louisiana.

George Balanchine choreographs. Victor Moore, Vera Zorina, and Irene Bordoni are in the cast. The show has 404 performances.

Sep 11 *Hold On To Your Hats* (NY—Shubert—Musical). An aging Al Jolson returns from Hollywood to share star-billing with Martha Raye, Jack Whiting, and Bert "Mad Russian" Gordon. Jolson plays the star of a radio show character like the Lone Ranger, whose fans expect him to foil the villain (Arnold Moss) in real life as well as on the airwaves. Music and lyrics are by Burton Lane and E. Y. Harburg, with "There's a Great Day Coming Manana" a hit. The show runs only 20 weeks because Jolson pleads poor health.

Sep 18 *Johnny Belinda* (NY—Belasco—Drama). Elmer Harris's melodrama centers on the character of a deaf-mute girl played by Helen Craig. There are 321 performances.

Oct 1 *Boys and Girls Together* (NY—Broadhurst—Revue). Ed Wynn studs his show with sight-gags, crazy inventions, and general nonsense. Albertina Rasch choreographs; Sammy Fain provides music; Veronica and Irene Sharaff create the costumes. Among those present are Jane Pickens, the La Varres, the De Marcos, and Dorothy Koster. The show wins 191 repetitions.

Oct 5 *Journey to Jerusalem* (NY—National—Drama). Maxwell Anderson's play depicts the life of Jesus when he was 12. Sidney Lumet, Arnold Moss, and Karl Malden are in the cast. There are only 17 performances.

Oct 10 *It Happens on Ice* (NY—Center—Revue). The Center Theatre is rebuilt for this ice show produced by Sonia Henie. (She does not perform.) The revue has a

The Fifth Column

split run of 276 performances. The spectacle and the skating proves such a draw that ice revues are to occupy this theatre for some years.

Oct 18 *George Washington Slept Here* (NY—Lyceum—Comedy). George S. Kaufman stages this farce he's crafted with Moss Hart. It deals with country people taking advantage of city folk's interest in restoring "historic" houses. The cast includes Percy Kilbride, Mabel Taliaferro, Dudley Digges, and Ernest Truex. The show runs 173 performances.

Oct 25 *Cabin in the Sky* (NY—Martin Beck—Musical). Ethel Waters, as Petunia Jackson, gets a second chance for her dying husband, Little Joe (Dooley Wilson), to go through the Pearly Gates—designed by Boris Aronson. George Balanchine stages, with the Katherine Dunham Dancers and the J. Rosamond Johnson Singers on hand. The story is Lynn Root's; the music and lyrics are the work of Vernon Duke and John LaTouche. The show runs almost

five months. "Taking a Chance on Love" becoming a hit.

Oct 30 *Panama Hattie* (NY—46th Street—Musical). Formerly one of the friendly girls of the Canal Zone, Hattie (Ethel Merman) has reformed and wants to win the affection of the little girl (Joan Carroll) who she hopes will be her step-daughter. Their duet, "Let's Be Buddies," is a high point in Cole Porter's score. Herbert Fields and B. G. DeSylva devise the plot. The show has 501 repetitions.

Nov 26 *The Corn Is Green.* See L premiere, 1938.

Dec 23 *Old Acquaintance* (NY—Morosco—Comedy). John Van Druten's plot conflict is between two women-novelists, Katherine (Jane Cowl) and Mildred (Peggy Wood), whose friendship is strained when Mildred's daughter (Adele Langmire) captures the interest of Katherine's lover (Kent Smith). This plays 170 times. On Dec 18, 1941, the play opens in London at the Apollo, with Edith Evans and Muriel Pavlow in the leads.

Dec 25 *Pal Joey* (NY—Ethel Barrymore—Musical). John O'Hara devises the book, with music and lyrics by Rodgers and Hart for this fable of Joey, a hoofer and a heel, who takes advantage of the women attracted to him. Gene Kelly and Vivienne Segal play the leading roles. "Bewitched Bothered and Bewildered," "Take Him," and "I Could Write a Book" are hits. There are 374 performances. Some critics are displeased with Joey's lack of morality. The play opens at London's Princes on March 31, 1954 with Harold Lang in the lead. There are 245 performances.

Dec 26 *My Sister Eileen* (NY—Biltmore—Comedy). Joseph Fields and Jerome Chodorov adapt Ruth McKenny's stories about her and her sister's adventures in New York. Shirley Booth and Jo Ann Sayers play the girls. Staged by George S. Kaufman, the show lasts 865 performances. It opens at London's Savoy on Sep 22, 1943, with Coral Browne and Sally Gray in the leads. Here it runs nearly eight months.

Dec 30 *Flight To the West* (NY—Guild—Drama). Elmer Rice stages his own play about the confrontation between Nazism and democracy. Paul Henried and Hugh Marlowe appear in this Playwrights Company production. It runs 17 weeks.

"None but an author who was also an actor, could have written this distinguished play, for in its background there is a more authentic rendering of the magic of the stage than can be found in hundreds of plays which have dealt directly with theatrical life. . . . Mr. Emlyn Williams' chief business is to make a study of the dependence of a once famous, now fecklessly dissolute and half-forgotton actor upon his daughter. . . . Each stage of this narrative carries us securely to the next, and at no time does the narrative crack. The humour throughout is as sound as the sentiment and the total impression is that the dialogue, situation, and acting have been welded with beautiful firmness. . . . ," reports *The Times.*

March 7 *Cousin Muriel* (L—Globe—Drama). Clemence Dane's play is staged by Norman Marshall with an impressive cast including Edith Evans, Alec Guinness, Frederick Leister, and Peggy Ashcroft.

March 15 *Beyond Compere* (L—Duchess—Revue). Ronald Frankau's title is a pun on what Americans call the Master of Ceremonies. Frankau stages and performs as well, supported by Rene Roberts, Hilary Allen, Max Kirby, Gerry Fitzgerald, and others. The show has a run of 133 performances.

April 5 *Rebecca* (L—Queen's—Drama). Daphne Du Maurier adapts her novel of suspense and terror for the stage. George Devine directs, with Margaret Rutherford, Owen Nares, and Celia Johnson in major roles. The play runs nearly 23 weeks.

April 11 *New Faces* (L—Comedy—Revue). Eric Maschwitz presents some fresh new talents. Among the faces are Jeremy Hawk, Bill Fraser, Sidney Bromley, Charles Hawtrey, Frith Banbury, Hazel Jennings, Zoe Gail, and Joan Eddowes. Jack Strachey composes the tunes. The show has an 8-month run.

April 17 *Up and Doing* (L—Saville—Revue). Among the talents in this show are Cyril Ritchard, Binnie Hale, Stanley Holloway, Graham Payn, Patricia Burke, and Leslie Henson, who co-directs with Robert Nesbitt. Douglas Furber and others have devised the show, with a Manning Sherwin score. It earns 171 performances.

May 13 *Present Arms* (L—Prince of Wales's—Musical). Fred Thompson's book and the songs by Frank Eyton and Noel Gay make possible a 7-month run for this show, staged by Harry Sylvester. Among the performers are Phyllis Monkman, George Gee, Max Wall, Billy Bennett, and Evelyn Dall.

July 31 *Cottage To Let* (L—Wyndham's—Drama). Geoffrey Kerr's thriller deals with German spy who tries to steal an important scientific discovery. Alastair Sim, Gillian Lind, and Leslie Banks appear. There are 105 showings.

Aug 1 *Margin for Error.* See NY premiere,

1940   BRITISH PREMIERES

Jan 11 *Funny Side Up* (L—His Majesty's—Musical). Stanley Lupino stages and stars in this show he's assembled. Assisting him are Florence Desmond, Sally Gray, Carol Raye, Arty Ash, Bernard Clifton, and others. There is a 27-week run.

Jan 16 *Follow My Leader* (L—Apollo—Comedy). Athole Stewart plays King Stefan of Neurasthenia in this play by Terence Rattigan and Anthony Maurice. Stewart stages such talents as Francis Sullivan, Frith Banbury, Eric Chitty, and Walter Hudd.

Feb 21 *The Light of Heart* (L—Apollo—Comedy). Emlyn Williams directs his play, casting such performers as Angela Baddeley, Anthony Ireland, Megs Jenkins, and Godfrey Tearle. It has a run of four months.

1939.

Sep 9 *Uniform Theatre* (L—Garrick—Revue). This is an entertainment for His Majesty's Forces and war-workers, performed by Seymour Hicks, Margaretta Scott, Chris Sands, Mark Hambourg, and others.

1940 REVIVALS/REPERTORIES

Jan At the Dublin Gate Theatre, the 13th season continues with a modern-dress *Hamlet*, followed by Micheal mac-Liammoir's *Where Stars Walk*. Revivals include Ibsen's *Peer Gynt*, Bronte's *Wuthering Heights*, and Balderston/Squire's *Berkeley Square*. Hamilton's *Gaslight* is also staged by Hilton Edwards, co-founder of the theatre with mac-Liammoir. Following production of Johnston's *The Dreaming Dust*, the troupe tours to Cork, Limerick, Waterford, and Belfast. All the Dublin stagings, except the *Hamlet*, are played at the Gaiety Theatre, as is the revival of *Where Stars Walk*, offered in April after the Irish tour.

Jan 16 Arthur Shields directs and Robert Edmond Jones designs a popular revival of Sean O'Casey's *Juno and the Paycock* which runs 13 weeks on Broadway at the Mansfield Theatre. Sara Allgood, Shields, Barry Fitzgerald, and Effie Shannon are in the company.

Feb 12 Donald Wolfit opens a series of Shakespeare revivals at London's Kingsway Theatre. *The Merchant of Venice* is the initial offering, with Wolfit as Shylock. On Feb 15, he plays Malvolio in *Twelfth Night*. On the 16, he plays the prince in *Hamlet*, with Rosalind Iden as Ophelia. *Much Ado About Nothing*, on Feb 20, features Wolfit and Rosalinde Fuller. He plays Petruchio to Fuller's Katherina in *The Taming of the Shrew* on March 6.

March 5 At London's Haymarket Theatre, John Gay's *The Beggar's Opera* is revived, staged by John Gielgud, with Michael Redgrave and Audrey Mildmay.

March 12 At London's Unity Theatre, Sean O'Casey's *The Star Turns Red* is staged by John Allen, with what is described as an "anonymous cast."

March 20 *The White Horse Inn*, with a score by Benatsky and Stolz, is revived at London's Coliseum, despite the fact that Britain is now at war with Austria, the locale of this show. Prince Littler stages.

March 25 Ferenc Molnar's *Liliom* is revived on Broadway at the 46th Street Theatre for seven weeks, with Ingrid Bergman and Burgess Meredith.

April 9 Wycherley's Restoration comedy, *The Country Wife*, is revived at London's Little Theatre. Miles Malleson directs, with Alec Clunes and Hermione Baddeley featured.

April 10 At London's Gate Theatre, the play is Basil Bartlett's *The Jersey Lily*, staged by Norman Marshall. Hermione Hannen plays the title-role of Lily Langtry. Leo Genn and Paul Henried are also in the cast.

April 15 At London's Streatham Hill Theatre, George Bernard Shaw's *In Good King Charles' Golden Days* is presented, staged by H. K. Ayliff. Ernest Thesiger plays Charles II, with Cecil Trouncer as Isaac Newton, Herbert Lomas as George Fox, Eileen Beldon as Nell Gwynn, and Irene Vanbrugh as Catherine of Braganza. On May 9, the play moves to the New Theatre.

April 15 At the Old Vic Theatre in London, Lewis Casson and Harley Granville Barker revive *King Lear*, with John Gielgud in the title-role. On May 29, Marius Goring and George Devine co-direct the revival of *The Tempest*, with Gielgud and Jessica Tandy as Prospero and Miranda.

April 23 *Measure for Measure* opens the season in Stratford-upon-Avon at the Shakespeare Memorial Theatre. B. Iden Payne is director of the festival, but he invites Baliol Holloway to stage both *As You Like It* and Goldsmith's *She Stoops to Conquer*. Other plays offered include *The Merry Wives of Windsor*, *The Merchant of Venice*, *Hamlet*, *King John*, and *The Taming of the Shrew*. Despite the rigors of wartime, the season lasts until Sep 7. A notice in the theatre reads: "By order of the Police, persons can under no circumstances be admitted to performances at the theatre unless they have their gas masks."

May 2 The Theatre Guild produces William Saroyan's *Love's Old Sweet Song*, the saga of a woman's love trials and economic tribulations. Jessie Royce Landis is featured. There are 44 performances at New York's Plymouth Theatre.

May 9 Laurence Olivier brings a slightly expanded version of his London Old Vic production of *Romeo and Juliet* to Broadway at the 51st Street Theatre. Even with Vivian Leigh opposite him as Juliet, the production doesn't win fans, running only 36 performances.

May 17 Jean Cocteau's *Les Parents Terribles*, translated by Caroline Francke, is staged by Norman Marshall at London's Gate Theatre. Henry Oscar, Martita Hunt, Mary Hinton, Cyril Cusak, and Vivienne Bennett make up the cast.

May 30 Henrik Ibsen's *Ghosts*, with the Greek actress Katina Paxinou as Mrs. Alving, opens at the Duchess Theatre in London.

June 10 George Bernard Shaw's *The Devil's Disciple* is revived at the Golder's Green Hippodrome. On this night at the Q Theatre, Susan Glaspell and Norman Matson's *The Comic Artist* is also revived. At the Streatham Hill Theatre, Oscar Asche's *Chu Chin Chow* opens, in a revival directed by Robert Atkins and Joseph Fenston. On July 3, it moves to the Palace Theatre for a run of nearly five months. On July 24, *The Devil's Disciple* transfers to the Piccadily Theatre.

July 25 London theatre in wartime is relying more and more on revues and revivals. Tonight the revival is *High Tem-*

The Corn is Green

perature, by Avery Hopwood and Wilson Collison. On July 27, it's Dodie Smith's *Dear Octopus* at the Adelphi Theatre. At the Shaftesbury Theatre, on Aug 20, *The Chocolate Soldier* comes back to life. On Aug 27, at the Westminster Theatre, J. B. Priestley's *Cornelius* is revived, with a new actor, Derek Bogaerde (Dirk Bogarde), in the cast. On Aug 30, Sutton Vane's *Outward Bound* returns to the London stage at the New Theatre.

July 27 At the Open Air Theatre in Regent's Park, Robert Atkins' production of *A Midsummer Night's Dream* opens, with Francis Sullivan as Bottom. This is the only summer show in this theatre.

Aug 9 William Cottrell has been named artistic director of the Oregon Shakespeare Festival, an annual summer outdoor performance venture founded by Angus Bowmer in Ashland, Oregon. In this brief summer season, running only till the 24th, *As You Like It* and *The Comedy of Errors* are revived. New stagings are *The Merry Wives of Windsor* and *Much Ado About Nothing*.

Sep 5 Jean Cocteau's *The Infernal Machine* opens for a brief engagement at London's Arts Theatre. Peter Glenville, Jeanne de Casalis, and Leueen MacGrath are in the cast.

Sep 16 Maxwell Anderson's *The Masque of Kings* launches the 14th season of the Dublin Gate Theatre, currently playing at the Gaiety. Other plays of the season include Du Maurier's *Rebecca*, Selous' *...No Traveller Returns...*, Shakespeare's *A Midsummer Night's Dream*, Robinson's *Roly-Poly*, Dance's *Granite*, and a holiday show, *Snapdragon*.

Oct 3 Robert Atkins revives Shakespeare's *All's Well That Ends Well* at London's Vaudeville Theatre. Peter Glenville is Bertram, with Catherine Lacey as Helena. On Oct 23, Atkins offers *Henry IV, Part 1*, playing Falstaff to Glenville's Prince Hal.

Oct 17 First produced in London in 1892, Brandon Thomas' farce, *Charley's Aunt*, earns 233 performances in this New York revival, with Jose Ferrer wearing skirts to impersonate the real Donna Lucia (Nedda Harrigan). Joshua Logan stages.

Oct 22 The Negro Playwrights Company presents Theodore Ward's *Big White Fog*, the tale of the miseries of an educated black who in 1922 sees Marcus Garvey's promises of a new black republic in Africa as the only hope of escaping from prejudice and oppression. Canada Lee has the lead. Offered at New York's Lincoln Theatre, the production runs two months.

Oct 29 The Theatre Guild produces *Suzanna and the Elders* by Lawrence Langner and Armina Marshall. It tells the story of a woman involved in a eugenically-oriented colony in early 19th century America. Haila Stoddard plays the woman. Presented at the Morosco in New York, it has only 30 showings.

Palace Theatre

Dec 14 The distinguished German director, Erwin Piscator, now in exile, stages his modernization of Shakespeare's *King Lear*, with music by Henry Cowell, for Studio Theatre, a group affiliated with his Dramatic Workshop at the New School for Social Research. On March 24, the production is *The Circle of Chalk*, a classical Chinese drama, staged by James Light. On June 3, Piscator supervises Robert Klein's staging of *Any Day Now*, by Philip Yordan.

Dec 23 Today, the Coliseum offers *Aladdin*—also performed from Dec 26 at the Golder's Green Hippodrome. Other holiday shows are *Where the Rainbow Ends* (New), *Berkeley Square* (Vaudeville), *The Merry Wives of Windsor* (Strand), and *Mother Goose* (Streatham Hill), representing a drastic reduction in the number of Christmas productions, compared with peacetime years.

1940 BIRTHS/DEATHS/DEBUTS

March 19 English costume and scenic designer Aubrey Hammond (b. 1893) is dead. Hammond designed revue settings for C. B. Cochran and Andre Charlot, as well as for numerous films. He was also a poster designer and book illustrator.

March 25 Swedish film actress Ingrid Bergman makes her New York City stage debut as Julie in Ferenc Molnar's *Liliom* at the 44th Street Theatre.

April 5 Stage and screen actor John Wray (b. 1888) is dead at age 52. Wray made his first appearance on stage at the Girard Avenue Theatre in Philadelphia in 1911 as Gustave in *Camille*. His Broadway credits include Fritz Winchelman in Channing Pollock's *The Enemy* and Joe Prividi in Hugh Stange's *Tin Pan Alley*.

April 7 Actor William Faversham (b. 1868) dies in Bay Shore, Long Island. Faversham made his first appearance on the New York stage in the Union Square Theatre in 1887. He subsequently became a member of Charles Frohman's Empire Theatre Company. In 1934 he toured as Jeeter Lester in *Tobacco Road*.

May 29 Actress Mary Anderson (b. 1859) dies in Worcestershire, England. Anderson made her first appearance at age 16 playing Juliet. In 1887 she appeared at London's Lyceum Theatre in *The Winter's Tale*, in which she was the first actress to double the parts of Perdita and Hermione. She retired in 1890. She is the author of *A Few Memories* (1896) and *A Few More Memories* (1936).

June 16 American novelist, playwright, and poet DuBose Heyward (b. 1885) dies in Tryon, North Carolina. With his wife Dorothy, Heyward dramatized his novel *Porgy*, which won the 1927 Pulitzer Prize. Other plays are *The Brass Ankle* and *Mamba's Daughters*.

Nov 16 German-born American theatre manager, owner, and impresario Martin Beck dies in New York at age 71. In addition to building the New York theatre which bears his name, Beck also built the Palace and the State Lake Theatres in Chicago. He brought the D'Oyly Carte Opera country to America for their 1934 engagement.

Dec 1 American stage and screen actor Charles J. Richman (b. 1870) dies in the Bronx, New York. Richman appeared with Augustin Daly's company from 1896 until Daly's death in 1899. In 1934 he played Frank Mason in *Jig-Saw* for the Theatre Guild. Richman began his film career in 1934.

Dec 21 Novelist and playwright F. Scott Fitzgerald (b. 1896) dies in Hollywood. Fitzgerald gained recognition for his novels and stories of the 1920s. His play, *The Vegetable; or, From President to Postman*, appeared in 1923.

Dec 26 Producer-manager Daniel Frohman (b. 1851) dies in New York City. Frohman first went into management on his own in 1885 when he acquired the old Lyceum Theatre in New York. When the theatre closed, he became manager of the new one bearing that name. In 1911 he published *Memories of a Manager*, which was followed in 1935 by *Daniel Frohman Presents*.

1940 THEATERS/PRODUCTIONS

A patent is granted in Britain to the Thomson-Houston Company for a device which uses an electro-magnetic field to create the illusion of invisible suspension.

A U.S. patent is granted to George Solkover for his method suggesting an outdoor scene with a body of water, in which a mirrored surface reflects the scenic background.

Jan 13 Producer-director Earl Carroll introduces the use of microphones and electronic amplification on the Broadway stage. The occasion is the opening of *Earl Carroll's Vanities* at New York's St. James.

April 10 Basil Bartlett's play, *The Jersey Lily*, about Lily Langtry and shown in club theatre performance, cannot be given a license for public performance. The Lord Chamberlain does not wish offense to be offered the Royal Family.

June 2 On the day following the close of the 1939–40 Broadway season, the *NY Times* is able to report the major statistics. There have been some 84 productions, in the following categories: musicals (7), revues (8), revivals (9), dramas and comedies (60). This is the *NY Times'* count and may vary from other reports. At this time, producers do not have to make public disclosures of financing and gains or losses on their shows, so the season's successes continue to be measured by the number of performances beyond the 100-mark, still considered a respectable run. Some shows run a year, however, and do not recoup their investment. Number of performances does not indicate how many seats have been sold each time. Some shows, especially musicals, cost initially a great deal to mount. Such shows often cost much more to run per week—large casts, musicians, added scenery and stage-hands—than one-set, small-cast dramas. According to *NY Times* reports, Hollywood studios have spent some $3 million acquiring screen rights for shows current on Broadway.

June 15 At the end of the 1939–40 Broadway theatre season, the ten *Best Plays* on critic Burns Mantle's annual list are: Sherwood's *There Shall Be No Night*, Anderson's *Key Largo*, Kingsley's *The World We Make*, Lindsay and Crouse's *Life With Father*, Kaufman and Hart's *The Man Who Came To Dinner*, Thurber and Nugent's *The Male Animal*, Saroyan's *The Time of Your Life*, Raphaelson's *Skylark*, Boothe's *Margin for Error*, and Osborn's *Morning's At Seven*. Both the Pulitzer Prize and the Drama Critics' Circle Award are won by Saroyan's comedy.

Aug 15 Fire destroys most of the costumes and damages the facade and backstage of the Oregon Shakespeare Festival in Ashland. It's the middle of the season, so contemporary costumes must be used to finish out the festival schedule. The damaged theatre will be torn down during World War II, when the festival is suspended.

Sep 7 The Blitz forces the closing of London's Shaftesbury Theatre.

Sep 24 Fire-bombs gut St. George's Hall, in London.

Sep 24 The Queen's Theatre on Shaftesbury Avenue in London is badly damaged by bombs. The current production, now forced to close, is *Rebecca* with Celia Johnson and Margaret Rutherford.

Nov 24 For the first time in New York's theatrical history, many legitimate theatres begin giving Sunday performances. Before this date, the Winter Garden, the Selwyn, and the Century have offered Sunday evening variety shows, but these have been special vaudeville programs, not performances of the regular legitimate attraction.

Daniel Frohman

Jan 10 *Arsenic and Old Lace* (NY—Fulton—Comedy). Joseph Kesselring's affectionate comedy thriller about two nice but demented old ladies, who gently poison lonely old men to free them of burdensome lives, features Josephine Hull and Jean Adair. John Alexander, Boris Karloff, and Allyn Joslyn are also in the cast. The show wins 1,444 performances and becomes an amateur and stock favorite. On Dec 23, 1942, it opens in London's Strand with Lilian Braithwaite and Mary Jerrold as the kindly killers. It runs 1,337 performances.

Jan 12 *Mr. and Mrs. North* (NY—Belasco—Comedy). Owen Davis dramatizes the *New Yorker* stories of Frances and Richard Lockridge (who is drama critic for the *NY Evening Sun*) for a run of 163 performances. Albert Hackett and Peggy Conklin play the sleuthing Norths on the track of a murderer. This play also becomes a stock favorite.

Jan 23 *Lady in the Dark* (NY—Alvin—Musical). Moss Hart provides the text for this show with score by Kurt Weill and lyrics by Ira Gershwin. Gertrude Lawrence stars as a successful fashion magazine editor who relates her dreams to her psychoanalyst. She sings "The Saga of Jenny" and "My Ship." Danny Kaye is in the cast as a photographer-suitor. Irene Sharaff and Hattie Carnegie create the costumes. The show runs for 467 performances.

Feb 5 *Liberty Jones* (NY—Shubert—Comedy). Philip Barry devises an allegory about the illness of Liberty, uncurable by the quack-doctors of Education, Law, Divinity, and Letters, and menaced by evils at home and black and brown-shirts from abroad. Paul Bowles provides music; Lew Christiansen, choreography. Nancy Coleman plays Liberty, with John Beal as her U.S. Navy saviour. This Theatre Guild offering has only 22 performances.

Feb 12 *Claudia* (NY—Booth—Comedy). Rose Franken's domestic drama of the child-wife Claudia (Dorothy McGuire), who matures in understanding and responsibility, is a success not only with women's audiences, but with the major critics as well. Mantle selects it as a "Best Play." The show runs for 722 performances. It has 558 London performances, opening at the St. Martin's on Sep 17, 1942, with Pamela Brown as Claudia.

March 24 *Native Son* (NY—St. James—Drama). Paul Green and Richard Wright adapt Wright's novel of a black man who accidently kills a white woman. Canada Lee and Anne Burr head the cast. It runs 114 performances. The drama is shown in London at the Boltons Theatre beginning Feb 20, 1948. Robert Adams has the lead.

April 1 *The Watch on the Rhine* (NY—Martin Beck—Drama). Herman Shumlin produces and directs Lillian Hellman's tense confrontation between an underground fighter and a Nazi sympathiser. Paul Lukas and George Coulouris are featured. The production, which critics see as less propagandistic than previous dramas about Nazism, runs nearly 48 weeks. On April 22, 1942, it opens in London at the Aldwych, with Charles Goldner and Anton Walbrook. It runs 673 performances.

April 21 *The Beautiful People* (NY—Lyceum—Comedy). William Saroyan's play deals with a woman who believes that the mice which throng her family's San Francisco house spell out her name in flowers. Betsy Blair and Eugene Loring appear. The play, which is much admired by some critics but scorned by others, runs 15 weeks.

Sep 10 *The Wookey* (NY—Plymouth—Drama). Frederick Brennan writes this play about a tugboat skipper who hates war but changes his attitude after rescuing men at Dunkirk. Edmund Gwenn appears. The show runs four months.

Oct 1 *Best Foot Forward* (NY—Ethel Barrymore—Musical). John Cecil Helm provides the book and Hugh Martin and Ralph Blane the music and lyrics for this story of a Hollywood starlet who comes to a local prom. George Abbott directs and Gene Kelly provides the dances. "Buckle Down Winsocki" is a hit. Gil Stratten, Jr., and Rosemary Lane have the leads. The show runs ten months.

Oct 22 *Candle in the Wind* (NY—Shubert—Drama). The Theatre Guild joins with the Playwrights' Company to present Maxwell Anderson's story of a woman who tries to help her lover escape from Nazi-occupied France. Helen Hayes, Lotte Lenya, and Joseph Wisemen are in the cast. It runs for 95 performances.

Oct 29 *Let's Face It* (NY—Imperial—Musical). Cole Porter's music and lyrics dress up the Herbert and Dorothy Fields' libretto, based on *The Cradle Snatchers*. Eve Arden, Vivian Vance, Benny Baker, Mary Jane Walsh and Nanette Fabray are featured in this tale of women who think their husbands are cheating on them. There are 547 performances. The show opens on Nov 19, 1942, at London's Hippodrome, with a cast including Rona Riccarde, Zoe Gail, Joyce Barbour, John Clifford, Bobby Howes, and Pat Kirkwood. It runs almost 11 months.

Nov 5 *Blithe Spirit*. See L premiere, 1941.

Nov 10 *Spring Again* (NY—Henry Miller—Comedy). Grace George is featured in this show about a woman who finally ends her husband's boasting. The play, by Isabel Leighton and Bertram Bloch, has 241 performances.

LADY IN THE DARK

Nov 12 *Theatre* (NY—Hudson—Comedy). Guy Bolton adapts the W. Somerset Maugham novel as a vehicle for Cornelia Otis Skinner, as an actress who wants to show her public that melodrama is not her only talent. An aging actress has a fling with her ex-husband's male secretary to bolster her ego. The production runs nearly nine weeks in New York, after which Skinner takes it on tour.

Nov 18 *Junior Miss* (NY—Lyceum—Comedy). Jerome Chodorov and Joseph Fields adapt Sally Benson's *New Yorker* series about teenage sub-debs for the stage. Patricia Peardon plays the lead. Moss Hart stages the show which runs 710 performances. On March 24, 1943, it opens in London at the Saville with Joan White. There are 514 showings.

Nov 26 *Hope for a Harvest* (NY—Guild—Drama). The Theatre Guild and the stars, Fredric March and Florence Eldridge, think well enough of this Sophie Treadwell play about the hopes and failures of some rural Californians to bring it to Broadway after encouraging responses in Boston, Baltimore, and Pittsburgh. There are 38 performances.

Dec 1 *Sons O' Fun* (NY—Winter Garden—Revue). Olsen and Johnson offer a new collection of nonsense, amiable vulgarity, and vaudeville routines. Carmen Miranda and Ella Logan are featured. Songs are by Jack Yellen, Sammy Fain, and Will Irwin. There were 742 showings.

Dec 5 *Angel Street.* See L premiere, 1939.

Dec 25 *Banjo Eyes* (NY—Hollywood—Musical). Eddie Cantor returns from the West Coast to play Erwin Trowbridge, the greeting-card writer who talks to winning

BLITHE SPIRIT

horses in his dreams. Vernon Duke provides the score, with lyrics by John LaTouche and Harold Adamson for this adaption of *Three Men on a Horse*. Virginia Mayo, the DeMarcos, Audrey Christie, and Lionel Stander are on hand for the show's 126 performances.

Dec 27 *Clash By Night* (NY—Belasco—Drama). Clifford Odet's new play centers on a husband who finally realizes that the man to whom he has opened his house is having an affair with his wife. Lee J. Cobb, Joseph Schildkraut, and Tallulah Bankhead are featured. The show runs only six weeks.

1941   BRITISH PREMIERES

March 5 *Apple Sauce* (L—Palladium—Revue). George Black's revue, tried out earlier in a suburban venue, wins 462 showings in the West End. Charles Henry directs the ensemble, which includes Max Miller, Florence Desmond, Vera Lynn, Jean Carr, Jack Stanford, Terry Conlin, and others.

March 27 *No time for Comedy.* See NY premiere, 1939.

June 5 *Rise Above It* (L—Comedy—Revue). Leslie Julian Jones devises this show, which earns a run of nearly 30 weeks. Henry Kendall directs the performers, among whom are Hermione Baddeley, Wilfrid Hyde-White, Billy Thatcher, Hermione Gingold, and Kendall himself.

July 2 *Blithe Spirit* (L—Piccadilly—Comedy). Noel Coward's tale of the hapless husband handling two wives—one a ghost—features Margaret Rutherford, Kay Hammond, Cecil Parker, and Fay Compton. It wins a long run of 1,997 perfor-

mances. The show opens in New York at the Morosco on Nov 5, 1941, with Clifton Webb, Mildred Natwick, Leonora Corbett, and Peggy Wood in the cast. There are 657 performances.

Aug 21 *Fun and Games* (L—Princes—Revue). Douglas Furber devises the show, aided by Frank Collins, Frith Shephard, and Richard Hearne, with music by Manning Sherwin. Performers include Vera Pearce, Carol Raye and Sydney Howard. The show runs nine months.

Oct 9 *The Nutmeg Tree* (L—Lyric—Drama). Irene Hentschel stages Margery Sharp's play, which runs nearly 34 weeks. Yvonne Arnaud is featured.

Oct 29 *Jupiter Laughs* (L—New—Drama). James Mason stages A. J. Cronin's play about the treatment of neurosis. Mason plays a lead.

Oct 30 *Other People's Houses* (L—Ambassadors'—Comedy). Lynn Dexter's play is about a woman who welcomes another

woman she wrongly thinks is the last domestic servant left in that part of the country. Marie Lohr, Rene Ray and Phyllis Dare are in the cast. There are 173 performances.

Nov 19 *Get a Load of This* (L—Hippodrome—Musical). This show is labelled a "surprise musical." Robert Nesbitt stages James Hadley Chase's book, with songs by Val Guest (lyrics) and Manning Sherwin (music). In the large cast are Vic Oliver, Celia Lipton, Charles Farrell, and Jack Allan. It runs 698 performances.

Dec 4 *The Man Who Came To Dinner.* See NY premiere, 1939.

Dec 10 *The Morning Star* (L—Globe—Drama). Emlyn Williams directs and has the lead in this play he has written about professional and personal problems of a medical student in London during the Blitz. It runs 474 performances. The play opens on Broadway at the Morosco on Sep 14, 1942, with Gregory Peck as the young student. The show lasts just three weeks.

Dec 17 *Gangway* (L—Palladium—Revue). Americans Ben Lyon and Bebe Daniels head the cast of this George Black show, staged by Robert Nesbitt. It has 535 performances. Also in the ensemble are Rona Riccardo, Lamar and Rosita, Tommy Trinder, Teddy Brown, and Anne Zeigler.

Dec 18 *Old Acquaintance.* See NY premiere, 1940.

Dec 23 *Warn That Man* (L—Garrick—Drama). Vernon Sylvaine's play, staged by Richard Bird, earns a run of 11 months. Among the players are Max Adrian, Gordon Harker, Ethel Coleridge, Judy Kelly, Stanley Groome, and Rosamund Paget.

Jan 6 Donald Wolfit, following his Christmas *Merry Wives* at London's Strand Theatre, offers now an *Othello* in which he plays the title role. On Jan 8, he plays Richard in *Richard III*. On Jan 11, Wolfit plays the prince in *Hamlet*, His wife Rosalind Iden is the female lead in each play. For a change of pace on the 18th, he plays Giovanni in John Ford's Jacobean drama, *'Tis Pity She's a Whore*. Wolfit brings back *Othello* on Jan 25.

Feb 17 The Dublin Gate Theatre's 14th season continues, playing at the Gaiety Theatre, with Micheal macLiammoir's *Dancing Shadow*. Other shows include Denham/Percy's *Ladies in Retirement*, Ardrey's *Thunder Rock*, Sears' *The Forced Marriage*, and Collis' *Marrowbone Lane*, Balderston/Squire's *Berkeley Square*, Smith's *The Drunkard*, and Shakespeare's *Hamlet*, all of which are revivals. The ensemble then tours three of the productions to Cork.

March 6 J. B. Priestley's *When We Are Married* is revived at London's Vaudeville Theatre. This year a number of recently produced plays are brought back to fill wartime stages or, after a brief closure, are transferred to other West End theatres. Some of these are *Once a Crook*, *Thunder Rock*, *New Faces*, *Shepherd's Pie*, *Women Aren't Angels*, *Up and Doing*, *The Light of Heart*, and *Cottage To Let*.

March 11 Katharine Cornell revives George Bernard Shaw's *The Doctor's Dilemma* on Broadway at the Shubert Theatre. The production runs 15 weeks.

April 12 *Much Ado About Nothing* opens the annual Shakespeare season at Stratford-upon-Avon in the Memorial Theatre. *Richard II* is the "birthday play." Festival director B. Iden Payne has Andrew Leigh stage *Julius Caesar*, while Baliol Holloway directs Sheridan's *The Rivals*. Other plays include *Twelfth Night*, *The Taming of the Shrew*, *The Tempest*, *Romeo and Juliet*, and *The Merchant of Venice*. The season runs until Sep 13.

June 10 The venue is London's Savoy Theatre. The D'Oyly Carte Opera Company presents its Gilbert & Sullivan productions. *The Gondoliers* opens tonight. On June 12, *Trial by Jury* and *The Pirates of Penzance* are played. *The Mikado* opens on June 13. On June 19, the operetta is *Patience*. *Iolanthe* is offered on June 20.

July 1 In Southwark Park, Robert Atkins presents his production of *The Taming of the Shrew* in the Open Air Theatre. On July 15, the play is *Twelfth Night*. On Aug 4, Atkins and his players have moved from Southwark Park to the summer Shakespeare festival's usual home, the Open Air Theatre in Regent's Park, where they present *Shrew* again. On Aug 19, the play is *Henry V*.

July 7 At London's New Theatre, Tyrone Guthrie and Lewis Casson co-direct this Old Vic revival of *King John*, with Ernest Milton as the monarch. On July 16, Sybil Thorndike plays the title role in *Medea*.

July 21 *This Sceptered Isle* is G. Wilson Knight's dramatization of "Shakespeare's call to Great Britain in time of war."

ANGEL STREET

Among the performers are Knight, Henry Ainley, Will Redgrave, Joan Simpson, and Diedre O'Brien.

Oct 5 At the Gaiety Theatre, the Dublin Gate Theatre opens its 15th season with Behrman's *No Time for Comedy*, followed by Bernard Shaw's *Caesar and Cleopatra*, Barrie's *Quality Street*, Johnston's *The Old Lady Says "No!"*, and a holiday treat, *Harlequinade*.

Oct 5 Billy Rose produces *Fun To Be Free*, a patriotic pageant-revue by Ben Hecht and Charles MacArthur, at Madison Square Garden. The music is by Kurt Weill; many stars and celebrities donate their talents.

Nov 11 Maurice Evans and Judith Anderson appear in *Macbeth* at Broadway's National. There are 131 performances.

Dec 2 Michael Chekhov stages and designs sets and costumes for this revival of *Twelfth Night*, with Beatrice Straight as Viola. It lasts two weeks on Broadway at the Little Theatre.

Dec 20 Erwin Piscator's Studio Theatre of the New School for Social Research opens Ferdinand Bruckner's *The Criminals* for a two-week run. It is staged by Sanford Meisner, with Lili Darvas, Herbert Berghof, and Paul Mann. Piscator's group offers four plays this season, one of which, *Nathan the Wise*, moves to Broadway. Notable is the Piscator version of Tolstoy's novel, *War and Peace*, which will have memorable productions later in Europe and America.

Dec 22 Christmas in time of war this year finds London theatres offering more children's entertainments than last. *Little Women* is revived at the Westminster Theatre. At the Players' Theatre, *Whittington Jnr. and His Cat* is followed by a "Grand Harlequinade," especially devised by M. Willson Disher. On Dec 24, three shows open: *Peter Pan* (Adelphi), with Alastair Sim as Captain Hook; *Babes*

BANJO EYES

in the Wood (Stoll), and Donald Wolfit's *A Midsummer Night's Dream* (Strand). Other holiday productions are *Jack and the Beanstalk* (Coliseum), *Jack and Jill* (Palace), *Puss in Boots* (Wimbledon), *Aladdin* (Richmond), *Cinderella* (Golder's Green Hippodrome), and *Humpty-Dumpty* (Streatham Hill).

1941 BIRTHS/DEATHS/DEBUTS

Jan 5 Actress Carol Channing makes her stage debut as Bobby in Marc Blitzstein's opera, *No for an Answer*—the first of three "experimental" performances on Sunday evenings—at the Mecca Temple in New York, The New York City Center.

Jan 13 Irish novelist, poet, and dramatist James Joyce (b. 1882) dies in Zurich. He was an admirer of Ibsen; Joyce's earliest publication is an essay on "Ibsen's New Drama" which appeared in a *Fortnightly Review* of 1900. Among his many literary works is a play, *Exiles*, written in 1918.

Feb 14 English stage and screen actor Jerrold Robertshaw (b. 1866) is dead. Robertshaw toured with Ben Greet in the 1890's and made his London appearance in 1898 as Trebonius in *Julius Caesar*. He subsequently toured with his own company in England and with Julia Marlowe in America. In 1933 Robertshaw played Jo Stengel in *Dinner at Eight* at London's Palace Theatre.

March 7 American actor Julian Eltinge (b. 1883) dies in New York. Eltinge (William Dalton) was chiefly known as a female impersonator. From 1904 until his retirement in 1930, he appeared in a number of successful plays and films. In 1940 he returned to the stage and night clubs. The Julian Eltinge Theatre, built on 42nd Street in 1910, was named for him.

March 8 American novelist and playwright Sherwood Anderson (b. 1876) dies in Panama. Among Anderson's best known works are *Winesburg, Ohio* and *Triumph of the Egg*, both of which he adapted for the stage.

June 26 American playwright Arthur F. Goodrich (b. 1878) dies in New York. Goodrich wrote *Caponsacchi, Richelieu,* and *A Journey by Night*, among other plays.

July 3 American producer Sam H. Harris (b. 1872) dies in New York. Harris' first theatrical venture was *The Gay Morning Glories*, a burlesque which toured the United States. In association with George M. Cohan, he produced *Little Johnny Jones, Forty-Five Minutes from Broadway,* and *Get-Rich-Quick Wallingford*. Harris also produced the 1936–37 Pulitzer Prize winning *You Can't Take It With You*.

July 12 Critic-novelist and dramaturg John Lahr is born in Los Angeles to actor Bert Lahr and wife Mildred.

July 20 Actor-manager Lew Fields (b. 1867) dies in Beverly Hills. Fields entered into partnership with Joseph Weber at the age of nine. In 1885 they established their own company, writing and acting in burlesques of the serious drama of the day (*Cyranose, Quo Vass Iss?*). After their careers diverged, Fields opened his own theatre. He retired in 1930.

Nov 11 Canadian born actor-director John Ireland makes his Broadway debut as the Sergeant and First Murderer in *Macbeth* at the National Theatre after a successful cross-country tour as Captain Hook in a Clare Tree Major Children's Theatre production of *Peter Pan*.

Dec 13 English stage and screen actress Minnie Rayner (b. 1869) is dead. Rayner made her first appearance on the regular stage at London's Comedy Theatre in 1882 as Little Hans in *Rip Van Winkle*. She played in various touring productions of Gilbert and Sullivan and the Bandmann Opera Company. Rayner's film career began in 1912.

May 12 German bombs damage the Holborn Empire Theatre in London, which is forced to close.

June 1 This year, the Broadway season officially closes on May 31, followed today by the *NY Times'* statistics. There have been 71 productions, divided thus: musicals (7), revues (6), revivals (10), and dramas and comedies (48). The *NY Times* lumps these together as "plays." Hollywood studios continue to acquire Broadway scripts. Warner Brothers pays $175,000 for *Arsenic and Old Lace*; 20th Century-Fox pays $150,000 for *Tobacco Road*; Paramount agrees to pay $288,000 for the rights to *Lady in the Dark*. The

LEW FIELDS

annual ten *Best Plays* in critic Burns Mantle's estimation are: Green and Wright's *Native Son*, Hellman's *Watch on the Rhine*, Williams' *The Corn Is Green*, Hart's *Lady in the Dark*, Kesselring's *Arsenic and Old Lace*, Fields and Chodorov's *My Sister Eileen*, Rice's *Flight to the West*, Franken's *Claudia*, Davis' *Mr. and Mrs. North*, and Kaufman and Hart's *George Washington Slept Here*.

June 16 The Gate Theatre Studio on Villiers Street in London is damaged in the Blitz.

Fall With the opening of the new Broadway season, outstanding stage-directors can expect a fee of $3,000 and from 1 to 3% of the gross receipts.

1941 THEATERS/PRODUCTIONS

A U.S. patent is given to Anton Grot for simulating a body of water on stage by means of constantly changing light and shadow patterns.

Jan 10 A remote lighting switch, controlled by actors, is used for the first time on the New York stage for *Arsenic and Old Lace* at the Fulton Theatre.

April 16 London's Little Theatre suffers heavy bomb damage. Restoration is not undertaken.

April 17 The Blitz demolishes London's Shaftesbury Theatre.

May London's historic Old Vic Theatre, hit by bombs, can no longer be used by the Old Vic Company. The theatre will not be rebuilt and ready for occupancy until 1950, when it will reopen on Nov 14. During the war years, the troupe will tour the provinces extensively, with London seasons presented in the West End at the New Theatre. From 1942 to 1946, the Old Vic's producing center will be the Playhouse in Liverpool.

May 12 German bombs damage the Kingsway Theatre.

Feb 1 *Of V We Sing* (NY—Concert—Revue). Alex Cohen helps the American Youth Theatre produce this fledgling show; the "V" stands for Victory. Songs and sketches are by many, including Alex North and Bea Goldsmith. On stage are Betty Garrett, Phil Leeds, Daniel Nagrin, and Curt Conway. There is some lively jitterbugging and a "Brooklyn Cantata." The show, done earlier Off Broadway, runs nearly ten weeks.

March 12 *Priorities of 1942* (NY—46th Street—Revue). Top price at matinees is $1, with $2 top at night. This show runs through the season, with such vaudeville favorites as Phil Baker, Lou Holtz, Willie Howard, and Hazel Scott.

April 7 *The Moon Is Down* (NY—Martin Beck—Drama). John Steinbeck adapts his novel of the German Occupation of Norway for the stage. Whitford Kane, Ralph Morgan, Russell Collins, Lyle Bettger, and Otto Kruger are in the cast. There are 71 performances. On June 8, 1943, the play opens at London's Whitehall with a cast including Ducan Ross, Paul Scofield, and Lewis Casson. It has 112 showings.

May 1 *Harlem Cavalcade* (NY—Ritz—Revue). Ed Sullivan produces and co-directs this black vaudeville with Noble Sissle. Even with Sissle, Flournoy Miller, the Harlemaniacs, and Amanda Randolph, the show runs only six weeks.

May 20 *Uncle Harry* (NY—Broadhurst—Drama). Thomas Job's play about a man who can't convince anyone he has murdered his sister features Joseph Schildkraut and Eva LeGallienne. There are 430 performances. It opens at London's Garrick Theatre on March 29, 1944, stage by Michael Redgrave who also plays Harry. There are 122 performances.

June 3 *By Jupiter* (NY—Shubert—Musical). Richard Rodgers and Lorenz Hart base this show on *The Warrior's Husband*, the tale of crafty Greeks ending Amazonian control over their men. This is the last Rodgers and Hart collaboration. Ray Bolger, Benay Venuta, Vera-Ellen, and Constance Moore are among the cast.

June 24 *Star and Garter* (NY—Music Box—Revue). Producer Mike Todd brings back burlesque, with Gypsy Rose Lee and Bobby Clark as his headliners. Music is provided by Irving Berlin, Harold Arlen, and Harold Rome, among others, but the songs aren't new. The show runs 609 performances.

July 4 *This Is the Army* (NY—Broadway—Revue). Irving Berlin's musical salute to the American soldier is scheduled for a four-week stay, but popular demand extends this to 12 weeks. The show goes on tour til 1945, making a great profit for Army Emergency Relief. Berlin revives and performs his World War I hit from

THIS IS THE ARMY

YipYip Yaphank, "How I Hate To Get Up In The Morning." New are the title song, "American Eagles," "I'm Getting Tired So I Can Sleep," and "I Left My Heart At the Stage Door Canteen." On Nov 10, 1943, it opens at London's Palladium for a limited run.

Sep 10 *Janie* (NY—Henry Miller—Comedy). Janie (Gwen Anderson) is a Junior Miss who invites a whole company of Army trainees to her house when her parents are away. Josephine Bentham and Herschel Williams' play runs for 642 performances.

Sep 16 *Show Time* (NY—Broadhurst—Revue). Originating on the West Coast, this revue features George Jessel, Ella Logan, Jack Haley and the dancing DeMarcos. It runs for 342 performances, playing 12 times a week.

Sep 28 *Wine, Women and Song* (NY—Ambassador—Revue). Impressario Max Liebman combines vaudeville, burlesque, and revue. Jimmy Savo, Herbie Faye, Margie Hart, and Pinkie Lee are in the cast. The show runs 150 performances, playing twice a day.

Oct 7 *The Eve of St. Mark* (NY—Cort—Drama). At the request of the National Theatre Conference, Maxwell Anderson writes a war drama which can be performed with a minimum of production effects. After the success of nearly 100 productions around the nation, Anderson's colleagues of the Playwrights' Company bring it to Broadway with William Prince, Aline MacMahon, and Matt Crowley. There are 307 performances. On July 4, 1943, it opens at London's Scala Theatre, presented by the Theatre Unit of the Special Service Section, Central Base Section S.O.S., E.T.O. (European Theatre of Operations).

Oct 22 *The Damask Cheek* (NY—Playhouse—Comedy). John Van Druten and Lloyd Morris write this comedy about a girl who comes to America to find a husband. Flora Robson appears. The show runs nearly three months. On Feb 2, 1949 the play opens in London at the Lyric with a cast including Claire Bloom, Jane Baxter, and Bill Travers.

Oct 28 *Rosalinda* (NY—44th Street—Musical). In exile, Max Reinhardt and his son, Gottfried, keep the splendors of his famed productions in Central Europe alive with this adaptation of his 1929 Berlin mounting of *Die Fledermaus*, which his son and John Meehan, Jr., have adapted for Broadway. Dorothy Sarnoff is Rosalinda, and George Balanchine chorergraphs. There are 521 performances.

Nov 18 *The Skin of Our Teeth* (NY—Plymouth—Comedy). Thornton Wilder's fantastic saga of the family of man from the Ice Age onward into the future proves highly controversial, but it wins the Pulitzer Prize and a 45-week run. Tallulah Bankhead and Fredric March are featured with Montgomery Clift, E. G. Marshall, and Dick Van Patten. The NY Times reports that the theme is "presented with pathos and broad comedy, with gentle irony and sometimes a sly self-raillery . . ." It also announces "Miss Bankhead is magnificent . . . On May 16, 1945, the play opens in London at the Phoenix with Vivien Leigh, Cecil Parker, and Joan Young. Laurence Olivier directs.

Dec 30 *The Doughgirls* (NY—Lyceum—Comedy). Joseph Field's play details some of the comings and going of self-important men, military and otherwise, and the women who know how to manipulate them. Doris Nolan and Arlene Francis are in the cast. There are 671 performances.

1942 BRITISH PREMIERES

March 2 *Moscow Bells* (L—Coliseum—Revue). Billed as an Anglo-Russian Spectacle, this show is directed by Boris Nevolin and choreographed by Nadejda Nikolaeva-Legat.

March 11 *Happidrome* (L—Prince of Wales's—Revue). There are 224 performances for this Robert Nesbitt-directed show. Among the talents are Tessie O'Shea and the Happidrome Girls.

March 26 *Skylark*. See NY premiere, 1939.

April 16 *Full Swing* (L—Palace—Musical). Jack Hulbert plays Jack Millett in this show he's staged and also written with the aid of Arthur Macrae and Archie Menzies. George Posford provides the score. Also among the cast members are Cicely Courtneidge, Nora Swinburne, Keneth Kent, and Gabrielle Brune. The production wins 468 performances.

April 22 *The Watch on the Rhine*. See NY premiere, 1941.

April 30 *Fine and Dandy* (L—Saville—Revue). Robert Nesbitt stages this show, which he's created with Firth Shephard. Manning Sherwin provides the score, but there are other songs and sketches as well. It runs 43 weeks, with a company including Leslie Henson, Stanley Holloway, Dorothy Dickson, and Douglas Byng.

May 8 *Big Top* (L—His Majesty's—Revue). Herbert Farjeon's show wins a run of over 17 weeks. A number of composers provide tunes. In the cast are Fred Emny, Cyril Ritchard, and Beatrice Lillie, among others.

June 4 *Sky High* (L—Phoenix—Revue). Walter Crisham directs and acts in this show which has 149 performances. He's joined by an ensemble including Naunton Wayne, and the two Hermiones—Baddeley and Gingold.

July 30 *No Orchids for Miss Blandish* (L—Prince of Wales's—Drama). Robert Nesbitt helps James Hadley Chase adapt his popular gangster novel for the stage. Linden Travers has the title role. There are 203 performances.

July 31 *Murder Without Crime* (L—Comedy—Drama). J. Lee Thompson's play, known earlier as *To Fit the Crime*, now has a run of 49 weeks in this Henry Cass staging. Peter Croft, Joyce Heron, Raymond Lovell, and Margaret Johnson are the entire cast.

Aug 6 *Wild Rose* (L—Princes—Musical). The music is Jerome Kern's, with the text of Guy Bolton and Clifford Grey. It runs nearly 26 weeks, staged by Robert Nesbitt. Linda Gray plays Lillian Russell, with Jack Morrison as Diamond Jim Brady.

Aug 12 *Flare Path* (L—Apollo—Drama). Terence Rattigan's drama of divided affections in wartime, as pilots train to protect Britain, wins a long run of 670 performances. Anthony Asquith directs a cast which includes Adrianne Allan, Gerard Hinze, Jack Watling, and Phyllis Calvert.

Sep 3 *Men in Shadow* (L—Vaudeville—Drama). Mary Haley Bell writes this story of English saboteurs in occupied France. John Mills is featured. The production runs for nearly 49 weeks.

Sep 17 *Claudia*. See NY premiere, 1941.

Sep 29 *Waltz Without End* (L—Cambridge—Musical). Bernard Grun has adapted and arranged selections from Chopin for this tale by Erich Maschwitz, staged by Jack Buchanan. Ivor Sheridan plays Chopin. The show runs for 23 weeks.

Oct 21 *The Little Foxes*. See NY premiere, 1939.

Oct 22 *DuBarry Was a Lady*. See NY premiere, 1939.

Nov 7 *Best Bib and Tucker* (L—Palladium—Revue). George Black assembles the material and Robert Nesbitt stages it for a run of 490 performances.

Nov 19 *Let's Face It*. See NY premiere, 1941.

Dec 16 *The Petrified Forest*. See NY premiere, 1935.

Dec 23 *Arsenic and Old Lace*. See NY premiere, 1941.

1942 REVIVALS/REPERTORIES

Jan Ken Murray launches his *Blackouts* at the El Capitan Theatre, north of Hollywood and Vine, in Los Angeles. The show, which undergoes periodic changes, becomes a local institution, running during World War II and beyond for a total of seven years, two months, and two days, or 3,844 performances. Marie Wilson is a voluptuous major attraction, as is the MC Murray, with his cigar, bow-tie, and wisecracks. Later, Murray moves to TV, taking some of his best acts with him.

Jan 6 Donald Wolfit continues at the Strand Theatre in London with a series of Shakespearean productions. Tonight, it's *The Merchant Venice*. On Jan 15, he plays the lead in *Richard III*. *Hamlet* is the play for Jan 20. On Feb 10, he offers *The Merry Wives of Windsor*.

Jan 29 Katina Paxinou, the "First Lady" of the Greek National Theatre, now in American exile, appears on Broadway at the Longacre Theatre as Henrik Ibsen's *Hedda Gabler*. There are only 12 performances, despite favorable reviews.

Feb 10 Frederick Lonsdale's comedy, *On Approval*, is revived at London's Aldwych Theatre. On the same day, at the Victoria Palace, the sporting musical, *Twenty-To-One*, is revived. This continues the wartime trend of revivals. Other revivals this spring include *Volpone* (St. James's, March 3), *The Doctor's Dilemma* (Haymarket, March 4), *The Dancing Years* (Adelphi, March 14), *Blossom Time* (Lyric, March 17), *School for Slavery* (Westminster, March 18), *Other People's Houses* (Phoenix, March 19), *The Maid of the Mountains* (Coliseum, April 1), *Whiteoaks* (Comedy, April 16), *Immortal Gar-*

ROSALINDA

den (Westminster, May 1), *Rebecca* (Strand, May 21), and *Rookery Nook* (St. Martin's, May 23).

March 2 The 15th season of the Dublin Gate Theatre, now playing at the Gaiety Theatre, continues with O'Neill's *Mourning Becomes Electra*. Other plays include Coward's *Blithe Spirit*, Carney's *The Doctor's Boy*, Williams' *The Light of Heart*, macLiammoir's *Where Stars Walk* (revival), a Thorndike/Casson Recital, *Summer Harlequinade*, and Gay's *The Beggar's Opera*.

March 27 Brett Warren stages *Salute To Negro Troops*, a pageant of black history in America. It has a week-long run at New York's Apollo/Harlem, having been first shown at the Cosmopolitan Opera House.

April 4 This is B. Iden Payne's last season as director of the Shakespeare Memorial Theatre in Stratford-upon-Avon. It opens with *A Midsummer Night's Dream*. *The Winter's Tale* is the "birthday play." Other productions include *As You Like It*, *The Merchant of Venice*, *Hamlet*, *Macbeth*, *The Tempest*, *The Taming of the Shrew*, and Sheridan's *The School for Scandal*. The season lasts until Sep 12.

April 27 To benefit Army and Navy charities, the American Theatre Wing War Service, Inc., revives Shaw's *Candida* for a few matinees. But the cast—Mildred Natwick, Stanley Bell, Raymond Massey, Dudley Digges, Katharine Cornell, and Private Burgess Meredith—is so impressive and effective, the production runs two weeks, with a further week in Washington.

May 20 Alec Clunes directs a production of Clifford Odets' *Awake and Sing* at London's Arts Theatre. Richard Attenborough, Lilly Kann, and Vivienne Bennett are featured. The play transfers to the Cambridge Theatre on Aug 5. On June 10, Clunes and his Arts Theatre Group offer *Twelfth Night*, with Clunes, Jean Forbes-Robertson, Donald Pleasance, and Russell Thorndike.

June 8 It's Gilbert & Sullivan time again, and this D'Oyly Carte London engagement is at the Prince's Theatre. *The Gondoliers* is the opening show. On June 15, *Trial by Jury* and *The Pirates of Penzance* open. On June 18, *Iolanthe* is revived. On June 22, Darrell Fancourt plays the title-role in *The Mikado*. On June 29, *Patience* is presented. The company finishes its engagement with *The Yeoman of the Guard* on July 2.

June 9 Revivals continue in London. Tonight it's Margaret Mayo's *Baby Mine* at the Westminster Theatre. On June 24, it's W. Somerset Maugham's *Rain* at St. Martin's Theatre. *Macbeth* is revived at the Piccadilly Theatre, with John Gielgud in the title-role and also staging on July 8. On July 16, at the Stoll Theatre, *Rose Marie* is revived. Frederick Valk plays the main role in the Old Vic's *Othello* on July 22

at the New Theatre. On Aug 3, the Vic's *The Merry Wives of Windsor* comes to the New. *The Man With a Load of Mischief* opens at the Mercury Theatre on Aug 5. On Aug 11, at the Q Theatre, *Nurse Cavell* is revived. On Aug 21, at the Wimbledon Theatre, it's Maugham's *Home and Beauty*.

July 16 In Regent's Park in London at the Open Air Theatre, the summer Shakespeare season begins with *Twelfth Night*, staged by Robert Atkins. Dulcie Gray plays Maria. On July 23, *A Midsummer Night's Dream* has Atkins both as its director and its Bottom. On Aug 5, *The Taming of the Shrew* takes the stage.

Aug 17 William Saroyan opens his Saroyan Theatre on Broadway at the Belasco, but the first bill is the last, running just one week. He offers *Across the Board on Tomorrow Morning*, in which Canada Lee plays a waiter in a New York nightclub who places a bet on a horse called Tomorrow Morning and philosophizes on life as seen in the club. Also on the program is *Talking To You*, in which Lee is a fighter, Blackstone Boulevard, who cannot hit opponents who he senses are good people. Saroyan stages, with designs by Cleon Throckmorton.

Sep 9 In London's West End, the spate of play revivals continues. At the Strand Theatre, *Night of the Garter*, by Avery Hopwood and Wilson Collison has a revival. On Sep 16, *The Belle of New York* comes back to the Coliseum. On the 18, it's *A Man With Red Hair*, based on Hugh Walpole's novel, by Benn W. Levy, produced at the Ambassadors' Theatre. Robert Atkins presents *The Merchant of Venice* at the Westminster Theatre on the 23. On Sep 30, at the Mercury Theatre, Ibsen's *Hedda Gabler* is revived. *Lilac Time* comes to the Stoll Theatre on Oct 13. At the Phoenix Theatre, the next day, Wilde's *The Importance of Being Earnest* returns with John Gielgud. On the 23, Atkins brings *Henry IV, Part 1* to the Westminster Theatre.

Oct 5 The Dublin Gate Theatre, still playing at the Gaiety Theatre, opens its 16th season with Greenwood/Gow's *Love on the Dole*, followed by Shaw's *The Man of Destiny*, O'Neill's *The Emperor Jones*, Kaufman/Hart's *The Man Who Came To Dinner*, Collis' *The Barrel Organ*, and Schauffler's *Parnell*. On Dec 26, the ensemble returns to the Gate Theatre, opening with a holiday entertainment, *Jack-in-the-Box*.

Nov 10 The Theatre Guild present's Philip Barry's *Without Love*, a play about a living arrangement that ends in love. Elliott Nugent and Katharine Hepburn are featured. After a tour, the show has 113 performances on Broadway.

Nov 11 More revivals this month, with Vernon Sylvaine's *Aren't Men Beasts* opening tonight at London's Garrick Theatre, followed on the 12 by Maugham's

SKIN OF OUR TEETH

Home and Beauty at the Playhouse. On the 24 at the Mercury Theatre, Congreve's Restoration comedy, *The Way of the World* is revived, staged by Ashley Dukes. On Nov 27, Robert Atkins, having recently played *Part 1*, follows with *Part 2* of *Henry IV*.

Nov 24 Paul Muni returns from Hollywood to recreate the leading role in Elmer Rice's *Counsellor-at-Law*, which he created in 1931. Rice stages. The show runs for over 32 weeks.

Nov 29 Erwin Piscator's group at the New School for Social Research presents Dan Jame's *Winter Soldiers* at the Studio Theatre in New York. This play about Russian resistance to the German advance on Moscow wins the Sidney Howard Memorial Award and is named among the *Best Plays* by Burns Mantle.

Dec 21 Katharine Cornell revives Chekhov's *The Three Sisters* on Broadway for a run of more than 15 weeks. Judith Anderson and Gertrude Musgrove complete the trio.

Dec 23 It's almost Christmas, so the Victoria Palace opens its pantomime, *Babes in the Wood*, with a bevy of Lupinos—Wallace, Lupino Lane, and Lauri Lupino Lane. Adele Dixon is Robin Hood. At the Westminster Theatre, Robert Atkins revives *A Midsummer Night's Dream*. On the 24, *Mother Goose* opens at the Coliseum, with Norman Evans as a pantodame Mother Goose. J. M. Barrie's *The Professor's Love Story* opens at the Q Theatre, while *Cinderella* bows at the Stoll Theatre, and *Peter Pan* opens at the Winter Garden. Other holiday pantomimes or revivals include *Humpty-Dumpty* (Golder's Green Hippodrome), Boucicault's *The Streets of London* (Orpheum, Golder's Green), *Jack and Jill* (His Majesty's), *Dick Whittington and His Cat* (Wimbledon), *The Drunkard* (Arts), *The Romance of David Garrick* (St. James's), another *Cinderella* (Streatham Hill), and *Rebecca* (Ambassadors').

Dec 29 The Theatre Guild produces Clifford Odets' Americanized version of Konstantin Simonov's *The Russian People* at the Guild Theatre. This story of Soviet resistance to the Nazis features Herbert Berghof, Luther Adler, and Eduard Franz in the large cast. It runs five weeks.

1942 BIRTHS/DEATHS/DEBUTS

May 16 American producer Morris Gest (b. 1881) dies in New York City. Gest brought Nikita Balieff's *Chauve-Souris* to America in 1922 for the first of many engagements, followed by the Moscow Art Theatre in 1923. His great success, Max Reinhardt's *The Miracle*, was produced the following year.

May 26 Ralph Alswang makes his Broadway debut as designer of the setting for Louis Vittes' comedy, *Comes the Revelation*, at Jolson's Theatre.

June 10 English actor, playwright, and producer Stanley Lupino (b. 1894) dies in London. Lupino was in variety with an acrobat troupe and in pantomime for many years at Drury Lane. He was also seen in revue and musical comedy and was the author of several plays. His volume of reminiscences, *From the Stocks to the Stars*, was published in 1934.

June 29 Actor John Barrymore (b. 1882) dies in Hollywood. The youngest of the Barrymores, he first appeared in Sudermann's *Magda* in 1903 at the Cleveland Theatre in Chicago. In 1922 he electrified New York with his *Hamlet* for a run of 101 performances. In later years he appeared mainly in films and on radio. His *Confessions of an Actor* was published in 1926.

July 25 English actor Tom Reynolds (b. 1866) is dead. Reynolds was a member of Sir Henry Irving's company from 1889 to 1905. On the death of Sir Henry, he joined H. B. Irving and remained with him as stage manager and principal comedian for 11 years.

Sep 2 Director, producer, and actor Ned Wayburn (b. 1874) dies in New York. Wayburn appeared in vaudeville where he allegedly originated "ragtime" piano playing. He founded the Ned Wayburn Dancing, Singing, and Dramatic Schools and composed the first "ragtime" song, *Syncopated Sandy.*

Sep 3 Producer, playwright, and drama critic Harrison Grey Fiske (b. 1861) dies in New York City. Fiske, former president and editor of the *NY Dramatic Mirror*, wrote a number of plays, among which are *Fontenelle, Hester Crewe, The Privateer,* and *The District Attorney.* He was married to the late actress Minnie Maddern Fiske.

Oct 20 American stage and screen actress May Robson (b. 1865) dies in Beverly Hills. From 1893–96 Robson was engaged at the Empire Theatre under Charles Frohman. She made her debut as a "star" in 1907 in Philadelphia as Aunt Mary Watkins in *The Rejuvenation of Aunt Mary.* Robson began her film career in 1926.

Oct 22 Actress Brenda de Banzie makes her London debut as Mme. La Duchesse de Vilandelle in Cole Porter's *Du Barry Was a Lady* at His Majesty's Theatre. She has appeared with repertory groups in Manchester, Bradford, Birmingham, and Nottingham.

Nov 5 Actor-playwright-composer-producer George M. Cohan (b. 1878) dies in New York. Son of vaudevillians, Cohan first appeared with his parents and sister as The Four Cohans. Apart from his own plays, he also starred with success in O'Neill's *Ah, Wilderness!* and the musical comedy *I'd Rather be Right.* His autobiography, *Twenty Years on Broadway and the Years it Took to Get There* was published in 1925.

Dec 12 American actress Helen Westley (b. 1879) dies in Middlebush, New Jersey. After several years in stock, Westley appeared with the Washington Square Players in 1915. She joined the Theatre Guild in 1919, to play Donna Sirena in *Bonds of Interest,* and from that date until 1936 appeared only in Guild productions.

1942 THEATERS/PRODUCTIONS

Owing to the war, production at the Liverpool Playhouse has ceased. The directors of the Liverpool Repertory Theatre decide to lease the theatre to London's Old Vic Company, whose historic house has been bombed in 1941. This gives the Old Vic a provincial center from which to tour its productions. In 1946, the Old Vic will vacate the Liverpool home.

Furthering the cause of Irish drama and the Irish language, Dublin's Abbey Theatre this year begins producing plays in Gaelic as well as in English.

Jan 28 The Theatre Royal, Bristol, is sold at auction for £10,500.

Feb On what was once the "Theatre Block" on West 42nd Street, the Republic and the Eltinge Theatres, once proud homes of legitimate drama but over a decade now housing burlesque shows, lose their licenses for such performances. Film programs will replace the bump-and-grind artistes.

March 1 The Stage Door Canteen, set up by theatre people to entertain servicemen passing through New York, opens in the basement of the 44th Street Theatre.

April 21 The Provincial Theatre Council is constituted today. Its functions are similar to those of the London Theatre Council, established in 1935. It represents the Theatrical Management Association and British Actors' Equity Association, regulating relations between managers and artists, ensuring that the Standard Contract, approved by the Council is maintained. All contracts between managers and performers, whether for a provincial tour, membership in a provincial repertory ensemble, or for work in a suburban theatre, must be approved by the Council and receive a Certificate of Registration.

May 31 The *NY Times*, considering the Broadway season closed on May 30, publishes its production-count for 1941–42: there have been 87 shows, divided into musicals (6), revues (2), revivals (15), variety shows (4), ice shows (1), operettas (1), return engagements (1), and plays—both comedies and dramas (57). *Life with Father* continues strong, a holdover from the 1939–40 season. *My Sister Eileen* and *Arsenic and Old Lace* have survived well from last season. Hollywood studios have spent a total of $1,122,500 for Broadway plays, shows that didn't reach New York, and even for some unproduced scripts.

June 15 The exigencies of wartime have obvious effects on casting—actors are being drafted; on production—some materials are scarce or rationed; and on playwriting—Burns Mantle and other critics find the quality diminished, so there is no Drama Critics' Circle Award and also no Pulitzer Prize for the current Broadway season. Among the 60 dramas produced, Mantle still manages to find ten worthy of inclusion in his *Best Plays*, but with difficulty. He notes that some fellow-critics are calling this "the worst theatre season in all the city's history," but discounts that as the usual love of superlatives. Revivals are popular. The annual ten *Best Plays* chosen by Mantle, are the following: Koch and Huston's *In Time To Come*, Steinbeck's *The Moon Is Down*, Coward's *Blithe Spirit*, Chodorov and Fields' *Junior Miss*, Anderson's *Candle in the Wind*, Rotter and Vincent's *Letters to Lucerne*, Raphaelson's *Jason*, Hamilton's *Angel Street*, Job's *Uncle Harry*, and Treadwell's *Hope for a Harvest*.

Dec 18 Although he is ill, the producer of the revue, *Wine, Women, and Song*, is ordered to jail. He has been found guilty of presenting illegal burlesque in his revue. The license of New York's Ambassador Theatre, as a result, is revoked for a year.

Jan 7 *Something for the Boys* (NY—Alvin—Musical). Cole Porter provides the music for this show, with book by Herbert and Dorothy Fields. Ethel Merman stars as a woman whose Texas ranch is off-limits to the Army. There are 422 performances. On March 20, 1944, the show opens in London at the Coliseum for a short run.

Jan 14 *Dark Eyes* (NY—Belasco—Comedy). Eugenie Leontovich and Elena Miramova act in their own play about three Russian actresses (Ludmilla Toretzka is the third), penniless in New York, but looking for an angel for a play they've written. The play wins 230 performances.

Jan 29 *The Patriots* (NY—National—Drama). Sidney Kingsley's play about the troubles of the Founding Fathers wins the Drama Critics' Circle Award as the best play of the season. The play has, however, only 173 showings. Among the cast are Raymond Edward Johnson, Madge Evans, and Cecil Humphreys.

March 3 *Harriet* (NY—Henry Miller—Drama). Florence Ryerson and Colin Clements write this play about Harriet Beecher Stowe. Helen Hayes stars. It runs for 47 weeks.

March 17 *Kiss and Tell* (NY—Biltmore—Comedy). Joan Caulfield appears in F. Hugh Herbert's play about teenagers growing up. The show runs for 956 performances, with three companies on the road next season. The play also becomes a popular radio serial. In London, it opens at the Phoenix on Aug 1, 1945, with Tilsa Page as Corliss Archer.

March 31 *Oklahoma!* (NY—St. James—Musical). Rodgers and Hammerstein base their sensationally successful musical on Lynn Riggs' *Green Grow the Lilacs*. They center it on the love and marriage of Laurey (Joan Roberts) and Curly (Alfred Drake). Howard DaSilva is Jud Fry, the menacing farm-hand who tries to come between them. Also in the cast are Celeste Holm (Ado Annie), Lee Dixon (Will Parker), Joseph Buloff (Ali Hakim), and Betty Garde (Aunt Eller). With 2,248 performances, a number of touring companies, many foreign productions, and endless stock, amateur and college stagings, this is one of the great hits of the American musical theatre. Agnes de Mille's ballets, especially the innovative "Dream Ballet" in which Laurey sees her love of Curly and her fear of Jud in a surreal vision, inaugurates a new era of dance on the Broadway stage. In *Oklahoma!* sophistication, often present in Rodgers's shows, is replaced by simplicity, honesty, and directness. The integration of song and story, though lacking in many earlier American musicals, is not an innovation, even for these collaborators. But critics consider

KISS AND TELL

it so. Memorable in the popular score are "Oh, What A Beautiful Morning," "The Surrey With The Fringe On Top," "Kansas City," "I Cain't Say No," "People Will Say We're In Love," "Out Of My Dreams," "All Er Nuthin'!," and the title song. Rouben Mamoulian stages for the Theatre Guild, with sets and costumes by Lemuel Ayers and Miles White. In its earliest version, this show has been called *Away We Go*. Initially produced for $75,000, it grosses millions of dollars. "There is more comedy in one of Miss de Mille's gay little passages than in many of the other Broadway tom-tom beats together. . . . Mr. Rodgers score's never lack grace, but seldom have they been so integrated as this for 'Oklahoma!' . . ." says, Lewis Nichols, of the *NY Times*. The show comes to London's Drury Lane on April 30, 1947, with Howard Keel and Betty Jane Watson leading the cast. It has a long run of 1,543 performances.

April 1 *The Ziegfeld Follies of 1943* (NY—Winter Garden—Revue). This show is considered shabby by some critics, and it is constantly in danger of being interrupted by Milton Berle, its star, getting involved in the other acts. The show achieves 553 performances.

April 14 *Tomorrow the World* (NY—Ethel Barrymore—Drama). James Gow and Arnaud d'Usseau write this story of an unreformed Hitler Youth who comes into a

democratic household. Skippy Homeier plays the boy. The cast also includes Nancy Nugent, Shirley Booth, and Ralph Bellamy. The show has 500 performances. The drama opens in London at the Aldwych on Aug 30, 1944, with David O'Brien as the boy.

May 4 *Sons and Soldiers* (NY—Morosco—Drama). Irwin Shaw writes this tale of a woman, told she might die if she has children, who dreams of her children's future. Geraldine Fitzgerald is featured with Gregory Peck, Stella Adler, and Karl Malden. Max Reinhardt stages and directs. There are only 22 performances.

June 16 *Those Endearing Young Charms* (NY—Booth—Comedy). Edward Chodorov writes this story of a woman who falls in love with a soldier on leave. Virginia Gilmore and Zachary Scott are the couple. The show has only 61 performances.

June 17 *Early To Bed* (NY—Broadhurst—Musical). Thomas "Fats" Waller composes the score and George Marion, Jr., the libretto for this show about goings-on in a bordello. Richard Kollmar, Muriel Angelus, John Lund, Jane Deering, and Choo Choo Johnson are featured. The show runs 48 weeks.

Aug 2 *The Army Play-By-Play* (NY—Martin Beck—Drama). Five prize-winning one-act plays from the Enlisted Men's Contest, sponsored by producer John

Golden and Special Services of New York's 2nd Service Command, are given a five-week run. They are *Where E'er We Go*, by Pfc. John O'Dea; *First Cousins*, by Cpl. Kurt Kazner; *Button Your Lip*, by Pfc. Irvin Neiman; *Mail Call*, by Air Cadet Ralph Nelson, and *Pack Up Your Troubles*, by Pfc. Alfred Geto.

Aug 3 *The Two Mrs. Carrolls* (NY—Booth—Comedy). Paul Czinner and Robert Reud produce this vehicle for Elizabeth Bergner. The play depicts a woman who is being slowly poisoned by her husband. Victor Jory and Irene Worth are also in the cast. The show achieves 585 performances.

Sep 8 *Laugh Time* (NY—Shubert—Revue). From the West Coast Fred Finklehoffe and Paul Small bring in this collage of talents: Ethel Waters, Bert Wheeler, Frank Fay, and Buck and Bubbles, the black dance duo. It runs nearly 16 weeks.

Sep 15 *A New Life* (NY—Royale—Drama). Elmer Rice's new play about the birth of a baby to a woman who thinks her husband has been killed in the war features Betty Field. The production lasts nine weeks.

Oct 7 *One Touch of Venus* (NY—Imperial—Musical). Mary Martin is Venus, a statue come to life, interested in the naive barber (Kenny Baker) who's awakened her. With the help of music and lyrics by Kurt Weill and Ogden Nash ("Speak Low") and two Agnes de Mille ballets—"Forty Minutes for Lunch" and "Venus in Ozone Heights"—Venus realizes that neither the city nor suburbia are right for a goddess. Nash and S. J. Perelman base the book on F. Anstey's tale, *The Tinted Venus*. The show runs for 567 performances.

Nov 15 *The Innocent Voyage* (NY—Belasco—Comedy). The Theatre Guild gets only a five-week run from Paul Osborn's adaptation of Richard Hughes' novel, *A High Wind in Jamaica*, in which some children find themselves on a pirate-ship. The children include Dean and Guy Stockwell; the adults, Clarence Derwent, Arvid Paulson, Herbert Berghof, and Oscar Homolka.

Nov 29 *Lovers and Friends* (NY—Plymouth—Drama). Dodie Smith's British plot spans two world wars but concerns the love, marriage, boredom, cheating, divorce, and reconciliation of two people, played by Raymond Massey and Katharine Cornell. Considering the casting, the 21-week run is surprising. Guthrie McClintic directs, with sets and costumes by the London designers, Motley.

Dec 2 *Carmen Jones* (NY—Broadway—Musical). Using George Bizet's music, Oscar Hammerstein II provides the lyrics for this variation on *Carmen*. Major roles in this all-black musical are double-cast to permit the non-operatic Broadway performance schedule. Carmen: Muriel Smith or Muriel Rahn; Joe: Luther Saxon or Na-

poleon Reed. The show runs 503 performances.

Dec 8 *The Voice of the Turtle* (NY—Morosco—Comedy). John Van Druten writes this charming tale of wartime romance between a young army man and an as-

piring Broadway actress. Margaret Sullavan, Audrey Christie, and Elliott Nugent are the entire cast. The show runs 1,557 performances. It comes to London's Piccadilly on July 9, 1947, where it has less than 100 performances.

1943   BRITISH PREMIERES

March 11 *Brighton Rock* (L—Garrick—Drama). Graham Greene's novel comes to the stage in this version by Frank Harvey, staged by Richard Bird. Among the cast are Virginia Winter, Richard Attenborough, Hermione Baddeley, Dulcie Gray, and Harcourt Williams.

March 12 *It's Foolish But It's Fun* (L—Coliseum—Revue). Jimmy Nervo and Teddy Knox head the cast, with Phyllis Stanley, Pamela Foster, Lulu Dukes, Bruce Carfax, and Toni Lupino also on hand. Douglas Furber's show achieves 469 performances.

March 18 *Strike a New Note* (L—Prince of Wales's—Revue). There are 661 showings of this revue, staged by Robert Nesbitt. Jill Manners, Sid Field, Jerry Desmonde, Bernard Hunter, Leni Lynn, and Zoe Gail are among the performers.

March 24 *Junior Miss*. See NY premiere, 1941.

March 30 *La-Di-Da-Di-Da* (L—Victoria Palace—Musical). Stanley Lupino's farcical musical earns 318 performances. Lu-

pino Lane and Wallace Lupino are in the company.

April 21 *They Came To a City* (L—Globe—Drama). J. B. Priestley's play has a 35-week run. In the company are John Clements, Googie Withers, Renee Gadd, Raymond Huntley, A. E. Matthews, and Mabel Terry-Lewis, among others.

April 29 *Present Laughter* (L—Haymarket—Comedy). Noel Coward stages his play about a popular London stage star with woman-trouble. He also has the leading role. Others in the cast are Joyce Carey, James Donald, and Dennis Price. The comedy opens on Broadway at the Plymouth on Oct 29, 1946, with Clifton Webb as the actor. It runs nearly five months.

May 25 *Shadow and Substance* (L—Duke of York's—Drama). Paul Vincent Carroll's Irish play, staged by Hugh Hunt, has a cast including Joyce Redman, Denis Carey, Megs Jenkins, Malcolm Keen, Mona Harrison, and Tony Quinn, among others.

VOICE OF THE TURTLE

MAX REINHARDT

May 27 *Magic Carpet* (L—Princes—Revue). Robert Nesbitt stages this show by Douglas Furber and Austin Melford, with music by Manning Sherwin and lyrics by Val Guest. The show runs 23 weeks.

June 3 *Hi-De-Hi* (L—Palace—Revue). Flanagan and Allen, Eddie Gray, Florence Desmond, and Roberta Huby, are in the cast. This show runs over 42 weeks.

June 8 *The Moon Is Down.* See NY premiere, 1942.

June 10 *Sweet and Low* (L—Ambassadors'—Revue). Hermione Gingold heads the ensemble in this Charles Hickman-directed show. With Brenda Bruce, Edna Wood, Mary Irwin, Graham Penley, Bonar Colleano, and others, it has a run of 33 weeks.

June 17 *The Lisbon Story* (L—Hippodrome—Musical). Harry Parr-Davis writes the music and Harold Purcell supplies the plot for this story of allies and enemies confronting each other on neutral territory. The cast includes Jack Livesey, Eleanor Fayre, Patricia Burke, Noele Gordon, and Albert Lieven. The show runs 492 performances.

July 22 *It's Time To Dance* (L—Winter Garden—Musical). Douglas Furber and Arthur Rose write this story of a peer trying to become a gossip writer while engaged in crime detection. Jack Buchanan stars. The show runs eight months.

Aug 18 *Sunny River* (L—Piccadilly—Musical). The score is by Sigmund Romberg; the book by Oscar Hammerstein II, and the staging by Maxwell Wray, but the run is not long. Among the large cast are Helen Lawrence, Evelyn Laye, and Bertram Wallis.

Sep 1 *Pink String and Sealing Wax* (L—Duke of York's—Drama). Roland Pertwee's play of murder and suicide features Iris Hoey, Margaret Barton, Dorothy Hyson, and David Horne. It runs 45 weeks.

Sep 8 *The Wingless Victory.* See NY premiere, 1936.

Sep 20 *Ten Little Niggers* (L—Wimbledon—Drama). Agatha Christie adapts her novel of the same name for the stage. Among the cast in this thriller of attrition by death are Terence de Marney, Henrietta Watson and Hilda Bruce-Potter. After this tryout, the production moves on Nov 17, to the St. James's Theatre, where it has a run of over eight months. The mystery opens at the Broadhurst in New York on June 27, 1944, under the title *Ten Little Indians.* Claudia Morgan, J. Pat O'Malley, Nicholas Joy, and Estelle Winwood are in the cast. A success, it has 426 performances.

Sep 22 *My Sister Eileen.* See NY premiere, 1940.

Sep 23 *Something in the Air* (L—Palace—Musical). Jack Hulbert directs this show, also playing the role of Jack Pendleton. Manning Sherwin provides music for the lyrics of Harold Purcell and Max Kester, with a book by Arthur MacRae, Archie Menzies, and Hulbert. Also in the company are Cicely Courtneidge, Gabrielle Brune, and Jean Gillie. The show runs 42 weeks.

Oct 14 *Acacia Avenue* (L—Vaudeville—Comedy). Mabel and Denis Constanduros write this play suggesting the conversational bromides and banalities of lower middle-class life after the war. The cast includes Megs Jenkins, Dorothy Hamilton, and Doris Rogers. The show runs 29 weeks.

Oct 26 *The Love Racket* (L—Victoria Palace—Musical). Stanley Lupino devises the book for this show, with a score by Noel Gay. Lyrics come from Frank Eyton, Leslie Gibbs, Basil Thomas, and Barbara Gordon. The cast includes Peggy Carlisle, Finley Currie, Roy Royston, and Arthur Askey. The show runs over ten months.

Nov 9 *Arc de Triomphe* (L—Phoenix—Musical). Ivor Novello creates the book and the score and helps Christopher Hassall with the lyrics for this show about an opera singer who must choose between love and a career. The cast includes Maidie Andrews, Harcourt Williams, and Mary Ellis. There are 222 performances.

Nov 10 *This Is the Army.* See NY premiere, 1942.

Dec 15 *There Shall Be No Night.* See NY premiere, 1940.

Dec 24 *While the Sun Shines* (L—Globe—Drama). Terence Rattigan's play about soldiers on leave in London features Michael Wilding, Brenda Bruce, Jane Baxter, and Ronald Squire. It runs 1,154 performances. It has only 39 showings in New York, opening at the Lyceum on Sep 19, 1944.

1943　REVIVALS/REPERTORIES

Jan 16 At London's Prince of Wales's Theatre, *The Desert Song* is revived. On March 4, *The Merry Widow* lives again at His Majesty's Theatre. At the Stoll Theatre, on April 17, *Show Boat* comes to life again as well. On April 23, at the Winter Garden, the revival is *The Vagabond King.*

Jan 25 Donald Wolfit brings his Shakespeare productions to London's St. James's Theatre. Tonight he offers *King Lear,* in which he plays the title-role. On Jan 27, *Twelfth Night* is revived, with the Wolfit Malvolio interpretation.

Feb 4 Walter Ellis's farce, *A Little Bit of Fluff,* is revived in the West End at the Ambassadors' Theatre. On Feb 11, Emlyn

Williams revives Turgenev's *A Month in the Country* in his own adaptation at St. James's Theatre. On March 10 at the Lyric Theatre, J. M. Barrie's *What Every Woman Knows* is revived. On the 16th at the Westminster Theater, Ibsen's *Hedda Gabler* comes back. On March 18, at the Cambridge Theatre, Bernard Shaw's *Heartbreak House* is played. On April 8, at the Phoenix Theatre, it's Congreve's *Love for Love*. *Rebecca* comes back on April 26 at the Scala Theatre.

Feb 16 Despite the loss of its London home, the Old Vic company continues active, touring from its temporary Liverpool Center, the Playhouse. Tonight in London at the New Theatre, it opens its revival of *The Merchant of Venice*, with Frederick Valk as Shylock. Other productions the Old Vic will offer Londoners include John Drinkwater's *Abraham Lincoln* on Apr 13, Konstantin Simonov's *The Russians* on June 10, and Peter Ustinov's *Blow Your Own Trumpet*, on Aug 11, all shown at the Playhouse.

March 8 The Dublin Gate Theatre continues its 16th season, returning to the Gaiety Theatre for Shakespeare's *Antony and Cleopatra*. Other plays include Kaufman/Hart's *The Man Who Came To Dinner* (revival), the Capeks' *The Insect Play*, Besier's *The Barretts of Wimpole Street*, Ibsen's *Ghosts*, and Shaw's *Captain Brassbound's Conversion*. The company then tours Ireland.

April 17 Milton Rosmer assumes leadership of the Shakespeare Memorial Theatre in Stratford-upon-Avon, opening the annual season with *Twelfth Night*. *Henry V* is the "birthday play." Dorothy Green, long an admired actress of leading Shakespearian roles at the theatre, directs *The Winter's Tale*. Peter Creswell stages *King Lear*. Baliol Holloway directs both *A Midsummer Night's Dream* and *The Merry Wives of Windsor*. *Othello* and Sheridan's *The Critic* are also played. The season closes on Sep 11.

May 6 At London's Whitehall Theatre, Eugene Brieux's *Damaged Goods* is revived. Revivals continue popular elsewhere also. At the Comedy Theatre on May 12, the Hicks-Dukes version of *Vintage Wine* opens, followed on May 18 at the Westminster Theatre by Lonsdale's *The Last of Mrs. Cheyney*. At the Scala Theatre on May 26, *Peg O' My Heart* is resuscitated. Donald Wolfit directs and plays the title-role in Moliere's *The Imaginary Invalid* at the Westminster Theatre on June 1. On June 7 at the St. James's Theatre, Becque's *Parisienne* is revived. Ibsen's *Ghosts* revives on June 25 at the Duke of York's Theatre. On June 29, Donald Wolfit opens *The Master Builder*—playing the title-role—at the Westminster Theatre.

June 7 The summer season of plays opens in Regent's Park at the Open Air Theatre, with *As You Like It*, staged by Robert At-

kins. On June 14, Bridie's *Tobias and the Angel* is played. *Lady Precious Stream* is revived on July 12. On July 26, *As You Like It* returns, followed by *The Tempest*, staged by Atkins, on August 3. *Love's Labour's Lost* opens on Aug 16.

Aug 4 Lehar's *The Merry Widow* is revived on Broadway at the Majestic Theatre for a ten-month run. European stars Marta Eggerth and Jan Kiepura sing the leads. George Balanchine choreographs. This Central European work is a success at a time when Americans are at war with the Third Reich.

Sep 2 Constance Garnett's translation of Chekhov's *Uncle Vanya* is seen in this revival at London's Westminster Theatre. Other fall revivals include Masefield's *The Tragedy of Nan* at the Mercury Theatre on Sep 30; Barrie's *The Admirable Crichton* on Oct 28 at His Majesty's Theatre; on Nov 16, Wilde's *An Ideal Husband* is revived at the Westminster; Farquhar's *The Recruiting Officer* is brought back at the Arts Theatre.

Sep 20 The Dublin Gate Theatre opens its 17th season with a revival of Merijkowski's *Tzar Paul*, playing at the Gaiety Theatre. Other shows include Kennedy/Dean's *The Constant Nymph*, Sheridan's *The School for Scandal*, O'Neill's *Anna Christie*, Williams' *Night Must Fall* (the

last three revivals all), and Drinkwater's *Abraham Lincoln*, for which the troupe returns to the Gate Theatre, where it also presents the holiday show, *Masquerade*.

Oct 19 The Theatre Guild revives Shakespeare's *Othello*, with Paul Robeson as the Moor, for a 37-week run on Broadway at the Shubert Theatre.

Nov 17 Richard Rodgers revives and revises *A Connecticut Yankee*. He produces at Broadway's Martin Beck Theatre, with a cast including Vivienne Segal, Dick Foran, and Vera Ellen. The revival has a 17-week run.

Dec 23 The holiday season is ushered in with the pantomime of *Humpty Dumpty* at London's Coliseum. At the Queen's Theatre, the entertainment is *Claudius, the Bee*. On Dec 24, *The Sleeping Beauty* opens at the Streatham Hill Theatre. At the Golder's Green Hippodrome, the panto is *Mother Goose*, an old favorite by J. Hickory Wood, while the Cambridge Theatre revives Barrie's *Peter Pan*. At the Scala, the gala is *Alice in Wonderland* and *Alice Through the Looking-Glass*. On Dec 27, two *Cinderellas* open, one at the Wimbledon Theatre, the other at His Majesty's. At the Winter Garden, *Where the Rainbow Ends* is shown, with *Jack and Jill* presented at the King's Hammersmith.

1943   BIRTHS/DEATHS/DEBUTS

Jan 13 Irene Dailey makes her Broadway debut as "Shotput" in Wilfred Pettitt's melodrama, *Nine Girls*, at the Longacre Theatre.

Jan 23 American drama critic and author Alexander Woollcott (b. 1887) dies in New York. Woollcott served as critic for the *NY Times*, the *NY Herald*, and the *Sun*. He later devoted himself to broadcasting, lecturing, and writing. His books include *Mr. Dickens Goes to the Play*, *Enchanted Aisles*, and *As You Were*.

March 31 Dancer-actress Bambi Linn makes her Broadway debut as a dancer in the chorus of *Oklahoma!* at the St. James Theatre.

April 1 Actress Cavada Humphrey makes her New York City debut as Esther in John Drinkwater's biblical play, *A Man's House*, at the Blackfriar's Guild.

April 3 Stage and screen actor Conrad Veidt is dead at age 50 in Los Angeles.

June 1 British actor Leslie Howard (b. 1893) is presumed dead when his plane is shot down between Lisbon and London. After many successful roles in London, Howard came to New York where he appeared in *Outward Bound*, *The Green Hat*, *Berkeley Square*, *The Petrified Forest*, *Hamlet*, and others. He also wrote the play, *Murray Hill*, produced in London, and *Tell Me the Truth*, later rewritten as

Elizabeth Steps Out. His film career began in 1930.

June 16 American playwright Bayard Veiller (b. 1869) dies in New York. A former newspaperman, Veiller made a specialty of mystery dramas; notably, *Within the Law*, *The Thirteenth Chair*, and *The Trial of Mary Dugan*. In his later years he became a movie executive. His autobiography, *The Fun I've Had*, was published in 1941.

June 17 Set and lighting designer George Jenkins designs his first New York production, the musical comedy *Early to Bed*, by George Marion and Thomas Waller, at the Broadhurst Theatre.

July 12 British-American actress Cissie Loftus (b. 1876) dies in New York City. Lostus, daughter of variety artist Marie Loftus, appeared at the Oxford Music Hall in London in 1893. In the early 1900s she played in a number of straight plays with Modjeska, Frohman, and Sothern. From 1902–15 she alternated between England and America, playing in vaudeville and burlesque.

July 16 American drama critic John Anderson (b. 1896) dies in New York. Anderson became drama critic of the New York *Evening Post* in 1924 and later joined the New York *Journal-American*. He is author of *Box Office* and *The American*

Theatre.

July 17 American actor Arthur Byron (b. 1872) is dead. Son of players Oliver Doud Byron and Kate Byron, the actor first appeared in his father's company in 1889. Later he played with Sol Smith Russell and John Drew respectively. Byron toured with Maude Adams in *What Every Woman Knows* in 1910. A notable film career began in 1932.

Oct 31 Actor, manager, and stage director Max Reinhardt (b. 1873) is dead. Reinhardt founded the Salzburg Festival in 1920 where he made many notable productions including *Jederman* and *Faust*. In 1934 he produced both the stage and film versions of *A Midsummer Night's Dream* in Hollywood.

1943 THEATERS/PRODUCTIONS

March 31 Getting *Oklahoma!* to Broadway and the St. James Theatre hasn't been easy. The producers, the 25-year-old Theatre Guild, after a poor season in 1941–42, have had only $30,000 in the bank. Steinway Hall auditions by Rodgers, Hammerstein, Alfred Drake, and Joan Roberts haven't found many backers. Ten days from the New Haven opening, auditions are held in the rehearsal studio. Capitalized at $150,000, only $83,313 is needed to get the show to Broadway. Columbia Pictures, offered a 50% share, gives only $15,000. Howard Cullman, famed as a judge of hits and successful backer, refuses to invest. Many of the 25 who do have to be pressured by Guild officers. The show is seen by some as "too clean to succeed." Mike Todd says: "No gags, no gals, no chance." Opening in New Haven as *Away We Go*, the show doesn't excite the critics. "Helburn's Folly," some call it, referring to the Guild's Theresa Helburn, who ardently believes in the musical.

May 11 The Theatre Royal, Bristol, handsomely restored, reopens. Dating from 1766, it is the oldest in England.

May 30 The current Broadway season will officially close tomorrow, but the *NY Times* has the statistics for 1942–43 ready now: of 77 productions, 43 have been plays; nine, musicals; five, revues; ten, revivals; four, return engagements; one, ice show; five, variety shows. Hollywood studios are estimated to have paid out some $3 million for screen rights to Broadway shows and other plays.

June 15 Burns Mantle notes a curiosity about wartime plays on Broadway: the public avoids them, especially the more realistic ones. In the 1941–42 season, only two of the eleven war plays produced found favor, and they were the least noisy. In the season of 1942–43, there are 12 war plays on record, of which only one has been really successful: Anderson's *The Eve of St. Mark*. Mantle also points out the relatively new phenomenon of the long run and the intermediate run. In the "good old days," *Way Down East* and *The Old Homestead* achieved their long runs by extensive national touring. *Abie's Irish Rose* and *Tobacco Road* begin the trend of long runs on Broadway, now reinforced by a number of popular plays. In the current season there have been ten less new plays produced than last season, but 21 of them are hits, as opposed to 17 in 1941–42. The ratio is still about one hit for every three flops. With the close of the wartime Broadway season Mantle chooses his annual ten *Best Plays*. They are: Kingsley's *The Patriots*, Anderson's *The Eve of St. Mark*, Wilder's *The Skin of Our Teeth*, James' *Winter Soldiers*, Gow and d'Usseau's *Tomorrow the World*, Ryerson and Clements' *Harriet*, Fields' *The Doughgirls*, Van Druten and Morris' *The Damask Cheek*, Herbert's *Kiss and Tell*, and Rodgers and Hammerstein's *Oklahoma!* Wilder's play wins the Pulitzer Prize; Kingsley's, the Drama Critics' Circle Award.

Sep 29 Dark for seven years, Broadway's intimate Bijou Theatre re-opens tonight, handsomely refurbished. The play is *All for All*, a reworking of Aaron Hoffman's 1923 farce, *Give and Take*. In Feb 1982, bulldozers will crush the Bijou to make way for a new multi-story Portman Hotel.

Oct 11 In Glasgow, Scottish playwright James Bridie has formed a new theatre company, to win repute as the Glasgow Citizens' Theatre. Tonight in the Athenaeum Theatre, the troupe presents its first production, Bridie's play, *Holy Isle*.

Nov 20 At the invitation of the U.S. Air Force's Commander, General Hap Arnold, Moss Hart—though allergic to flying—covers 28,000 miles in a bomber, going around the nation to visit training camps, to tell the story of pilot-training and the esprit of America's flyers. He writes the play, *Winged Victory* in three weeks and stages it in 17 days, using a cast of 350 servicemen, chosen from 7,000 applicants, with 41 service wives and 9 professional actresses. Hart waives all royalties, giving them to Army Emergency Relief. David Rose composes the music and conducts; Leonard DePaur directs the chorus. It plays at New York's 44th Street Theatre.

Dec 11 The New York City Center of Music and Drama opens, with Artur Rodzinski conducting the New York Philharmonic. Lawrence Tibbett and Bidu Sayo are also on the program. On Dec 20, Sidney Kingsley's *The Patriots* is revived here for a week, with Walter Hampden as Thomas Jefferson.

MECCA AUDITORIUM

Jan 3 *Over 21* (NY—Music Box—Comedy). Ruth Gordon writes and appears in this play about a glamorous actress married to an Army officer in wartime. The play runs nearly 28 weeks.

Jan 5 *Ramshackle Inn* (NY—Royale—Comedy). Zasu Pitts plays Belinda Pryde, who buys a haunted inn. The ghosts are gangsters; there are also some murders and a few FBI agents to complicate matters. The show wins a 27-week run, confounding critics who find little to admire in George Batson's script.

Jan 24 *The Duke in Darkness* (NY—Playhouse—Drama). *Angel Street's* author, Patrick Hamilton, tells the costumetale of a duke imprisoned for five years, pretending to be blind until he escapes. Alex Cohen and Joe Kipness produce for a three-week run.

Jan 26 *Wallflower* (NY—Cort—Comedy). Reginald Denham and Mary Orr write this romantic comedy about a shy girl. Joel Martson and Mary Rolfe play leads. The show runs over six months.

Jan 28 *Mexican Hayride* (NY—Winter Garden—Musical). Mike Todd produces this Cole Porter show—with book by Herbert and Dorothy Fields. The musical, about a female American bullfighter and a man who sets up an illegal lottery in Mexico, features such songs as "I Love You" and "Count Your Blessings." June Havoc and Bobby Clark have the leads. The show runs 481 performances.

Feb 2 *Decision* (NY—Belasco—Drama). Edward Chodorov's play exposes the corruption of a U.S. senator and his newspaper-editor henchman, who have fomented a raceriot in a war plant and go on to destroy an honest school official who stands up to them. It runs 20 weeks.

Mar 14 *Jacobowsky and the Colonel* (NY—Martin Beck—Comedy). Oscar Karlweis plays the resourceful Jew Jacobowsky, who helps the blustering colonel (Louis Calhern) escape from France to fight the Nazis from England. Annabella plays the beautiful Marianne. S. N. Behrman's adaptation of the Franz Werfel novel earns a run of 111 performances. Elia Kazan stages for the Theatre Guild. On June 6, 1945, the play opens in London at the Piccadilly Theatre, with Michael Redgrave as the colonel and Karel Stepanek as Jacobowsky.

Mar 31 *Mrs. January and Mr. X* (NY—Belasco—Comedy). Billie Burke is featured in Zoe Akins' tale of a rich widow who wants to see what it would be like to live under communism. Frank Craven and Barbara Bel Geddes are also in the cast. The play runs just over five weeks.

April 5 *Chicken Every Sunday* (NY—Henry Miller—Comedy). Julius and Philip Epstein adapt Rosemary Taylor's popular

THE SEARCHING WIND

novel about a woman who runs a boarding house. Mary Phillips and Rhys Williams are in the cast. The show runs nearly ten months. On June 20, 1945, it opens at London's Savoy for a short run.

April 8 *Follow the Girls* (NY—Century—Musical). Phil Charig, Dan Shapiro, and Milton Pascal provide the music and lyrics. Guy Bolton, Eddie Davis, and Fred Thompson write the book about a burlesque queen who runs a serviceman's canteen. Gertrude Niesen and Jackie Gleason are featured. The show runs beyond the season. On Oct 25, 1945, the show opens in London at his Majesty's Theatre for a run of 572 performances.

April 12 *The Searching Wind* (NY—Fulton—Drama). Lillian Hellman's play is considered by a number of critics the best serious drama of the season. With the advantage of hindsight, she exposes the evasions and conciliations in high places in America and elsewhere which made Mussolini and Hitler possible. The cast includes Dudley Digges, Cornelia Otis Skinner, Montgomery Clift, Dennis King, and Barbara O'Neil, among others. The play runs nearly ten months.

April 24 *Helen Goes To Troy* (NY—Alvin—Musical). Erich Wolfgang Korngold provides the music and Gottfried Reinhardt and John Meehan, Jr., the libretto for this version of Offenbach's *La Belle Helene*. Jarmila Novotna, of the Metropolitan Opera, is Helen. The show runs only three months.

May 3 *Pick Up Girl* (NY—48th Street—

Drama). Elsa Shelley's play about a 15-year old who has social disease but who's to sort out her life at Bellevue and a reform-school runs six months. In London, it's first shown at a club theatre on May 13, 1946, followed by public performances beginning on July 23.

June 22 *Hats Off To Ice* (NY—Center—Revue). Ice-shows are becoming a fixture at Rockefeller Center's smaller theatre. This successful one is produced by Sonja Henie and Arthur Wirtz. Carol Lynne and Freddie Trenkler head the ensembles.

June 27 *Ten Little Indians*. See L premiere (*Ten Little Niggers*), 1943.

Aug 1 *School for Brides* (NY—Royale—Comedy). Warren Ashe plays Jeff O'Connor who creates a brides' school, using his fashion-models as the pupils. Frank Gill, Jr., and George Carleton Brown's play runs for 375 performances.

Aug 2 *Catherine Was Great* (NY—Schubert—Comedy). Mae West plays a comically sexy and insatiable Empress of Russia in this play she's based on some known historical facts and on some wild fantasy. The show runs for 191 performances.

Aug 21 *Song of Norway* (NY—Imperial—Musical). Lawrence Brooks plays Edvard Grieg in this fictionalized account of his life by Homer Curran, based on a book by Milton Lazarus. The music is Grieg's. George Balanchine choreographs with a large number of artists from the Ballet Russe de Monte Carlo in the cast. The show has 860 performances. It opens in London at the Palace on March 7, 1946, with John Hargreaves in the lead. There it wins 526 showings.

Aug 30 *Anna Lucasta* (NY—Mansfield—Drama). Philip Yordan's play about a former prostitute comes to Broadway after being tried out by the American Negro Theatre. Hilda Simms has the title role. The show runs for 957 performances. On Oct 29, 1947, the play opens at His Majesty's in London with Hilda Simms repeating her role. The production gets 423 performances.

Sep 5 *Last Stop* (NY—Barrymore—Comedy). Erwin Piscator stages Irving Kaye Davis's farce about rebellion in an old ladies' home. It runs three weeks.

Sep 12 *Star Time* (NY—Majestic—Revue). Benny Fields and Lou Holtz head the bill in Paul Small's show, with the dancing DeMarcos (Tony and Sally) also on hand. The production runs 15 weeks.

Sep 19 *While the Sun Shines*. See L premiere, 1943.

Oct 4 *Soldier's Wife* (NY—Golden—Drama). Rose Franken's play dealing with the problems facing husbands and wives separated by the war runs nearly eight months. Martha Scott and Myron McCormick have the leads. On Aug 26, 1946, the play opens at the Duchess in London with Katherine Rogers heading the cast.

Oct 5 *Bloomer Girl* (NY—Shubert—Musical). Richard Arlen composes the music and E.Y. Harburg the lyrics for this story of a liberated women in the mid-19th century. Agnes de Mille choreographs a Civil War ballet. Celeste Holm and Margaret Douglass are featured. The show has 654 performances.

Oct 19 *I Remember Mama* (NY—Music Box—Comedy). Mady Christians plays Mama in John Van Druten's adaptation of the popular book by Kathryn Forbes, *Mama's Bank Account*, depicting the trials and joys of a Norwegian family in San Francisco in 1910. Joan Tetzel is her daughter, Katrin, believing in Mama's non-existent bank account. Marlon Brando makes his Broadway debut as brother Nels. Oscar Homolka is crusty Uncle Chris. Producers Rodgers and Hammerstein have a run of 714 performances. Christians repeats her role and also stages in London, where the show opens on March 2, 1948 at the Aldwych.

Oct 25 *Snafu* (NY—Hudson—Comedy). Billy Redfield is featured as a brave soldier who has trouble readjusting to civilian life. Louis Solomon and Harold Buchman write this play which runs nearly five months.

Nov 1 *Harvey* (NY—48th Street—Comedy). Mary Chase's farce about a lovable drunk who thinks he sees a huge white rabbit stars Frank Fay. The show runs 1,775 performances and remains a favorite with stock and amateur companies. The play wins the Pulitzer Prize in 1945. *Harvey* opens in London at the Prince of Wales's on Jan 5, 1949, with Sid Field in

ON THE TOWN

the lead. On this side of the Atlantic, there are 610 performances.

Nov 23 *The Man Who Had All the Luck* (NY—Forrest—Drama). Arthur Miller's drama about a man who comes to realize that his luck is a result of careful planning and hard work earns some admiring critical comments but is shown just four times. Karl Swenson is in the lead.

Nov 23 *The Late George Apley* (NY—Lyceum—Comedy). John P. Marquand's Pulitzer Prize novel is adapted by Marquand and George S. Kaufman, who also stages. Leo G. Carroll plays the proper Bostonian, fighting a genteel battle against change in his world. The production enjoys 385 performances.

Dec 6 *A Bell for Adano* (NY—Cort—Drama). Paul Osborn adapts John Hersey's Pulitzer Prize-winning novel for the stage. In this production Frederic March plays Major Joppolo, the American officer who tries to help recently defeated Italians begin life again. There are 304 performances. The play opens in London at the Phoenix on Sep 19, 1945, with Robert Beatty as the Major.

Dec 7 *Seven Lively Arts* (NY—Ziegfeld—Revue). The phrase is that of arts-critic Gilbert Seldes. Billy Rose stocks this show with performers such as Beatrice Lillie, Bert Lahr, Benny Goodman, Alicia Markova, Anton Dolin, Doc Rockwell, Bill Tabbert, and Dolores Gray. It is a melange of such creative talents as Igor Stavinsky, Moss Hart, George S. Kaufman, Hassard Short, Jack Donohue, Maurice Abravanel, Robert Shaw, Norman Bel Geddes, and Valentina. The top price for opening-night tickets is an unheard-of $24, but there's free champagne. The show runs 23 weeks.

Dec 13 *Dear Ruth* (NY—Henry Miller—Comedy). Norman Krasna writes this comedy about a girl who discovers she has a devoted beau, thanks to letters her sister has been sending him in her name. Virginia Gillmore has the title role. The show runs 683 performances. It opens in London at the St. James's on Feb 28, 1946, with Dulcie Gray in the lead.

Dec 23 *Laffing Room Only* (NY—Winter Garden—Revue). Ole Olsen and Chic Johnson join the Shuberts to bring forth another sequel to *Hellzapoppin*. With its songs by Burton Lane, the show achieves 233 performances. Olson and Johnson lead the madness.

Dec 28 *On the Town* (NY—Adelphi—Musical). Leonard Bernstein composes the score, with book and lyrics by Betty Comden and Adolph Green. It celebrates "New York, New York" and three servicemen's search for Miss Turnstiles (Sono Osato). The show is based on Jerome Robbins' popular modern ballet, *Fancy Free*, and Robbins creates two effective ballets for this production. Green plays one of the service trio—John Battles and Chris Alexander are the others. Nancy Walker is a cab-driver; Comden an anthropology student. There are 463 performances. " 'On the Town' is the freshest and most engaging musical show to come this way since the golden day of 'Oklahoma!' Everything about it is right. It is fast and it is gay, it takes neither itself nor the world too seriously, it has wit," reports Lewis Nichols of the NY Times.

Dec 29 *Trio* (NY—Belasco—Drama). Dorothy Baker and her husband Howard adapt her novel about Ray Mackenzie's successful attempt to free attractive Janet Logan (Lois Wheeler) from the domination of an older woman friend (Lydia St. Clair), who then kills herself. Richard Widmark plays the man who comes between them, directed by Bretaigne Windust. After 67 performances, responding to complaints of outraged moralists and church pressure-groups, New York's License Commissioner refuses to renew the Belasco's license until the play is withdrawn. Critic Burns Mantle finds the play legitimate and effective as a treatment of "the unhealthy subject of Lesbianism."

McCracken's play about a good housewife gallantly struggling with the familiar shortages and emergencies of wartime. It runs 740 performances.

Oct 12 *It Depends What You Mean* (L—Westminster—Drama). James Bridie's play receives 189 performances. The characters come from different walks of life, but each has initials such as B.A., M.P., D.B.E., and R.A.S.C. following his name. Alastair Sim, Angela Baddeley, Wilfrid Hyde-White, and Margaret Barton are in the company.

Nov 28 *Strike it Again* (L—Prince of Wales's—Revue). The cast includes Wendy Toye, Roberta Huby, Sid Field, Jerry Desmonde, Billy Dainty, Pauline Black, and Stella Moya. The show runs for 438 performances.

Dec 20 *Love in Idleness* (L—Lyric—Comedy). Alfred Lunt stages Terence Rattigan's popular play about a woman whose radical son by an earlier marriage has some strong feelings about her forceful, capitalist husband. Lynn Fontanne is the woman and Lunt the husband. It runs 213 performances. On Jan 23, 1946, the play arrives at New York's Empire under the title *O Mistress Mine*. Lunt and Fontanne repeat their roles. The show achieves 452 performances.

1944 BRITISH PREMIERES

Jan 26 *The Druid's Rest* (L—St. Martin's—Comedy). Emlyn Williams writes and directs this play, in which Richard Burton plays. It runs nearly 23 weeks.

Feb 3 *A Soldier for Christmas* (L—Wyndham's—Drama). Reginald Beckwith's play runs nearly 23 weeks. Robert Beatty plays the soldier in the title role.

Feb 17 *Sweeter and Lower* (L—Ambassador—Revue). This is the second edition of *Sweet and Low*, earning a long run of 870 performances. Hermione Gingold heads the cast, with Edna Wood, Bonar Colleano, Yvonne Jacques, and others in the company.

March 15 *This Was a Woman* (L—Comedy—Drama). Joan Morgan's play about a strong-willed, destructive housewife who is forced to yield to the will of her son runs nearly 48 weeks. It was tried out at the Q Theatre in January under the title *The Dark Potential*.

March 20 *Something for the Boys*. See NY premiere, 1943.

March 29 *Uncle Harry*. See NY premiere, 1942.

June 7 *The Last of Summer* (L—Phoenix—drama). Kate O'Brien and John Perry write this story of a polite but deadly battle between a woman who was jilted in her youth and the daughter of the man who jilted her. The cast includes Ada Reeve, Fay Compton, and Lally Bowers.

Aug 1 *Is Your Honeymoon Really Necessary?* (L—Duke of York's—Comedy). E. Vivian Tidmarsh's farce about a man who embarks on a second honeymoon without being sure he has divorced his first wife features Ralph Lynn and Enid Stamp-Taylor. It runs 980 performances.

Aug 30 *Tomorrow the World*. See NY premiere, 1943.

Sep 6 *The Banbury Nose* (L—Wyndham's—Drama). Peter Ustinov's play has a run of 101 performances. Various Banburys are played by Roger Livesey, Eric Maturin, Alan Trotter, Ursula Jeans, and Philip Hillman.

Sep 21 *Three's a Family* (L—Seville—Comedy). Phoebe and Henry Ephron write this light play about an over-large family. There are 317 performances.

Oct 3 *Happy and Glorious* (L—Palladium—Revue). The Dagenham Girl Pipers are featured in this George Black show, which achieves a long run of 938 performances. Robert Nesbitt stages, with Tommy Trinder, Zoe Gail, Victor Standing, Elisabeth Welch, and others.

Oct 4 *No Medals* (L—Vaudeville—Drama). Fay Compton is featured in Esther

1944 REVIVALS/REPERTORIES

Jan 10 At the New York City Center of Music and Drama, Thornton Wilder's *Our Town* is revived for three weeks, with Marc Connelly as the Stage Manager. Montgomery Clift and Martha Scott are George and Emily Gibbs. Jed Harris oversees the production. On Feb 7, *Porgy and Bess* is revived by Cheryl Crawford. On May 17, *The New Moon* is revived for seven weeks.

Jan 25 Margaret Webster and Carly Wharton revive Chekhov's *The Cherry Orchard* for three months on Broadway at the National Theatre. Eva LaGallienne plays Lyubov Andreyevna and shares staging tasks with Webster.

Jan 27 John Gielgud stages this revival at London's Apollo Theatre of *The Cradle Song*, by the Spanish playwrights, Gregorio and Maria Martinez Sierra. Wendy Hiller, Yvonne Mitchell, and Muriel Aked are in the cast.

Feb 10 At London's Arts Theatre, John Masefield's *The Witch*, adapted from a Norwegian drama, is revived, staged by Catherine Lacey. On March 9, Alec Clunes stages Peter Powell's *The Two Children*. On April 7, Shaw's *The Philanderer* is revived by Henry Cass. Moliere's *Doctor Without Medicine* (*Doctor in Spite of Himself*) and *Les Precieuses Ridicules* are presented at the Arts, the first in English, the second in French, by a largely French cast. On May 26, Sheridan's 18th century reworking of a Vanbrugh Restoration comedy, *The Trip to Scarborough* (originally *The Relapse*), opens. On June 22, the play is *The Sulky Fire*, by Jean-Jacques Bernard, followed on July 20, by a revival of John Drinkwater's *Bird in Hand*, staged by Alec Clunes. On Aug 17, Goldoni's *Mistress of the Inn*, adapted by Clifford Bax as *Mine Hostess*, opens.

Feb 11 Starved for more Gilbert & Sullivan revivals, New Yorkers flock to ten of the most popular of the comic operas at the Ambassador Theatre on Broadway. Louis Kroll is the musical director for the 54 performances.

Feb 12 At the New Theatre in London, director Tyrone Guthrie, revives *Hamlet*, with Robert Helpmann as the melancholy Dane in this Old Vic production, conceived by Michael Benthall, now on active duty. The play is cut to ensure a 9:30 p.m. final curtain.

Feb 15 Eugene O'Neill's *Desire Under the Elms* continues the 17th season of the Dublin Gate Theatre, followed by Bronte's *Jane Eyre*, Farrell's *Guardian Angel*, and Bridie's *Mr. Bolfrey*.

Feb 16 Donald Wolfit returns to London to present a season of Shakespeare at the Scala Theatre. *The Merchant of Venice* opens the run, with stage-director Wolfit

ROYAL SHAKESPEARE THEATRE— STRATFORD UPON AVON

playing Shylock as usual. On Feb 19, he plays the title-role in *Richard III*. On the 22, he's Othello, followed on the 29th, by *As You Like It*, in which he appears as Touchstone. He's Hamlet on March 7, and King Lear on March 11. *Volpone's* title-role offers him a change of pace on March 21. On April 4, he plays Malvolio in *Twelfth Night*.

Apr 5 At His Majesty's Theatre in London, the old musical, *The Lilac Domino* is revived. On April 21, *Jill Darling*, with Vivian Ellis' score, is revived at the Winter Garden Theatre. On May 23, *The Student Prince* is revived at the Stoll Theatre, followed on May 24 by *A Night in Venice* at the Cambridge Theatre. On the next evening, *The Quaker Girl* is revived at the Coliseum. At the Saville Theatre on June 14, a modern version of Emmerich Kalman's *The Gipsy Princess* is staged.

Apr 8 Robert Atkins takes over the control of the Shakespeare Memorial Theatre in Stratford-upon-Avon from Milton Rosmer. *The Merchant of Venice* opens the season today. This staging and productions of *Macbeth*, *Hamlet*, and *The Taming of the Shrew* have just been "tried-out" in a two-week engagement at the Theatre Royal, Bristol preceded by another two-week booking at the Grand Theatre, Croydon. *Hamlet* is the "birthday play." Other plays include *As You Like It*, *A Midsummer Nights Dream*, *Richard II*, and Johnson's *Volpone*. When the season closes on Sep 16, the company returns to Bristol with three plays from the repertory.

May 29 At the Open Air Theatre in Regent's Park, the summer play season opens with *The Winter's Tale* with Cicely Byrne and Vivienne Bennett as Hermione and Paulina. On June 19, *Lady Precious Stream* returns. *Twelfth Night* is presented on July 10.

May 29 At London's Lyric Theatre, Hammersmith, Walter Hudd directs a revival of Thomas Dekker's *The Shoemakers' Holiday*, playing Master Hammon himself. The same evening, Shaw's *The Millionairess* is revived at the Q Theatre. On June 15 at the Savoy Theatre, Frederick Lonsdale's *The Last of Mrs. Cheyney* is revived, staged by Tyrone Guthrie. On July 31, at the Lyric, Hammersmith, Stephen Thomas stages *Macbeth*, with Ernest Milton in the title-role. Esther McCracken's recent success, *Quiet Week-End*, is returned to the West End at Wyndham's Theatre on Aug 1. On the 23rd, Drinkwater's *Bird in Hand* transfers to St. Martin's.

Aug 31 Ralph Richardson plays the title-role in the Old Vic's revival of Ibsen's *Peer Gynt*, opening in London at the New Theatre in a Tyrone Guthrie staging. On Sep 5, Shaw's *Arms and the Man* opens with the Old Vic's Margaret Leighton, Sybil Thorndike, Laurence Olivier, among others. On Sep 13, Olivier plays the title-role in *Richard III*. John Burrell directs both plays.

Sep 11 The Dublin Gate Theatre opens the 18th season with Kesselring's *Arsenic and Old Lace*, followed by a revival of Bronte's *Wuthering Heights*. In October, the company tours Cork, playing Limerick in November. On Dec 26, they are back at The Gate Theatre, with *Punchbowl*.

Sep 14 Musical revivals continue, with His Majesty's offering a recent rediscovery, *The Lilac Domino*. On the 19, the Coliseum revives *The Merry Widow*, with Madge Elliott as Sonia and Cyril Ritchard as Prince Danilo. On Oct 5, the recently produced Jack Hulbert show, *Something in the Air*, is revived at the Palace Theatre. *The Lisbon Story* comes back on Oct 17, at the Stoll Theatre. On the 19th, *Merrie England* is revived at the Winter Garden Theatre. *A Night in Venice* returns on Nov 28, to the Phoenix Theatre. *The Love Racket* comes back for Christmas on Dec 23 at the Adelphi Theatre.

Sep 14 George Bernard Shaw's *Fanny's First Play* comes back to life at the Arts Theatre in London. On Oct 31 at the Lyric, Hammersmith, Shaw's *Too True To Be Good* is revived, staged by Ellen Pollock. She also directs the Nov 14 revival of *Candida* on the stage, as well as *Village Wooing*, on Nov 28, when Michael Golden directs *The Dark Lady of the Sonnets* on the double-bill. They co-direct *Pygmalion* on Dec 12, with Pollock as Eliza and Golden as Higgins.

Sep 16 Some recent productions are transferred or revived. Tonight it's J. B. Priestley's *How Are They At Home?*, with some cast changes for the Apollo Theatre. At the Phoenix Theatre, Pertwee's *Pink String and Sealing Wax* returns on Sep 25. At the Playhouse Theatre on Oct 6, *A Soldier for Christmas* is revived with cast changes. On Nov 9 at the same theatre, McCracken's *Quiet Week-End* is revived.

Sep 26 Revivals of older modern plays and classics also continue popular. St. John Ervine's *Jane Clegg* opens tonight at the Lyric, Hammersmith. At the Haymarket Theatre, W. Somerset Maugham's *The Circle* is revived on Oct 11. The next night, Congreve's *Love for Love* comes to that stage, staged by John Gielgud. On Oct 13, Gielgud plays Hamlet at the Haymarket. On Oct 19 at the Arts Theatre, Maugham's *The Breadwinner* is revived. On November 1, Noel Coward's *Private Lives* opens at the Apollo Theatre, revived by John Clements. On Nov 23, Arthur Wing Pinero's *The Magistrate* is revived at St. Martin's Theatre. On the next night, Eugene O'Neill's *Anna Christie* is offered at the Arts Theatre.

Sep 27 Revivals continue at the New York City Center of Music and Drama. Helen Hayes appears for 11 performances as Harriet Beecher Stowe in the Ryerson Clements' *Harriet*. Operetta revivals (*The Merry Widow*) and operas, produced by

242

the Center Opera Company, follow. On Dec 12, for the holiday season, *Little Women* is revived.

Oct 31 In *Embezzled Heaven* at New York's National, Ethel Barrymore plays a lonely, religious cook who pays for her nephew's education, hoping he'll become a priest and pray for her. He becomes instead a crook, but the disappointed cook makes a pilgrimage to Rome where the Pope makes all things right for her. The Theatre Guild production has only 52 performances.

Dec 16 The holiday season is here, so pantomimes, musicals, and revivals open for limited runs. At the Stoll Theatre, Barrie's *Peter Pan* opens, with Frances Day as Peter. On Dec 22, at the Coliseum, Emile Littler's panto, *Goody Two Shoes*, opens. At the St. James's today *The Glass Slipper* is the holiday piece. At His Majesty's Theatre, Nervo and Knox appear in *Babes in the Wood*. At the Queen's Theatre, Lewis Carroll's two *Alice* books come to the stage. On Dec 23, *Cinderella* opens at the Winter Garden, with *The Sleeping Beauty* at the Golder's Green Hippodrome, and *The Love Racket* at the Adelphi Theatre. Other offerings are *Robinson Crusoe* at the Wimbledon Theatre, *Cinderella* at the King's Hammersmith, and *Alice in Wonderland* at the Palace Theatre. Sheridan's 18th century comedy, *The*

SING OUT SWEET LAND

Critic, is revived at the Arts Theatre.

Dec 27 At New York's National the Theatre Guild wins a 13-week run with *Sing Out Sweet Land*, a pageant of America's music, assembled by Walter Kerr, with special score and conducting by Elie Siegmeister. Alfred Drake, Burl Ives, Bibi Osterwald, Juanita Hall, and Philip Coolidge are in the ensemble.

in transit, servicemen stationed nearby. Never, says Mantle, have so many poor plays sold for such good money. In commercial—not artistic—terms, there are 14 strong hits, 6 moderate successes, against 50 failures. Nine successes of previous seasons continued popular. This past season has 20 more productions than last; Hollywood writers are bringing unsold film ideas back to Broadway, says Mantle. The success-ratio seems to be one hit to three flops. Mantle's annual list of ten *Best Plays* for the Broadway season just completed includes: Hart's *Winged Victory*, Van Druten's *The Voice of the Turtle*, Hellman's *The Searching Wind*, Chodorov's *Decision*, Gordon's *Over 21*, Franken's *Outrageous Fortune*, Behrman's *Jacobowsky and the Colonel*, Anderson's *Storm Operation*, Shelley's *Pick-Up Girl*, and Osborn's *The Innocent Voyage*.

Aug 31 The Old Vic's new *Peer Gynt* production is the first presented in London under the new managing triumvirate which has taken over the directorship of the Old Vic Theatre Company from Tyrone Guthrie: Ralph Richardson, Laurence Olivier, and John Burrell. They announce a policy of playing repertory rather than limited runs. The Liverpool Playhouse is the company's wartime center, the historic Old Vic Theatre having been bombed in 1941.

Nov 6 The Shuberts, afraid of legal action against the production of *Trio*, which might harm one of their theatres, refuse the Cort for booking. The *NY Times* notes that *Trio* will open at the Belasco Theatre instead, despite potential objections to the play's lesbian theme.

1944 BIRTHS/DEATHS/DEBUTS

April 4 American philanthropist Irene Lewisohn dies in New York City. Lewisohn and her sister, Alice, built and endowed the Neighborhood Playhouse in New York. She and Aline Bernstein founded the Museum of Costume Art on Fifth Avenue in 1937.

Apr 17 English comedian and playwright Arthur Rigby (b. 1870) is dead. Rigby was a leading turn in the principal music halls for many years. He subsequently toured in his own sketches and revues. Rigby co-authored, with Stanley Lupino, *Love Lies*, *Room For Two*, and *Sporting Love*.

Sep 10 American playwright Arthur Richman (b. 1886) is dead. Richman was president of the society of American Dramatists and Composers from 1925–27. Among his plays of the 1920s were *Ambush*, *A Serpent's Tooth*, *The Awful Truth*, *A Proud Woman*, and *Heavy Traffic*. His *The Season Changes* was produced in 1936.

Oct 22 American stage and screen actor Richard Bennett (b. 1873) dies in Los Angeles. Bennett made his stage debut in 1891 as Tombstone Jake in *The Limited Mail*. He appeared as Cyrano in *Cyrano de Bergerac* at the Martin Beck Theatre in New York in 1935. He is the father of actresses Constance, Barbara, and Joan Bennett.

Nov 10 English actor-playwright Ferdinand Gottschalk (b. 1858) is dead in London. Gottschalk began his career in Toronto in 1887 appearing with Rosina Vokes in *Which is Which?*

1944 THEATERS/PRODUCTIONS

June 4 The *NY Times* presents its annual account of the Broadway season, which closed officially on May 31. There have been 93 productions divided in this way: plays (55), musicals (11), revues (4), operettas (1), revivals (18), and "others" (4). Film-rights sales have totaled some $2,503,000.

June 15 Surveying the statistics and the quality of the past Broadway season, drama critic Burns Mantle humorously observes that in this third war-year the theatre season might also be considered a war casualty. Not at the box-office, of course, as New York is crowded with businessmen, war-workers, servicemen

Jan 3 *The Hasty Heart* (NY—Hudson—Drama). Richard Basehart plays a dying Scots loner in a British military hospital in Southeast Asia for 207 performances of John Patrick's play, directed by Bretaigne Windust.

Jan 18 *Rebecca* (NY—Barrymore—Drama). Daphne Du Maurier has adapted the play from film and radio versions of her novel. Diana Barrymore, Florence Reed, and Bramwell Fletcher are directed by Clarence Derwent for a run of only 20 performances.

Jan 27 *Up in Central Park* (NY—Century—Musical). Currier and Ives lithographs and Boss Tweed inspire this Sigmund Romberg musical, with book by Herbert and Dorothy Fields. It runs 504 performances.

March 13 *Foolish Notion* (NY—Martin Beck—Comedy). Philip Barry's new script achieves a 13-week run, with Tallulah Bankhead, directed by John C. Wilson. Henry Hull, Donald Cook, and Mildred Dunnock are in the cast.

March 14 *Dark of the Moon* (NY—46th Street—Drama). Richard Hart and Carol Stone appear in this play attributed to Howard Richardson and William Berney, which runs 320 performances.

March 20 *Kiss Them for Me* (NY—Belasco—Comedy). Frederic Wakeman's *Shore Leave* becomes a play by Luther Davis, with Judy Holliday, Richard Widmark, and Paul Ford in the cast. There are 111 performances.

March 31 *The Glass Menagerie* (NY—Playhouse—Drama). Tennessee Williams's "memory-play" of frustrated lives wins praise from critics for its poetic vision and for the triumphant comeback of Laurette Taylor as the impoverished Amanda Wingfield, a faded Southern belle remembering the glories of the past. Eddie Dowling is her son, Julie Haydon her daughter, and Anthony Ross the gentleman caller. The play runs for 561 performances. Lewis Nichols of the *NY Times* calls Taylor's acting "completely perfect." Louis Kronenberger, in *PM* writes "As a play, I think there is a great deal wrong with it. But I recommend it without qualms, because it makes interesting and sometimes absorbing theatre, and because Laurette Taylor is giving in it one of the most remarkable and fascinating performances in many seasons. . . . beyond the fact that Mr. Williams isn't really master of his rather showy (and derived) devices, I think he has asked oddity to do work that simple artistry can do far better. . . ." The play opens at Londons Haymarket on July 28, 1948, with Helen Haye as Amanda. Phil Brown, Frances Heflin, and Hugh McDermott are in the cast. There are 109 performances.

April 19 *Carousel* (NY—Majestic—Musical). Molnar's *Liliom* is now a musical by Richard Rodgers and Oscar Hammerstein II. John Raitt and Jan Clayton head the cast. Choreography by Agnes de Mille. The Theatre Guild production wins 890 performances. The hit comes to London's Drury Lane on June 7, 1950, with Margot Moser, Iva Withers, Marjorie Mars, Bambi Linn, and Stephen Douglas. It has only 199 showings.

July 18 *Marinka* (NY—Winter Garden—Musical). Emmerich Kalman, an exile in America, composes a score for George Marion, Jr., and Karl Farkas' libretto. The show runs nearly 21 weeks.

Sep 25 *You Touched Me* (NY—Booth—Comedy). Montgomery Clift and Edmund Gwenn appear with Marion Stewart in Tennesse Williams and Donald Windham's collaboration, based on a D.H. Lawrence story, which plays 109 times.

Sep 26 *Deep Are the Roots.* (NY—Fulton—Drama). This Arnaud d'Usseau and James Gow play features Gordon Heath and Barbara Bel Geddes and is staged by Elia Kazan for 477 performances.

Nov 10 *Are You With It?* (NY—Century—Musical). Harry Revel scores this show about a man who joins a carnival, with Johnny Downs and Joan Roberts. This book, by Sam Perrin and George Balzer, is appealing enough to run 267 performances.

Nov 14 *State of the Union* (NY—Hudson—Comedy). Howard Lindsay and Russel Crouse are inspired by Wendell Wilkie, and their play, with Ralph Bellamy and Ruth Hussey, becomes a big hit, running 765 performances, under Bretaigne Windust's direction. The play wins the Pulitzer Prize.

Nov 29 *Strange Fruit* (NY—Royale—Drama). Lillian Smith's adaptation of her novel (with her sister's help) has Eugenia Rawls, Murray Hamilton, and Ralph Meeker in the cast, directed by Jose Ferrer. The play lasts 60 performances.

Dec 14 *Dream Girl* (NY—Coronet—Comedy). Elmer Rice stages his play with his wife, actress Betty Field, in the lead for 348 performances.

Dec 21 *Billion Dollar Baby* (NY—Alvin—Musical). Betty Comden and Adolph Green recreate the 1920's with a score by Morton Gould. Joan McCracken is directed by George Abbott, with Jerome Robbins' choreography. The show runs 220 performances.

Dec 27 *Home of the Brave* (NY—Belasco—Drama). Arthur Laurents' play earns only 69 performances but has admiring critics. He wins $1,000 from the American Academy of Arts and Letters for this war play, with Joseph Pevney in a leading role.

Jan 4 *See How They Run* (L—Comedy—Comedy). Philip King's farce wins a run of 589 performances as staged by Henry Kendall, with George Gee, Joan Hickson, Joan Sanderson, Beryl Mason, and Ronald Simpson.

Jan 10 *The Years Between* (L—Wyndham's—Drama), Daphne DuMaurier's play earns a run of 617 performances. Among the cast are Clive Brook, Henrietta Watson, Nora Swinburne, and Allan Jeaves. Irene Hentschel directs.

Feb 7 *Emma* (L—St. James's—Drama). Jane Austen's heroine is played by Anna Neagle in this stage version by Gordon Glennon.

Feb 22 *Madame Louise* (L—Garrick—Comedy). Vernon Sylvaine's farce has a run of 51 weeks, with Lesley Brook, Robertson Hare, and Constance Lorne among the cast, directed by Richard Bird.

March 1 *Three Waltzes* (L—Prince's—Musical). The music is by Oscar Straus but Diana Morgan's book is unGerman. Lyrics are by Robert MacDermot. The show is staged by Norman Marshall and runs almost six months.

March 14 *Great Day* (L—Playhouse—Drama). Lesley Storm's play, staged by Henry Kendall, has a cast including Olga Lindo, Elsie Randolph, Dorothy Dewhurst, and Winifred Evans.

March 22 *The Assassin* (L—Savoy—Drama). Irwin Shaw's American drama does not earn a long run. Barry Morse, Guy Verney, Patricia Hicks, and Charles Quartermain are among the players.

March 29 *The Gaieties* (L—Winter Garden—Revue). Hermione Baddeley and Leslie Henson head this ensemble, directed by Henson and Freddie Carpenter. It runs nearly 23 weeks.

March 31 *Appointment with Death* (L—Piccadilly—Drama). Agatha Christie makes a play from her novel. Terence de Marney directs. On April 9, her new play, *Hidden Horizon*, is tried out at the Wimbledon Theatre.

April 1 *The Shop at Sly Corner* (L—St. Martin's—Drama). Edward Percy's thriller wins 863 performances. Henry Kendall directs Cathleen Nesbitt and Keneth Kent.

April 10 *Lady from Edinburgh* (L—Playhouse—Comedy). Sophie Stewart is

Christabel in Aimee Stuart and L. Arthur Rose's play. As staged by Charles Hickman, it earns a run of 557 performances.

April 12 *The Wind of Heaven* (L—St. James's—Drama). Emlyn Williams directs his play and also performs, with Dilys Parry. There are 268 performances.

April 21 *Perchance to Dream* (L—Hippodrome—Musical). Ivor Novello calls his new show a "musical romance." He plays two roles for director Jack Minster, and it has a very long run of 1,022 performances. Margaret Rutherford is also in the cast.

May 16 *The Skin of Our Teeth.* See NY premiere, 1942.

May 17 *The Night and the Music* (L—Coliseum—Revue). Robert Nesbitt and Joan Davis devise this spectacular revue, which achieves a run of 686 performances.

June 6 *Jacobowsky and the Colonel.* See NY premiere, 1944.

June 21 *Sweet Yesterday* (L—Adelphi—Musical). Jack Hulbert stages this musical romance by Philip Leaver. Score is by Kenneth Leslie-Smith and lyrics by Max Kester and James Dyrenforth. The show runs just over six months.

June 27 *Duet for Two Hands* (L—Lyric—Drama). Mary Hayley Bell's play, staged by husband John Mills, also in the cast, runs 364 performances.

July 12 *The Cure for Love* (L—Westminster—Drama). Walter Greenwood's play has 220 performances, staged by H.K. Ayliff. Robert Donat and Renee Ascher-son are in the cast.

July 18 *The First Gentlemen* (L—New—Drama). Robert Morley, Frances Waring, and Wendy Hill are directed by Norman Marshall in Norman Ginsbury's Regency play. It runs 654 performances.

Aug 1 *Kiss and Tell.* See NY premiere, 1943.

Aug 6 *For Crying Out Loud* (L—Stoll—Revue). Nervo and Knox head the ensemble in this show directed by Val Guest. It runs 11 months.

Aug 28 *Sigh No More* (L—Piccadilly—Revue). Noel Coward stages his revue, with Cyril Ritchard, Madge Elliott, and Joyce Grenfell among the cast. The show earns a run of almost 27 weeks.

Sep 12 *Big Boy* (L—Saville—Musical). There are 174 performances of this show with a book by Douglas Furber, Fred Emney and Max Kester. Carol Gibbons scores Furber's lyrics.

Sep 19 *A Bell for Adano.* See NY premiere, 1944.

Oct 11 *Fine Feathers* (L—Prince of Wales's—Revue). Robert Nesbitt stages this show he's created, which runs 578 performances.

Oct 25 *Follow the Girls.* See NY premiere, 1944.

Nov 22 *Under the Counter* (L—Phoenix—Musical). There are 665 performance of this show, with a book by Arthur Macrae. The score is by Manning Sherwin, and Harold Purcell provides the lyrics. Jack Hulbert directs.

GLASS MENAGERIE

and Cleopatra (the "birthday play"), and *Henry VII*.

April 6 At London's Unity Theatre, Nazi persecution of the Jews is dramatized in Ted Willis' *The Yellow Star*, staged by the author.

June 11 At the King's Theatre, Hammersmith, a D'Oyly Carte season of Gilbert & Sullivan opens, including *The Gondoliers, Iolanthe, The Mikado, Yeoman of the Guard, Patience* and *The Pirates of Penzance.*

June 11 *The Private Life of the Master Race*, Bertolt Brecht's collection of short plays about life under the Nazis is staged in New York at the Pauline Edwards Theatre.

June 12 In London in the Regent's Park Open Air Theatre, the Shakespeare season opens with *As You Like It*, staged by Eric Capon. George Hayes plays Shylock in *The Merchant of Venice*, and *A Midsummer Night's Dream* will complete the season.

June 12 Ibsen revivals are popular this summer in London. *Little Eyolf* plays the Embassy; *A Doll's House* is scheduled for the Arts; and *Rosmersholm* will be at the Torch.

July 2 The Comedie Francaise comes to London, bringing six plays with them: *Le Barbier de Seville, L'Impromptu de Versailles, Ruy Blas, Tartuffe, Les Boulingrins*, and *Phedre*.

Sep 5 Shaw's *Getting Married* is revived at London's Arts Theatre, staged by Judith Furse. James Joyce's *Exiles* is produced at the Torch. Other London revivals this month are Pinero's *The Thunderbolt*, Chekhov's *The Marriage Proposal*, Maeterlinck's *The Winter of Our Discontent*, Sheridan's *School for Scandal* and *The Rivals*.

Sep 24 Micheal macLiammoir, co-founder with Hilton Edwards of the Dublin Gate Theatre, adapts Dickens' *A Tale of*

1945 REVIVALS/REPERTORIES

Jan 1 At the New York City Center, Eva LeGallienne plays the lead in her production of *The Cherry Orchard. You Can't Take It With You, Carmen Jones*, and Paul Robeson's *Othello* are all offered this spring at popular prices, per City Center policy.

Jan 16 Jasper Deeter's Hedgerow Theatre comes to Off-Broadway's Cherry Lane Theatre for nearly a month with four plays.

Jan 16 At London's New Theatre The Old Vic's revival of *Uncle Vanya*, with Olivier, Richardson, Redman, Leighton, and Thorndike joins the repertory. Other revivals seen this season will be *Midsummer Night's Dream, Quality Street, Saint Joan, When We Dead Awaken, Easter*, and *The Duchess of Malfi*.

Jan 17 Avery Hopwood's old farce about the timid professor who finds himself in a Turkish bath on Ladies Night comes back as *Good Night Ladies* at New York's Royale Theatre. It runs almost ten weeks.

Jan 25 Margaret Webster adapts and stages Shakespeare's *The Tempest* with Vera Zorina as Ariel and Arnold Moss as Pros-pero. Canada Lee is Caliban. It has an impressive 100-performance run at the Alvin Theatre in New York.

Jan 25 *Panama Hattie*, recently premiered, now reopens in New York for 100 performances. Bebe Daniels is still Hattie. Other musical revivals are *The Quaker Girl, Gay Rosalinda (Die Fledermaus)*, with Ruth Naylor and Cyril Ritchard, and *Irene*, with Pat Taylor.

Feb 12 Donald Wolfit opens a short season of Shakespeare at London's Winter Garden. *Macbeth, The Merchant of Venice*, and *Much Ado About Nothing* are the repertory.

Feb 19 The 18th season of the Dublin Gate Theatre continues with Wilde's *The Picture of Dorian Gray*. Other shows will be Job's *Uncle Harry*, *Othello*, Coward's *Blithe Spirit* and Quintero's *A Hundred Years Old*. The troupe tours Northern Ireland in June.

March 31 Robert Atkins directs *Much Ado About Nothing* at Stratford's Memorial Theatre. Other productions this season will be *Twelfth Night, Othello*, Antony

Two Cities to open the 19th season. Other plays include Wilder's *The Skin of Our Teeth*, Wilde's *An Ideal Husband*, Hellman's *The Watch on the Rhine* and Housman Granville Barker's *Prunella*, for the holidays.

Sep 26 At London's New Theatre, Nicholas Hannen plays the title-role in this Old Vic revival of *Henry IV, Part 1*, to be followed on October 3 by *Part 2*. Laurence Olivier, Sybil Thorndike, Ralph Richardson, and Margaret Leighton are also cast. John Burrell stages. On Oct 18, the classical revival consists of a double bill: Sophocles' *Oedipus Rex*, in Yeats' translation, and Sheridan's *The Critic*. Olivier and Thorndike appear in the former. Olivier plays Mr. Puff in Sheridan's satire.

Oct 9 Thomas Job's reworking of Zola's *Therese Raquin* called *Therese*, opens for three months at the Biltmore in New York. May Whitty plays the title role.

Oct 10 *Hamlet* is revived at London's Arts Theatre, staged by Judith Furse, with Alec Clunes as the prince. Olga Lindo and Dorothy Primrose are Gertrude and Ophelia.

Oct 11 *This Way to the Tomb!*, Ronald Duncan's masque with an anti-masque is staged by E. Martin Browne. Robert Speaight, Norman Tyrell, Frank Napier, and Eileen Vine, are among the players.

Oct 16 Montgomery and Stone's 1906 *The Red Mill* is revived in New York for 531 performances, almost twice as long as the original run. Stone's daughters are involved, as co-producer and performer.

Nov 12 At the New York City Center, Margaret Webster opens the season of play and musical revivals with her staging of *The Tempest*. *Little Women*, *The Desert Song*, and *Carmen Jones* follow.

Nov 22 At London's St. Martin's Theatre, W. Somerset Maugham's *The Sacred Heart* is revived by Geoffrey Wardwell, and on Dec 6, Emlyn Williams revives his *Spring, 1600* in a revised version. He directs the cast, impersonating Shakespeare's neighbours and colleagues at the Globe Theatre.

Dec 13 Maj. Maurice Evans brings his streamlined GI *Hamlet* to the Columbus Circle Theatre for 131 performances, after touring for American soldiers in the South Pacific. Cuts include the Gravedigger's scene and Ophelia's burial. George Schaefer stages.

Dec 15 The holiday season arrives with the opening of Barrie's *Peter Pan* at the Scala Theatre, with Celia Lipton as Peter. At the Duke of York's Theatre, on December 19, the play is *The Land of the Christmas Stockings*. The next day at St. James's Theatre, *The Glass Slipper* is on, complete with a Harlequinade and direction by Robert Donat and Stephen Thomas. Other holiday shows are *Aladdin* (Cambridge, Golder's Green Hippodrome, and King's, Hammersmith), *Mother Goose* (Wimbledon), *The Sleeping Beauty* (Grand, Croydon), *Treasure Island* (Granville), and *Cinderella* (Adelphi), with Bud Flanagan directing and playing Buttons.

Dec 20 The American Negro Theatre presents a double-bill, *Home Is the Hunter*, by Samuel Kootz, and *On Strivers' Row*, by Abraham Hill, in their own playhouse in Harlem.

Dec 26 It's a holiday first in Dublin: the Abbey Theatre presents a Christmas pantomime in Gaelic.

1945 BIRTHS/DEATHS/DEBUTS

July 19 Anglo-American playwright Edward Knoblock (b. 1874) dies in London. His credits include: *Kismet*, *Marie-Odile*, *Milestones* (with Arnold Bennett), *The Good Companions* (with J.B. Priestley) and an adaptation of Baum's *Grand Hotel*.

Aug 26 Austrian novelist-dramatist Franz Werfel (b. 1890) dies in Beverly Hills. His most successful contribution to the theatre was his adaptation of his novel, *Bocksgesang* (*Goat Song*).

Oct 18 American playwright Hatcher Hughes dies in New York City at age 62. A professor of playwrighting at Columbia University, Hughes won the 1924 Pulitzer Prize for *Hell Bent for Heaven*.

Oct 19 Actor-director John Lithgow is born in Rochester, New York.

Oct 20 *New York Times* theatre caricaturist Al Hirschfeld conceals his daughter's name, NINA, in his drawings, and reveals how many times it appears with a numeral after his signature.

Nov 11 Jerome Kern (b. 1885) dies in New York City. His classic *Show Boat* was written in 1927, in collaboration with Edna Ferber. His *Roberta* and *Very Warm for May* were hits of the 1930's.

Nov 21 Robert Charles Benchley (b. 1889) dies in New York. Critic for *Life* magazine and *The New Yorker*, he retired in 1939 to devote his time to film acting.

Nov 22 Czechoslovakian-born Franz Allers conducts for the first time on Broadway. Lerner and Loewe's *The Day Before Spring* is the show.

Nov 25 American actress Doris Keane (b. 1881) dies in New York City. Her 1903 New York debut and 1907 London debut led to early successes including *The Happy Marriage*, *The Lights O' London*, *Anatole*, and *Romance*.

Dec 30 American actor Glenn Hunter is dead at 52. He first appeared with the Washington Square Players in 1916, and scored successes as Merton Gill in *Merton of the Movies* and in the title role of *Young Woodley*.

1945 THEATERS/PRODUCTIONS

Among the British patents granted this year is a theatre-related one to J. Currie for a waterfall apparatus, in which water is pumped to a tank at the top, running downward through a series of falls, pools and streams to a bottom tank and then recirculated.

Drama critic and journalist Otis Guernsey discovers that of the 16 outraged New York ministers who have signed a petition against showing *Trio* at the Belasco, only one, John S. Bonnell, has seen the play.

Feb 25 Paul Moss, Mayor LaGuardia's Commissioner of Licenses, closes the production of *Trio*, which deals with a lesbian theme.

Embattled Commissioner of Licenses Paul Moss insists he has the right to censor what is presented on New York's stages. Both he and Mayor LaGuardia will soon be out of office. The new mayor will be more tolerant of theatre fare.

June 3 The *NY Times* today sums up the season just ended: 95 productions, including 10 musicals, 66 plays, 2 revues and 2 operettas. Screenrights sales totaled $3,740,000.

June 7 The Sadler's Wells Theatre re-opens with Benjamin Britten's opera *Peter Grimes*. Closed since September 1940, the theatre has served as a public shelter during the war.

June 15 For the Broadway season of 1944–1945, Burns Mantle selects ten scripts which he believes are the "Best Plays." They are Osborn's *A Bell for Adano*, Van Druten's *I Remember Mama*, Patrick's *The Hasty Heart*, Williams' *The Glass Menagerie*, Chase's *Harvey*, Kaufman and Marquand's *The Late George Apley*, Franken's *Soldier's Wife*, Yordan's *Anna Lucasta*, Barry's *Foolish Notion*, and Krasna's *Dear Ruth*.

June 15 This past season, New York has seen 83 new plays with some 24 of them rated commercial hits. Customary top ticket price for musicals is $6, but some opening nights have cost $8 or $12. There are 14 holdovers from the previous season and six major revivals.

Sep 11 The Glasgow Citizens' Theatre, founded in 1943 by playwright James Bridie, moves to its own house, the Royal Princess's Theatre, which was opened in 1878 as Her Majesty's Theatre. The opener is J.B. Priestley's *Johnson over Jordan*.

Sep 22 Robert Atkins resigns after two years of leadership of the Shakespeare Memorial Theatre in Stratford-upon-Avon.

Jan 22 *The Magnificent Yankee* (NY—Royale—Comedy). Louis Calhern plays Oliver Wendell Holmes in Emmett Lavery's drama based on Holmes' life. Dorothy Gish plays Fanny Holmes. Arthur Hopkins directs; There are 160 performances.

Jan 23 *O Mistress Mine.* See L premiere (*Love in Idleness*), 1944.

Feb 4 *Born Yesterday* (NY—Lyceum—Comedy). Judy Holliday makes an immediate hit with critics and public as a crook's seemingly dumb blonde mistress who rapidly masters the basics of American economics and government to expose him. Garson Kanin writes this play which also features Paul Douglas. There are 1,642 performance. The show comes to the West End on Jan 23, 1947. In this production at the Garrick, Yolanda Donlan plays the blonde. The show runs over 42 weeks.

Feb 6 *Lute Song* (NY—Plymouth—Musical). Raymond Scott writes the score and Sidney Howard and Will Irwin the libretto for this show based on an old Chinese tale. Mary Martin is featured as the loving wife who travels many miles to find her husband (Yul Brynner), cut off from her by court edict and married to a princess' daughter against his will. "Mountain High—Vally Low" is a memorable song from the show. The production runs 18 weeks. *Lute Song* comes to London's Winter Garden on Oct 11, 1948, with Dolly Haas and Brynner.

Feb 27 *Truckline Cafe* (NY—Belasco—Comedy). Despite a cast that includes Richard Waring, Virginia Gilmore, Marlon Brando, and Karl Malden, Maxwell Anderson's play about an American soldier and his wife lasts just 2 weeks. Harold Clurman stages.

March 7 *Three To Make Ready* (NY—Aldelphi—Revue). There are 327 showings of this musical revue. Ray Bolger, Brenda Forbes, and Gordon MacRae are among the cast. John Murray Anderson and Margaret Webster direct.

March 30 *St. Louis Woman* (NY—Martin Beck—Musical). Ruby Hill deserts her man for a winning jockey in this musical version of Arna Bontemps and Countee Cullen's novel, *God Sends Sunday,* with score by Harold Arlen and lyrics by Johnny Mercer. Pearl Bailey is also in the show which has 113 performances. Rouben Mamoulian stages.

April 18 *Call Me Mister* (NY—National—Revue). Army red-tape, southern racial prejudice, and other topics are satirized in sketches in this long-running (734 performances) revue. Betty Garrett and Jules Munshin are among the cast; Harold Rome provides songs and lyrics; Robert Gordon stages.

May 8 *On Whitman Avenue* (NY—Cort—Drama). Canada Lee plays a black war veteran who rents an apartment in a white neighborhood in Maxine Woods' drama, staged by Margo Jones. It has 150 showings.

May 16 *Annie Get Your Gun* (NY—Imperial—Musical). Irving Berlin provides words and music for the book, by Herbert and Dorothy Fields, in which the naive, boastful sharpshooter Annie Oakley (Ethel Merman) learns to lose to colleague Frank Butler (Ray Middleton), if she's to have him as a husband. Rodgers and Hammerstein produce. Among the popular songs are "There's No Business Like Show Business" and "The Girl That I Marry." The show achieves 1,147 performances. On June 7, 1947, it opens in London at the Coliseum with Delores Gray as Annie Oakley. There it has 1,304 performances.

May 31 *Around the World* (NY—Adelphi—Musical). Orson Welles' version of Jules Verne's *Around the World in 80 Days* with Welles in the cast, has a small-scale train wreck, a circus, exotic settings, and score by Cole Porter. But it lasts only 75 performances.

Sep 5 *A Flag is Born* (NY—Alvin—Drama). Paul Muni stars (replaced during the 15-week run by Luther Adler) and Marlon Brando is in the cast of this Ben Hecht and Kurt Weill collaboration about Jewish hopes for a homeland in Palestine.

Oct 9 *The Iceman Cometh* (NY—Martin Beck—Drama). Eugene O'Neill's play, set in a bar where a cross-section of life's failures come to bolster their illusions, runs only 17 weeks. James Barton, Dudley Digges, and E.G. Marshall are in the cast. On Jan 29, 1958, the play opens in London at the Arts Theatre and transfers on March 29 to the Winter Garden. Jack MacGowran and Ian Bannen are in the cast.

Oct 29 *Present Laughter.* See L premiere, 1943.

Oct 31 *Happy Birthday* (NY—Broadhurst—Comedy). The *NY Daily News* calls Anita Loos' play, about a quiet librarian (Helen Hayes) in pursuit of a nice young man, "junk" but has raves for Hayes. Joshua Logan directs; Rodgers and Hammerstein produce and provide some songs. It has 564 performances.

Nov 18 *Joan of Lorraine* (NY—Alvin—

THREE TO MAKE READY

Drama). A "radiant" Ingrid Bergman (*NY Herald-Tribune*) stars in Maxwell Anderson's drama about a group of actors rehearsing a play depicting the martyrdom of St. Joan. Sam Wanamaker and Kevin McCarthy are in the cast. Margo Jones stages the 199 performances.

Nov 20 *Another Part of the Forest* (NY—Fulton—Drama). Lillian Hellman creates a sequel, though set in an earlier period, to her successful play *The Little Foxes.* Patricia Neal is Regina. Mildred Dunnock and Leo Genn also appear in this 23-week run. Hellman stages.

Nov 26 *No Exit* (NY—Biltmore—Drama). Claude Dauphin, Annabella, and Ruth Ford play soul-searching characters confined to a room in Hell in Paul Bowles' adaptation of Jean-Paul Sartre's existentialist drama. It runs only 4 weeks.

Dec 3 *Years Ago* (NY—Mansfield—Comedy). Frederic March wins the first Tony Award for Best Actor in this Ruth Gordon play, based on her experiences as a budding playwright. Florence Eldridge costars. Garson Kanin, Gordon's husband, stages the 26-week run.

Dec 26 *Beggar's Holiday* (NY—Broadway—Musical). Duke Ellington provides the music for this John LaTouche adaptation of *The Beggar's Opera.* Alfred Drake and Zero Mostel are in the cast. Nicholas Ray stages. It has 108 performances.

1946   BRITISH PREMIERES

Feb 14 *The Time of Your Life.* See NY premiere, 1939.

Feb 19 *The Guinea-Pig* (L—Criterion—Drama). Robert Flemyng heads the cast of Warren Strode's play, which has 561 performances. Rachel Gurney and Denholm Elliott are among the cast, directed by Jack Minster. A teacher fights tradition to give poor boys the chance to attend his public (private) school.

Feb 26 *Red Roses for Me* (L—Embassy—Drama). Humor and tragedy combine in Sean O'Casey's play about the Irish labor disputes of 1913. Ethel O'Shea and Kieron O'Hanrahan are in the cast. On May 28, the play transfers to the New Theatre. On Dec 28, 1955, it opens at New York's Booth with Kevin McCarthy, E.G. Marshall, Ann Dere, Virginia Bosler, and Whitford Kane in the cast. John O'Shaughnessy directs. Designs are by Howard Bay and Ballou. It has a short run of 29 performances.

Feb 28 *Dear Ruth.* See NY premiere, 1944.

March 6 *Fifty-Fifty* (L—Strand—Comedy). Larson Brown bases his farce on a play by Aaron Hoffman, and wins 513 performances. Beryl Baxter and David Langton are in the cast.

March 7 *Song of Norway.* See NY premiere, 1944.

March 14 *Evangeline* (L—Cambridge—Musical). Frances Day plays the title-role and with Val Guest co-directs Romney Brent's musical adaptation of the novel *Nymph Errant.*

March 19 *Murder on the Nile* (L—Ambassadors'—Drama). Agatha Christie's thriller opens in the West End in this Claud Gurney staging. Helen Haye plays Miss Ffolliot-Ffoulkes; Joanna Derrill is Christina Grant; Ronald Millar plays Smith, and Vivienne Bennett is Jacqueline de Severac. As *Hidden Horizon*, it opens in New York on Sep 19, 1946, with Diana Barrymore. There are only 12 showings.

March 20 *Make It a Date* (L—Duchess—Revue). Max Wall and Pat Kildare are in the cast of this musical revue which has 140 performances. Wall also provides some of the material.

April 11 *Here Come the Boys* (L—Saville—Revue). Jack Hulbert and Bobby Howes head the cast, and Hulbert stages with Jevan Brandon-Thomas. The mix of music and sketches earns a run of 41 weeks.

April 20 *National Velvet* (L—Embassy—Drama). Enid Bagnold's play will become a film classic. In this Anthony Hawtrey staging, Tilsa Page plays the horse-loving Velvet Brown, with Marie Löhr as her mother.

April 20 *High Time* (L—Palladium—Revue). Comic actress and singer Tessie O'Shea and Nat Jackley head this Robert Nesbitt revue and win a run of 570 performances.

April 24 *Better Late* (L—Garrick—Revue). Beatrice Lillie and other members of the cast have a 26-week run in Leslie Julian Jones' revue.

April 30 *Our Town.* See NY premiere, 1938.

May 3 *No Room at the Inn* (L—Winter Garden—Drama). Freda Jackson plays a cruel and sluttish landlady who darkens the lives of children evacuated to her house during the war, in Joan Temple's well-received play which has a run of 425 performances. Anthony Hawtrey directs.

May 9 *Sweetest and Lowest* (L—Ambassadors'—Revue). This third edition of *Sweet and Low*, with Hermoine Gingold and Henry Kendall among the cast, has 791 performances. Charles Zwar provides the score for Alan Melville's sketches and lyrics. Charles Hickman stages.

May 23 *The Winslow Boy* (L—Lyric—Drama). Terence Rattigan's new play depicts a father who tries to clear his son, a naval cadet wrongly accused of forgery. Frank Cellier plays the father. There are 476 performances. On Oct 29, 1947, the drama opens at Broadway's Empire with Alan Webb in the role. The Theatre Guild production runs 27 weeks.

May 30 *Protrait in Black* (L—Piccadilly—Drama). Diana Wynyard, Hugh Williams, and Ronald Squire animate Ivan Goff and Ben Roberts' play. Squire also directs. There are 116 performances.

June 12 *Grand National Night* (L—Apollo—Drama). " . . . first rate theatre," is the *Times* verdict on Dorothy and Campbell Christie's play about a man (Leslie Banks) who plots the murder of his drunken wife. Hermoine Baddeley plays two roles: the wife and her sister. It runs almost 34 weeks.

July 17 *Big Ben* (L—Adelphi—Musical). Wendy Toye stages A.P. Herbert's book, with Vivian Ellis' music. Carole Lynne heads the cast. The show has 172 performances.

Aug 14 *Clutterbuck* (L—Wyndham's—Comedy). Benn W. Levy's play about men remembering former affairs wins 366 performances. Gorden Bell has the title role. Constance Cummings and Naunton Wayne are also in the cast. The comedy opens at New York's Biltmore on Dec 3, 1949, for a 27-week run. Charles Campbell is Clutterbuck, with Ruth Ford, Ruth Matteson, and Tom Helmore also in the cast.

Aug 26 *Soldier's Wife.* See NY premiere, 1944.

Aug 28 *Message for Margaret* (L—Westminster—Drama). Flora Robson plays the title-role in James Parrish's play which has 208 performances. Parrish directs.

Sep 2 *Fools Rush In* (L—Fortune—Comedy). Glynis Johns and Bernard Lee are among the cast of Kenneth Horne's comedy, which runs almost 30 weeks. Richard Bird stages.

Sep 3 *But for the Grace of God* (L—St. James's—Drama). Frederick Lonsdale's play, with a cast including Mary Jerrold and A.E. Matthews, is staged by Leslie Armstrong. It runs 25 weeks.

Sep 26 *The Shephard Show* (L—Prince's—Revue). Devised by Firth Shephard, staged by Wendy Toye, with songs by Harry Parr

JOAN OF LORRAINE

Davis and lyrics by Harold Purcell, this revue runs nearly 22 weeks. Marie Burke and Gavin Gordon are in the cast.

Oct 1 *An Inspector Calls* (L—New—Drama). J.B. Priestley's play about a family implicated in the death of a factory girl has an Old Vic cast including Julien Mitchell, Alec Guinness, Marian Spencer, and Ralph Richardson. It premieres at New York's Booth Theatre on Oct 21, 1947, with Thomas Mitchell and Melville Cooper in the cast. The play runs three months.

Oct 11 *Piccadilly Hayride* (L—Prince of Wales's—Revue). Music and comedy, devised by Dick Hurran and Phil Park, win a run of 778 performances. Entertainers Sid Field, Terry Thomas, and Jerry Desmonde head the troupe.

Oct 17 *The Night and the Laughter* (L—Coliseum—Revue). Comic Bud Flanagan heads the company of this revue, devised by Robert Nesbitt (who also stages) and Joan Davis. It runs 21 weeks.

Dec 19 *Pacific 1860* (L—Drury Lane—Musical). Mary Martin plays a singer who much choose between love and a career in Noel Coward's period musical. Staged by Coward, the show has 129 performances.

Dec 24 *The Man From The Ministry* (L—Comedy—Comedy). There are 221 performances of Madeleine Bingham's play. Staged by Anthony Parker, the cast is headed by Beryl Mason and Clifford Mollinson.

Jan 5 At New York's Ziegfeld Theatre, Oscar Hammerstein II revives *Showboat*, the musical with a cast including Carol Bruce, Jan Clayton, and Charles Fredericks.

Jan 9 Bobby Clark adapts Moliere's *Le Bourgeois Gentilhomme* and achieves 77 performances in the title role.

Jan 15 The Theatre Guild Shakespearean Repertory Company bows at the Cort Theatre in New York with a revival of *The Winter's Tale*. In the large cast are Romney Brent, Jessie Royce Landis, and a relatively new face, Jo Van Fleet. The show runs five weeks.

Jan 17 Angela Baddeley plays Nora in Henrik Ibsen's *A Doll's House*, revived in London at the Winter Garden Theatre. On March 13, Ibsen's *The Lady from the Sea* is offered at the Arts Theatre, staged by Judith Furse.

Feb 13 Donald Wolfit and his Shakespeare troupe return to London with a season at the Winter Garden Theatre. Tonight, it's *Othello*, with Wolfit in the title-role. On the 14, he's Falstaff in *The Merry Wives of Windsor*. *Hamlet* opens on the 15. On Feb 16, *Twelfth Night* is played at the matinee, with *The Merchant of Venice* in the evening. On the 18, the play is *Cymbeline*, followed on the next day by *King Lear*. On March 18, he brings *Macbeth* into the repertory.

Feb 18 Katharine Cornell, returning from playing for the troops in Europe, brings back a new version of the Antigone legend she's discovered in Paris. Jean Anouilh's *Antigone* makes subtle parallels between King Creon's harsh rule and the Nazi rulers in France. Cedric Hardwick is Creon to her Antigone. Her husband, Guthrie McClintic, directs. The production lasts two months. It's followed, on April 3, by a revival of Shaw's *Candida*, with Cornell and Marlon Brando as the poet Marchbanks.

Feb 19 Bristol's Theatre Royal, built in 1766 and now the oldest surviving theatre in England, re-opens as the Bristol Old Vic's home, under the artistic direction of Hugh Hunt and the sponsorship of London's Old Vic and the Arts Council. The opening production is Farquhar's Restoration comedy, *The Beaux' Stratagem*. Players include Pamela Brown and Yvonne Mitchell.

Feb 25 Continuing its 19th season, the Dublin Gate Theatre offers a revival of the Kaufman and Hart *The Man Who Came To Dinner*, followed by Shakespeare's *The Merchant of Venice*, Shaw's *Pygmalion*, macLiammoir's *Ill Met by Moonlight*, and Bell's *Duet for Two Hands*.

March 1 At London's King's Theatre, *Romeo and Juliet* opens, directed by Clare Harris, with Basil Langton and Renee Asherson. On March 7, the company plays Shaw's *Saint Joan*. On March 19, Langton directs Paul Vincent Carroll's Irish play, *The Wise Have Not Spoken*. He plays John Tanner in Shaw's *Man and Superman* on April 9. On May 7, *In Time To Come*, an American play by Howard Koch and John Huston is presented with Lewis Casson and his wife, Sybil Thorndike. On June 11, Thorndike is Clytemnestra in Euripides' *Electra*.

March 19 Robert Ardrey's American play, *Casey Jones*, about a courageous railroad engineer, opens at London's Unity Theatre.

March 20 Judith Guthrie reworks Leonid Andreyev's *He Who Gets Slapped*. Even with Tyrone Guthrie's direction, this revival at Broadway's Booth Theatre for the Theatre Guild lasts only 46 performances. Dennis King plays the mysterious and suicidal hero.

April 20 In this first postwar season, Barry Jackson takes charge of the annual festival at the Shakespeare Memorial Theatre at Stratford-upon-Avon. Eric Crozier's production of *The Tempest* opens today. A different director is engaged for each play: *Cymbeline* (the "birthday play," staged by Nugent Monck), *Love's Labour's Lost* (Peter Brook), *Henry V* (Dorothy Green), *As You Like It* (H. M. Prentice), *Macbeth* (Michael MacOwan), *Doctor Faustus* (Walter Hudd), and *Measure for Measure* (Frank McMullan, an American). Paul Scofield makes his debut with the company.

April 25 William Butler Yeats' symbolic poetic drama, *Resurrection*, is presented in London at the Mercury Theatre, with Eileen Vine, Robert Speaight, Alan Wheatley and Frank Napier. *A Phoenix Too Frequent*, a verse-drama by a new

CLUTTERBACK

playwright, Christopher Fry, is the other half of the double-bill. E. Martin Browne stages both productions.

May 6 London's Old Vic Theatre Company begins an engagement at New York's Century Theatre, with performances of Shakespeare's *Henry IV, Part 1 and Part 2*. Laurence Olivier plays Hotspur. Also in the company are Margaret Leighton, and Ralph Richardson. On May 13, the troupe offers *Uncle Vanya*, with Olivier and Richardson. On May 20, Olivier plays Sophocles' *Oedipus* and Sheridan's *The Critic*.

May 13 Elsa Shelley's American play (1944) *Pick-Up Girl*, a topic of the times, thanks to the influx of American servicemen, as well as the mobilization of the British fighting-men, opens at London's New Lindsey Theatre, staged by Peter Cotes. On July 23, it moves to the Prince of Wales's Theatre for a run of 21 weeks. The approval of Queen Mother Mary of the Cotes production helps win the Lord Chamberlain's permission for the transfer.

May 30 It's time for summer Shakespeare in London's Regent's Park. At the Open Air Theatre, Robert Atkins stages *As You Like It*. On June 28, *Troilus and Cressida* is staged. *A Midsummer Night's Dream* opens on July 16.

June 2 The Repertory Players present Menander's comedy, *The Arbitration*, in Gilbert Murray's translation, at London's New Theatre staged by Charles LeFeaux. On the next day, at the Wimbledon Theatre, Tolstoi's *Redemption* is revived, with Donald Wolfit. On June 4, Alec Guinness offers his stage adaptation of Dostoevsky's *The Brothers Karamazov* at the Lyric, Hammersmith. Peter Brook directs. Guinness and Donald Pleasance play leads.

June 18 *Crime and Punishment*, adapted by Rodney Ackland, is staged at the Wimbledon Theatre by Anthony Quayle. Edith Evans and John Gielgud play the leading roles. On June 26, the production moves to the New Theatre.

July 1 With Gilbert Sullivan's *Iolanthe*, the D'Oyly Carte Opera Company opens its London season at the King's Theatre, Hammersmith. On July 3, *The Gondoliers* is presented, followed on the 4th by *The Mikado*. *The Pirates of Penzance* opens on July 5, with *The Yeoman of the Guard* programmed for July 11. On July 15, the show is *Patience*.

July 3 At London's Arts Theatre, Bernard Shaw's *Don Juan in Hell* is revived, with Alec Clunes. On July 16, Jean-Paul Sartre's *Vicious Circle*, is staged by Peter Brook, with Alec Guinness and Beatrix Lehmann. On Aug 7, Shaw's *The Apple Cart* is staged by Jack Hawkins, who also plays King Magnus.

July 24 At the St. James's Theatre in London, John Dryden's Restoration comedy, *Marriage a la Mode*, is revived, staged by

CANDIDA

John Clements. Clements and his wife Kay Hammond play the leading roles.

Aug 5 The 20th season of the Dublin Gate Theatre opens at the Gaiety Theatre with *. . . And Pastures New*, by Micheal macLiammoir and Dick Forbes. Other productions include Du Maurier's *Trilby*, Sophocles' *Oedipus the Tyrant*, and Shaw's *Don Juan in Hell*.

Aug 8 Johann Strauss' *Die Fledermaus* is revived in London at the Prince's Theatre, under the title of *Gay Rosalinda*.

Sep 3 Richard Brinsley Sheridan's comedy, *The Scheming Lieutenant; Or, St. Patrick's Day*, is revived at London's Art Theatre. At the Coliseum tonight, John Milton's masque of *Comus*, with music by Handel, is also revived, with Mona Inglesby's International Ballet. Other revivals this month include Maugham's *The Constant Wife* at the Arts on Sep 10, Helen Jerome's version of Charlotte Brontë's *Jane Eyre* at the Embassy Theatre on the same night, and Wilder's *The Skin of Our Teeth* at the Piccadilly Theatre on the 11th. This is the Laurence Olivier production, with Vivian Leigh as Sabina.

Sep 4 Jean Cocteau's *The Eagle Has Two Heads*, adapted by poet Ronald Duncan, opens at London's Lyric Theatre, staged by Murray MacDonald, with Eileen Herlie. On Sep 16, Duncan's *This Way To the Tomb*—with music by Benjamin Britten—bows at the Garrick Theatre.

Sep 4 At Broadway's Royale Theatre, Charles MacArthur stages a revival of *The Front Page* which he wrote with Ben Hecht. In the cast are Lew Parker and Arnold Moss. The show runs ten weeks.

Sep 24 Laurence Olivier stages and acts the title-role in *King Lear*, opening the Old Vic season in London at the New Theatre. On Oct 1, J. B. Priestley's *An Inspector Calls* joins the repertory. Edmond Rostand's *Cyrano de Bergerac* is revived on Oct 24, with Ralph Richardson as Cyrano to Margaret Leighton's Roxanne. Tyrone Guthrie directs.

Oct 3 *Our Betters*, vintage Maugham, is

revived in London at the Playhouse Theatre, with Cathleen Nesbitt. Other Oct revivals include Allan Turpin's adaptation of Henry James' *The Turn of the Screw* at the Arts Theatre, on Oct 23; Constance Cox's version of Thackeray's *Vanity Fair*—with Claire Luce as Becky—at the Comedy Theatre on the 29th, and T. S. Eliot's *The Family Reunion* at the Mercury Theatre on Oct 31.

Oct 14 There are 228 performances of this revival of Oscar Wilde's *Lady Windermere's Fan* at Broadway's Cort Theatre. Cecil Beaton designs the stylish production. Penelope Ward and Cornelia Otis Skinner are among the cast.

Oct 15 Elizabeth Bergner fascinates critics—and disappoints her fans—in the title role of John Webster's gory Jacobean tragedy, *The Duchess of Malfi*. Her husband, Paul Czinner, produces it on Broadway at the Barrymore Theatre. There are 38 performances.

Oct 16 Renee Asherson and Robert Donat head the cast in Shakespeare's *Much Ado About Nothing*, staged by Fabia Drake at London's Aldwych Theatre.

Oct 17 An all-black cast presents Gilbert Seldes' adaptation of Aristophanes' Greek comedy, *Lysistrata*, on Broadway at the Belasco Theatre. In the ensemble are Pearl Gaines and Sidney Poitier. It closes after only four performances.

Oct 26 J. M. Synge's *The Playboy of the Western World* is revived at the Booth Theatre in New York with Burgess Meredith in the lead. Others in the cast include Maureen Stapleton and Julie Harris. Staged by Guthrie McClintic, it runs ten weeks.

Nov 5 Strindberg's *There Are Crimes And Crimes*, in a version by Graham Rawson, is staged by Esme Percy at London's New Lindsey Theatre. On Nov 6, Herman Heijermanns' Dutch play, *The Rising Sun*, is revived at the Arts Theatre, directed by Beatrix Lehmann. On the 19th, *Mrs. Dane's Defense*, by Henry Arthur Jones, is revived at the Q Theatre. That night, Tom Robertson's *Caste* is revived at the Lyric, Hammersmith. Christopher Fry's recently produced *A Phoenix Too Frequent* is revived on Nov 29 at the Arts Theatre, with Paul Scofield in the cast. On the 21st, Maugham's *Lady Frederick*, with Coral Browne, is revived at the Savoy Theatre.

Nov 6 Eva Le Gallienne, determined to

realize her dream of a classical repertory company in New York, tries again this season at the International Theatre, with the American Repertory Theatre, in association with Margaret Webster and Cheryl Crawford. Shakespeare's *Henry VIII* opens the season with a five-week run. Victory Jory is supported by LeGallienne, Webster, and Eli Wallach, among others. On Nov 8 James Barrie's *What Every Woman Knows* opens, but only 21 performances are supported by subscribers. On Nov 12 Ibsen's *John Gabriel Borkman* receives a LeGallienne staging, with Jory, LeGallienne, and Webster in the cast. This also has 21 showings. On Dec 19, with the revival of Shaw's *Androcles and the Lion*, Ernest Truex appears as Androcles. It is a modest success, with a run of five weeks. The play is preceded by Sean O'Casey's *A Pound on Demand*. This is followed on Feb 27, by a revival of Sidney Howard's *Yellow Jack* for 21 showings, staged by Martin Ritt.

Nov 19 The Theatre Guild produces George Kelly's play *The Fatal Weakness* at New York's Royale. Ina Claire heads the cast. The show has 119 performances.

Dec 18 The annual spate of London holiday pantomimes and revivals opens with *The Land of the Christmas Stocking* at the Duke of York's Theatre. On Dec 20, *Peter Pan* is revived at the Scala Theatre, with *Mother Goose* opening at the Casino. On the 21, *Dick Whittington* opens at the Alexandra Theatre, Stoke Newington, as well as at the Finsbury Park Empire. On the same day, two *Cinderellas* open; one at the Players' Theatre, the other at the Golder's Green Hippodrome. Later holiday treats include *Treasure Island* (Whitehall), *Aladdin* (Wimbledon), *Red Riding Hood* (Adelphi), *King Stag* (Lyric, Hammersmith), *Jack and the Beanstalk* (Grand, Croydon; King's, Hammersmith), and, at the Winter Garden, *The Wizard of Oz*, with songs by Harold Arlen and Yip Harburg.

Dec 20 Glen Byam Shaw stages a revival of Shakespeare's *Antony and Cleopatra* in London at the Piccadilly Theatre, with Godfrey Tearle, Edith Evans and Anthony Quayle.

Dec 25 Jean Dalrymple revives *Burlesque* by Arthur Hopkins and George Watters, with Bert Lahr. Hopkins directs. The show has 439 performances at New York's Belasco Theatre.

1946 BIRTHS/DEATHS/DEBUTS

Jan 10 Composer, performer, and song publisher Harry von Tilzer (b. 1872) dies in New York. A charter member of ASCAP, von Tilzer founded his own publishing firm in 1902.

Feb 5 Actor-author George Arliss (b. 1868) dies in London. Best remembered for roles

in *The Darling of the Gods*, *Disraeli*, and *The Green Goddess*, Arliss is also the author of several plays and an autobiography, *Up the Years from Bloomsbury* (1927).

Aug 31 Author, actor, and producer Harley Granville Barker (b. 1877) dies in Paris.

Barker appeared in a variety of productions in the early 1900's. In 1907 he co-authored (with William Archer) *A National Theatre: Scheme and Estimates.* He produced the premiere of Shaw's *Androcles and the Lion* in 1913. His later fame rests chiefly on the 5-volume series, *Prefaces to Shakespeare.*

Sep 17 American playwright and drama critic Clayton Hamilton (b. 1881) dies in New York. Hamilton's most successful play is *The Better Understanding,* (with Augustus Thomas). His books include *Problems of the Playwright, Theory of the Theatre,* and *So You're Writing a Play!*

Dec 25 Actor W. C. Fields (b. 1879, William Claude, Dukinfield) dies in Pasadena, California. Fields made his New York debut in 1898 in a comedy juggling routine and soon became a vaudeville star. From 1915–21, he appeared as a comedian in the *Ziegfeld Follies.* He turned exclusively to movies in 1931.

Dec 28 American playwright and composer Brian Hooker is dead in New London, Connecticut at age 66. Hooker translated *Cyrano de Bergerac* for the successful 1923 Walter Hampden production. With W. H. Post, he adapted *The Squaw Man* as the libretto of the musical, *White Eagle.*

1946   THEATERS/PRODUCTIONS

1946 F. Shipman is granted a patent in Britain for his arrangement of reflecting surfaces set in a V-shape, the open section toward the audience, with scenic elements to the reflected placed in the apex.

1946 A U.S. patent is granted to Walter Spohn for a cinema screen with door or window openings permitting live actors to interact with the filmed sequences.

1946 In Britain, *Amateur Stage* begins publication as a monthly.

1946 Since 1942, London's Old Vic ensemble has been using the Playhouse in Liverpool as a provincial center from which to tour its productions around the country. Its own historic home was bombed in 1941 and will not be ready for the company's use until 1950. In the meantime, the New Theatre in the West End is being used for the Old Vic's London seasons, as it has been during wartime by the Old Vic and the Sadler's Wells Opera and Ballet ensembles.

Jan Britain's Lord Chamberlain directs playwright T. B. Morris to contact surviving members of the Rossetti family to make sure they don't object to his drama about Dante Gabriel Rossette, artist and poet, *We Dig for the Stars.* The play is already being cast by co-producers C. B. Cochran and Lord Anthony Vivian. At first Rossetti relatives agree not to block production. Soon after, Morris receives a telegram: "Please suspend exhumation play writing," as he later reports to Richard Findlater in *Theatrical Censorship in Britain.*

Jan 14 The Players' Theatre in London opens as a censorship-free private club with a program of *Late Joys.*

Feb At the historic Theatre Royal in Bristol, a permanent repertory company, the Bristol Old Vic, is established.

March Hurt and angered at the critical rejection of his new play, *Truckline Cafe,* Maxwell Anderson pays for an ad in the NY Times. "The public is far better qualified to judge plays than the men who write reviews for our dailies," he insists. "It is an insult to our theatre that there should be so many incompetents and irresponsibles among them."

April Century Lighting introduces to American theatres the CI (Century Izenour) lighting control system. New developments included in this system are the use of thyratron tubes, proportional corssfading, and presetting capabilities for up to ten scenes in advance.

May Peter Cotes, operating London's New Lindsay Theatre Club, finds the Lord Chamberlain adamant about deletions of some offensive words—"syphillis," "abortion," and "miscarriage"— in the text of the American drama, *Pick-Up Girl.* Cotes is seeking a license for public performance. On her 79th birthday, Queen Mary attends. Elsa Shelley's play is then licensed with no changes.

June In August, Michigan, Jack and Betty Ragotzy found The Barn Theatre, an Equity Resident Summer Stock playhouse.

June 1 Burns Mantle's annual list of ten "*Best Plays*" for the 1945–46 Broadway season includes the following: Lindsay and Crouse's *State of the Union,* Laurents' *Home of the Brave,* d'Usseau and Gow's *Deep Are the Roots,* Lavery's *The Magnificent Yankee,* Anouilh's *Antigon,* Rattigan's *O Mistress Mine,* Kanin's *Born Yesterday,* Rice's *Dream Girl,* Sherwood's *The Rugged Path,* and Irwin and Howard's *Lute Song. State of the Union* wins the Pulitzer Prize.

June 2 The 1945–46 Broadway season ended on May 31. The *NY Times* reports that the number of productions has dropped from last season's high of 95 to a low of 79. There were plays (46), musicals (13), revues (2), revivals (11), and "others" (7). There is a "low water mark" for productions—less than ten performances in this category are two intriguing titles: *Woman Bites Dog* and *Marriage is for Single People.*

July 15 The *Maid in the Ozarks* at New York's Belasco Theatre is advertised as "the worst play in the world," and lives up to its billing, say most critics. It lasts 13 weeks only through a forced run. Jules Pfeiffer is the producer and director.

Aug The Arts Council of Great Britain is formed this month to continue in peacetime work begun in 1940 by the Council for the Encouragement of Music and the Arts (CEMA). In 1947, the Council will be granted a Royal Charter. It receives an annual government grant, though operates as an independent organization. The Secretary of State for Education and Science is responsible in the Cabinet for the arts vote and appointment of the Council's members who govern its policies and disbursements. It has three main objects: 1) to develop knowledge and practice of the arts; 2) to increase accessibility of the arts to the British public, and 3) to advise and cooperate with departments of the national government and local authorities on these goals. Drama, opera, dance, and music, and other arts, will be supported. Eventually, Scotland and Wales will have their own Councils.

W.C. FIELDS

Oct 14 The London Casino, closed since 1940 because of the blitz, is re-convested to a theatre and opens with *Pick-Up Girl.*

Nov 6 With the opening of the American Repertory Theatre's sumptuous revival of Shakespeare's *Henry VIII,* financial difficulties are already menacing Eva Le-Gallienne's latest effort to establish repertory theatre in New York. There is no second season.

Dec 19 London's Theatre Royal, Drury Lane, previously closed because of war damage, re-opens with Noel Coward's *Pacific 1860.*

Jan 10 *Finian's Rainbow* (NY—46th Street—Musical). E.Y. Harburg and Fred Saidy have devised this fantasy which satirizes a variety of American foibles and prejudices. Albert Sharpe is Finian, who's stolen a pot of gold from a leprechaun (David Wayne) planning to bury it near Fort Know in hope of accumulating riches. Burton Lane provides the score. Among the popular songs are "How Are Things in Glocca Mora?" and "Look To the Rainbow." The show has 725 performances. On Oct 21, 1947, it opens at London's Palace with Patrick J. Kelly and Alfie Bass. Despite its success in America and the popularity of most of its songs, the show doesn't reach the 100-performance mark.

Jan 29 *All My Sons* (NY—Coronet—Drama). Arthur Miller's drama depicts a dishonest airplane manufacturer who must face the fact that his own son's death is the result of his defective engines. Arthur Kennedy and Ed Begley are featured. The play, which wins the Drama Critics' Circle Award, runs 41 weeks. On May 11, 1948, it opens in London at the Lyric, Hammersmith. Joseph Calleia is the manufacturer. On June 16 the production moves to the Globe Theatre where it runs for 110 performances.

Feb 4 *John Loves Mary* (NY—Booth—Comedy). In Norman Krasna's farce, John (William Prince) loves Mary (Nina Foch) but marries Lily (Pamela Gordon) who loves Fred (Tom Ewell). There's a reason, of course, and it's revealed for 423 performances. Joshua Logan stages.

Feb 8 *The Story of Mary Surratt* (NY—Henry Miller—Drama). Dorothy Gish plays the boarding-house keeper in whose home Booth planned Lincoln's assassination. John Patrick's play suggests her execution may have been a miscarriage of justice. Though it has only 11 performances, it is chosen as one of Burns Mantle's "Best Plays."

March 13 *Brigadoon* (NY—Ziegfeld—Musical). Alan Jay Lerner concocts a fantasy of a mythical Scottish village which appears out of the Highland mists every hundred years. The score, by Frederick Loewe, includes such numbers as "The Heather on the Hill" and "Almost Like Being In Love." Agnes de Mille creates the dances. The cast includes David Brooks, George Keane, James Mitchell, Marion Bell, and Pamela Britton. The show runs for 581 performances and is later often revived. Lerner and Loewe's show opens in London at His Majesty's on April 14, 1949. Philip Hanna, Hiram Sherman, Patrica Hughes, and Bunty Kelley are in the cast. It has 685 performances.

March 19 *The Eagle Has Two Heads.* See L premiere, 1947

April 3 *Barefoot Boy With Cheek* (NY—Martin Beck—Musical). Max Shulman's musical about college radicals has music by Sidney Lippman and lyrics by Sylvia Dee. Nancy Walker, William Redfield, and Red Buttons play 108 performances. George Abbott stages.

May 1 *The Telephone/The Medium* (NY—Barrymore—Musical). Marie Powers plays a fraudulent medium in composer/librettist Gian Carlo Menotti's new work which runs nearly 27 weeks. *The Telephone* is Menotti's curtain-raiser about a young man trying to propose to a girl whose line is always busy.

May 28 *Icetime of 1948* (NY—Center—Revue). Freddie Trenkler heads a new ice-skating extravaganza, produced by Sonja Henie and Arthur Wirtz, which has 422 performances.

Sep 29 *The Heiress* (NY—Biltmore—Drama). Ruth and Augustus Goetz adapt Henry James's novel, *Washington Square*. Basil Rathbone appears with Wendy Hiller and Peter Cookson. The play has 410 performances. It opens in London at the Haymarket on Feb 1, 1949, with Ralph Richardson, Peggy Ashcroft, and James Donald. Here it wins 644 performances.

Oct 1 *Command Decision* (NY—Fulton—Drama). William Wister Haines' drama about a U.S. Air Force commander and the wrenching decisions he has to make, has 408 performances. Paul Kelly and James Whitmore head the cast.

Oct 9 *High Button Shoes* (NY—Century—Musical). Stephen Longstreet adapts his partly autobiographical novel of life in New Brunswick in 1913. Jule Styne and Sammy Cahn provide the music. Jerome Robins choreographs. Among the cast are Nanette Fabray and Phil Silvers. The show has 727 performances. The musical premieres at London's Hippodrome on Dec 22, 1948, with Kay Kimbler, Lew Parker

and Joan Heal in the cast. It runs nine months.

Oct 10 *Allegro* (NY—Majestic—Musical). A smalltown doctor (James Battles) who goes to the big city is the hero of Rogers and Hammerstein's new musical, which runs for 315 performances. Lawrence Langner and Theresa Helburn stage. Agnes de Mille choreographs.

Oct 21 *An Inspector Calls.* See L premiere, 1946.

Oct 22 *The Druid Circle* (NY—Morosco—Drama). John Van Druten's new play, about a repressed headmaster and his influence on two students, has only 70 performances. Leo G. Carroll and Ethel Griffies are in the cast. Van Druten directs.

Oct 29 *The Winslow Boy.* See L premiere, 1946.

Nov 4 *For Love or Money* (NY—Henry Miller—Comedy). A charming young girl (June Lockhart) wins the love of an aging leading-man (John Loder) in F. Hugh Herbert's comedy, which runs 33 weeks. Harry Ellerbe stages.

Nov 18 *Eastward in Eden* (NY—Royale—Drama). Though it runs only 2 weeks, John Chapman chooses Dorothy Gardner's play, about an imagined romance between poet Emily Dickinson (Beatrice Straight) and Dr. Charles Wadsworth (Onslow Stevens), as one of the year's ten "Best Plays." Ellen Van Volkenburg stages.

Dec 3 *A Streetcar Named Desire* (NY—Barrymore—Drama). Tennessee Williams' southern tale of a woman's gradual mental disintegration features Jessica Tandy, Kim Hunter, and Marlon Brando. The production has 855 performances. Williams' play wins the Pultizer Prize and the Drama Critics' Circle Award. "Out of poetic imagination and ordinary compassion, he [Williams] has spun a poignant and luminous story," reports Brooks

BAREFOOT BOY WITH CHEEK

HIGH BUTTON SHOES

Atkinson of the NY Times. The show premieres in London at the Aldwych on Oct 11, 1949, with Vivien Leigh, Bonar Colleano, and Renee Asherson. Lawrence Olivier directs. It runs 41 weeks.

Dec 11 *Angel in the Wings* (NY—Coronet—Revue). Elaine Stritch sings "Bongo, Bongo, Bongo, I don't want to leave the Congo," in Paul and Grace Hartman's music and comedy revue, which runs beyond the season.

1947   BRITISH PREMIERES

Jan 23 *Born Yesterday.* See NY premiere, 1946.

Jan 29 *Jane* (L—Aldwych—Comedy). W. Somerset Maugham's story of a woman who resolves some romantic impasses becomes a play thanks to S.N. Behrman. Yvonne Arnaud has the title role. It runs over 34 weeks. In New York the show opens at the Coronet on Feb 1, 1952, with Edna Best. There are 100 performances.

Feb 12 *The Eagle Has Two Heads* (L—Haymarket—Drama). Shown last September at the Lyric, Hammersmith, Jean Cocteau's play now moves to the West End. Eileen Herlie plays an unhappy queen. James Donald is the rebel who comes to kill her and stays to love. The production runs 170 performances. On March 19, the drama opens in New York at the Plymouth in Ronald Duncan's adaptation. Tallulah Bankhead and Helmut Dantine are featured. There are just 29 performances.

March 7 *Now Barabas . . .* (L—Vaudeville—Drama). Jill Bennett is in the cast of William Douglas Home's new play, which has 130 showings. Colin Chandler stages.

March 7 *Romany Love* (L—His Majesty's—Musical). The music is Victor Herbert's, but the songs are the work of Robert Wright and George Forrest, who created *Song of Norway.* The "gypsy" script is by Henry Myers.

April 5 *Here, There, and Everywhere* (L—Palladium—Revue). Hy Hazell and comedian Tommy Trinder are among the headliners of this new Robert Nesbitt revue. It wins a run of 466 performances.

April 26 *Bless the Bride* (L—Adelphi—Musical). Vivian Ellis provides score for A.P. Herbert's musical play which wins 886 performances. Singing star Georges Guetary heads the cast. Wendy Toye stages.

April 27 *Together Again* (L—Victoria Palace—Revue). The popular Crazy Gang (Flanagan, Nervo and Knox, Naughton and Gold) earns a memorable run of 1,566 performances in this revue, staged by Alec Shanks. The *Times* calls them "irresistible."

April 30 *Oklahoma!* See NY premiere, 1943.

May 30 *Edward, My Son* (L—His Majesty's—Drama). Robert Morley and Noel Langley write this play about a father who has spoiled his son and now threatens to spoil his grandson. Morley, Peggy Ashcroft, John Robinson, and Leueen MacGrath are in the cast. The production has 787 performances. On Sep 30, 1948, it opens in New York at the Martin Beck with Morley again playing the father. The cast is largely the same as in the London production. The play runs nearly 33 weeks.

June 4 *Ever Since Paradise* (L—New—Comedy). Roger Livesey and Ursula Jeans head the cast of J.B. Priestley's new play, which he calls an "entertainment." Priestley stages for 165 performances.

June 5 *Life With Father.* See NY premiere, 1939.

June 7 *Annie Get Your Gun.* See NY premiere, 1946.

June 20 *Noose* (L—Saville—Drama). Michael Hordern and Nigel Patrick have a run of nearly 22 weeks in Richard Llewellyn's thriller, staged by Reginald Tate.

July 8 *Deep Are the Roots.* See NY premiere.

July 9 *The Voice of the Turtle.* See NY premiere, 1943.

July 11 *The Crime of Margaret Foley* (L—Comedy—Drama). Kathleen O'Regan plays the title-role in Percy Robinson and Terence de Marney's mystery thriller. Author de Marney is also in the cast. Anthony Hawtrey directs; there are 210 performances.

July 16 *Trespass* (L—Globe—Drama). Emlyn Williams directs and stars in his new play, which he calls a ghost story. Francoise Rosay and Leon Quartermaine are also in the cast. It runs almost five months.

July 22 *Peace in Our Time* (L—Lyric—Drama). England under German occupation is the subject of Noel Coward's new play. *The Times* calls it " . . . melodrama, wearing the cap of sophisticated comedy." Alan Webb directs a cast which includes Elspeth March, Bernard Lee, and Kenneth More.

July 30 *Dr. Angelus* (L—Phoenix—Drama). Alastair Sim directs James Bridie's new play, and acts the title-role. George Cole and Archie Duncan are also in the cast. It has a run of almost 25 weeks.

Aug 15 *The Linden Tree* (L—Duchess—Drama). Husband-and-wife Sybil Thorndike and Lewis Casson head the cast of J.B. Priestley's play, and earn a run of 422 performances. Michael MacOwan stages.

Aug 27 *The Chiltern Hundreds* (L—Vaudeville—Comedy). Popular actor A. E. Matthews and Marjorie Fielding play the leads in William Douglas Home's play which runs for 651 performances. Colin Chandler stages.

Sept 4 *Tuppence Coloured* (L—Lyric, Hammersmith—Revue). Comic actress Joyce Grenfell, singer Elisabeth Welch, and Max Adrian, are among the cast of Laurier Lister's new revue, which transfers to the West End's Globe Theatre on Oct 15, where it runs 34 weeks.

Oct 21 *Finian's Rainbow.* See NY premiere, 1947.

Oct 23 *Starlight Roof* (L—Hippodrome—Revue). A young Julie Andrews is in the company, headed by comedian Vic Oliver and muscial comedy actress Pat Kirkwood, of this revue staged by Robert Nesbitt. It earns a run of 649 performances.

Oct 29 *Anna Lucasta.* See NY premiere, 1944.

Nov 13 *Outrageous Fortune* (L—Winter Garden—Comedy). Veteran farceurs Ralph Lynn and Roberston Hare win a run of almost eight months in Ben Travers' new farce, staged by Charles Hickman.

Dec 2 *The Blind Goddess* (L—Apollo—Drama). Honor Blackman and Basil Radford are in the cast of Patrick Hastings' play, which draws audiences for 123 performances. Charles Hickman directs.

Jan 1 The new year opens with a revival of Ibsen's *The Master Builder*, at London's Arts Theatre. On Jan 22, Tom Robertson's *Caste* is revived at the Duke of York's Theatre.

Jan 9 With a score added by Kurt Weill, Elmer Rice's *Street Scene* (1929) returns to Broadway at the Adelphi Theatre for a run of 148 performances. Poet Langston Hughes provides the lyrics. The opera eventually enters the repertory of the New York City Opera.

Jan 14 Continuing its London season at the New Theatre, the Old Vic ensemble opens Jonson's *The Alchemist*, with Alec Guinness as Abel Drugger and Joyce Redman as Doll Common. John Burrell directs. Guinness plays the title-role in *Richard II*, opening April 23 to salute Shakespeare's birthday. Ralph Richardson stages the Old Vic revival.

Jan 21 Victor Herbert's *Sweethearts* (1943) has some plot revisions to permit comedian Bobby Clark to make the story more manic. John Kennedy's staging has a nine-month run at Broadway's Shubert Theatre.

Feb 4 Suddenly, there's a spate of Irish plays in London. Tonight at the Lyric, Hammersmith, Walter Macken's *Galway Handicap* opens, staged by Irene Hentschel. At the Arts Theatre, Paul Vincent Carroll's *The Wise Have Not Spoken*, staged by Basil Langton, is presented. On Feb. 5, the Dublin Gate Theatre ensemble offers *Ill Met by Moonlight* at the Vaudeville Theatre.

Feb 18 Shaw's five-part epic, *Back To Methuselah*, is revived at London's Arts Theatre. Tonight, Part 1 is presented, staged by Noel Willman. On Feb 19, Parts 2 and 3 are played. On Feb 25, Part 4 is

produced, followed by Part 5 on March 4.

Feb 18 From Britain comes Donald Wolfit to New York's Century Theatre with an Elizabethan repertory. He opens with *King Lear* but critics are not kind. Also offered are *As You Like It*, *Hamlet*, *The Merchant of Venice*, and *Volpone*, for a total of 23 performances.

March 3 Oscar Wilde's *The Importance of Being Earnest* is revived on Broadway at the Royale Theatre by the Theatre Guild with John Gielgud staging and playing John Worthing. It runs ten weeks.

March 3 Paul Vincent Carroll's Irish drama *The White Steed* opens at London's Embassy Theatre. Siobhan McKenna is in the cast. The production moves to the Whitehall Theatre on March 24.

March 6 John Webster's Jacobean tragedy, *The White Devil*, is revived at the Duchess Theatre in London, staged by Michael Benthall. Margaret Rawlings, Robert Helpmann, and Martita Hunt are in the cast.

March 8 Ivor Novello's popular musical, *The Dancing Years*, is revived at London's Casino Theatre.

March 12 In this American revival of Oscar Straus' *The Chocolate Soldier*, Frances McCann and Keith Andes play the romatic leads for 70 performances. George Balanchine choreographs.

April 5 The Shakespeare Memorial Theatre at Stratford-upon-Avon opens this year's season with Peter Brook's production of *Romeo and Juliet*. From last season, *Doctor Faustus*, *Love's Labour's Lost*, and *Measure for Measure* return. New are Walter Hudd's staging of the "birthday play," *Twelfth Night*; Norman Wright's

The Tempest, Hudd's *Richard II*, Nugent Monck's *Pericles*, and Michael Benthall's *The Merchant of Venice*.

April 5 In need of a play to sustain their American Repertory Theatre subscription season, Eva LeGallienne, Margaret Webster, and Cheryl Crawford revive the LeGallienne Civic Repertory production of *Alice in Wonderland*. It has an extended run of 100 performances.

April 9 Donald Wolfit brings his company to London's Savoy Theatre, and opens with Jonson's *Volpone*. On April 12, *The Merchant of Venice* is presented. On April 21, *King Lear* is the play. *Othello* opens on April 24, and *Hamlet* on April 29. On May 8, the play is *Twelfth Night*.

April 15 Clive Brook stages a revival of Molnar's *The Play's The Thing* at London's Lyric, Hammersmith. It moves to the St. James's Theatre on May 19. On the next night, at the Haymarket Theatre, Noel Coward's *Present Laughter* is revived, staged by Coward, who plays opposite Joyce Carey. On April 22, at the Boltons Theatre, Madge Pemberton's play about Napoleon's son, *The King of Rome*, is shown. On April 24, the popular revue, *1066 And All That*, is revived for 188 performances.

May 3 William Inge's *Farther Off from Heaven* opens, the first production of the Margo Jones Theatre in Dallas.

May 22 Summer Shakespeare in the Open Air Theatre in London's Regent's Park begins with *Twelfth Night*, with Robert Atkins staging. On June 23, Atkins revives the Chinese classic, *Lady Precious Stream*. *A Midsummer Night's Dream* follows on July 22.

May 26 Following the success of his Oscar Wilde revival at the Royale Theatre, John Gielgud resurrects Congreve's *Love for Love* on Broadway, which runs for six weeks. The cast includes Adrianne Allan, Pamela Brown, and Gielgud, who also stages. Rex Whistler creates the settings.

June 9 Eugene O'Neill's sea-play, *S. S. Glencairn*, is revived in London at the Mercury Theatre, staged by Robert Henderson. Other revivals this month include Shaw's *Pygmalion* at the Lyric, Hammersmith, with Alec Clunes on June 18; and James Bridie's *A Sleeping Clergyman* at the Criterion Theatre, with Robert Donat and Margaret Leighton on June 19.

July 15 At the New York City Center, a newly formed City Theatre Company opens a summer season with a revival of Dion Boucicault's adaptation of Washington Irving's tale, *Rip Van Winkle*. Herbert Berghof has also tinkered with the story and directed it. It runs two weeks.

July 17 In Williamsburg, Virginia, *The Common Glory* premieres. Paul Green's historical drama, about the War for Independence, is shown annually, with a

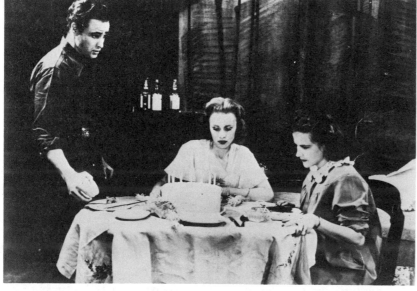

STREETCAR NAMED DESIRE

break between 1963 and 1965.

July 21 The D'Oyly Carte Opera Company arrives at London's Sadler's Wells Theatre for a summer season of their Gilbert & Sullivan repertoire. *Trial by Jury* and *The Pirates of Penzance* are on tonight's program. The company presents *The Gondoliers, The Mikado, The Yeoman of the Guard, Patience,* and *Iolanthe.*

July 30 Bertolt Brecht's *Galileo Galilei* has its world premiere in Los Angeles at the Coronet Theatre with John Houseman and Norman Lloyd producing and Charles Laughton—who's worked on the script's English version closely with Brecht in the title-role. Every seat for the four-week run has been sold.

Aug 8 In Ashland the Oregon Shakespearean Festival re-opens after a wartime hiatus with *Hamlet,* staged by Frank Lambrett-Smith. Festival founder Angus Bowmer stages the remaining three plays: *Love's Labour's Lost, Macbeth,* and *The Merchant of Venice.*

Aug 24 In the Scottish capital of Edinburgh, the first Edinburgh International Festival opens today. Eventually, it will offer each season major theatre, dance, music, and opera ensembles from many lands, as well as encourage the development of the "Fringe Festival" and concurrent art exhibitions and other events. The Edinbrugh Tattoo, an impressive spectacle of military music, will also be an allied attraction. This summer, the Old Vic Theatre Company comes from London to present two productions. The first *The Taming of the Shrew,* is directed by John Burrell, with Trevor Howard. *Richard II* is staged by Ralph Richardson, with Alec Guinness the king; Louis Jouvet also brings his company from the Theatre de L'Athenee in Paris to the Festival, opening with Moliere's *L'Ecole des Femmes.* Their second play is Giraudoux's *Ondine.* This season also sees the establishment of the Edinburgh Film Festival, a complementary event. The Sadler's Wells Ballet presents *The Sleeping Beauty,* with Margot Fonteyn, Beryl Grey, and Frederick Ashton. Mozart's *Le Nozze di Figaro* and Verdi's *Macbeth* are also on the program, brought from the Glyndebourne Festival.

Sep 18 Donagh MacDonagh's Irish play, *Happy As Larry,* staged by Denis Carey, earns a run of 100 performances at London's Mercury Theatre. On Dec 16, it moves to the Criterion Theatre. The play is preceded by a revival of Sean O'Casey's *A Pound on Demand.*

Sep 22 Micheal macLiammoir's *Portrait of Miriam* is produced by the Dublin Gate Theatre, now in its 21st season. Also shown are Johnston's *The Old Lady Says "No!"* and Shaw's *John Bull's Other Island.*

Oct 2 Walter Hudd stages a revival of *Richard II* at His Majesty's Theatre, London. Among the cast are Robert Harris, Beatrix Lehmann, and Donald Sinden. On Oct 6, Peter Brook stages a revival of *Romeo and Juliet.* Paul Scofield is Mercutio. On Oct 8, Hudd stages *Twelfth Night,* with Scofield as Sir Andrew Aguecheek.

Oct 8 On Broadway at the large Alvin Theatre, Maurice Evans directs Shaw's *Man and Superman* for an impressive 37-week run. Frances Rowe is in the cast.

Oct 8 At London's Princes Theatre, Hugh Miller stages a revival of *The DuBarry.* On Oct 30, at the Q Theatre, *The Picture of Dorian Gray* is revived. W. Somerset Maugham's *Smith* is also revived the same night at the Arts Theatre. At the Torch Theatre on Oct 31, Ibsen's *The Wild Duck* is revived.

Oct 20 Robinson Jeffers' poetic adaptation of Euripides' tragedy, *Medea,* with Judith Anderson and John Gielgud becomes a big success in New York at the National Theatre. Gielgud also stages. The production runs nearly 27 weeks.

Nov 4 At London's New Theatre, The Old Vic Season opens with Shakespeare's *The Taming of the Shrew,* staged by John Burrell, with Trevor Howard, and Patricia Burke. On Nov 18, *Richard II,* staged by Ralph Richardson, opens with Alec Guinness as the king. On Dec 3, the company presents Shaw's *Saint Joan* in a Burrell staging. Celia Johnson, and Alec Guinness.

Nov 26 Katharine Cornell and Godfrey Tearle enjoy a four-month run in this revival of Shakespeare's *Antony and Cleopatra,* on Broadway at the Martin Beck Theatre. Guthrie McClintic stages a cast including, Eli Wallach, Charlton Heston, and Maureen Stapleton.

Dec 7 Bertolt Brecht's epic theatre-piece *Galileo* has six performances, sponsored by the Experimental Theatre (ANTA) at New York's Maxine Elliott Theatre. Charles Laughton, who has translated and appeared in Los Angeles in the play, is Galileo. Joseph Losey directs

Dec 16 Revivals continue in London with Arthur Wing Pinero's *Mid-Channel* opening at the Q Theatre, staged by Peter Cotes. The next evening, Anthony Quayle opens his staging of Vanbrugh's *The Relapse,* with Cyril Ritchard and Paul Scofiled. On Dec 18, *Macbeth* is revived at the Aldwych, staged by the young American director, Norris Houghton. Michael Redgrave is his Macbeth.

Dec 21 Barrie Stavis offers his vision of the life of Galileo, *Lamp At Midnight,* produced by the New Stages company at the New Stages Theatre in New York. This production is an answer to the Experimental Theatre, which has chosen to present the same subject, as viewed by a foreign author, Bertolt Brecht, in the same season. Stavis' play runs till February.

Dec 29 Britain's D'Oyly Carte Opera Company arrives at the Century Theatre in New York for a 17-week run of Gilbert & Sullivan repertory.

Dec 29 *Cinderella,* with comedian Arthur Askey as Buttons, opens the holiday pantomine season. Emile Littler stages this show he's devised for the Casino Theatre in London. On the 23rd, *Treasure Island* opens at St. James's Theatre, while *Daddy Long-Legs* is revived at the Comedy Theatre. *Peter Pan* bows at the Scala Theatre. On the 24th, a number of shows open: *Where the Rainbow Ends* (Empire, Kilburn), *Jack and the Beanstalk* (Golder's Green Hippodrome), *Babes in the Wood* (Princes), *The Wizard of Oz* (Strand), *Charley's Aunt* (Palace), and *Alice Through the Looking-Glass* (Q). On Boxing Day, more shows open: *Mother Goose* (Trocadero/Elephant and Castle), *Babes in the Wood* (Richmond), *More Just William* (Palladium), and *Dick Whittington* (Troxy).

EVER SINCE PARADISE